St, J

Speculative Markets

Speculative Markets

Sarkis J. Khoury
University of Notre Dame

Macmillan Publishing Company
New York
Collier Macmillan Publishers
London

Macmillan Publishing Company
866 Third Avenue, New York, New York 10022

Collier Macmillan Canada, Inc.

Library of Congress Cataloging in Publication Data

Khoury, Sarkis J.
  Speculative markets.

  Includes index.
  1. Speculation. 2. Investments. 3. Put and call transactions. 4. Interest rate futures. 5. Stock index futures. I. Title.
  HG6015.K48 1984   332.64'5   83–11317
  ISBN 0–02–362850–2

Printing:1 2 3 4 5 6 7 8   Year:4 5 6 7 8 9 0 1 2

ISBN 0-02-362850-2

To the United States of America:
A veritable Land of Opportunity

Preface

The revolution in the financial markets has increased the complexity as well as the opportunities in these markets. Professional money managers have adjusted well to the changes and have been able to capitalize on the opportunities they presented. Many questions remain unanswered, however. Although the fundamentals of each of the new instruments are quite well understood, their full implications have yet to be sorted out. For example, little is known about how and to what extent the futures market affects the cash market of the underlying commodity. Little is also known about how the proliferation of futures and options contracts affects the efficiency and stability of the financial system and consequently the efficiency and stability of other sectors of the economy.

An unfortunate thing with regard to these developments is that the classroom remains well behind Wall Street in integration of the new instruments into a well-developed investment program which should serve as a foundation for an investment course. The evidence is seen in practically every investment textbook published before 1983. Their emphasis is almost strictly on stocks and bonds with a sparse discussion of the instruments analyzed in this text.

Several professors of investments have recognized the problem, however, and moved swiftly to bridge the gap between Wall Street and the classroom. New courses have been introduced. They are typically designated as Investment II, Advanced Investments, or Speculative Markets. The materials used in these courses consist of several articles and chapters of different books, each dealing separately with each topic in this book. The end result is that no comprehensive source of information is available to the student in these courses. Additionally, several of the new instruments such as interest options and stock index futures have not been treated thoroughly in any article or book that is readily available to faculty and students, which creates a peculiar problem in their discussion.

This text attempts to remedy the situation by integrating the various speculative instruments into one text and by summarizing both academic and trade literature on their developments and implications. While this procedure may not answer all the questions, it should at least give an indication of how far we have come. The text will in

addition summarize the various strategies that are being used by investors and speculators in the financial markets. All of this is done with minimum reliance on mathematical and statistical skills. The reader must note, however, that a consistent level of rigor across topics is impossible. There simply is little research on diamonds, art, and gold.

The contents of this text have been used successfully in my speculative markets classes with excellent feedback from the students. I hope your experience will be as positive as mine and I look forward to receiving your comments, whatever their nature.

ACKNOWLEDGEMENTS

The writing of a book on speculative markets is especially difficult because of the diversity and extremely technical nature of the subjects and the lack of sufficiently rigorous materials on several issues and strategies. The literature on speculative markets continues to evolve at a very rapid pace, making the writing of a book like this a very risky and laborious venture. The journey through the maze of papers and books on various speculative vehicles would have been very lonely, if not impossible, without the help of many persons of good will and tremendous competence and energy. I owe very special thanks to Mike Granito for his support and encouragement. His patience was severely tested with some of my outlandish ideas. For this I am thankful. Two persons without whose help this work would have been impossible deserve special thanks: Todd Hooper and Jane Herbstritt. Their commitment and intelligence are truly amazing. They worked far beyond the call of duty. Special thanks are owed to Professors Gerald Jones of Notre Dame, Georges Courtadon of N.Y.U., Owen Gregory of the University of Illinois/Chicago, Raymond Chiang of the University of Florida, Robert Kolb of the University of Miami, and to Joyce Khoury and Mike Kvalvik.

Very special thanks go to Thomas M. Pugliese and Brian Ledley for their tolerance and exceptional assistance in editing. My thanks also go to Eileen Schlesinger and Chip Price of Macmillan, and to many anonymous referees. Professor Shantaram Hegde made valuable comments on two chapters. For this I am very grateful.

The generosity of the persons named above was not sufficiently high, however, to allow me to shift any blame for errors in fact or procedure onto their shoulders.

SARKIS J. KHOURY

Contents

CHAPTER

6

PART
THREE **International Dimensions**

CHAPTER
7

PART
FOUR **Precious Stones, Collectibles, and Gold**

CHAPTER
8

Speculative Markets

Speculative Markets: Developments and Scope

1.1 AN OVERVIEW

The transformation in the securities market in the last ten years can be mildly described as revolutionary. Never in the financial history of the United States have so many choices been available to investors, hedgers, and speculators. Many new contracts were introduced, particularly in the second half of the 1970s. Some met with remarkable success while others found limited success. The balance went through the market's revolving doors into oblivion because of insufficient market interest and lack of liquidity.

The financial environment of the 1970s and the early 1980s could be characterized by one word: uncertainty. The volatility of markets during those years was unprecedented, sending portfolio managers looking for cover. All markets, whether labor, financial, or commodities, experienced dramatic changes in the behavior of prices. Unemployment rates were rising simultaneously with inflation rates, producing stagflation, a situation thought impossible only a few years earlier. Currency markets experienced unprecedented gyrations (see Figure 1.1) as central banks decided to let exchange rates float in 1973. The flexible exchange rate system did not turn out to be the disaster most predicted. New instruments like currency futures contracts and currency options[1] emerged to supplement the forward market and provide additional hedging tools.

Figure 1.2 illustrates the volatility of some short-term and long-term interest rates. The debt markets witnessed unprecedented volatility in the 1970s, which continues today. The largest average weekly fluctuation in 13-week T-bill auction rates was recorded in 1974. The size of the fluctuation was 33.4 basis points. Futures contracts on debt instruments were introduced one year later, in 1975, on the Chicago Board of Trade (CBT)

---

[1] A futures contract is an obligation to buy or sell a specified amount and quality of a commodity (physical or financial) at some future date at a price negotiated today.

An option is a contract which gives the buyer the right to purchase (call) or sell (put) 100 shares of stock or a designated amount of a financial instrument, or a futures contract on a financial instrument or commodity at a designated price anytime during the limited life of the contract.

FIGURE 1.1. Effective exchange rates (change in tradeweighted rates from March 1973 levels).

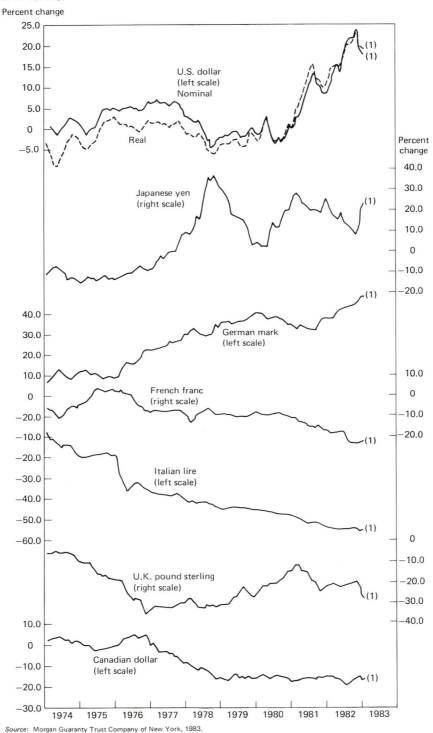

Percent change

U.S. dollar
(left scale)
Nominal

Real

Percent change

Japanese yen
(right scale)

German mark
(left scale)

French franc
(right scale)

Italian lire
(left scale)

U.K. pound sterling
(right scale)

Canadian dollar
(left scale)

Source: Morgan Guaranty Trust Company of New York, 1983.

FIGURE 1.2. **The cyclical behavior of yields.**

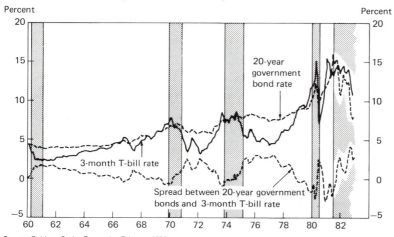

Source: Goldman Sachs *Economics*, February 1983.

to allow portfolio managers to cope with this new phenomenon of "high interest rate volatility."

The volatility of the stock market was no less dramatic (see Figure 1.3). New highs of the Dow Jones Industrial Average (DJIA) and record volume on the New York Stock Exchange were set. Between August 1982 and February 1983 the DJIA appreciated by 37.5 percent with wide historic daily fluctuations both on the upside and the downside in the interim. In dollar terms the market rise, measured by the Wilshire 5,000 Equity Index—which is the total value of all stocks listed on the New York Stock Exchange, the American Stock Exchange, and the actively traded shares on the over-the-counter market—translates into an increase of $354.131 billion between February 11, 1982 and February 11, 1983 ($1.539 trillion on February 11, 1983). This rally was broad and deep. Stock volume in December 1982 (1.682 billion) was almost 70 percent higher than it was in December 1981 (0.959 billion). For the year as a whole, stock volume in 1982 was almost four times the 1975 volume and 38 percent higher than that of 1981 (see Table 1.1). The record daily volume on the New York Stock Exchange was reached on November 4, 1982 with 149,385,480 shares traded, a total equal to the number of shares traded in all of 1915. An all-time new high for the DJIA was recorded on June 16, 1983 with the average at 1248.30. Many analysts expected this record to be broken again, and shortly thereafter it was.

On the macroeconomic level, conditions of the early 1980s produced the worst recession since the depression of the 1930s, further eroding consumer confidence and increasing the riskiness of markets. Two of many indicators of uncertain economic times are business and bank failures. During the week of February 3, 1983, 690 business firms failed compared with 449 for the same period only one year earlier. Forty-two banks failed in 1982. The latest major bank failure took place on February 15, 1983 when the United American Bank of Knoxville was declared insolvent by the Tennessee banking authorities. This represented the fourth largest bank failure in the history of U.S. commercial banking. When banks, the traditional symbol of stability and economic strength, fail at the rate they have been, uncertainty and the need to cope with it increase. Add to bank failures the record losses posted by Ford, International Harvester, Pan Am, and a host of other

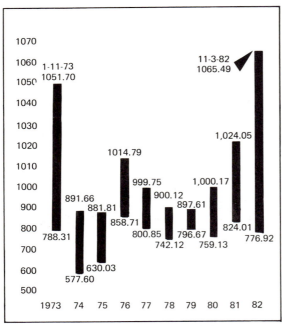

FIGURE 1.3. Behavior of Dow Jones industrials, 1973–1982 and during 1982.

Source: Associated Press, November 4, 1982.

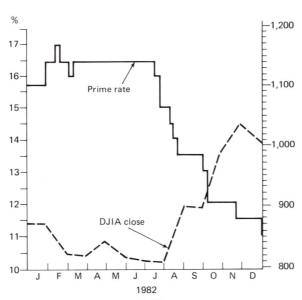

Source: The Wall Street Journal, January 3, 1983.

TABLE 1.1
Stock Volume and Institutional Participation

Year	Volume (in Billions of Shares)	Percent of Volume Transacted by Institutions
1982	16.5	41
1981	11.9	31.8
1980	11.4	29.2
1979	8.2	26.5
1978	7.2	22.9
1977	5.3	22.4
1976	5.4	18.7
1975	4.7	16.6

Source: New York Stock Exchange, Inc., February 1983.

companies, and an unemployment rate approaching 11 percent, and you will have a better understanding of the underlying reasons for investors' wariness.

1.2 OTHER MAJOR DEVELOPMENTS

Several dramatic developments have and continue to exert powerful influence on the U.S. economy and the performance of financial and commodities markets. Space allows us to mention only a few.

The emergence of financial centers ("super-markets") changed the method of delivering financial services. Acquisition of Dean Witter by Sears and of Shearson by American Express are but two examples. Recent acquisition of the discount brokerage house Charles Schwab & Co. by the Bank of America and purchase of Rose & Co. of Chicago by Chase Manhattan Bank and internal expansions by banks like Security Pacific National, Citicorp, Chemical Bank, and Citizens and Southern National Bank into the brokerage industry are further examples of the integrated approach to delivery of financial services. These developments and innovative products introduced by Merrill Lynch, such as the Cash Management Account, effectively reduced the impact of certain regulations and the force of the Glass-Steagall Act of 1933, which was intended to separate banking from investment banking.

Negotiated commissions, inaugurated on May 1, 1975, produced a new industry (discount brokers) and increased the efficiency of securities markets. Also of great significance was the enactment of the Employment Retirement Income Security Act on Labor Day 1974. ERISA provided greater impetus to the expansion of pension funds. Their assets currently approximate $300 billion.

A tax law and an SEC ruling also helped shape the securities industry. The Economic Recovery Tax Act of 1981, intended to spur saving and investment, produced the largest tax cut in U.S. history. SEC Rule 415 (shelf registration) was issued by the SEC on March 10, 1982. The rule governs registration of securities to be offered and sold on a delayed or continuous basis in the future. Rule 415 brought new opportunities in investment banking, increased competition in the industry, and made it easier and cheaper, some claim, for corporations to issue debt and equity securities. These effects will continue if Rule 415 becomes a permanent feature of investment banking.

All of the changes in securities markets brought them new vitality, which was enhanced by explosive technology in communications. Today 30 million individuals own stocks directly. They are younger and less affluent on the average and have a much wider array of investment vehicles to choose from than ever before, as well as a multitude of information sources on every aspect of every investment vehicle.

1.3 THE NEW PRODUCTS

The proliferation of financial instruments continues at a fast pace. No quarter seems to go by without an introduction or an announcement about a new product to be introduced on one of the exchanges or on several of them. Prior to 1972 stocks, bonds, and commodities were practically the only game in town. Those trained to handle these three vehicles had to do some quick learning as new ones were introduced and as the pace of their introduction quickened. As a result of innovations, the make-up of the financial market has become very dynamic. The lazy, the inept, and the unsophisticated will find it very hard, if not impossible, to survive in this infinitely more complex new environment.

The 1970s and the early 1980s saw the emergence and disappearance of many investment vehicles. The first financial futures contract was introduced on May 16, 1972 by the Chicago Mercantile Exchange. It covered currencies. There were originally contracts on British pounds, Canadian dollars, Deutsche marks, Japanese yen, Mexican pesos, and Swiss francs. The first listed option contract was introduced by the Chicago Board Options Exchange (CBOE) on April 26, 1973. Several other futures and option contracts were to follow, with various degrees of success.

Tracing the development of the futures and option contracts on the Chicago Board of Trade alone is indicative of the evolving nature of financial futures and interest options (options on interest-bearing or zero coupon bonds or on futures contracts thereon). Table 1.2 reports the activity per contract and its day of introduction. As the reader can see, several contracts such as GNMA futures contracts on GNMA itself, 30- and 90-day commercial paper futures contracts, and four- to six-year Treasury notes futures contracts were never able to generate a consistently high level of interest. The CBT's most successful contract is the futures contract on Treasury bonds. Volume in this contract rose from 32,101 contracts traded in 1977—the first year the contract was introduced—to 16,739,695 contracts in 1982, and the interest continues to grow. This contract is by far the most active financial futures contract on any exchange.

To further illustrate the pace of innovation in the futures and options markets, we report those contracts which were introduced in 1982 and early 1983 on the various exchanges.

First to do so, the CBT introduced options on T-bond futures contracts on October 1, 1982 after a long legal battle with the Chicago Mercantile Exchange (CME). In March 1983, the CBT introduced an option on the Value Line Stock Index futures contract that will be traded on the floor of the Kansas City Board of Trade. The only other contract planned for 1983 by the CBT is one on a physical commodity: silver. Options on agricultural commodities may follow after 1983.

The CME introduced the S&P 500 futures contracts on January 28, 1983. On July 14, 1983 the CME added a new futures contract on a mini S&P, the S&P 100.

The CBOE was not to be denied participation in these new markets. It began trading T-bond options on October 22, 1982 and plans to introduce options on GNMAs during

TABLE 1.2
CBT Financial Futures

Year Underlying Instrument to Futures Contract (Date Contract Was Introduced)	Annual Volume (No. of Contracts)	Year Underlying Instrument to Futures Contract (Date Contract Was Introduced)	Annual Volume (No. of Contracts)
1975		*1980*	
GNMA—collaterized Depository Receipt (CDR) (Oct. 20, 1975)	20,125	GNMA (CDR)	2,326,292
		GNMA (CD)	12,619
		T—bonds	6,489,555
1976		4- to 6-year T-notes	449
GNMA (CDR)	128,536	90-day CP	15,996
		30-day CP	67
1977		*1981*	
GNMA (CDR)	422,421	GNMA (CDR)	2,292,882
T-bonds (Aug. 22, 1977)	32,101	GNMA (CD)	175
90-day commercial paper (CP) (Sept. 26, 1977)	3,553	T-bonds	13,907,988
		4- to 6-year T-notes	2,721
		90-day CP	49
1978		30-day CP	0
GNMA (CDR)	953,161	*1982*	
GNMA—actual certificate (Sept. 12, 1983)	6,527	GNMA (CDR)	2,055,648
		GNMA (CD)	0
T-bonds	555,350	T-bonds	16,739,695
90-day CP	18,767	4- to 6-year T-notes	0
		10-year T-notes (May 4, 1982)	881,325
1979		90-day CP	0
GNMA (CDR)	1,371,078	30-day CP	0
GNMA (CD)	77,365	Option on T-bond futures (Oct. 1, 1982)	118,772
T-bonds	2,059,594		
90-day CP	39,072		
30-day CP (May 14, 1979)	1,292		
Treasury Notes–4 to 6 years (June 25, 1979)	11,599		

Source: The Chicago Board of Trade, March 1983.

1984. On Friday, March 11, 1983 the CBOE introduced an option on 100 stocks dubbed the CBOE 100 Index and later renamed Standard & Poor's 100 Options. Options on the S&P 500 were introduced on July 1, 1983.

After an unsuccessful try at trading futures contracts, the American Stock Exchange introduced 13¾ T-notes options on October 22, 1983. It also introduced T-bill options

(13-week) on November 5, 1982 and 10½ T-note options on November 8, 1982. In March of 1983, Amex began trading an option on the Amex Index.

Some of the regional exchanges also participated in the trend. The Philadelphia Exchange began trading options on foreign currencies on November 22, 1982. The Kansas City Board of Trade was the first to introduce futures contracts on stock indexes (the Value Line in this case) on February 24, 1982. The CME followed with its futures contract on the S&P 500 and the New York Futures Exchange paced the innovations with its futures contract on the New York Stock Exchange Index introduced on May 6, 1982.

All of these instruments increased the complexities of financial markets and simultaneously the opportunities therein. This meant more extensive training for investment advisors, new strategies for portfolio managers, a redefinition of investment courses in colleges and universities and introduction of new courses under titles like Advanced Investment and Speculative Markets.

1.4 COPING WITH THE CHANGES

Changes in the market place led to a complete revamping of training programs at all brokerage houses and investment banking houses throughout the United States and in major foreign capitals. Helping in the education process were the exchanges on which the new vehicles were traded. The Chicago Board of Trade is in the lead through its Education and Publication Services Department, headed by the aggressive Lloyd Besant. This department also helped in retraining various university professors by providing them with literature, inviting them to seminars, sponsoring several research projects, and permitting access to CBT's massive data files.

Universities were slow in adapting to the changes. Investment textbooks began only recently to discuss the new instruments and then only at the introductory level. Now more sophistication is coming gradually into the classroom so that academia can catch up with Wall Street and LaSalle Street. Some universities decided early, with the help of financial institutions and the exchanges, to stay at the forefront of developments in the financial markets, however. Two excellent examples are *The Center for the Study of Futures Markets* at Columbia University and the *Salomon Brothers Center for the Study of Financial Institutions* at the Graduate School of Business Administration, New York University. The *Food Research Institute* at Stanford University continues to provide excellent studies and data on futures markets.

Books like this one represent initial steps on the road to integrating the seemingly divergent issues and investment vehicles and to make hedging/speculative vehicles a standard diet for finance and economics students at the undergraduate and graduate levels. More help is coming from college administrators who accept the changes and support research projects and courses in areas of futures, options, real estate, and other investment/speculative markets.

1.5 A PREVIEW OF THE CHAPTERS TO FOLLOW

The objective of the chapters to follow is to present an integrated, comprehensive treatment of the subjects under examination. Valuation models for the various vehicles are introduced. Some are slightly complex mathematically but should be examined if only to understand the relevant determining variables. Various strategies, some quite advanced,

for certain instruments and across instruments are presented along with ample, real examples.

Chapter 2 presents the basics of stock options. Two valuation models for call and put options are presented. A brief discussion of other forms of options such as warrants and stock rights is also presented.

Advanced options strategies are discussed in Chapter 3. They include combinations, spreads, arbitrage, and tax implications of option strategies. Likely consequences of each strategy are explored in detail.

Chapter 4 introduces interest options with a discussion of an existing instrument and another to be introduced by the Chicago Board of Trade (the GNMA option). Various strategies that can be used with these vehicles are discussed in detail.

Chapter 5 examines developments in commodities futures markets, and strategies that can be used in these markets. Some advanced strategies are discussed. Efficiency of the commodities markets and methods for pricing commodities futures contracts are also discussed and some definitive conclusions are presented.

Chapter 6 looks at financial futures, stock index futures, and their options. Several strategies are presented as well as methods for pricing some of these instruments. Efficiency of these markets and their influence on the underlying cash market and tax implications are examined.

Chapter 7 covers the foreign exchange markets: spot, forward, futures, and options. Ample examples are provided. The determinants of spot exchange rates are examined in detail as are the various hedging, arbitrage, and speculative strategies.

Chapter 8 considers investing in gems and collectibles, their fit in portfolios, and pitfalls and advantages of making them an integral part of an investment program.

Chapter 9 looks at various ways of investing in gold, factors influencing the price of gold, and the nature of and strategies in the gold futures market.

Chapter 10 examines various methods for participating in the real estate market. A comprehensive method for evaluating a real estate project is presented in addition to the tax consequences of real estate investment.

CONCLUSION

This chapter sets the tone of those chapters to follow. It provides an overview of major developments of the 1970s and 1980s and of various methods of coping with them. The dynamism and complexity of the financial and commodities markets are illustrated and made comprehensible in the chapters to follow.

PART
ONE

Stock and
Interest Options

CHAPTER 2

Fundamentals of Stock Options

2.1 AN OVERVIEW

The trading of options contracts had been going on for years before the Chicago Board Options Exchange (CBOE) began trading listed options on April 26, 1973. The market was an over-the-counter market with brokers attempting to match buyers and sellers.

Growth of options trading since 1973 has been phenomenal. From 1,119,177 contracts traded in 1973 and 5,682,907 contracts traded in 1974 options volume grew to 137,264,816 in 1982. Four exchanges—The CBOE, The American Stock Exchange, Inc., The Philadelphia Stock Exchange, Inc., and The Pacific Stock Exchange, Inc.—are currently participating in the vitality of the options market. Distribution of trading volume on the four exchanges appears in Table 2.1. In 1982, 55 percent of options trading was on the floor of the CBOE. The Amex options market was consistently a respectable second in terms of volume. The regional exchanges accounted for 17 percent of total volume. The distribution of the volume of trade by month and the size of open interest (number of contracts outstanding) on the CBOE are shown in Table 2.2.

The success of stock options led to the introduction of options on interest-bearing instruments and on futures contracts in 1982 and in 1983, respectively. These new options have met with considerable market acceptance as documented in the chapters to follow.

This chapter will concentrate on the simple strategies in options and on the pricing of call and put options. We leave the advanced options strategies and other option-related issues to Chapter 3.

2.2 DEFINITIONS

Option

An option is a contract that carries privileges and obligations and is executed at the discretion of its holder.

TABLE 2.1
Option Volume on All Exchanges

	1982	1981	1980	1979	1978
Total Share Volume:	137,264,816	109,405,782	96,728,546	64,264,863	57,231,018
CBOE share (in percent)	55.2	52.6	54.7	55.1	59.9
American Exchange	28.2	31.9	30.0	27.2	25.1
Philadelphia Exchange	9.8	9.1	8.0	7.7	5.7
Pacific Exchange	6.8	6.4	5.7	6.0	5.7
Midwest Exchange	—	—	1.6	4.1	3.5

Source: The Chicago Board Options Exchange, private release, February 1983. (CBOE has permitted use of this table, but has not participated in the preparation of this book and is not responsible for its contents.)

TABLE 2.2
Contract Volume and Open Interest in Contracts 1982–Equity Options (CBOE)

Time Period	All Classes Trading Days	Total	Daily Average	Volume High Day	Date	Low Day	Date	Open Interest Total Contracts
Jan.	20	6,343,617	317,181	411,457	15	207,827	22	3,799,786
Feb.	19	5,085,320	267,648	313,436	23	192,660	26	3,683,268
Mar.	23	6,359,726	276,510	427,691	9	183,704	30	3,681,911
Apr.	21	4,485,143	213,578	317,125	16	170,606	30	3,308,187
May	20	4,172,022	208,601	258,461	26	159,415	24	3,244,372
June	22	5,344,816	242,946	318,608	9	181,291	25	3,534,450
July	21	5,360,226	255,249	339,878	15	175,673	23	3,467,577
Aug.	22	8,361,187	380,054	596,181	18	215,676	2	4,251,058
Sept.	21	7,074,092	336,862	538,803	3	144,846	27	5,074,761
Oct.	21	8,882,289	422,966	666,457	12	232,480	4	4,991,928
Nov.	21	7,095,594	337,885	531,386	4	148,950	26	5,290,745
Dec.	22	7,157,573	325,344	—	—	—	—	5,610,671
Total for 1982		75,721,605	299,295					

Source: Chicago Board Options Exchange. Released January 1983. (CBOE has permitted use of this table, but has not participated in the preparation of this book and is not responsible for its contents.)

15

Call Option

An American call option gives its buyer, for a price called a premium, a right (option) to purchase at any time during the specified life of the contract 100 shares of the underlying security at a set price—the striking price (or exercise price). A European call has the same characteristics as an American call except that it is exercisable only upon expiration.

Put Option

A put option gives its buyer, for a price called a premium, the right to sell at any time during the specified life of the contract 100 shares of the underlying security at a set price—the striking price.

2.3 THE OPTIONS CLEARING CORPORATION

The Options Clearing Corporation (OCC) is owned equally by its clearing members: the Chicago Board Options Exchange, Inc.; the American Stock Exchange, Inc.; the Philadelphia Stock Exchange, Inc.; and the Pacific Stock Exchange, Inc.

The OCC serves as a clearing agency by interposing itself between the buyer and the seller of the option without interfering in the market mechanism for price determination. Buyers and sellers, through their brokers, arrive at the option price (premium) on the floor of the participating exchange. What the OCC does is, in effect, to make the buyer's contract not with the seller but rather with the OCC. The same applies to the seller, whose commitments are now to the OCC and not the buyer.

Options contracts traded by clearing members are issued by the OCC with their set expiration time and exercise price (striking price). Market price of the option as well as transactions costs are determined by the market. Each type of option is assigned to one of three expiration-month cycles: the January-April-July-October cycle, the February-May-August-November cycle, or the March-June-September-December cycle. A contract expiring in any of these months requires that notice of exercise be given to the OCC by 11:59 P.M. eastern standard time on the Saturday immediately following the third Friday of the expiration month. Each option has one striking price (price at which the underlying stock could be bought in a call or sold in a put), and one expiration date. A common stock can, therefore, have many options with different striking prices and different expiration dates written on it.

Standardization of the terms of options issued by the OCC, as well as issuance of the option contract by the OCC—which substitutes its ability to deliver on its commitments for that of the issuer—were intended to facilitate trading in the secondary market. Investors with option positions can choose to close out their positions at any time before the expiration date of their options simply by reversing the original position [sell if they had bought; buy if they had sold (written)].[1]

The OCC determines the exercise price of an option in the following manner: for a

---

[1] Selling an option is frequently referred to as writing an option. In this case, the option writer stands ready to buy the stock from the option holder in case of a put and to sell the stock to the option holder in case of a call at a fixed price during a specified period of time.

given expiration month, OCC selects two exercise prices surrounding the market price (e.g., 35 and 40 for a stock selling at 38). It then introduces new contracts with different striking prices as warranted by the movements of the market price of the stock—a new contract with a striking price of 30 if the market price of the stock falls to 32. New exercise prices may be set for one month or for every month of the expiration month cycle.[2] The usual intervals between striking prices are 5 points ($5) for stocks trading below $50 a share, 10 points for stocks trading between $50 and $200, and 20 points for securities trading above $200.

Upon receipt of an exercise notice from an option holder, the OCC, with a pool of options it can call on to answer the notice, selects at random on a first-in/first-out basis or on any other basis that is fair and equitable from among all clearing member accounts with outstanding obligations on options with the exact characteristics as those being exercised. The clearing member, in turn, selects at random from the accounts of its clients with outstanding obligations on the option that is being exercised. The chosen client (the option seller or writer) would, therefore, have to deliver a security (100 shares per option contract) in the case of a call or buy a security in the case of a put. The terms for delivery are exactly as specified on their contract except for adjustments because of dividends, distributions, stock splits, recapitalizations, or reorganizations with respect to the underlying security. No adjustment is made for the declaration or payment of cash distributions. Stock splits, stock dividends, and other stock distributions increase the number of underlying shares and accordingly reduce the striking price of the option. If the underlying security were split two for one, a call option covering 100 shares with a striking price of $30 would turn into two options of 100 shares each at a striking price of $15. The number of options was adjusted in this case because the adjustment in the underlying security resulted in a new round lot. If not, the number of outstanding options would remain the same, with a different number of underlying shares and a different striking price. If a three-to-two stock dividend is declared, an option on 100 shares of stock with a $60 striking price becomes an option on 150 shares with a striking price of $40.

There are two classes of options: one class consisting of all the calls on an underlying stock and the other of all the puts on the same underlying stock. Options are opened for trading in rotation. As trading in the underlying stock opens on any exchange, the options on that stock then go into opening rotation on the options exchange. Once traded, options require settlement in one day: the trade settles on the next business day after the trade.

Investors with interest in the options market are limited by the OCC as to the size of their position. No single investor or group of investors acting in concert may own more than an aggregate (on all clearing member exchanges combined) of 1,000 puts and calls on the same side of the market in the underlying security. A call sold is on the same side of the market as a put purchased. Also restricted is the number of options contracts which can be exercised in a particular time period. The limit is set by the exchange.

We advise the reader to examine the OCC prospectus for additional details on the issues covered above and other pertinent issues. The prospectus is available free of charge from any brokerage house.

---

[2] For additional information on this and many issues relating to options, the reader should consult the prospectus of the OCC.

TABLE 2.3
Listed Options Quotations (January 13, 1983)

Most Active Options

CHICAGO BOARD OPTIONS EXCHANGE

	Sales	Last	Chg.	N.Y. Close
CALLS				
Teldyn Jan150	6491	2 5-16	+13-16	144⅛
I B M Jan100	5858	1 11-16	+ ⅛	98¼
Teldyn Jan140	5672	7½	+ 3	144⅛
Am Tel Jan65	4428	1	+ 7-16	65½
Eas Kd Jan85	4105	⅞	− 1	82⅞
PUTS				
Eas Kd Jan85	3102	2⅞	+15-16	82⅞
Teldyn Jan140	2668	2 7-16	−1 9-16	144⅛
I B M Jan95	2561	13-16	− ¼	98¼
Eas Kd Jan80	2443	9-16	+ ¼	82⅞
Teldyn Jan130	1781	½	− ¾	144⅛

AMERICAN STOCK EXCHANGE

	Sales	Last	Chg.	N.Y. Close
CALLS				
Proc G Jan95	4716	16	− 3	110⅝
Proc G Jan100	2954	10⅞	− 1⅝	110⅝
Dig Eq Jan100	2933	3¼	+ 1⅛	100¾
Proc G Jan90	2455	21½	− 2½	110⅝
Tandy Jan50	1795	1⅞	+ 7-16	50⅜
PUTS				
Dig Eq Jan90	968	3-16	− 3-16	100¾
Dig Eq Jan100	949	2¼	− ¾	100¾
Dig Eq Jan95	875	¾	− 9-16	100¾
Dig Eq Apr90	761	4	− ⅝	100¾
Tandy Jan50	656	1 7-16	−1 1-16	50⅜

PHILADELPHIA STOCK EXCHANGE

	Sales	Last	Chg.	N.Y. Close
CALLS				
DomeM Aug20	2839	6¼	+ ¾	20½
La Lnd Feb30	1918	15-16	....	26⅞
La Lnd Feb25	1780	2⅞	....	26⅞
DomeM May20	1762	4½	+ ⅜	20½
DomeM Feb20	1260	2½	+ ⅜	20½
PUTS				
La Lnd Feb20	585	1-16	....	26⅞
Bendix Feb75	500	⅝	+ ¼	84
Comsat Jan55	400	1-16	....	75⅜
Comsat Jan60	400	1-16	....	75⅜
DomeM May20	378	3¾	+ ⅛	20½

PACIFIC STOCK EXCHANGE

	Sales	Last	Chg.	N.Y. Close
CALLS				
ShellO May45	1119	1¾	− ⅛	40¾
Wang B Apr35	1109	3	− ⅛	32¾
D Sham Jan25	778	½	− 1-16	25⅛
Wang B Jan30	653	3	− ½	32¾
DorchG Feb10	510•	2⅞	+ 9-16	12½
PUTS				
Wang B Jan27½	790	1-16	....	32¾
Wang B Apr30	686	2	+ ⅛	32¾
Un Oil Jan30	404	13-16	+ 1-16	29⅝
Lockhd Mar80	361	3½	− ⅜	83⅛
Wang B Jan30	348	¼	....	32¾

Chicago Board

Option & NY Close	Strike Price	Calls—Last			Puts—Last		
		Jan	**Apr**	**Jul**	**Jan**	**Apr**	**Jul**
Alcoa	25	8¼	8½	r	1-16	9-16	r
33¼	30	3	4½	5	1-16	1½	2
33¼	35	3-16	1⅞	3	1⅞	r	4¾
Am Tel	50	r	15½	s	1-16	⅛	s
65½	55	10⅜	10¾	11	1-16	⅜	r
65½	60	5⅝	6⅜	7	1-16	1 1-16	2⅛
65½	65	1	2¾	3¾	⅝	2¾	3¾
65½	70	s	1¼	1¾	s	r	6
Atl R	30	15½	r	r	r	r	r
44⅝	35	10	11	r	r	5-16	13-16
44⅝	40	4¾	6	8	1-16	1⅛	1⅝
44⅝	45	⅝	2⅝	3¾	⅞	3⅛	3¼
44⅝	50	1-16	1⅜	3	5	6	r
44⅝	55	r	⅝	r	r	r	r
Avon	20	r	r	r	r	⅛	r
29⅝	25	4⅞	5⅛	6⅛	r	r	1⅜
29⅝	30	5-16	2	2⅝	⅝	2 7-16	2½
29⅝	35	s	⅝	1⅛	s	r	r
BankAm	15	6½	r	7	r	r	r
21⅝	20	1⅝	2¼	3⅛	⅛	¾	1¼
21⅝	25	1-16	⅝	1	r	r	r
21⅝	30	r	5-16	½	r	r	r
Beth S	15	r	6½	r	r	⅛	r
21¼	20	1⅜	2⅝	3⅝	⅛	1	1½
21¼	25	1-16	15-16	1½	3	r	r
Burl N	40	22¼	r	s	r	r	s
62¼	45	17¼	18	18	r	r	r
62¼	50	12	r	14	r	⅝	r
62¼	55	7¼	8¾	10	r	1½	2¾
62¼	60	2½	5¼	6⅞	½	3	r
62¼	65	7-16	3⅜	4¾	r	5¾	6
CIGNA	40	5½	r	r	r	r	r
45½	45	1⅛	3¼	4	¾	r	r
45½	50	⅛	1⅜	2⅝	r	r	r
Citicp	25	r	11	s	r	5-16	s
35⅞	30	6	6¾	r	r	r	1 1-16
35⅞	35	1⅝	3½	4¼	11-16	2¼	2 13-16
35⅞	40	⅛	1⅜	2¼	3⅞	5	r
35⅞	45	r	11-16	r	r	r	r
Delta	30	13	13¼	14½	s	s	s
42½	40	2⅞	s	s	s	s	s
42½	35	8	9	r	1-16	1	1¼
42½	40	s	6	7⅜	¼	2 5-16	3
42½	45	⅝	3⅛	4⅝	2¾	4½	r
42½	50	3-16	1 9-16	4	r	r	r
Eas Kd	70	13¾	r	s	r	1	s
82⅞	75	8¾	11¾	s	1-16	2	s
82⅞	80	3½	7⅝	r	9-16	4	5½
82⅞	85	⅞	5	7¼	2⅞	6¼	7¾
82⅞	90	3-16	3¼	5⅝	7⅛	9	10⅜
82⅞	95	1-16	2	4¼	11⅞	r	r
82⅞	100	1-16	1	3	17	r	r
Eckerd	25	¼	1⅝	3	r	r	r
23¾	30	r	⅝	1½	r	r	r
Engelh	25	11	r	r	r	r	r
35⅞	30	6¼	6½	8	r	r	r
35⅞	35	1 3-16	3⅞	5	⅝	2½	r
Exxon	25	5⅝	5¾	r	1-16	3-16	⅜
30⅝	30	¾	1⅝	2 3-16	3-16	1 3-16	1⅝
30⅝	35	1-16	⅜	11-16	r	r	r
FedExp	40	39½	40½	s	1-16	⅛	s
79½	45	34¾	36	s	1-16	⅛	s
79½	50	30	30	s	r	5-16	s
79½	55	25	26¾	r	r	½	1¼
79½	60	20	21⅝	22¾	1-16	⅞	1⅞
79½	65	14¾	17¾	20	1-16	1⅞	2½
79½	70	10	14	r	⅛	3	4⅝
79½	75	5¾	10¾	13¾	½	4⅞	6½
79½	80	2 1-16	7½	10½	2 5-16	6⅞	9
Fluor	15	9	9⅝	10½	r	r	r
24¼	20	4¼	5	5½	r	¾	1½
24¼	25	½	2¼	3⅛	1¼	2⅝	3⅛
24¼	30	s	¾	r	s	r	r
Gt Wst	15	10¼	10¼	s	r	r	s
24⅝	20	5	6	6¾	r	r	1
24⅝	25	15-16	2⅜	3½	⅝	r	r
Halbtn	25	13⅛	r	r	r	r	r
37⅞	30	8	8¾	r	r	r	r
37⅞	35	2⅞	4½	6	1-16	1⅞	2½
37⅞	40	7-16	2⅜	3¾	2¾	4½	r
Hitachi	30	6	r	r	r	r	2½
35⅝	35	⅞	r	r	r	r	r
35⅝	40	s	1½	r	s	r	r
Homstk	20	41¾	r	s	r	r	s
61¾	25	r	36⅜	s	1-16	⅛	s
61¾	30	31	32	s	r	⅛	s
61¾	35	26½	27½	28	r	r	⅝
61¾	40	21½	22	24⅜	1-16	7-16	⅞
61¾	45	16¾	17¾	20	r	¾	1⅜
61¾	50	12¼	14	16⅛	1-16	1½	2⅝
61¾	55	7¼	11	13½	¼	2 13-16	4⅛
61¾	60	s	8½	11	s	5⅜	6¾
61¾	65	s	6½	9	s	7¾	9⅛

Option & NY Close	Strike Price	Calls—Last			Puts—Last		
		Jan	**Apr**	**Jul**	**Jan**	**Apr**	
39¼	45	s	11-16	1¼	s	6	r
Xerox	25	r	15¼	s	r	r	s
40¾	30	10½	r	r	r	¼	11-16
40¾	35	5⅞	6½	r	r	¾	1⅜
40¾	40	1⅜	3⅜	4⅜	11-16	2¾	3½
40¾	45	1-16	1⅜	2⅜	4⅜	5⅝	6½
		Feb	**May**	**Aug**	**Feb**	**May**	**Aug**
Amdahl	20	r	r	s	r	½	s
31¾	25	7¼	8¾	r	⅜	1½	2
31¾	30	3½	5½	r	1 11-16'	3¼	r
31¾	35	1 3-16	3	4½	4¼	r	6
A E P	15	r	4	r	r	r	r
19	20	1-16	⅜	11-16	r	r	r
Am Hos	35	4½	r	r	⅝	r	r
38⅜	40	1	r	3¾	2⅝	3¾	5
38⅜	45	3-16	1¼	2⅜	r	r	r
A M P	45	r	r	s	1-16	r	s
73	60	13⅞	r	r	r	r	r
73	65	r	r	r	1	r	r
73	70	r	8	r	r	r	r
73	75	2⅝	5½	r	4½	6¾	r
Bally o	25	2	r	s	r	r	s
Baxter	30	r	s	s	1-16	s	s
47½	45	4½	r	r	⅞	2¼	r
47½	50	1 1-16	2 9-16	r	2¾	r	r
47½	55	3-16	1¼	r	r	r	r
Blk Dk	15	4	4¼	r	r	r	r
18⅝	20	½	1⅜	2⅛	r	r	r
Boeing	15	r	r	s	1-16	r	s
36⅝	20	16⅝	16¾	s	1-16	r	s
36⅝	25	11¾	11¾	r	1-16	5-16	r
36⅝	30	6⅞	7½	8¼	⅛	⅞	1⅝
36⅝	35	2 9-16	4⅛	5⅛	1⅛	2¼	3⅜
36⅝	40	11-16	1⅞	2 15-16	r	5	r
Bois C	25	r	r	s	1-16	r	s
40¼	30	10½	r	r	r	r	r
40¼	35	r	6¾	7¼	9-16	r	r
40¼	40	2½	4	r	2⅛	r	r
40¼	45	1	r	r	r	6	r
C B S	45	r	r	s	3-16	r	s
58¾	50	r	r	s	9-16	r	s
58¾	55	5	6¾	r	1 9-16	3¼	r
58¾	60	r	4⅜	r	r	r	r
58¾	65	r	2½	3¾	r	r	r
CapCit	65	60	s	s	1-16	s	s
124½	70	55⅛	r	s	⅛	r	s
124½	75	51⅛	r	s	r	r	s
124½	80	45	r	s	⅛	r	s
124½	85	40⅛	r	s	⅛	r	s
124½	110	r	r	r	2½	5	r
124½	120	9¼	r	r	5⅜	r	r
124½	130	3¾	r	r	r	r	r
124½	140	1¼	5⅜	r	r	r	r
Cessna	15	9½	10¼	s	r	r	s
24⅜	20	4½	r	r	r	r	1½
24⅜	25	1¼	2¼	r	2	2 15-16	r
24⅜	30	3-16	r	1⅝	r	r	r
Coke	35	13½	r	s	r	r	s
48	40	8¾	r	11	⅛	⅝	r
48	45	4	5½	r	⅞	1¾	2½
48	50	1¼	2⅝	4½	2⅞	4	r
48	55	⅝	1¼	2½	6¼	r	r
Colgat	15	r	5⅜	r	r	r	r
19⅞	20	⅝	1⅜	2	⅞	1⅜	r
19⅞	25	⅛	½	⅞	r	r	r
Cmw Ed	20	r	6¼	r	r	r	r
26⅛	25	1⅜	1 13-16	2¼	⅛	9-16	15-16
26⅛	30	1-16	⅛	7-16	r	r	r
CtIIII	15	r	r	r	⅛	5-16	r
21	20	1⅝	2¾	3½	¾	1⅜	2
21	25	5-16	13-16	1⅜	4¼	4¼	r
C Data	20	21½	r	s	r	r	s
41½	25	16	16½	s	1-16	r	s
41½	30	10¾	r	s	⅛	⅞	s
41½	35	7¼	8¼	9⅝	11-16	1¾	r
41½	40	3⅝	5¾	6½	1⅞	3⅝	r
41½	45	1 3-16	3⅜	r	r	6⅞	r
CornGl	50	23½	r	s	r	9-16	s
72½	55	r	20	r	3-16	r	1½
72½	60	13¼	14¾	r	r	r	r
72½	65	8½	10½	r	⅞	2¼	r
72½	70	4½	7	8¼	2	4	r
72½	75	s	4	5½	s	6	r
Datapt	10	10	r	s	r	⅛	s
20	15	5¼	6½	7¼	¼	¾	1 1-16
20	20	1¾	3⅛	3¾	1⅜	2 9-16	3⅛
20	25	⅜	1 7-16	2 7-16	r	r	r
Diebld	45	r	r	s	r	¼	s
81¾	55	r	r	s	1-16	⅝	s
81¾	60	23½	r	s	⅛	r	s
81¾	65	r	r	r	⅜	r	r
81¾	70	13¾	r	r	⅞	3	r
81¾	75	9	r	r	1¾	4½	r
81¾	80	5¾	9½	12½	4	7	r
81¾	85	s	6½	r	s	r	r

Option & NY Close	Strike Price	Calls—Last			Puts—Last		
		Feb	**May**	**Aug**	**Feb**	**May**	**Aug**
60	65	s	2½	r	s	6¾	r
J Walt	25	12¼	r	s	r	r	s
37⅛	30	7½	r	r	r	r	r
37⅛	35	2⅞	4¾	r	¾	r	r
37⅛	40	1⅛	2⅝	r	r	r	r
WarnCm	25	5½	7	8⅛	7-16	1 7-16	2
29⅝	30	2¼	4¼	5½	2 5-16	3⅝	4⅝
29⅝	35	15-16	2⅝	3⅝	6	7	7¾
29⅝	40	7-16	1 9-16	2⅝	10¼	10½	11
29⅝	45	3-16	1 1-16	1⅝	15¼	14⅝	r
29⅝	50	⅛	9-16	1¼	20¼	r	r
29⅝	55	1-16	7-16	⅞	25¼	r	r
29⅝	60	1-16	¼	⅝	29⅞	r	r
Willms	15	4¼	4⅞	5¼	r	r	¾
19⅛	20	13-16	1¾	2½	1⅞	r	r
19⅛	25	⅛	½	s	r	r	s
		Mar	**Jun**	**Sep**	**Mar**	**Jun**	**Sep**
Apache	10	2	3	3⅛	½	r	1
11½	15	5-16	⅞	1	r	r	r
BrisMy	50	r	s	s	1-16	s	s
65¾	60	7½	r	10	13-16	2	r
65¾	65	3¾	6	r	2⅜	r	r
65¾	70	2	3¾	5½	5¾	r	r
65¾	75	¾	2 1-16	r	r	r	r
Bruns	25	2⅛	3½	4¼	1⅛	r	r
26⅛	30	¾	1½	r	r	5	r
Celan	40	11½	r	r	5-16	r	r
49¼	45	4¾	r	r	1¾	r	r
49¼	50	2½	r	r	2½	r	r
49¼	55	1 1-16	1¾	r	r	r	r
Chamln	15	10½	r	r	r	r	r
24⅞	20	5	r	r	3-16	r	r
24⅞	25	1¼	2½	3¼	1⅜	2	r
24⅞	30	5-16	⅞	1½	r	r	r
CompSc	15	3⅛	r	r	⅞	r	1¼
17¼	20	¾	1⅝	r	3¼	r	r
17¼	25	¼	r	s	r	r	s
Dow Ch	15	13¾	s	s	r	s	s
28⅞	20	8⅞	r	r	⅛	r	r
28⅞	25	4¼	5⅛	5½	½	r	r
28⅞	30	1 5-16	2½	3	2 7-16	3⅜	3⅜
28⅞	35	¼	11-16	1¼	r	r	r
Esmark	55	r	r	r	2¼	r	r
59¼	60	3½	r	r	r	r	r
Esmk o	40	18	r	s	r	r	s
Ford	20	r	s	s	1-16	s	s
38⅝	25	14	15½	s	1-16	¼	s
38⅝	30	9½	r	r	5-16	11-16	1 3-16
38⅝	35	5⅛	7	8	1 5-16	2	r
38⅝	40	2 7-16	4¼	5	3½	4	r
38⅝	45	⅞	2⅜	3⅝	6⅞	7½	r
Gen El	70	28½	r	s	¼	r	s
96⅞	75	23⅜	r	s	5-16	r	s
96⅞	80	19	r	s	7-16	1	s
96⅞	85	13½	r	17	⅞	1⅞	3
96⅞	90	9	11½	r	1⅞	r	r
96⅞	95	6	r	r	3⅞	5¾	r
96⅞	100	3¾	6¾	r	6¾	r	r
96⅞	110	1	3	5	r	r	r
G M	40	24⅛	s	s	1-16	s	s
64	45	19	r	s	1-16	⅜	s
64	50	14	15	s	3-16	r	s
64	55	9⅝	11¼	12¼	⅝	1⅝	r
64	60	5¾	7¾	9¼	1⅞	3⅛	4⅜
64	65	2 13-16	5	6¼	3⅞	5⅝	r
Glf Wn	15	2 15-16	3½	3⅞	r	r	r
17½	20	5-16	⅞	1 3-16	r	r	r
HughTl	15	8⅜	8¾	r	⅛	¼	r
23⅜	20	4	5	5⅞	⅜	1¼	1⅝
23⅜	25	1⅝	2 11-16	3⅜	3	3⅝	4
I T T	25	7⅛	r	r	r	r	½
31⅝	30	2¼	2¾	3⅜	r	1 3-16	r
31⅝	35	½	1	1¼	r	r	r
K mart	15	9	s	s	r	s	s
23⅝	20	4¼	4⅞	5	½	⅞	1
23⅝	25	1	2	2¾	2½	2¾	r
23⅝	30	5-16	⅝	s	r	r	s
Lifemk	40	1½	3	r	r	r	r
35¾	45	¾	r	s	r	r	s
Litton	40	17	17¾	s	1-16	½	s
57⅛	45	12½	r	r	7-16	r	r
57⅛	50	8¼	10¼	11	1 1-16	2½	4½
57⅛	55	4¾	6⅝	r	2 9-16	4½	r
57⅛	60	2½	4½	r	r	r	r
57⅛	34⅜	22⅝	s	s	r	s	s
57⅛	49	9	s	s	r	s	s
MaryK	40	r	r	s	⅝	1⅜	s
54½	45	r	r	r	1⅜	3	4
54½	50	7½	r	r	3	5	6½
54½	55	4¾	r	r	5	r	r
54½	60	2⅝	4⅞	r	r	r	r
McDn o	53⅜	6¾	r	s	1⅜	2⅛	s
Mc Don	50	r	r	12¾	⅝	r	r
57⅝	55	5⅝	r	9	2	r	r
57⅝	60	2⅝	4½	r	4¼	r	r

TABLE 2.3 (*Continued*)

I B M	55	43¾	s	s	r	s	s
98¼	60	38¾	38⅞	s	1-16	r	s
98¼	65	34¼	34	s	r	1-16	s
98¼	70	28⅜	29¼	s	r	3-16	s
98¼	75	23⅝	24½	25¼	r	⅜	15-16
98¼	80	18⅝	20⅛	21¾	1-16	¾	2
98¼	85	13⅝	15⅝	17½	1-16	1½	3⅛
98¼ ↔	90	8¾	12⅝	15	1-16	2¾	4½
98¼	95	4⅝	9⅛	12	13-16	4⅝	7
98¼	100	1 11-16	6¾	9⅜	2¾	7½	9¼
In Min	35	⅞	2	3½	r	2⅜	r
In Pap	35	17¼	r	s	r	r	s
52	40	11⅞	r	r	r	r	r
52	45	7¼	8	8⅞	r	1	2¼
52	50	2⅜	4	r	½	2	r
52	55	¼	2	2⅝	r	4½	r
John J	35	13¾	14	r	r	r	r
48¾	40	9	9¼	10½	1-16	½	r
48¾	45	3⅞	5¾	7	⅛	1⅜	1 9-16
48¾	50	½	2¾	4¼	1¾	3¼	3¾
48¾	55	s	1⅛	2 1-16	s	6½	r
Kerr M	25	5	6	r	r	⅝	1
29⅝	30	9-16	2⅜	3½	1 1-16	2½	r
29⅝	35	⅛	1 1-16	2	r	r	r
Loral	35	r	10¼	r	r	r	r
44½	40	4½	6¾	r	r	r	r
44½	45	⅞	3¾	r	r	3¼	r
44½	50	r	2	r	r	6¾	r
Merck	60	24	r	s	1-16	r	s
84½	65	20⅜	r	s	r	r	s
84½	70	14¼	r	s	1-16	r	s
84½	75	r	r	r	r	1⅛	r
84½	80	5	8⅜	11	⅜	2 15-16	r
84½	85	1½	5	7¾	1⅞	5	r
84½	90	⅜	2¾	4½	6½	6¾	r
M M M	55	r	23⅝	s	r	⅛	s
78⅜	60	18½	19	s	r	⅜	s
78⅜	65	13½	14	r	r	¾	r
78⅜	70	8⅜	10	11½	1-16	1¾	r
78⅜	75	3⅝	6¾	r	¼	3	r
78⅜	80	⅝	3⅝	5¾	2¼	5¼	r
Monsan	65	r	19¼	s	r	r	s
82⅞	70	14	r	15	r	¾	r
82⅞	75	9	10½	11¾	r	1 15-16	r
82⅞	80	3	7	8⅝	¼	2¾	r
82⅞	85	1	3⅞	r	3	5⅝	r
82⅞	90	¼	2½	4⅝	r	7¾	r
Nw Air	30	r	r	r	r	⅜	r
45⅜	35	10½	11¼	r	r	⅜	1¼
45⅜	40	r	r	r	r	1½	r
45⅜	45	1⅛	r	r	1⅛	3⅝	r
45⅜	50	⅛	2⅜	r	r	6⅜	r
45⅜	55	r	1⅛	3⅛	r	9½	r
PaineW	30	s	r	r	s	⅜	r
41⅜	35	r	r	8	1-16	1⅞	r
41⅜	40	1¾	5	6	⅜	3⅛	r
41⅜	45	7-16	3	4	r	6¼	r
PalW o	33¾	7	r	r	r	r	r
41⅜	37½	3⅝	r	7½	r	r	r
41⅜	41¼	9-16	4	r	r	r	r
Pennz	25	11¾	11¾	r	1-16	3-16	r
36⅞	30	6⅞	7⅜	8	1-16	7-16	1
36⅞	35	2 3-16	3¾	4¾	¼	1¾	2⅞
36⅞	40	¼	1 11-16	2⅝	3⅛	4⅝	5½
36⅞	45	1-16	s	s	8¼	s	s
Pepsi	30	s	r	7½	s	r	⅞
35½	35	⅞	3⅛	4	7-16	2 1-16	2¾
35½	40	1-16	1⅛	2⅛	4¼	4¾	5¼
35½	45	r	9-16	1 3-16	9¼	r	r
35½	50	1-16	3-16	r	r	r	r
Polar	15	13½	r	s	r	r	s
28⅜	20	8⅛	8¾	r	r	⅜	r
28⅜	25	3¼	4½	5⅜	1-16	1⅛	1¾
28⅜	30	5-16	1 15-16	2⅞	1⅞	3½	r
Sabn o	30	10½	11	r	r	r	r
36⅝	35	5⅝	r	r	1-16	r	r
18⅜	40	1¼	r	r	r	r	r
Sabine	20	s	1	r	s	r	r
SouPac	35	4¾	r	r	r	r	r
39⅞	40	¾	2¾	r	r	2¾	r
39⅞	45	r	1	r	r	r	r
Sperry	25	9	9½	r	1-16	r	11-16
34⅛	30	4⅛	5⅛	6	r	⅞	r
34⅛	35	⅜	2⅛	3¼	1⅜	3	r
34⅛	40	1-16	15-16	1⅜	r	r	r
Squibb	35	9¾	r	s	r	r	s
44½	40	5	6	r	r	¾	1½
44½	45	½	2½	3¾	⅞	2½	r
44½	50	1-16	1	2¼	r	r	r
44½	55	r	⅜	r	r	r	r
StorTec	15	9⅜	9¾	r	r	5-16	r
24⅛	20	4⅛	5⅝	6¼	1-16	1	1⅝
24⅛	25	⅝	2½	4	1⅜	3	3⅞
24⅛	30	1-16	1	2 1-16	r	r	6
Teldyn	65	77½	r	s	r	⅛	s
144⅛	70	72⅞	r	s	1-16	r	s
144⅛	75	69½	r	s	1-16	r	s
144⅛	80	63	64⅝	s	1-16	5-16	s
144⅛	85	58	60	s	1-16	r	s
144⅛	90	55½	55	s	1-16	⅝	s
144⅛	95	49	51¾	s	r	13-16	s
144⅛	100	43¾	45	s	1-16	1⅛	s
144⅛	110	34½	36½	40	1-16	2¼	4¼
144⅛	120	25	29½	36	3-16	4½	7
144⅛	130	15¾	23½	27	½	7¼	11
144⅛	140	7½	17½	22⅜	2 7-16	11	15¾
144⅛	150	2 5-16	12⅛	18	8	16½	r
Tex In	80	56	r	s	r	r	s
137½	85	52	r	s	1-16	7-16	s
137½	90	47	r	s	r	9-16	s
137½	95	42	r	s	1-16	¾	s
137½	100	36	r	r	1-16	1¼	2 9-16
137½	110	27	30	r	1-16	2⅝	r
137½	120	17	23	r	⅛	4½	r
137½	130	8½	17½	21½	1	8¼	12
137½	140	2⅞	12	r	5¼	13¾	r
137½	150	½	7½	13	14⅛	20½	r
137½	160	1-16	4⅞	8⅜	r	r	r
Upjohn	45	r	6½	7½	r	1¼	r
50½	50	1¼	3⅜	4¾	1	2¾	r
50½	55	¼	1½	r	r	6	r
Weyerh	30	10⅛	10¼	r	r	⅜	⅝
39¼	35	4¾	5⅝	r	1-16	¾	r
39¼	40	½	2½	3¼	⅞	2½	r
FptMcM	10	r	11¼	r	r	r	r
21⅝	15	6½	7	7⅜	1-16	⅜	9-16
21⅝	20	2¼	3½	4¼	¾	1¾	2 3-16
21⅝	25	s	1½	2½	s	4½	r
GnAOil	30	13⅞	r	r	r	r	r
44	35	8⅞	9	r	9-16	¾	r
44	40	4	4	4	3½	r	r
44	45	¼	⅜	r	8⅜	8⅛	r
44	50	1-16	r	r	12¼	r	r
Gn Dyn	20	14¼	s	s	r	s	s
34⅜	25	9½	10	r	1-16	¼	11-16
34⅜	30	5¼	6¼	6¾	9-16	1 5-16	2¼
34⅜	35	1⅞	3½	4½	2⅛	3¾	r
34⅜	40	⅜	1½	s	6	r	s
Gen Fd	35	3¼	3¾	r	7-16	r	r
37¼	40	½	r	r	3⅛	3½	r
37¼	45	⅛	¾	r	r	r	r
37¼	50	1-16	r	r	r	r	r
Harris	20	r	r	s	1-16	r	s
40½	30	11	r	r	r	r	r
40½	35	6¼	7¾	r	⅜	r	r
40½	40	2¼	4¼	r	1	r	r
40½	45	s	2	3⅜	s	r	r
Hewlet	40	37	r	s	1-16	r	s
77¾	45	32½	33¼	s	1-16	r	s
77¾	50	27½	28	s	1-16	r	s
77¾	55	22⅝	r	s	⅛	11-16	s
77¾	60	17½	r	s	⅛	1⅜	s
77¾	65	r	r	r	½	2⅜	r
77¾	70	9⅜	12½	r	1⅛	3⅜	r
77¾	75	6	9⅜	11⅞	2½	5½	7
77¾	80	3¼	6¾	9¾	5½	r	r
77¾	85	1⅝	4¾	7¾	8½	r	r
H Inns	25	r	15	s	r	¼	s
38⅝	30	9¾	r	r	1-16	⅝	⅞
38⅝	35	4⅝	7	7½	9-16	1¾	r
38⅝	40	1½	3⅜	4	2⅝	3½	r
Honwll	60	34½	r	s	1-16	5-16	s
92⅞	70	23¼	25	s	3-16	1¼	s
92⅞	75	18¾	r	s	⅜	2⅜	s
92⅞	80	14¾	r	r	⅞	3½	5
92⅞	85	10	14	r	1 15-16	5⅛	r
92⅞	90	7⅛	11	r	3⅝	6¾	r
92⅞	95	4¾	8¾	11¾	6	r	r
92⅞	100	2 11-16	6¼	r	9¼	r	r
92⅞	110	13-16	3¾	5½	17	r	r
Humana	40	6	7⅛	9	½	1⅝	r
45	45	2	4⅜	6½	2⅛	3¾	r
45	50	¾	2	4	r	6¼	r
In Flv	25	r	r	r	½	r	r
27½	30	7-16	r	r	r	r	r
Manvil	10	2¼	3⅛	s	⅜	½	s
12	15	½	1 3-16	s	r	r	s
Medtrn	40	15⅛	15½	s	r	1⅛	s
53⅝	45	8⅞	r	r	r	1⅝	r
53⅝	50	5	r	r	r	r	r
53⅝	55	2⅜	r	r	r	r	r
53⅝	60	r	r	4	r	r	r
Mobil	20	r	6	6	r	¼	r
25¾	25	1⅜	2 1-16	2 11-16	⅝	r	1¾
25¾	30	3-16	⅝	1 1-16	r	r	r
N Semi	15	12⅛	r	r	1-16	⅜	r
27	20	7½	8¼	9¼	¼	1 1-16	1⅝
27	25	3⅛	5	5½	1⅜	2¾	3¼
27	30	15-16	2 7-16	3⅝	4	4½	r
Nthrop	45	28½	r	s	⅛	r	s
75⅛	50	r	25½	s	r	r	s
75⅛	55	19	r	r	¼	r	r
75⅛	60	15¼	r	r	½	r	r
75⅛	65	11⅝	r	r	1¼	r	r
75⅛	70	8	10¼	r	1⅞	4½	r
75⅛	75	5	r	r	3¾	6¼	r
75⅛	80	3	6	8	r	r	r
Occi	15	r	6	r	1-16	¼	½
20⅞	20	1 5-16	2	2 7-16	7-16	r	1⅝
20⅞	25	⅛	7-16	15-16	r	r	r
Ow Ill	25	4⅛	r	r	r	r	r
28⅞	30	1	2	r	r	r	r
28⅞	35	s	r	⅞	s	r	r
Raythn	35	r	r	r	⅛	r	r
45½	40	6	7½	r	r	1¼	r
45½	45	2½	4½	r	1 9-16	3½	r
45½	50	¾	2¼	3⅞	r	6⅝	r
Rynlds	45	6	r	r	r	r	r
51	50	2¼	4½	r	r	r	r
51	55	½	1⅜	3	r	r	r
Rockwl	35	10⅜	r	s	1-16	9-16	s
45¼	40	5⅞	6¾	r	¾	1¾	2½
45¼	45	2	3⅝	r	2¼	3⅝	5
45¼	50	⅜	1½	r	r	r	6½
Safewy	40	r	r	r	r	r	1⅝
44¼	45	1 11-16	3	r	r	r	r
Slumb	25	24¼	23¾	s	r	r	s
48½	30	19¼	r	s	r	r	s
48½	35	14	14¼	r	1-16	r	r
48½	40	9⅜	r	11½	3-16	11-16	1⅜
48½	45	5	7	8¼	11-16	2	r
48½	50	2⅛	4⅜	5¾	2¾	4⅝	5½
48½	55	s	2 5-16	4	s	r	r
Skylin	15	r	r	s	1-16	r	s
24⅞	20	5⅝	r	r	r	r	¾
24⅞	25	1⅜	2⅞	3⅞	1¼	2⅜	r
24⅞	30	½	1 7-16	r	r	r	r
Southn	15	1 3-16	1 5-16	1 7-16	r	r	r
16¼	20	r	1-16	r	r	r	r
St Ind	35	9¾	r	r	r	9-16	1
44⅜	40	5	6½	7⅛	9-16	1½	2½
44⅜	45	1 11-16	3¼	4¼	2½	3⅝	4½
44⅜	50	⅜	1½	2⅜	r	6½	r
Tidewt	20	r	9	r	r	r	r
27⅞	25	3⅞	6	r	⅝	1¾	r
27⅞	30	1¼	3¼	4⅝	r	r	r
U A L	20	11⅞	r	s	r	r	s
31½	25	7½	8	r	5-16	1½	2 3-16
31½	30	3⅜	4¾	r	1½	3	r
31½	35	15-16	2¼	3½	4½	5¼	r
31½	40	3-16	1	2	r	r	r
U Tech	35	25⅞	s	s	1-16	s	s
60	40	21	r	s	1-16	r	s
60	45	15⅝	15¾	s	r	r	s
60	50	10⅞	r	12⅛	r	r	r
60	55	6¼	7¾	r	¾	2¼	r
60	60	2⅝	4½	5¾	2⅜	4	r
57⅝	65	1	2½	4½	r	r	[illegible]
57⅝	70	½	1⅝	s	r	r	s
Mid SU	15	13-16	15-16	1⅛	r	⅜	½
15½	20	1-16	r	⅛	4½	r	r
N C R	50	42	s	s	⅛	s	s
91½	55	37⅛	s	s	¼	s	s
91½	60	r	r	s	r	½	s
91½	65	r	r	s	¼	¾	s
91½	70	r	25¾	s	½	1¼	s
91½	75	18	r	r	1	2½	r
91½	80	14¾	17	r	2	4	r
91½	85	10¾	14½	r	3½	r	r
91½	90	7½	10½	14	5¼	7¾	r
91½	95	5½	8¾	12¼	7¾	9¾	r
91½	100	3⅛	6¼	s	10	r	s
NorSo	50	r	r	r	r	1 9-16	r
56	55	3½	r	r	r	3¾	5
56	60	2	3	r	r	r	r
56	70	r	¾	s	r	r	s
NorTel	60	r	r	r	1	r	r
74	70	7¾	r	r	r	6	r
74	75	5¼	r	r	r	r	r
Nw Ind	30	10⅜	10¾	r	r	r	r
39⅞	35	6	r	r	⅞	1¾	r
39⅞	40	2⅝	4¼	5	2¾	4¼	r
39⅞	45	1 1-16	2⅜	3	r	r	r
39⅞	50	½	s	s	r	s	s
39⅞	55	¼	s	s	r	s	s
39⅞	60	⅛	s	s	r	s	s
Parady	20	r	s	s	1-16	s	s
42	30	12	r	s	r	r	s
42	35	8	r	10½	1⅛	r	r
42	40	4½	6½	r	2¾	r	r
42	45	2 7-16	4½	5¾	6	7	r
42	50	1¼	2½	s	r	r	s
42	55	r	1¾	s	r	r	s
R C A	20	3⅛	4⅛	5	11-16	r	1⅜
22⅜	25	⅞	1⅝	2½	3	3¼	3½
22⅜	30	¼	⅝	s	r	r	s
RalPur	15	3	3⅝	3⅞	3-16	r	r
17⅞	20	½	1 1-16	1 9-16	r	3	r
Revlon	25	8	r	r	¼	r	r
31¾	30	2 15-16	r	r	⅞	r	r
31¾	35	¾	1¾	2⅝	r	r	r
Rolm	35	r	r	s	½	r	s
49⅝	40	10⅞	r	s	13-16	r	s
49⅝	45	7¼	8½	r	2	2⅝	r
49⅝	50	4¼	5¾	r	4¼	5	r
49⅝	55	2	4	r	r	r	9
Sears	20	8½	8½	s	r	¼	s
28½	25	4¼	4⅞	5½	9-16	1⅛	1½
28½	30	1½	2 9-16	3⅛	2½	3½	3¾
28½	35	⅜	1	1¾	6⅜	r	r
SwAir	55	5	7¼	r	r	r	r
55½	60	2⅞	5	r	r	7⅞	r
SupOil	20	10¼	11¼	r	⅛	r	¾
30⅛	25	6	7⅜	r	½	1½	2
30⅛	30	3	4⅝	5⅝	2 7-16	3¾	4
30⅛	35	1 7-16	2 13-16	3¾	r	6¾	r
Syntex	40	9	10	r	r	1½	r
47⅞	45	4¾	r	9	1⅝	r	r
47⅞	50	2⅝	4½	r	4¼	r	r
47⅞	55	1¼	r	5	r	r	r
47⅞	60	⅜	1⅞	s	r	r	s
47⅞	65	¼	1 3-16	s	r	r	s
Tektrn	35	r	r	s	r	¼	s
63⅛	45	17¾	r	s	r	r	s
63⅛	50	14¼	r	r	r	r	r
63⅛	55	10⅜	r	r	1⅜	r	r
63⅛	60	r	7⅞	r	2⅜	3⅝	r
63⅛	65	3⅝	r	r	4⅝	r	r
Toys	30	r	15	s	7-16	⅞	s
43	35	9½	11¾	r	⅞	2⅛	3
43	40	r	r	r	2½	r	r
43	45	3¼	6	r	4½	r	r
43	50	1⅜	r	5	7¾	r	r
43	55	⅝	2¼	s	r	r	s
43	60	r	1¼	s	r	r	s
Viacom	30	2	4⅜	r	r	r	r
29⅞	35	1	r	r	r	r	r
WalMrt	25	22⅜	s	s	r	s	s
46⅜	27½	20	s	s	r	s	s
46⅜	35	12	r	s	r	r	s
46⅜	40	r	r	r	1¼	r	r
46⅜	45	4¾	r	r	2½	r	r
46⅜	50	2⅝	5¼	r	5¼	r	r
46⅜	55	1¼	3¼	4¼	r	r	r

Total call vol. 190,752 Call open int. 4,103,853
Total put vol. 76,190 Put open int. 2,029,352

r – Not traded. s – No option offered. o – Old.
Last is premium (purchase price).

Source: The Wall Street Journal, January 14, 1983.

2.4 BUYING CALL OPTIONS

Call options, as mentioned earlier, are traded on four different exchanges, all of which are members of the OCC. Call options transactions are reported regularly in *The Wall Street Journal,* as shown in Table 2.3. The first column refers to the underlying security and the closing price of the stock; the second column refers to the exercise or striking price—the price at which the options buyer may acquire the stock from (in the case of a call) or may sell the stock to (in the case of a put) the options writer; the January heading refers to the option's expiration month (as does April); and so on. Last refers to the option's price per one underlying share, but since options normally cover 100 shares, the price should be multiplied by 100 to arrive at the market price per call. An *r* entry in a column indicates that an options contract for that expiration month did not trade. An *s* entry indicates that the option is not available. An *o* indicates that the old last is the purchase price. The IBM call option (indicated by → in Table 2.3) has a striking price of $90, with a market price of $875 for the January contract and $1,262.50 for the April contract; no July IBM call contract with a striking price of $55 or $60 was available on January 14, 1983. The January IBM put with a $90 striking price could be purchased for $6.25 on January 14, 1983, while the underlying stock is selling for $98.25.

To put the numbers in Table 2.3 in an historical perspective we offer Table 2.4. Average call premiums in 1981 were $417 and average put prices $323 for the same year. Call buyers entered orders to buy 7.3 contracts on the average in 1981 and put buyers averaged 7.0 puts per transaction.

In-the-Money Call

A call is "in-the-money" if the market price of the stock exceeds the striking price, that is, if the call can be profitably exercised. The investor will gain by calling the

TABLE 2.4
Historical Average Premium and Average Contract Size

	Average Premium per Contract				Average Number of Contracts per Trade		
Year	All Classes	Calls	Puts	Year	All Classes	Calls	Puts
1981	$390	$417	$323	1981	7.2	7.3	7.0
1980	527	588	265	1980	6.1	6.0	6.5
1979	392	403	329	1979	6.0	5.8	7.2
1978	420	419	429	1978	5.3	5.3	5.7
1977*	322	318	389	1977*	5.1	5.1	5.3
1976	420	—	—	1976	4.1	—	—
1975	446	—	—	1975	3.5	—	—
1974	294	—	—	1974	3.4	—	—
1973	402	—	—	1973	2.6	—	—

* Put trading began on June 3, 1977. Only calls were traded prior to that time.

Source: The Chicago Board Options Exchange, *Market Statistics,* 1982. (CBOE has permitted use of this table, but has not participated in the preparation of this book and is not responsible for its contents.)

stock at the striking price and selling it in the marketplace for a higher sum. The higher the differential, the deeper in-the-money the call option is.

At-the-Money or Close-to-the-Money Call

A call is "close-to-the-money" when the striking price approximates the market price of the stock.

Out-of-the-Money Calls

Calls are "out-of-the-money" if the striking price of the call is higher than the market price, that is, if an exercise of the call will result in a loss. The greater the differential, the deeper out-of-the-money the option is.

The differential between the striking price and the market price of the security is of considerable importance. An out-of-the-money option commands a lower price. The deeper out-of-the-money an option is, the lower its price. The differential between the prices also affects the risk profile of the option and the movement in the price of the option in relation to the movement in the price of the underlying stock. A closer examination of these and related issues follows later in this chapter.

Puts are in- or out-of-the money for reasons opposite to those of calls.

Why Buy Calls

Call options are bought for several reasons, primarily for leverage and risk limitation.

Calls for Leverage

A call option on JAK (a hypothetical company) stock expiring in July with a striking price of $50, JAK/July/50 call, selling for $500 allows for substantial leverage potential. If the market price on the underlying stock is $55, the purchase of 100 shares will require a total commitment of $5,500 or the equivalent of the cost of 11 options. If the stock advances to $60 and the option to $10, the profits are

Stock Position		**Call Position**	
Loss	Profit	Loss	Profit
	$6,000 − $5,500 = $500		($1,000 − $500) × 11 = $5,500

To simplify the presentation, the profit figures ignore taxes and transaction costs. The rate of return on the stock position is $500/$5,500 or approximately 9 percent. That on the option position is $5,500/$5,500 or 100 percent. Clearly the investor should prefer the option position under those circumstances. If, on the other hand, the share price remains constant or actually falls during the life of the option, the loss on the option position is 100 percent of the invested capital, while it is much smaller or negligible on the stock position. The leveraged position must, therefore, be looked at very carefully.

The reader may already have observed that call buyers have a more complex task with regard to future predictions of movements in stock prices. Not only must they predict the direction of the market price of the underlying security but also the timing of the appreciation in the value of the security. The accretion in the value of the security

must occur during the life of the option and must be substantial enough to cover the cost of the option and to ensure the desired rate of return.

Calls to Limit Trading Risk

A JAK/July/50 call purchased for $500 becomes profitable (assuming conversion) if the stock trades at over $55, say $58 (see Figure 2.1). An investor watching the charts on JAK may arrive at the conclusion that the stock has hit a resistance level and may decide to sell his or her call (bought at 50) and simultaneously short the stock at 58. Using this strategy, however, the investor stands to lose a considerable sum if the price of JAK continues to rise instead of fall. The extent of the loss is theoretically unlimited. If, instead, the investor keeps the call option and goes short, the risk is reduced considerably. If the stock continues to appreciate, the call will appreciate in value, offsetting the loss on the short position. Once the price of the stock pierces the resistance level, the short position is closed. If the stock drops in price, the loss on the call is limited by its premium at the time of purchase ($500). The $500 is the maximum loss. Therefore, if the stock falls below 50, the gains on the short position will more than offset the losses on the call. The real value of the call, however, is increased through repeated trades against the protection it provides.

A short position at 58 followed by a cover and a simultaneous long position at 51, a sale of the long position and a short sale at 60 followed by a cover and a long position at 52, and finally a sale of the long position (optimal) and a sale of the option contract for 54 at its expiration date for $200 would produce considerable profits. This obviously assumes almost perfect foresight on the part of the investor. Needless to say, the presence of the call emboldens the investor to a great degree.

Calls to Release Cash

An investor with 20-point appreciation in a security may wish to sell the security because of a cash need and replace his or her long position in the stock with a call in order to continue participating in the expected upside potential (see Figure 2.2). At 70, the stock is sold for $7,000 (assume 100 shares). Simultaneously, a call is purchased for $800, reducing the gross proceeds (before deduction of taxes and commissions) to $6,200. If the stock continues to appreciate, the investor would hope to recover the cost of the premium and even make a profit. If the stock price declined instead, the maximum loss would be the price of the call.

FIGURE 2.1.

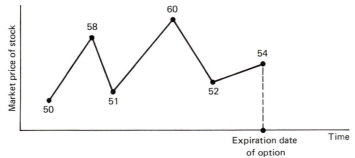

FIGURE 2.2.

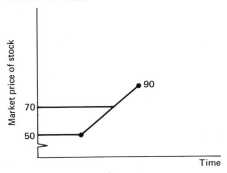

Calls to Protect Principal

A call is a substitute, although potentially an expensive one, for a long position in the stock. Instead of going long on 100 shares of JAK selling at 50, an investor may choose to buy a JAK/December/50 contract for $500. The difference, $4,500, will be kept in a bank, invested in money market instruments like T-bills, or used for other purposes. This advantage must be balanced by the following sobering considerations:

1. Unless the stock price rises by more than five points (assuming compulsory conversion, however unrealistic) there would be no profit in the call position, while a positive return would have been realized in a long position in the stock.

2. If the stock price stays at 50 during the life of the call option, the call position expires and is worthless, incurring a loss of $500. A long position in the stock would have zero loss unless the opportunity costs of tying up the principal (funds committed to the purchase of a stock) were accounted for.

3. If a stock price falls by more than five points by the option expiration date, the loss on the call position is the maximum $500, but the loss limit on the long position in the stock could theoretically reach $5,000. An investor wishing to limit this loss could, however, place with his or her broker a stop-loss order at 45, which means that if this stock trades at or through 45, the order becomes a market order and the stock will be sold at the next bid. This is true for securities listed on the New York Stock Exchange. Stocks listed on the American Stock Exchange will trade at the limit of the stop order. If that limit is passed and the stock is not sold, the investor would have to adjust the price limit if the stock were to be sold. Therefore, while the stop order offers considerable downside protection, it does not limit the maximum loss the investor would suffer. Given the trading rules on the floor of the New York Stock Exchange, however, a sale significantly below 45 is not likely.

Hence our conclusion is that a stop order does offer a reasonable level of protection when compared with a call.

Calls to Protect Short Positions

As discussed earlier in this section, a call is useful in keeping the loss in a short position to a maximum set by the call premium. The profit on the short position is reduced, however, by that premium. The profit on a 100-share unprotected short position in

XYZ at 60 will be $2,000 if the stock trades at 40 but $1,400 if the position is protected by a call costing $600. With an uncovered position, the loss is theoretically unlimited if the XYZ appreciates in value (a limit defined by the investor's level of rationality and wealth does exist, however). The call limits the loss to the size of the premium. The reader should note that the options market permits various levels of protection at obviously different costs depending on the striking price of the call, the life of the call, and the relationship between the market price of the underlying security and the striking price of the call—that is, on whether a given call is out-of-the-money, at-the-money, or in-the-money. Referring back to Table 2.1, an investor with a short position in IBM in January 1983 can protect it by purchasing IBM/Jan/85 (in-the-money call because the market price of IBM, 98¼, is higher than the striking price of the option, 90) or by purchasing an IBM/Jan/90, which is less in-the-money and closer to being at-the-money; or an IBM/Jan/95, which is almost at-the-money; or an IBM/Jan/100, which is out-of-the-money. The investor can also consider the April and July 1983 maturities with different striking prices. Given the maturity date, the less in-the-money the option is, the lower its cost. Therefore, the higher the level of the desired protection the higher the cost ceteris paribus. The purchase of an in-the-money option and particularly a deep in-the-money option is consequently not a desirable hedging strategy. The more risk-averse an investor is, the closer to the money he or she would want to be, particularly when the striking price is equal to that price at which the short position was established. The reader should be better able to conceptualize this discussion after reading the section on the determinants of call-option premiums.

Calls for Psychological Sustenance

An investor with a long position in the JAK Corporation established at 60 may panic and sell the stock if the market price drops to 50, for example. The worst psychological pains would be felt if the stock were sold only to return back to 60 and beyond. A call position, established on the basis of expectations at the time of purchase, would permit the investor to ride out downward slumps in the price of the underlying security for two major reasons:

1. The maximum loss that the investor can sustain, regardless of how low the price of the underlying security falls, is limited to the price of the option (the premium).

2. The fact that the price of an option does not fall to zero if the stock drops substantially in price—provided that a considerable portion of the life of the option has not expired—is an added advantage. The time premium will provide a cushion. More on this later.

The investor is therefore, more likely to "stick it out" if he or she owns a call option instead of a long position in the underlying security.

Calls to Fix the Price of a Security to Be Purchased in the Future

An investor expecting a dramatic rise in the price of a security but unable to purchase it now would buy a call on the security with a maturity coinciding with the date of receipt of expected funds. If the investor's price expectations materialized, he or she would purchase the underlying security for a total cost equal to the striking price plus

the call premium plus the additional transactions costs. If the expectations did not materialize, the investor would simply sell the call option at a loss or allow it to expire.

Vector Representation of a Call Position

One easy way to track the effect of price movements in the underlying security on the profitability (or lack thereof) of a security or an option position is through the utilization of a vector notation. The vector here is a column vector with two of three possible entries: +1, 0, and −1. The first entry in the vector (the first row) represents the effect of a price rise in the underlying security. The second or last row represents the effect of a price drop in the security. A long position in a stock is, therefore, represented by the vector $\begin{bmatrix} 1 \\ -1 \end{bmatrix}$, since the investment rises by one point when the stock appreciates by one point and falls by one point when the stock falls by one point. A short position in a stock has the opposite signs from those of a long position $\begin{bmatrix} -1 \\ 1 \end{bmatrix}$.

A long call position is represented by $\begin{bmatrix} 1 \\ 0 \end{bmatrix}$. If the market price of the underlying security increases, the call will realize a profit (gross profit), but a decrease in the price of the security will result only in a loss of the cost of the call (zero gross loss) without any further liability. The cost of the call is considered here as a sunk cost. The vector representation ignores the premium paid in any of the instruments. Alternatively and more accurately, the vector notation for a call looks at profits in a call position resulting from a change in the price of the stock before accounting for the premium.

The vector representation should prove a very useful tool, as we shall see later, in the analysis of the consequences of various option combinations and strategies.

2.5 WRITING (SELLING) CALL OPTIONS

The call writer is on the opposite side of a call buyer in terms of attitude toward risk and expectations about the future. Call writers seek a reasonable rate of return (in addition to that earned on the security alone) on their capital and are willing to sell options only on securities for which price movements are not expected to be substantial. Otherwise, call writers would be better off maintaining a long position in the security. A security with considerable upside potential will realize a greater return if held long instead of being held as an underlying security to an option. Call option writers seek to capitalize on the option price and particularly on the time premium that favors them and not the option buyer.

The preceding presupposes that the call writer owns the underlying security; that is, he or she has a "covered" position. Call options can also be written "naked" (meaning no underlying security). The writer of a naked option would be assuming a greater risk if the price of the underlying security rose substantially. To deliver against the naked call, the writer would purchase the security at a higher price than that prevailing at the time the contract was sold and would deliver against the call option at the striking price. In the event of a price decline, the writer of a naked option would realize the full premium on the call because the option holder would choose not to exercise his or her option. A covered option writer, on the other hand, would see the premium received reduced, if not eliminated, by the loss on the long position in the underlying

security in the event of a price decline. Later on, we shall examine other alternatives to owning the underlying security in a covered option—alternatives consisting of owning a warrant, a call option, or a security convertible into the underlying stock. What is important to remember, however, are the risk characteristics faced by the writer of a naked call. His or her income is limited to the size of the call premium, but the possible losses are theoretically limitless.

We now examine the motives for writing a call.

Writing a Call Option for Income

An investor (individual, corporation, pension fund, mutual fund, and so forth) with a long position in JAK, Inc. could choose to write a call on the stock in order to improve dividend income. Many possibilities exist. The investor can frequently choose from many maturity dates and striking prices. Given JAK's market price, the size of the premium will be determined, among other things, by the investor's choice of maturity and of the striking price.

Consider the following case:

JAK's market price	$50
Call striking price	$55
Call maturity	three months
Call premium	$2

If the market price of JAK does not exceed $55, the call premium will be realized in full because the call buyer would simply not exercise the call. If the market price exceeds $55, but is less than $57 ($55 + $2), the call buyer would exercise the call (or sell it on the options exchange) in order to recoup portions of the call premium. If the market price exceeds $57, the option buyer will exercise the option (or sell it) and realize a profit (gross profits before commissions).

From the perspective of the option writer, the possibilities are as follows:

1. Stock remains at $50. The return on the sale of a call contract is equal to the premium received: $200. The annualized rate of return = ($200/$5,000) × 4 = 16%.

2. Stock advances beyond $55 to $70. The return is still $200 if commissions, dividends, and taxes are ignored. The investor, however, no longer owns the stock, for it was called away. The opportunity loss is enormous. If a call had not been written on JAK, the investor would have realized a gain equal to $70 − $50 = $20 per share.

3. The stock declines to $40. The investor, though still realizing the $200 in premium, now holds an asset that has depreciated by $1,000 (based on 100 shares). The $200 received merely cushions the loss.

In conclusion, the covered call writer would forego the possibility of price appreciation and assume the risk of a price decline against the receipt of the call premium. This conclusion must be tempered by the nature of the investor's expectations. The investor expected little movement in the price of the security at the time the contract was sold, was not averse to losing the stock at a price higher than current market value [$50 + $2 (premium)], and is willing to hold onto the stock even if it dropped to $40. If at $40 or anywhere below $50 the investor revises his or her expectations and decides

the stock is no longer worth holding, the stock can be sold and the investor can assume a naked position. Another conclusion worth remembering comes from Fischer Black:

> *It is not correct to say that an investor can increase his rate of return by writing call options against his stock. In fact, he reduces his "expected return" because he creates a position that is equivalent to selling some of his stock. He creates a position in which he will come out ahead only if the stock doesn't move very much. He will come out behind if the stock moves a lot.*
>
> *The only way the writer can improve expected return and retain the same exposure to small stock movements is to buy more stock and write overpriced options against his dated stock position. The hedge ratio tells how much more stock to buy. If this hedge ratio is 0.50, then writing options against a stock position cuts its exposure in half; so the investor should double his stock position and write overpriced calls on all of it.* [3]

A discussion of the hedge ratio follows later in the chapter.

The preceding discussion assumes that the only way to cover a short call position is by a long position in the underlying security. There are other ways, such as a long position in a convertible bond or in a convertible preferred bond which can be converted at the option of its holder to the equity security underlying the short call. In this case two factors must carefully be considered:

1. The conversion ratio of the convertible bond—that is, to how many shares can the bond be converted. If that number is 20, then the short call seller would need five bonds to cover the 100-share obligation.

2. The premium over conversion value, that is, the market price of the convertible bond minus its value if immediately converted (conversion ratio x current market price of stock) divided by the conversion value. The higher this conversion premium, the more the bond characteristic of the convertible bond dominates its value and the less the influence of stock price movements is on the value of the convertible bond. Since the short call holder is a conservative investor, he or she would want the value of the convertible bond to follow reasonably the price of the stock. The choice, therefore, should be of a bond with low (no higher than 15 to 20 percent) premium over conversion value.

The advantages of this form of covering are that the yield on convertible bonds is usually higher than on an equal investment in common stock and the transactions costs on convertible bonds are lower than those on common stock.

The other assumption we made in analyzing the consequences of a covered short call is that the writer remains wedded to his position or to the underlying security until expiration date. Few experienced writers do this. One strategy is simply to close the short call by buying a long call (not necessarily with the same striking price or expiration date) or, in the event of a price decline that is expected to continue, to sell the underlying stock. Other strategies are referred to as rolling actions which are very useful follow-up strategies.

---

[3] **Fischer Black,** "Fact and Fantasy in the Use of Options." *Financial Analysts Journal* (July–August 1975), p. 3.

A covered call writer may "roll down" when the price of the underlying stock falls or "roll up" when that price rises.

Rolling down involves the sale of another call on the underlying stock with a lower striking price. The premium received provides some protection against further price weakness. If that weakness does not materialize, the call writer would earn the premium, which could offset some or all of the book loss resulting from the price decline against the initial position. Rolling down, we must note, does not have to be done against every short call. Partial rolling down may be optimal in certain cases.

The effect of a rolling down is to reduce, generally, the maximum profit potential of a covered short call. By rolling down the option writer is committing himself to selling the stock at a strike price lower than the one he originally was willing to accept. The results would be beneficial if the stock price were to weaken or rise not beyond the new strike price plus the last premium received. If the stock price rises beyond this level the covered call writer would have been better off not rolling down.

An example of a roll down would be to write a new call option with a striking price of 40 if the third scenario in our covered call position materializes.

A roll up follows a rise in the price of the underlying stock. It is achieved by buying back the call originally sold and selling a new one with a higher striking price. The total risk of the covered writer increases because of the additional commitment of funds resulting from the repurchase of the first call and because the new break-even point on the short position (new strike price − premium received) is higher than it originally was.

When the same data are used for the writer of a naked option, the results are as follows:

1. Stock remains at $50. The returns are $200, but no funds are tied up in the purchase of the underlying security. However, brokerage houses require that a sum set by the margin requirement (established by the Federal Reserve Board) be maintained in the account of the naked option writer. In the JAK's case, this sum will be $5,000 × 30% (current margin requirement) = $1,500.[4] This total is less than the sum that would have been tied up had the stock been purchased outright on margin (the margin requirement in this case is 50 percent). An additional saving is realized from the commission that would have been owed in the long position. The returns on the stock must be reduced by the interest costs on the borrowed funds ($5,000 − $1,500) and by the commissions (on the sale of a call).

2. The stock goes up to $70. The writer of a naked option would have to purchase the stock at $70 in order to deliver it against the call when exercised or equivalently buy a call similar to the one sold to offset the open position. The loss is $2,000 − $200 = $1,800. The call writer may choose to close his position considerably earlier

---

[4] Actually the margin requirement is calculated as follows: 30 percent of the value of the underlying stock ± amount in the money minus premium received (margins for exchange members are significantly less). Example:

$5,000 × 30%	$1,500
Less out-of-the-money credit	−500
	$1,000
Less premium received	−200
Total commitment	**$ 800**

It must be noted that 80 percent of the naked margin can be posted in interest-yielding T-bills.

than the $70 level on the underlying security. This decision may be enhanced by the marking to the market required by the brokerage house. This simply means that whenever the price of the stock rises, the brokerage house asks the option writer to deposit more funds in his or her margin account to keep the value of the deposit at 30 percent of the market value of the security. A naked call writer may get fed up with frequent requests for additional funds and decide to close the position.

The common strategy is usually to place a stop-buy order at a stop price corresponding to the maximum loss the naked writer is willing to tolerate. Our naked writer may well have placed such an order at 65 when the call was established. Yet another alternative would have been to buy a call with a different striking price and/or maturity to provide some protection in the event expectations do not materialize. The purchased call will obviously have to be out-of-the-money.

3. Stock goes down to $40. This is the best of all worlds for the writer of a naked option. The return is $200, there are excess funds in the margin account, and there is no book or real loss on the underlying security.

In conclusion, an investor with limited financial resources should avoid writing naked options.

Writing a Call Option to Hedge

The premium received from writing a call option serves as a cushion against a price decline in the underlying security. The larger the premium, the greater the cushion.

Writing a Call Option to Improve on Market

An investor with little hope of an upward price movement in a given stock may sell a call on the stock. The current market price on the stock plus the option premium constitute a new price that is only realizable through the option market. If the stock price advances, the investor happily sells the stock. If the price remains the same, the investor is even happier. Gloom sets in with a price decline. The stock will not be called away from the investor. However, the premium received provides a cushion. The investor with a depreciated security may choose to sell yet another call on it, further cushioning the loss or reducing the cost of the security.

One additional advantage, to be elaborated later, stems from tax considerations. The premium received on an exercised option is added onto the price of the security and is, therefore, subject to captial gains taxes. If the option is not exercised or is closed out on the option exchange, then the premium is taxed as ordinary income. This represents an additional incentive to use the option market as a mechanism for selling at above the current market price. The premium from an exercised option is equivalent, from a tax point of view, to an appreciation in the market value of the security.

Vector and Graphic Representations

The vector representation for writing a call is $\begin{bmatrix} -1 \\ 0 \end{bmatrix}$. An increase in the price of the security results in a loss on the sale of a call, while a decline results in no loss. The loss on the sale of the call represents the call writer's foregone gain on the long position or, more accurately, the realized loss on a naked position.

Graphically, buying and writing a call can be shown as in Figure 2.3. In Figure

FIGURE 2.3.   Buying and writing a call.

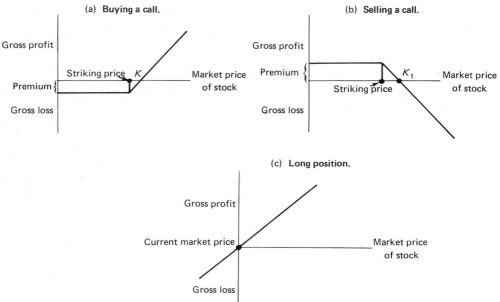

2.3a, the call buyer will lose the premium (before commissions and other charges) in its entirety until the market price of the stock reaches the striking price. Beyond that point, the call buyer begins to recoup the premium on a one-to-one basis (one point appreciation in the market price of the security means a one-point reduction in the cost of the premium). Once K is reached, profits continue to accumulate.

The writer of the call (see Figure 2.3b) will earn the premium and will continue in an advantageous position until the stock price falls below K_1. At that point, the investor wishes that the option had never been sold or simply that a long position in the stock had been assumed.

Both option strategies should be compared with the long position in the stock market depicted in Figure 2.3c.

2.6 THE DETERMINANTS OF THE CALL PREMIUM

The major theoretical breakthrough in the identification and quantification of the determinants of call premiums did not come until 1973, in a study by Fischer Black and Myron Scholes in the May–June issue of the *Journal of Political Economy*. The paper, entitled "The Pricing of Options and Corporate Liabilities," presented a theoretical valuation formula for options and laid the foundation for a deluge of literature on option pricing, efficiency of option markets, and trading strategies in the marketplace. We shall examine the Black-Scholes (B&S) model in considerable detail. We will first look at some of the intuitive determinants of option pricing.

Option Premium Determinants

The connection between options and the underlying stock is of considerable importance in the determination of options premiums. More specifically, the current market price of the stock in relation to the striking price is a major determinant. The lower the

FIGURE 2.4. **Relationship between market price and option premium.**

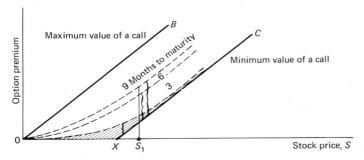

market price in relation to the striking price—that is, the more out-of-the-money the option is—the less valuable it is. The more in-the-money the option is, the more valuable it is and the higher the premium.

Market Price of Stock and Call Premium

The relationship between the market price of the stock and the option premium is shown in Figure 2.4. The maximum price for an option is shown by *OB*, because an option with an infinite life would be equivalent to a common stock. Along *OB*, every point of appreciation in the price of a stock brings a point of appreciation in the value of the call. This is the maximum appreciation possible.

The lower limit, the minimum value of a call, is shown by *XC* (parallel to *OB*) in Figure 2.4. Every point along *XC* represents the difference between the market price of the stock S and the striking price X. $S - X$ is referred to as the relative price of intrinsic value. The price of an option is always greater than or equal to zero even if the intrinsic value is negative. No one is going to pay you for buying his or her option.

The option price must, therefore, be somewhere between *OB* and *XC*, as shown by the broken lines in Figure 2.4. These lines show that the price of an option is greater than the intrinsic value and always tends towards it. To the left of X, $S - X < 0$ and the option is out-of-the-money. At or around X, the option is at-the-money. To the right of X, the option is in-the-money. The farther to the right of X the stock price, the deeper in-the-money the option. The outstanding issue still is: What determines the shape of the broken lines? A few theorems should aid in providing the answer.

Theorem 1.[5] **The rate of increase in the price of an option W is approximately half that of the underlying security when $S = X$.**

Theorem 2. **The excess of market price of an option over its intrinsic value $W - (S - X)$ increases with the price of the underlying security S when $S < X$ and decreases with the price of the underlying security when $S > X$.**

---

[5] This and the theorems to follow are based on the work of **Claude G. Henin** and **Peter J. Ryan**, *Options*, Lexington Books, Lexington, Mass., 1977. (Differentiating the Black and Scholes model with respect to stock price shows that the rate would be exactly one half only when S is slightly less than X, as we shall present later).

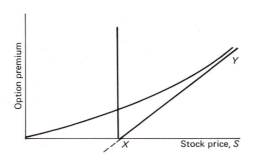

FIGURE 2.5. Graphic depiction of Theorem 2.

This theorem is best explained using Figure 2.5. Up to X, the excess $W - (S - X)$ is rising (excess equals W if $S - X \leq 0$). Beyond X, the excess decreases. Correspondingly, the option premium rises at a slow rate up to X and at a faster rate beyond X when the option is in the money. At point Y, when the option is well in the money, the option premium rises on an almost one-to-one basis with the stock price. This is the nature of the beast. When the stock price is close to zero, it is far from the striking price. That is, a large appreciation in the price of the security must take place before the option buyer expects to break even.

Theorem 3. **The excess on an option is symmetrical about the strike (exercise) price.**

Theorem 4. **The option on a stock commands a higher price than another option on the same stock if the striking price is lower. The difference in the price of the options is lower than that in the striking prices.**

Time and Call Premium

The three courses shown by the broken lines in Figure 2.4 illustrate the relationship between time and the call premium. From the perspective of the option buyer, the longer the life of the option, the larger the probability that the stock price will move sufficiently to allow a profit on the position to be realized. Hence the willingness to pay more for an option that has a longer maturity, *ceteris paribus*. From the perspective of the option seller, the longer the life the larger the probability that the option will be exercised and a loss on the underlying security incurred. The option writer will therefore demand a higher premium.

The option price can therefore be generalized, although incompletely, as follows:

$W =$ intrinsic value (relative price) + time premium

An out-of-the-money option with a zero or close to zero relative price would have a positive value. The longer the remaining life of the option, the larger the time premium and the larger the price of the option. The brackets in Figure 2.4 corresponding to a stock price of S_1 represent the time premium. The shaded area in Figure 2.4 represents the time premium, given different stock prices, for an option with three months to maturity. The longer the remaining life, the larger the time premium. To the left of X the time premium is the call premium. As $S - X$ approaches zero, the time premium approaches W; the option has no intrinsic value. From Figure 2.4 we can also observe that the shorter the remaining life of the option, the more the price of the option moves

in congruence with the stock price. Another conclusion to be drawn from Figure 2.4 is that the rate of decrease in the option price accelerates as the option approaches the date of expiration.

Call Premium and Stock Volatility

Common stocks that have a history of wide price fluctuations (Polaroid and Teleprompter, for example) command higher call premiums because the probability of those options becoming profitable is higher. Table 2.5 shows the differences in price volatility among three NYSE-listed securities.

The covariance between the rate of return on a stock and that on a market index normalized by the variance of the rates of return on the market index is a measure of volatility referred to as the *beta (β) coefficient.* The importance of this measure lies in the fact that in times of generally rising stock prices, there is an increased interest in option ownership; consequently prices for options are higher, since option writers are less interested in supplying option contracts. If stock prices are generally falling, option writers are ready to supply larger numbers of option contracts, while option buyers are not so interested. The result is lower option prices. Stocks with high variances, therefore, command higher prices for options written on them than those with lower variances if stock market prices are generally rising, and vice versa.

It is instructive at this point to differentiate between the volatility of the underlying security and that of the option itself. The volatility of the option is usually larger than that of the underlying stock because of the leverage offered by options. The further in-the-money an option is, the more consistent its volatility with that of the stock. Figure 2.6 shows the volatility of the option market as measured by the CBOE Call Option Index. A comparison of Figure 2.6 with Figure 2.7 (with slight adjustment) will show the volatility of the options market relative to that of the stock market as measured by the Standard & Poor's Composite Index.

Call Premium and Interest Rates

The risk/return tradeoff in the option market must be compatible with the tradeoffs on alternative investment opportunities with similar profiles. When interest rates are rising, options premiums tend to move upward; when interest rates are falling, options premiums move downward.

F. Black and M. Scholes (B&S) argue that the option premium is a function of the risk-free rate.[6] The basis of the argument is that option buyers, by following a certain hedging strategy, can establish a risk-free position. This is done by taking a long position in the stock and a short position in a certain number of options. This number is equal to

$$\frac{1}{W_1(S,t)}$$

where $W_1(S,t)$ is the partial first derivative of the option price with respect to the normal density function with respect to the first argument of the function S. For a

---

[6] **Fischer Black** and **Myron Scholes,** "The Pricing of Options and Corporate Liabilities." *Journal of Political Economy,* vol. 81 (May–June 1973), pp. 637–654.

TABLE 2.5
Price Ranges for Six NYSE-Listed Securities

General Electric Co. (GE)

		I	II	III	IV
1981	high	69⅛	69⅞	63¾	60⅜
	low	59⅛	61⅝	51⅛	53⅛
1980	high	57½	52	58⅛	63
	low	44	44½	51⅛	51½
1979	high	50⅜	51⅝	56¾	52¼
	low	45½	46⅞	49⅛	45
1978	high	49⅝	54⅞	57⅝	53⅞
	low	43⅝	45⅞	49⅞	45¾
1977	high	55⅞	57¼	56½	52¾
	low	49	47⅞	50⅜	47⅜

General Foods Corporation (GF)

		I	II	III	IV
1981	high	34¾	35	32¾	32⅞
	low	30	30¾	27¾	28¾
1980	high	34¼	31⅞	32¼	31
	low	23½	24¼	29⅝	27⅞
1979	high	36¾	33⅜	37	36⅞
	low	31⅞	28¼	31	31⅞
1978	high	31½	33	35	35¼
	low	26½	27¼	31⅜	30⅜
1977	high	33	35½	36⅛	33⅞
	low	29	31	32¼	29

General Motors Corporation (GM)

		I	II	III	IV
1981	high	56⅛	58	53⅛	46½
	low	43⅞	51⅜	42⅝	33⅞
1980	high	55¾	49½	58⅞	54⅛
	low	44	39½	46⅜	40⅜
1979	high	59⅜	61¾	65⅞	64⅞
	low	53⅛	56⅜	54⅞	49⅜
1978	high	62½	66⅞	66½	65½
	low	57⅛	59¼	58	53¾
1977	high	78½	71	70¾	70⅞
	low	66⅜	65⅞	64¾	61⅛

Great Western Financial Corp. (GWF)[1]

		I	II	III	IV
1981	high	19⅛	18⅜	16¾	16
	low	14¼	14⅝	13⅜	12
1980	high	22⅛	22¾	23½	21
	low	14	15⅜	16⅜	16⅜
1979	high	20⅛	25½	27¾	26½
	low	15¾	16¾	23	18¼
1978	high	15⅜	19⅛	23⅛	21⅝
	low	12⅛	14⅛	18¼	15⅜
1977	high	16⅛	16⅞	16¾	16⅝
	low	13½	13⅜	13⅞	14

Gulf + Western Industries, Inc. (GW)[2]

		I	II	III	IV
1981	high	17¾	22⅛	20	17½
	low	14	16¾	14⅜	15⅜
1980	high	17¾	18⅝	20⅞	19¼
	low	11⅛	12⅞	16⅛	15
1979	high	12¼	12¼	14½	15¾
	low	11⅛	11¼	11½	10⅞
1978	high	10⅝	12⅝	13	12
	low	8¾	10	10⅞	9
1977	high	14¾	11⅞	11	9⅞
	low	11⅛	10¼	8⅞	8

Halliburton Co. (HAL)[3]

		I	II	III	IV
1981	high	84½	76	70½	60¼
	low	69	53¾	44⅛	47⅛
1980	high	54¾	58⅜	69⅝	86½
	low	41	44¼	54⅞	64⅞
1979	high	37½	36⅛	42⅜	42½
	low	29⅞	32⅛	32½	35⅞
1978	high	32¾	34⅜	39¼	37¾
	low	27½	27¼	29¾	29⅜
1977	high	32½	33⅝	33⅜	32⅞
	low	27¼	27⅜	28¼	29⅛

1. Adjusted for 3/2 stock split March 19, 1979.
2. Adjusted for 5/4 stock split April 30, 1980.
3. Adjusted for 2/1 stock split December 26, 1980.

Source: Chicago Board Options Exchange, *Market Statistics, 1982.* (CBOE has permitted use of this table, but has not participated in the preparation of this book and is not responsible for its contents.)

FIGURE 2.6. CBOE composite option indices.

Source: Ghicago Board Options Exchange, *Market Statistics,* 1982.

FIGURE 2.7. Standard & Poor's price index (quarterly averages).

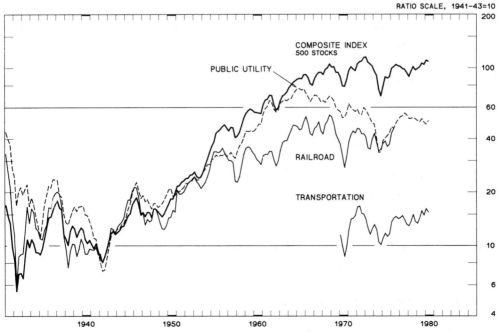

Source: Board of Governors of the Federal Reserve System, *1980 Historical Chart Book,* 1981.

normal probability distribution with mean zero and a standard deviation equal to one, $N(d_1)$ gives the probability that a deviation less than S will take place.

The hedge ratio is, therefore, the ratio of the change in the option value to that in the value of the underlying stock. A partial first derivative equal to 0.19 means that if the price of the stock goes up or down by $1, the value of the option goes up or down by $0.19. Therefore, a long position in the stock combined with a short position of $1/0.19 = 5.26$ options (the hedge ratio) results in a neutral hedge—a hedge that is risk free and earning the risk-free rate if the option market is operating efficiently. The reader should note that the amount expended on the long position is not necessarily equal to that committed to the short position.

It must be noted and emphasized that the neutral hedge strategy is merely a theoretical possibility. The hedge ratio requires continuous hedging as the price of the underlying stock changes. Very few investors follow their portfolios that closely. Transaction costs can become prohibitive if a continuous hedging strategy is pursued. Furthermore, the hedge ratio requires divisibility that is not present in the options market; no one is going to sell 26 percent of an option. These realities have led to the utilization of the call-money rate instead of the risk-free rate in the price determination equation of a call option. The call rate[7] is deemed more representative of arbitrageurs' costs and incomes.

From the preceding discussion and based on the assumptions above, it can be concluded that the price of an option contract is determined as follows:

$$W = f(S, X, \sigma^2, t, r, D)$$

where $W =$ option price

$X =$ strike price

$S =$ price of the underlying stock

$\sigma^2 =$ volatility of the stock price measured by the instantaneous variance of the rate of return on the stock

$t =$ life of the options contract

$r =$ the risk-free rate of interest

$D =$ dividend yield on the stock

$$\frac{\delta W}{\delta S} > 0, \frac{\delta W}{\delta X} < 0, \frac{\delta W}{\delta \sigma^2} > 0, \frac{\delta W}{\delta t} > 0, \frac{\delta W}{\delta r} > 0, \frac{\delta W}{\delta D} < 0$$

The B&S model conveniently drops dividends as a determinant of the options price and deals with non-dividend-paying stocks or with stocks on which the options expire prior to the ex-dividend date.

2.7 THE BLACK-SCHOLES CALL-VALUATION MODEL

The development of the B&S model requires considerable mathematical sophistication. We shall, therefore, content ourselves with a discussion of the main features of the model and pay little attention to the details.

---

[7] The call rate is the rate paid by brokerage firms to their bankers.

Assumptions of the B&S Model

The assumptions of the B&S model are

1. Efficient securities markets.
2. No dividends on the underlying stock.
3. No transactions costs.
4. No restrictions on short selling.
5. The option is of the European type—exercisable only at maturity.[8]
6. Stock prices follow a random walk. Stock prices are log-normally distributed so that the continuously compounded one-period rates of return are normally distributed with a known constant variance. The variance rate is proportionate to the square of the stock price.
7. A known and constant rate of interest.

If we start with the value of a hedged portfolio,

$$V_H = SQ_s + WQ_w \tag{2.1}$$

where Q_s = number of shares in the hedged position

Q_w = number of option contracts in the hedged position

Black and Scholes took the total derivative of Equation 2.1 and, using techniques borrowed from physics, arrived at the call-valuation equation:

$$W(S,t) = S \times N(d_1) - e^{-r\tau} X \times N(d_2)$$

$$d_1 = \frac{\ln(S/X) + r\tau}{\sigma\sqrt{\tau}} + \frac{1}{2}\sigma\sqrt{\tau}$$

$$d_2 = d_1 - \sigma\sqrt{\tau} \tag{2.2}$$

When all the variables are as previously defined except

$\tau = t - T = $ time to maturity = life of the option − time elapsed

$N(\cdot) = $ cumulative standard normal distribution

$N(-\infty) = 0$, $N(0) = 0.5$, and $N(\infty) = 1$

Note: If t were equal to infinity, the price of the option should equal that of the underlying stock—an option on the assets of the corporation.

---

[8] R. C. Merton, "Theory of Rational Option Pricing." *Bell Journal of Economics and Management Science*, vol. 4 (1973), pp. 141–183. In this article **Merton** shows that if the underlying security pays no dividend, the option on it will never be exercised prior to the expiration date. This makes the B&S model applicable to American options on stocks that do not pay dividends. Whether exercised at expiration date or before, the value of the American option can only be equal or greater than that of a European call option. The American option offers an additional advantage—the option to exercise any time before the expiration date.

Example

Calculate the theoretical value of an option on a security with a market price of $40, a striking price of $35, and a maturity of three months ($\tau = 3$ mo $= \frac{1}{4}$ year). The annual risk-free rate is 8 percent and the instantaneous variance of the stock price is equal to 20 percent.

Answer

$$d_1 = \frac{\ln(40/35) + 0.08(0.25)}{\sqrt{0.2} \quad \sqrt{0.25}} + \frac{1}{2} (\sqrt{0.2}) \ (\sqrt{0.25})$$

$$= \frac{0.13348 + 0.02}{(0.447) \ (0.5)} + \frac{1}{2} (0.447) \ (0.5)$$

$$= 0.799$$

$$d_2 = 0.799 - 0.447\sqrt{0.250} = 0.5755$$

where $N(d_1)$ = cumulative probability from $-\infty$ to 0.799

$\qquad\qquad$ = 0.7881 (using Table 2A.1 in the appendix to this chapter)

$\qquad N(d_2)$ = 0.7174 (interpolating from Table 2A.1)

Therefore

$$W(S, t) = 40(0.7881) - e^{-0.08(0.25)}35(0.7174)$$

$$= 31.52 - 24.61 = \textbf{\$6.91} \text{ per share}$$

The value of the call contract on 100 shares is therefore equal to $691 (6.91 $\times$ 100).

The reader may wish to calculate option prices for various stock prices with the values of the remaining variables held constant. If the resulting call prices are plotted, we get Figure 2.8.

In the preceding example, all the values are available in the financial press with the exception of the instantaneous variance. One way of estimating the size of the variance is to set the right-hand side of Equation 2.2 equal to the actual current market price of the option and calculate the implied variance.[9] The accurate gauging of the size of the variance is important, for the B&S option model is very sensitive to the volatility variable. One additional comment worth making relates to the risk-free variable. It is customary to use the average bid-and-ask price on a U.S. Treasury bill with equivalent maturity date. This method, however, does not always yield a satisfactory answer.

It must further be noted once again that the B&S model applies to nondividend-paying stocks. Many attempts[10] have been made to adjust the model for dividend payouts.

---

[9] **M. Parkinson,** "Option Pricing: The American Put." *Journal of Business* (January 1977), pp. 21–36. H. Latane and R. J. Rendleman, Jr., "Standard Deviations of Stock Price Ratios Implied in Option Prices." *Journal of Finance* (May 1976), pp. 369–382.

[10] **M. Brennan** and **E. Schwartz,** "The Valuation of American Put Options." *Journal of Finance,* vol. 32, no. 2 (May 1976), pp. 449–462. **R. J. Rendleman** and **B. J. Bartter,** "Two State Option Pricing." Working paper, Northwestern University, Evanston, Ill., (1978). R. Roll, "An Analytical Valuation Formula for Unprotected Call Options With Known Dividends." *Journal of Financial Economics,* vol. 5 (1977), pp. 251–258. R. Geske, "The Pricing of Options with Stochastic Yield." *Journal of Finance* (May 1978), pp. 617–625.

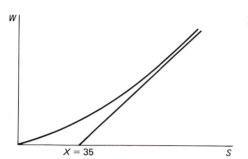

FIGURE 2.8. Plot of call prices.

The mathematics, particularly in R. Roll's paper, are complex and the efforts did not produce a neat, closed-form solution.

The easiest method for adjusting the B&S model for dividend payment was suggested by F. Black.[11] It simply requires that the option value be calculated using a stock price reduced by the present value of the dividend payment on the underlying stock.

F. Black further suggested an easy method for adjusting the B&S model to deal with the possibility of early exercise. All that is needed is to recalculate the value of the option assuming it is exercised just before the ex-dividend date.

2.8 Call Valuation—An Alternative Approach

A much simpler model for the valuation of call options on common stocks was developed by R. Rendleman and B. Bartter.[12] The model is derived algebraically and yields results consistent with those of B&S. The model was dubbed the two-state option pricing model (TSOPM).

The understanding of TSOPM requires the understanding of the uses of call options and put options as hedging tools which were discussed earlier in the chapter. A short position in the stock is protected either by a long call or a short put. A long position in the stock is protected by a long put or a short call. The achievement of a perfect hedge depends on the use of the appropriate hedge ratio, that is, the appropriate number of options against a given position in the stock.

Assume that:

$H^+ =$ returns per dollar invested if the stock rises in price between period $t - 1$ and t. This is the $+$ state.

$H^- =$ returns per dollar invested if the stock falls in price between period $t - 1$ and t. This is the $-$ state.

There are only two states $+$ and $-$; the stock rising in price or falling. In both states:

$V^+ =$ end of period value of the option if the $+$ state obtains

$V^- =$ end of period value of the option if the $-$ state obtains

$\alpha =$ number of option units to be held in the portfolio per \$1 invested in the stock. α can be positive (a long position) or negative (a short position)

$W_{t-1} =$ price of option

[11] F. Black, "Fact and Fantasy in the Use of Options." *Financial Analysts Journal,* vol. 31 (July/August, 1975) pp. 36–72.

[12] Richard J. Rendleman, Jr. and Brit J. Bartter, "Two-State Option Pricing," *Journal of Finance,* vol. 34, no. 5 (December 1979), pp. 1093–1110.

A riskless portfolio in our construct would consist of a position in a stock requiring a commitment of $1 minimally (or any multiple thereof) and the appropriate number of options (α) purchased at price W_{t-1}. If α is properly chosen the portfolio payoffs would be the same whether the stock rises or falls in price.
Therefore

$$H_t^+ + \alpha V_t^+ = H_t^- + \alpha V_t^- \tag{2.3}$$

Solving equation (2.3) for α — the number of units of the option per $1 invested in common stock, we get:

$$\alpha = \frac{H_t^- - H_t^+}{V_t^+ - V_t^-} \tag{2.4}$$

At time $t - 1$ the total value of the portfolio is simply the value of the stock (assumed $1) plus the value of the options used to protect it: αW_{t-1}. This value must be the present value of the expected future value of the portfolio at time t whether the $+$ state or the $-$ state obtains.
Therefore

$$1 + \alpha W_{t-1} = \frac{H_t^+ + \alpha V_t^+}{1 + r} \tag{2.5}$$

The discounting is done at the risk-free rate because the position is riskless.
Replacing α in (2.5) by its value in (2.4) we can solve for the price of the option

$$W_{t-1} = \frac{V_t^+ (1 + r - H_t^-) + V_t^- (H_t^+ - 1 - r)}{(H_t^+ - H_t^-)(1 + r)} \tag{2.6}$$

Equation 2.6 is the TSOPM. It can be used to price American call and put options as well as European call and put options. To see how both calls and puts are priced by TSOPM, a distinction must be made between the value of the option and its market price. At any point in time the value of the option is the larger value of its market price or its value exercised. In mathematical terms this value is expressed as:

$$V_t = \max(W_t, \text{VEX}_t) \tag{2.7}$$

where $\text{VEX}_t =$ value of the option exercised at time t.
Therefore

$\text{VEX}_t = S_t - X$ for all t in the case of an American call
$\text{VEX}_t = X - S_t$ for all t in the case of an American put

The value is determined by the extent to which the call or the put are in-the-money.
To further understand the model assume there are only two individuals in the option market, John wishing to sell an option and Jill wishing to buy. If both John and Jill can agree on the exact magnitude of the price change then they will definitely agree

on the option price. To illustrate this, assume that current market price is $50, the option matures in one period, and the current risk-free rate is 9 percent. John and Jill agree on the following:

Stock	Option		Stock	Value of Option
		$+$ 55		5
$50	W_o			
		$-$ 45		0
$t = 0$			$t = 1$	

With the above scenario and values we can arrive at the price of the option using Equation 2.6:

$$W_o = \frac{5(1 + 0.09 - 0.90) + 0(1.10 - 1 - 0.09)}{(1.10 - 0.90)(1 + 0.09)}$$

$$= \frac{0.95}{0.218} = \$4.35$$

$$H^+ = \frac{55}{50} = 1.10, \qquad H^- = \frac{45}{50} = 0.90$$

The above model is deterministic and also unrealistic. John and Jill may not know the exact values for H^+ and H^-, which is typically the case, considering the behavior of stock prices. An estimation procedure for H^+ and H^- will, therefore, have to be devised. The model suggested by R&B amounts to a (possibly biased, with a trend) two-state random walk process using a binomial distribution as an approximation procedure for arriving at option prices. That procedure can be illustrated using a two-period model.

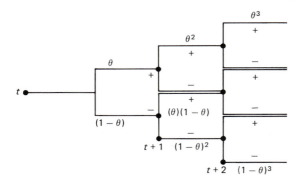

Starting at period t the price of the underlying stock could rise or fall $\left(\begin{bmatrix} + \\ - \end{bmatrix}\right)$. The probability of a rise is θ, of a fall is $1 - \theta$. At time $t + 1$, the stock price could again rise or fall if it had risen at time t or rise or fall if it had fallen at time t. However, the fact that it had risen or fallen at time t is assumed to influence in no

way the probabilities of a rise or a fall at time $t + 1$. The probabilities are independent. Thus the probability of a rise-rise is θ^2, that of a rise-rise-rise is θ^3, and that of a fall-fall-fall is $(1 - \theta)^3$.

In this construct, John and Jill will simply have to agree on the possible size of the $+$ or $-$ change in the stock price and on θ. If the option price consists of T periods, $T + 1$ possible stock prices would emerge which would be log-normally distributed (for large T's) with mean μ and variance σ^2.

The mean of the distribution of returns is calculated by

$$\mu = T[h^+\theta + h^-(1 - \theta)] = T[(h^+ - h^-)\theta + h^-] \tag{2.8}$$

The variance of the distribution of returns is calculated by

$$\sigma^2 = T(h^+ - h^-)^2\, \theta(1 - \theta) \tag{2.9}$$

where $\theta =$ probability that the price of the stock will rise in any period
$$h^+ = \ln(H^+)$$
$$h^- = \ln(H^-)$$

Given that John and Jill can agree on an H^+, H^-, and a θ value, and given a value for T, we can calculate the market price of the call or the put by using Equation 2.6. We must note that given the value of μ, σ, θ, and T we can arrive at the implied values of H^+ and H^- using the following equations:

$$H^+ = \exp\left(\frac{\mu}{T}\right) + \left(\frac{\sigma}{\sqrt{T}}\right)\sqrt{\frac{1 - \theta}{\theta}} \tag{2.10}$$

$$H^- = \exp\left(\frac{\mu}{T}\right) - \left(\frac{\sigma}{\sqrt{T}}\right)\sqrt{\frac{\theta}{1 - \theta}} \tag{2.11}$$

Example
Assume:

$$H^+ = 1.10$$
$$H^- = 0.95$$
$$\theta = 0.50$$
$$T = 100 \text{ (option life} = 100 \text{ days. Each day is considered a period in this example.)}$$
$$h^+ = \ln(1.10) = .0953$$
$$h^- = \ln(0.95) = -0.0513$$

Therefore

$$\mu = 100[(0.0953 + 0.0513)0.50 - 0.0513] = 2.20$$
$$\sigma^2 = 100(0.0953 + 0.0513)^2(0.50)(0.50) = 0.54$$

implied

$$H^+ = \exp\left[\left(\frac{\mu}{T}\right) + \left(\frac{\sigma}{\sqrt{T}}\right)\sqrt{\frac{1-\theta}{\theta}}\right]$$

$$= \exp\left[\left(\frac{2.20}{100}\right) + \left(\frac{0.54}{10}\right)\sqrt{\frac{0.50}{0.50}}\right] = e^{0.076} = 1.079$$

$$H^- = \exp\left[\left(\frac{2.20}{100}\right) - \left(\frac{0.54}{10}\right)\right] = e^{-0.032} = 0.968$$

$$W_o = \frac{V_t^+(1 + r - H_t^-) + V_t^-(H_t^+ - 1 - r)}{(H_t^+ - H_t^-)(1 + r)}$$

If we assume an $r = 9\%$ and a current market price of 50, the price of the call option will be

$$W_o = \frac{3.95(1 + .09 - .968) + 0(1.079 - 1 - .09)}{(1.079 - .968)(1 + .09)} = \$4.$$

where	value of $H_t^+ = 53.95$	$H_t^- = 48.4$
	$V_t^+ = 3.95(53.95 - 50)$	$V_t^- = 0$

We must note that W_o represents not the result of the interaction between a John and a Jill in the market place (as we have simplified), but the result of all the expectations of all the "Johns" and the "Jills" in the market.

Rendelman and Bartter tested their model on various calls and put options and found it to be consistent with the adjusted Black and Scholes model.

Investment Implications

The B&S model is of considerable help in the setting of investment strategy. The model can be used in identifying options that are overpriced (market price, B&S option price) or underpriced. Black cautions us, however, that

> The actual prices on listed options tend to differ in certain systematic ways from the values given in the formula. Options that are way out-of-the-money tend to be overpriced, and options that are way into-the-money tend to be underpriced. Options with less than three months to maturity tend to be overpriced. [13]

Black offered three possible explanations for this observation: (1) the volatility variables, (2) taxes, and (3) leverage. None of these explanations was satisfactory to Black, nor are they to others.

---

[13] **Fischer Black,** *Financial Analysts Journal,* p. 8.

2.9 EMPIRICAL TESTS

The first test of the B&S option pricing model was conducted by Black and Scholes[14] using the diaries of an option broker from 1966 to 1969 (a period predating the CBOE). They were able to select 2,039 six-month calls and 3,052 straddle contracts. Using the commercial paper rate continuously compounded (for r), their own estimate of σ, and assuming no transactions costs, they calculated W and the hedge ratio on a daily basis. Based on this, Black and Scholes were able to calculate the "realized excess dollar return" on each hedge for each day and sum over 766 trading days to arrive at a "portfolio excess dollar return." Four portfolios were developed using accurately (according to the model) priced options as well as overpriced and underpriced options. Overpriced options were sold and underpriced options were bought.

Regressing the excess dollar portfolio return on the returns on the S&P Composite Index, they were able to verify that β, systematic risk of the hedged portfolio, was not significantly different from zero; that is, the actions are uncorrelated. Whether or not a profit was realized in the options market depended on whether ex post variances (using past stock prices) or ex ante variances (estimate the variance over the holding period) were used. The profits realized using the ex post estimate of the variance were insignificant and, in fact, disappeared when transactions costs were introduced.

Black and Scholes concluded that "the model tends to overestimate the value of an option on a high variance security and . . . tends to underestimate the value of a low variance security."[15]

Dan Galai, following in the footsteps of his professor, tested the B&S model using a different and better data base from the CBOE.[16] Galai used the same type of test as Black and Scholes but adjusted the hedged option position on a daily basis. Again, overpriced options were sold and underpriced options were bought. Two tests were conducted using an ex post hedging test (using end-of-previous-day closing prices to establish option positions) and various estimates of the volatility variable were made. Each estimate was assumed to remain constant during the life of the option. Galai's tests resulted in the following conclusions:

1. Significant excess returns can be earned using ex post data.
2. Transactions costs (1 percent) eliminate any excess returns.
3. Nonmembers of the CBOE cannot consistently beat the market.
4. The B&S model performed best when its specifications were adhered to.

Both tests, that of Black and Scholes and Galai's, show that the B&S model does price options accurately and that the options markets were efficient.

A more recent test of the B&S model was made by J. Macbeth and L. Merville.[17]

---

[14] **Fischer Black** and **Myron Scholes,** "The Valuation of Option Contracts and a Test of Market Efficiency." *Journal of Finance,* vol. 27 (May 1972).

[15] Ibid., pp. 415–417.

[16] **Dan Galai,** "Tests of Market Efficiency of the Chicago Board Options Exchange." *Journal of Business,* vol. 50 (April 1977), pp. 167–197.

[17] **James D. Macbeth** and **Larry J. Merville,** "An Empirical Examination of the Black-Scholes Call Option Pricing Model." *Journal of Finance,* vol. 34, no. 5 (December 1979), pp. 1173–1186.

The authors' conclusions were exactly the opposite of those of Black.[18] Macbeth and Merville found—using daily closing prices for CBOE-traded options on AT&T, Avon Products, Eastman Kodak, Exxon, IBM, and Xerox between December 31, 1975, and December 1976—that:

1. The B&S model predicted prices are on average less (greater) than market prices for in-the-money (out-of-the-money) options.

2. With the lone exception of out-of-the-money options with less than ninety days to expiration, the extent to which the B&S model underprices (overprices) an in-the-money (out-of-the-money) option increases with the extent to which the option is in-the-money (out-of-the-money), and decreases as the time of expiration decreases.

3. B&S model prices of out-of-the-money options with less than ninety days to expiration are, on average, greater than market prices, but there does not appear to be any consistent relationship between the extent to which these options are out of the money or the time to expiration.[19]

The conflicting results were attributed by the authors largely to the nonstationary variance (σ^2 changing through time) used in the B&S model (the σ used in calculating d_1).

The most recent evidence on the accuracy of the B&S model was presented by William E. Sterk.[20] The test conducted covered the two methods for adjusting the B&S model for dividend payments: Black's method and the more complex Roll method. Sterk's findings are the opposite of those of Macbeth and Merville and reconfirm the evidence presented by Black and Scholes in their original paper. The biases can be made to disappear, however.

> *When the implied standard deviations calculated using the technique developed by Macbeth and Merville are used, the Roll model is seen to alleviate both the in-the-money and the out-of-the-money biases.*[21]

The evidence presented thus far suggests that great care should be exercised in arriving at option prices, particularly in arriving at a definite conclusion as to whether or not an option contract is overpriced.

2.10 PUTS

Definitions

A put is an option to sell 100 shares of an underlying security (commodity) at a designated price (the striking price) during a specified period of time.

In-The-Money Put

A put is in-the-money—that is, it is profitable to exercise—if the market price of the underlying stock is below the striking price. The put holder can purchase the underlying security on the market and sell it at the higher striking price to the put writer.

---

[18] **F. Black,** *Financial Analysts Journal,* pp. 36–72.

[19] **Macbeth** and **Merville,** p. 1185.

[20] **William Sterk,** "Tests of Two Models for Valuing Call Options on Stocks with Dividends," *The Journal of Finance,* vol. 37, (December 1982), pp. 1229–1237.

[21] Ibid., p. 1236.

Out-of-the-Money Put

A put is out-of-the-money if the market price of the underlying security is higher than the striking price. The exercise of the put will result in a loss.

Why Buy Puts?

Put trading did not become prevalent on the CBOE until 1980. Prior to this date, only a handful of puts were listed on the CBOE. To understand the usefulness of puts, the trader has to shift into reverse from the call option case.

Puts for Leverage

An investor expecting the price of JAK Inc. to fall can either sell the stock short or buy a put on the security. If the stock price was $50, the investor would have to commit either the required minimum for a margin account ($2,000), for short sales are usually affected in the margin account, or 30 percent of the value of the stock, whichever is higher.

If the stock goes down to $40 after one month, the profits from the short position, assuming 100 shares, would be

Original market price	$5,000
Current market price	4,000
Gross profits	$1,000

The return on the invested capital is $1,000/$2,000 = 50 percent. Annualized, it is equal to 50 × 12 = 600 percent. This obviously assumes no transactions costs.

If, instead, the investor bought five puts at $400 each for a total commitment of $2,000, the profits would be as follows:

Gross profit per option:	$1,000 − $400 = $600
Total gross profit:	$600 × 5 = $3,000

The return on the invested capital is $3,000/$2,000 = 150 percent, an annualized return of 1,800 percent. The numbers would double if the total commitment were $4,000, the full price of the shares.

This illustrates the tremendous leverage possibilities of puts. Lest our enthusiasm for puts lead us astray, we must examine the opposing side. Leverage is great when the market forces lead prices in the desired direction, but it is disastrous if things go wrong. Consider the situation of the stock rising to $55 in three months.

The investor with five puts would lose $2,000—that is, 100 percent of his or her investment. The loss in the short position in the stock would have been 50 percent of investment capital ($1,000/$2,000).[22]

---

[22] The loss in percentage terms would be lower because additional margin would have been required of the investor as the market moved in an unfavorable direction. The additional margin is required because the investor is "marked to market."

The preceding assumes that the investor does not initiate a closing sale transaction prior to the expiration date of the option. The investor may well decide to sell the puts prior to expiration in order to reduce the loss. The puts can also be exercised. The preferred way for closing out the position is a function of transactions costs, taxes, and margin requirements.

Puts to Protect a Long Position

An investor with a long position in JAK Inc. (actual or contemplated) may choose to buy a put to eliminate the downside risk on the stock. The maximum loss if the stock falls in price is the price of the put. If the put is purchased, profits begin to accrue only after the price of the put is earned. If stock is selling at $50 when a put is purchased against it for $400, profits begin to accrue after the stock price reaches $54. This protection is usually sought on volatile securities and is the only effective protection against a long position. No insurance company sells policies protecting investors against the whims of the market. The investor buying a put to protect an existing long position in the stock may negate certain tax benefits. This issue will be discussed later in the chapter.

Puts to Protect Book Profits

An investor owning a security with a cost basis of $50 and a market value of $80 may choose to purchase a put in order to lock in the book profit (minus the put premium). If the stock price continues to move upward, the put may be sold or be allowed to expire. Taxes are an important consideration here. As we shall explain later, the purchase of the put will eliminate the holding period on the stock for tax purposes. The holding period begins again when the put position is closed.

Puts for Limited-Risk Trading

An investor wishing to trade a volatile security and wary about not being able to guess the turns in the market may purchase a put for protection.

At 80 (Figure 2.9), the investor may wish to buy a put (or short the stock). At 60, he or she will sell the put, go long and buy a put with a lower striking price. At 90, sell the long position and go short. The short position is unprotected, however. This may lead the investor to a decision to simply close out the long position at 90 and

FIGURE 2.9.

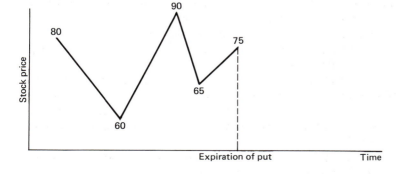

wait for the stock to come back down to 65. At 65, the investor goes long once again, protected by the put position in the event the stock continues to depreciate. And so the process continues until the option expires. The preceding assumes that the investor has guessed the turns in the stock prices correctly. Furthermore, as we shall later see, many other strategies are also possible.

Puts for Psychological Sustenance

An investor with a short position in a security may panic if its price appreciates by a certain number of points and may therefore decide to close out the position. A put owner, knowing the maximum size of the loss (the put premium), would wait out the stock until, with luck, its trend reversed. The closing of the short position may occur and the investor may only later discover that the stock price has dropped considerably. Additional pressure is put on the short position in the security by the brokerage house. As the price of the stock appreciates, the short seller is marked to the market—that is, asked to deposit more money, further increasing the commitment and the pressure to close the position.

Vector Representation

A put buyer position is represented by the vector $\begin{bmatrix} 0 \\ 1 \end{bmatrix}$. If the stock appreciates, there is no loss on the put. The cost of the put is a sunk cost. If the price of the underlying security drops by one point, the put will appreciate by a point ($+1$).

A long put position, it must be observed, is equivalent to a short position in the stock and a long position in a call option.

Short Stock		Buy Call		Buy Put
$\begin{bmatrix} -1 \\ 1 \end{bmatrix}$	$+$	$\begin{bmatrix} 1 \\ 0 \end{bmatrix}$	$=$	$\begin{bmatrix} 0 \\ 1 \end{bmatrix}$

Put Versus a Stop-Loss Order

Protection against a loss in a newly established long position and the protection of book profits in a long position is securable through the purchase of a put. The market, however, affords the investor another avenue for protection that requires no initial commitment of funds. This avenue is the stop-loss order. An investor with a long position, for example, may ask his or her broker to place a stop-loss order at five points below the current market price. If the market price falls to five points below market or through this threshold, the stop order becomes a market order (remains a limit order for stocks listed on the American Stock Exchange) and is sold at the bid, which can be much lower than the price limit set by the investor. The investor will obviously be distraught if the stock price rebounds up immediately after the stop order is executed. By contrast, the put gives the trader a considerable amount of flexibility, but at a price. The stop order is more rigid but does not require the commitment of funds. The additional advantages of a stop order stem from the fact that its time horizon can be indefinite, while a put has a fixed and short life, and that it can be used against odd-lot security holdings. Puts are available on round lots only.

We can, therefore, conclude that the choice between puts and stop orders is a matter of investor biases, risk preferences, and other considerations.

2.11 WRITING PUTS

The put writer, like the call writer, is primarily interested in earning premium income. Against the premium, he or she is committed to purchasing the underlying security at the striking price any time it is "put" to him or her by the option buyer during the life of the contract.

Puts to Earn Premium Income

The put writer must be bullish on the underlying stock or, at worst, expect it not to decline in price before a commitment is made. Otherwise the losses in the event of a price decline will equal those realized on a long position adjusted for the put premium received.

Consider the case of an investor who sold a three-month put on JAK Inc. for $250 with a striking price of $45. The current market price of JAK is $45. The investor does not hold a long position. The three situations outlined below are possible.

Situation 1: Stock Appreciates (Assume to $55)

The holder of the put will obviously not exercise it. The put writer realizes the full premium. If we assume a 30 percent margin requirement, the rate of return is equal to[23]

$$\frac{\$250}{(\$4{,}500 \times 30\%)} = \frac{\text{call premium}}{\text{funds committed}} = \textbf{18.51\% per quarter}$$

or an annualized rate of 18.51 × 4 = 74.04%.

These results must be compared with the outright ownership of the stock, a real alternative given that the investor is bullish on the security.

The returns on a long position (assuming 100 shares) are

$$\frac{\$5{,}500 - \$4{,}500}{(\$4{,}500 \times 50\%)} - \begin{array}{c}\text{interest costs on} \\ \text{borrowed funds} \\ \text{(assume market rate} = 15\%)\end{array} =$$

$$\left(\frac{\$1{,}000}{\$2{,}250} \times 100\right) - \left(15\% \times \frac{1}{4}\right) = \textbf{40.69\%}$$

or an annualized rate of 40.69% × 4 = 162.76%.

Hindsight shows that the investor would have been better off holding a long position.

Situation 2: Stock Remains at $45

If the stock remained at $45, the put writer would simply realize the full amount of the premium.

---

[23] This is the amount the investor must keep on deposit with his broker. The exact amount actually equals 30 percent of the value of the stock plus the amount in-the-money or minus the amount out-of-the-money less the proceeds from the sale of the put.

Situation 3: Stock Falls to $35

At $35 the put holder will have a profitable option. Exercising the option means that the option writer would acquire a security with a $35 market value at the striking price of $45. There is a loss of $750 ($1,000 − $250 premium received) on the position. The implications of these results for the put writer are not to write a put unless he is willing to own the security under those circumstances.

Puts to Acquire a Stock

The put writer here sells the put in the hope that it will be exercised—that the price of the underlying security will, in fact, drop. If the writer's expectations materialize, he or she would succeed in buying a stock at a price lower than that prevailing at the time the put was written. The obvious contradictions are that the investor who expects a temporary correction in the price of the stock would still go through with the sale of the option when it would have been wiser simply to wait. If the stock appreciated in price the put would not be exercised and the put writer collects the full put premium.

Vector and Graphic Representation

The put writer's position is summarized in the following vector $\begin{bmatrix} 0 \\ -1 \end{bmatrix}$, which indicates that the position would realize zero profit (before considering the put premium) if the stock appreciated by a point and would lose a point for every point depreciation in the value of the underlying security. This position is equivalent to a long position in the stock against which a call has been written.

$$\underset{\text{Long}}{\begin{bmatrix} 1 \\ -1 \end{bmatrix}} \quad + \quad \underset{\text{Write Call}}{\begin{bmatrix} -1 \\ 0 \end{bmatrix}} \quad = \quad \underset{\text{Write Put}}{\begin{bmatrix} 0 \\ -1 \end{bmatrix}}$$

This vector presentation assumes that the put sold is naked, that is, the put writer does not own the security. If the put writer owns the underlying stock, a put may well be sold with the expectation of improving cash flow on a stock position held for long-term appreciation. The expectations are obviously that the stock will not drop in price or actually go up. Graphically, the put position is illustrated by Figure 2.10.

Figure 2.10a shows the position of a put buyer. The buyer begins to recover the cost of the put when the striking price is reached. Profits are realized below K. The position of the put option writer is shown in Figure 2.10b. Losses are incurred below point K on the stock price axis. The writer would obviously be averse to a price decline—an event for which the options buyer is hoping, if not praying.

The put positions are to be contrasted with the short position depicted in Figure 2.10c.

Pricing Puts

The logic applied to the pricing of a call should be reversed if one is to understand the pricing of put options. Figure 2.11 shows how the put price is related to the stock price, the term to maturity, and the striking price.

The straight line beginning at point X on the horizontal axis represents the minimum

FIGURE 2.10. Graphic depiction of put position

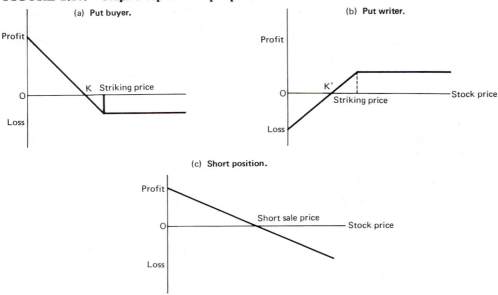

(a) Put buyer.

(b) Put writer.

(c) Short position.

value of a put. At *X*, the striking price is equal to the stock price. Below *X*, $S - X$ is negative, that is, the put is in-the-money. The put holder can buy the stock at the market price and "put" it to the put writer at the higher striking price. At *X*, the put is just in-the-money. To the right of *X*, the put is out-of-the-money. The put holder will not exercise the put; that is, the put writer will realize the full premium.

Figure 2.11 shows two curves for puts with differing maturities. The explanations

FIGURE 2.11. Put price in relation to stock price, term to maturity, and striking price.

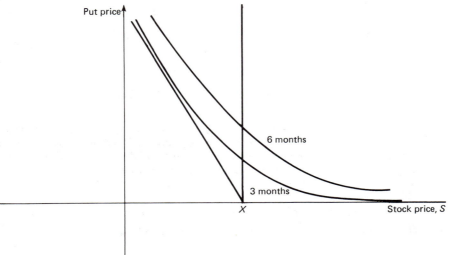

of the curvature are essentially similar to those of a call. The longer the life of the option, the higher the values of the put. The appreciation of the value of the put in relation to the price of the stock is closer to a one-to-one basis the more in-the-money the put option is and the closer it is to its expiration date. At *X*, the rate of increase in the put price is half the rate of depreciation in the price of the stock.

Put-Valuation Formula[24]

Consider an investor with a long position in the stock. In order to establish a riskless position in the security, the investor would sell a call and buy a put. Using a vector notation, the risk-free position is as follows:

Long Position		Sell Call		Buy Put		Risk-free Position[25]
$\begin{bmatrix} 1 \\ -1 \end{bmatrix}$	$+$	$\begin{bmatrix} -1 \\ 0 \end{bmatrix}$	$+$	$\begin{bmatrix} 0 \\ 1 \end{bmatrix}$	$=$	$\begin{bmatrix} 0 \\ 0 \end{bmatrix}$

The cash outlay required for the establishment of a risk-free position is equal to

$$C = V + P - W$$

where C = total cash outlay

  V = price of stock × number of shares bought (assume 100)

  P = put premium

  W = call premium

Since the investor's position is risk-free, a broker or bank should be willing to loan him V dollars at the risk-free rate i, thereby avoiding the commitment of any of the investor's funds. The total interest cost is Vi. The present value of the interest costs is $Vi/(1 + i)$. Therefore, the profit resulting from a risk-free arbitrage operation is equal to

$$W - \frac{Vi}{1 + i} - P = \Pi_f$$

where Π_f = risk-free profit.

In a perfect market, Π_f should equal zero. That is, as the arbitrage process starts

---

[24] The discussion is based on **Hans R. Stoll**, "The Relationship between Put and Call Option Prices." *Journal of Finance*, vol. 24, (December 1969), pp. 801–829; and **J. P. Gould** and **D. Galai**, "Transactions Costs and the Relationship Between Put and Call Prices." *Journal of Financial Economics*, vol. 1 (1974), pp. 105–129. An alternative and more rigorous derivation was provided by **Michael Parkinson** in "Option Pricing: The American Put." *Journal of Business* (January 1977), pp. 21–35.

[25] A risk-free position can also be established starting with a short position in the stock.

Short Position		Write Put		Buy Call		Risk-free Position
$\begin{bmatrix} -1 \\ 1 \end{bmatrix}$	$+$	$\begin{bmatrix} 0 \\ -1 \end{bmatrix}$	$+$	$\begin{bmatrix} 1 \\ 0 \end{bmatrix}$	$=$	$\begin{bmatrix} 0 \\ 0 \end{bmatrix}$

and continues, $\Pi_f > 0$, the sale of the call exerts downward pressure on their price, and the purchases of the puts places an upward pressure on their price, causing Π_f to move toward zero. Therefore

$$W - \frac{Vi}{1+i} - P = 0 \tag{2.12}$$

and

$$W - P = \frac{Vi}{1+i} \tag{2.13}$$

dividing Equation 2.13 through by V, we get

$$\frac{W}{V} - \frac{P}{V} = \frac{i}{1+i} \cong i$$

Therefore, the difference between the relative value of a call (W/V) and the relative value of a put (P/V) is approximately equal to the risk-free rate. In order to calculate the put premium, an investor only has to consider the call premium and the risk-free rate.

Another method for pricing put options is to use the Two-State Option Pricing Model (TSOPM) introduced earlier in this chapter. We reintroduce Equation 2.6 and use it on a simple example

$$P_o = \frac{V_t^+ (1 + r - H_t^-) + V_t^- (H_t^+ - 1 - r)}{(H_t^+ - H_t^-)(1 + r)}$$

Assume:

Stock Price	Put Option		Stock	Put Option
		+	110	0
100	P			
	t	−	90	10

$$t = 1$$

and assume: $r = 0.09$. Therefore

$$P_o = \frac{0(1 + 0.09 - 0.90) + 10(1.10 - 1 - 0.09)}{(1.10 - 0.90)(1.09)} = \frac{0.1}{0.218} = \textbf{\$0.46}$$

A more complex derivation of the put premium would proceed along the same lines as those of the call option presented earlier.

We now look at the relationship between stock and options markets.

2.12 OPTIONS AND STOCK, ANOTHER LINKAGE

The dependence of options prices on the behavior of stock prices was discussed earlier in this chapter. The question we address here is whether a net benefit accrues to the trader in the stock market from observing the behavior of the option on the underlying stock of interest. The answer appears to be yes. Our discussion will rely on the work of S. Manaster and R. Rendleman, Jr.[26]

Manaster and Rendleman set out to test, using the B&S model, whether stock prices implied in the option risk premiums are the same as those observed in the stock market. Using data on 172 stocks and their listed options covering the period April 26, 1973 to June 30, 1976 (805 trading days) M&R found, taking dividends into consideration, that by observing the options market additional information not contained in stock prices can be derived. Actual stock prices were expected to move in the direction of implied prices as actual prices adjusted to their equilibrium level which is better approximated by the implied price. This is so because option markets appear to discount more relevant information or the same information at a faster pace. The stock market appears to lag behind the options market in the discounting of new information by up to 24 hours. The lag, however, was not sufficiently large so as to allow for significant arbitrage opportunities between the options and stock markets.

We now look at a new option covering a multitude of stocks.

The S&P 100

On Friday, March 11, 1983, the CBOE introduced options (calls and puts) on the CBOE 100 index. This index was renamed the S&P 100 index in June 1983. The option calls for a cash settlement off a market-weighted index of 100 stocks. The index includes names like IBM, General Motors, AT&T, and Eastman Kodak.

The index was well received. Interest in the then-nearest contract (the June contract) was high from the starting bell. One reason for the interest is that this instrument is yet another vehicle for betting on the direction of the market with limited financial exposure. The maximum that could be lost in a long position is the premium paid. Another reason is that an option on the S&P 100 allows for the unbundling of risk. Since the index is made up of 100 stocks from different industries, it succeeds in eliminating firm-specific risk (present in an option on a single stock) and industry risk. The latter risk derives from factors specific to an industry such as regulation, technology gap, foreign competition, and so forth. Firm-specific risk and industry risk can be eliminated through portfolio diversification. One hundred stocks assure this. The risk that the S&P 100 hedges against is, therefore, the market or systematic risk—a risk that is common to all stocks but in varying degrees. An option on a single stock allows for the transference of all three risks combined: market risk, industry risk, and firm-specific risk. Two of these risks can be eliminated by portfolio diversification.

The S&P 100 is a creation of the CBOE. Each option on the index represents $100 times the value of the index. If the index is at 110, its value is $11,000. Various maturities and striking prices are available. The contract months are March, June, September,

---

[26] **Steven Manaster** and **Richard Rendleman, Jr.,** "Option Prices as Predictors of Equilibrium Stock Prices," *The Journal of Finance,* vol. 37, (September 1982), pp. 1043–1057.

and December. The expiration date in the contract month is, as in options on individual stocks, the Saturday following the third Friday of the expiration month. Exercise prices are set at five-point intervals around the current value of the index and new exercise prices are added as the value of the index changes significantly upward or downward. Options below 3 are quoted in increments of $\frac{1}{16}$ ($2\frac{1}{16}$, for example, is equal to $2.0625 \times 100 = \$206.25$) and those above 3 are quoted in $\frac{1}{8}$ increments. The value of the index is continuously updated by the CBOE.

The settlement of options of the S&P 100 is in cash. The exerciser of the option receives that amount by which the option is in-the-money. That is, the exerciser receives the difference between [the strike price $\times$ 100] and [closing index value on exercise date $\times$ 100].

The uses of options of the S&P 100 are similar to those of options on individual stocks. S&P 100 options are used for speculative and hedging purposes.

Speculators could use S&P 100 options to bet on the direction of the stock market since the 100 shares making up the index are quite representative of all the shares in the market. A call will be purchased and a put will be sold if expectations are bullish, and a put will be purchased and a call sold if expectations are bearish.

Portfolio managers with diversified portfolios would use the S&P 100 (and the S&P 500) to hedge market risk, or to generate additional income. A portfolio manager concerned with a downturn in stock prices could buy a put or puts on the S&P 100 hoping that the realized profits (if any) from the put would offset the book losses in the portfolio, or would write a call on the S&P 100. If expectations do not materialize the put(s) premium may be lost in its (their) entirety. The reader should refer to the discussion earlier in the chapter for a profile on the consequences of the various hedge positions. We now look at a long-term option available on certain stocks.

2.13 WARRANTS

A warrant is a long-term option to buy a certain number of shares of the issuing company's stock at a specified price during a given period of time. This option is issued by the Corporation.

Use of Warrants

Warrants are usually issued by corporations as "sweeteners" to debt and preferred stock issues. Their inclusion in debt issues is intended to lower the interest costs to the firm, to reduce if not eliminate the restrictive covenants in the indenture agreement, and/or to facilitate the sale of the issue. A warrant attached to a bond is equivalent to a convertible bond. This equity feature allows bondholders to participate in the growth of the issuing corporation. If the growth is realized and reflected in a higher market price for the stock and hence the warrant, the warrant holder may be motivated to exercise the warrant. This exercise is equivalent to the corporation issuing new stock at the option price, a price higher than that prevailing at the time the warrant was issued.

From the point of view of the investor, a warrant allows for the following:

1. *Leverage.* The price of a warrant is a fraction of the price of the stock. The investor can, therefore, using the same dollar amount that would have been committed to the purchase of common stock, be able to participate in the growth of more shares

by buying warrants. The extent of the leverage depends on the relationship between the price of the warrant and the price of the stock.

2. *Limited-risk trading.* This results from the lower financial commitment required for warrants versus common stock.

3. *Protecting a short position in the stock.* Warrants protect a short position against rising stock prices in a fashion not too dissimilar from call options. The protection comes from the fixed option price at which the stock can be purchased. Warrants, however, may be much more costly and less flexible than listed options. There is only one striking price and one maturity, and few companies have warrants outstanding.

Warrants Versus Calls

The supply of warrants is limited to the financial needs of a certain corporation in relation to the capital markets requirements. It exists and it expands by corporate fiat. The supply of call options, on the other hand, is determined by market forces. The expansion of this supply has no impact on the number of shares outstanding. As calls are exercised, a mere transfer of ownership of existing shares from a stockholder to an investor occurs. The exercise of a warrant results in a net increase in the number of shares outstanding, with the attending issue of ownership distribution to existing stockholders.

Other differences lie in unequal margin requirements and commission costs and in the fact that warrants have a much longer maturity than any available call option. Indeed, warrants may have unlimited lives because the Internal Revenue Service provided the issuing corporations with the incentive to extend the warrant life. In 1971, the IRS rules that the proceeds from the sale of warrants become taxable income to the issuing corporation if the warrants expire worthless. In order to escape payment of taxes, issuing corporations extended the expiration data on their warrants, leaving those with a long warrant position delighted and those with a short warrant position depressed. The extension breathes life into the warrant and hence its value.

Valuation of Warrants

The theoretical value of a warrant is equal to

$$W_t = (S - OP)N \tag{2.14}$$

where W_t = theoretical value of a warrant

S = market price of stock

OP = option price of stock

N = number of shares to which the warrant can be converted

Note that W_t would be negative if $OP > S$. This is not possible because a warrant selling at a negative price implies that the buyer is receiving money from the seller. We thus concentrate on warrants with positive prices.

The market price of a warrant is ordinarily larger than the theoretical value. Leverage and the life of the warrant account for this difference. As in the call case, the higher the price of the stock, the higher the price of the warrant. The relationship between

FIGURE 2.12. Theoretical vs. market value of a warrant.

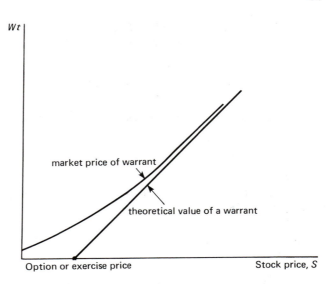

the price of the warrant and the price of the stock converges beyond the option price, as shown in Figure 2.12. The reader may want to compare Figure 2.8 with Figure 2.12.

Warrants are transferable securities and are traded like stocks. Some warrants are listed on the major exchanges, others are traded over the counter. The popularity of warrants as financing vehicles seems to be waning. No research has yet been completed on what impact, if any, the options market has had on the warrant market.

2.14 STOCK RIGHTS

A stock right is an option given existing stockholders to buy a certain number of shares of a new stock issue. Stock rights are technically referred to as "stock subscription warrants." A stockholder receives a right for every share held. Stock rights have a limited life and are transferable.

Use of Rights

Stock rights are used by the issuing corporation to induce existing stockholders to purchase new shares of stock, allowing them in the process to maintain their proportionate ownership in the company. The subscription price (price at which the right holder can purchase a new share of stock) is lower than the market price of stock.

An investor uses stock rights the same way warrants are used. Typically, stock rights have a much shorter maturity than warrants.

Value of Rights

The value of one stock right is derived as follows:

$$SR = \frac{S - SP}{M + 1}$$

where SR = price of a stock right
$\quad\quad\quad S$ = market price of one stock with rights on
$\quad\quad\quad SP$ = subscription price
$\quad\quad\quad M$ = number of rights required to purchase one share of stock

The 1 in the denominator is added because the numerator is inflated by the price of one stock right.

Example

What is the value of one right if the market price of one share (rights on) is $55, the subscription price is $50, and it takes four rights to acquire a new share of stock?

$$SR = \frac{55 - 50}{4 + 1} = \$1$$

The holder of one share of stock needs four rights valued at $4 and $50 in cash in order to acquire a share of stock valued at $55. The net saving is $1 or the price of one right. Hence, the addition of 1 in the denominator.

If the stock goes "ex-right" (the holder of the stock no longer receives a right for a share held), its price will drop by the theoretical value of a right, to $54. The theoretical value of one right remains the same as is calculated as follows.

$$SR = \frac{S' - SP}{M}$$

where S' = market price of stock ex-rights.

$$SR = \frac{54 - 50}{4} = \$1$$

Some corporate statutes have preemptive rights clauses requiring the company to give existing stockholders preferential treatment (in terms of access and price). Rights, therefore, allow existing stockholders to keep their proportionate ownership in the corporation, if they so desire, and prevent management from selling new stocks at prices that would effectively disenfranchise existing stockholders. One additional benefit worth noting is that stock rights enjoy a lower margin requirement, hence they have an even larger leverage potential.

CONCLUSIONS

In this chapter we have provided the basics of stock options. Hedgers, investors, and speculators in the options market have found other means of using options successfully, however. These strategies and other options considerations are covered in the chapter to follow.

QUESTIONS

1. The April 21, 1983, issue of *The Wall Street Journal* gave the following option prices on IBM.

Option & NY Close	Strike Price	Calls—Last			Puts—Last		
		Jul	Oct	Jan	Jul	Oct	Jan
IBM	75	$40\frac{1}{4}$	s	s	$\frac{1}{16}$	s	s
$114\frac{3}{4}$	80	$35\frac{1}{2}$	s	s	$\frac{1}{16}$	s	s
$114\frac{3}{4}$	85	$30\frac{1}{2}$	s	s	$\frac{1}{8}$	s	s
$114\frac{3}{4}$	90	$25\frac{7}{8}$	$26\frac{3}{4}$	s	$\frac{5}{16}$	$1\frac{1}{16}$	s
$114\frac{3}{4}$	95	21	23	s	$\frac{1}{2}$	$1\frac{5}{16}$	s
$114\frac{3}{4}$	100	$16\frac{1}{2}$	$18\frac{3}{4}$	$20\frac{1}{4}$	$1\frac{1}{8}$	$2\frac{1}{8}$	$\frac{13}{16}$
$114\frac{3}{4}$	110	$9\frac{1}{8}$	12	$14\frac{3}{8}$	$3\frac{1}{2}$	$5\frac{1}{4}$	$6\frac{1}{8}$
$114\frac{3}{4}$	120	$4\frac{1}{4}$	$7\frac{1}{8}$	$9\frac{1}{4}$	$8\frac{3}{8}$	$9\frac{3}{4}$	$10\frac{3}{4}$

   a. Which options are in-the-money?
   b. Which options are out-of-the-money?
   c. Which option would you use to protect a long position if you were very concerned about an adverse price movement in IBM? What type of risk does this put option protect you against?
   d. Which option would you use to protect a short position if you were somewhat unsettled about market conditions?
   e. Why would the July/95 put have a positive value?

2. How are intervals between striking prices set?

3. What function does the Options Clearing Corporation perform?

4. How can calls be used to limit trading risk (assuming an investor has gone short on a stock)?

5. The vector representation of a call is $\begin{bmatrix} 1 \\ 0 \end{bmatrix}$. What does this reveal about the potential loss of the option buyer?

6. From a risk perspective, what is the difference between "naked" and "covered" call option writing?

7. An option trader resells a call option that she bought in-the-money. If the price of the underlying stock has not moved, can she still lose out on the option investment? (Ignore transactions costs).

8. Two calls have the same striking price but different maturities. How does one explain the additional value of the call with nine months to maturity over the call with three months to maturity?

9. Why would an option on a security with a high beta coefficient tend to have a higher premium than options written on securities with lower betas?

10. Many of the assumptions of the B&S model are questionable. What are their implications for the validity of the model itself?

11. How is writing a call similar to buying a put? How is it dissimilar? What are the vector representations of each position?

12. What are the costs/benefits of a put versus a stop-loss order to reduce downside risk on a long position in a stock?

13. An investor who is bullish on a stock may choose to write a put versus taking a long position in the stock. Why?

14. Compare and contrast a warrant to a call.

15. Delineate specifically the risk associated with writing put and call options to generate income.

16. You are a manager of a pension fund. Under what conditions would you add options to your portfolio? Justify your decision, given your fiduciary responsibility.

17. List the various ways of using call and put options.

18. Stagnant equity markets have historically dampened investors' enthusiasm for committing funds to equity securities. How might the option market have changed this reluctance?

19. An investor has a long position in a stock and a long position in a put. Does he have a perfectly hedged position? If not, what would he need to do in order to achieve such a position?

20. "The relationship between the price of a call and that of a put is complex." Comment.

21. How does the size of dividends affect the price of call options? Why?

22. What type of risk does the S&P 100 hedge against? Why?

PROBLEMS

1. Mrs. Trader buys a call option for $400 on Oct. 1, 1982, and exercises it one month later to acquire a round lot of DGO stock at $45/share. Assume Mrs. Trader is in the 50 percent tax bracket. What is the cost of the stock for tax purposes? If she sells the stock for $5,500 on Oct. 10, 1983, what will her tax liability be? What if she waits to sell until Nov. 10, 1983?

2. Mr. Investor, optimistic about WJM stock (current price: $44/share) is considering these two strategies (assume no margin buying):
   a. Buy 100 shares of WJM
   b. Buy WJM/3 mo./40 selling for $500
   What is the profit and annualized return on each of these two strategies if WJM moves up to $50? WJM moves up to $45? WJM retreats to $40?

3. Mrs. Investor owns 100 shares of Kinnare Cube Company stock selling at $83/share; Mr. Speculator does not. They both write call options on KCC stock with a

striking price of $85 and receive a $750 premium. Calculate the gain/loss for each if KCC stock moves to $88/share.

4. RGH stock is known to have a hedge ratio of 0.25. How could an investor who owns one round lot of the stock construct a "neutral hedge"? What would his return be if markets are efficient?

5. Use the B&S model to calculate the theoretical value of a MES/3 mo./40 call option. MES stock is selling at $50, has a dividend yield of 3 percent, and a σ^2 of 0.36. The risk-free rate is 6 percent.

6. Use the B&S model to estimate the σ^2 of a KWO/6 mo./45 call option; KWO is selling at $52 and has a dividend yield of 5 percent. The risk-free rate is 8 percent and the option sells for 12¼. (Hint: You will have to use trial and error.) Can the values given here be useful, and sufficient, to arrive at an option price using TSOPM? Why?

7. What is the value of one right if the market price of one share (rights on) is $31, the subscription price is $25, and it takes five rights to acquire one new share of stock?

Cumulative Probability Distributions

Table 2.A1

Values of $N(x)$ for Given Values of x for a Cumulative Normal Probability Distribution with Zero Mean and Unit Variance

x	$N(x)$	x	$N(x)$	x	$N(x)$	x	$N(x)$	x	$N(x)$	x	$N(x)$
		−1.00	.1587	1.00	.8413	−2.00	.0228	.00	.5000	2.00	.9773
−2.95	.0016	− .95	.1711	1.05	.8531	−1.95	.0256	.05	.5199	2.05	.9798
−2.90	.0019	− .90	.1841	1.10	.8643	−1.90	.0287	.10	.5398	2.10	.9821
−2.85	.0022	− .85	.1977	1.15	.8749	−1.85	.0322	.15	.5596	2.15	.9842
−2.80	.0026	− .80	.2119	1.20	.8849	−1.80	.0359	.20	.5793	2.20	.9861
−2.75	.0030	− .75	.2266	1.25	.8944	−1.75	.0401	.25	.5987	2.25	.9878
−2.70	.0035	− .70	.2420	1.30	.9032	−1.70	.0446	.30	.6179	2.30	.9893
−2.65	.0040	− .65	.2578	1.35	.9115	−1.65	.0495	.35	.6368	2.35	.9906
−2.60	.0047	− .60	.2743	1.40	.9192	−1.60	.0548	.40	.6554	2.40	.9918
−2.55	.0054	− .55	.2912	1.45	.9265	−1.55	.0606	.45	.6736	2.45	.9929
−2.50	.0062	− .50	.3085	1.50	.9332	−1.50	.0668	.50	.6915	2.50	.9938
−2.45	.0071	− .45	.3264	1.55	.9394	−1.45	.0735	.55	.7088	2.55	.9946
−2.40	.0082	− .40	.3446	1.60	.9452	−1.40	.0808	.60	.7257	2.60	.9953
−2.35	.0094	− .35	.3632	1.65	.9505	−1.35	.0885	.65	.7422	2.65	.9960
−2.30	.0107	− .30	.3821	1.70	.9554	−1.30	.0968	.70	.7580	2.70	.9965
−2.25	.0122	− .25	.4013	1.75	.9599	−1.25	.1057	.75	.7734	2.75	.9970
−2.20	.0139	− .20	.4207	1.80	.9641	−1.20	.1151	.80	.7881	2.80	.9974
−2.15	.0158	− .15	.4404	1.85	.9678	−1.15	.1251	.85	.8023	2.85	.9978
−2.10	.0179	− .10	.4602	1.90	.9713	−1.10	.1357	.90	.8159	2.90	.9981
−2.05	.0202	− .05	.4801	1.95	.9744	−1.05	.1469	.95	.8289	2.95	.9984

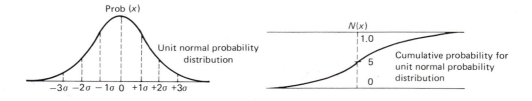

Prob (x)

Unit normal probability distribution

$-3\sigma \ -2\sigma \ -1\sigma \ 0 \ +1\sigma \ +2\sigma \ +3\sigma$

$N(x)$

1.0

.5

0

Cumulative probability for unit normal probability distribution

3 | Advanced Option Strategies and Considerations

3.1 INTRODUCTION

The options market is becoming increasingly complex, in the process multiplying potentially profitable opportunities. This chapter focuses on most of the strategies employed by options traders and on the necessary elements of an options program. We begin our discussion with combinations.

3.2 COMBINATIONS

The variety of investment opportunities available to the sophisticated investor in the options market is practically limitless. We begin the sorting out with the various combinations that can be developed by using puts and calls. First, a few definitions.

A combination is the purchase or sale of a call and a put with different (or similar) striking prices or maturities or both.

A straddle is a combination of a put and a call with the same striking price and maturity. Both options are on the same side of the market (long or short).

3.3 BUYING STRADDLES

Call buyers are optimistic about the direction of the price of the underlying security. Unless their expectations materialize , they would not realize a profit on the long call position. The opposite is true for put buyers. A problem presents itself if the direction of the market price of the security is unpredictable or the news that could cause a certain price movement is unpredictable. An example of the latter was, to pull an episode from corporate history, the announcement by Polaroid that the company would produce its own films for use in Polaroid instant cameras (these films were previously bought from Eastman Kodak). If all the bugs in the production process and in the quality of the film are worked out, the stock would experience a substantial price appreciation; if not, the stock would suffer a significant price decline. The question, therefore, was how an investor could bet on the outcome and simultaneously minimize the cost of

the bet. Straddles offered just such an alternative. The call offered a profit potential if the price rose, and the put offered a profit potential if the price fell. We now summarize the various motivations for buying straddles.

Straddles for Leverage

An investor who is expecting a major change in the price of a security but is uncertain about the direction would purchase a straddle. A price change in either direction that will allow the investor to recoup the unprofitable side of the straddle would result in a profit. Such possibilities are not as rewarding and as risk-limiting outside the option market. Given the uncertainty about the direction of the price movement, a long position in the stock offers no downside protection, a short position offers no protection against price appreciation, and a combination of both a short and a long position offers a zero profit opportunity. The losses (gains) on the long position would offset the gains (losses) on the short position.

An investor can, however, close out either of the positions as soon as the direction of the market is determined. In so doing, the investor does not capitalize on the full increase or decrease in the price of the stock (a somewhat analogous position to that of a straddle) but, most importantly, remains open to the possibility of price reversals. These possibilities are very real if the evidence on the random walk theory is correct. This theory argues that there are no observable trends in the market that allow an investor to realize a gain from any filter rule, regardless of the nature of the filter. Protection, however, is not costless.

The leverage provided by a straddle results from the small financial commitment it requires when compared with a position in the underlying stock. A straddle on JAK/Dec/50 selling for $7 requires a commitment of $700 plus commission costs. A commitment to a long, short, or combined position in the stock would require an investment of at least 50 percent of the price of the security. If the current market price is $50, the minimum commitment would be $2,500 on one side of the market, over three times that of a straddle.

While leverage can be very lucrative in the event of a major price change, we must voice a caution about the negative side: If there is *no* movement in the price of the stock, the investor will lose the full premium or 100 percent of the capital invested in the straddle. The losses in percentage terms are large (small in dollar terms) up to the neighborhood of the break-even point. This point is determined by the striking price on the straddle $\pm$ the premium. A JAK/Dec/50 straddle selling at $700 has break-even points of 43 (50 $-$ 7) and 57 (50 $+$ 7). Below 43, the put is well in-the-money and hence profitable; beyond 57, the call is well in-the-money and is profitable. The extent to which an option is in-the-money or out-of-the-money depends, as stated earlier, on the relationship between the striking price and the market price on the underlying security. If the straddle premium of $700 were distributed $300 and $400 for the put and the call respectively and the current market price of the stock is $55, then the call is $5 in-the-money ($S - X = 5$) and the put is $5 out-of-the-money ($X - S = -5$). The profit on the call option is equal to $100; the loss on the put is $300 if the straddle is exercised. The put price does not drop to zero, however, if the straddle has some time left to run before expiring. The positive put premium in this case is time premium, as was suggested earlier.

An investor who is more optimistic than pessimistic about the prospects for a stock

may wish to purchase a straddle with an in-the-money call and a put that is out-of-the-money. A rather pessimistic investor may purchase a straddle with an in-the-money put and an out-of-the-money call. The length of the life of the straddle purchased would depend on the expected speed of adjustment in the stock price. The structuring of the straddle strategy depends on the investor's expectations, risk profile, and budget size.

Straddles for Aggressive Trading

An investor wishing to be protected against unexpected movements in the price of a stock, given a position in the stock, would buy a straddle. The option position would allow for a more aggressive posture.

Consider the hypothetical stock price pattern shown in Figure 3.1. An investor owning a straddle (premium = $1,200) with $S = 60$ would be protected by the put had he or she bet on a long position and the price dropped to 50.

A short position at 60 would result in a $1,000 gross profit (on 100 shares) excluding commission; it would bring a profit on the put and a loss on the call (equal to its cost) if the stock fell to 50. If at 50 the investor believed that the price of the stock was about to rebound and would be unlikely to return to this level, he or she would close out the short position, go long on the stock, and possibly decide to close out the put side of the straddle. This latter course is referred to as "lifting a leg." If this were done, the investor would have guessed the market correctly (see Figure 3.1) and would reap substantial profits. Lifting a leg exposes the investor to downside risk, however, in the event of a continuing price decline. If the straddle position were kept intact and the long position was closed, the appreciation from 50 to 90 would obviously cover the full cost of the straddle. Once this was achieved, the investor could trade with impunity. The investment is zero, and no matter what the direction of the stock, a profit will accrue on the straddle because its cost has been recovered. A long position will be doubly profitable (long + call) if the stock moves as expected; a short position will be doubly profitable (short + put). The ideal—an unrealistic expectation—based on Figure 3.1, is to lift a leg (the put) at 50, go long, sell at 90 and go short, cover at 70 and go long, and close out the long position and/or the call position at 80 when the option expires.

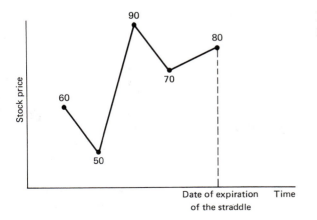

FIGURE 3.1. Hypothetical stock price pattern.

FIGURE 3.2. **Position of the straddle buyer.**

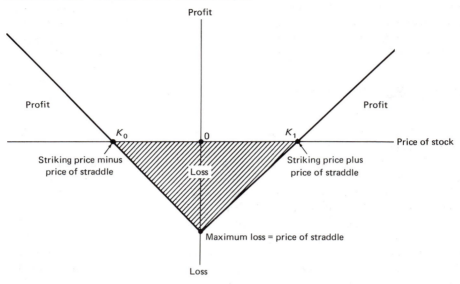

Vector and Graphic Representation

The vector representation of a straddle is as follows:

Call   Put   Straddle

$$\begin{bmatrix} 1 \\ 0 \end{bmatrix} + \begin{bmatrix} 0 \\ 1 \end{bmatrix} = \begin{bmatrix} 1 \\ 1 \end{bmatrix}$$

A point appreciation in the price of the stock causes a point appreciation in the value of the call (before accounting for the premium); a point drop in the price of the stock brings about a point appreciation in the value of the put.

The position of the straddle buyer is shown graphically in Figure 3.2, which shows the straddle position realizing a gain beyond K_1 and below K_0. The maximum loss (100 percent of the premium) is realized at point 0, where there is no movement in the price of the stock (striking price = market price).

3.4 WRITING STRADDLES

The straddle writer makes a commitment to purchase a stock at the striking price during the life of the option (against the put) and to sell a stock at the same striking price during the same time period (against the call).

The commitment of the straddle writer can be made against a position in the underlying security or against no position (a naked straddle). No matter what position the straddle writer has in the stock, he seeks a return—the ceiling on which is defined by the size of the straddle premium. The maximum return is realized if the market price of the underlying security is equal to the striking price. Any deviation (+ or −) from the striking price would mean a dollar return lower than the full premium (minus the double commission incurred upon the sale of the straddle). A loss would result, however,

TABLE 3.1
Straddle Opportunities in IBM, Quoted
Jan. 14, 1983[a]

Option	Expiration Dates		
	January	April	July
IBM 90	8¾	12⅝	15
IBM 90*P*[b]	¹⁄₁₆	2¾	4½
IBM 95	4⅝	9⅛	12
IBM 95*P*	¹³⁄₁₆	4⅝	7
IBM 100	1¹¹⁄₁₆	6¾	9⅜
IBM 100*P*	2¾	7½	9¼

[a] IBM market price = 98¼

[b] *P* = put

if the price of the stock appreciated or depreciated by an amount greater than the size of the premium.

The option market currently allows for varied straddle-writing opportunities on several securities. Turning to Table 3.1, we can see that in the case of International Business Machines, Inc. nine straddle-writing opportunities present themselves.

The maximum premium could be earned on the longest maturity of IBM 90. The straddle writer must be aware, however, of the fact that the longer the commitment is outstanding, the longer the position is exposed to price fluctuations which could lead to a loss in the position.

In addition to the choice of maturity and striking price, given the security, the straddle writer has an additional choice between a covered position and a naked position.

Writing Covered Straddles

The writer of a covered straddle assumes a position with different risk/return features from those of the writer of naked options. This, we shall examine in detail.

A covered straddle position should be assumed if and only if the writer is prepared to sell shares when the stock appreciates in price and the call is exercised. The writer must also be ready to buy additional shares when the stock drops in price and the put is exercised. A rise in the price of the stock could leave the writer with no position in the security and a decline could leave him or her with twice the original position. The possibility that both sides of the straddle could be exercised prior to expiration should not be discounted, however.

Consider an April straddle position involving the following (from Table 3.1):

Buy 100 IBM at 98¼
Sell IBM/April/95 at 9⅛
Sell IBM/April/95*P* at 4⅝

The proceeds from the sale of the straddle are $912.50 + $462.50 = $1,375.

The amount of capital committed (with 50 percent margin requirement on the stock and 30 percent on the put) is outlined below.

For Stock

98¼ × 100 = $9,825.00

Margin requirement = $9,825 × 50% = $4,912.50

For the Put Option

The margin requirement on the put is 30 percent of the market price of the underlying stock ± the difference between the market price and the striking price (+ if the put is in-the-money, − if the put is out-of-the-money)

(9,825 × 30%) − [(98¼ − 95) × 100] =	$2,622.50
Total ($4,912.50 + $2,622.50)	7,535.00
Less premium received 13¾ × 100	−1,375.00
Capital commitment (investment)	**$6,160.00**

The figures above do not account for the commissions; one on the stock, one on the call, and a third on the put.

If the stock appreciates in price, to 105 for example, the call will be exercised. The straddle writer would lose the stock and earn just the call premium or $912.50 (a lower sum than could have been earned on a straight long position) minus the loss on the stock because of the exercise of the call (98¼ − 95 = 3¼). If the appreciation continues during the life of the straddle, the put becomes worthless and the straddle writer could have earned a total of 10½ points (13¾ − 3¼) or $1,050/$6,160 ≅ 0.17 (from January 14 to the Saturday following the third Friday of April).

If the stock reverses its upward direction and falls to but not below 95, the put will not be exercised and the returns to the straddle writer are similar to the previous case.

If the stock price declines below 95, the put will be in the money and its holder will exercise it. The straddle writer is, once again, the owner of the stock which could produce more loss if the market continues to weaken.

If the stock price started out in a downward direction, the straddle writer would see the put exercised against him or her. If the stock price falls to 80 and the put is exercised at this level, the writer would now own a depreciated asset (the original stock) and an overvalued asset (the new shares of stock). The returns from the sale of the straddle are as follows:

Loss on old stock: 98¼(100) − 80(100) =	$1,825
Loss on new shares: 95(100) − 80(100) =	1,500
Total loss	$3,325
Less the premium received	1,375
Loss	**$1,950**

This loss is a book loss (realized loss) if the straddle expires with the stock trading at 80 on an investment of $6,160, or a rate of approximately 32 percent.

One way to reduce this loss is to close out the stock position before the stock price reaches 80. Another course, an optimum course for the minimization of a loss resulting from a decline in the price of the underlying security, is to write a naked straddle. This strategy, however, could backfire if the stock appreciates substantially over 98¼.

Writing a Naked Straddle

Writing a naked straddle would obviously reduce the size of the total initial commitment, for the writer would not have to pay for a long position in the stock and for the commission thereon.

The capital commitment on a naked straddle is equal to 30% of the value of the underlying security:

$$(98\tfrac{1}{4} \times 100) \times 30\% = \$2,947.50$$

± the larger of the amount in (out) of the money on the call or the put.

The put is $3\tfrac{1}{4}$ out-of-the-money; the call is $3\tfrac{1}{4}$ in-the-money. Therefore an additional sum is required, equal to $3\tfrac{1}{4} \times 100$, or $325.00

Additional sum	325.00
Total investment (2,947.50 + 325)	$3,272.50
Minus premium on straddle	1,375.00
Required initial commitment (before commission)	**$1,897.50**

The position of the naked straddle writer can best be shown as in Figure 3.3.

The best position for the writer of a naked straddle is when the stock price is at 95, the striking price. At 95, neither the call nor the put are exercisable and the option writer realizes the full straddle premium. At another point, less than the full premium is realized and a loss is, in fact, possible depending on the size of the deviation from 95 in relation to the size of the premium received.

Consider the option writer's position if the stock appreciates to 110. The call, well in-the-money, will be exercised. The writer of a naked straddle would have to purchase the stock in the open market at 110 and deliver it to the option holder. This means buying a stock at 110 and simultaneously selling it at 95. The loss will exceed the premium received on the straddle. This position should be contrasted with that of a covered straddle. A stock price rise to 110 results in a realization of the full premium on the straddle (assume that the stock remains above 95 up to the expiration date).

If the price of the stock falls to 80, the put will be exercised. The straddle writer now holds an $80 stock for which $95 was paid. The loss is equal to

Loss on acquired shares (put to the writer)	$1,500
Less premium received	$1,375
Loss	$ 125

FIGURE 3.3. Position of writer and naked straddle.

Loss	Profit range	Loss
81 1/4		108 3/4
(95 − 13 3/4)		(95 + 13 3/4)

The $125.00 loss is realized on an investment of $1,897.50 or a rate of 125/1,897.50 = 7%. This loss is significantly lower than that realized on the covered straddle position (32 percent). In addition, the writer of a naked straddle holds only 100 shares as opposed to 200 shares held by the writer of a covered option. This position reduces the risk associated with the naked option by one half should the market weakness persist.

We can summarize, therefore, by stating that a naked straddle position, while loss-minimizing in a lean market, could be devastating in a bullish market. The loss from an upward movement in the price of the security is theoretically limitless unless the straddle writer closes out the position at a certain "acceptable" loss level by either buying a call or buying the stock to deliver against the outstanding call commitment.

If the stock price remains at or around 95, the naked straddle position is superior to that of a covered straddle. These tradeoffs must be weighed carefully if the straddle writer is to realize any positive return on investment.

Vector and Graphic Representation

The vector representation of a straddle sale position is as follows:

Write Put   Write Call

$$\begin{bmatrix} 0 \\ -1 \end{bmatrix} + \begin{bmatrix} -1 \\ 0 \end{bmatrix} = \begin{bmatrix} -1 \\ -1 \end{bmatrix}$$

A one-point movement (+ or −) in the price of the underlying stock would result in a one-point loss on a short straddle position (before accounting for the premium).

Graphically, the straddle writer position can be depicted as in Figure 3.4, in which the put is exercisable to the left of K_3. The loss that could result from the newly established long position is limited (the stock could fall only to zero). Beyond K_5, the loss that could result from an exercised call is theoretically limitless. There is no upward limit to the price of a security. The constraining forces are time, the nature of the

FIGURE 3.4.   Straddle writer's position.

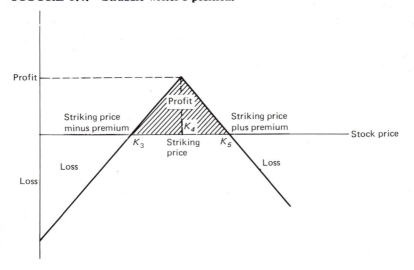

market, and the psychology of the straddle writer—the ability to withstand the pressures to cover a given position. From Figure 3.4 we can also see that the maximum return is realized at K_4, the striking price. The straddle writer earns the full value of the premium at K_4. It is unrealistic to expect, however, that a straddle-writing strategy would result in earning the full premium.

3.5 BUYING COMBINATIONS

A combination, once again, is made up of a call and a put with different striking prices, different maturities, or both.

Referring back to Table 3.1, we can identify 81 possible combinations: consisting of nine calls, each combinable with any of the nine puts ($9 \times 9 = 81$).

The combination buyer, like the buyer of a straddle, is seeking protection no matter what the direction of the price of the underlying security. The nature of the protection is considerably different from that offered by the straddle and the range of choice is vastly superior (81 versus 9; see Table 3.1).

A combination buyer uses a combination for the same purposes as a straddle buyer, but starting with a different prognosis. While straddle buyers admit to their inability (or unwillingness) to predict the direction of the market at the time the straddle is bought, combination buyers bet that the stock will go up or down with a certain probability in mind. Given that the probability is not equal to one, combination buyers would seek protection with a call (if they were betting on a stock price decline) or with a put (if they were betting on a stock price rise). The lower the probability that the direction of the market will be in accordance with expectations, the larger the sum the investor would be willing to commit to the protection. That is, the lower the probability is, the further in-the-money (or the less out-of-the-money) a call option is bought to protect a short position; and the lower the probability, the further in-the-money (or the less out-of-the-money) a put is bought to protect a long position in the underlying security.

Consider the case of an investor who expects a considerable decline in the price of IBM. The expected decline will be realized, he or she reasons, no matter what the attitude of the U.S. government might be toward the export of high technology. U.S. policymakers are expected to announce a new policy concerning the exportation of computers and software. The investor expects that the policy will be very restrictive and consequently the investor will either sell IBM short, buy a put, or do both. Concerned, however, with the possibility that not very restrictive measures on exports could be announced, coupled with stimulative measures for the U.S. computer industry, the investor may wish to purchase protection using a long call position. The higher the probability of lenient measures, the more the investor would pay for a call.

The investor may pick an IBM/April/100 selling at 6¾ and an IBM/July/100P selling at 9¼. The call option is out-of-the-money (IBM is trading at 98¼) and the put is in-the-money; hence, the movement in its price will roughly coincide with the movement in the price of the stock. If the policy announcement is made and is favorable to the investor's position, and if IBM drops in price from 98¼ to 90, an investor holding a combination plus a short position in the stock would realize 8¼ points on the put portion of the combination and another 8¼ points on the short position. The only costs are the commissions, the cost of the call (6¾), and the interest costs on the margined short position in the stock.

Opposite expectations would have produced an opposite strategy. An in-the-money call option and an out-of-the-money put option would have been purchased. The range of opportunities (in or out of the money) is quite substantial. The reader should be able to produce various combination strategies to fit various expectations.

3.6 SELLING COMBINATIONS

A short combination position is established to earn a desired rate of return. The size of the return depends on the behavior of the underlying stock, on the distribution of the combination premium between the put and the call, and on how far the two options are in- or out-of-the-money. A combination writer who is unable to predict the direction of the market, but who is willing to place a higher probability on a price decline, would want a lower limit on the profit range (consult Figure 3.5.) This would obviously allow the writer to keep a larger portion of the premium if the price of the stock follows the expected direction. The wide range of combination opportunities that are available in the marketplace does allow the combination writer to set the desired profit range. The lower profit limit on a combination (the break-even price on the downside) is equal to the striking price on the put minus the total premium received. The upper limit (the break-even price on the upside) is equal to the striking price on the call plus the premium on the combination.

The sale of IBM/April/100*P* and an IBM/April/95 (see Table 3.1) would produce the following range:

$$(100 - (9\tfrac{1}{8} + 7\tfrac{1}{2}) \text{ to } (95 + 16\tfrac{5}{8})$$

or

$$83\tfrac{3}{8} \text{ to } 111\tfrac{5}{8}$$

Below 83⅜ or over 111⅝ the investor loses money. The lowest possible limit that can be extracted from Table 3.1 is through the sale of an IBM/July/90*P* and the sale of IBM/July/100. The lower limit in this case is $90 - 13\tfrac{7}{8}(4\tfrac{1}{2} + 9\tfrac{3}{8}) = 76\tfrac{1}{8}$. The upper limit is 113⅞.

The resulting combination here consists of two out-of-the-money options and thus provides a considerable protection against small price fluctuations. If IBM falls in price from 98¼, the combination writer would have 22 points (98¼ − 76¼) before a loss in the short combination position. If the stock rises in price, there is a 15⅝ point

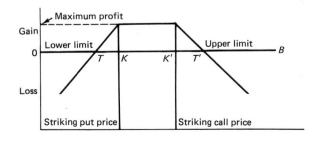

FIGURE 3.5. Combination writer's position.

(113⅞ − 98¼) protection. The ideal situation, therefore—as in the case of a straddle—is for the price of the underlying security not to change at all or not to change substantially. Thus the price will remain within the range set by the striking call price and the striking put price if they are different.

In the case above where the maximum limit was established, it must be noted that only 9⅜ + 4½ or 13⅞ was collected as premium. The writer could have picked another combination that would have yielded a much larger premium income. However, there is a price to pay. The larger the premium, the smaller the profit range and the greater the risk. This situation is depicted in Figure 3.5. *KK'* represents the maximum profit range and *TT'* the no-loss range.

A combination writer should therefore be very careful in selecting a combination. While the combination allows for considerable room for error, it does not eliminate risk altogether.

We have thus far spoken of a naked short combination position. This position can obviously be covered by a long position in the underlying security. The considerations are very similar to those discussed under covered straddles, with the necessary adjustment to account for the added flexibility that combinations introduce in the investment process.

3.7 SYNTHETIC COMBINATIONS

If a put on a given security is not available on the option exchanges, a combination can still be created through the sale of two calls with different striking prices against a long position in the stock.

Consider the case of the investor interested in writing a combination on JAK Inc., but who is unable to sell the put side through the option exchanges. The resolution lies in the creation of a synthetic combination where two calls with different striking prices are written, as follows:

Market price JAK Inc.	46
JAK/Sept/45	4
JAK/Sept/50	2

As previously discussed, the maximum profit from this position is realized when the stock price remains between $45 and $50. Therefore, an investor expecting a considerable movement (more than five points, in this case) in the price of the stock should not consider writing a synthetic combination.

The synthetic combination position with a long position in the stock is equivalent to the conventional naked combination sale. Using the vector notation, we can see why:

Long Position **Write Call** **Sell Put**

$$\begin{bmatrix} +1 \\ -1 \end{bmatrix} \quad + \quad \begin{bmatrix} -1 \\ 0 \end{bmatrix} \quad = \quad \begin{bmatrix} 0 \\ -1 \end{bmatrix}$$

Sell Put **Sell Call**

$$\begin{bmatrix} 0 \\ -1 \end{bmatrix} \quad + \quad \begin{bmatrix} -1 \\ 0 \end{bmatrix} \quad = \text{naked combination}$$

The margin requirement for the synthetic combination is equal to (using the current 50 percent margin requirement on a long stock position and a 30 percent margin requirement on a naked call) the following:

Long Stock Position

Stock margin requirement		
50% × 46 × 100 =	$2,300	
Less premium on covered call	400	
		$1,900

Naked Call

30% of stock price (30% × 46 × 100)	=	$1,380	
Less out-of-the-money credit			
(50 − 46) × 100	=	−400	
Less call option premium		−200	780
Total investment			**$2,680**

The maximum profit, as mentioned earlier, is realized if the price of the stock remains between $45 and $50. This profit is equal to the size of the premium collected, or $400 + $200 = $600. Let us now consider the results from a stock price decline or appreciation.

1. Stock declines to 40. Both calls will be worthless, hence not exercised, if the stock price is at $40. The writer of a synthetic combination earns the $600 in premiums but loses $600 on the long stock position.

2. Stock appreciates to 50. One call is profitable (that with a $45 exercise price) to the holder, and the other is at-the-money and hence not worth exercising. The call with the lower striking price will be exercised and the stock will be called away from the investor. His or her income is $600.

3. Stock appreciates to 70. Both calls are profitable at 70. The investor would have to deliver stock against one of the calls and purchase 100 shares of JAK Inc. at a $70 market price. Before calculating the profit/loss position, we must mention that as the price of JAK Inc. rises, the synthetic combination writer would be marked to the market for the naked call position and asked to deposit additional funds in the margin account. Also, the writer always has the option of closing the position either by buying a call on JAK Inc. or by purchasing another 100 shares of JAK Inc.

The profit/loss position at $70 is calculated as follows:

Loss on the covered call position (46 − 45) =	$ 100
Loss on the naked call position (70 − 50) =	2,000
Total loss	$2,100
Minus premium received	600
Loss	**$1,500**

This loss does not account for transactions costs, which are larger for synthetic combinations than for conventional combinations because of the additional commission charges

on the long stock position. Also, the loss does not include the interest charges on the debit balance from the margin requirements on the stock and on the naked call position. The debit balance on the latter position increases as the price of the stock rises.

We can, therefore, observe that the combination writer is advised to stick with conventional combinations on stocks with minimum expected price movements and to use synthetic combinations only if conventional combinations are not possible.

3.8 Spreads

Definitions

Spread

A spread is the simultaneous purchase and sale of option contracts of the same class (put or call) on the same underlying security. The option bought has a different striking price and/or a different expiration month from the option sold. The spread is the difference between the premium received and the premium paid.

Bull Spread

A bull spread is established when the investor "buys" a spread, that is, the investor pays more (less) premium for the call (put) option bought than is collected in premium on the option sold. As its name implies, a bull spread is established when an investor expects an advance in the price of the underlying stock. In the call case, the bull spread results in a debit to the investor's account; in the put case, in a credit to the investor's account. In both cases, however, the investor is buying the option with the lower striking price and is selling the option with the higher striking price.

Bear Spreads

A bear spread is established when the investor "sells" a spread, that is, paying less (more) premium for the call (put) option bought than is collected in premium on the option sold. As its name implies, a bear spread is established when an investor expects a decline in the price of the underlying stock. In the call case, the bear spread results in a credit to the investor's account. In the put case, the spread results in a debit to the investor's account. In both cases, however, the investor is buying the option with the higher striking price and is selling the option with the lower striking price.

Vertical Call Spreads

Vertical (sometimes referred to as "price") call spreads involve the purchase of a call contract at one price and the simultaneous sale of a call contract on the same stock, with both option contracts having the same maturity but a different striking price. Referring back to Table 3.1, the reader can observe that for a given maturity, striking prices are listed vertically. Hence the designation "vertical." Vertical call spreads can be bullish or bearish.

Vertical Bull Call Spread

The raison d'etre of spreads is the establishment of a perfectly hedged position—not a riskless position, we must remember—that reduces the risk associated with a long or a short position and allows the investor a reasonable rate of return with only minor

TABLE 3.2
Summary of Spread Opportunities

	February	May	August
UAL 20[a]	11⅞	r	s
UAL 20 *P*	r	r	s
UAL 25	7½	8	r
UAL 25 *P*	⁵⁄₁₆	1½	2³⁄₁₆
UAL 30	3⅜	4¾	r
UAL 30 *P*	1½	3	r
UAL 35	¹⁵⁄₁₆	2¼	3½
UAL 35 *P*	4½	5¼	r
UAL 40	³⁄₁₆	1	2
UAL 40 *P*	r	r	r

[a] *P* = put; *r* = not traded; *s* = no option offered.

movements in the price of the underlying security. The spread position is best understood using the vector notation:

Buy Call   Write Call   Spread

$$\begin{bmatrix} 1 \\ 0 \end{bmatrix} + \begin{bmatrix} -1 \\ 0 \end{bmatrix} = \begin{bmatrix} 0 \\ 0 \end{bmatrix}$$

The zero entries in the spread vector represent profits before the premium is accounted for. The size of the premium paid in a vertical bull call spread is the maximum amount at risk. The call spread, therefore, limits the risk to the differential between premium received and premium paid.

On a given day, we can observe all possible spread opportunities involving a certain stock, such as United Air Lines (UAL) by merely inspecting *The Wall Street Journal*. Assume that the opportunities on UAL are like those summarized in Table 3.2.

An investor bullish on UAL would, based on Table 3.2, have several vertical call spreads to choose from. The choice, then, would depend on the investor's level of risk aversion, on how bullish he or she is, and on the size of the financial commitment the investor wishes to make. With UAL trading at 31½, the investor settles on the following:

Buy UAL/Feb/20	$1,187.50
Sell UAL/Feb/25	−750.00
Investment (maximum loss)	$ 437.50

Being bullish on UAL, the investor buys the option with the greater potential (the one more in-the-money) and sells the option with the lesser potential (the one less in-the-money)—which requires a financial commitment. We now explore the impact of stock price movements on the spread position while we ignore commissions and tax considerations.

Stock Remains at 31½

Since both options are in the money, they will be profitable for exercising or for closing out by entering a closing sale (purchase) transaction. The exercise would result in the following:

Profit in long call position   (3,150 − 2,000) = $1,150
Loss on the short position   (3,150 − 2,500) =   −650
Gross profit   **$ 500**
Profit = 500 − 437.5 = $62.50 or a return of 62.50/437.50 = 14.29%

Stock Appreciates to 40

The results are as follows:

Exercise the long position at a cost of $2,000 (striking price) + $1,187.50 (option premium) =	$3,187.50
Short position is exercised against us. (The stock we now own (from the exercise of the long call) is effectively being sold at the striking price + option premium). $2,500 (striking price) + $750 (option premium) =	$3,250.00
Gross profit	$ 62.50
or a return of 14.29% (62.50/437.50)	

Therefore, the maximum profit in a spread position is established in advance. It is simply equal to: [(striking price on short position) + (option premium received)] − [(striking price on long position) + (option premium paid)].

Stock Falls to 15

At 15, both the short and the long call positions are out-of-the-money (the market price is below both striking prices). Neither option will be exercised. The maximum loss is the differential in the premiums of $437.50. By establishing a bullish vertical call spread position, the investor therefore knows in advance the maximum gain and the maximum loss. Since the investor expects the stock price to rise, he or she expresses satisfaction with the 14.29 percent return (for one month) on a $437.50 investment in a spread.

The Alternatives

A bullish investor in United Air Lines (UAL) has various options for participating in an upward stock price movement. He can establish a long position in the stock—which offers an unlimited upward potential, a maximum loss potential equal to the price of the stock, and requires a financial commitment equal to at least 50 percent of the market price of the stock—or (31.5) (100) × 50% = $1,575. The investor can buy a call that would offer a substantial appreciation potential, which is limited by the movement in the price of the stock during the life of the option. The call also limits the potential loss to the size of the call premium ($1,187.50). While the vertical call option spread position limits the upside potential to only $62.50, it also limits the downside loss to $437.50 (compared with $1,187.50 for the call position and $3,150 for the long stock position). The reduction of exposure is, therefore, not without its costs.

The maximum profit is $62.50 and the maximum loss is $437.50—the difference between the premium paid and the premium received (Figure 3.6). This assumes that both options are not exercised prior to maturity. If the investor receives an exercise notice against the short position in the spread, he or she would be left with a net long

FIGURE 3.6.   Graphic representation of vertical call option.

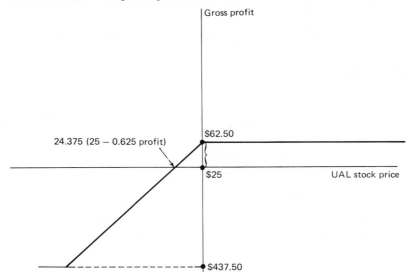

position in the call option. The maximum loss may obviously be larger in this case. The investor can meet an exercise notice in various ways: (1) by delivering a stock that is already owned, (2) by buying a stock in the open market, (3) by borrowing a stock and delivering it (establish a short position in the stock), or (4) by exercising the long side of the spread. The decision depends on the circumstances. If the long side of the spread is out-of-the-money or is substantially less in-the-money than the short position, it would have a larger time-premium component—which will be lost immediately upon the exercise. The investor should, therefore, be very careful in assessing opportunities.

Closing one side of the spread is sometimes deliberately done by the investor. In this case, the strategy is referred to as "lifting a leg." This is done when the investor anticipates a weakness in the price of the stock after a dramatic move—which results in a substantial profit in one side of the spread. An anticipated temporary weakness in the price of the stock may lead the investor to lift a leg on the long call position. In so doing he or she turns the short position into a naked short position. This position requires additional investment equal to 30 percent of the market price of the underlying security plus or minus the appropriate adjustment. Then the investor must reestablish the long call position once the market moves in the expected direction and reaches the desired level. In so doing, the investor is undoing the spread and automatically increasing the chance of a loss. The investor is well advised not to forget the reasons for establishing the spread position in the first place. This, however, should not suggest that the optimal position is to remain wedded to the spread position, no matter what the developments in the market may be.

Vertical Bull Call Spread Worksheet

A very convenient tool for evaluating and understanding spreads is the worksheet, as shown in Table 3.3.

Vertical Bear Call Spread

In a vertical bear call spread, the difference (+) between the premium received and the premium paid determines the profit limit (as compared to the loss limit in the vertical bull call spread). The maximum loss is determined as follows:

(Striking price on short position + premium received)
− (striking price on long position + premium paid)
= maximum loss

An investor bearish on UAL for example, would assume a position opposite that discussed in the previous section. For example

Sell	UAL/Feb/20	$1,187.50
Buy	UAL/Feb/25	− 750.00
Credit		$ 437.50

The $437.50 credit represents the maximum profit. The maximum loss = ($2,000 + $1,187.50) − ($2,500 + $750) = ($62.50)

Let us now examine the effects of changes in the price of the underlying stock.

Stock Remains at 31½

At 31½, both options are exercisable. The exercise of the short option against our investor results in a gain of

($2,000 + $1,187.50) − $3,150 = $37.50

TABLE 3.3
Vertical Bull Call Spread Worksheet

		Option Price	Stock Price
Sell	UAL/Feb/25	7½	31½
Buy	UAL/Feb/20	11⅞	31½

1. Money at risk = 11⅞ − 7½ = 4⅜
2. Maximum profit potential = difference in exercise prices − money at risk = (25 − 20) − 4⅜ = ⅝
3. Risk/reward = (1.)/(2.) = 4⅜/⅝
4. Break-even point = money at risk + exercise price of option bought = 4⅜ + 20 = 24⅜
5. Percent change in the price of the underlying security needed to reach break-even point (24⅜ (break-even point) − 31½ (price of stock))/31½ = 22.62% (decrease)

The exercise of the long call position by the investor would yield a loss equal to

$3,150 − ($2,500 + $750) = ($100)
Net loss = $100 − $37.50 = **($62.50)**

Stock Appreciates to 40

At 40, both options are exercisable.

Loss on short position = $2,000 + $1,187.50 − $4,000 = ($812.50)
Gain on long position = $4,000 − $3,250.00   =   750.00
Net Loss   (**$ 62.50**)

Stock Falls to 15

At 15, both options are out-of-the-money and neither will be exercised. The spread holder would have earned the full premium differential, or $437.50.

The Alternatives

A bearish investor could have chosen to establish a short position in UAL, sell a naked UAL call, or buy a put on UAL instead of the spread. While all these possibilities increase the return, they also increase the exposure of the investor. Hence the importance of establishing a position that carefully takes one's risk profile and financial resources into consideration.

Graphic Representation

The United Airlines vertical call spread can be visualized by referring to Figure 3.7. As it shows, the maximum loss is realized when the price of the underlying stock exceeds $25. The maximum gain is realized at or below the lower of the two striking prices in the spread.

Vertical Bear Call Spread Worksheet

As in the case of the vertical bull call spread, a worksheet on the vertical bear callspread is of considerable usefulness to the investor. (See Table 3.4.)

Vertical Put Bull Spreads

To understand vertical put spreads, the reader must reverse the logic used in the case of vertical call spreads.

As in the vertical call bull spread, the vertical put bull spread involves the purchase of the option with the lower striking price and the sale of the option with the higher striking price. While this results in a debit balance in the call case, a credit balance would result in the put case. An example should make the point clear.

FIGURE 3.7. United Air Lines vertical call spread.

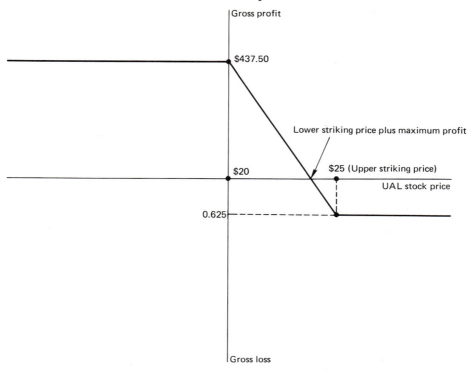

TABLE 3.4
Vertical Bear Call Spread Worksheet

	Option Price	Stock Price
Buy UAL/Feb/25	7½	31½
Sell UAL/Feb/20	11⅞	31½

1. Maximum profit potential = difference in option premiums

$$= 11\tfrac{7}{8} - 7\tfrac{1}{2} = 4\tfrac{3}{8}$$

2. Money at risk = difference in exercise prices − (1)

$$= 5 - 4\tfrac{3}{8} = \tfrac{5}{8}$$

3. Risk/reward $= \dfrac{\tfrac{5}{8}}{4\tfrac{3}{8}}$

4. Break-even point = (1) + exercise price of option sold

$$= 4\tfrac{3}{8} + 20 = 24\tfrac{3}{8}$$

5. Percent change in the price of the underlying security needed to reach break-even point =

$$\frac{31\tfrac{1}{2} \text{ (price of stock)} - 24\tfrac{3}{8} \text{ (break-even point)}}{31\tfrac{1}{2}} = 22.62\%$$

Referring to Table 3.2, an investor bullish on UAL would

Buy	UAL Feb/25P	$\frac{5}{16}$
Sell	UAL Feb/35P	$4\frac{1}{2}$
Credit		$\mathbf{4\frac{3}{16}}$

The reader should be able to verify, as is shown in detail in the preceding section, what the impact of expected and unexpected changes in the price of the underlying security would be. Briefly, if the price of the underlying security rises (to 40 from its current level of 31½), both put options will be worthless and the investor would earn the full $4\frac{3}{16}$. If the stock price remains at 31½, the put option with the 35 striking price is profitable and the other is worthless. The stock will be put to the investor at 35 while its market value is only 31½, a loss of 3½ that practically wipes out the credit of $4\frac{3}{16}$. If the stock falls in price to 15, for example, then both options are in-the-money and the investor would lose $5\frac{13}{16}$, which is equal to the difference in the striking prices minus the credit. This sum is also equal to the loss on the short position $(35 - 15 = 20)$ minus the gain on the long position $(25 - 15)$ and minus the credit $4\frac{3}{16}$.

Vertical Put Bear Spread

In a vertical put bear spread, the investor undertakes the opposite of the vertical put bull spread, that is, buying the put with the high striking price and selling the put with the low striking price.

Buy	UAL Feb/35P	$4\frac{1}{2}$
Sell	UAL Feb/25P	$\frac{5}{16}$
Debit		$\mathbf{4\frac{3}{16}}$

This debit represents the maximum loss. The maximum gain is equal to the difference in exercise prices minus the debit, or $10 - 4\frac{3}{16} = 5\frac{13}{16}$, yielding a risk–reward ratio of $4\frac{3}{16}/5\frac{13}{16}$. This ratio is much more advantageous than that of the vertical put bull spread, and the underlying strategy should be adopted if the probability of an appreciation in the price of the security is equal to that of a depreciation.

Horizontal Call Spreads

Horizontal call spreads are also referred to as "calendar" or "time" spreads. The "horizontal" connotation derives from the fact, as shown in Table 3.2, that the time to maturity is listed horizontally. The options bought/sold have the same striking price but different maturities. The investment considerations are essentially the same as those of vertical spreads with one major qualification: the time premium. Two options with equal striking prices but different maturities would have different premiums because of the time-premium component. The reader should recall the discussion in the preceding chapter, where it was shown that

$$W = \text{relative price (intrinsic value)} + \text{time premium}$$

As an option approaches its expiration date, the time premium approaches zero. The longer the maturity, the higher the time premium. The fundamental reason for using horizontal spreads is that the time value of the near option diminishes more rapidly than that of the distant option. That is why the investor is more likely to sell the near option, buy the distant option, and establish a bullish horizontal spread.

Horizontal Bull Call Spreads

From Table 3.2, we can see the various horizontal spread opportunities available on UAL. Once again, a bullish spread should result in a debit balance in the investor's account. Assume that the investor settles for the following:

Sell	UAL/Feb/35	$^{15}\!/_{16}$
Buy	UAL/May/35	2¼
Debit		**1$^{5}\!/_{16}$**

With UAL trading at 31½, both options are out-of-the-money; that is, an exercise would result in an immediate loss to the holder of a call spread. If, by the end of the third week in February, UAL is trading at 35, the short side is worthless but the long side still has three months to go and may be selling at, say, 3.5. If the stock advances to 40, both options are profitable. The short side would be exercised against the investor for a loss of $500 [(40 − 35) (100)] and the long side of the spread would realize a profit larger than $500 because the option still has three months to run and the spread has widened. If the UAL/May/35 is currently selling at 6¾ and the investor decides to close out the position, his or her profit would be as follows:

Profit on long position − loss on short position
$$= (6\tfrac{3}{4} - 2\tfrac{1}{4}) - (5 - {}^{15}\!/_{16}) = {}^{7}\!/_{16}$$

The profit is $^{7}\!/_{16}$ points on an investment of 1$^{5}\!/_{16}$ points.

The investment represents the amount at risk or the maximum loss, assuming the spread is kept intact until both options expire and the investor does not decide to lift a leg temporarily or permanently. The maximum profit is, therefore, realized at the striking price. Graphically, the horizontal call spread can be depicted as in Figure 3.8.

Horizontal Bear Call Spreads

The strategy here is the opposite of a horizontal bull call spread. Two problems must be pointed out.

1. As indicated earlier, the time premium favors the option with the longer life. The option sold in this case was the short position.

2. Since the option bought is shorter in life, its exercise or expiration would leave the investor with a short call position. This would require approximately a 30 percent margin and would leave the investor open to the risks discussed in Chapter 2, in the section on naked call options.

Graphically, the horizontal bear call spread is depicted in Figure 3.9.

FIGURE 3.8. **Graphic representation of horizontal bull call spread.**

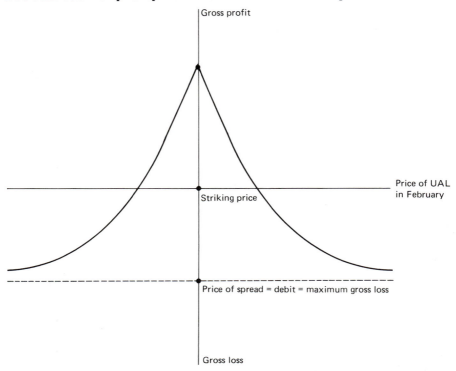

FIGURE 3.9. **Graphic representation of horizontal bear call spread.**

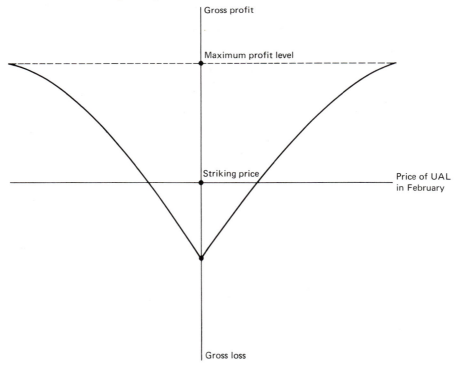

Diagonal Spreads

Diagonal spreads involve the purchase of an option and the sale of another on the same underlying stock, with the options having different striking prices and different maturities.

Diagonal spreads offer substantial additional flexibility to the investor in the formulation of strategy and in the determination of the risk/reward ratio. One possible diagonal spread that can be established on UAL, given bullish expectations, is

Buy	UAL/May/25	8
Sell	UAL/Feb/35	$^{15}/_{16}$
Debit		$7^{1}/_{16}$

The call option sold has a shorter maturity. This is advantageous, because the opposite position would mean that toward the end of February the spread position would reduce to a naked short call position. This strategy necessitates funds to meet the margin requirements.

Again, the debit represents the maximum loss. The maximum gain is equal to the difference in the exercise prices minus the debit, or $2^{15}/_{16}$ points. Needless to say, if the investor is not satisfied with this risk/reward ratio, he or she can easily find a diagonal spread on UAL or on another suitable stock to accomodate his or her needs.

Other Sophisticated Spreads

The spread opportunities in the marketplace are almost limitless. The more capable and imaginative the investor, the more interesting and complex the spread formations. We shall discuss a few of the more prevalent types of sophisticated spreads.

Sandwich Spreads

Sandwich spreads are a combination of bull and bear spreads on the same stock, having the same expiration month, but different striking prices. These spreads necessarily involve four options: two on the long side at both ends of the striking price range and two on the short end sandwiched between the long positions. An example, shown below, can be developed from Table 3.2.

Buy	1	UAL/Feb/20	11⅞
Sell	2	UAL/Feb/30	6¾
		(3⅜ each)	
Buy	1	UAL/Feb/40	$^{3}/_{16}$
Debit			$5^{5}/_{16}$

On certain securities, sandwich spreads can be so structured that the out-of-pocket cost is zero (before commissions are accounted for). The sandwich spread has a profit potential as long as UAL trades in the 20–40 range.

Consider a stock price at 30 toward the end of February. The short positions will be worthless. The UAL/Feb/20 earns 10 points. The UAL/Feb/40 is worthless. The net profit (before commissions) is equal to $10 - 5\frac{5}{16} = 4\frac{11}{16}$. This is the maximum profit.

The UAL falls in price to 15, none of the options is in the money. The investor has lost $5\frac{5}{16}$. If UAL rises in price to 45, all the options are profitable to exercise. The profit goes to the option holder and the option writer loses money. The profits could equal

Profit on UAL/Feb/20	25
Loss on UAL/Feb/30	−30
Profit on UAL/Feb/40	5
Net Profit	**0**

Again the investor loses $5\frac{5}{16}$, the cost of the sandwich spread (the debit).

Had the investor structured a sandwich spread requiring no investment, he or she could earn a substantial return—the maximum of which is realized at 30, the median point in the striking price range. There could be no better risk/reward ratio than this. Below the lowest striking price, losses are zero, as they are above the highest striking price. Anywhere between the low and the high striking price, profits are realized on a zero investment.

Butterfly Spreads

The butterfly position is opposite that of a sandwich spread. Here the investor is short the options with striking prices on both ends of the spread range, and is long on the options with the median striking price. Expectations here are for a major movement in the price of the underlying security. Otherwise a net loss or a zero gain will result from the butterfly position.

It is left as an exercise to the reader to develop an example from Table 3.2 and to measure the consequences of a price decline below the lowest striking price, a price rise above the highest striking price, and a situation of no price change.

Neutral Volatility Spreads

Assume the following is determined in February 1983 about the March 1983 option on Bristol Meyers:

Delta for March/65 = 95
Delta for March/70 = 62

The delta factor is a measure of the extent to which the movement of an option price tracks that of the underlying stock. In the case of March/65, a one-dollar movement in the price of the stock produces a $0.95 move in the price of the option. A neutral volatility spread would be

Sell 2 March/65
Buy 3 March/70

Words of Caution

Although spreading is potentially lucrative, it has several disadvantages:

1. The most serious disadvantage lies in the execution of the spread order. Both sides of the spread must be executed simultaneously, otherwise there is no execution.

2. While our calculations show profits on certain positions under certain assumptions, those profits can disappear if commissions are accounted for.

Tests run by M. Gombola, R. Roenfeldt, and P. Cooley show that investors trying to beat the market by using various spread strategies were not successful once commissions were subtracted from the anticipated arbitrage profits. The options market was, once again, shown to be efficient. In the authors' words, "For those arbitrage positions with available price information at expiration, profits were barely sufficient to cover commission costs at the rate of 0.25 per underlying share. Profits after commissions were sufficiently small to provide only a minimal return for the average investor."[1]

3. The market for certain options is thin. This means that the volume is not large enough to allow a spread to be executed.

4. Our preceeding calculations did not take another major transaction cost into consideration, namely, taxes. The tax implications of a spread or any option position are serious enough to require consultation with competent tax attorneys or accountants. If taxes are accounted for, certain option positions may lose their attractiveness.

3.9 ARBITRAGE OPPORTUNITIES IN THE OPTIONS MARKET

Arbitrage opportunities that use options abound. We shall cover some of the prevalent ones. We must first note that arbitrageurs play a very important role in the options markets. Their activities help bring prices into equilibrium, thus improving the efficiency of the market. The evidence of their contributions lies in the profitability of their operations. Several investment banks have very profitable arbitrage departments, which attest to their ability to identify opportunities and to capitalize on them. Their operating costs are essentially fixed. Thus marginal transactions costs for arbitrage positions are approximately equal to zero. The individual investor is not as fortunate because what appears as a profitable arbitrage opportunity to him could well evaporate after transactions costs are accounted for. In the examples to follow, transactions costs will be ignored. All the data in the arbitrage strategies are based on Table 2.3 in the preceding chapter.

Basic Call Arbitrage

A basic call arbitrage attempts to take advantage of the difference between the value of a call exercised and its market value. It is the simplest form of arbitrage.

An example of this is a basic call arbitrage available on January 14, 1983.

---

[1] **Michael J. Gombola, Rodney L. Roenfeldt, and Philip L. Cooley,** "Arbitrage Opportunities and Pricing Efficiency in CBOE Options." Unpublished paper, University of Connecticut School of Business, p. 11.

Data

Market price of Homestake Mining	61¾
Market price of Homestake Mining/Jan/30	31

Strategy

Buy call at 31
Exercise call and buy stock at 30
Sell stock at 61¾
Profit from strategy is $61¾ - 61 (30 + 31) = ¾$ of a point.

Basic Put Arbitrage

A basic put arbitrage achieves a similar objective as a basic call arbitrage.

Data

Market price of Bethlehem Steel	21¼
Market price of Bethlehem Steel/January/25P	3

Strategy

Buy put at 3
Buy stock at 21¼
Exercise the put, that is, sell the stock at 25.
Profit from strategy is: $25 - (21¼ + 3) = ¾$ of a point.

Conversions

A conversion consists of a long position in the stock, a long put position, and a short call position with the same strike price and maturity as the put. Conversions attempt to capitalize on an unwarranted difference between call and put prices.

Data

Market price of Eastman Kodak	82⅞
Market price of Eastman Kodak/Jan/75P	¹⁄₁₆
Market price of Eastman Kodak/Jan/75	8¾

Strategy

Buy Stock at	82⅞
Buy Eastman Kodak/Jan/75P	¹⁄₁₆
Sell Eastman Kodak/Jan/75	8¾

The cost of the long positions is $82⅞ + ¹⁄₁₆ = \$82^{15}\!/_{16}$
$$-8^{12}\!/_{16}$$
$$\$74^{3}\!/_{16}$$

The reader should note that the conversion is the purchase of a put and the simultaneous sale of a synthetic put. Chapter 2 showed that a synthetic put is the sum of a short position in the stock and a long call position.

Long Put   Short Stock   Long Call   Short Put   Long Stock   Short Call

$$\begin{bmatrix} 0 \\ 1 \end{bmatrix} = \begin{bmatrix} -1 \\ 1 \end{bmatrix} + \begin{bmatrix} 1 \\ 0 \end{bmatrix} \text{ and } \begin{bmatrix} 0 \\ -1 \end{bmatrix} = \begin{bmatrix} 1 \\ -1 \end{bmatrix} + \begin{bmatrix} -1 \\ 0 \end{bmatrix}$$

Synthetic Put

The conversion consists of a purchase of the left side and a sale of the right side with intent to capitalize on any diversion between two equivalent positions.

Since the net cost ($74\frac{3}{16}$) is less than the strike price of the options (75), there exists a locked-in profit of $75 - 74\frac{3}{16}$ or $\frac{13}{16}$ of a point. To see why, assume that the price of Eastman Kodak goes to 90. The call is very much in-the-money and can be exercised. The call option writer receives ($75 + 8\frac{3}{4}$) or $83\frac{3}{4}$ for the long shares he delivers against the option position. He paid $82\frac{7}{8}$ for the stock and $\frac{1}{16}$ for the now worthless put for a total of $82\frac{15}{16}$. The profit is $83\frac{3}{4} - 82\frac{15}{16} = \frac{13}{16}$.

This example ignores dividends that could increase cash inflows and the opportunity cost of carrying the long stock position, the real interest cost if the position was bought on margin.

Reverse Conversions

A reverse conversion is, as its name implies, the opposite of a conversion. It is profitable if the proceeds from the short position in the stock and the put are higher than the striking price of the options.

Data

Market price of Xerox	40¾
Market price of Xerox/Jan/45P	4⅝
Market price of Xerox/Jan/45	$\frac{1}{16}$

Strategy

Sell stock short at	40¾
Sell Xerox/Jan/45P	4⅝
Buy Xerox/Jan/45	$\frac{1}{16}$

The reverse conversion is, therefore, a purchase of a synthetic put and the sale of a put.

Total credit of reversal is $45\frac{5}{16}$; $40\frac{6}{8}$ from stock sale and $4\frac{5}{8}$ from the put sale, less $\frac{1}{16}$ from the call purchase. Since $45\frac{5}{16}$ is greater than the striking price of 45, there is a locked-in profit of $\frac{5}{16}$ of a point.

The general and comprehensive formulae for calculating profits on conversions and reverse conversions are:

Profit from conversions = Strike price + call premium − stock price − put premium + dividends (if any) − carrying costs (if margined)

Profit from reverse conversions = Proceeds from short stock position + put premium − strike price − call premium + carrying charges (if any) − dividends (if any).

The arbitrageur here should not forget transactions costs if they are significant.

The Box Spread

The box spread is an attempt to capitalize on an inefficient pricing of vertical spreads. It consists of a long position in a bull call spread and a short position in a bear put spread. These two spreads are equivalent, as was demonstrated earlier. They both result in a net commitment of funds. If total funds committed are less than the difference in strike prices, a risk-free profit opportunity exists. Here is an example.

Data

Market price of Coca-Cola Company	48
Market price of Coca-Cola/Feb/45	4
Market price of Coca-Cola/Feb/55	⅝
Market price of Coca-Cola/Feb/55*P*	6¼
Market price of Coca-Cola/Feb/45*P*	⅞

Strategy

Buy a bull call spread		
Buy Coca-Cola/Feb/45	4	
Sell Coca-Cola/Feb/55	− ⅝	
Net bull call spread cost		3⅜
Buy a put bear spread		
Buy Coca-Cola/Feb/55*P*	6¼	
Sell Coca-Cola/Feb/45*P*	− ⅞	
Net bear put spread cost		5⅜
Total cost of box spread		8¾

The value of the box spread when the options expire will simply equal the difference in strike prices:

$$55 - 45 = 10$$

The gross profit accruing to the arbitrageur is $10 - 8¾ = 1¼$ from "buying the box." These profits are guaranteed, provided that all buying and selling of options is done simultaneously at the designated prices.

Dividend Arbitrage

A dividend arbitrage is intended to capitalize on a dividend paid on a stock during the life of a put option that is sold on the stock. Here is an example.

Data

Market price of Atlantic Richfield	44⅝
Market price of Atlantic Richfield/Jan/50*P*	5

Strategy

Wait until the ex-dividend date and exercise the put.
The profit from this strategy is 1 point calculated as follows:

Profit on the exercise of the put: $50 - 44\frac{5}{8} =$	$5\frac{3}{8}$
Dividend collected	$\frac{5}{8}$
Total inflow	6.0
Minus cost of put	5.0
Profit	**1.0**

This profit can disappear if carrying and transactions costs care accounted for. The carrying costs on $4,962.50 [$4,462.50 (stock) + $500 (put)] are $99.25 assuming 12% annual interest cost.

"Interest-Play" Arbitrage

An interest play arbitrage is a reverse conversion without the short position in the put. Its purpose is to earn interest income on the net proceeds from the short sales that exceed any loss from the exercise of the call option. The call purchased is an in-the-money call. Here is an example.

Data

Market price of Ford Motor Co.	$38\frac{5}{8}$
Market price of Ford/March/25	14
Prevailing short-term rates	12%

Strategy

Sell Ford short at	$38\frac{5}{8}$
Buy Ford/March/25	14
Invest net proceeds at	12%

The net proceeds are $3,862.50 − $1,400 (price of call) = $2,462.50.

At 12% annual interest rate, the net interest income on $2,462.50 invested between January 14, 1983 and the third Saturday of March is $55.40. The loss from the exercise of the call option is $\frac{3}{8}$ or $37.50. The profit from the strategy is $55.40 − $37.50 = $17.90. The profit is locked in, as any loss on the short stock position is offset by the profit on the long call position and vice versa.

Several other arbitrage strategies are used. The more recent is between the options market and the futures market. An example is a conversion between the interest option market and the interest futures market. Here the strategy consists of a long put + short call + a long futures contract against what is an equivalent position: a short futures position. The three chapters to follow explain this strategy.

We now review the major tax considerations for options.

3.10 OPTIONS CONTRACTS AND THE TAX LAWS

The tax treatment of option positions is both straightforward and complex. The level of complexity depends on the nature of the position, its timing, its horizon, its intended purpose, and the method of closing it out.

We shall examine the tax implications for both sides of the market—the buy and

the sell sides—and we shall examine techniques for deferring or reducing tax liability through the options market.[2]

Taxes on Long Positions

An option is a capital asset, provided that the underlying stock that is owned currently or prospectively is treated as a capital asset. Options held for over a year qualify for the preferential long-term capital gain treatment. Otherwise, gains or losses are treated as short-term gains or losses. Such is usually the case, for options have maturities of less than one year.

The tax treatment of options depends on whether they are exercised, sold, or allowed to expire.

Exercise

The call holder becomes the owner of the underlying stock upon the exercise of the option. The cost of the option is simply added to the striking price of the stock to determine the tax basis for the stock. The holding period on the stock begins with the acquisition of the stock and not with the acquisition of the option.

The put holder disposes of a stock upon exercising his or her option and receives the striking price. For tax purposes, receipts are the striking price minus the cost of the put. Put holders, however, must be careful of certain factors that could have considerable impact on their tax liability.

The acquisition of a put is considered a short sale by the Internal Revenue Service because, like the short sale, the put buyer is contracting to sell a stock at a fixed price. If the put buyer establishes a long position in the underlying stock during the same day—that is, "marries" the stock to the put—the short sale rule will no longer apply. The tax implications of the latter case are that exercise of the put option produces long- or short-term gains or losses on the stock position, depending on the holding period. If a substantially identical stock is purchased during the holding period of the put or was held for one year or less prior to the acquisition of the put, then any gain

---

[2] The economic Recovery Tax Act of 1981 includes in Title V, "Tax Straddles," provisions that significantly change the tax treatment of spreads and straddles in various kinds of personal property. (Title V also makes a number of changes that are not limited to straddles, such as requiring all "regulated futures contracts" to be marked to market at the end of each year, with unrealized gains or losses taken into account at a special tax rate. Another change eliminates provisions that previously permitted securities dealers to defer for 30 days identifying those securities that are held in an investment account. Title V provides that certain short-term government obligations will be traded as capital assets.) The straddle provisions, together with the mark to market provisions applicable to regulated futures contracts, are designed to eliminate the opportunity for a taxpayer to use a loss to reduce taxes if the taxpayer has an unrealized gain in a position that is "offsetting" to the loss position. These provisions prevent the use of such losses either to defer income from year to year or to convert ordinary income to long-term capital gains. Another provision of the legislation disallows any deduction from carrying charges allocable to personal property that is part of a straddle. Offsetting positions, which are termed "straddles" for purposes of the legislation, are those where one or more positions substantially diminish the risk of another position. The reader is strongly advised to consult with a tax advisor with regard to straddles and spreads, and The Chicago Board Options Exchange memo to members, 8/19/81.

from the exercise of the put is a short-term capital gain and any loss is a short-term capital loss. This is so even if the total holding period of the stock (holding period prior to purchase of the put plus the holding period beginning with the purchase of the put and ending with its exercise) exceeds one year. An owner of a long stock position between January 1, 1980 and January 5, 1981 would have a short-term capital gain (loss) if he or she purchased a put at any time between January 1, 1980 and January 1, 1981. Effectively, the purchase of the put eliminates the holding period of the underlying stock and transforms realized gains into short-term capital gains. The holding period on the underlying stock begins to run on the earliest of (1) the sale date of the stock, (2) the put exercise date, (3) the put sale date, or (4) the put expiration date.

Sale

The sale of a call will produce long-term (short-term) capital gains or losses if the call is held for more than a year (a year or less). Considering the maturity distribution of listed options, capital gains or losses will always be short-term.

The sale of a put is equivalent to closing a short position, if a substantially identical asset was held short-term prior to the acquisition of the put or was bought during its life. Resulting gains or losses are short-term capital gains or losses. If a put option in a "married" position is sold, then the gains or losses are also short-term, given the maturity schedule of listed options.

Expiration

A listed call that expires unexercised results in a short-term capital loss equal to the call premium. The same is true for a put. However, a "married" put that goes unexercised produces neither long- nor short-term capital losses. Its cost is added to the tax basis of the stock.

Taxes on Short-Option Positions

The premium received by an option writer is not taxable income until the option is exercised or until it expires. If the option expires, the premium is treated as a short-term capital gain. If the option is exercised, the premium is used to reduce the cost of the underlying stock in the put case or to add to the striking price received in the call case.

If the option writer chooses to close out a commitment by entering into a closing transaction, the difference between the premium received and the premium paid is a short-term capital gain or loss.

The short-sale rule—section 1233(6) of the Internal Revenue Code—does not apply to a short option position. A call written against a long stock position does not change the holding period of the underlying stock.

Special Tax Considerations and Strategies

A straddle is taxed on the basis of each of its components, the put, and the call. Special tax rules apply to spreads. The net tax liability is the sum of the liabilities of the component parts.

Investors adjusting their portfolios at the end of the tax year must be careful with the use of options. An investor who sells a security at a loss at the end of the tax year is disallowed the tax loss deduction if he or she reacquires the stock or an option thereon anytime during a period beginning 30 days prior to the sale and ending 30 days after the sale. This is considered a "wash sale." Such are the special considerations. Investors can, however, use options to reduce their tax burden in any given tax year.

Options can be used to convert short-term gains into long-term gains. An investor who wishes to sell a stock held for less than a year and wants to avoid paying taxes on short-term capital gains would write a call option against his or her stock position. The life of the call will be long enough to ensure that the holding period on the stock is longer than a year. The premium received on the call would be added to the striking price of the stock when the option is exercised. The call writer obviously hopes that the call will not be exercised before the holding period on the stock (which begins with the purchase date of the stock) exceeds one year. The reader is reminded that the maximum tax on long-term capital gains is 20 percent.

Another beneficial outcome can accrue to the investor from the above strategy. By writing a call against a long stock position, an investor is shifting taxable income from one year to the next. This may be predicated upon the expectation that next year some capital losses may be incurred to neutralize the capital gains and to reduce, if not eliminate, the taxes due on the sale of capital assets.

The potential problem with this strategy lies in the fact that call options may be exercised well before their expiration date. The investor may still be better off than he or she was prior to writing the option. The sale of the option earned a premium that would have been foregone had the option market been overlooked. Moreover, if the investor wishes to hold on to shares so that gains will be realized in the following year, he or she would purchase shares in the marketplace and deliver them against the call. This produces a short-term capital loss, which can offset current capital gains or offset current income on a one-to-one basis up to $3,000.

Another tax strategy available to a put holder with a profit in the position involves the exercise of the put by using borrowed stock for delivery. This is equivalent to a short sale. In so doing, the put holder postpones the payment of taxes on the profit in the put from one year to the next. The short sale, the reader may recall, can only produce short-term capital gains or losses.

Tax considerations and strategies can be quite complex. An option investor should seek competent professional help when in doubt.

3.11 FIDUCIARIES DISCOVER OPTIONS

Until recently, professional money managers have avoided options. Many believed, and some still do, that options are not consistent with prudent money management and are nothing more than a gimmick or a gamble similar to a poker game where the house gets the lion's share of the money gambled. It is believed by some that options are a tool invented by brokers in order to further line their pockets. Many new developments are beginning to win several converts to the options market. These developments were summarized in the September 22, 1980 issue of *The Wall Street Journal:*

> *In March, the Securities and Exchange Commission ended a long moratorium on increasing the number of stock issues against which options can be traded*

on exchanges. The comptroller of the currency, who regulates national banks, and the Department of Labor, which oversees pension funds, have issued statements expressing no objections to options trading that is consistent with portfolio diversification and yield objectives.

Last month, Gov. Edmund Brown of California signed an Act permitting insurance companies in the state to trade in options. Elsewhere, state insurance commissioners have removed some regulatory restrictions on options trading by insurance companies. . . .

These developments follow two other major events that set the stage for the acceptance of options trading. The first was the passage of the Rostenkowski Bill (HR 3052) in 1976, which changed the definition of unrelated business to exclude premiums from options trading. The second was the clarification of the Employee Retirement Income Security Act (ERISA) provided by the courts, showing option writing to be prudent and desirable, and by the Department of Labor, which emphasizes the "whole portfolio" approach instead of the "single investment" approach in the evaluation of fiduciary conduct.

Money managers are well advised to consider selling call options on stocks they wish to continue holding but consider fully priced currently. Puts should also be considered by money managers expecting major weaknesses in the market. No wholesale recommendation can be made, however. Every portfolio manager has a different strategy or portfolio investment requirements. However, no portfolio manager should reject options as an element in the process of maximizing return and minimizing risk of portfolios.

3.12 OPTION STRATEGY—BROAD OUTLINES

The development of an investment strategy requires the setting of investment goals and the full realization of one's financial position. An investor with little cash reserves, poor health and minimal life insurance, an inadequate housing arrangement, and other glaring shortages should avoid the stock and option markets.

With the needed financial resources justifying entry into the capital markets, an investor is well advised to adopt a portfolio strategy in which options have a constructive role to play. The ad hoc arrangements and the "looks good" approach inevitably lead to financial setbacks.

From a portfolio perspective and with a certain attitude toward risk, the investor can best devise the option strategy most suitable for his or her needs and tax bracket. The characteristics of the most prevalent options strategies are summarized in Table 3.5. The choice depends on the special circumstances of the investor and on the perceived risk of each position. The reader should remember from the discussions throughout the chapter that the options markets are so flexible that they allow the investor a wide range of possibilities in structuring the desired risk/return tradeoff: an income-oriented combination, a short put, and/or a short call. A short-run speculative strategy could ordinarily restrict the investor to a long position in a call or in a put. There obviously exist other strategies, as indicated earlier.

These strategies, however, or the choice among them, constitute the second level in the investment decision-making process. As the reader is aware by now, there are several ways of acquiring an option on the stock. The first level in the choice process consists,

TABLE 3.5
Characteristics of Strategies

Strategy	Nature of Strategy	Desired Action of Stock at Expiration	Risk	Gain Potential
Write naked puts	High risk/ high return	Up (above strike)	Substantial but limited to price of stock minus premium received	Limited to option premium
Write covered calls	Moderate risk/ moderate return	Unchanged	Substantial but limited to price of stock minus premium received	Limited to premium
Write naked calls	High risk/high return	Down (below strike)	Unlimited	Limited to premium
Write covered straddles	Moderate risk/ moderate return	Band between strike prices	Limited downside	Dual premium
Write naked straddles	High risk/ moderate return	Band between strike prices	Unlimited upside but limited downside	Dual premium
Buy puts	High risk/ high return	Down	Limited but may lose entire premium	Limited but substantial
Buy calls	High risk/ high return	Up	Limited but may lose entire premium	Unlimited
Buy straddles	High risk/ moderate return	Above call or below put striking price	Limited but may lose entire premium	Unlimited

Source: Financial World, January 15, 1979 p. 80.

therefore, of choosing between a long position in the stock (a stock being an option on the assets of the corporation), a long position in a convertible bond (an option—a much longer-term option than is available with the listed options—on the stock of the company), a long position in a convertible preferred stock, and a long position in a warrant or in a stock right. This obviously assumes that all or some of these instruments are available on each company that is being considered for investment purposes. After mentioning this, we should not lose sight of the fact that options offer much flexibility as well as a high level of liquidity and that they are becoming available on an increasing number of stocks. Furthermore, options may be the least costly and the quickest, if not the only, way for hedging a stock position.

An investor seeking income from an investment should consider alternative income-producing vehicles such as government bonds, corporate bonds, dividend-paying stock, convertible stocks, and others that offer good if not better risk/return opportunities in certain cases.

Having settled on the options route, the investor must have a mechanism for surveying market opportunities. Many investment houses have devised both simple and very sophisticated techniques for sifting through the options market and identifying those options consistent with certain specifications. Tables 3.6 and 3.7 summarize the opportunities in straddles and bull spreads. The operator specifies the time range—that is, the acceptable range for the life of the option. He also sets the minimum and maximum price for the straddle (Table 3.6), and whether he or she wishes to have deviations from the theoretical value (as determined by the B&S model) included in the output. The outputs are shown in both tables, with the necessary footnotes. From all the stocks on which options are sold, those listed are the only ones that meet the specifications of the investor. The remaining decision requires a choice among those available opportunities.

These computer outputs are available to the public, generally at little or no cost. They are useful for certain purposes, but not for all. An investor wishing to hedge a long or a short position in a stock has little if any freedom in the choice of the option to be used.

No matter what the expressed purpose for using options, an investor is best advised to consult his or her options broker, to do frequent homework, and to consult competent, professional tax advisors.

TABLE 3.6
Straddles

Time range in days (min, max) 0, 190 (days)
Straddle price range (min, max) 0.25, 3
Theoretical values (yes = 1/no = 0) 1
6/30/80

Jan Series 1

Stock[a]		Exch[b]	Option		Price	In-COMM[c]	%-N-VAL[d]	Down[e]	Up[e]
ASH	38.500	NX	JLY	40.0	2.687	0.130	130.33	37.31	42.68
BOL	43.875	NA	JLY	45.0	2.187	0.496	82.65	42.81	47.18
STK	15.125	NX	OCT	15.0	2.906	0.236	130.81	12.09	17.90

Jan Series 2

Stock		Exch	Option		Price	In-COMM	%-N-VAL	Down	Up
ACD	48.125	NX	JLY	50.0	2.937	0.462	84.06	47.06	52.93
AH	25.687	NX	JLY	25.0	1.593	0.510	129.74	23.40	26.59

Source: E. F. Hutton & Co., New York, 1980.

[a] The stock symbol (ASH, etc.) is followed by the current stock price. ASH is the sticker tape symbol for Ashland Oil, BOL for Bausch & Lomb, STK for Storage Technology, ACD for Allied Chemical, and AH for Allis-Chalmers.

[b] Exchange is NX = New York Stock Exchange; NA = American Stock Exchange.

[c] In-COMM = commission cost = $0.13 \times 100 = \$13$.

[d] %-N-VAL = percent duration from the theoretical value determined by the B&S model. Overvalue (>100%) indicates sell, undervalue (<100%) indicates buy.

[e] Down = stock price − price (premium); up = stock price + price (premium).

TABLE 3.7
Bull Spread

Time range in days (min, max) 0, 115 (days)
Price range (min, max) 0, 7
Ratio of spread (buy, sell) 1, 1
In/out of the money (in, out) 105, 85
06/30/80

Stock[a]		Exch[b]	Long		Short		Debit[c]	B.E.[d]	In-COMM[e]
ACD	48.125	NX	JAN	45.0	JLY	50.0	6.56	52.08	0.520
ACD	48.125	NX	JLY	45.0	JLY	50.0	2.93	48.41	0.475
ACD	48.125	NX	OCT	45.0	JLY	50.0	5.06	50.56	0.504
ACD	48.125	NX	JAN	45.0	OCT	50.0	4.12	49.45	0.331
ACD	48.125	NX	OCT	40.0	OCT	50.0	5.87	46.22	0.349
ACD	48.125	NX	OCT	45.0	OCT	50.0	2.62	47.94	0.316
AH	25.687	NX	JAN	25.0	JLY	30.0	2.59	27.75	0.159
AH	25.687	NX	JLY	25.0	JLY	30.0	1.03	26.16	0.135
AH	25.687	NX	OCT	25.0	JLY	30.0	2.21	27.37	0.153
AH	25.687	NX	JAN	25.0	OCT	30.0	2.06	27.62	0.557
AH	25.687	NX	OCT	25.0	OCT	30.0	1.68	27.23	0.552

Source: E. F. Hutton & Co., New York, 1980.

[a] ACD is a stock symbol for Allied Chemical. AH is a stock symbol for Allis-Chalmers.

[b] NX = New York Stock Exchange.

[c] Debit = required financial commitment to the bull spread.

[d] B.E. = break-even point on the bull spread.

[e] In-COMM = required commission on a bull spread. For the first row, it equals 0.52 × 100 = $52.

3.13 IMPACT OF OPTIONS MARKET

Several studies on the impact of options trading on the value of the underlying stock have been undertaken, the most extensive of these having been done by Robert R. Nathan Associates.[3] These studies concluded that there were no systematic effects of options trading—including effects of the exercise of options during the expiration week— on price behavior of the underlying stocks. In fact, these studies showed that optioned stocks had narrower bid/ask spreads and experienced less price volatility. G. N. Naider disputed the finding related to volatility and concluded that the decline in volatility on the stock examined by R. Nathan was caused by cyclical market movements.[4] Furthermore, Naider formed evidence of increased relative volatility of CBOE stocks.

---

[3] Robert R. Nathan Associates, Inc., *Review of Initial Trading Experience at the Chicago Board Options Exchange,* Chicago Board Options Exchange, December 1974; *Analysis of Volume and Price Patterns in Stocks Underlying CBOE Options from December 30, 1974 to April 30, 1975,* Chicago Board Options Exchange, July 1975; *Analysis of Volume and Price Patterns in Stocks Underlying CBOE Options from December 31, 1975 to January 16, 1976.* Chicago Board Options Exchange, February 1976.

[4] **G. N. Naider,** "The Effect of Option Trading on Variability of Common Stock Returns." Paper presented at the Annual Meeting of the Southern Finance Association, 1977.

Many other studies have attempted to measure the effect of options trading on the capital markets' operational and allocational efficiencies. The studies we have surveyed suffer from lack of quality data and/or from deficiencies in the statistical techniques employed. We believe that the evidence is not conclusive and that further research is needed in this area as far as investors are concerned. A voluminous study undertaken by the SEC concludes by stating that

> *In general, the Options Study found that options can provide useful alternative investment strategies to those who understand the complexities and risks of options trading. . . . The Options Study found numerous instances of sales practice abuses in which registered representatives told investors of possible rewards they might expect from options without simultaneously warning them of the risks inherent to options trading. Often inadequately trained registered representatives recommended options strategies to their customers which it is doubtful that the salesmen, much less their customers, understood.*[5]

These findings further point out the need for investors to have a strategy; to do their homework thoroughly, taking, among other things, taxes and transactions costs into account; and to keep a watchful eye on developments affecting the underlying security.

CONCLUSIONS

Advanced options strategies are not for amateurs. Complex as they may seem, options strategies can be mastered with some effort. They represent yet another vehicle for improving return and lowering risk. Such strategies should be used as part of an overall portfolio strategy and not to the exclusion of everything else.

QUESTIONS

1. (This question covers material from Chapters 2 and 3). The Friday, April 22, 1983, edition of *The Wall Street Journal* carried the following options quotations:

Option & NY Close	Strike Price	Calls–Last			Puts–Last		
		Jun	*Sep*	*Dec*	*Jun*	*Sep*	*Dec*
GM	50	14¾	S	S	1–16	S	S
64½	55	9½	11½	11½	¼	1	1½
64½	60	5⅝	7¾	8⅝	15–16	2½	2⅞
64½	65	2⅝	4½	6¼	3	4½	5
64½	70	11–16	2¾	S	6	7¼	S

---

[5] Securities and Exchange Commission. *Report of the Special Study of the Options Markets to the Securities and Exchange Commission.* Washington, D.C. December 22, 1978.

   a. Which puts and calls are in the money? Which are out of the money?

   b. Which of the call options would you purchase if you were very bullish? Which put options? Why?

   c. Which of the options would you pick if you held a long position about which you felt rather but not very comfortable?

   d. What combination (one) would be best to establish if you were very bullish on GM? Which combination would be best if you were very bearish?

   e. Do you see any spread opportunities? How would you segregate between them depending on your expectations?

   f. How and when would you use the GM/Sep/65?

   g. Construct a butterfly spread. Explain your decision and the conditions under which it will work.

   h. Which option (one) would you choose to write if your outlook on GM were bearish between now and June? Why?

   i. Why does the GM/June/70 sell at a positive price?

   j. Which variables influence option prices? How? Why?

   k. Pick a straddle to write if you were mildly bullish on GM. Explain your selection.

2. What are the expectations of an investor who buys a straddle? Why could he or she not profit outside the options market? What are the straddle writer's expectations?

3. An options trader constructs a vertical put bear spread by purchasing a DGO April/60P for $12 and writing a DGO April/45P for $1. DGO is currently selling for $50/share. What is the maximum potential loss? What is the maximum potential gain? What is the risk/reward ratio? Evaluate the ratio of this position.

4. Given: on April 22, 1983, the current price of SRB stock was 61½ and cost of options (s.p. = strike price) was as follows:

	Call			**Put**		
s.p.	*Apr*	*Jul*	*Oct*	*Apr*	*Jul*	*Oct*
50	13¼	15½	16¼	¼	½	1
55	6½	8½	9½	¼	1¼	1½
60	4	5½	6¼	2	2½	3
65	1½	3¼	4½	5½	6¼	7

Develop strategies for two types of investors: a conservative (risk-averse) investor and a speculator. Present the potential profit for that investor with $2,500 in cash and $10,000 worth of government securities (remember capital requirements for option positions) under each of the following cases:

   a. Expect SRB to increase to 70 by July.

   b. Expect SRB to retreat to 50 by July.

   c. Forthcoming R&D announcement will cause SRB either to advance sharply or decline sharply by July.

   d. Expect SRB to remain static, near 60, until July.

3. A "strap" is a combination of two calls and one put with the same striking price and exercise date. What does the buyer of a strap believe about the movement of the underlying stock?

4. An options trader establishes a bull spread by purchasing a call (put) and by selling a call (put) on the same security. Which option will he or she buy (the one with the lower or higher striking price)? How will he or she profit?

5. Many brokerage houses now use what is known as a "reverse conversion strategy" to profit. It involves selling a stock short, investing the proceeds at money market rates, and hedging the short position by writing a put and buying a call in the option market. How does the investor hope to profit from the reverse conversion strategy? What potential drawbacks do you see to such a strategy? To which market participants is this strategy available? What type of stocks would best suit a reverse conversion? What is the vector representation for the investor?

6. What are the major drawbacks of spreads?

7. What should a potential options trader consider before entering the options market?

8. R. R. Nathan Associates' studies show minimal impact of options upon the price of the underlying security. What would be the implications of opposite findings?

9. From the information in Question 1, construct at least three combinations and show the profit and loss ranges for each.

10. The tax law treats a call option differently depending on whether it is exercised. What is that difference from the perspective of the option buyer and the option seller?

11. Do you see any arbitrage opportunities from the table in Question 1?

12. Construct a graph depicting possible profit/loss outcomes for an investor who writes a naked straddle on a stock selling at $45 share. He receives $450 for writing a 90-day call with a striking price of 45, and $350 for writing a 90-day put with the same striking price (ignore transactions costs). How much capital would he have to commit? What is the most he could hope to earn?

13. An options trader constructs a vertical put bear spread by purchasing a DGO April/60P for $12 and writing a DGO April/45P for $1. DGO is currently selling for $50/share. What is the maximum potential loss? What is the maximum potential gain? What is the risk reward ratio? Evaluate the ratio of this position.

CHAPTER
4 | Interest Rate Options

4.1 An Introduction to Interest Options

The interest options market was still in its infancy stage as of early 1983. Some market observers are predicting a rosy future, others are much more skeptical.

The volatility of interest rates in the late 1970s and early 1980s is well documented in Chapter 6. The unprecedented movement in interest rates and consequently in the price of debt instruments sent portfolio managers scurrying for a shelter to protect income and principal. The first instrument for such protection was provided by financial futures contracts which are discussed in detail in Chapter 6. On October 1, 1982, the Chicago Board of Trade introduced another instrument for hedging interest rate risk: the T-bond option contract. Several exchanges joined the fray with a multitude of contracts most of which have been approved but not yet traded.

Three national exchanges currently trade interest options: the Chicago Board of Trade (CBT), the Chicago Board Options Exchange (CBOE), and the American Stock Exchange (AMEX). The Chicago Mercantile Exchange, which is very active in the financial futures market, remains on the sideline. The CME introduced an option on the S&P 500 on January 28, 1983. This option constitutes the CME's total involvement (actual and expected) in the option market.

The Chicago Board of Trade (CBT), ordinarily very innovative and aggressive, introduced the first interest option on T-bonds futures contracts on October 1, 1982 after a long legal battle with the CBOE over options on GNMA securities. The fate of interest options was in the hands of the courts and of the U.S. Congress for a long time. The issues were: (1) Is a GNMA Option a security or a commodity? and (2) Does the SEC or the Commodity Futures Trading Commission (CFTC) have jurisdiction over the GNMA options?

The controversy began on February 26, 1981, when the SEC gave the Chicago Board Options Exchange (CBOE) approval for the issuance, clearance, and exercise of GNMA options under Section 19 (b) (2) of the Securities Exchange Act of 1934. Worried about its competitive edge to the CBOE, The Chicago Board of Trade (CBT) filed a suit

against the CBOE and the SEC. The CBT alleged that the SEC had no authority to grant approval because a GNMA option is not a security but rather a commodity.

On August 7, 1981, the CBT moved the Court of Appeals for a stay, which was granted in October 1981. All trading on the CBOE in GNMA options was thus suspended.

In December 1981, John Shad, chairman of the SEC, and Phillip Johnson, chairman of the CFTC, while attempting to avert legal complications, reached an agreement that gave the SEC exclusive jurisdiction over nonstock options, subject to Congressional approval. The Shad/Johnson agreement was soon to be negated. The Court of Appeals ruled in favor of the CFTC on March 25, 1982. The court declared that the SEC has no regulatory authority over nonstock options and prohibited the CBOE from trading mortgage-backed options without approval from the CFTC.

On April 7, 1982, the SEC and the CBOE asked the court to reconsider its decision. In the petition that was filed, the SEC and CBOE argued that if the decision were allowed to stand, it would seriously disrupt the securities industry and the regulatory process. Further complications clouding the future of nonstock options came as a result of expiration of the regulatory authority of the CFTC. The future of the CFTC was uncertain because some members of Congress considered it unnecessary and because some critics considered its recent performance less than admirable. The charge by the General Accounting Office that the CFTC's review of futures trading was inadequate was not very helpful either.

The issues were resolved by keeping the CFTC and finding a way to please both the CBT and the CBOE. The Commodities Futures Trading Commission (CFTC), which

TABLE 4.1
Contract Volume 1982—T-Bond Options

Time Period	Trading Days	Total	Daily Average	High Day	Date	Low Day	Date
All Classes							
Oct*	6	2,224	371	1020	22	155	26
Nov	21	5,850	279	1238	24	31	19
Dec	22	6,060	275				
Total for 1982	49	14,134	288				
Call Classes							
Oct*	6	1,436	239	614	22	103	28
Nov	21	4,402	210	703	24	19	2
Dec	22	4,548	207				
Total for 1982	49	10,386	212				
Put Classes							
Oct*	6	788	131	406	22	28	26
Nov	21	1,448	69	535	24	12	2
Dec	22	1,512	69				
Total for 1982	49	3,748	76				

* Trading began October 22, 1982.

Source: Chicago Board of Options Exchange, January 1983. (CBOE has permitted use of this table and Table 4.2, but has not participated in the preparation of this book and is not responsible for its contents.)

TABLE 4.2
Open Interest in T-Bond Options
Contracts

1982	Calls	Puts	Total
October	585	374	959
November	2,849	1,380	4,229
December	1,583	694	2,277

Source: Chicago Board of Options Exchange, January 1983.

regulates the CBT, permitted the CBT to trade only one interest option—but not on a cash T-bond. The CBT chose T-bond options on a treasury bond futures contract (see Chapter 6). The introduction of the option has been successful. Average trading volume in the first four months was in the 1500–2000 contracts range, and open interest (number of contracts outstanding) averaged 13,000 contracts.

The CBOE, which is regulated by the Securities Exchange Commission (SEC), began trading T-bond options on October 22, 1982.

The activity in this contract in the first three months of trading is shown in Table 4.1. The open interest in both classes (calls and puts) of T-bond options is shown in Table 4.2.

The CBOE has also received SEC approval to trade GNMA options. When trading begins—scheduled for 1984—it will be the only exchange offering such a contract. The CBT is barred from introducing a GNMA option. The CBOE carefully monitors the growth and the acceptability of the T-bond option contract before going ahead with the GNMA option contract.

The AMEX introduced options on 13¾ Treasury notes on October 22, 1982, on 13-week Treasury bills on November 5, 1982, and on 10½ T-notes on November 8, 1982. On June 20, 1983 the AMEX began trading options on $100,000 T-notes and $1,000,000 T-bills. Other options on Treasury notes and bills with different coupons and sizes are also traded on the AMEX today. The activity level in the interest options contracts offered by the AMEX remains low but impressive. The AMEX was still paying for advertising space in *The Wall Street Journal* to report prices and open interest on most of its option contracts.

This chapter will concentrate on two options contracts, namely, one currently contemplated by the CBOE—the GNMA option contract, and the other currently traded on the CBOE—the T-bond option contract. The option contracts on T-notes and T-bills will also be discussed briefly.

4.2 Definitions

Options confer rights to buy (sell) a specified amount of a security (commodity) at a specified price within a designated time period.

Futures contracts, on the other hand, are obligations to buy (sell) commodities (securities) at a specified price, time, and place.

A GNMA option is a contract issued by the Options Clearing Corporation that gives the holder the right to buy (a call option) or to sell (a put option) at a specified yield $100,000 principal balance of GNMA pass-through securities on or before a set date. For this right a price (premium) is paid.

A T-bond option contract, similarly, gives the holder the right to buy (a call) or to sell (a put) $100,000 principal amount of T-bonds any time during its life.

A miniseries T-bond options contract covers $20,000 principal amount and carries similar privileges.

The current T-bill option traded on the AMEX gives its holder the right to buy (a call) or to sell (a put) $200,000 principal amount of 13-week U.S. T-bills any time during its life.

The Options Clearing Corporation has authorized, however, the issuance of large ($1,000,000 principal) and small ($200,000) 13-week T-bill options, and large ($500,000 principal) and small ($100,000) 26-week T-bill options.

The T-note option contract is the same as a T-bond contract except it covers shorter term Treasury obligations.

4.3 GNMA Options

The discussion of interest options covers the basic features of the contracts, their advantages, the controversy surrounding them, the potential users and uses of the contract, and the tax implications. We begin with a discussion of GNMA securities.

Government National Mortgage Association Securities (GNMA) and the GNMA Option Market

GNMA interest options are options on $100,000 ($\pm$ 2.5 percent) of GNMA passthroughs. These GNMA passthroughs are so named because periodic payments on these securities, covering both interest and principal, are "passed through" to the holder of GNMA securities. GNMA passthroughs represent a pro rata share in a pool of mortgages. This pool is typically assembled by a mortgage banker and is guaranteed as to interest and principal by GNMA, an agency of the Department of Housing and Urban Development. GNMA securities are backed by the full faith and credit of the U.S. government. The mortgages in the pool are insured by the Federal Housing Authority (FHA) or the Farmers Home Administration (FMHA), or guaranteed by the Veterans Administration (VA). The minimum size of the pool is $500,000. The mortgages assembled must be on homes in one geographic area, and must have the same mortgage rate and the same maturity. The pool of mortgages is then submitted to GNMA for approval upon which shares in the pool are sold to the public or to institutions. The mortgage banker continues to service the mortgages by issuing monthly checks to the shareholders. As the mortgage payments are received by the mortgage banker he simply prorates the net value (gross value — bankers' commissions) among the shareholders. GNMA guarantees the shareholders that their payments will be made on the promised date regardless of whether the initial mortgagee defaults on the loan. If the mortgage payments' date coincides with that of the GNMA, the GNMA securities are referred to as GNMA passthroughs, and if the dates are different the securities are referred to as modified passthroughs. The minimum denomination for a GNMA passthrough is $25,000.

Two problems could arise in the delivery of GNMA securities against the option contract. They result from:

1. The nonhomogeneity of the coupon rates on outstanding GNMAs.
2. The fact that GNMAs are declining balance instruments.

This means that at a point in time when delivery is required, the principal balance on the GNMA securities held may not be equal to the standard $100,000 principal balance required for delivery against the option contract.

We now discuss these two problems.

The Coupon Rate

The discussion of the acceptable coupon rate for delivery against an option contract requires an understanding of the "current production rate." This rate is the maximum coupon rate on GNMA securities and is one-half percent below the maximum FHA/VA mortgage rate. The production rate is not constant and consequently the value of the GNMA securities is not constant.

For a GNMA security to be deliverable against an option contract, the production coupon rate must be equal to or less than the current production rate. If the coupon rate is higher than the production rate, the older coupon will continue to be deliverable for a period equal to 45 days or the expiration settlement date, whichever is longer.

It can be said, therefore, and particularly for the near contracts, that any coupon rate is deliverable against the option position. To allow for standardization, and thus for easy comparability among the deliverable GNMA securities, the Chicago Board Options Exchange (CBOE) allows for delivery of various coupons using yield equivalence. The CBOE is one of the exchanges on which interest options contracts will be traded. The other is the Chicago Board of Trade. Deliverable GNMAs, under the yield equivalence method, are priced to provide the same yield to maturity as an 8 percent GNMA. This serves to fix a specific yield on a GNMA option contract as opposed to a specific price. The utilization of such a system expands the number of deliverable GNMAs. To otherwise restrict the deliverable GNMAs to a certain coupon rate is to decrease the depth of the market and thus its liquidity. The CBOE publishes the set of Tables shown in Table 4.3 to help translate a certain coupon rate into an 8 percent equivalent.

To illustrate how yield equivalence is applied, we consider the case where the contractual market yield on GNMA is 15.65 percent. At this yield to maturity, an 8 percent GNMA would be quoted at 60 (or $600 per $1,000 face value). If the production rate on the GNMA held is 12 percent, the adjusted exercise price is 80.06 (fractions in 32nds on Table 4.3). Therefore, if the strike (exercise) price on an interest option is 60, the effective exercise price is then 80.06, if a GNMA bearing a 12 percent coupon rate is delivered against the option contract.

The exercise price contracted for is a nominal exercise price based on the delivery of a GNMA with an 8 percent coupon. The effective exercise price depends on the coupon rate of the GNMA that is being delivered. Thus, the cheapest deliverable GNMA against an interest option position is almost always that with the highest market yield. The reasons can be seen in the following example.

Coupon on Deliverable GNMA (%)	Exercise Price Yield (%)	Nominal Strike (Exercise) Price	Effective Exercise Price	Market Yield (%)	Market Price
8	14.84	63*	63	14.53	64–6
10	14.84	63	73–10	14.95	72–27
13	14.84	63	89–12	15.16	87–24

* This price, like every price in Table 4.3, is based on the assumption that the GNMA has a life of 30 years with a balloon payment in the 12th year.

TABLE 4.3. GNMA Yield and Price Equivalent Table

8% GNMA		ADJUSTED EXERCISE PRICES FOR ALTERNATIVE COUPON RATES								
STRIKE PRICE	YIELD PREPAID 12 YRS	6%	6¼%	6½%	6¾%	7%	7¼%	7½%	7¾%	STRIKE PRICE
50	18.885	41-27	42-27	43-27	44-27	45-27	46-28	47-29	48-30	50
51	18.517	42-23	43-23	44-23	45-24	46-25	47-27	48-28	49-30	51
52	18.160	43-18	44-19	45-20	46-22	47-23	48-25	49-27	50-29	52
53	17.815	44-14	45-15	46-17	47-19	48-21	49-23	50-26	51-29	53
54	17.479	45-10	46-12	47-14	48-16	49-19	50-22	51-25	52-28	54
55	17.153	46-06	47-08	48-11	49-14	50-17	51-20	52-24	53-28	55
56	16.836	47-01	48-04	49-08	50-11	51-15	52-19	53-23	54-27	56
57	16.528	47-29	49-01	50-04	51-08	52-13	53-17	54-22	55-27	57
58	16.227	48-25	49-29	51-01	52-06	53-11	54-16	55-21	56-26	58
59	15.935	49-21	50-25	51-30	53-03	54-08	55-14	56-20	57-26	59
60	15.650	50-17	51-22	52-27	54-01	55-06	56-12	57-19	58-25	60
61	15.372	51-13	52-18	53-24	54-30	56-04	57-11	58-18	59-25	61
62	15.102	52-09	53-15	54-21	55-27	57-02	58-09	59-17	60-24	62
63	14.837	53-05	54-11	55-18	56-25	58-00	59-08	60-16	61-24	63
64	14.579	54-01	55-08	56-15	57-22	58-30	60-06	61-15	62-23	64
65	14.326	54-29	56-04	57-12	58-20	59-28	61-05	62-14	63-23	65
66	14.080	55-25	57-00	58-09	59-17	60-26	62-03	63-13	64-22	66
67	13.839	56-21	57-29	59-06	60-15	61-24	63-02	64-11	65-22	67
68	13.603	57-17	58-25	60-03	61-12	62-22	64-00	65-10	66-21	68
69	13.372	58-13	59-22	61-00	62-10	63-20	64-31	66-09	67-21	69
70	13.146	59-09	60-18	61-29	63-07	64-18	65-29	67-08	68-20	70
71	12.924	60-05	61-15	62-26	64-05	65-16	66-28	68-08	69-20	71
72	12.707	61-01	62-12	63-23	65-02	66-14	67-26	69-07	70-19	72
73	12.495	61-29	63-08	64-20	66-00	67-12	68-25	70-05	71-19	73
74	12.286	62-25	64-05	65-17	66-29	68-10	69-23	71-05	72-18	74
75	12.082	63-21	65-01	66-14	67-27	69-08	70-22	72-04	73-18	75
76	11.881	64-17	65-30	67-11	68-24	70-06	71-20	73-03	74-17	76
77	11.685	65-13	66-26	68-08	69-22	71-04	72-19	74-02	75-17	77
78	11.491	66-09	67-23	69-05	70-20	72-02	73-17	75-01	76-16	78
79	11.302	67-05	68-20	70-02	71-17	73-00	74-16	76-00	77-16	79
80	11.115	68-02	69-16	70-31	72-15	73-30	75-14	76-31	78-15	80
81	10.932	68-30	70-13	71-28	73-12	74-28	76-13	77-30	79-15	81
82	10.752	69-26	71-09	72-26	74-10	75-27	77-11	78-29	80-14	82
83	10.575	70-22	72-06	73-23	75-07	76-25	78-10	79-28	81-14	83
84	10.401	71-18	73-03	74-20	76-05	77-23	79-09	80-27	82-13	84
85	10.230	72-14	73-31	75-17	77-03	78-21	80-07	81-26	83-13	85
86	10.062	73-10	74-28	76-14	78-00	79-19	81-06	82-25	84-12	86
87	9.896	74-07	75-25	77-11	78-30	80-17	82-04	83-24	85-12	87
88	9.733	75-03	76-21	78-08	79-27	81-15	83-03	84-23	86-11	88
89	9.572	75-31	77-18	79-06	80-25	82-13	84-01	85-22	87-11	89
90	9.414	76-27	78-15	80-03	81-23	83-11	85-00	86-21	88-10	90
91	9.259	77-24	79-11	81-00	82-20	84-09	85-31	87-20	89-10	91
92	9.105	78-20	80-08	81-29	83-18	85-08	86-29	88-19	90-10	92
93	8.954	79-16	81-05	82-26	84-16	86-06	87-28	89-18	91-09	93
94	8.805	80-12	82-02	83-23	85-13	87-04	88-26	90-17	92-09	94
95	8.659	81.09	82.30	84.20	86-11	88-02	89-25	91-16	93-08	95
96	8.514	82-05	83-27	85-18	87-09	89-00	90-24	92-15	94-08	96
97	8.371	83-01	84-24	86-15	88-06	89-30	91-22	93-15	95-07	97
98	8.231	83-29	85-21	87-12	89-04	90-28	92-21	94-13	96-07	98
99	8.092	84-26	86-17	88-09	90-02	91-26	93-19	95-13	97-06	99
100	7.955	85-22	87-14	89-07	90-31	92-25	94-18	96-12	98-06	100
101	7.820	86-18	88-11	90-04	91-29	93-23	95-17	97-11	99-05	101
102	7.687	87-15	89-08	91-01	92-27	94-21	96-15	98-10	100-05	102

TABLE 4.3. (*Continued*)

8% GNMA		ADJUSTED EXERCISE PRICES FOR ALTERNATIVE COUPON RATES								
STRIKE PRICE	YIELD PREPAID 12 YRS	8¼%	8½%	8¾%	9%	9¼%	9½%	9¾%	10%	STRIKE PRICE
50	18.885	51-02	52-04	53-06	54-08	55-10	56-13	57-16	58-19	50
51	18.517	52-02	53-05	54-07	55-10	56-13	57-16	58-20	59-23	51
52	18.160	53-03	54-06	55-09	56-12	57-16	58-20	59-23	60-28	52
53	17.815	54-03	55-07	56-11	57-14	58-19	59-23	60-27	62-00	53
54	17.479	55-04	56-08	57-12	58-17	59-21	60-26	61-31	63-04	54
55	17.153	56-04	57-09	58-14	59-19	60-24	61-29	63-03	64-08	55
56	16.836	57-05	58-10	59-15	60-21	61-27	63-00	64-07	65-13	56
57	16.528	58-05	59-11	60-17	61-23	62-29	64-04	65-10	66-17	57
58	16.227	59-06	60-12	61-19	62-25	64-00	65-07	66-14	67-21	58
59	15.935	60-06	61-13	62-20	63-27	65-03	66-10	67-18	68-25	59
60	15.650	61-07	62-14	63-22	64-29	66-05	67-13	68-21	69-30	60
61	15.372	62-08	63-15	64-23	65-31	67-08	68-16	69-25	71-02	61
62	15.102	63-08	64-16	65-25	67-01	68-10	69-19	70-29	72-06	62
63	14.837	64-09	65-17	66-26	68-04	69-13	70-22	72-00	73-10	63
64	14.579	65-09	66-18	67-28	69-06	70-15	71-26	73-04	74-14	64
65	14.326	66-10	67-19	68-29	70-08	71-18	72-29	74-08	75-18	65
66	14.080	67-10	68-20	69-31	71-10	72-21	74-00	75-11	76-22	66
67	13.839	68-11	69-21	71-00	72-12	73-23	75-03	76-15	77-27	67
68	13.603	69-11	70-22	72-02	73-14	74-26	76-06	77-18	78-31	68
69	13.372	70-12	71-23	73-03	74-16	75-28	77-09	78-22	80-03	69
70	13.146	71-12	72-24	74-05	75-18	76-31	78-12	79-25	81-07	70
71	12.924	72-13	73-26	75-07	76-20	78-01	79-15	80-29	82-11	71
72	12.707	73-13	74-27	76-08	77-22	79-04	80-18	82-00	83-15	72
73	12.495	74-14	75-27	77-09	78-24	80-06	81-21	83-04	84-19	73
74	12.286	75-14	76-29	78-11	79-26	81-09	82-24	84-07	85-23	74
75	12.082	76-15	77-29	79-12	80-28	82-11	83-27	85-11	86-27	75
76	11.881	77-15	78-30	80-14	81-30	83-14	84-30	86-14	87-31	76
77	11.685	78-16	79-31	81-15	83-00	84-16	86-01	87-18	89-03	77
78	11.491	79-16	81-00	82-17	84-02	85-19	87-04	88-21	90-07	78
79	11.302	80-16	82-01	83-18	85-04	86-21	88-07	89-24	91-10	79
80	11.115	81-17	83-02	84-20	86-06	87-23	89-10	90-28	92-14	80
81	10.932	82-18	84-03	85-21	87-07	88-26	90-13	91-31	93-18	81
82	10.752	83-18	85-04	86-23	88-09	89-28	91-15	93-03	94-22	82
83	10.575	84-19	86-05	87-24	89-11	90-31	92-18	94-06	95-26	83
84	10.401	85-19	87-06	88-26	90-13	92-01	93-21	95-09	96-30	84
85	10.230	86-19	88-07	89-27	91-15	93-04	94-24	96-13	98-02	85
86	10.062	87-20	89-08	90-28	92-17	94-06	95-27	97-16	99-05	86
87	9.896	88-20	90-09	91-30	93-19	95-08	96-30	98-20	100-09	87
88	9.733	89-21	91-10	92-31	94-21	96-11	98-01	99-23	101-13	88
89	9.572	90-21	92-11	94-01	95-23	97-13	99-04	100-26	102-17	89
90	9.414	91-22	93-12	95-02	96-25	98-16	100-07	101-30	103-21	90
91	9.259	92-22	94-13	96-04	97-27	99-18	101-09	103-01	104-25	91
92	9.105	93-23	95-14	97-05	98-29	100-20	102-12	104-04	105-29	92
93	8.954	94-23	96-15	98-07	99-31	101-23	103-15	105-08	107-00	93
94	8.805	95-24	97-16	99-08	101-00	102-25	104-18	106-11	108-04	94
95	8.659	96-24	98-17	100-09	102-02	103-27	105-21	107-14	109-08	95
96	8.514	97-25	99-18	101-11	103-04	104-30	106-23	108-17	110-11	96
97	8.371	98-25	100-19	102-12	104-06	106-00	107-26	109-21	111-15	97
98	8.231	99-26	101-19	103-13	105-08	107-02	108-29	110-24	112-19	98
99	8.092	100-26	102-20	104-15	106-10	108-05	110-00	111-27	113-23	99
100	7.955	101-27	103-21	105-16	107-12	109-07	111-03	112-30	114-26	100
101	7.820	102-27	104-22	106-18	108-13	110-09	112-05	114-02	115-30	101
102	7.687	103-27	105-23	107-19	109-15	111-12	113-08	115-05	117-02	102

TABLE 4.3. (*Continued*)

8% GNMA		ADJUSTED EXERCISE PRICES FOR ALTERNATIVE COUPON RATES								
STRIKE PRICE	YIELD PREPAID 12 YRS	10¼%	10½%	10¾%	11%	11¼%	11½%	11¾%	12%	STRIKE PRICE
50	18.885	59-22	60-25	61-28	63-00	64-04	65-07	66-11	67-15	50
51	18.517	60-27	61-31	63-02	64-07	65-11	66-15	67-19	68-24	51
52	18.160	62-00	63-04	64-09	65-13	66-18	67-23	68-28	70-01	52
53	17.815	63-05	64-09	65-14	66-20	67-25	68-30	70-04	71-10	53
54	17.479	64-09	65-15	66-20	67-26	69-00	70-06	71-12	72-18	54
55	17.153	65-14	66-20	67-26	69-01	70-07	71-14	72-20	73-27	55
56	16.836	66-19	67-26	69-00	70-07	71-14	72-21	73-28	75-04	56
57	16.528	67-24	68-31	70-06	71-13	72-21	73-29	75-04	76-12	57
58	16.227	68-29	70-04	71-12	72-20	73-28	75-04	76-12	77-21	58
59	15.935	70-01	71-10	72-18	73-26	75-03	76-11	77-20	78-29	59
60	15.650	71-06	72-15	73-24	75-01	76-10	77-19	78-28	80-06	60
61	15.372	72-11	73-20	74-29	76-07	77-17	78-26	80-04	81-14	61
62	15.102	73-15	74-25	76-03	77-13	78-23	80-01	81-12	82-22	62
63	14.837	74-20	75-30	77-09	78-19	79-30	81-09	82-20	83-31	63
64	14.579	75-25	77-04	78-14	79-26	81-05	82-16	83-27	85-07	64
65	14.326	76-30	78-09	79-20	81-00	82-11	83-23	85-03	86-15	65
66	14.080	78-02	79-14	80-26	82-06	83-18	84-30	86-11	87-23	66
67	13.839	79-07	80-19	81-31	83-12	84-25	86-06	87-18	89-00	67
68	13.603	80-11	81-24	83-05	84-18	85-31	87-13	88-26	90-08	68
69	13.372	81-16	82-29	84-11	85-24	87-06	88-20	90-02	91-16	69
70	13.146	82-20	84-02	85-16	86-30	88-12	89-27	91-09	92-24	70
71	12.924	83-25	85-07	86-22	88-04	89-19	91-02	92-17	94-00	71
72	12.707	84-30	86-12	87-27	89-10	90-26	92-09	93-25	95-08	72
73	12.495	86-02	87-17	89-01	90-16	92-00	93-16	95-00	96-16	73
74	12.286	87-06	88-22	90-06	91-22	93-07	94-23	96-08	97-24	74
75	12.082	88-11	89-27	91-12	92-28	94-13	95-30	97-15	99-00	75
76	11.881	89-15	91-00	92-17	94-02	95-20	97-05	98-22	100-08	76
77	11.685	90-20	92-05	93-22	95-08	96-26	98-12	99-30	101-16	77
78	11.491	91-24	93-10	94-28	96-14	98-00	99-19	101-05	102-24	78
79	11.302	92-29	94-15	96-01	97-20	99-07	100-25	102-12	103-31	79
80	11.115	94-01	95-20	97-07	98-26	100-13	102-00	103-20	105-07	80
81	10.932	95-05	96-25	98-12	100-00	101-19	103-07	104-27	106-15	81
82	10.752	96-10	97-30	99-17	101-05	102-26	104-14	106-02	107-23	82
83	10.575	97-14	99-02	100-23	102-11	104-00	105-21	107-10	108-31	83
84	10.401	98-18	100-07	101-28	103-17	105-06	106-28	108-17	110-06	84
85	10.230	99-23	101-12	103-01	104-23	106-13	108-02	109-24	111-14	85
86	10.062	100-27	102-17	104-07	105-29	107-19	109-09	110-31	112-22	86
87	9.896	101-31	103-22	105-12	107-02	108-25	110-16	112-07	113-29	87
88	9.733	103-04	104-26	106-17	108-08	109-31	111-22	113-14	115-05	88
89	9.572	104-08	105-31	107-23	109-14	111-06	112-29	114-21	116-13	89
90	9.414	105-12	107-04	108-28	110-20	112-12	114-04	115-28	117-20	90
91	9.259	106-16	108-09	110-01	111-25	113-18	115-10	117-03	118-28	91
92	9.105	107-21	109-13	111-06	112-31	114-24	116-17	118-10	120-04	92
93	8.954	108-25	110-18	112-11	114-05	115-30	117-24	119-17	121-11	93
94	8.805	109-29	111-23	113-17	115-10	117-04	118-30	120-24	122-19	94
95	8.659	111-01	112-27	114-22	116-16	118-10	120-05	121-31	123-26	95
96	8.514	112-06	114-00	115-27	117-22	119-16	121-11	123-06	125-02	96
97	8.371	113-10	115-05	117-00	118-27	120-23	122-18	124-14	126-09	97
98	8.231	114-14	116-09	118-05	120-01	121-28	123-24	125-20	127-16	98
99	8.092	115-18	117-14	119-10	121-06	123-03	124-31	126-27	128-24	99
100	7.955	116-23	118-19	120-15	122-12	124-09	126-05	128-02	129-31	100
101	7.820	117-27	119-24	121-20	123-17	125-15	127-12	129-09	131-07	101
102	7.687	118-31	120-28	122-25	124-23	126-21	128-18	130-16	132-14	102

TABLE 4.3. (*Continued*)

8% GNMA		ADJUSTED EXERCISE PRICES FOR ALTERNATIVE COUPON RATES								
STRIKE PRICE	YIELD PREPAID 12 YRS	12¼%	12½%	12¾%	13%	13¼%	13½%	13¾%	14%	STRIKE PRICE
50	18.885	68-19	69-23	70-28	72-00	73-04	74-09	75-13	76-18	50
51	18.517	69-29	71-01	72-06	73-11	74-16	75-21	76-26	77-31	51
52	18.160	71-06	72-11	73-17	74-22	75-28	77-01	78-07	79-13	52
53	17.815	72-15	73-21	74-27	76-01	77-07	78-13	79-20	80-26	53
54	17.479	73-25	74-31	76-05	77-12	78-19	79-25	81-00	82-07	54
55	17.153	75-02	76-09	77-16	78-23	79-30	81-05	82-13	83-20	55
56	16.836	76-11	77-18	78-26	80-02	81-09	82-17	83-25	85-01	56
57	16.528	77-20	78-28	80-04	81-12	82-21	83-29	85-05	86-14	57
58	16.227	78-29	80-06	81-14	82-23	84-00	85-09	86-18	87-27	58
59	15.935	80-06	81-15	82-24	84-02	85-11	86-20	87-30	89-07	59
60	15.650	81-15	82-25	84-02	85-12	86-22	88-00	89-10	90-20	60
61	15.372	82-24	84-02	85-12	86-23	88-01	89-12	90-22	92-01	61
62	15.102	84-01	85-11	86-22	88-01	89-12	90-23	92-02	93-13	62
63	14.837	85-10	86-21	88-00	89-12	90-23	92-03	93-14	94-26	63
64	14.579	86-18	87-30	89-10	90-22	92-02	93-14	94-26	96-06	64
65	14.326	87-27	89-08	90-20	92-00	93-13	94-25	96-06	97-19	65
66	14.080	89-04	90-17	91-30	93-11	94-24	96-05	97-18	98-31	66
67	13.839	90-13	91-26	93-07	94-21	96-02	97-16	98-30	100-11	67
68	13.603	91-21	93-03	94-17	95-31	97-13	98-27	100-09	101-24	68
69	13.372	92-30*	94-12	95-27	97-09	98-24	100-06	101-21	103-04	69
70	13.146	94-07	95-21	97-04	98-19	100-02	101-17	103-01	104-16	70
71	12.924	95-15	96-31	98-14	99-29	101-13	102-29	104-12	105-28	71
72	12.707	96-24	98-08	99-24	101-08	102-24	104-08	105-24	107-08	72
73	12.495	98-00	99-17	101-01	102-17	104-02	105-19	107-03	108-20	73
74	12.286	99-09	100-26	102-11	103-28	105-13	106-30	108-15	110-00	74
75	12.082	100-17	102-03	103-20	105-05	106-23	108-09	109-26	111-12	75
76	11.881	101-26	103-12	104-29	106-15	108-01	109-20	111-06	112-24	76
77	11.685	103-02	104-20	106-07	107-25	109-12	110-30	112-17	114-04	77
78	11.491	104-10	105-29	107-16	109-03	110-22	112-09	113-28	115-16	78
79	11.302	105-19	107-06	108-25	110-13	112-00	113-20	115-08	116-27	79
80	11.115	106-27	108-15	110-03	111-23	113-11	114-31	116-19	118-07	80
81	10.932	108-03	109-24	111-12	113-00	114-21	116-09	117-30	119-19	81
82	10.752	109-12	111-00	112-21	114-10	115-31	117-20	119-09	120-30	82
83	10.575	110-20	112-09	113-30	115-20	117-09	118-31	120-20	122-10	83
84	10.401	111-28	113-18	115-08	116-29	118-19	120-09	121-31	123-22	84
85	10.230	113-04	114-26	116-17	118-07	119-29	121-20	123-11	125-01	85
86	10.062	114-12	116-03	117-26	119-17	121-07	122-30	124-21	126-13	86
87	9.896	115-21	117-12	119-03	120-26	122-18	124-09	126-01	127-24	87
88	9.733	116-29	118-20	120-12	122-04	123-28	125-19	127-12	129-04	88
89	9.572	118-05	119-29	121-21	123-13	125-06	126-30	128-23	130-15	89
90	9.414	119-13	121-05	122-30	124-23	126-16	128-09	130-01	131-26	90
91	9.259	120-21	122-14	124-07	126-00	127-25	129-19	131-12	133-06	91
92	9.105	121-29	123-23	125-16	127-10	129-04	130-29	132-23	134-17	92
93	8.954	123-05	124-31	126-25	128-19	130-13	132-08	134-02	135-28	93
94	8.805	124-13	126-07	128-02	129-29	131-23	133-18	135-13	137-08	94
95	8.659	125-21	127-16	129-11	131-06	133-01	134-28	136-23	138-19	95
96	8.514	126-29	128-24	130-20	132-15	134-11	136-07	138-02	139-30	96
97	8.371	128-05	130-01	131-29	133-25	135-21	137-17	139-13	141-09	97
98	8.231	129-13	131-09	133-05	135-02	136-30	138-27	140-24	142-20	98
99	8.092	130-21	132-17	134-14	136-11	138-08	140-05	142-02	143-31	99
100	7.955	131-29	133-26	135-23	137-20	139-18	141-15	143-13	145-11	100
101	7.820	133-04	135-02	137-00	138-30	140-28	142-26	144-24	146-22	101
102	7.687	134-12	136-10	138-09	140-07	142-05	144-04	146-02	148-01	102

TABLE 4.3. (*Continued*)

8% GNMA		ADJUSTED EXERCISE PRICES FOR ALTERNATIVE COUPON RATES								
STRIKE PRICE	YIELD PREPAID 12 YRS	14¼%	14½%	14¾%	15%	15¼%	15½%	15¾%	16%	STRIKE PRICE
50	18.885	77-23	78-28	80-00	81-05	82-10	83-15	84-20	85-25	50
51	18.517	79-05	80-10	81-15	82-21	83-26	85-00	86-06	87-11	51
52	18.160	80-19	81-24	82-30	84-04	85-10	86-17	87-23	88-29	52
53	17.815	82-00	83-07	84-13	85-20	86-26	88-01	89-08	90-14	53
54	17.479	83-14	84-21	85-28	87-03	88-10	89-17	90-25	92-00	54
55	17.153	84-27	86-03	87-11	88-18	89-26	91-02	92-10	93-17	55
56	16.836	86-09	87-17	88-25	90-01	91-10	92-18	93-26	95-03	56
57	16.528	87-22	88-31	90-08	91-16	92-25	94-02	95-11	96-20	57
58	16.227	89-04	90-13	91-22	93-00	94-09	95-18	96-28	98-05	58
59	15.935	90-17	91-27	93-05	94-14	95-24	97-02	98-12	99-22	59
60	15.650	91-30	93-09	94-19	95-29	97-08	98-18	99-29	101-07	60
61	15.372	93-12	94-22	96-01	97-12	98-23	100-02	101-13	102-24	61
62	15.102	94-24	96-04	97-15	98-27	100-06	101-17	102-29	104-09	62
63	14.837	96-06	97-17	98-29	100-09	101-21	103-01	104-13	105-25	63
64	14.579	97-19	98-31	100-11	101-24	103-04	104-17	105-29	107-10	64
65	14.326	99-00	100-12	101-25	103-06	104-19	106-00	107-13	108-27	65
66	14.080	100-12	101-26	103-07	104-21	106-02	107-16	108-29	110-11	66
67	13.839	101-25	103-07	104-21	106-03	107-17	108-31	110-13	111-27	67
68	13.603	103-06	104-20	106-03	107-17	109-00	110-14	111-29	113-12	68
69	13.372	104-19	106-02	107-16	108-31	110-15	111-30	113-13	114-28	69
70	13.146	105-31	107-15	108-30	110-14	111-29	113-13	114-28	116-12	70
71	12.924	107-12	108-28	110-12	111-28	113-12	114-28	116-12	117-28	71
72	12.707	108-25	110-09	111-25	113-10	114-27	116-11	117-28	119-12	72
73	12.495	110-05	111-22	113-07	114-24	116-09	117-26	119-11	120-28	73
74	12.286	111-18	113-03	114-20	116-06	117-23	119-09	120-27	122-12	74
75	12.082	112-30	114-16	116-02	117-20	119-06	120-24	122-10	123-28	75
76	11.881	114-10	115-29	117-15	119-02	120-20	122-07	123-25	125-12	76
77	11.685	115-23	117-09	118-28	120-15	122-02	123-21	125-08	126-28	77
78	11.491	117-03	118-22	120-10	121-29	123-17	125-04	126-24	128-12	78
79	11.302	118-15	120-03	121-23	123-11	124-31	126-19	128-07	129-27	79
80	11.115	119-27	121-16	123-04	124-25	126-13	128-02	129-22	131-11	80
81	10.932	121-08	122-28	124-17	126-06	127-27	129-16	131-05	132-26	81
82	10.752	122-20	124-09	125-30	127-20	129-09	130-31	132-20	134-10	82
83	10.575	124-00	125-22	127-11	129-01	130-23	132-13	134-03	135-25	83
84	10.401	125-12	127-02	128-24	130-15	132-05	133-28	135-18	137-09	84
85	10.230	126-24	128-15	130-05	131-28	133-19	135-10	137-01	138-24	85
86	10.062	128-04	129-27	131-18	133-10	135-01	136-24	138-16	140-07	86
87	9.896	129-16	131-07	132-31	134-23	136-15	138-07	139-31	141-22	87
88	9.733	130-28	132-20	134-12	136-04	137-29	139-21	141-13	143-06	88
89	9.572	132-08	134-00	135-25	137-18	139-10	141-03	142-28	144-21	89
90	9.414	133-20	135-13	137-06	138-31	140-24	142-17	144-11	146-04	90
91	9.259	134-31	136-25	138-18	140-12	142-06	143-31	145-25	147-19	91
92	9.105	136-11	138-05	139-31	141-25	143-20	145-14	147-08	149-02	92
93	8.954	137-23	139-17	141-12	143-07	145-01	146-28	148-22	150-17	93
94	8.805	139-03	140-03	142-25	144-20	146-15	148-10	150-05	152-00	94
95	8.659	140-14	142-10	144-05	146-01	147-28	149-24	151-19	153-15	95
96	8.514	141-26	143-22	145-18	147-14	149-10	151-06	153-02	154-30	96
97	8.371	143-06	145-02	146-30	148-27	150-23	152-20	154-16	156-13	97
98	8.231	144-17	146-14	148-11	150-08	152-04	154-01	155-30	157-27	98
99	8.092	145-29	147-26	149-23	151-21	153-18	155-15	157-13	159-10	99
100	7.955	147-08	149-06	151-04	153-02	154-31	156-29	158-27	160-25	100
101	7.820	148-20	150-18	152-16	154-14	156-13	158-11	160-09	162-08	101
102	7.687	149-31	151-30	153-29	155-27	157-26	159-25	161-23	163-22	102

TABLE 4.3. (*Continued*)

8% GNMA		ADJUSTED EXERCISE PRICES FOR ALTERNATIVE COUPON RATES								
STRIKE PRICE	YIELD PREPAID 12 YRS	16¼%	16½%	16¾%	17%	17¼%	17½%	17¾%	18%	STRIKE PRICE
50	18.885	86-30	88-04	89-09	90-14	91-19	92-24	93-30	95-03	50
51	18.517	88-17	89-23	90-28	92-02	93-08	94-14	95-20	96-25	51
52	18.160	90-03	91-09	92-16	93-22	94-28	96-03	97-09	98-16	52
53	17.815	91-21	92-28	94-03	95-10	96-17	97-24	98-31	100-06	53
54	17.479	93-07	94-15	95-22	96-30	98-05	99-13	100-20	101-28	54
55	17.153	94-25	96-01	97-09	98-17	99-25	101-01	102-09	103-17	55
56	16.836	96-11	97-20	98-28	100-05	101-13	102-22	103-30	105-07	56
57	16.528	97-29	99-06	100-15	101-24	103-01	104-10	105-19	106-28	57
58	16.227	99-15	100-24	102-02	103-11	104-21	105-31	107-08	108-18	58
59	15.935	101-00	102-10	103-20	104-30	106-09	107-19	108-29	110-07	59
60	15.650	102-18	103-28	105-07	106-18	107-28	109-07	110-18	111-28	60
61	15.372	104-03	105-14	106-25	108-05	109-16	110-27	112-06	113-18	61
62	15.102	105-20	107-00	108-12	109-23	111-03	112-15	113-27	115-06	62
63	14.837	107-05	108-18	109-30	111-10	112-22	114-03	115-15	116-27	63
64	14.579	108-23	110-03	111-16	112-29	114-10	115-22	117-03	118-16	64
65	14.326	110-08	111-21	113-02	114-15	115-29	117-10	118-23	120-05	65
66	14.080	111-25	113-06	114-20	116-02	117-16	118-30	120-11	121-25	66
67	13.839	113-09	114-24	116-06	117-20	119-03	120-17	121-31	123-14	67
68	13.603	114-26	116-09	117-24	119-07	120-21	122-04	123-19	125-02	68
69	13.372	116-11	117-26	119-10	120-25	122-08	123-24	125-07	126-22	69
70	13.146	117-28	119-12	120-27	122-11	123-27	125-11	126-27	128-11	70
71	12.924	119-13	120-29	122-13	123-29	125-14	126-30	128-14	129-31	71
72	12.707	120-29	122-14	123-31	125-15	127-00	128-17	130-02	131-19	72
73	12.495	122-14	123-31	125-16	127-01	128-19	130-04	131-21	133-07	73
74	12.286	123-30	125-16	127-02	128-19	130-05	131-23	133-09	134-27	74
75	12.082	125-14	127-01	128-19	130-05	131-23	133-10	134-28	136-14	75
76	11.881	126-31	128-17	130-04	131-23	133-10	134-29	136-15	138-02	76
77	11.685	128-15	130-02	131-21	133-08	134-28	136-15	138-02	139-22	77
78	11.491	129-31	131-19	133-07	134-26	136-14	138-02	139-22	141-10	78
79	11.302	131-15	133-03	134-23	136-12	138-00	139-20	141-09	142-29	79
80	11.115	132-31	134-20	136-09	137-29	139-18	141-07	142-28	144-16	80
81	10.932	134-15	136-04	137-26	139-15	141-04	142-25	144-14	146-04	81
82	10.752	135-31	137-21	139-11	141-00	142-22	144-12	146-01	147-23	82
83	10.575	137-15	139-05	140-27	142-18	144-08	145-30	147-20	149-10	83
84	10.401	138-31	140-22	142-12	144-03	145-26	147-16	149-07	150-30	84
85	10.230	140-15	142-06	143-29	145-20	147-11	149-02	150-25	152-17	85
86	10.062	141-31	143-22	145-14	147-05	148-29	150-20	152-12	154-04	86
87	9.896	143-14	145-06	146-30	148-22	150-14	152-07	153-31	155-23	87
88	9.733	144-30	146-23	148-15	150-08	152-00	153-25	155-17	157-10	88
89	9.572	146-14	148-07	150-00	151-25	153-18	155-11	157-04	158-29	89
90	9.414	147-29	149-23	151-16	153-10	155-03	156-29	158-22	160-15	90
91	9.259	149-13	151-07	153-00	154-26	156-20	158-14	160-08	162-02	91
92	9.105	150-29	152-23	154-17	156-11	158-06	160-00	161-27	163-21	92
93	8.954	152-12	154-07	156-01	157-28	159-23	161-18	163-13	165-08	93
94	8.805	153-27	155-23	157-18	159-13	161-08	163-04	164-31	166-26	94
95	8.659	155-11	157-06	159-02	160-30	162-25	164-21	166-17	168-13	95
96	8.514	156-26	158-22	160-18	162-14	164-11	166-07	168-03	169-31	96
97	8.371	158-09	160-06	162-03	163-31	165-28	167-24	169-21	171-18	97
98	8.231	159-24	161-21	163-19	165-16	167-13	169-10	171-07	173-04	98
99	8.092	161-08	163-05	165-03	167-00	168-30	170-27	172-25	174-22	99
100	7.955	162-23	164-21	166-19	168-17	170-15	172-13	174-11	176-09	100
101	7.820	164-06	166-04	168-03	170-01	172-00	173-30	175-29	177-27	101
102	7.687	165-21	167-20	169-19	171-18	173-17	175-15	177-14	179-13	102

Source: Chicago Board Options Exchange.

The data provided on page 106 is derived from Table 4.3 and from published quotations on GNMA as of June 17, 1982. The deliverable coupons were available on that day and the market yields and prices are actual yields and prices. Columns 2, 3, and 4 are from Table 4.3. From this data one can see that the optimal delivery would be that of the highest coupon bond. The reasons are that if the 8 percent coupon bond is delivered, the investor would be delivering his GNMAs that are worth $64\%_{32}$ at 63 (a loss of $1\%_{32}$). If the 10 percent coupon is delivered, the net profit from delivery is $(73^{10}\!\!/_{32}) - (72^{27}\!\!/_{32}) = 15/32$. If the 13 percent coupon rate is delivered, the profit from delivery would be $(89^{12}\!\!/_{32}) - (87^{24}\!\!/_{32}) = 1^{20}\!\!/_{32}$. In general, therefore, the higher coupon GNMA should be the instrument delivered against the option position.

The Declining Principal

Every payment on a GNMA passthrough, whether it is straight or modified, consists of two components, namely, interest and principal. The early payments on mortgages consist primarily of interest payments, while the later payments consist primarily of principal payments. Thus, over time, the interest component of a fixed periodic mortgage payment is decreasing, while the principal component is increasing. This means that as time passes, the outstanding balance of the mortgage decreases and converges to zero by the balloon payment or by the maturity date. This situation creates a problem, however. The outstanding balance on a GNMA may not be equal to the required $100,000 for delivery against an interest option contract at the appropriate point in time.

To alleviate this problem, the option exchanges permit delivery of GNMAs whose principal balance falls in the $100,000 ± 2.5% range, that is, a principal value between $97,500.01 and $102,499.99. If the deliverable GNMA has an outstanding balance below $100,000 but one that is above the lower end of the range, the difference is made up by a cash adjustment referred to as "appropriate differential." A similar procedure is followed if the remaining principal exceeds $100,000. In this latter case, additional cash (principal − $100,000) is released to the trader making the delivery. GNMAs with principal balances outside the acceptable range are not deliverable against the GNMA option contract.

Other Characteristics of GNMA Options and Option Markets

GNMA options are purchased and sold by investors through a brokerage house and commissions are charged on both the buy and the sell side. Trading is done in the margin account or in the cash account. Naked option writing—a position not covered by a long position in the underlying asset—spreads, and straddles are all established in the margin account. The full cost of a put or a call is paid in cash within seven business days of the transaction date if a long (buy) position is established. The payment for a put or a call is received in cash if a short (sell) position is established. This is true regardless of the account (cash or margin) in which the trade is made.

A long position in the GNMA security itself, namely a cash position, could be established in the cash or the margin account. A portion of the investment could be borrowed by the investor. In accordance with Regulation T, the initial margin requirement is 15 percent of the principal amount. Up to 85 percent can be borrowed and the maintenance margin is 10 percent of the principal amount. The maintenance margin represents that

value below which the equity in a GNMA position is not allowed to fall. If it does fall, the investor will be called upon to commit additional cash.

Types of Positions

Two positions may be established in the GNMA option market: a long position or a short position. A long position is a purchase of a call—the right to buy $100,000 of GNMAs at a set price anytime during a specified time period—or a put—the right to sell. A short position in a call, on the other hand, represents a commitment to sell $100,000 of GNMA securities at a set price anytime during a specified time period. A short position in a put also represents a commitment to buy (take delivery of) $100,000 of GNMA securities at a set price anytime during a designated period. The characteristics, uses, risks, advantages, and disadvantages of long and short positions in interest options will be explored in detail later in this chapter.

Maturity Terms/Dates

The maturity terms on GNMA options are 3, 6, 9, 12, and 15 months in length. The maturity months on the CBOE are March, June, September, and December. The exact maturity date is the Saturday before the second Wednesday of the expiration month.

Exercise (Strike) Prices

The exercise prices are set at two-point intervals in terms of an 8 percent deliverable GNMA. Additional exercise prices are introduced as yields on the underlying GNMAs fluctuate. The reader should note that yields and prices are inversely related.

Accrued Interest

The holder of a GNMA call and the writer (the seller-holder of a short put position) of a GNMA put are likely to take delivery of GNMA securities from the writer of a call or the holder of a put, respectively. When delivery is consummated, the party receiving the GNMA securities is obligated to pay the exercise price that is adjusted to reflect the 8 percent yield equivalence of the delivered coupon plus accrued interest from the first day of the exercise month up to but not including the settlement day in the exercise month.

Option Market Operations

The option market is a centralized location where trading in standardized contracts takes place within the rules and regulations of the exchange. Exchanges which currently trade interest options use the open auction system where traders standing in a designated pit use open outcry and hand signals to buy and sell contracts.

   The key operators on the floors of the exchanges are the floor brokers and the market makers. Floor brokers fill the orders of their own customers and those of the customers of their employer-firm. They cannot trade for their own account on the same day they trade for clients. Market makers, on the other hand, trade for their own account and may establish long and/or short positions. They are charged by the exchange with the

FIGURE 4.1.

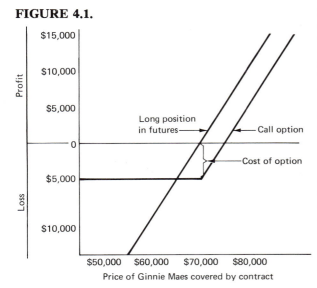

Profit

$15,000

$10,000

$5,000

Long position
in futures →   ← Call option

0

← Cost of option

$5,000

Loss

$10,000

$50,000 $60,000 $70,000 $80,000

Price of Ginnie Maes covered by contract

Futures vs. options. Option buyers have a safety net: they never lose more than they pay for the option—in this example $5,000 for a call. By contrast, there is no limit to what a futures player could lose. The option holder's profit, however, will always be lower than the profit in futures, by an amount equal to the option's cost. In this example, provided by First Boston Corp., the securities underlying both the futures contract and the call are assumed to be Ginnie Mae pass-throughs with $100,000 in outstanding mortgages and an 8% coupon. Although the options will not begin trading until the fall, First Boston's analysts figure $5,000 is about what a 15-month call to purchase these Ginnie Maes at $70,000 would have cost a few months ago when they were selling for $70,000 and yielding 13%. (Chart by Patricia Byrne. *Fortune* Magazine; 1981.)

maintenance of a fair and orderly market. This may require the establishment of a position that is not consistent with the expectations of the market maker.

The options markets are highly competitive and very liquid, though risky (Figure 4.1).

Risks in GNMA Options

Interest options carry the same type of risks as stock options do. The risks differ considerably from a long position to a short position, and from a speculative long position to a hedged long position. The highest risks are connected with uncovered long positions and naked short positions. Among the risks to watch for are

1. The possibility of losing the entire investment (the premium) in a put or a call. This loss can be realized in a very short time period.

2. The more volatile interest rates are, the more volatile the options become. Interest rates have been very volatile in recent years.

3. The writer of a GNMA call may not be able to deliver the GNMAs held if their principal drops below a certain value. GNMA monthly cash flows consist of both interest and principal payments. As principal payments are made, the outstanding balance drops and in certain cases below the limit allowed for delivery. This renders the GNMAs held unacceptable for delivery, which may necessitate the purchase of the requisite number of bonds in the open market.

4. The newness of the GNMA option market will continue to present liquidity risk until the contract achieves a sufficiently high daily volume.

Other risks are also present. They are inherent in the strategy employed in the options market, as we shall demonstrate later.

Pricing GNMA Options

The pricing of GNMA options should not be different from the pricing of stock options according to Black and Scholes, the authors of the stock option pricing model.[1] Despite very strong similarities, researchers have yet to arrive at a closed form solution for pricing GNMA options. Cox, Ingersoll and Ross[2] have arrived, however, at a closed form solution (a solution yielding a unique answer) for the evaluation of a European call option (an option exercisable only upon maturity) on a default-free pure discount bond.

The factors influencing stock option (call) prices (see Chapter 2) are:

$$C = f(S, \sigma^2, X, T, R_f)$$

where C = market price of a call option

       S = price of the underlying security

     σ^2 = volatility of the stock price measured by the instantaneous variance of the stock rate of return

     X = striking price

     T = life of option contract

    R_f = risk-free rate

The signs of the partial first derivatives are

$$\frac{\partial C}{\partial S} > 0, \frac{\partial C}{\partial X} < 0, \frac{\partial C}{\partial \sigma^2} > 0, \frac{\partial C}{\partial T} > 0, \frac{\partial C}{\partial R_f} > 0$$

The reasons for R_f are that an options trader can establish a perfectly hedged position in the options market by using an appropriate hedge ratio, and realize the risk-free rate. The other relationships should be easy to rationalize. These independent variables must be similarly incorporated in the pricing of GNMA call options.

While the variables influencing interest options are identifiable, mainly interest rates and time to expiration, the complete solution to the model has yet to be derived. A significant effort has been made by Georges Courtadon. We discuss Professor Courtadon's contributions which apply to options on default-free coupon-bearing cash instruments at the end of this chapter.

In-the-Money, Out-of-the-Money Options

In-the-money and out-of-the-money are nomenclature peculiar to the options market. They merely indicate whether the option (put or call) is profitable to exercise or not.

A call is in-the-money when the market price of the security exceeds the striking

---

[1] F. Black and M. Scholes, "The Pricing of Options and Corporate Liabilities," *Journal of Political Economy* (May/June 1973), 637–659.

[2] J. Cox, J. Ingersoll, and S. Ross, "A Theory of the Term Structure of Interest Rates," Research Paper no. 468, Graduate School of Business, Stanford University (August 1978).

price $(S > X)$. This is so because the trader can exercise his call at X and can sell the acquired securities at the higher market price.

A call is out-of-the-money if $S < X$. An exercise of the call will result in a loss. The price of a call that is out-of-the-money is obviously lower than that which is in-the-money. No one wants to pay a high price for an instrument that would lose money if converted. The question, therefore, deals with the positive premium on an out-of-the-money call. The answer lies in the following equation:

$$C = \text{intrinsic value} + \text{time premium}$$

The intrinsic value deals with the difference between S and $X(S - X)$. An out-of-the-money call has theoretically a negative intrinsic value. However, the option value does not drop below zero because no one is going to pay another for selling him an option. The time premium is always greater than or equal to zero. The longer the time to maturity is, the higher the time premium. The reason lies in the fact that with a longer life, the probability of an advantageous price movement is higher than it would be with a short-lived contract.

The put case is the reverse of that of a call. A put is in-the-money if the striking price (X) exceeds the market price (S). In this case the put holder would buy at the lower market price and sell at the higher striking price. If $X < S$, the put is out-of-the-money. The exercise of such a put results in a loss the size of which depends on the magnitude of the difference. Out-of-the-money GNMA put options are obviously cheaper than in-the-money options. Hedgers and speculators are careful to gauge the extent to which a put (call) is in- or out-of-the-money for that influences the magnitude of the risk assumed and the cost of the hedge. This will become apparent later in this chapter.

Interest Options Strategies

Strategies using interest options are essentially similar to those using stock options. Our problem, however, lies in the fact that interest options are not currently traded although stock options are. It is necessary, therefore, to create fictitious interest options

TABLE 4.4
GNMA Call Prices (May 19, 1982)

Striking Price	Maturity Months				
	June	Sept.	Dec.	March	June
56	7–20*	8–24	10–05	11–01	12–00
58	5–14	6–18	7–31	8–31	9–30
60	3–00	4–04	5–19	6–20	7–20
62	1–00	2–02	3–17	4–18	5–16
64	00–24	1–24	2–27	3–18	4–06
66	00–16	1–14	2–11	2–30	3–16
68	00–08	1–02	1–31	2–16	3–00

* Fractions are in $\frac{1}{32}$.

TABLE 4.5
GNMA Put Prices (May 19, 1982)

Striking	Maturity Months				
Price	*June*	*Sept.*	*Dec.*	*March*	*June*
56	00–10*	00–26	1–09	1–28	1–31
58	00–15	1–07	1–27	2–15	2–24
60	00–20	1–20	2–15	3–09	3–22
62	3–30	4–30	5–25	6–17	6–30
64	6–29	7–28	8–20	9–10	9–26
66	8–30	10–16	11–10	11–31	12–00
68	11–12	12–04	12–11	12–17	12–22

* Fractions are in $\frac{1}{32}$.

TABLE 4.6
Spot GNMA Prices (May 19, 1982)

	GNMA Issues		
Rate	Bid	Asked	Yld
8.00	65.14	65.30	14.10
9.00	69.16	70.00	14.38
9.50	71.24	72.80	14.47
10.00	74.30	74.19	14.55
11.00	79.60	79.14	14.66
11.50	81.18	81.26	14.72
12.50	86.22	86.30	14.78
13.00	89.30	89.11	14.84
13.50	91.19	91.27	14.88
14.00	93.11	93.19	15.07
15.00	97.19	97.27	15.28
16.00	102.50	102.13	15.43

Source: The Wall Street Journal, May 19, 1982.

prices to better illustrate the strategies on both the long and the short side. The fictitious call and put prices appear in Tables 4.4 and 4.5, respectively. The spot GNMA prices as of May 19, 1982 are shown in Table 4.6.

All strategies presented below are based on the following assumptions:

1. All deliverable GNMA securities have a $100,000 principal balance.
2. If the GNMA coupon rate is not specified, it is assumed to equal 15 percent.
3. Higher coupon bonds are indeed the cheapest to deliver against a short call position.

We now look at the various strategies using GNMA call options.

Strategies in GNMA Calls (Long Positions)

GNMA calls are used in a variety of ways, each with its risk/reward characteristics. We now examine these uses.

Calls for Leverage A GNMA/March/64 call selling at 3–18 offers substantial leverage potential when compared with 11.5 percent GNMAs selling for 81–26 on May 19, 1982 and yielding 14.72 percent. The spot purchase of three (3) GNMA securities, assuming a 10 percent margin requirement and ignoring transaction costs, would require an investment of:

$$(\$81,812.50) \times 10\% \times 3 = \$24,543.75$$

For about the same amount, seven (7) GNMA/March/64 calls may instead be purchased. If interest rates decline and the 11.5 percent GNMAs rise to 84–24, the profit from the cash position would equal:

$$[(84\text{--}24) - (81\text{--}26)] \times 3 = (2\text{--}30) \times 3$$
$$= 8\text{--}26 \text{ or } \$8,812.50$$

However, had the investor purchased 7 GNMA/March/64 calls for $(3\text{--}18) \times 7 = \$24,937.50$ and the interest rate decline occurred before the March expiration date, the price of the call may have risen to 6–18 and the resulting profit would equal:

$$[(6\text{--}18) - (3\text{--}18)] \times 7 = (3\text{--}00) \times 7 = 21\text{--}00 \text{ or } \$21,000$$

The increase in the price of the underlying security may not be entirely reflected in the value of the GNMA option because of the decrease in the time premium imbedded in the option price. The rates of return on the cash and options position are:

Cash Position   *Option Position*

$$\frac{8,812.50}{24,543.75} \approx 36\% \qquad \frac{21,000}{24,937.50} \approx 84\%$$

Clearly, if the investor correctly anticipates price movements, the options position is much more rewarding than the cash (spot) position in the underlying security. One must remember, however, that while leverage may be rewarding when expectations materialize, it can be devastating when expectations do not. The investor could conceivably lose his entire investment by the options expiration date.

Calls to Limit Trading Risk. A mortgage banker or a bond dealer may use GNMA call options as a cushion in trading GNMA securities. Consider the price pattern shown in Figure 4.2. It represents interesting opportunities to traders. For example, on May 19, 1982 a mortgage banker might expect an increase in GNMA rates and, therefore, sell short one 14-percent GNMA security selling at 93–11 and yielding 15.07 percent. Simultaneously, the banker would buy a December/GNMA/62 call selling for 3–17, to protect the short cash position. If GNMA securities prices do not drop to 91 as

FIGURE 4.2.

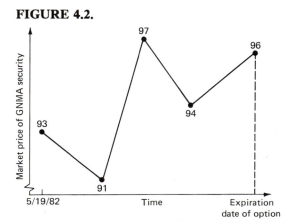

shown in Figure 4.2, and remain, say, at 93, the maximum loss in the options position is limited to the call premium paid or $3,531.25. This is, therefore, the maximum cost for protecting a short position for a period equal to the life of the call option.

If the price for the 14 percent GNMA security rises to 97–03 and the GNMA/Dec/62 call rises to 7–01, the loss of $3,750 from the short position (97–03 − 93–11 = 3–24) will be partially offset by the $3,500 gain from the option (7–01 − 3–17 = 3–16). Because the presence of the call emboldens the investor to a great degree, the real value of the call is increased through repeated trades against the protection it provides. Thus, an excellent strategy would include a short position at 93, protected by the call option, a cover and simultaneous long position at 91, a sale of the long position and a short position at 97. This sequence is followed by a cover and a long position at 94, finally ended by the sale of the long position at 96 and the expiration of the option. This strategy, of course, assumes perfect foresight on the part of the investor. If this foresight existed, the purchase of the call—indeed the option market in its entirety—would not be necessary.

Calls to Release Cash. An investor in need of the cash presently tied up in GNMA securities, but wishing to participate in anticipated upward price movement, may sell his GNMAs and purchase a call. Thus, on May 19, 1982, the investor may sell his 14 percent GNMA security, yielding 15.07 percent for 93–11 and buy a GNMA/Dec/62 call for 3–17. The proceeds from the sale of the GNMA, ignoring transaction costs and taxes, will be reduced by the size of the call premium: (93–11) − (3–17) = 89–26. If the 14 percent GNMA prices rise, the investor will profit from appreciation in the call. If the 14 percent GNMA price remains constant or falls, the loss is limited to the size of the premium, namely $3,531.25.

Calls to Fix Yields. A pension fund manager who expects to switch his current T-bond holdings for GNMAs sometime in the near future is obviously concerned about the probability of falling yields and may purchase a GNMA call with a maturity that coincides with the rollover date. For example, if the manager holds T-bonds that will be sold in September, he may purchase a GNMA/Sept/62 call option for 2–02 or $2,062.50. When the GNMA call matures in September, assuming that the cheapest deliverably GNMA is the 16 percent coupon, the manager may

1. Receive, say, $110,000 from his T-bonds, which he uses to take delivery of GNMA securities against the call. If the price of a 16 percent GNMA has risen to 109–27, the call is exercised at $104,281.25 (the adjusted exercise price assuming $100,000 principal balance) plus transactions costs. The acquisition price represents a yield to maturity equal to 15.102%. The amount saved through the call option equals

$$109\text{–}27 - [(104\text{–}09) + (2\text{–}02)] = 3\text{–}16 \text{ or } \$3,500$$

2. If the proceeds from the T-bonds are, say, $90,000, the manager would not be able to take delivery of the 16 percent GNMA bonds. In this case, he would sell the call and buy the appropriate GNMA (appropriate in terms of coupon and maturity) in the spot market. The spot market allows obviously for greater flexibility. For example, if the 13 percent GNMA rises from 89–11 on May 19, 1982 to 94–24 on September 14, 1982, and the GNMA/Sept/62 increases in value to 6–23, the manager would acquire the 13 percent GNMA at a cost of:

$$94\text{–}24 - [(6\text{–}23) - (2\text{–}02)] = 90\text{–}03$$
$$= \$90,093.75$$

The sum saved is equal to the call premium:

$$(94\text{–}24) - (90\text{–}03) = (6\text{–}23) - (2\text{–}02) = 4\text{–}21$$
$$= \$4,656.25$$

Calls for Psychological Sustenance. Calls allow for much greater flexibility to traders and more room for second guessing. A trader who is worried about the direction of yields may take an action that he/she would later regret. For example, if a trader sells a long position with the expectation that yields would rise, only to see them fall instead, he or she could miss a substantial gain. Had the trader held a call option, he or she would have been more tenacious, perhaps because the maximum loss is known and fixed. He or she is unlikely to sell the call unless a definite market trend sets in.

We now look at the short side of call options. A multitude of objectives can be served through short call positions. We begin with the discussion of the most common one.

Short Call Positions

Writing Call Options for Income. Selling a call option is selling someone the right to purchase $100,000 of GNMA securities from the seller at a specified yield during a specified time period.

Writing call options could supplement the cash flows from coupons on a long GNMA security. From the call options listed in Table 4.4, the investor may wish to write (sell) the GNMA/Sept/64 call and receive 1–24 or $1,750. The call option sold is out-of-the-money. The investor could have chosen an in-the-money or a less out-of-the-money option at the cost of an increased probability of the option being exercised against him, that is, an increased probability of giving up the securities he holds.

Selling a call option while the trader(s) holds a long position in the underlying security is referred to as covered call writing. The option seller could also sell a naked call. In this case no position is held in the underlying security. The risk/return profile differs considerably from the covered to the naked call position as we shall demonstrate.

The covered call option sold above for 1–24 could produce the following results under different states of the world.

1. If the 15 percent GNMA drops in price from 97–19 to 95–03, the entire premium would be earned by the option writer because it is not profitable to exercise the option. The covered option holder would now hold a depreciated asset. Thus, the premium earned would be conceptualized as one way to cushion a slide in GNMA prices.

2. If the 15 percent GNMA does not change in price, the entire call premium would be earned by the option writer.

3. If the 15 percent GNMA prices rise above the exercise price, the call writer might:

    (a) purchase a GNMA/Sept/64 call option to offset the short position.

    (b) deliver his securities if an exercise notice is assigned to him. The effective sale price of the GNMA position is the exercise price plus the call premium.

If GNMA prices had appreciated considerably, the option writer would have missed any price appreciation in excess of the striking price plus the premium. The loss here is an opportunity loss. Had the investor written a naked call, the consequences would have been different.

A drop in GNMA prices produces gains equal to the call premium. This is the ideal position for the naked option writer. Equally advantageous is a no-change-in-price.

An appreciation in GNMA prices, on the other hand, results in a loss of part or all the call premium, and possibly in a net (real) loss to the option writer. The reason is that the option writer would have to buy at the higher market price and sell (deliver) at the lower striking price.

Writing a Call Option to Hedge. A mortgage banker holding 11.5 percent GNMAs on May 19, 1982 and expecting a rise in GNMA yields would sell a call option to cushion the price drop. This is an alternative to selling the GNMA securities now and buying them later, assuming a sale is indeed possible.

The sale of, say, a GNMA/March 83/62 call for 4–18 would compensate for the entire loss if the GNMA prices drop to 77–00. A larger price drop would produce a book loss that exceeds the call premium. A sufficient price appreciation, however, could lead to the GNMA securities being called away from the option writer unless an offsetting call option is purchased. If the securities are called away, the full call premium is earned.

Writing Call Options to Improve on Market. A mortgage banker wishing to sell GNMA holdings at above current market prices would write the appropriate call and hope it is exercised against him. If 11.5 percent GNMAs are held and GNMA/Dec/64 is sold for 2–27, the mortgage banker would happily sell his GNMAs if prices rise to 83–05. If the price does not change, the GNMAs are sold and the call premium is added to the sale price. The sale proceeds are equal to

$$(81\text{--}18) + (2\text{--}27) = 84\text{--}13.$$

A price decline to, say, 77–13 would not allow for the exercise of the call. The price decline [(81–18) − (77–13) = 4–05] is larger than the call premium received (2–27). The sale of the call has partially cushioned the price drop.

Strategies in GNMA Puts

Long GNMA put positions have a multitude of uses. Their analysis requires the reader to think in a manner opposite that of a call.

Puts for Leverage. A put, being an option to sell a stock at a specified price during a specified period, allows the holder to take advantage of a price decline. The put holder would buy at the lower market price and sell at the striking price. In this regard, a put is equivalent to a short position in the underlying security. A margin requirement of 10 percent on GNMA securities translates into a $9,784.38 deposit on $100,000 of 15 percent GNMAs selling for 97–27 on May 19, 1982. For the $9,784.38, a trader may wish to purchase six (6) GNMA/Sept/60 puts at 1–20 each. If the price of the 15 percent GNMAs falls to 91–11 by August 20, 1982 and the put price rises to 4.30, the results are

Profits on the short cash position = (97–27) − (91–11) = 6–16 or $6,500
Profits on the long put position = [(4–30) − (1–20)] × 6 = 19–28 or $19,875

The rates of return are then equal to

$$\text{Short cash position} = \frac{6,500}{9,784.38} = 0.66$$

$$\text{Long put position} = \frac{19,875}{9,750} = 2.04$$

A price increase, however, could lead to the loss of the entire investment in the puts. Leverage can be disastrous if expectations do not materialize.

Short positions in the cash market require an uptick before they are established. One of the advantages of puts is that they do not have such a requirement. Another advantage is that the commission costs on puts are lower than those in the cash market. One of the disadvantages, however, is that the put holder must be able not only to anticipate the price decline but its magnitude, and the time period in which it will occur as well.

Puts to Protect Long Positions. A mortgage banker with a long position in 13.5 percent GNMAs may wish to protect it with a GNMA put option. The extent of protection depends on the banker's expectations and his resources. The less out-of-money and the more in-the-money the put option is, the more expensive the protection. On May 19, 1982 13.5 percent GNMAs sold for 91–19. The purchase of a GNMA/March '83/62 put for 6–17, a slightly out-of-the-money option, would guarantee that the maximum loss on the GNMA cash position would be $6,531.25, the price of the put. The banker, however, foregoes the first 6–17 points of appreciation if an interest rate decline occurs. Protection is not a free good.

Puts for Limited Risk Trading. A bond trader operating in a very volatile market may wish to protect long positions with a put. The put may be used for protection against several trades in which long positions are established.

Puts for Psychological Sustenance. GNMA put options may embolden the trader and prevent him from taking premature actions. An unsettled GNMA market may lead a trader to close the position at the slightest rise in price. A put option with its loss ceiling encourages the trader to hang on to the position. No one enjoys closing a short position only to see prices fall precipitously immediately thereafter.

Short Put Positions

We now look at the short side of put options. Short put positions, like their call counterpart, are primarily used to generate income.

Puts to Earn Premium Income. The put writer expects constant or rising prices for GNMAs. A mortgage banker may sell a GNMA/December/60 put for 2–15. The adjusted exercise price for a 16 percent GNMA or for a 60 option is 101–07. The market price is 102–13. One of the following cases could obtain:

1. If 16 percent GNMAs rise to 104–21 before December, the holder of the put will obviously not exercise his option. The put writer realizes the entire option premium. The gross rate of return to the put writer is equal to—assuming a 10 percent margin requirement—the deposit on the total commitment of the option seller,

$$\frac{2,470}{102,406.25 \times 0.10} = 0.24$$

From this return, commission costs must be deducted.

2. If 16 percent GNMAs remain at 102–13, the put will still not be exercised and the entire premium of \$2,470 will be kept by the option writer.

3. If the 16 percent GNMA falls to 96–29, the put will be exercised and the writer (if naked) will be forced to pay 101–07 for an asset with a market value of only 96–29. The loss would equal

$$[(101–07 - 96–29)] - (2–15) = 1–27 \text{ or } \$1,843.75$$
book loss on asset   premium   net
acquired   received   loss

If the put writer is forced to buy an 11 percent GNMA that sells for 70–03, the loss would equal:

$$[(75–01) - (70–03)] - (2–15) = 2–15 \text{ or } \$2,468.75$$

Puts to Acquire a Security. The put writer hopes, if he wishes to acquire a position in the underlying security, that the put will be exercised. If a mortgage banker, for example, sells a GNMA/June '82/60 put, which is an out-of-the-money option, he hopes the price of the 15 percent GNMA will fall below the adjusted exercise price of 95–29. Thus, if the price of the GNMA falls to 94–00, the put will be exercised. If the price remains at its May 19, 1982 price of 97–19, the put writer can purchase the GNMA in the cash market. His cost is lessened somewhat by the 00–20 put premium. If the price rises, however, the put will not be exercised and the writer will be forced to purchase the GNMA in the cash market. Although the writer will keep the entire

premium, he may be forced to pay considerably more for the GNMA than he would have if he had purchased it when it was first considered.

Put options with different striking prices and maturities could have been considered by the put writer. The higher the premium received, the larger the probability of exercise against the short put position. High premiums indicate, therefore, a greater interest in acquiring the underlying security. We now move to a discussion of combinations and straddles.

Combinations

A combination is the simultaneous purchase of a put and a call with different striking prices and/or maturities. Both the call and the put could be in- or out-of-the-money. The strategy depends largely on the investor's expectations (and sanity).

Combinations are used by investors who are uncertain about the direction of the market but wish to participate in the market nonetheless. A combination allows for protection regardless of the direction of price movements. Some price expectations are reflected in the type of combination established, however. A mortgage banker who is uncertain about the direction of monetary policy and its attending impact on interest rates, but is leaning toward a tightening of monetary policy, would buy the following combination (at 16% coupon):

GNMA/Dec/62	3–17	out-of-the-money
GNMA/June '83/62*P*	6–30	in-the-money
Total cost of the combination	**10–15**	

If the 16 percent GNMAs fall from 102–13, their market price on May 19, 1982, to 94–21 by July 31, 1982, the put would appreciate from 6–30 to 14–22, a 7–24 point appreciation. The profit on the combination position would equal (14–22) − (10–15). This profit assumes that the call expires worthless and transactions costs are nil.

The reader may feel that an open put position (not covered by a call) would have been much better than a combination. The cost of the call would have been avoided. This is hindsight, however.

A long combination position can also be used for speculative purposes. An investor expecting a vigorous movement in GNMA prices could be interested in a combination. Whether the call or the put purchased is in-the-money or out-of-the-money would depend on the degree of certainty with regard to the direction of the price movement.

Short Combinations.
A short combination position is established by investors expecting minor or no changes in prices. The objective is to realize a reasonable rate of return on the invested capital. The riskiness of the position depends on the chosen options (in- or out-of-the-money) and on whether the call portion is covered or not.

A mortgage banker may sell the following combination (assume 16% GNMA):

GNMA/Sept/60	4–04	in-the-money
GNMA/Dec/62P	5–25	in-the-money
Total premium received	**9–29**	

The choice of a put that is more in-the-money than the call indicates that the mortgage banker is relatively bearish. The no-loss range for this combination writer is

  62–(9–29) to 60 + (9–29)

or

  52–3 to 69–29

The combination seller would lose money below 52–3 or over 69–29. The maximum profit, that is, the full combination premium, is earned if GNMA prices remain in the 60 to 62 range—between the call striking price and the put striking price. If the striking prices are adjusted to reflect the fact that a 16 percent GNMA will be delivered against the position, the range (see Table 4.3) would be:

  91–10 to 114–06

The adjusted striking prices are 101–07 for the call and 104–09 for the put. The entire premium will be earned if the market price of GNMAs remains between 101–07 and 104–09.

Straddles

A straddle is a special case of a combination in which the striking price and the maturity month of the put are the same as those of the call. Again, we look at the long and the short side of straddles.

Long Straddles. A trader who is uncertain about the impact of a to-be-announced government policy could buy a straddle to protect a cash GNMA position or simply to speculate in the options market. He could buy:

GNMA/Sept/60	4–04	in-the-money
GNMA/Sept/60P	1–20	out-of-the-money
	5–24	

The loss range on this straddle is (101–07) ± (5–24). That is, if by the expiration of the straddle, GNMA prices remain between 95–15 and 106–31, the trader will incur a loss equal to a portion or the total value of the premium paid. A long straddle position must be established, therefore, only when a vigorous move in the price of the underlying security is expected.

Straddles can be used as a protective shield for an aggressive trading strategy in the cash GNMA market. Assume the price pattern shown in Figure 4.3. Assume also that the following straddle is established:

GNMA/Dec/62	3–17	in-the-money
GNMA/Dec/62P	5–25	out-of-the-money
Total premium paid	**9–10** or $9,312.50	

FIGURE 4.3.

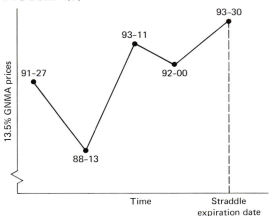

A short position in the GNMA cash market established at 91–27 produces profits if GNMA prices in fact drop to 88–13. Additional profits will be realized on the put side of the straddle. If net profits equal or exceed the total straddle premium, the investor can then trade with impunity. A long position will be protected by the put and a short position by the call. The protection is provided without the "drag" caused by the price of the opposite (unprofitable) option. That is, a put, while protecting a long position, does not compensate for the loss of the call premium. This is so because the call becomes out-of-the-money in a down market and the maximum price movement in the put cannot exceed that of the cash GNMA.

The trader can successively establish a long position at 88–13 that is protected by the put portion of the straddle, sell the long position, establish a short position at 93–11 that is protected by the call, cover, and go long at 92–00. Then the trader can sell both the call and the long position at 93–30. This is obviously an idealized situation. No investor we are aware of has such perfect foresight. The example, however, illustrates the possibilities that a long straddle offers.

Short Straddles. Straddles may be written naked or covered. The maximum return from a short straddle position is realized when the GNMA market price equals the striking price. This return is equal to the straddle premium. A loss is incurred if GNMA prices rise above the striking price plus the straddle premium, or fall below the striking price minus the straddle premium. The risk/return tradeoffs vary considerably depending on whether the short straddle position is naked or is covered.

Covered Straddles. On May 19, 1982 a trader who expected no major price fluctuations in GNMA securities could have sold the following straddle on the 14 percent GNMA securities he held.

Sell	GNMA/Sept/62	2–02	at-the-money
	GNMA/Sept/62P	4–30	at-the-money
	Total premium received	**7–00**	

The current GNMA cash price is 93–19. The results under varying states of the world are:

1. If 14 percent GNMA prices rise to 103–13 by July 18, 1982, the call will be exercised and the straddle writer would have to deliver the cash GNMAs held. The straddle writer would earn the full premium but would realize an opportunity loss if prices continued their upward trend. This sequence of events assumes that the GNMAs held are deliverable against the call position.

2. If prices fall to 84–00, the put will be exercised and the straddle writer would have to buy a security valued at 84–00 for 93–13. The book loss = (93–13) − (84–00) = 9–13. The book loss increases as prices continue their slide. The cushion is provided by the premium collected on the straddle. Any loss incurred here is a real loss, not an opportunity loss.

3. Ideally, the straddle writer wishes to see no change in GNMA prices. A constant price leads to the maximum return, namely, the full premium.

We now look at naked straddles.

Naked Straddles. A straddle is naked if the call is not covered by a long GNMA position. We now examine the consequences of a naked straddle under different states of the world.

1. If GNMA prices rise significantly during the life of the straddle, the writer would have to deliver GNMA securities which he does not own. This requires the purchase of GNMAs at the higher market price and their delivery at the lower striking price. The loss here is a real loss cushioned by the premium received on the now worthless put and the call premium. If for some reason prices turn around and begin to decline, the put may move into-the-money and the straddle writer, now a put writer, may realize yet another loss. Straddle writers should not hang onto their positions longer than necessary, particularly when market conditions are very unsettled. All losses in this case are real (explicit) losses.

2. If GNMA prices fall significantly, the put will be exercised. This means that the investor would purchase securities at a price higher than the prevailing market price. The straddle writer can always offset his position by buying a straddle or by closing only the put side in this case.

3. If prices remain relatively constant and the writer is neither forced to buy nor to deliver a GNMA, he would earn the entire premium less transactions costs.

Straddles are not easy to handle or understand. Their ramifications could be complex. We now discuss an even more interesting and popular option position, the spread.

Spreads

A spread is the simultaneous purchase and sale of calls (puts) of different maturities and/or striking prices. Two types of spreads can generally be distinguished: vertical call (put) spreads and horizontal (time) call (put) spreads.

Vertical spreads are so called because they involve a position in call (put) contracts of the same contract month but different striking prices. The prices are listed vertically as shown in Tables 4.4 and 4.5.

Horizontal spreads are so called because they involve the same striking price but different maturity months. Maturity months are listed horizontally. (See Tables 4.4 and 4.5.) We now examine the various types of spreads.

Vertical Spreads. Two types of vertical spreads can be established—vertical bull call (put) spreads, and vertical bear call (put) spreads. A vertical bull call spread requires a net commitment of funds, whereas the put counterpart results in a net receipt of funds. A vertical bear call spread, on the other hand, results in a net receipt of funds. The opposite is true for vertical bear put spreads.

Vertical Bull Call Spreads. Vertical bull call spreads involve a long position in a call that is more in-the-money or less out-of-the-money and a short position in another. A spread of this type might involve:

Buy GNMA/Dec/56	10–05
Sell GNMA/Dec/60	5–19
Net commitment	**4–18**

If at expiration the 16 percent GNMA remains at 102–13 and both options are exercised:

Profit (loss) on long call: 102–13
                           (95–03)   7–10

Profit (loss) on short call: (102–13)
                               101–07   (1–06)
                                                  6–04

Profit = 6–04 − 4–18 = 1–18 or $1,562.50

If at expiration the 16 percent GNMA has risen to 110–00 and both options are exercised

Profit (loss) on long call: 110–00
                           (95–03)   14–29

Profit (loss) on short call: (110–00)
                               101–07   (8–25)
                                                    6–04

Profit = 6–04 − 4–18 = 1–18 or $1,562.50

If GNMA prices drop to 90–00, neither option would be profitable and the spreader would lose the entire premium or $4,562.50.

When dealing with spreads, it is best to develop a worksheet.

Worksheet

		16% GNMA Price
Buy GNMA/Dec/56	10–05	102–13
Sell GNMA/Dec/60	5–19	102–13

1. Money at risk. 10–05 − 5–19 = 4–18 or $4,562.50
2. Max profit potential: (101–07 − 95–03) − 4–18 = 1–18 or $1,562.50

3. Risk/reward = $4,562.50/1,562.50 ≅ 2.92
4. Breakeven point = 95–03 + 4–18 = 99–21
5. Percent Δ in price of GNMA needed to reach breakeven.

$$(99–21 - 102–13)/102–13 = \mathbf{0.027 \text{ or } -2.7\%}$$

It is instructive here to give an example of a vertical put bull spread.

Buy GNMA/Dec/58P	1–27
Sell GNMA/Dec/62P	5–25
Net receipt	**3–30**

We now turn our attention to the vertical bear spread.

Vertical Bear Call Spread. A vertical bear call spread might involve:

Buy GNMA/Sept/60	**4–04**
Sell GNMA/Sept/56	**8–24**
Net receipt	**4–20**

If at expiration the 16 percent GNMA remains at 102–13 and both options are exercised:

Profit on long call	102–13	
	(101–07)	1–06
Loss on short call	(102–13)	
	95–03	(7–10)
		(6–04)

Profit (loss) = (6–04) + 4–20 = (1–16) or − $1,500

If at expiration the 16 percent GNMA appreciates to 110–00 and both options are exercised:

Profit on long call	110–00	
	(101–07)	8–25
Loss on short call	(110–00)	
	95–03	(14–29)
		(6–04)

Profit (loss) = (6.04) + 4–20 = (1–16) or −$1,500

If GNMA depreciates to 90–00, neither option will be exercised and the profit would equal the net premium received, namely, 4–20 or $4,625.

The worksheet for a vertical bear spread looks as follows:

Worksheet		
		16% GNMA Price
Buy GNMA/Sept/60	4–04	102–13
Sell GNMA/Sept/56	8–24	102–13

1. Max profit potential $= 8\text{--}24 - 4\text{--}04 = 4\text{--}20$ or \$4,625
2. Money at risk $=(101\text{--}07 - 95\text{--}03) - 4\text{--}20 = 1\text{--}16$ or \$1,500
3. Risk/reward $= 1\text{--}16/4\text{--}20 = 0.32$ or 32%
4. Breakeven point $= 4\text{--}20 + 95\text{--}03 = 99\text{--}23$
5. Percent Δ in price of 16% GNMA needed to reach breakeven.

$$[-(102\text{--}13) + (99\text{--}23)] \Big/ (102\text{--}13) = -0.026 \text{ or } -2.6\%$$

It is instructive here to give an example of a vertical put bear spread.

Buy GNMA/March/62P	6–17
Sell GNMA/March/58P	2–15
Net commitment	**4–02**

We now discuss horizontal spreads.

Horizontal Call Spreads. Horizontal spreads can be of the bull or bear variety.

Horizontal Bull Call Spreads. A horizontal (or calendar or time) bull call spread might involve (for 16% coupon):

Buy GNMA/Dec/62	3–17	out-of-the-money
Sell GNMA/Sept/62	2–02	out-of-the-money
Net commitment	1–15	

If the 16 percent GNMA price rises to only 104–09 by the expiration of the September option, the September call will be worthless. The December call, however, still has three months to go and may be selling at 3–00. Profits would equal $(3\text{--}00) - (1\text{--}15) = 1\text{--}17$ or \$1,531.25.

If prices rise to 110–00, both calls could be exercised or covered with a short December and a long September call. At expiration of the September option, the September call would be worth 5–23 (110–00 − 104–09). Since the December option has—in addition to its intrinsic value of 5–23—three months of time premium, it would be worth more, say 9–26.

Profit on long position	Loss on short position	Net Profit
$[(9\text{--}26) - (3\text{--}17)]$ −	$[(5\text{--}23) - (2\text{--}02)]$	$= 2\text{--}20$ or \$2,625.

If the price for 16 percent GNMAs remains constant or falls to 100–00 at the expiration of the September option, this call will be worthless. The December call still retains three months of time premium and as long as it can be sold for 1–15 or more, the investor will not lose money.

Horizontal Bear Call Spreads. A horizontal bear call spread might involve (for all coupons):

Buy GNMA/Sept/58	6–18	in-the-money
Sell GNMA/March '83/58	8–31	in-the-money
	2–13	

If 16 percent GNMA prices fall to 94–05, the September option will not be exercised. The March '83 option will retain slight value, say 00–31. The attainable profit would equal (2–13) − (00–31) = 1–14 or $1,437.50. The farther the prices of GNMAs fall, the less the March '83 option will be worth and the greater the profit (maximum at 2–13).

If 16 percent GNMA prices increase to 105–00 at the expiration of the September option, a trader who exercises this call would make a profit of (105–00) − (98–05) = 6–27.

However, the March '83 call would be worth more than 6–27 because the option has a remaining life of six months. Thus, if GNMA/March '83/58 is worth 9–31, the profit or loss would equal:

$$-(9\text{–}31) + (6\text{–}27) + (2\text{–}13) = -(00\text{–}23)$$

If the March '83 option is worth 9–08 or more, the investor will incur a net loss.

If 16 percent GNMAs remain constant at the expiration of the September call, this option will be worth (102–05) − (98–05) = 4–00. Again, however, the more distant call will be worth more. If the March '83 call is worth less than 6–13, the investor will still make a profit (ignoring transaction costs). If the March '83 call is worth more than 6–13, the investor will incur a loss.

More sophisticated spreads, such as sandwich spreads (two short calls at one striking price surrounded by a long call at the immediately lower striking price and another long call at the immediately higher striking price) and butterfly spreads (two long calls at one striking price surrounded by a short call at the immediately lower striking price and another short call at the immediately higher striking price), are also used. Their discussion is beyond the scope of this book. We now look very briefly at the tax consequences of interest options.

Federal Tax Aspects of GNMA Options

The tax treatment of GNMA options differs from the treatment of stock options or futures contracts. GNMA options have a maximum term of fifteen months and, therefore, create an opportunity for the holder of the option to realize either long or short term capital gain or loss treatment upon disposition. Because of their maximum term of nine months, stock options produce only short-term capital gain or loss taxable as ordinary income. Interest rate futures, like all commodities, need to be held only six months to qualify for long-term capital gain or loss treatment. In this respect futures are more attractive than either GNMA or stock options.

The taxation of interest options depends on whether they are long or short and on whether they are exercised, covered, or allowed to expire.

As investors devise more intricate investment strategies using GNMA options, the tax consequences of such strategies become more complex. For example, when an investor uses straddles or a combination of a put and call with the same striking price and maturity, the tax treatment of this offsetting position falls under Section 1092 of the Internal Revenue Code. A loss with respect to one position of a straddle is allowable only to the extent that the loss exceeds unrecognized gains with respect to the other offsetting position. Under the law, an offsetting position is said to occur when there is a "substantial diminution of risk of loss from holding one position by reason of the

investor's holding one or more other positions."[3] Vehicles used for the reduction of risk under Section 1092 may include another GNMA option, a GNMA security or a futures or forward contract to acquire or sell a GNMA security or other types of personal property—such as T-bills, T-bonds, other evidences of indebtedness, commodities, and futures including forward contracts and options relating to futures.

The provisions for wash sales and short sales under the Internal Revenue Code also apply to GNMA options transactions. The applicable wash sale rule provides that no capital loss shall be recognized for tax purposes if the investor purchases substantially identical securities during a period 30 days before or 30 days after the sale in which a loss was realized. The short sales provision of the Code prohibits the conversion of short-term capital gains to long-term capital gains by selling short or acquiring a put for property substantially identical to property held for one year or less. Additionally, the conversion of a short-term capital loss to a long-term capital loss by selling short property substantially identical to property held for more than one year is disallowed.

The tax consequences of interest options are quite complex. Competent professional advise should be sought.

4.4 T-BOND, T-BILL OPTIONS

T-bond options are a late 1982 phenomenon and carry similar privileges as GNMA options. The character of the underlying security is different, however.

A Treasury bond option covers a specific issue of T-bonds—long-term (more than 10 years) obligations of the U.S. government. Option series are generally introduced two business days after the U.S. Treasury auctions T-bonds. Only one expiration cycle (e.g., March–June–September) is introduced against a given Treasury auction. Up to five different expiration months may be introduced simultaneously with expirations extending from 1 to 15 months. New expiration months are not added (as in the case of common stocks) as old ones expire. Another T-bond option must take place before another expiration cycle in introduced.

T-bond options, like stock options, expire on the Saturday after the third Friday of the expiration month. Exercise prices are introduced in such a way so as to bracket the prevailing market prices with increments of 2 points. If, for example, the current market price is 100½, striking prices of 98 and 102 will be introduced. More striking prices will be added as changes in the market price of the underlying instrument warrant it. T-bond options, as Table 4.7 shows, are quoted in terms of points and $\frac{1}{32}$nds of a point. The minimum fluctuation is $\frac{1}{32}$. For example, the March 1983 14 percent T-bond option quoted on the CBOE (see Table 4.7) on January 14, 1983 is valued at 5.14. Each of the 5 points is equal to 1 percent of the underlying principal or $1,000 on a standard contract. The 5.14 is, therefore, equal to $(5\% \times 100,000) + (14\frac{1}{32}\% \times 100,000) = 5,000 + 437.50 = \$5,437.50$. A $\frac{1}{32}$ of a point on a standard contract is equal to $31.25 and to $6.25 on a minicontract ($20,000 in principal amount).

The futures exchanges place a limit on the size of positions established by a trader or a group of traders. The limit on the 14 percent T-bond issue due in the year 2011 is, for example, $100 million of principal on an initial issuance of $1 to $2 billion. The limits are adjusted depending on the size of the issue and the conditions of the market.

---

[3] The Options Clearing Corporation. *Prospectus GNMA Put and Call Options,* 1981, p. 29.

TABLE 4.7.

Interest Rate Options

Thursday, January 13, 1983

For Notes and Bonds, decimals in closing prices represent 32nds; 1.1 means 1 1/32. For Bills, decimals in closing prices represent basis points; $5 per .01

American Exchange

U.S. TREASURY NOTE—$20,000 principal value

Underlying Issue	Strike Price	Calls—Last			Puts—Last		
		Mar	June	Sept	Mar	June	Sept
13¾ note	116	2.8	....	....	....	....	....
due 5/15/92	120	0.16	3.0	....	....	....	....
		Mar	June	Sept	Mar	June	Sept
10½ note	96	5.21	....	....	....	0.24	....
due 11/15/92	100	2.0	....	....	1.4	....	....
	104	....	1.4	....	....	....	....

13-WEEK U.S. TREASURY BILL—$200,000 principal value

Strike Price	Calls—Last			Puts—Last		
	Mar	June	Sept	Mar	June	Sept
91	....	....	....	....	.26	....
92	....	....	.76	.20	....	....
93	....	.22	....	....	1.12	....

Total call vol. 804 Call open int. 3698
Total put vol. 122 Put open int. 1528

Chicago Board Options Exchange

U.S. TREASURY BOND—$100,000 principal value

Underlying Issue	Strike Price	Calls—Last			Puts—Last		
		Mar	June	Sept	Mar	June	Sept
14% bond	122	5.14	....	....	....	....	....
due 11/11	124	3.17	....	....	1.12	....	....
	126	2.28	....	....	....	....	....
	128	1.15	....	....	....	....	....
	130	1.2	....	....	....	....	....
		Mar	June	Sept	Mar	June	Sept
10⅜% bond	96	3.30	....	....	....	2.6	....
due 11/12	100	1.18	....	....	....	4.2	5.10
	104	....	1.10	....	....	....	....

Total call vol. 266 Call open int. 2322
Total put vol. 82 Put open int. 1044

Treasury Issues

Thursday, January 13, 1983

Mid-afternoon Over-the-Counter quotations; source on request.

Decimals in bid-and-asked and bid changes represent 32nds; 101.1 means 101 1/32. a-Plus 1/64. b-Yield to call date. d-Minus 1/64. n-Treasury notes.

Treasury Bonds and Notes

Rate	Mat. Date		Bid	Asked	Bid Chg.	Yld.
13⅝s,	1983	Jan n	100.7	100.11	− .1	4.30
8s,	1983	Feb n	99.31	100.3	.....	6.58
14⅞s,	1991	Aug n	122.14	122.22	+ .9	10.75
14¼s,	1991	Nov n	119.18	119.26	+ .12	10.72
14⅝s,	1992	Feb n	122.2	122.10	+ .10	10.71
13¾s,	1992	May n	117.18	117.26	+ .12	10.69
4¼s,	1987-92	Aug	86.14	86.30	+ .13	6.07
7¼s,	1992	Aug	82.25	83.25	+ .7	9.91
10½s,	1992	Nov n	101.14	101.22	+ .8	10.22
4s,	1988-93	Feb	85.24	86.8	+ .13	5.83
6¾s,	1993	Feb	78.24	79.8	+ .4	10.07
7⅞s,	1993	Feb	85.13	85.29	− .5	10.14
7⅞s,	2002-07	Nov	79.2	79.10	+ .4	10.18
8⅜s,	2003-08	Aug	82.9	82.17	+ .7	10.33
8¾s,	2003-08	Nov	84.21	84.29	+ .9	10.45
9⅛s,	2004-09	May	87.28	88.4	+ .9	10.46
10⅜s,	2004-09	Nov	98.19	98.27	+ .9	10.50
11¾s,	2005-10	Feb	107.26	108.2	+ .10	10.78
10s,	2005-10	May	95.14	95.22	+ .7	10.48
12¾s,	2005-10	Nov	115.25	116.1	+ .8	10.84
13⅞s,	2006-11	May	125.8	125.16	+ .9	10.85
14s,	2006-11	Nov	126.22	126.30	+ .11	10.82
10⅜s,	2007-12	Nov	99.14	99.22	+ .4	10.41

U.S. Treas. Bills

Mat. date	Bid Discount	Asked Discount	Yield	Mat. date	Bid Discount	Asked Discount	Yield
-1983-				5- 5	7.73	7.63	7.92
				5-12	7.74	7.64	7.94
1-20	8.18	8.02	8.14	5-19	7.75	7.63	7.94
1-27	8.11	7.99	8.12	5-26	7.75	7.65	7.98
2- 3	7.72	7.60	7.73	6- 2	7.75	7.65	7.99
2-10	7.64	7.48	7.62	6- 9	7.75	7.65	8.00
2-17	7.63	7.49	7.64	6-16	7.75	7.65	8.01
2-24	7.68	7.52	7.69	6-23	7.74	7.64	8.02
3- 3	7.65	7.53	7.71	6-30	7.74	7.64	8.04
3-10	7.68	7.54	7.73	7- 7	7.73	7.67	8.05
3-17	7.68	7.54	7.74	7-14	7.70	7.66	8.06
3-24	7.68	7.56	7.77	8-11	7.77	7.65	8.07
3-31	7.71	7.57	7.80	9- 8	7.77	7.65	8.09
4- 7	7.69	7.61	7.85	10- 6	7.81	7.71	8.18
4-14	7.66	7.62	7.87	11- 3	7.86	7.76	8.27
4-21	7.72	7.62	7.88	12- 1	7.84	7.74	8.28
4-28	7.72	7.62	7.90	12-29	7.79	7.75	8.33

Source: The Wall Street Journal, January 14, 1983.

If a delivery is opted for against T-bond option contracts, it is much more restricted than in the case of futures contracts. Only a T-bond carrying a specific rate and expiring at a specified time is deliverable against the option unless the Option Clearing Corporation (OCC) allows for the delivery of another bond when conditions in the cash market warrant.

The issue of delivery is much more critical in the case of T-bills. Writers of T-bill options cannot always be certain of acquiring the needed number of T-bills to meet their obligation to deliver. The T-bill option is not written against a specific T-bill issue as in the case of T-bond options, but rather is written against the current T-bills with 13 or 26 weeks to maturity beginning with the exercise date. Since the supply of such bills is not very predictable, securing the needed T-bills should delivery be required could be problematic. The exercise settlement date is ordinarily the Thursday of the week following the week when the exercise notice is assigned to the option writer. This is so because the U.S. Treasury Department auctions its bills on Monday of the exercise week and issues them the following Thursday.

A writer of an option is provided additional flexibility in that she may deliver not only newly issued 13-week T-bills but also 26-week and 52-week T-bills with 13 weeks left until maturity.

We now discuss various call and put strategies using T-bonds, T-notes, and T-bills options. Several of these select strategies have been covered earlier in this chapter. We repeat them for further illustration.

Interest Calls

Table 4.7 shows the available call options on T-bonds, T-notes, and T-bills on the CBOE and the AMEX as of January 14, 1983. The relative thinness of the three markets restricts the number of strategies that can be devised. We therefore concentrate on some of the more straightforward ones while we recognize that all the strategies presented for GNMA options are also relevant here.

Buying Calls

The purchase of calls can serve various useful purposes, some speculative and others risk reducing.

Calls for Leverage. On January 14, 1983, the ask price on 14 percent T-bonds (due 11/2011) was 126.30. The purchase of two such bonds on margin would require $25,387.50 (10 percent of total market value). Alternatively, an investor could acquire two T-bond options expiring in March 1983 with a striking price of 126 for 2.28 or $2,875 each, and have a claim on the same amount of principal. Or, alternatively, intent on committing the same amount of resources, $25,387.50, he could purchase nine call options. If, by February 18, 1983, interest rates have fallen and the bid price on the cash T-bond has risen to 127.22, and the call option price has reached 3.18, the profits would be:

Bond Position	**Call Position**
2(127.22 − 126.30) = 1.16	(3.16 − 2.28) × 9 = 0.20 × 9
or $1,500	or $5,625
A gross return of **5.9%**	A gross return of **21.7%**

The above calculations ignore transactions costs and taxes to simplify the presentation. If, however, interest rates had remained constant or had risen, the option investor could have lost all of his investment. The loss in the cash position, however, would have been small or negligible.

Leverage is evidently a worthwhile strategy if expectations prove to be correct, and potentially a devastating strategy if not.

Calls to Release Cash. An investment banker may be in need of cash and be forced to sell a 10⅜ percent T-bond (due 11/12), even though he anticipates falling interest rates and rising bond prices. He could satisfy both his cash need and the desire to participate in the bond appreciation by selling the bond at the bid price of 99.14, or $99,437.50, and simultaneously buying a March call, with a striking price of 96, for

3.30 or $3,937.50. Thus, $95,500 is freed and if the bond price rises sufficiently, the investment banker could realize considerable profits in his position. If interest rates rise, the maximum loss would be equal to the price of the call, namely $3,937.50.

Calls to Protect a Short Position. As discussed earlier, a call can be used to limit the loss on a short position to the size of the call premium. The profit for a short position on a 10½ percent T-note (due 11/15/92), with a principal value of $20,000, would be $687.50 if the security was sold short on 1/14/83 for $20,287.50 and covered on 3/18/83 at $19,600. The profit would be reduced to $287.50 if on 1/14 a March T-note call, with a striking price of 100, was purchased for 2.0 or $400 to protect the short position and the option expired worthless. The reader should note that despite the thinness (limited open interest) of the market, there are still several levels of protection available to the investor. Instead of the March 100 call, the investor could have chosen the March 96 call. This would have cost $1,131.25—and on 3/18/83, since the T-note is selling for 98 or $19,600, the March 96 call would be worth $400. The net cost of protection would equal $731.25 ($1,131.25 − $400), and the net loss on the short T-note position would be $43.75 ($687.50 − $731.25). Finally, the investor could have purchased the June 104 call for $225. On 3/18/83, this option would have three months left to maturity and might be worth $50. Thus, the net cost of the protection would be $175 and the net profit would equal $512.50. In retrospect, the out-of-the-money call was the best choice.

Writing Interest Call Options (The Short)

A short call position is generally a conservative investment strategy. The exceptions are many, however, as we shall demonstrate.

Writing a Call Option for Income. A pension fund manager with $100,000 in Treasury notes in her portfolio could choose to write calls on them in order to improve the coupon income. Through this strategy the fixity of cash flows from interest-bearing instruments is shattered. For example, the pension fund manager could sell five June 120 T-notes calls on the 13¾ percent note (due 5/15/92) for $600 × 5 = $3,000. If the market price of T-notes remains at or below the 120 striking price until the expiration of the calls in June, the manager would have earned the entire $3,000 premium. If the market price of the T-notes exceeds 120 but remains below 123 (120 + 3), the call buyer would exercise the call (or sell it on the option market) in order to recoup part of the call premium. Thus, the income from the option writing program is positive, but less than the $3,000. If, on the other hand, the market price exceeds 123, the fund manager retains the $3,000 premium but will suffer an opportunity loss the size of which depends on the difference between the new price and 123. The call holder would realize the profit. The short position has a ceiling on returns during the life of the option.

Had the fund manager written a naked T-note call option (options written without a long position in the underlying security) the results could be drastically different. If the same five calls are sold and the price of the T-notes remains below 123, the short would again realize the entire $3,000 premium. Additionally, the fund manager would not have tied up over $100,000 (or the margin requirement thereon) in the underlying security. If the price rises to 121.5, the short may have to sell T-notes to the call

buyer at 120. Since he does not own the underlying security, he would have to purchase them at 121.5 and sell them at 120. The premium income would be reduced by the amount of the loss (1.5 points or $1,500).

A rise in the market price of spot T-notes to, say, 127 is very detrimental to the naked short position. The loss on the transaction would equal (127,000 − 120,000) − 3,000 (premium) = $4,000.

Writing a Call Option to Hedge. The premium received from writing a call option serves as a cushion against a price decline in the underlying security. Thus, an investment banker holding a $100,000 14 percent T-bond could write any of the available five calls against this position. Clearly, the March 122 call provides the greatest cushion.

Writing a Call Option to Improve on the Market. An investment banker holding a 10⅜ percent T-bond (due 11/12), with a market price of $99,437.50, and little chance of appreciation may sell a March 96 call for $3,937.50. In essence, through the options market the investment banker has created a new price for the T-bond equal to $103,375 ($99,437.50 + $3,937.50). If the T-bond appreciates, the banker happily sells the security. If the price remains the same, he will be even happier. If, however, the price of the bond falls, the security will not be called away from the investment banker. The premium, however, will cushion the fall in price or, assuming stable prices, would augment the coupon income on the bond.

Interest Puts

Interest put options can also serve very useful speculative and hedging purposes.

Buying Puts

Puts to Protect a Long Position. An investor with a long position in one 10½ percent note (due 11/15/92), may purchase a put to protect against a price decline from the current $20,287.50. He might acquire a March 100 put option for $225. If the price of the Treasury-note rises, the appreciation is offset by the $225 premium paid. If the price remains constant, the option could be sold at a loss or allowed to expire. The maximum loss is equal to the premium paid. If the market price of the T-notes falls to between 100.00 and 99.25 ($20,000 and $19,956) part of the premium is recouped. If the market price of the T-note falls below 99.25, to, say, 92.16, the investor will be able to sell a security worth $18,500 for $20,000. Thus, his gross profit equals $20,000 − $18,500 − $225 = $1,275.

Puts to Protect Book Profits. A pension fund manager holding 14 percent T-bonds (due 11/11) with a cost basis of 118, and a market value of 126.22, may choose to purchase a put in order to lock in the book profit (minus the put premium). Hence, by purchasing a March 128 put option for $1,468.75, he locks in a book profit equal to $8,687.50.

Puts for Leverage. An investor who expects interest rates to rise can either sell a 14 percent T-bond (due 11/11) short or buy a put on the security. If the bond were selling for 126.22 on 1/14/83 and assuming a 10 percent margin requirement on short

sales, the short position would require a commitment of $12,668.75. A March 124 put would require only $1,375, however. Hence, the investor could acquire nine puts for less than the margin requirement on $100,000 of T-bonds. If the T-bond market ask price falls to 121.13 and the put rises to 3.20 the profits would be:

Bond Position	**Put Position**
$126.22 - 121.13 = 5.09$	$9(3.20 - 1.12) = 9(2.08)$
or	or
$5,281.25	$20,250.00
For a return of **41.7%**	For a return of **163.6%**

Clearly, however, if bond prices rise, the results could be disastrous—especially for the put position. If the T-bond market price rises to 129.06 and the put expires worthless, the loss in the cash market would equal:

$$129.06 - 126.22 = 2.16 \text{ or } \$2,500.$$

The loss for the put position would be the entire premium. For example, $9 \times 1.12 =$ $12,375. Thus, the loss in the put position is much greater than in the cash position. It is important to remember, however, that the loss in the put position is limited to the premium. The loss in the cash position could have been significantly higher had interest rates dropped more drastically.

Writing Puts

Puts to Earn Premium Income. The put writer believes that interest rates will fall or at worst remain constant. Consider the case of an investor who sold a naked March 100 put on 10½ percent T-note (due 11/15/92) for 1.4 on January 14, 1983. Given the T-note price of 101.22 for that day, the following three situations may arise later on, say, March 14, 1983:

1. T-note price rises to 103.22. The holder of the put will obviously not exercise it. The put writer realizes the full premium. His return would be

$$\frac{1.\frac{4}{32}\% \text{ of } 20,000 \text{ or } \$225}{101.\frac{22}{32}\% \times (10\% \times 20,000)} = \frac{\text{put premium}}{\text{funds committed}} = \textbf{11.1\%}$$

or an annual rate of $11.1 \times 6 = 66.6\%$

The results may be compared with the outright ownership of the T-note, a real alternative given his bullish attitude.

$$\frac{103.22 - 101.22}{101.22 \times 10\%} = 19.7\% \text{ or } 118\% \text{ annually}$$

Thus, in retrospect, a long position would have been more profitable.

2. T-note price remains at 101.22. The put writer would simply realize the full premium and his return would again be 66.6 percent annually.

3. T-note price falls to 98.22. The put owner should have a profitable option. Thus the put writer's loss would equal $262.50 [$(1.\frac{10}{32}\%) (\$20,000)$] since he would have

to pay 100 for a security worth 98.22. The loss is cushioned by the put premium of $225 for a net loss of $262.50 − $225 = $37.50.

Puts to Acquire a Security. An option writer hoping to acquire a stock at below the prevailing market price could write a put option to achieve his goal. Here, if a June 96 put is written on a 10½ percent note (due 11/15/92), a premium of $150 will be received. If the price of the security remains above 96, the writer realizes the premium. If, however, the price will in fact drop below 96, to say, 94, he will acquire $20,000 of T-notes at an apparent loss of $250 (400 − 150). However, on January 14, when the option was written, a long position in the T-note would have required a purchase of note at 101.22. Thus, he has in fact used the put to lower the purchase price of the security.

We now look at a new model for pricing options on interest bonds.

4.5 THE PRICING OF OPTIONS ON DEFAULT-FREE BONDS

The pricing of options on default-free bonds began with a very technical and mathematically involved paper by J. Cox, J. Ingersoll, and S. Ross (CIR) titled: "A Theory of the Term Structure of Interest Rates" published as a research paper by the Graduate School of Business, Stanford University, in August 1978. In this paper CIR derive a model for the valuation of discount bonds and of options on discount bonds.

When interest rates are known with certainty, a bond issued at time t, having a maturity T, and a face value of $\$a$ would be valued as follows:

$$P(r,t,T) = ae^{-(T-t)R} \tag{4.1}$$

where R = market rate of interest.

When interest rates are variable—increasing or decreasing deterministic interest rates—and stochastic (random), the valuation of discount bonds becomes much more complex. Using several assumptions about production opportunities and the utility function of investors, CIR arrived at the following discount bond valuation equation.

$$P(r,t,T) = A(t,T)\, e^{-B(t,T)R} \tag{4.2}$$

where $A(t,T) \equiv \left[\dfrac{2\gamma\, e^{[(\kappa+\lambda+\gamma)(T-t)]/2}}{(\gamma+\kappa+\lambda)(e^{\gamma(T-t)}-1)+2\gamma} \right]^{2\kappa\mu/\sigma^2}$

$\qquad B(t,T) \equiv \dfrac{2(e^{\lambda(T-t)}-1)}{(\gamma+\kappa+\lambda)(e^{\gamma(T-t)}-1)+2\gamma}$

$\qquad\qquad \gamma \equiv \sqrt{(\kappa+\lambda)^2 + 2\sigma^2}$

$\qquad\qquad \mu \equiv$ mean value of interest rates

$\qquad\qquad \kappa \equiv$ speed of adjustment parameter when $R \neq \mu$

$\qquad\qquad \lambda \equiv$ "market risk" parameter = covariance of interest rate with wealth.

$\qquad\qquad \sigma^2 \equiv$ interest rate variance.

Equation 4.2 basically says that bond prices are a decreasing function (convex) of μ, the speed of adjustment κ, and the interest rate variance σ^2.

Armed with the discount bond valuation equation, CIR proceeded to derive a closed form valuation model for a European call option (an option exercisable only upon maturity) on this bond. The results were:

$$W(R,t,T;\tau,E) = P(R,t,\tau)\chi^2[2R^*(\phi + \theta + B(T,\tau)];$$
$$\frac{4\kappa\mu}{\sigma^2}, \frac{2\phi^2 R \, e^{\gamma(T-t)}}{\phi + \theta + B(T,\tau)} - E\,P(R,t,T)\chi^2[2R^*(\phi + \theta)];$$
$$\frac{4\kappa\mu}{\sigma^2}, \frac{2\phi^2 R e^{\gamma(T-t)}}{\phi + \theta} \qquad\qquad (4.3)$$

where
$$\gamma \equiv \sqrt{(\kappa + \lambda)^2 + 2\sigma^2}$$

$$\phi \equiv \frac{2\gamma}{\sigma^2(e^{\gamma(T-t)} - 1)}$$

$$\theta \equiv (\kappa + \lambda + \gamma)/\sigma^2$$

$$R^* \equiv \frac{\log\left(\dfrac{A(T,\tau)}{E}\right)}{B(T,\tau)}$$

$\quad$ = interest rate below which the option will be exercised

$\chi^2(\cdot)$ = noncentral chi-square distribution function.

τ = length of option life

E = striking price of the option. The other variables are as defined earlier.

Equation 4.3 simply says that the value of a call option on a discount bond is a function of the price of the underlying security $P(R,t,\tau)$. The price is weighted by a noncentral χ^2 distribution with $\dfrac{2\kappa\mu}{\sigma^2}$ degrees of freedom and a noncentrality parameter equal to $(2\phi^2 Re^{\gamma(T-t)})/[\phi + \theta + B(T,\tau)]$, minus the present value of the exercise price $EP(R,t,T)$ weighted by a χ^2 distribution with $(4\kappa\mu)/(\sigma^2)$ degrees of freedom and a noncentrality parameter equal to $(2\phi^2 Re^{\gamma(T-t)})/(\phi + \theta)$. The weighting by the χ^2 distribution is intended to account for the uncertainty about interest rates. This equation is very similar to the Black and Scholes model (see Chapter 2) with one exception. B&S assumed that rates of returns on stocks are normally distributed while interest rates according to CIR have a chi-square distribution. The correct solution to the valuation model depends on the accurate gauging of the values of the parameters.

This valuation model can be expanded to apply to coupon-bearing bonds if one recognizes that a coupon bond may be viewed as a collection of discount bonds with each coupon payment representing the maturity value of a discount bond. Work on this problem is currently underway at New York University.

An alternative formulation of valuation model for an option on a coupon-bearing bond was advanced by G. Courtadon. His model is discussed next.

4.6 THE VALUATION OF AN OPTION ON A COUPON-BEARING BOND

Building on the work of CIR and on the work of D. Vasicek,[4] E. Schwartz,[5] R. J. Rendleman and B. J. Bartter,[6] Georges Courtadon[7] of New York University developed a model for pricing options on default-free coupon bearing bonds.

The assumptions of Courtadon are similar to those of Black and Scholes (B&S) (see Chapter 2) with one important addition. While B&S arrived at a closed form solution to their option pricing model independent of the preferences of investors, Courtadon's model was utility dependent. Courtadon assumed that the individuals in the market place behaved so as to maximize an expected time additive utility of consumption where the utility function $U(d,t)$ is of the following form:

$$U(d,t) = f(t) \log d$$

where t = time

d = optimal consumption rules

With these assumptions and with the additional assumption that the movement of the rate of interest can be described by a diffusion process—a process with a continuous time path—Courtadon was able to arrive at a valuation model for European call and put options (options exercisable only at expiration date) and for American call and put options (options exercisable anytime between the contract date and expiration date). The interest-generating process chosen by Courtadon was that of constant expectations or a mean-reverting process. This process implies that the interest rate (R_t) is a random variable whose mean value remains constant over time.

$$R_t = \alpha + \epsilon_t \tag{4.4}$$

where α = normal, mean level of the rate of interest

ϵ_t = random disturbance term with zero expected value

This process generates serially correlated (dependent) time series of interest rate changes.

The Courtadon model we present does not allow for a closed form solution, but requires the utilization of a simple numerical method to arrive at the value of a call or a put.

The valuation equations for American call and puts options are:

---

[4] **D. Vasicek,** "An Equilibrium Characterization of the Term Structure," *Journal of Financial Economics,* (November 1977).

[5] **E. Schwartz,** "The Valuation of Warrants: Implementing a New Approach," *Journal of Financial Economics,* vol. 4, (1977), pp. 79–93.

[6] **R. J. Rendleman, Jr.,** and **B. J. Bartter,** "The Pricing of Options on Debt Securities," *Journal of Financial and Quantitative Analysis,* (March 1980).

[7] **Georges Courtadon,** "The Pricing of Options on Default-Free Bonds," *Journal of Financial and Quantitative Analysis,* vol. 17, (March 1982), pp. 75–100.

Call Valuation

$$\tfrac{1}{2}\beta^2 r^2 \frac{\partial^2 W_c}{\partial R^2} + (\kappa(\mu - R) + \lambda\beta R) \frac{\partial W_c}{\partial R} - R W_c - \frac{\partial W_c}{\partial \tau} = 0 \qquad (4.5)$$

Subject to

$$W_c(R,0) = \max[U(R,T) - E, 0] \qquad (4.5a)$$

$$W_c(\infty,\tau) = 0 \qquad (4.5b)$$

$$W_c(R,\tau) = Max[U(R,T+\tau) - E, W_c(R,\tau)], \text{ for } \tau > 0 \qquad (4.5c)$$

where W_c = value of an American call option
               $= W_c(R,\tau)$
          R = nominal rate of interest
          τ = length of option period
          $\beta^2 R^2$ = infinitesimal variance of the mean reverting process
          β = the standard deviation of the rate of change in interest rates $(\partial R/R)$
          κ = speed of adjustment
          μ = mean level of the rate of interest
          λ = nonnegative constant representing the market price of risk for default-free bonds
          $U(R,T)$ = value of default-free bond with T periods to maturity from the day of the option expiration.
          E = Interest option exercise price

Equation 4.5a represents the "initial condition" at time zero; the value of the option is the proceeds from conversion $U(R,T) - E$.

Equation 4.5b represents the boundary condition, that is, the price of the call option, no matter what the time to maturity, will be zero as $R \rightarrow \infty$. As $R \rightarrow \infty$, $U(R,T)$ approaches zero (given the inverse relationship between bond prices and interest rates) and, correspondingly, the value of the option.

Equation 4.5c represents the condition for early exercise. If $(U(R,T+\tau) - E)$—the value of the option exercised exceeds the value of the option not exercised—the investor would exercise the option. Otherwise he or she will hold onto it.

Put Valuation

The valuation model for an American interest put option is

$$\tfrac{1}{2}\beta^2 R^2 \frac{\partial^2 W_p}{\partial R^2} + (\kappa(\mu - R) + \lambda\beta R) \frac{\partial W_p}{\partial R} - R W_p - \frac{\partial W_p}{\partial \tau} = 0 \qquad (4.6)$$

Subject to

$$W_p(R,0) = \max[E - U(R,T),0] \tag{4.6a}$$

$$W_p(\infty, \tau) = E \tag{4.6b}$$

$$W_p(R,\tau) = \max[E - U(R,T+\tau), W_p(R,\tau)], \text{ for } \tau > 0 \tag{4.6c}$$

where W_p = value of an American put option and all the variables are as defined earlier.

The switching in the position of $U(R,T)$ and E as compared with the call case is due to the fact that the reverse thinking applies to put from that of calls. As $R \rightarrow \infty$ the value of the underlying T-bonds approaches zero and the value of the put option is the exercise price minus zero or simply E. Thus, the boundary condition $W_p(\infty, \tau) = E$ — Equation 4.6b.

From the valuation equations the investor expects to arrive at a unique value of a call or a put like that reported in *The Wall Street Journal* which represents the equilibrium option price in the market. The Courtadon model allows for a unique price once all the parameters are assigned unique values. The problem does not lie in finding a value for each parameter but rather in finding the appropriate value.

The search for a solution can best be explained diagramatically. Since W_c is a function of two independent variables, R and τ, a graphical presentation can be easily made. (See Figure 4.4.)

Thus, given a value for each of the parameters, (κ, μ, β, λ, E), and assuming $\tau = 0$ and a known value for r or $s = 1/1(1 + R)$, we can easily calculate W_c once the

FIGURE 4.4.

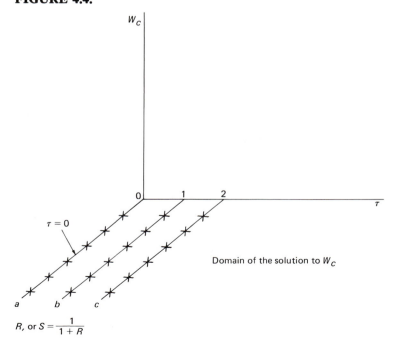

Domain of the solution to W_c

TABLE 4.8
Value of a Ten-Year Default-Free Bond and of the Corresponding American Options for a Maturity of the Options of One Year and

	$\kappa=.1$	$\mu=.06$	$\beta=.4$	$\lambda=0.0$	$\phi=.08^*$	$E=1.0$	
R	.0309	.0526	.0753	.0989	.1236	.1494	.1765
$u(R, 10)$	1.34167	1.22242	1.11461	1.01670	.92750	.84603	.77149
$w_c (R, 1)$	.34167	.22242	.12807	.06997	.03619	.01790	.00855
$w_p (R, 1)$	.00004	.00184	.01280	.04062	.08766	.15397	.22851

	$\kappa=.1$	$\mu=.08$	$\beta=.2$	$\lambda=0.0$	$\phi=.08$	$E=1.0$	
R	.0309	.0526	.0753	.0989	.1236	.1494	.1765
$u(R, 10)$	1.28230	1.17020	1.06860	.97613	.89171	.81448	.74369
$W_c(R, 1)$	.28230	.17020	.08902	.04421	.02084	.00945	.00416
$W_p (R, 1)$	.00012	.00378	.02083	.05736	.11309	.18552	.25631

	$\kappa=.1$	$\mu=.08$	$\beta=.4$	$\lambda=0.0$	$\phi=.08$	$E=1.0$	
R	.0309	.0526	.0753	.0989	.1236	.1494	.1765
$u(R, 10)$	1.26644	1.14509	1.03389	.93217	.83931	.75470	.67776
$W_c (R, 1)$	.26644	.14509	.04486	.00774	.00080	.00006	.00000
$W_p (R, 1)$	.00000	.00030	.01273	.06930	.16069	.24530	.32224

	$\kappa=.1$	$\mu=.08$	$\beta=.4$	$\lambda=0.0$	$\phi=.08$	$E=1.05$	
R	.0309	.0526	.0753	.0989	.1236	.1494	.1765
$u(R, 10)$	1.28230	1.17020	1.06860	.97613	.89171	.81448	.74369
$W_c (R, 1)$	.23230	.12160	.05534	.02381	.00978	.00390	.00152
$W_p (R, 1)$	.00041	.00843	.03683	.08779	.15829	.23552	.30631

* ϕ = size of coupon on T-bond

differential Equation 4.6 is transformed into a difference equation (to allow for discrete values). The various values for W_c associated with $\tau = 0$ and different R or S values are shown by the red Xs along Oa in Figure 4.4. Those values of W_c associated with $\tau = 1$ are shown by the X's along $1b$, and so forth.

The utilization of S instead of R transforms an unbounded interval in R, $0 \le R \le \infty$ into a bounded interval in S, $0 \le S \le 1$ making the calculations and the graphical representation possible.

Courtadon arrived at option values, by way of example, for one year on an 8 percent ten-year T-bond with a $1,000 par value and a $1,000 exercise price. The results are shown in Table 4.8. The reader should note the sensitivity of the results to the values of R and to those of the parameters.

CONCLUSION

Interest options are complex but useful instruments. They are excellent vehicles for hedging and for speculation. Any trader should minimally understand the contents of this chapter before venturing into the options market.

This chapter focused on options on cash interest-yielding instruments. Options have been introduced on futures contracts on interest-yielding instruments. We shall discuss them at the end of the chapter on financial futures after the introduction of both commodity and financial futures contracts.

QUESTIONS

1. For what reasons would an investor participate in the interest options market instead of the interest futures market?

2. Which GNMA calls listed in Table 4.4 are in-the-money? Which are out-of-the-money? Which GNMA puts listed in Table 4.3 are in-the-money? Which are out-of-the-money?

3. What are the differences in the risk-reward characteristics of a long call position (naked) as compared to a short call position?

4. Give an example of how a long and a short position in interest rate puts may be used. What are the investors' primary motives, hopes, and fears for these positions?

5. Compare a long combination position with a long spread position. Include the risk-reward characteristics of each.

6. Construct a vertical bear spread from Tables 4.4 and 4.7, and complete a worksheet for every position.

7. What is the function of the clearing corporation in the interest options? What are the guarantees offered by the clearing corporation on interest options and what protection is actually provided by these guarantees?

8. What is the likely effect of interest rate options on the financial futures market? Give reasons for your conclusion.

9. Given the relationship between a deliverable bond and the current production rate, how would interest options influence the cash bond market? If the production rate drops from 17 percent to 16 percent for how long will a 16.5 percent coupon bond be deliverable? For how long will a 15.5 percent coupon bond be deliverable?

10. Upon what coupon rate are the GNMA interest options exercise prices based? If a GNMA security is to be delivered against a GNMA option, how much fluctuation in the principal balance is allowed before a cash adjustment is required?

11. What are the main differences and similarities between interest options and interest futures?

12. Why are interest options so hard to price?

13. Discuss the Courtadon method for pricing interest options. Compare it to the Black and Scholes model.

CHAPTER 5 | Commodity Futures

5.1 AN OVERVIEW

The preceding chapters dealt with various hedging tools for stocks and bonds. This chapter adds another hedging and speculative tool, the futures contract. Specifically, the commodity futures contract is the subject of this chapter.

5.2 FUTURES CONTRACT—DEFINED

A futures contract is a commitment to deliver or accept delivery, at a designated time in the future, of a specified quantity and quality of a commodity at an auction price determined at the time the contract is entered into.

Definitions of terms related to futures contracts appear in the appendix of this chapter.

5.3 THE ORIGIN OF COMMODITY FUTURES CONTRACTS

Futures contracts began as forward contracts where buyers and sellers agreed to sell or take delivery of a specified quality and quantity of a commodity at a specified future date.

The use of forward contracts became a necessity once spot markets proved their inability to handle excess supply or excess demand for commodities. For example, the dumping of excess grain in the Chicago River[1] and its sale as animal feed became a common practice among wheat producers who were unable to sell their harvest in the spot market because of excessively low prices and the absence of adequate storage facilities.

The forward contract was only a partial answer to the problem. While it matched buyers with sellers so that farmers were assured a sale at a certain price and users were assured an adequate supply of commodities at a known price, the forward contract was unable to provide a mechanism for hedging price risks because of sudden price changes. Another problem was that the forward contract did not have a secondary market—that is, the forward contract was not liquid. The forward contract was merely

---

[1] See the *Commodity Trading Manual* of the Chicago Board of Trade, 1980.

a mechanism for making delivery of the actual commodity at a designated point in time in the future. The forward commodity market was simply a cash market with a deferred delivery. A forward contract does not require a commitment of funds at the time it is entered into or during its life.

The first "centralized" market in futures contracts began with the establishment of the Chicago Board of Trade (CBT) in 1848. At its inception the CBT was a businessman's association and was more Pickwickian than commercial. The first futures contract was traded in the mid 1870s.

5.4 ORGANIZATION OF FUTURES MARKETS

Today there are eleven commodity exchanges: the Chicago Board of Trade; the Chicago Mercantile Exchange with its important division, the International Monetary Market; the Coffee, Sugar, and Cocoa Exchange (New York); the Commodity Exchange, Inc. (New York); the Board of Trade of Kansas City, Missouri, Inc.; the Mid-American Commodity Exchange (Chicago); the Minneapolis Grain Exchange; the New York Cotton Exchange; the Citrus Associates of the New York Cotton Exchange, Inc.; the Petroleum Associates of the New York Cotton Exchange, Inc.; and the New York Mercantile Exchange. The most significant commodity exchange and one of the most innovative is the Chicago Board of Trade. The volume of sales for the year 1982 as compared with 1981 for all the contracts traded on the CBT and the average daily volume per contract are shown in Tables 5.1 and 5.2 respectively.

TABLE 5.1
Chicago Board of Trade Volume of Sales January–December 1981, 1982

	Jan.–Dec. 1982	Jan.–Dec. 1981	Percentage Change
Wheat	4,031,584	4,511,934	− 10.7
Corn	7,948,257	10,674,986	− 25.5
Oats	424,595	370,103	+ 14.7
Soybeans	9,165,520	10,489,932	− 12.6
Soybean oil	3,049,313	3,047,490	+ 0.1
Soybean meal	2,784,423	3,039,633	− 8.4
Western plywood[a]	100,001	175,189	− 42.9
5,000 oz. silver	77,682	214,236	− 63.7
1,000 oz. silver	775,136	184,776	+319.5
New gold	19,515	14,749	+ 32.3
Treasury bonds	16,739,695	13,907,988	+ 20.4
Treasury bond options	118,772	—	—
CDR-GNMA	2,055,648	2,292,882	− 10.4
CD-GNMA	—	175	—
Domestic CD	145,360	158,920	− 8.5
90-day commercial paper	—	49	—
New Treasury notes	881,325	—	—
4–6 year notes	—	2,721	—
Unleaded regular gasoline	8,736	—	—
Total	48,325,562	49,085,763	− 1.6

[a] Includes old plywood in January; 1981 old plywood

Source: Chicago Board of Trade, Market Information Department

TABLE 5.2
Average Daily Volume of the Chicago Board of Trade by Month (reported in contracts)

	Yr.	Jan.	Feb.	Mar.	Apr.	May	Jun.	Jly.	Aug.	Sep.	Oct.	Nov.	Dec.
Wheat	82	15,996	17,061	15,842	15,297	15,166	16,498	19,177	18,071	16,741	12,744	18,479	
	81	17,666	15,889	15,769	12,708	14,001	19,765	21,529	19,574	17,459	16,559	23,403	19,291
Corn	82	28,116	35,686	31,587	30,500	27,547	32,168	28,379	32,290	29,784	30,848	46,341	
	81	46,304	47,316	45,779	49,735	38,671	43,503	49,624	47,801	34,533	28,427	39,132	36,164
Oats	82	1,667	1,944	1,776	2,033	1,815	2,254	2,009	1,990	1,440	1,077	1,276	
	81	1,189	1,792	1,174	1,299	1,205	1,474	1,139	1,282	1,114	1,313	2,649	2,009
Soybeans	82	31,201	36,814	38,936	40,355	35,170	38,595	36,519	34,750	30,448	38,227	42,823	
	81	55,314	42,887	43,603	43,664	39,134	43,061	43,825	37,117	34,532	37,154	37,649	39,431
Soy oil	82	10,956	12,927	11,244	12,370	13,884	12,303	12,023	12,498	12,403	9,305	15,369	
	81	11,608	12,162	10,812	12,097	11,095	12,490	16,140	11,128	11,440	10,863	11,403	13,279
Soy meal	82	10,982	12,532	10,339	12,713	9,847	11,090	10,451	10,231	9,466	11,478	11,669	
	81	12,471	10,689	10,041	12,108	10,919	13,402	13,719	11,490	13,158	9,982	12,142	13,835
Western plywood	82	450	827	514	635	342	461	240	308	209	252	211	
	81	N/T	N/T	N/T	35	24	21	47	105	92	279	277	581
New silver	82	982	1,235	1,878	1,287	1,005	1,077	2,123	2,965	4,463	5,390	7,995	
	81	N/T	N/T	648	522	613	570	797	760	1,335	1,168	1,396	1,179
Silver	82	313	365	329	226	304	214	224	377	296	320	463	
	81	1,405	962	962	959	724	1,378	676	978	804	415	459	630
Gold	82	15	81	81	97	72	123	127	113	75	64	93	
	81	267	95	95	68	64	21	21	18	14	11	13	6
Treasury bonds	82	63,320	68,740	61,473	57,245	70,410	56,956	52,067	75,886	70,211	78,285	77,262	
	81	40,321	45,714	44,359	47,566	56,188	49,744	49,174	56,737	62,566	58,594	84,575	62,628
GNMA CDR	82	9,441	9,691	7,940	6,390	7,963	7,104	7,037	10,122	8,118	10,398	7,179	
	81	8,561	8,418	8,475	9,633	10,570	8,570	7,365	7,440	9,040	8,816	12,112	9,216
Ten-year notes	82	N/T	N/T	N/T	N/T	8,644	4,911	5,293	7,255	4,709	4,448	3,659	
	81	N/T	N/T	N/T	N/T	N/T	N/T	N/T	N/T	N/T	N/T	N/T	N/T
Domestic Bank CD	82	1,109	1,196	2,062	1,506	634	197	83	8	40	1,273	1,250	
	81	N/T	N/T	N/T	N/T	N/T	N/T	2,626	1,541	1,769	[a]	[a]	699
Total	82	174,548	199,018	184,061	180,654	192,803	183,951	175,752	206,864	188,403	202,836	232,819	
	81	195,740	186,701	182,337	191,389	184,001	194,914	207,202	196,516	188,165	174,980	226,655	199,029

[a] Less than one contract a day

N/T–Not Trading

Source: Chicago Board of Trade, Market Information Department

151

Most of these exchanges are not-for-profit associations with limited memberships. Only an individual, generally, can be a member, but some exchanges allow partnerships, cooperatives, or corporations. A membership may be purchased as an investment, it may be leased, or it may be used by the holder to transact business on the floor of the exchange.

Settlements of day-to-day transactions on the exchanges are handled by the clearinghouses, which are either independent organizations or subsidiaries of the exchanges. The clearing corporation interposes itself between the buyer and the seller in each contract. The sale of a futures contract is effectively a sale to the clearing corporation, and a purchase of a futures contract is a purchase from the clearing corporation.

In addition, to preserve the liquidity and the integrity of the futures market, the clearing corporation clears margins. The margin requirements ("performance bonds" of sorts) on each futures contract are set by the exchanges on which the contracts are traded. Exchange members must post the required margin on their net short or long position on a daily basis. That is, if the net short (sell) position of a member is five contracts, that member would be required to deposit five times the margin requirements of one contract. Some exchanges do not allow for the netting of short positions against long positions and thus require separate margins on both the long and the short positions.

The settlement of the clearing margins is made daily, prior to the opening of trading the following day. The clearing member can use cash, government securities, stock in the clearing corporation, and letters of credit issued by an approved bank in meeting the margin call.

Under certain circumstances, the clearing corporation will vary the margin requirement. This is referred to as a variation margin call, which must be paid within an hour by using a certified check. Such calls are made when market conditions are very volatile.

Members with losses in their open positions are required to put up additional margin (maintenance margin). Those with gains will be able to withdraw the full amount of the profit.

The clearing corporation provides several additional services. Among them are market information and a systematic procedure for deliveries against the contracts. Less than 3 percent of commodity contracts are delivered against, yet detailed prescriptions for deliveries have been instituted by all the exchanges.

5.5 THE NATURE OF THE COMMODITIES FUTURES MARKETS

The success of the futures markets is evidenced by the explosive growth in the volume of trades and the frequent addition of new contracts.

The growth of futures contract trading is illustrated in Table 5.3. From 3.66 million contracts in 1960, trading grew to 101.1 million contracts in 1981. The distribution of these trades among the various commodities is shown in Table 5.4. Grain, oilseed products, metals, and financial futures contracts lead in terms of trading activity. In 1982 agricultural futures dominated the activity in futures markets. Only a slim percentage of contracts that are traded is ever delivered against, as shown in the bottom of Table 5.3. The dominant role in commodities futures is still played by the Chicago Board of Trade, as shown in Table 5.4, although the Chicago Mercantile Exchange is gaining rapidly.

The characteristics of futures contracts on some exchanges are shown in Table 5.5. Several entries in this table merit some discussion.

TABLE 5.3
Average Month-end/Open Interest, Estimated Number of Contracts Traded and Number of Contracts Settled by Delivery by Major Groups, All Markets Combined

Fiscal Year	Total	Grain	Oilseeds/ Products	Livestock/ Products	Foodstuffs	Industrial Materials	Metals	Financial Instruments	Currencies
Average Monthend Open interest (in contracts)									
1960	149,356	41,781[2]	39,906	—	50,592	7,088	9,989	—	—
1970	348,630	72,745[1]	86,809	47,457	59,784	4,455	77,380	—	—
TQ	888,080	189,604	172,809	52,329	73,873	37,148	350,556	5,483	6,278
1977	1,121,570	176,270	196,513	76,027	88,662	38,728	517,257	17,909	10,204
1978	1,385,112	209,751	203,352	121,126	77,133	44,146	649,805	57,221	22,578
1979	1,710,727	247,756	244,532	143,776	74,270	50,578	729,148	186,410	34,257
1980	1,489,360	289,159	249,306	126,881	117,765	61,538	400,483	190,966	52,262
1981	1,739,220	308,041	263,966	108,632	106,658	60,978	427,104	408,813	55,028
Number of Contracts Traded[2]									
1960	3,656,381	1,117,827[1]	1,434,368	—	875,592	129,601	98,993	—	—
1970	12,398,188	2,162,179[1]	3,676,702	3,431,947	1,960,894	56,057	1,110,409	—	—
TQ	9,546,331	2,749,329	2,696,595	1,204,492	535,198	382,151	1,875,335	63,602	39,629
1977	41,022,825	7,928,127	13,474,905	5,632,917	2,447,436	1,677,355	8,864,229	604,622	393,234
1978	53,222,321	10,227,983	14,037,111	8,501,774	2,335,210	1,785,649	13,393,704	1,595,363	1,345,527
1979	74,309,239	13,023,423	16,569,675	11,529,178	2,359,884	2,374,090	21,878,549	4,570,694	2,003,746
1980	82,691,169	18,287,003	15,691,770	11,807,659	5,314,210	3,559,799	14,099,125	10,212,968	3,718,635
1981	101,124,296	19,807,558	20,314,830	9,803,734	4,548,843	3,290,318	17,869,752	20,091,322	5,397,939
Number of Contracts Settled by Delivery									
1960	48,495	21,416	14,289	—	8,595	2,030	2,165	—	—
1970	76,908	15,948	14,774	7,516	9,404	1,862	27,404	—	—
TQ	98,565	21,317	32,789	1,561	3,725	4,316	33,763	—	722
1977	318,562	66,089	92,645	6,025	21,424	11,463	114,589	372	4,060
1978	314,315	56,974	52,219	5,931	15,966	8,164	160,916	2,267	8,830
1979	410,606	65,093	93,217	14,171	25,194	5,588	179,132	5,315	6,861
1980	598,898	65,998	170,748	15,088	29,798	7,189	254,679	21,350	22,544
1981	757,089	85,573	239,726	14,513	25,117	19,345	275,606	32,854	49,471

[1] Based on a standard 5,000-bushel contract.
[2] Figures from Futures Industry Association

Source: CFTC, *Annual Report*, 1981, p. 126.

TABLE 5.4
Contract Market Review/Estimated Average Month-end Open Interest, 12-Month Total Volume of Trading and Deliveries by Commodity for Fiscal Years Ending September 30, 1980 and September 30, 1981

Exchange/Commodity	Contract Unit	Monthend Open Interest (Contracts) 1979-80	1980-81	Volume of Trading (Contracts) 1979-80	1980-81	Total Contracts Settled by Delivery 1979-80	1980-81
Chicago Board of Trade (CBOT)							
Wheat	5,000 bu.	56,535	61,327	5,258,534	4,649,284	21,240	32,700
Corn	5,000 bu.	185,437	197,062	10,310,168	12,289,604	25,502	29,385
Oats	5,000 bu.	5,611	6,094	276,081	337,215	7,562	2,812
Soybeans	5,000 bu	125 351	133,125	9,364,201	12,403,133	111,477	83,470
Soybean Oil	60,000 lbs.	62,993	64,076	2,890,067	3,295,530	23,562	104,324
Soybean Meal	100 tons	52,745	56,036	2,583,817	3,457,384	32,037	45,248
Iced Broilers	30,000 lbs.	342	10	8,773	369	773	32
Plywood	76,032 sq. ft	4,097	3,733	160,411	175,228	2,180	4,190
Western Plywood[2]	76,032 sq. ft	–	486	–	6,421	–	254
Silver (Old)	5,000 oz.	44,062	24,725	517,912	262,369	18,777	7,954
Silver (New)[3]	1,000 oz.	–	5,198	–	105,228	–	3,035
Gold (Old)	3 Kg.	59	0	157	0	38	0
Gold (New)	100 oz.	4,120	1,591	73,692	30,380	1,708	816
U.S. Treasury Bonds	$ 100,000	86,824	242,966	4,845,972	11,973,459	16,407	24,911
Com. Paper Loan, 90-Day	$ 1,000,000	382	24	20,635	2,590	55	0
Com. Paper Loan, 30-Day	$ 3,000,000	17	0	125	1	7	0
U.S. T-Notes (4-6 Yrs)	$ 100,000	454	232	2,404	2,771	331	38
GNMA Mortgages (CDR)	$ 100,000	65,732	106,003	2,090,923	2,392,076	7,826	9,806
GNMA Mortgages (CD)[4]	$ 100,000	2,911	267	29,652	476	2,607	239
Domestic CD (90-Day)	$ 1,000,000	–	1,825	–	90,531	–	93
Total CBOT		697,672	904,782	38,433,524	51,474,049	272,089	349,307
MidAmerica Commodity Exchange (MACE)							
Wheat	1,000 bu.	3,891	3,772	526,710	359,070	1,355	1,698
Corn	1,000 bu.	5,753	8,631	365,193	618,367	2,111	4,984
Oats	1,000 bu.[5]	33	72	2,208	2,697	95	83
Soybeans	1,000 bu.	7,083	9,724	837,074	1,133,551	3,616	4,875
Live Hogs	15,000 lbs.	1,740	2,297	118,791	96,124	70	396
Live Cattle	20,000 lbs.	1,090	1,051	210,295	136,794	397	51
Silver	1,000 oz.	4,334	8,946	142,907	199,676	6,402	7,463
Gold	33.2 oz.	6,130	5,992	381,734	529,601	2,477	4,307
U.S. Treasury Bonds[6]	$ .50,000	–	10,373	–	10,373	–	0
Total MACE		30,054	50,858	2,584,912	3,086,253	16,523	23,857
Kansas City Board of Trade (KCBT) Board of							
Wheat	5,000 bu	24,499	23,802	1,201,532	1,204,161	6,065	11,552
Grain Sorghum	280,000 lbs.	–	0	–	295	–	0
Total KCBT		24,499	23,802	1,201,532	1,204,456	6,065	11,552
Minneapolis Grain Exchange (MGE)							
Wheat	5,000 bu.	7,400	6,089	346,577	330,161	2,068	2,221
Sunflower Seeds	100,000 lbs.	1,134	1,003	16,611	25,232	56	1,819
Total MGE		8,534	7,092	363,188	355,393	2,124	4,040
Chicago Mercantile Exchange (CME) and International Monetary Market (IMM)							
Feeder Cattle	42,000 lbs.	12,852	10,149	918,341	606,775	3,371	1,656
Live Hogs	30,000 lbs.	26,654	26,307	1,940,444	2,420,328	631	2,097
Pork Bellies, Frozen	38,000 lbs.	23,529	16,394	2,056,928	2,036,590	3,826	3,153
Live Cattle	40,000 lbs.	58,539	50,759	6,490,817	4,465,035	5,186	6,284
Broilers, fresh, frozen	30,000 lbs.	1,388	1,097	41,258	27,323	367	386
Russet Potatoes	80,000 lbs.	86	123	2,003	1,817	17	9
Shell Eggs	22,500 doz.	142	9	4,912	303	151	38
Lumber	100,000 bd. ft.	11,108	9,132	819,515	666,691	286	337
Stud Lumber	100,000 bd. ft.	224	42	2,626	476	85	58
Plywood[7]	152,064 sq. ft.	–	50	–	298	–	0
U.S. Silver Coins	$ 5,000	8	2	29	9	24	4
Gold	100 tr. oz.	52,918	70,455	2,273,148	2,952,856	21,240	16,148
Canadian Dollars	100,000	10,717	8,492	585,585	458,592	5,733	8,836
French Franc	250,000	13	96	110	1,598	6	140
Swiss Franc	125,000	9,748	9,496	753,701	1,219,039	4,194	8,795
Dutch Guilder	125,000	0	0	4	0	0	0
Deutsche Mark	125,000	10,240	11,598	772,948	1,485,124	3,436	9,969
Mexican Peso	1,000,000	2,790	1,985	19,818	18,005	730	760
Brit Pound Sterling	25,000	12,395	13,892	1,115,596	1,377,716	5,096	12,835
Japanese Yen	12,500,000	5,919	9,330	463,850	832,665	3,142	7,361
U.S. T-Bills (90-Day)	$ 1,000,000	28,520	37,304	3,043,994	5,072,432	2,592	5,613
U.S. T-Bills (1 year)	$ 250,000	210	1	1,040	8	234	2
U.S. T-Notes (4 year)	$ 100,000	255	0	1,588	0	114	0
Domestic CD (90 Day)[8]	$ 1,000,000	–	2,277	–	104,474	–	330
Total CME and IMM		268,255	278,989	21,308,255	23,748,154	60,461	84,813

TABLE 5.4 *(Continued)*

Exchange/Commodity	Contract Unit	Monthend Open Interest (Contracts) 1979-80	1980-81	Volume of Trading (Contracts) 1979-80	1980-81	Total Contracts Settled by Delivery 1979-80	1980-81
New York Mercantile Exchange (NYME)							
Imported Lean Beef	36,000 lb.	747	569	22,012	14,396	467	458
Round White Potatoes	50,000 lb.	6,925	7,539	278,655	356,829	88	299
Palladium	100 tr. oz.	2,061	2,410	61,741	43,153	1,152	2,113
Platinum	50 tr. oz.	8,078	8,999	431,349	486,950	7,638	15,698
U.S. Silver Coins	$ 10,000	347	16	7,487	216	2,737	185
Gold (new)	400 tr. oz	12	0	0	0	14	0
Gold (old)	1 Kg.	8	0	31	0	17	0
Canadian Dollars	100,000	24	0	22	0	6	0
No. 2 Heating, NY	42,000 U.S. Gal.	3,175	17,263	104,571	825,319	2,114	11,455
No. 2 Heating Oil	42,000 U.S. Gal.	–	395	–	1,148	–	0
Total NYME		21,377	37,191	905,868	1,728,011	14,233	30,208
New York Cotton Exchange and Associates (NYCE)							
Orange Juice, Fzn. Con.	15,000 lbs.	7,156	10,291	154,632	362,109	1,973	5,978
Cotton No.[2]	50,000 lbs.	42,934	29,487	2,472,650	1,610,081	2,513	3,026
Propane Gas	100,000 gal.	0	0	26	71	11	13
Total NYCE		50,090	39,778	2,627,308	1,972,261	4,497	9,017
Coffee Sugar & Cocoa Exchange (CSCE)							
Coffee "C"	37,500 lbs.	13,853	9,163	942,558	484,719	10,714	7,167
Sugar No. 11	112,000 lbs.	76,945	63,446	3,566,218	2,812,271	12,158	7,949
Sugar No. 12	112,000 lbs.	4,050	1,605	25,772	11,911	3,760	2,864
Cocoa	30,000 lbs.	5,559	0	250,215	0	937	0
Cocoa	10 metric tons	3,049	14,482	89,245	518,884	0	813
Total CSCE		103,456	88,696	4,874,008	3,827,785	27,569	18,793
Commodity Exchange, Inc. (COMEX)							
Zinc	60,000 lbs.	7	0	25	15	27	12
Silver	5,000 tr. oz.	62,096	29,858	1,260,941	1,089,109	50,332	38,988
Copper	25,000 lbs.	47,457	51,524	1,940,492	1,676,139	38,320	43,246
Gold	100 tr. oz	168,786	217,658	7,007,480	10,494,066	103,776	135,649
U.S. T-Bills (90-Days)	$ 1,000,000	476	122	83,348	21,645	645	653
GNMA Mortgage (CD)	$ 100,000	324	0	8,276	0	762	0
U.S. T-Notes (2 year)[10]	$ 100,000	–	799	–	47,624	–	2,769
Total COMEX		279,146	299,691	10,300,562	13,328,598	193,862	221,317
AMEX Commodities Exchange, Inc. (AMEX)							
U.S. T-Bills (90-Day)[11]	$ 1,000,000	165	0	640	0	146	0
GNMA Mortgages (CD)[12]	$ 100,000	2,138	0	10,123	0	1,128	0
U.S. T-Bonds[11]	$ 1,000,000	84	0	15,153	0	–	0
Total AMEX		2,387	0	25,916	0	1,274	0
New York Futures Exchange (NYFE)							
U.S. T-Bills (90-Day)	$ 1,000,000	542	358	15,738	26,480	–	1,328
U.S. T-Bonds	$ 100,000	1,932	5,445	43,357	255,527	–	1,899
Domestic CD (90-Day)[13]	$ 1,000,000	–	817	–	90,855	–	45
British Pound	25,000	226	74	3,560	3,829	108	426
Canadian Dollar	100,000	46	7	466	230	38	35
Deutsche Mark	125,000	29	4	114	147	16	15
Japanese Yen	12,500,000	22	6	121	91	–	27
Swiss Franc	125,000	93	48	2,740	903	39	272
Total NYFE		2,890	6,759	66,096	378,062	201	4,047
New Orleans Commodity Exchange (NOCE)							
Rice, Milled [14]	120,000 lbs.	–	607	–	8,213	–	62
Rice, Rough[15]	200,000 lbs.	–	585	–	8,491	–	76
Cotton[16]	50,000 lbs.	–	390	–	4,570	–	0
Total NOCE			1,582	–	21,274	–	138
Total all contracts		1,488,360	1,739,220	82,691,169	101,124,296	598,898	757,089

Source: CFTC, Annual Report 1981, pp. 127-131.

[1] Data were supplied by the Futures Industry Association, Inc.

[2] Trading began April 20, 1981.

[3] Trading began March 16, 1981.

[4] Trading began July 22, 1981.

[5] Contract unit reduced from 5,000 bushels to 1,000 bushels effective June 10, 1981.

[6] Trading began September 18, 1981.

[7] Trading began July 28, 1981.

[8] Trading began July 29, 1981.

[9] Trading began August 17, 1981.

[10] Trading began December 2, 1980.

[11] Contract market vacated February 2, 1981.

[12] Contract market vacated July 3, 1981.

[13] Trading began July 9, 1981.

[14] Trading began April 9, 1981.

[15] Trading began April 10, 1981.

[16] Trading began July 7, 1981.

TABLE 5.5
Trading Facts and Figures

Exchange	Commodity	Trading Months	Trading Hours (Central Time)	Contract Size	Price Quoted In	Minimum Price Fluctuation	Daily Limit
Chicago Board of Trade	Iced Broilers	Jan/Feb/Mar/Apr/ Sept/Oct/Nov	9:15-1:05	30,000 lbs	¢/lb	2.5/100¢/lb = $7.50	2¢ = $600
	Commercial Paper 90-Day	Mar/June/Sept/Dec	8:30-1:35	Face Value at maturity of $1,000,000	as an annualized discount	1/100 of 1% of $1,000,000 (1 basis point) = $50.00	50 pt = $1250 Points = $625
	Commercial Paper 30-Day	Mar/Jun/Sept/Dec	8:30-1:45	Face Value at maturity of $3,000,000	as an annualized discount	1 pt. = $50.00	25 pt. = $1,250
	Corn	Mar/May/July/Sept/ Dec	9:30-1:15	5,000 bu	¢/bu	1/4¢/bu = $12.50	10¢ = $500
	GNMA	Mar/May/Jun/Sept/ Oct/Nov/Dec	8:00-2:00	$100,000 principal	32nds/per point	1/32 point = $31.25	64/32 = $2,000
	Gold	All months	8:25-1:35	100 Troy Oz.	$/oz	10¢/oz = $10.00	$25 = $2,500
	Oats	Mar/May/July/ Sept/Dec	9:30-1:15	5,000 bu	¢/bu	1/4¢/bu = $12.50	6¢ = $300
	Plywood	Jan/Mar/May/July/ Sept/Nov	9:00-1:00	76,032 sq ft	$/thousand square feet	10¢/1000 sq ft. = $7.60 (1 pt = 76¢)	$7 = $532 (700 pts)
	Silver	Feb/Apr/June/Aug/ Oct/Dec	8:40-1:25	5,000 troy oz	¢/oz	1/10¢/oz = $5	40¢ = $2000
	Soybeans	Jan/Mar/May/July/ Aug/Sept/Nov	9:30-1:15	5,000 bu	¢/bu	1/4¢/bu = $12.50	30¢ = $1,500
	Soybean Meal	Jan/Mar/May/July/ Aug/Sept/Oct/Dec	9:30-1:15	100 tons (200,000 lbs)	$/ton	10¢/ton = $10	$10 = $1,000
	Soybean Oil	Jan/Mar/May/July/ Aug/Sept/Oct/Dec	9:30-1:15	60,000 lbs	¢/lb	1/100¢/lb = $6	1¢ = $600 (100 pts)
	Long-Term U.S. Treasury Bonds	Mar/June/Sept/Dec	8:00-2:00	Bonds with face value at maturity of $100,000 and coupon rate of 8%	32nds per point	1/32nd of a point = $31.25	64/32 = $2,000
	Wheat	Mar/May/July/Sept/ Dec	9:30-1:15	5,000 bu	¢/bu	1/4¢/bu = $12.50	20¢ = $1,000
	Silver	Feb/Apr/June/Aug/ Oct/Dec/	8:40-1:25	1,000 troy oz	¢/oz	1/10¢/oz = $1	40¢ = $400
MidAmerica Commodity Exchange	Corn	Mar/May/July/Sept/ Dec	9:30-1:30	1,000 bu	¢/bu	1/8¢/bu = $1.25	10¢ = $100
	Gold	Mar/Jun/Sept/Dec	8:25-1:40	33.2 (troy oz)	$/oz	2.5¢/troyoz = .83	$50 = $1,660
	Hogs	Feb/Apr/June/July/ Aug/Oct/Dec	9:15-1:05	15,000 lbs	¢/lbs	2.5/100¢/lb = $3.75 (1 pt = $1.50)	1.5¢ = $225 (150 pts)
	Oats	Mar/May/July/Sept/ Dec	9:30-1:30	5,000 bu	¢/bu	1/8¢/bu = $6.25	6¢ = $300
	Silver	Feb/Apr/June/Aug/ Oct/Dec/Spot	8:40-1:40	1,000 troy oz	¢/oz	5/100¢/oz = $.50	40¢ = $400
	Cattle	Jan/Feb/Apr/June/ Aug/Oct/Dec	9:05-1:00	20,000 lbs	¢/lb	2.5/100¢/lb = $5 (1 pt = $2)	1.5¢ = $300 (150 pts)
	Soybeans	Jan/Mar/May/July/ Aug/Sept/Nov	9:30-1:30	1,000 bu	¢/bu	1/8¢/bu = $1.25	30¢ = $300
	Wheat	Mar/May/July/Sept/ Dec	9:30-1:30	1,000 bu	¢/bu	1/8¢/bu = $1.25	20¢ = $200

156

TABLE 5.5 (*Continued*)

Exchange	Commodity	Trading Months	Trading Hours (Central Time)	Contract Size	Price Quoted In	Minimum Price Fluctuation	Daily Limit
Chicago Mercantile Exchange	Boneless Beef	Feb/Apr/June/Aug/ Oct/Dec	9:05-12:45	38,000 lbs	$/cwt	2.5/100¢/lb = $9.50 (1 pt = $3.80)	1.5¢ = $570 (150 pts)
	Broilers, Fresh	Feb/Apr/Jun/ Jul/Aug/Oct/Dec	9:10-1:00	30,000 lbs	¢/lb	2.5/100¢/lb = $7.50 (1 pt = $3.00)	2¢ = $600 (200 pts)
	Butter	Mar/May/Oct/Nov/Dec	9:25-12:35	38,000 lbs	¢/lb	2.5/100¢/lb = $9.50 (1 pt = $3.80)	1.5¢ = $570 (150 pts)
	Cattle, Feeder	Jan/Mar/Apr/May/ Aug/Sept/Oct/Nov	9:05-12:45	42,000 lbs	¢/lb	2.5/100¢/lb = $10.50 (1 pt = $4.20)	1.5¢ = $630 (150 pts)
	Cattle, Live	Jan/Feb/Apr/June/ Aug/Oct/Dec	9:05-12:45	40,000 lbs	¢/lb	2.5/100¢/lb = $10 (1 pt = $4)	1.5¢ = $600 (150 pts)
	Eggs, Shell (Fresh)	All Months except Aug	9:20-1:00	22,500 doz	¢/doz	5/100¢/doz = $11.25 (1 pt = $2.25)	2¢ = $450 (200 pts)
	Eggs, Frozen	Jan/Sept/Oct/Nov/ Dec	9:20-1:00	36,000 lbs	¢/lb	2.5/100¢/lb = $9 (1 pt = $3.60)	1.5¢ = $540 (150 pts)
	Eggs, Nest Run	All Months	9:20-1:00	22,500 doz	¢/doz	5/100¢/doz = $11.2o (1 pt = $2.25)	2¢ = $450 (200 pts)
	Hams, Skinned	Mar/July/Nov	9:10-1:00	36,000 lbs	¢/lb	2.5/100¢/lb = $9 (1 pt = $3.60)	1.5¢ = $540 (150 pts)
	Hogs	Feb/Apr/June/July/ Aug/Oct/Dec	9:10-1:00	30,000 lbs	¢/lb	2.5/100¢/lb = $7.50 (1 pt = $3)	1.5¢ = $450 (150 pts)
	Lumber	Jan/Mar/May/July/ Sept/Nov	9:00-1:05	100,000 board feet	$/thousand board ft	10¢/1,000 bd ft = $10 (1 pt = $1)	$5 = $500 (500 pts)
	Stud Lumber	Jan/Mar/May/July/ Sept/Nov	9:00-1:05	100,000 board feet	$/thousand board feet	10¢/1,000 bd ft = $10 (1 pt = $1)	$5 = $500 (500 pts)
	Milo	Mar/May/July/Sept/ Oct/Dec	9:30-1:15	400,000 lbs	$/cwt	2.5/100¢/cwt = $10 (1 pt. = $4.00)	15¢ = $600 (15 pts)
	Pork Bellies	Feb/Mar/May/July/ Aug	9:10-1:00	38,000 lbs	¢/lb	2.5/100¢/lb = $9.50 (1 pt = $3.80)	2¢ = $760 (200 pts)
	Potatoes, Russet Burbank	Jan/Mar/May/Nov	9:00-1:00	80,000 lbs	¢/cwt	1¢/cwt = $8 (1 pt. = $8.00)	50¢ = $400** (50 pts)
	Turkeys	Jan/Mar/May/Aug/ Oct	9:10-12:45	36,000 lbs	¢/lb	2.5/100¢/lb = $9 (1 pt = $3.60)	1.5¢ = $540 (150 pts)
International Monetary Market of the Chicago Mercantile Exchange	Copper	Jan/Mar/May/July/ Sept/Nov	8:45-1:15	12,500 lbs	¢/lb	10/100¢/lb = $12.50 (1 pt = $1.25)	5¢ = $625 (500 pts)
	Currencies: British Pound	Jan/Mar/Apr/Jun/ Jul/Sept/Oct/Dec & Spot	7:30-1:24	25,000 BP	¢/BP	.0005/lb = $12.50 (1 pt = $2.50)	5¢ = $1,250 (500 pts)
	Canadian Dollar	Jan/Mar/Apr/Jun/ Jul/Sept/Oct/Dec & Spot	7:30-1:22	100,000 CD	¢/CD	.0001/CD = $10 (1 pt = $10)	3/4¢ = $750 (75 pts)
	Dutch Guilder	Jan/Mar/Apr/Jun/ Jul/Sept/Oct/Dec & Spot	7:30-1:30	125,000 DG	¢/DG	.0001/DG = $12.50 (1 pt = $12.50)	.0100 = $1250 (100 pts)
	French Franc	Jan/Mar/Apr/Jun/ Jul/Sept/Oct/Dec & Spot	7:30-1:28	250,000 FF	¢/FF	5/1000¢/FF = $12.50 (1 pt = $2.50)	1/2¢ = $1,250 (500 pts)
	Deutschemark	Jan/Mar/Apr/Jun/ Jul/Sept/Oct/Dec & Spot	7:30-1:20	125,000 DM	¢/DM	.0001/DM = $12.50 (1 pt = $12.50)	.0100 = $1,250 (100 pts)
	Japanese Yen	Jan/Mar/Apr/Jun/ Jul/Sept/Oct/Dec & Spot	7:30-1:26	12,500,000 Yen	¢/Yen	.000001/Y = $12.50 (1 pt = $12.50)	.0001 = $1,250 (100 pts)
	Mexican Peso	Jan/Mar/Apr/Jun/ Jul/Sept/Oct/Dec & Spot	7:30-1:18	1,000,000 Peso	¢/Peso	.00001/P = $10 (1 pt = $10)	3/20¢ = $1,500 (150 pts)
	Swiss Franc	Jan/Mar/Apr/Jun/ Jul/Sept/Oct/Dec & Spot	8:45-1:13	125,000 SF	¢/SF	1/100¢/SF = $12.50 (1 pt = $12.50)	3/5¢ = $1,875 (150 pts)
	Gold	Jan/Mar/Apr/Jun/ Jul/Sept/Oct/Dec/ & Spot	8:25-1:30	100 troy oz	$/oz	10¢/oz = $10 1 pt = $1	$50 = $5,000 (5000 pts)
	U.S. Silver Coins	Mar/June/Sept/Dec	8:50-1:25	$5,000 (5 bags @ $1,000)	$/bag	$2/bag = $10 1 pt = $1	$150 = $750 (150 pts)

157

TABLE 5.5 (Continued)

Exchange	Commodity	Trading Months	Trading Hours (Central Time)	Contract Size	Price Quoted In	Minimum Price Fluctuation	Daily Limit
International Monetary Market of the Chicago Mercantile Exchange (cont'd.)	Treasury Bills 13 Weeks	Jan/Mar/Apr/Jun/ Jul/Sep/Oct/Dec	8:00-1:40	$1,000,000	Basis Point(IMM Index)	.01 1 basis point = $25	60 pts = $1,250 (60 pts)
	Treasury Bills 1 Year	Mar/June/Sept/Dec	8:15-1:35	250,000	Basis Point (IMM Index)	1 basis point = $25	50 pts = $1,250
	U.S. Treasury Notes Four Year	Feb/May/Aug/Nov	8:20-1:55	$100,000		01 (in 64ths of 1%) 1 pt. = $15.62	48 = $750
Commodity Exchange (Comex)	Copper	Jan/Feb/Mar/May/ July/Sept/Dec	8:50-1:00	25,000 lbs	¢/lb	5/100¢/lb = $12.50 (1 pt = $2.50)	5¢ = $1250 (500 pts)
	GNMA	Jan/Feb/Apr/July/ Oct/Dec	8:00-2:30	$100,000	$/³²₆₄	¹⁄₆₄ = $15.62	⁶⁴⁄₆₄ = $1,000
	Gold	Jan/Feb/Apr/June/ Aug/Oct/Dec	8:25-1:30	3 Kilo (100 troy oz)	$/oz	.10¢/oz = $10	$25 = $2500
	Silver	Jan/Feb/Mar/May/ July/Sept/Dec	8:40-1:15	5,000 troy oz	¢/oz	10/100¢/oz = $25.00	50¢ = $2500
	Treasury Bills	Feb/May/Aug/Nov	8:00-2:30	$1,000,000	Basis Point (Comex Index)	.01 = $25	60 pts = $1500
	Treasury Notes Two-Year	Mar/June/Sept/Dec	8:00-2:30	$100,000	$/³²₆₄	¹⁄₆₄ = $15.62	⁶⁴⁄₆₄ = 1,000
	Zinc	Jan/Feb/Mar/May/ July/Sept/Dec	9:15-11:45	60,000 lbs	¢/lb	5/100¢/lb = $30 (1 pt = $6.00)	3¢ = $1800 (300 pts)
New York Coffee Sugar & Cocoa Exchange	Cocoa	Mar/May/July/Sept/ Dec	8:30-2:00	10 metric tons	¢/ton	$1.00/ton = $10.00 (1 pt. = $10.00)	$88 = $880 (88 pts)
	Coffee "C"	Mar/May/July/Sept/ Dec	8:45-1:30	37,500 lbs	¢/lb	1/100¢/lbs = $3.75 (1 pt = $3.75)	4¢ = $1,500 (400 pts)
	Coffee "B"	Mar/May/July/Sept/ Dec	8:45-1:30	32,500 lbs	¢/lb	1/100¢/lb = $3.25 (1 pt = $3.25)	4¢ = $1,300 (400 pts)
	Sugar No. 11 (World)	Jan/Mar/May/July/ Sept/Oct	9:00-1:45	112,000 lbs	¢/lbs	1/100¢/lb = $11.20 (1 pt = $11.20)	½¢ = $560 (100 pts) (50 pts)
	Sugar No. 12 (Domestic)	Jan/Mar/May/July/ Sept/Nov	9:00-1:45	112,000 lbs	¢/lb	1/100¢/lb = 11.20 (1 pt = $11.20)	½¢ = $560 (50 pts)
New York Cotton Exchange	Cotton No. 2	All months	9:30-2:00	50,000 lbs	¢/lb	1/100¢/lb = $5 (1 pt = $5)	2¢ = $1,000 (200 pts)
	Crude Oil	Mar/June/Sept/Dec	8:50-1:20	5,000 barrels	¢/barrels	1/10¢/barrel = $5	25¢ = $1,250 (250 pts)
	Orange Juice	Jan/Mar/May/July/ Sept/Nov	9:15-1:45	15,000 lbs	¢/lb	5/100¢/lb = $7.50 (1 pt = $1.50)	5¢ = $750 (500 pts)
	Propane, Liquified	Jan/Mar/May/July/ Sept//Dec	8:45-1:35	100,000 gals	¢/gal	1/100¢/gal = $10 (1 pt = $10)	1¢ = $1,000 (100 pts)
New York Mercantile Exchange	Gold	Jan/Mar/May/ July/Sep/Dec	8:25-1:30	1 kilo (32 troy oz)	$/oz	20¢/oz = $6.40	$24 = $768
	Gold, 400 oz	Mar/June/Sept/Dec	8:25-1:30	400 oz bar (Four 100 oz bars) (12 or 13 kilo bars)	$/oz	5¢/oz = $20	$25 = $10,000
	Imported Boneless Beef	Jan/Mar/May/July/ Sept/Nov	9:15-12:45	36,000 lbs	$/100 lbs (or ¢/lb)	2¢/100 lbs = $7.20 (1 pt = $3.60)	$1.50 = $540 (150 pts)
	Oil, Heating No. 2	Jan/Feb/Mar/May/ July/Aug/Sept/ Nov/Dec	9:30-1:45	42,000 gal	¢/gal	$.0001/gal = $4.20	.02/gal = $840
	Oil Industrial No. 6	Jan/Feb/Mar/May/ July/Sept/Nov/Dec	9:35-1:43	42,000 gal	¢/gal	$.0001/gal = $4.20	.02/gal = $840
	Palladium	Jan/Apr/July/Oct	8:35-1:20	100 troy oz	$/oz	5¢/oz = $5	$6 = $360 (600 pts)
	Platinum	Jan/Apr/July/Oct	8:30-1:30	50 troy oz	$/oz	10¢/oz = $5	$20 = $1,000
	Potatoes, Maine and Round White	Mar/Apr/May/Nov	9:00-1:00	50,000 lbs	$/100 lbs (or ¢/lb)	1¢/100 lbs = $5 (1 pt = $5)	50¢ = $250 (50 pts)
	U.S. Silver Coins	Jan/Apr/July/Oct	8:40-1:15	$10,000 (10 bags @ $1,000)	$/bag	$1/bag = $10	$150 = $3,000 ($300 per bag)

Source: Archer Commodities, Inc., Chicago, 1981.

158

The trading months are select months of the year, occasionally every month, which best correspond to the nature of the demand by hedgers of a given commodity. The contract size is standard for each commodity. This guarantees uniformity and increases the liquidity of the contract.

The daily limit on each contract is not permanent and can change rather frequently, depending on market conditions. The daily limit is the maximum permitted price movement below or above the previous day settlement price. The daily limit differs from one contract to another and sometimes from one exchange to another. Another limit is on the "range." The "daily range" is frequently the same as the daily limit. If the limit is 1 cent and the range is 2 cents, a contract could trade up 1 cent and then fall by the 2 cents allowed by the daily range.

Missing from Table 5.5 is the margin requirement. For a wheat contract, for example, the margin requirement on the CBT is 20 cents per bushel or $1,000 per contract. This represents not a deposit on the contract but a performance bond. It is intended to at least cover the maximum allowable daily price fluctuation in the contract. A fall in the price of the contract calls for an additional commitment by the trader, and every rise (assuming a long position) releases cash to the trader. The settlement must be done daily. This should explain why commodities traders must have considerable liquidity in order to meet their margin calls should the market head in a direction opposite to their expectations.

Occasionally, the behavior of the price of a commodity may warrant revision of the margin requirements. The clearing corporation may call on its member firms to deposit additional margin under these circumstances. This margin call must be met by the member within one hour by using a certified check. The member firm in turn would require its customer to increase his margin.

5.6 TYPES OF ORDERS

The various types of orders available to commodity hedgers and speculators are:

Market Order

A market order is an order to buy or sell at the best available price—the market-determined price. A buy order is filled at the ask and a sell order is filled at the bid.

Limit Order

A limit order to buy is an order to buy at no more than a specific price. A limit order to sell is an order to sell at a price no lower than the specified price. There is no guarantee with this type order that the order will be filled, particularly in a fast-moving market.

Stop Order

A stop order can be placed on the buy as well as on the sell side of the market.

A buy stop order instructs the broker to buy when the market reaches the stop-order price. This type of order is placed above the current market price and is executed

as soon as the stop price is touched. The execution price may be equal to, less than, or greater than the stop-order price.

A stop order may also be a stop-limit order. Here both the stop price and the limit price must be specified. For example, the buyer may instruct the broker to "buy stop at $2.67 but don't give more than $2.69."

A sell stop order is placed below prevailing market price, usually to protect a profit in a long position or to limit loss. A seller may instruct a broker to sell at $2.65—the purchase price was equal to $2.75—in order to limit the loss to 10 cents.

A stop order may also be of the "trailing" variety. A trailing stop order moves with the market. A holder of a long position in corn, for example, may instruct the broker every day to place a sell order at a price below that day's closing price.

Scale Order

With a scale order the seller of a commodity can instruct his or her broker to sell x bushels of, say, corn at $2.60, sell y bushels at $2.70, and z bushels at $2.80, based on the belief that the corn market is in an uptrend.

Market-If-Touched Order

The market-if-touched (MIT) order is like a stop order. It allows substantially more leeway in the execution of the order. The order becomes a market order if the price is reached.

Take Your Time (TYT) Order

The take your time order is used when the trader wishes to give the floor broker the opportunity to use judgment in filling an order. However, the floor broker, unless negligent, cannot be held responsible if a good opportunity in the market is missed.

In addition, a trader may specify the time when an order is to be filled: "on close," "on opening," or at any other specified time during the trading hours.

5.7 THE FILLING OF AN ORDER

The order begins with a telephone call from the trader to the broker. The brokerage firm, using its teletype machine, wires the order in to the telephone center on the floor of the exchange. The order is then relayed to the appropriate commodity broker who looks for another broker on the opposite side of the transaction. Using "open outcry" and hand signals, the pit broker flashes the bid (if buying), hoping to receive a "sold" signal from a seller. Upon the receipt of such a signal, the order is completed. The broker then writes the agreed-upon price and the seller's initials on the order blank, endorses it, and throws it back for a messenger to pick up and return to the brokerage firm's floor telephone network operator. The telephone operator verifies the order and wires the information to the office where the order was initially placed. Upon receipt of the information that the order has been filled, the broker informs the client of the details of the transaction.

5.8 PRICE QUOTATIONS

Using sophisticated communications networks, the commodity exchanges report futures prices promptly and accurately. The Chicago Board of Trade has in place an advanced system called the Commodity Price Reporting System.

As soon as a transaction is consummated in the pit, a "market reporter" who is employed by the exchange records the time and price of the transaction and enters the price quotation in a computer terminal. The trade is validated automatically and is then flashed on screens throughout the country and transmitted to more than eighty foreign countries.

It must be noted that reported prices are not necessarily prices resulting from actual transactions. Prices may merely be indicators of bids and offers for which there were no takers.

The formats used by newspapers in reporting futures prices are not uniform. Table 5.6 is quoted from *The Wall Street Journal.* The first column under the corn futures, for example, indicates the various maturity months followed by the opening prices in cents per bushel ($2.54½), the high price for the day ($2.55½), the low price for the day ($2.53¼), and the closing (settlement) price of the day ($2.54¼). The settlement price is unique to futures trading. Unlike the stock market, the last price of the day may not be the closing price because closing in the futures market is not a point in time. It is, instead, a period of time (about 2 minutes) when a multitude of transactions could take place. The settlement price is usually calculated as the average of the highest and the lowest price during the closing period.

"Change" represents the net change from the previous day's closing price. "Open interest" indicates the number of unliquidated contracts (open buy and sell contracts) for a given contract month. It is similar to the number of shares issued by a corporation. The headline for each commodity: "Corn (CBT)—5,000 bu.; cents per bu." indicates the commodity (corn), the exchange on which it is traded (the Chicago Board of Trade), the contract size (5,000 bushels), and the basis of the price quotation (cents per bushel).

5.9 THE MAJOR OPERATORS IN THE FUTURES MARKETS

The operations of the exchange depend on the activities of hundreds of persons, each filling an assigned role or assuming a role. The manner in which these responsibilities are discharged has significant implications for market efficiency and liquidity.

The activities of speculators, some are members of the exchanges, have a pronounced effect on the efficiency and the liquidity of the markets. Speculators are professional risk takers trying to capitalize on their supposedly greater foresight into future price movements. Without the speculators, the futures market would not function. Three types of speculators play important roles on the various exchanges: the position trader, the scalper, and the spreader.

The position trader, using his or her own or borrowed capital, establishes a position in the futures market in the hope of capitalizing on advantageous price movements. The position is held for only a day, by the day traders, and usually for short periods of time by other position traders.

Scalpers trade for their own accounts in the pits of the exchanges and rarely hold positions for more than one day. They buy at the ask and sell at the bid, hoping to

TABLE 5.6
Future Prices (January 13, 1983)

—GRAINS AND OILSEEDS—

CORN (CBT)—5,000 bu.; cents per bu.

	Open	High	Low	Settle	Change	Lifetime High	Lifetime Low	Open Interest
Mar83	254½	255½	253¼	254¼	− 1¾	320¾	227½	68,632
May	264	264¾	262½	263¾	− 1¾	322½	236¼	31,065
July	271½	272½	270½	271½	− 1¾	316½	243	21,103
Sept	275	276	274¼	274¾	− 1¼	291	247	3,871
Dec	282	283¼	281¼	282¼	− 1¼	283¾	253	16,595
Mar84	291¾	293	290¾	292	− 1½	293¾	278½	1,200
May	298¼	299	297	297¾	− 1¾	299½	294½	47

Est vol 30,154; vol Wed 51,014; open int 142,513, +4,618.

OATS (CBT)—5,000 bu.; cents per bu.

	Open	High	Low	Settle	Change	Lifetime High	Lifetime Low	Open Interest
Mar83	172¼	173	170½	171	− 1¾	205	151½	2,831
May	180¼	180¾	177½	178¼	− 2¼	196	158½	1,155
July	187	188	185	185¼	− 2	188	163	543
Sept	190¾	191½	188	188½	− 2¾	191½	166	205
Dec	199	199	197½	198	− 1	199½	181	130

Est vol 1,103; vol Wed 2,151; open int 4,864, +198.

SOYBEANS (CBT)—5,000 bu.; cents per bu.

	Open	High	Low	Settle	Change	Lifetime High	Lifetime Low	Open Interest
Jan83	583½	585½	582	585	− ¼	783½	532½	3,505
Mar	592	595¾	591½	594½	− ½	744	547½	45,429
May	602	606	602	605	+ ¼	746	558½	15,285
July	610	614½	610	613¼	....	731½	556½	16,447
Aug	611½	615	611¼	613½	....	734½	566½	1,012
Sept	612	614	609½	612	+ ½	686½	567	929
Nov	613	616	612	615¼	+ ¼	640	568½	7,850
Jan84	625½	629	624½	627	....	629	594	162
Mar	639	642	639	642	+ 1	642	616	71

Est vol 32,498; vol Wed 48,908; open int 90,690, +2,279.

SOYBEAN MEAL (CBT)—100 tons; $ per ton.

	Open	High	Low	Settle	Change	Lifetime High	Lifetime Low	Open Interest
Jan83	183.00	183.70	182.10	183.60	+ .20	207.00	153.70	4,027
Mar	182.70	183.20	181.80	182.90	− .30	212.00	157.20	21,830
May	183.30	184.20	182.50	184.10	− .20	214.00	160.30	9,945
July	185.00	185.70	184.00	185.30	− .50	210.00	162.50	6,560
Aug	185.00	185.70	184.50	185.50	− .60	200.50	162.50	2,567
Sept	185.00	186.00	184.80	185.50	− 1.00	186.50	162.50	1,886
Oct	185.50	185.50	184.30	184.80	− .70	185.50	163.00	1,003
Dec	188.00	188.50	187.00	188.50	− .30	188.80	166.50	1,100
Jan84	....	....	....	187.50	+ .50	187.00	174.50	264
Mar	....	....	....	189.50	+ .50	189.00	179.50	31

Est vol 12,541; vol Wed 17,252; open int 49,213, +1,790.

SOYBEAN OIL (CBT)—60,000 lbs.; cents per lb.

	Open	High	Low	Settle	Change	Lifetime High	Lifetime Low	Open Interest
Jan83	16.30	16.50	16.28	16.38	+ .08	23.00	15.98	3,237
Mar	16.68	16.83	16.60	16.72	+ .07	22.90	16.31	28,675
May	17.10	17.22	17.01	17.11	+ .05	22.90	16.71	9,244
July	17.50	17.60	17.40	17.50	+ .04	23.20	17.08	5,054
Aug	17.55	17.70	17.55	17.65	+ .05	19.75	17.25	1,035
Sept	17.80	17.80	17.70	17.79	+ .04	20.00	17.38	978
Oct	17.85	18.00	17.85	17.94	+ .05	19.50	17.52	844
Dec	18.20	18.25	18.12	18.21	+ .01	18.81	17.82	715
Jan84	18.33	18.45	18.33	18.35	− .02	18.45	18.03	102
Mar	....	....	....	18.65	− .10	18.80	18.75	1

Est vol 11,288; vol Wed 12,036; open int 49,885, +969.

WHEAT (CBT)—5,000 bu.; cents per bu.

	Open	High	Low	Settle	Change	Lifetime High	Lifetime Low	Open Interest
Mar83	340	346	340	345¾	+ 4½	458	318½	20,781
May	349	353	348	352¾	+ 3½	444½	327¼	7,564
July	354	358½	354	358¼	+ 2¾	420	332½	6,336
Sept	365	368½	364¼	367¾	+ 2½	407½	341½	406
Dec	380	384¼	380	383¼	+ 2¼	391	356¼	529
Mar84	393½	396¼	393½	396	+ 2½	396¼	376	26

Est vol 18,048; vol Wed 24,089; open int 35,642, −914.

WHEAT (KC)—5,000 bu.; cents per bu.

	Open	High	Low	Settle	Change	Lifetime High	Lifetime Low	Open Interest
Mar83	378½	379¾	378	379½	+ 1¼	449½	343	16,556
May	371¼	373	371¼	373	+ 1½	410	345½	3,507
July	368	370	368	369½	+ 1¼	399½	345½	3,315
Sept		....	....	376	....	379	356	21
Dec	394	395	393	393	+ 1	395	380	46

Est vol 4,007; vol Wed 4,714; open int 23,445, +8.

WHEAT (MPLS)—5,000 bu.; cents per bu.

	Open	High	Low	Settle	Change	Lifetime High	Lifetime Low	Open Interest
Mar83	372¼	375¾	372¼	375¼	+ 2½	439½	369¼	3,474
May	378½	381¼	378½	380½	+ 1¼	418	372	1,401
July	378¼	385¼	384¼	385	+ ½	410¾	374	287
Sept	391	391½	390	390	+ ½	408½	379	163

Est vol 1,180; vol Wed 1,315; open int 5,325, +252.

BARLEY (WPG)—20 metric tons; Can. $ per ton

	Open	High	Low	Settle	Change	Lifetime High	Lifetime Low	Open Interest
Mar	103.50	104.50	103.50	103.90	+ .40	131.40	97.70	3,022
May	107.00	107.70	106.80	107.20	+ .10	126.60	100.70	2,962
July	109.70	110.00	109.60	109.60	− .20	116.30	103.50	1,673
Oct	....	....	....	112.00	+ .20	115.00	109.00	521

Est vol 1,090; vol Wed 1,349; open int 8,178, +128.

FLAXSEED (WPG)—20 metric tons; Can. $ per ton

	Open	High	Low	Settle	Change	Lifetime High	Lifetime Low	Open Interest
Mar	....	....	....	290.80	+ 2.50	368.50	281.00	468
May	294.50	296.50	294.00	296.50	+ 2.50	373.50	288.30	3,072
July	....	....	....	302.50	+ 2.50	375.00	296.00	288
Oct	....	....	....	308.00	....	....	....	3

Est vol 270; vol Wed 389; open int 3,831, +14.

RAPESEED (WPG)—20 metric tons; Can. $ per ton

	Open	High	Low	Settle	Change	Lifetime High	Lifetime Low	Open Interest
Jan	....	....	....	323.60	+ 1.10	369.70	309.10	459
Mar	325.50	327.70	325.00	326.10	+ .80	372.20	314.30	8,334
June	330.40	332.70	330.10	330.70	+ .30	366.00	322.30	3,478
Sept	334.00	334.00	333.10	333.40	+ 2.30	360.60	326.00	2,481
Nov	328.00	330.00	328.00	329.30	+ 2.30	347.00	324.30	1,838

Est vol 2,800; vol Wed 1,554; open int 16,590, −28.

RYE (WPG)—20 metric tons; Can. $ per ton

	Open	High	Low	Settle	Change	Lifetime High	Lifetime Low	Open Interest
Mar83	121.00	121.00	121.00	121.00	− .20	144.00	117.50	967
May	124.00	124.50	124.00	124.00	− .30	147.20	119.80	2,275
July	127.30	127.30	127.00	127.00	− .30	149.00	127.00	130

Est vol 270; vol Wed 121; open int 3,372, +14.

—LIVESTOCK & MEAT—

CATTLE—FEEDER (CME)—44,000 lbs.; cents per lb.

	Open	High	Low	Settle	Change	Lifetime High	Lifetime Low	Open Interest
Jan83	69.40	70.00	69.40	70.00	+ .50	69.70	62.75	418
Mar	68.40	69.20	68.30	68.97	+ .55	69.25	62.60	5,176
Apr	68.06	68.75	67.95	68.47	+ .27	68.95	62.95	2,262
May	67.00	67.55	66.80	67.27	+ .17	68.40	62.85	1,813
Aug	67.50	67.50	67.25	67.27	+ .12	67.90	62.75	255
Sept	66.50	66.60	66.40	66.60	+ .10	66.75	62.70	146
Oct	66.00	66.05	65.80	65.80	− .20	66.45	62.95	32
Nov	66.30	66.40	66.20	66.20	− .15	66.60	63.00	43

Est vol 2,585; vol Wed 2,228; open int 10,145, +217.

CATTLE—LIVE (CME)—40,000 lbs.; cents per lb.

	Open	High	Low	Settle	Change	Lifetime High	Lifetime Low	Open Interest
Feb83	60.85	61.47	60.55	60.85	− .05	64.55	54.87	20,616
Apr	61.25	61.97	61.10	61.77	+ .47	64.65	55.85	14,139
June	62.70	63.37	62.55	63.12	+ .37	65.50	58.02	8,558
Aug	61.20	61.70	61.15	61.55	+ .27	63.00	56.05	3,259
Oct	59.65	60.17	59.65	59.87	+ .25	60.12	55.60	1,166
Dec	61.00	61.50	61.00	61.37	+ .12	61.75	61.00	38

Est vol 17,874; vol Wed 13,037; open int 47,776, +483.

HOGS—LIVE (CME)—30,000 lbs.; cents per lb.

	Open	High	Low	Settle	Change	Lifetime High	Lifetime Low	Open Interest
Feb83	57.75	58.90	57.67	58.80	+ .87	61.25	43.00	21,297
Apr	54.50	55.90	54.40	55.80	+ 1.20	57.45	46.25	11,303
June	55.75	57.00	55.70	56.95	+ 1.00	57.17	48.00	7,450
July	55.60	56.55	55.55	56.50	+ .80	56.60	47.75	3,972
Aug	54.00	54.60	53.87	54.55	+ .62	54.60	45.75	1,822
Oct	49.70	50.40	49.60	50.35	+ .47	50.25	43.90	1,480
Dec	49.20	49.90	49.15	49.90	+ .25	50.25	41.10	391
Feb	49.00	49.00	48.50	48.50	− .62	49.40	44.70	61
Apr	47.50	47.50	47.15	47.50	+ .20	47.50	46.00	6

Est vol 14,341; vol Wed 10,857; open int 47,782, +140.

PORK BELLIES (CME)—38,000 lbs.; cents per lb.

	Open	High	Low	Settle	Change	Lifetime High	Lifetime Low	Open Interest
Feb83	83.35	85.75	83.35	85.75	+ 2.00	91.00	65.50	10,681
Mar	82.30	84.75	82.30	84.75	+ 2.00	88.32	65.45	3,817
May	81.80	83.90	81.80	83.90	+ 2.00	85.45	65.25	2,701
July	80.35	82.40	80.15	82.17	+ 1.60	81.65	65.25	3,347
Aug	78.00	79.85	77.75	79.50	+ 1.47	78.90	66.00	618
Feb84	67.80	68.00	67.60	67.85	+ .15	70.85	63.00	188
Mar	....	....	....	66.45	+ .45	69.00	62.02	60

Est vol 15,066; vol Wed 12,340; open int 21,412, +363.

—FOOD & FIBER—

COCOA (CSCE)—10 metric tons; $ per ton.

	Open	High	Low	Settle	Change	Lifetime High	Lifetime Low	Open Interest
Mar83	1,680	1,687	1,647	1,668	− 2	2,295	1,383	11,435
May	1,710	1,725	1,690	1,710	+ 13	1,900	1,438	5;871
July	1,745	1,748	1,720	1,735	....	1,897	1,475	2,512
Sept	1,775	1,775	1,750	1,765	− 1	1,817	1,527	1,803
Dec	1,800	1,800	1,790	1,795	− 5	1,818	1,560	1,429
Mar	1,832	1,850	1,832	1,830	− 5	1,850	1,638	9

Est vol 3,125; vol Wed 3,951; open int 23,059, +590.

CBT—Chicago Board of Trade; CME—Chicago Mercantile Exchange; CMX—Commodity Exchange, New York; CSCE—Coffee, Sugar & Cocoa Exchange, New York; CTN—New York Cotton Exchange; IMM—International Monetary Market at CME, Chicago; KC—Kansas City Board of Trade; MPLS—Minneapolis Grain Exchange; NOCE—New Orleans Commodity Exchange; NYFE—New York Futures Exchange, unit of New York Stock Exchange. NYM—New York Mercantile Exchange; WPG—Winnipeg Commodity Exchange.

COFFEE (CSCE)—37,500 lbs.; cents per lb.

	Open	High	Low	Settle	Change	Lifetime High	Lifetime Low	Open Interest
Mar83	130.49	130.50	128.10	128.16	− 1.71	142.49	106.00	3,844
May	125.25	125.80	123.60	123.62	− 1.13	135.40	103.51	2,272
July	121.25	122.00	120.45	120.45	− 1.30	130.50	102.00	1,694
Sept	119.75	119.75	118.00	118.25	− .58	126.50	101.00	1,111
Dec	117.30	117.30	116.25	115.90	− .45	123.00	98.00	514
Mar84	115.00	115.25	115.00	114.51	+ .13	121.75	113.50	110
May	113.00	113.00	113.00	112.00	....	115.00	111.50	20

Est vol 1,333; vol Wed 2,134; open int 9,565, +101.

COTTON (CTN)—50,000 lbs.; cents per lb.

	Open	High	Low	Settle	Change	Lifetime High	Lifetime Low	Open Interest
Mar83	66.75	67.15	66.40	66.72	+ .09	76.68	64.40	12,133
May	68.00	68.30	67.75	67.90	+ .13	77.50	65.80	5,447
July	69.05	69.25	68.75	68.90	+ .10	78.60	66.60	3,806
Oct	68.55	68.75	68.38	68.40	− .05	78.50	65.65	723
Dec	68.90	69.00	68.60	68.77	− .05	77.50	65.50	6,823
Mar84	70.03	70.03	70.03	70.03	....	70.55	67.10	179
May	....	....	....	70.73	+ .23	70.60	69.85	11

Est vol 4,500; vol Wed 5,570; open int 29,122, +624.

ORANGE JUICE (CTN)—15,000 lbs.; cents per lb.

	Open	High	Low	Settle	Change	Lifetime High	Lifetime Low	Open Interest
Jan83	116.20	117.40	116.20	116.20	+ 1.65	162.50	112.40	201
Mar	115.60	117.90	115.25	116.50	+ 2.10	163.25	111.80	4,645
May	116.20	118.25	115.90	117.00	+ 1.95	163.75	112.50	1,580
July	117.40	118.30	116.50	117.85	+ 1.55	142.20	113.85	796
Sept	117.20	119.20	117.00	118.75	+ 1.55	134.50	114.40	1,020
Nov	....	....	....	119.25	+ 1.45	131.95	116.40	243
Jan84	118.50	120.00	118.45	119.75	+ 1.65	132.50	116.25	363
Mar	....	....	....	120.25	+ 1.55	132.20	118.20	85
Mar	....	....	....	120.45	+ 1.55	119.20	119.20	5

Est vol 1,500; vol Wed 1,183; open int 8,866, +66.

POTATOES (NYM)—50,000 lbs.; cents per lb.

	Open	High	Low	Settle	Change	Lifetime High	Lifetime Low	Open Interest
Feb83	5.01	5.01	5.01	5.11	− .09	9.30	4.75	26
Mar	6.10	6.20	6.10	6.20	− .08	9.60	5.55	170
Apr	7.02	7.10	6.95	7.06	− .05	10.74	6.10	3,228

Est vol 334; vol Wed 161; open int 3,424, −87.

SUGAR—WORLD (CSCE)—112,000 lbs.; cents per lb.

	Open	High	Low	Settle	Change	Lifetime High	Lifetime Low	Open Interest
Mar	6.07	6.21	6.05	6.17	+ .07	15.15	6.05	31,696
May	6.46	6.63	6.44	6.61	+ .12	14.90	6.44	14,876
July	6.82	6.95	6.81	6.95	+ .09	13.41	6.81	7,487
Sept	7.19	7.37	7.19	7.28	+ .05	11.45	7.19	1,813
Oct	7.46	7.60	7.47	7.53	+ .04	11.13	7.40	9,778
Mar84	8.55	8.62	8.53	8.53	− .05	10.02	8.48	1,270
May	8.90	8.90	8.90	8.85	− .05	9.65	8.88	73

Est vol 15,986; vol Wed 11,178; open int 66,993, +360.

SUGAR—DOMESTIC (CSCE)—112,000 lbs.; cents per lb.

	Open	High	Low	Settle	Change	Lifetime High	Lifetime Low	Open Interest
Mar83	21.30	21.35	21.30	21.35	....	21.50	19.45	1,604
May	21.62	21.62	21.60	21.57	− .04	21.62	19.55	1,501
July	....	....	....	21.74	+ .01	21.75	20.45	1,710
Sept	....	....	....	21.71	....	21.70	20.50	870
Nov	21.27	21.27	21.10	21.22	− .05	21.33	20.80	947
Mar84	21.30	21.30	21.30	21.30	− .05	21.30	21.25	176
May	21.40	21.40	21.40	21.35	− .10	21.40	21.20	52

Est vol 563; vol Wed 244; open int 6,860, +5.

—METALS & PETROLEUM—

COPPER (CMX)—25,000 lbs.; cents per lb.

	Open	High	Low	Settle	Change	Lifetime High	Lifetime Low	Open Interest
Jan83	73.40	73.40	72.60	72.75	− .90	109.20	57.70	78
Feb	....	....	....	73.10	− .90	71.40	71.30	0
Mar	74.70	75.10	73.65	73.75	− .90	107.00	59.35	58,293
May	75.70	76.00	74.70	74.80	− .90	108.30	60.80	15,627
July	76.65	77.05	75.70	75.85	− .85	103.00	62.60	9,761
Sept	77.60	78.10	76.70	76.80	− .85	93.60	64.15	5,922
Dec	79.10	79.30	78.00	78.05	− .95	93.00	66.30	5,749
Jan84	79.60	79.95	79.45	78.50	− .95	89.50	66.90	812
Mar	80.50	80.95	79.70	79.45	− .95	90.40	68.00	3,955
May	81.40	81.60	80.50	80.40	− .95	84.70	69.00	1,737
July	82.50	82.70	82.30	81.35	− .95	83.10	70.70	1,122
Sept	83.60	84.00	82.80	82.30	− .95	84.10	73.20	1,462

Est vol 13,000; vol Wed 16,507; open int 104,518, +1,066.

GOLD (CMX)—100 troy oz.; $ per troy oz.

	Open	High	Low	Settle	Change	Lifetime High	Lifetime Low	Open Interest
Jan	491.50	491.50	486.50	488.30	− 1.80	491.50	408.00	48
Feb83	491.00	495.00	485.00	490.00	− 2.60	642.00	319.00	45,537
Mar	495.00	497.50	488.50	493.00	− 2.60	497.50	458.00	83
Apr	498.00	502.00	492.00	497.10	− 2.60	604.00	327.00	27,031
June	506.00	510.00	499.00	504.10	− 2.60	596.00	334.00	19,318
Aug	513.00	517.00	510.00	511.50	− 2.60	545.40	348.00	8,081
Oct	521.00	524.50	515.00	519.30	− 2.60	548.50	362.00	5,024
Dec	529.00	542.00	522.00	527.20	− 2.60	554.70	370.00	8,146
Feb84	536.00	537.00	531.00	535.20	− 2.60	557.00	389.00	5,954
Apr	545.00	545.00	543.50	543.50	− 2.60	569.00	385.50	2,562
June	555.00	555.00	555.00	551.90	− 2.60	580.00	409.00	1,029
Aug	566.00	566.00	566.00	560.40	− 2.60	566.00	470.00	405
Oct	576.00	576.00	569.00	569.20	− 2.60	576.00	515.00	136

Est vol 67,000; vol Wed 67,617; open int 123,354, +944.

GOLD (IMM)—100 troy oz.; $ per troy oz.

	Open	High	Low	Settle	Change	Lifetime High	Lifetime Low	Open Interest
Mar83	494.50	498.50	487.50	493.30	− 2.30	887.20	323.00	7,870
June	506.50	508.60	498.00	504.20	− 2.30	674.50	336.00	1,276
Sept	519.50	519.50	510.00	515.60	− 2.20	626.20	350.00	295
Dec	530.00	530.30	523.00	527.50	− 2.00	549.50	437.50	105
Mar84	....	....	....	539.90	− 1.70	535.00	454.70	11

Est vol 8,229; vol Wed 9,054; open int 9,557, +751.

HEATING OIL NO. 2 (NYM)—42,000 gal.; $ per gal.

	Open	High	Low	Settle	Change	Lifetime High	Lifetime Low	Open Interest
Feb	.8225	.8260	.8175	.8229	+ .0030	1.0340	.7965	7,186
Mar	.8060	.8075	.8005	.8044	− .0003	1.0200	.7790	8,615
Apr	.8060	.7890	.7825	.7869	+ .0002	1.0200	.7570	2,863
May	.7795	.7820	.7770	.7770	− .0023	1.0550	.7500	1,559
June	.7800	.7810	.7765	.7770	− .0020	.9220	.7510	409
July	.7800	.7815	.7750	.7767	− .0033	.9475	.7570	298
Aug	.7850	.7850	.7810	.7820	− .0030	.8200	.7775	27
Sept	.7925	.7925	.7925	.7925	− .0015	.8400	.7910	9
Oct	....	....	....	.8080	....	.8010	.8000	7
Nov	.8150	.8150	.8150	.8150	....	.8700	.8075	43
Dec	....	....	....	.8225	....	1.0090	.8125	49

Est vol 5,282; vol Wed 5,549; open int 21,065, −707.

PLATINUM (NYM)—50 troy oz.; $ per troy oz.

	Open	High	Low	Settle	Change	Lifetime High	Lifetime Low	Open Interest
Jan	484.00	484.00	474.00	477.80	+ 1.90	484.00	256.50	2,210
Feb	....	....	....	485.30	+ 3.10	384.00	365.00	2
Mar	488.00	488.00	472.00	485.30	+ 3.10	488.00	411.00	62
Apr	490.00	492.00	476.50	485.30	+ 1.40	492.00	263.00	13,464
July	496.00	498.00	484.50	493.30	+ 2.10	498.00	276.50	1,697
Oct	509.00	509.00	492.00	501.90	+ 2.50	509.00	298.50	1,052
Jan84	510.00	515.00	503.00	510.90	+ 2.80	515.00	325.00	129
Apr	519.50	528.00	519.00	520.10	+ 2.80	528.50	381.00	91

Est vol 6,020; vol Wed 5,900; open int 18,707, +677.

SILVER (CMX)—5,000 troy oz.; cents per troy oz.

	Open	High	Low	Settle	Change	Lifetime High	Lifetime Low	Open Interest
Jan83	1248.0	1264.0	1244.0	1253.0	+ 2.5	1264.0	518.0	240
Feb	1263.0	1270.0	1248.0	1258.0	+ 2.5	1270.0	965.0	54
Mar	1264.0	1278.0	1245.0	1267.0	+ 3.0	1278.0	533.0	23,224
May	1283.0	1297.0	1264.0	1286.4	+ 2.9	1449.0	550.0	6,287
July	1304.0	1317.0	1285.0	1306.4	+ 2.7	1350.0	563.0	3,255
Sept	1325.0	1340.0	1316.0	1326.4	+ 2.5	1340.0	587.0	1,274
Dec	1365.0	1380.0	1340.0	1358.0	+ 2.5	1380.0	615.0	1,632
Jan84	1377.0	1383.0	1377.0	1368.6	+ 2.5	1383.0	680.0	46
Mar	1398.0	1410.0	1373.0	1389.8	+ 2.5	1410.0	628.0	1,014
May	1425.0	1425.0	1414.0	1411.3	+ 2.5	1425.0	700.0	672
July	....	....	....	1433.3	+ 2.5	1429.0	962.0	350
Sept	1490.0	1495.0	1450.0	1455.5	+ 2.5	1495.0	1075.0	590

Est vol 28,000; vol Wed 24,872; open int 38,638, +650.

SILVER (CBT)—1,000 troy oz.; cents per troy oz.

	Open	High	Low	Settle	Change	Lifetime High	Lifetime Low	Open Interest
Jan83	1254.0	1254.0	1240.0	1259.0	+ 4.0	1259.0	908.0	11
Feb	1250.0	1270.0	1236.0	1264.0	+ 5.0	1503.5	530.0	7,626
Mar	1260.0	1280.0	1249.0	1273.0	+ 3.5	1280.0	1103.0	180
Apr	1272.0	1289.0	1256.0	1283.5	+ 4.5	1434.0	545.0	7,251
June	1294.0	1312.0	1275.0	1304.0	+ 6.0	1470.0	560.0	3,484
Aug	1317.0	1330.0	1295.0	1325.0	+ 6.0	1498.0	575.0	616
Oct	1335.0	1345.0	1325.0	1346.0	+ 7.0	1530.0	590.0	402
Dec	1360.0	1375.0	1335.0	1367.0	+ 8.0	1375.0	625.0	911
Feb84	1380.0	1400.0	1370.0	1388.0	+ 9.0	1400.0	639.5	143
Apr	1405.0	1430.0	1390.0	1409.0	+ 4.0	1430.0	654.0	634

Est vol 13,967; vol Wed 12,447; open int 21,258, +1,059.

—WOOD—

LUMBER (CME)—130,000 bd. ft.; $ per 1,000 bd. ft.

	Open	High	Low	Settle	Change	Lifetime High	Lifetime Low	Open Interest
Jan83	177.00	177.90	176.50	177.50	+ 1.00	205.50	139.00	456
Mar	193.20	193.20	191.20	192.50	+ .60	209.80	146.80	4,982
May	203.50	203.60	201.50	202.20	....	205.50	151.50	1,872
July	211.30	211.60	210.00	211.10	+ .10	214.00	158.00	1,183
Sept	215.30	215.30	214.30	215.00	+ .10	216.50	163.80	845
Nov	216.20	216.30	215.30	215.30	+ .30	216.50	168.00	444
Jan	216.00	221.60	221.00	210.00	....	222.10	179.00	90
Mar	225.70	225.80	225.00	225.00	....	227.00	206.50	18

Est vol 1,729; vol Wed 2,266; open int 9,890, +559.

PLYWOOD (CBT)—76,032 sq. ft.; $ per 1,000 sq. ft.

	Open	High	Low	Settle	Change	Lifetime High	Lifetime Low	Open Interest
Jan83	199.50	200.00	198.50	199.20	+ 1.00	218.60	157.00	112
Mar	202.50	203.00	201.70	202.90	+ 1.20	204.00	162.50	1,129
May	206.50	207.20	206.00	207.00	+ 1.50	208.50	167.00	267
July	211.60	211.60	210.60	211.00	+ .70	212.50	170.00	452
Sept	214.30	214.50	214.00	214.50	+ .70	216.50	185.00	59
Nov	217.70	217.70	217.70	217.70	....	218.50	206.50	33

Est vol 190; vol Wed 295; open int 2,052, −40.

Source: The Wall Street Journal, January 14, 1983.

capitalize on small movements in commodity prices and on the volume of their activity. Their willingness to take positions at prevailing bids and asks contributes enormously to the liquidity of the market.

Spreaders are speculators attempting to capitalize on "unnatural" or "unjustifiable" relationships between commodity prices. They may find opportunities in the differences in contract prices between maturity months for a given commodity, between the same maturity month of two different commodities, and between the same (or different) maturity months of a commodity futures contract and that of a derivative product (for example, between November soybeans and October soybean oil). The activities of spreaders allow for realignment of commodities futures prices and thus contribute to the efficiency of the market as long as their activities produce profits in the long run. Spread positions are discussed in greater detail later in this chapter.

Other individuals playing a critical role in the operations of the exchanges are the floor brokers who fill the orders of various clients, ranging from farmers to manufacturers to food exporters or importers to speculators.

5.10 THE ANALYTICAL APPROACHES TO COMMODITIES

Two schools of thought dominate commodities analysis as they do stock analysis. They are the fundamentalist school and the technical school.

The technical school believes in the same principles and uses the same techniques as those used for common stocks. Most commodities technicians pay considerable attention to moving averages and related forecasting tools, and frequently to the changes in the fundamentals of a commodity.

The fundamental school, on the other hand, concentrates its efforts on the factors influencing supply and demand and on the resulting impact on commodities prices. The interaction between supply and demand produces equilibrium prices. It is the departure from equilibrium prices that offers opportunities in the market place on which traders may capitalize.

To cover the supply and demand factors for every commodity is beyond the scope of this book. Instead, we shall undertake a brief analysis of the case of wheat.

Wheat

The supply of and demand for wheat are influenced by a variety of factors, some of which are predictable and quantifiable and others which are not. The major relationships in the wheat economy are shown in Figure 5.1.

The identification of the supply and demand factors and the evaluation of their relative importance is at the heart of fundamental analysis.

The sources of wheat supplies in the United States are current production, imports, old-crop carry-over, and government supply from accumulated inventory under various subsidy schemes administered by the U.S. Department of Agriculture. The most important source of supply is current production.

The wheat crop year runs from July 1 to June 30. During this period, seven grades of wheat are harvested: hard red winter, soft red winter, hard red spring, durum, red durum, white, and mixed wheat. About 75 percent of U.S. wheat production is in the form of hard red winter wheat. Hard wheat is used for bread, soft wheat for pastry.

In terms of yield per acre, the winter wheat is most productive. Winter wheat produces

FIGURE 5.1. Major relationships in the wheat economy.

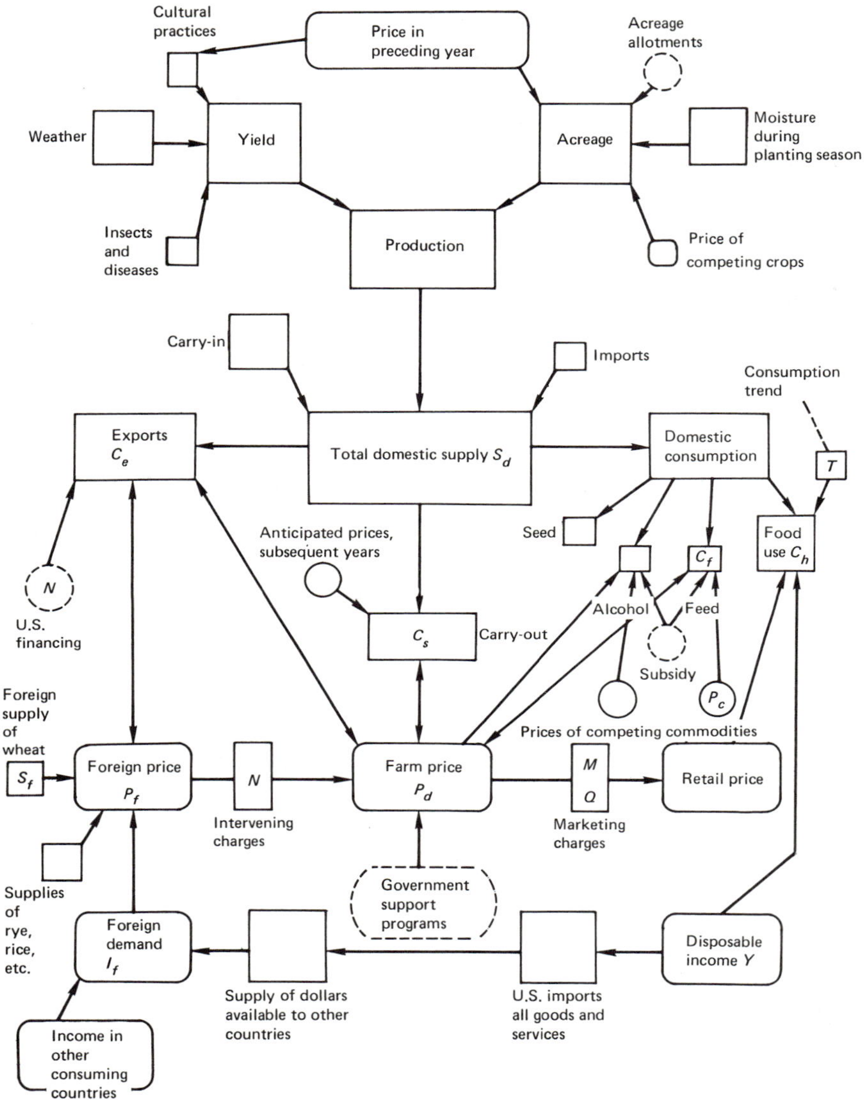

Source: The Demand and Price Structure for Wheat, Technical Bulletin 1136, U.S. Department of Agriculture, 1955, p. 12.

about 31 bushels per acre, spring wheat about 28 bushels, and durum wheat about 26 bushels. The average expected production of wheat, assuming no weather or other disasters, should equal the yield per acre (average of 28 bushels) multiplied by the number of acres expected to be planted (taking the Federal acreage diversion program and other limiting programs into consideration).

Since the wheat market is a world market, the supplies of other countries should also be estimated. The estimates by Merrill Lynch for the 1980–81 crop year per country are shown in Table 5.7. The U.S.S.R. leads all countries not only in wheat production, but also in wheat imports. Of all the wheat produced in the United States, about 60

TABLE 5.7
Total World Wheat Production, Export and Import by Countries (in million metric tons)

	1976/77	1977/78	1978/79	1979/80	ML[a] Estimates 1980/81
Production					
U.S.	58.3	55.4	48.9	58.3	64.3
Canada	23.6	19.9	21.1	17.2	18.7
Australia	11.7	9.4	18.1	16.1	10.0
Argentina	11.0	5.7	8.1	8.0	7.5
EC-9	39.1	38.4	47.6	46.1	51.3
U.S.S.R.	96.9	92.2	120.8	90.1	90.0
China	45.0	41.0	54.0	60.5	55.0
India	28.8	29.0	31.7	35.0	30.5
World	415.5	383.9	447.6	419.8	428.0
Export					
U.S.	26.1	31.5	32.3	37.2	41.5
Canada	12.9	15.9	13.5	15.0	15.0
Australia	8.5	11.1	6.7	15.0	10.5
Argentina	5.6	2.6	3.3	4.7	4.3
EC-9	4.9	5.0	8.0	9.8	12.0
World	63.1	73.1	71.9	85.4	90.0
Import					
Japan	5.5	5.8	5.7	5.6	5.5
U.S.S.R.	4.6	6.6	5.1	12.0	14.0
China	3.2	8.6	8.0	8.8	13.0
EC-9	4.4	5.5	4.6	4.5	4.5
East Europe	6.3	5.0	4.2	5.9	5.8
World	63.1	73.1	71.9	85.4	90.0

[a] ML = Merrill Lynch
Source: Merrill Lynch Pierce Fenner & Smith, Inc., Commodity Division.

percent is exported annually, 30 percent is milled into flour, and the remaining 10 percent is used for seeding and for animal feed.

The demand for U.S. wheat is predominantly a world demand for U.S. wheat exports. The United States is and has been the leading exporter of wheat in the world. The factors influencing this demand are as follows:

1. Wheat prices and the prices of substitutable commodities.
2. Income levels overseas and the availability of dollars in the importing countries, or the availability of credit.
3. The income and the price elasticity of demand for wheat. A demand function is price elastic if, for a small decrease in price, the quantity demanded increases sufficiently to increase the total revenue of the selling firm. Mathematically, this can be expressed as

$$\xi = \Delta Q / \Delta P \cdot P / Q$$

where ξ = price elasticity
Q = quantity,
P = price

if $\xi > 1$, the demand function is said to be elastic.

4. The nature of government programs.
5. A host of other factors such as taste, customs, tariffs, and so forth, which may not be possible to incorporate in an equilibrium model.

The problem to the fundamentalist is not only to isolate the relevant factors that bear on supply and demand, but also to determine their relative importance and the extent to which they are already reflected in observable spot prices.

It is this complexity of fundamental analysis and its susceptibility to error in fact or in judgment that drive many traders into technical analysis. Some traders have derived larger payoffs from studying the market itself (technical analysis) than from the elaborate and often imperfect study of supply and demand factors and the resulting "equilibrium prices." Having briefly looked at the determinants of spot prices, we now examine futures commodities prices.

5.11 THE DETERMINANTS OF COMMODITY FUTURES PRICES

The inability of those who produce, handle, and process commodities to purchase insurance for protection against value risks provided the impetus for the futures markets where hedgers can shift risk onto speculators.

The activities of three agents in the futures market must be understood in order to arrive at a method for rationalizing the process of determining futures prices. These agents are the hedger, the speculator, and the arbitrageur.

The hedger is primarily motivated by the security and not the profit derived from a futures transaction. A hedger protects a cash position against price declines through the sale of a futures contract. He gains protection against the possibility of increased costs of anticipated future purchases through the purchase of a futures contract. Examples of precisely how a hedge is achieved are provided later in this chapter.

A speculator, on the other hand, is motivated by the profits that are achieved through the successful prediction of price movements in a futures transaction. As compensation for the uncertainty of price expectations, the speculator charges a risk premium. Speculators expecting a price rise exceeding that suggested by a futures price would buy futures contracts. They would sell these contracts if their expectations were the opposite.

An arbitrageur capitalizes, among other things, on unjustifiable price differences over space (for example, between one market and another) or over time (between one maturity month and another). Pure arbitrage involves zero risk and no commitment of capital.

In addition to understanding the function of these three operators, we must understand the "basis."

The basis is the differential at a point in time between the futures price of a commodity and the cash or spot price of the same commodity. For example, if the July corn futures contract is trading at $2.70 and the spot price is $2.40, the basis is "30 under." Futures prices often exceed spot prices, but not always. The closer the spot price is to the higher futures price, the *stronger* the basis is said to be. The wider the difference, the *weaker* the basis. A strong basis (spot price close to or exceeding the futures price)

reflects excess demand for the commodity. In this case, the cash market is indicating its willingness to pay for spot delivery earlier than normal. A weak basis indicates that the market has a sufficient supply cash crop and is unwilling to make early storage payments. This weak basis usually occurs at harvest time when supplies are plentiful.

An understanding of the basis—that is, the relationship between futures prices and spot prices—requires an understanding of net carrying (storage) costs.

Let SP = spot price
FP = futures price
c = net carrying charges
$c = C - CY$

where C = carrying (storage) charges = interest costs + insurance costs + storage costs + loading and unloading charges associated with carrying a commodity inventory

CY is the convenience yield[2] or the benefits accruing from holding stock of a commodity today instead of the cash for purchasing that commodity tomorrow. The benefits manifest themselves in the form of lower costs of maintaining an output or sales level and in lower costs for varying the level of output by relying on existing stock as opposed to the purchase of stock as it is needed. The more specialized the commodity is, the greater the benefits will be.[3] The value of c could, therefore, be positive or negative depending on the relationship between C and CY. The concept of convenience yield can thus explain why deferred deliveries can be priced below or above near deliveries or spot delivery (the nearest delivery of all). Storage of commodities in this case will not be done exclusively on the basis of expected price appreciation, which implies that the price of a deferred delivery will always exceed that of nearer deliveries.

Therefore

$$FP - SP \gtreqless 0$$

If $FP - SP > 0 \Rightarrow$ contango[4]
$FP - SP < 0 \Rightarrow$ backwardation[4] or an *inverted market*

Which of the signs prevail in the equation above obviously depends on the value of c. Under conditions of certainty,

$$FP = SP + c$$

for if $FP < SP + c$, hedgers would be better off carrying their stock and selling it at the date that coincides with the maturity of the future contract instead of selling their

---

[2] See **Nicholas Kaldor,** "Speculation and Economic Stability," *Review of Economic Studies,* vol. 7, (1939–1940).

[3] See the excellent work of **Gerda Blau,** "Some Aspects of the Theory of Futures Trading," *Review of Economic Studies,* vol. 12, (1944–1945), pp. 1–30.

[4] These two terms were used by **Keynes** in an essay in the *Manchester Guardian Commercial* in 1923.

commodities forward for future delivery. The reverse strategy would be more profitable if $FP > SP + c$.

Under conditions of uncertainty, speculators would buy or sell futures contracts, depending on whether their expectations about future prices, EP, coincide with the maturity of the futures contract. If $EP > FP$, speculators would be long on the futures contract. That is, they would buy for future delivery and close (sell) the contract at a higher price in the future or take delivery of the commodity, an unlikely course, and sell it at the higher spot rate. A short position would be established by speculators if $EP < FP$. They sell at FP and close the position by buying at EP. Assuming their expectations materialize, profits will accrue to the speculators.

The hedgers would enter futures contracts to offset their current or expected cash position, independent of what the EP is going to be. Hedgers do not forecast EP and are only interested in shifting the risk that results from price fluctuations onto the speculators.

Those who make sure that the relationship between future prices and spot prices is in equilibrium are the arbitrageurs. They capitalize on any deviation between FP and $SP + c$.

If $FP - SP > c$, arbitrageurs would profit by selling futures, buying spot, and holding stock until delivery. If, on the other hand, $FP - SP < c$, arbitrageurs would pursue the opposite strategy; they would sell spot and buy futures. The arbitrage profit would equal $FP - SP - c$. If arbitrage is working perfectly, it would ensure, at least for a while, that equilibrium prices prevail—that is, $FP = SP + c$.

The above discussion on the determinants of futures prices is referred to as the *Price-of-Storage Theory*. This theory explains all the cases where $FP \gtreqless SP + c$:

> *the negative prices occur when supplies are relatively scarce. They then impose pressure on hedging merchandisers and processors to avoid holding unnecessarily large quantities out of consumption in the form of stocks which they can do without. Thus a negative price of storage makes available for consumption in a year of shortage, supplies which would otherwise be tied up in "convenience stocks."* [5]

If agricultural commodity supplies are plentiful, as they are around harvest time, the calculation of future prices—using wheat as an example—is made as follows (CBT):

1. Find the cash price (quoted daily in the *Wall Street Journal* and other sources) for a given type wheat deliverable against the contract.
2. Determine the storage and insurance rate per month per bushel.
3. Determine the interest-rate charge per bushel per month using the prime interest rate.
4. Add 2 and 3 to arrive at total carrying charge.
5. Add 4 and 1 to arrive at the appropriate future price of a bushel.

In the wheat case, the spot price of a bushel of No. 2 soft red wheat deliverable against KC futures contract was \$3.41½ on January 14, 1983.

---

[5] **Holbrook Working,** "The Theory of Price of Storage," *American Economic Review,* (December 1949), p. 1262.

1. Storage and insurance costs per month per bushel = 13.6¢.
2. Interest costs per month per bushel at a 12 percent prime rate = $0.12(\frac{1}{12}) \times 3.41\frac{1}{2} = 0.0342$
3. Total carrying charges = $0.0342 + 0.136 = 0.1702$
4. Total carrying charges per bushel until the maturity of the futures contract = $0.1702 \times$ number of months until delivery.

To determine the exact time period until delivery is difficult because delivery is at the option of the seller. The rules of the exchanges require that the last notice day for delivery be the next to the last business day of the delivery month. The oldest contract receives delivery first. The rules also state that no trading in the maturing contract may take place in the last seven business days.[6]

Since 97 percent of the contracts are not delivered against, it makes sense to price a contract up to the last business day on which it can be traded, which is March 22 in our case.

Thus, the time period left in the life of the contract is that period falling between January 14, 1983, and March 22, 1983, which is equal to 68 days. The adjusted carrying costs are equal to:

$0.1702 \times 68/30 = 0.386$

The future price = spot + carrying costs

$= \$3.41\frac{1}{2} + 0.386 = \textbf{\$3.80.}$

which approximates the settlement price on the March KC futures contract shown in Table 5.6 (p. 162).

We now discuss the theory of "normal backwardation" advanced by J. M. Keynes and by J. R. Hicks.[7]

Normal Backwardation

J. M. Keynes and J. R. Hicks argued that it is in the nature of the market to have the futures price lie below the expected spot price, whether the market is inverted ($SP > FP$) or is a carry market ($SP < FP$). The futures price is a downward-biased estimate of the expected price, and the futures price rises as the futures contract approaches its maturity date.

In this world the speculator is seen as providing a valuable service to the hedger, a service that warrants a positive price. The hedger wishes to shift the price (value) risk onto the speculator. To do so, he is willing to pay a price, a risk premium. The implication is that the net cost of hedging is always positive. It is possible, however, as we shall demonstrate later, that the gains (losses) in the futures market will more than offset

---

[6] Speculators, who avoid the possibility of a delivery, avoid long speculative positions in the nearby months after the first notice day. The first notice day is specified by the exchange and the notice is made by the seller.

[7] See **J. R. Hicks,** *Value and Capital,* ed. 2. Clarendon Press, Oxford, 1950, chap. 10, pp. 130–152.

the losses (gains) in the cash market. That is, hedgers can conceivably, and often do, realize a profit from the hedging transaction itself.

Stated differently, the normal backwardation theory looks at speculators as sellers of insurance to hedgers. Since hedgers, on the average, are net sellers of futures contracts (net short position), speculators must be net buyers of futures contracts.[8] In order to maintain a net long position, speculators charge a positive premium, which is equal to the difference between *EP* and *FP*. The speculator buys at *FP* and sells at *EP*. This premium should be the necessary inducement to the speculator to bear price risk. The determinants of this premium are summarized in Figure 5.2.

Would the theory of backwardation hold if we observe that the futures price exceeds the spot price? Keynes answered in the affirmative. Keynes "maintained that there is still backwardation because the expected spot price exceeds both the current spot price and the futures price."[9]

The normal backwardation theory relies on the following assumptions:

1. Speculators have net long positions in the commodity.
2. Speculators are not capable of forecasting expected spot prices.
3. Speculators are risk-averse.

Grauer and Litzenberger[10] (GL), however, have shown that risk aversion of speculators is neither necessary nor a sufficient condition for backwardation or contango. GL also showed that, in general, futures prices are not good predictors of spot prices.

The speculator (or anyone), the theory argues, could earn a profit simply by having a net long position in futures. He or she simply capitalizes on the upward trend in commodity prices, although unable to forecast expected spot prices. The larger the speculator's position is, the larger the profit. Even if markets were efficient this trend would exist because of the required risk premium, which is an increasing function of the life of the contract.

The acceptance or the rejection of the theory depends, according to Telser, on testing two implications of the theory:

> the first is that, on the average, long speculators should receive profits and short hedgers should suffer losses on their futures transactions. The long speculators' profits must be net of transactions costs. A second implication, the one explored here, is that there is an upward trend in futures prices as the contract approaches maturity. In their (Keynes and Hicks's) theory, the futures price is below the expected spot price by the amount of the insurance premium paid the long speculators by the short hedgers. This insurance premium is the remuneration for the risk of price changes. The risk of an unanticipated price change increases the farther away the maturity date of the futures contract is from the current date, assuming that it is more difficult to foresee the distant future. Since the risk premium is the excess of the expected spot prices

---

[8] See **Lester G. Telser**, "Reply," *Journal of Political Economy,* vol. 68, (August 1960).

[9] **Lester Telser**, "Futures Trading and the Storage of Cotton and Wheat," *Journal of Political Economy,* vol. 66, (June 1958), pp. 233–255.

[10] **F. L. A. Grauer** and **R. H. Litzenberger**, "The Pricing of Commodity Futures Contracts, Nominal Bonds, and Other Risky Assets Under Commodity Price Uncertainty." *Journal of Finance,* vol. 34 (1979), pp. 69–83.

FIGURE 5.2. **Summary of factors influencing the marginal risk premia of hedgers and speculators.**

Given: the degree of uncertainty of expectations and the degree of perfection, liquidity and security in the market.

A Hedger's →   ← A Speculator's

willingness to enter into risk commitments by contracting forward in the futures market (by either buying or selling futures)

in order to neutralize opposite risks in the cash market

in order to make a profit by risk bearing

will be the greater

1. The stronger the hedger's subjective aversion to risk.

2. The larger the size of his risk commitments *in the cash market* (i.e. the possible loss relatively to total assets);

3. The *less* definite his opinion on the expected price (EP), the more definite the hedger's opinion on EP, the greater his inducement to turn into a speculator by leaving his cash commitments unhedged;

4. The higher the expected degree of price variability in general for the standard grade as compared with the variability of the index of *all* other prices relevant to the trader;

5. The higher the proportion of hedgeable risks to nonhedgeable risks.

1. The *less* the speculator's subjective aversion to risk.

2. The *less* the size of his *total risk* commitments; (i.e., the possible loss relatively to total assets).

3. The *more* definite his opinion of the expected price (EP);

4. The greater the difference between the forward price (FP) and the expected price (EP).

Source: Gerda Blau, "Some Aspects of the Theory of Futures Trading," *The Review of Economic Studies,* vol. 12, (1944–1945), pp. 18–19.

over the futures price, this excess decreases as the futures contract approaches maturity. Under normal conditions, when the expected spot price is not expected to change, this implies that futures price rises as it approaches maturity. Although we cannot directly observe the expected spot price, the theory that the futures price is a biased estimate of the expected spot price can be tested

by observing whether there is an upward trend in the futures price as it approaches maturity [emphasis added].[11]

Telser tested the hypothesis that futures prices are unbiased predictors of expected spot prices and was unable to reject the null hypothesis. Futures prices did not display a trend.

Stone,[12] in an earlier study (1901), also found no evidence of bias, but a study by the Federal Trade Commission showed a downward bias in futures prices of wheat and corn but not of oats.[13]

Paul Cootner[14] presented evidence confirming the presence of risk premiums in several commodity futures contracts.

Charles Rockwell,[15] in a very extensive study covering the 1947–1965 period, found evidence of consistent price rises when speculators held *net short* positions, and that the tendency toward normal backwardation when speculators held a net long position was insignificant.

D. S. Miracle[16] was able to show that in the case of the egg futures market a bias in favor of Keynes's hypothesis was found during one period whereas the opposite results obtained in another.

These and other studies do not allow the researcher to convincingly confirm or deny the validity of the normal backwardation theory. This must await further evidence.

The Behavior of Futures Prices

The behavior of futures prices has been of interest to traders, regulators, and academicians. Traders are interested in price trends which allow for a trading rule that produces above-average rates of return. Regulators are also interested in efficiency because they want markets in which every trader feels confident that no one person or group of persons could expropriate his or her wealth because of superior ability to digest information or because of a hold on the market trading mechanism. The academic interest stems from the interest in fairness as well as efficient allocation of resources.

Before presenting the evidence on the behavior of futures prices, we should take note of the admonishments of Danthine[17] regarding the link between efficiency and martingale (the general case of a random walk) processes in the commodities case.

---

[11] Ibid., **Telser,** p. 243.

[12] U.S. 56th Congress, 2nd session, U.S. Industrial Commission Report (1900–1901), House Document 94.

[13] U.S. Federal Trade Commission, Report on Grain Trade, Washington, D.C., 1920–1926.

[14] **Paul Cootner,** "Speculation and Hedging," *Food Research Institute Studies,* Supplement 7 (1967), pp. 84–103.

[15] **Charles Rockwell,** "Normal Backwardation, Forecasting, and the Returns to Commodity Futures Traders," *Food Research Institute Studies,* Supplement 7 (1967), pp. 107–130.

[16] **D. S. Miracle,** "The Egg Futures Market: 1940 to 1966," *Food Research Institute Studies* (1972), pp. 269–292.

[17] **J. P. Danthine,** "Martingale, Market Efficiency, and Commodity Prices," *European Economic Review,* vol. 10 (1977), pp. 1–17.

Danthine argued that nonrandom processes may be observed in an inefficient commodities market because of commodity shortages and diminishing marginal rate of transformation over time. The presence of price trends is generally equated with market inefficiency.

The first study suggesting that futures prices follow a random process was completed by H. Working[18] in 1958. Futures prices were found to be nearly random. Houthakker[19] found evidence of trends in the prices of corn and wheat futures during 1921–39 and 1947–56. L. H. Rocca[20] and W. C. Labys and C. W. J. Granger[21] found evidence in support of a martingale process—a process requiring uncorrelated price changes but not a common distribution for price changes that the random walk model requires.

T. F. Martell and B. P. Helms,[22] using data covering every transaction on several commodities, found evidence of serial dependence. Similar evidence was found by S. Khoury and G. Jones[23] with a very important difference. Using per-transaction data on soybean contracts covering every contract month between February 13, 1981 and July 14, 1981, Khoury and Jones found evidence of serial dependence. However, that serial dependence disappeared after one-half hour of trading. Four tests were used and they all yielded the same results. The tests were the equal probability test, the runs test, the serial correlation test, and the spectral analysis test. The presence of serial correlation in the per-transaction data for every contract month suggests net benefit from being a floor trader.

Several studies tested for nonlinear dependencies in futures prices. The latest we are aware of is by R. Leuthold.[24] Using spectral analysis and filter rules tests on cattle contracts between 1965 and 1970, Leuthold found evidence of excess profit opportunities even after accounting for commission costs.

Additional evidence is offered by the market and the market participants. The great success of several research houses offering technical analysis on commodities, the sales of books on technical analysis, the heavy use of moving averages by market traders, the market movements which have no relation to underlying supply and demand factors, and the profitability of arbitrage departments in many investment houses are all examples of people trying to capitalize on market inefficiencies which appear to be frequent and repetitive.

[18] H. Working, "A Theory of Anticipatory Prices," Reprinted in *Selected Writings,* Chicago Board of Trade, pp. 33–43.

[19] H. S. Houthakker, "Systematic and Random Elements in Short-Term Price Movements," *American Economic Review,* vol. 51 (1961), pp. 164–1672.

[20] L. H. Rocca, "Time Series Analysis of Commodity Futures Prices," University of California, Berkeley, Unpublished Ph.D. dissertation (1969).

[21] W. C. Labys and C. W. J. Granger, *Speculation, Hedging, and Commodity Price Forecasts,* D. C. Heath Co., Lexington, Mass., 1970.

[22] T. F. Martell and B. P. Helms, "A Reexamination of Price Changes in the Commodity Futures Market," *International Futures Trading Seminar,* vol. 5, Chicago Board of Trade (1978), pp. 136–159.

[23] S. J. Khoury and G. Jones, "Daily Price Limits on Futures Contracts: Nature, Impact, and Justification," Working Paper, University of Notre Dame (1983).

[24] R. M. Leuthold, "Random Walk and Price Trends: The Live Cattle Futures Market," *Journal of Finance,* vol. 27 (1972), pp. 879–889.

5.12 THE USES OF COMMODITIES FUTURES CONTRACTS

Commodities futures contracts have proved and continue to prove their utility to various economic agents and to the economy as a whole. The dramatic increase in commodities futures contracts traded on the various exchanges (Table 5.1) is a strong indicator of the merits of futures trading. Commodities futures are used by hedgers, speculators, and arbitrageurs.

Hedging with Commodities Futures

Producers, processors, and marketers of actual physical commodities have found a refuge from price risk in the futures market. This market has permitted them to shift risk onto the speculators.

Abraham Kamara, in an excellent survey article on futures markets, identified four basic categories of hedging strategies:

1. Carrying charge hedging—is done simultaneously with the holding of commodity stocks for direct profit from storage; the hedger speculates on the basis—i.e., the spot—futures price differential.

2. Operational hedging—is done to facilitate operations in a merchandising or processing business. The benefits depend on the existence of a high correlation between changes in spot prices and changes in futures prices over very short intervals day to day or even intraday.

3. Selective hedging—the hedging of commodity stocks according to price expectations when hedgers may hedge incompletely or overhedge according to circumstances.

4. Anticipatory hedging—also guided by price expectations. Used by producers or processors as a substitute for a merchandising contract that will be made later, with the purpose of taking advantage of the current futures price.[25]

The essence of hedging is to take a position in the futures market opposite that in the cash market. If a farmer is actually or prospectively long on 1,000,000 bushels of wheat, he would sell (short)[26] 200 contracts (each wheat futures contract covers 5,000 bushels on the CBT) in the wheat futures markets. Since cash and futures prices tend to move in tandem because they are influenced by the same supply/demand factors, whatever gains (losses) are realized in the futures market will offset the losses (gains)

---

[25] **Abraham Kamara,** "Issues in Futures Markets—A Survey." Working Paper Series CSFM-30, Center for the Study of Futures Markets, Columbia University, New York, March 1982, p. 2.

[26] A short position in the futures market, unlike its counterpart in the stock market, does not require the borrowing of a commodity for delivery to the buyer. The reasons are that the contract does not require delivery until maturity date and that almost all buyers never intend to take delivery of the commodity. There is no "equity" in a futures margin position as there is in a stock margin.

in the cash market and the farmer will have locked in a price for his wheat. This obviously assumes that the farmer holds the futures contract until maturity. Otherwise, the gains (losses) on the futures market may be larger or smaller than the losses (gains) in the cash market depending on how futures prices move in relation to cash prices (that is, depending on the change in the basis.)

The basis, as discussed earlier, is the difference between the futures price and the cash price. As the maturity date of a futures contract approaches, the futures contract would approximate more and more the cash contract. That is why a cash contract is a special case of a futures contract where the delivery period shrinks to one day. Therefore, the farther away from maturity one is, the larger, *ceteris paribus,* the size of the basis will be. Also, the farther away from maturity, the greater the instability in the basis—given changes in supply and/or demand. The stability of the basis is of considerable significance to the hedger if the futures contract is not going to be carried to maturity—that is, if the futures contract is not going to be delivered against or the hedger accepting delivery on it.

Since 97 percent or more of futures contracts are never delivered against, the behavior of the basis becomes of paramount importance. We now look at the impact of changes in the basis on a long hedge and on a short hedge. Before doing so, let us quote from the *Commodity Trading Manual* of the Chicago Board of Trade:

> *By counterbalancing his cash position with an opposite and equivalent position in the futures market, a hedger replaces the risk of price fluctuation with risks of a change in the relationship between the cash price and the futures price of a commodity, thus the importance of the basis.*

Long Hedge

A long hedge is used by the processor, seller, exporter, or user of a commodity. The objective is to "fix" the purchase price of a commodity between the consideration date and the actual purchase date.

A cereal manufacturer anticipating a need for 40,000 bushels of wheat in April 1983 could buy them today and store them until April, or alternatively he can wait until April to buy them in the spot (cash) market. The latter option would leave the manufacturer exposed to price risk. By April the price of wheat could be higher. To gain protection against a price increase, the manufacturer would hedge in the futures market. The process is as follows:

Cash Market

January 17, 1983
Expect 40,000 bushels of wheat in April 1983. Current price per bushel is equal to $3.4150.

April 15, 1983
Buy 40,000 bushels, spot market price (assumed) $3.5000.

Futures Market

January 17, 1983
Buy eight* May futures contracts (CBT) at per bushel $3.5275.

April 15, 1983
Sell (to offset) eight May futures contracts at $3.675.

Results

Opportunity loss = $3.5000 − $3.4150   Actual gain = $3.675 − $3.5275
             = $0.085   = $.1475

Net gain per bushel = 0.1475 − 0.0850 = **$0.0625**

* The matching of the size of the cash position, with that of the futures position is referred to as a *naive hedge*. This type hedge is not always optimal.

Had the opportunity loss equalled the actual gain, the hedge would be a "perfect" hedge.

The net gain on the hedge results from the fact that the basis has weakened; that is, the difference between the futures price and the cash price has widened, $FP >> SP$. Had the basis remained the same, the net gain would be zero. Had the basis strengthened, the net gain could have become negative, and the hedge would not have been as effective as the manufacturer would have wished. We now look at the effects of a stronger basis:

Cash Market   **Futures Market**

April 15, 1983   April 15, 1983
Cash Price = $3.55   Futures Price = $3.62

Results

Opportunity loss = $3.55 − $3.415   Actual gain = $3.62 − $3.5275
             = $0.135   = $0.0925

Net loss = $0.0925 − 0.1350 = **($0.0425)**

Thus, in this case, the strengthening of the basis has produced a net loss. The hedge is not a very effective one.

The Short (Selling) Hedge

A farmer expecting to harvest and sell his wheat in July 1983 is obviously concerned with the price of wheat falling from its current levels. If satisfied with the current price levels and wishing to at least lock them in, the wheat farmer would hedge in the futures market by selling futures contracts to offset the long expected cash position. The process is as follows:

Cash Market   **Futures Market**

January 17, 1983   January 17, 1983
Expect to harvest and sell 10,000 bushels   Sell two July futures contracts (CBT) at
  of wheat. $3.5825 per bushel (Table 5.6)
No actual position in the cash market.
Current cash price for wheat = $3.415

July, 1983

Sell 10,000 bushels at $3.35[27]

Buy (to offset) two July futures contracts at $3.40.

Results

Opportunity loss = $0.065   Actual gain = $0.1825

Net gain = 0.1825 − 0.065 = **$0.1175**

The net gain in this short hedge results from the strengthening of the basis. This is precisely the opposite result obtained in a long hedge with a strengthening basis. Similarly, a weakening basis will diminish, if not eliminate, the effectiveness of a short hedge.

Had the basis weakened, the farmer might have decided to roll the hedge forward, that is, close out the hedge in the July contract, and establish a new short position in another contract month where the basis is expected to strengthen. Meanwhile, he holds onto his wheat longer with the attendant storage costs.

Thus far we have concentrated on hedging in the wheat market. Hedges in other markets work in essentially the same way. To cover hedging for each commodity is beyond the scope of this book.

Before we move to a discussion on spreads, we shall list the other advantages of hedging to, for example, a farmer.[28] In addition to reducing price risk and locking in the basis, they are:

1. Improve the chances for a bank loan if not for lower interest rates. A hedged crop is a "safer" crop from a banker's perspective.
2. Set a ceiling on production costs. An example is the cost of feed to a hog farmer.
3. Allow for better production plans as prices fluctuate and as the demand for the crop fluctuates.
4. Stabilize profit margins through hedging production costs and the sale price of the final product.
5. Since the futures market is a costless tool for price discovery of expected spot prices, this should help the farmer plan his sales (sell now versus sell tomorrow).
6. Extend the selling season through the sale of a crop yet to be harvested in the futures market.
7. Reduce inventory levels. Futures contracts are an excellent vehicle for farmers with insufficient storage capacity and with a desire to minimize the holding of an inventory stock while maintaining an access (a commitment) to the commodity.

We now look at an increasing popular investment/speculative strategy.

---

[27] It must be noted that the difference between the futures price and the spot price represents the cost of delivering wheat against the futures contract. If the farmer had the wheat that is acceptable for delivery against the futures contracts, and if that wheat was in the location designated by the exchange, he would have simply chosen to deliver the harvested wheat against the futures contract and would have effectively locked in the futures price back on November 24, 1981.

[28] Based on *Professional Hedging Handbook,* Mid-American Commodity Exchange, Chicago, pp. 6–7.

Spreads

A spread represents a simultaneous long position in one futures contract and a short position in another. A spread is established in order to take advantage of expected changes in the relationships between different futures prices.

The popularity of spreads stems from two basic features:

1. Spreads have a lower price risk than an outright position in a futures contract, for the same market factors influence the short position as the long position.
2. The margin requirements on spreads are lower than those on an equivalent but separate positions in the futures market.

There are four basic types of spreads—the intermonth spread, the intermarket spread, the intercommodity spread, and the commodity/product spread.

Intermonth Spreads

Experience with commodities indicates that, for a given set of events, near-month contracts gradually appreciate in price more than do distant ones. This is so for most commodities although recent evidence suggests the contrary.[29] Thus, a bull spread calls for a long position in the near month and a short position in the distant month. The bear spread, on the other hand, calls for a short position in the near month and a long position in the distant month.

The results of the spread, as in the financial futures case, would depend on whether the market were inverted—price of near contract P_N > price of distant contract P_D— or noninverted—$P_N < P_D$—and on whether the spread strengthened or weakened. We now discuss spread strategies when markets are noninverted and when they are inverted.

$P_D > P_N$ or Noninverted Market

Bear Spread

Figure 5.3 shows the behavior of the spread between July 82 soybean and November 82 soybean during November 1981. An astute trader could have capitalized on at least the major swings in the spread. With the expectation that the spread will weaken from its level on January 14, 1982, the trader may wish to

---

[29] **Paul A. Samuelson,** in a classic article titled "Proof That Properly Anticipated Prices Fluctuate Randomly" in *Industrial Management Review* vol. 6 (1965), pp. 120–123, advanced a theory stating that the volatility of futures price changes per unit of time increases as the time to maturity decreases. The empirical evidence provides weak support for this theory. The latest study by **Ronald W. Anderson,** "The Determinants of the Volatility of Futures Prices" in Columbia University Working Papers Series (December 1981), showed that Samuelson's theory applies only to a few commodities.

FIGURE 5.3. Behavior of the spread between July 82 soybean and November 82 soybean.

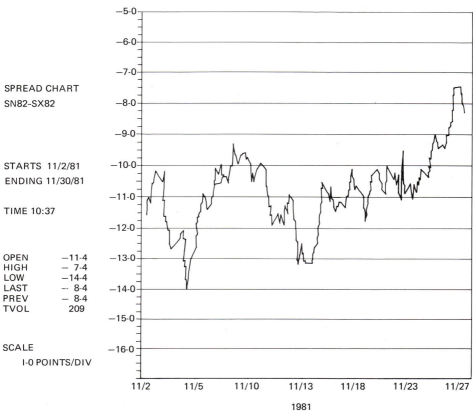

SPREAD CHART
SN82-SX82

STARTS 11/2/81
ENDING 11/30/81

TIME 10:37

OPEN	−11-4
HIGH	− 7-4
LOW	−14-4
LAST	− 8-4
PREV	− 8-4
TVOL	209

SCALE
  1-0 POINTS/DIV

1981

January 17, 1983

Sell one (or more) July soybean at   613¼

Buy one (or more) November soybean at   615¼

$$P_D - P_N = 2$$

If the trader's expectations materialize, in, say, six weeks, he would reverse the positions and realize profit on this bear spread.

February 28, 1983

Buy one July soybean at   600

Sell one November soybean at   607

$$P_D - P_N = 7$$

Profits/Losses

Profit on short position = 613.25–600 = $0.1325
Loss on long position = 615.25–607 = 0.0825
Net profit   **$0.0500**

The profits result from the weakening in the spread from 2 to 7. The spread strengthens as it approaches zero in a noninverted market.

Bull Spread

A bull spread would be established if the spreader expected the spread to strengthen. It requires a long position in the near contract and a short position in the distant.

January 17, 1983

Buy July soybean   613¼

Sell November soybean   615¼

$\longrightarrow P_D - P_N = 2$

February 28, 1983

Sell July soybean   620

Buy November soybean   620

$\longrightarrow P_D - P_N = 0$

Profits/Losses

Profit on long position	$0.0675
Loss on short position	0.0475
Net profit	**$0.0200**

These profits accrued as a result of a strengthening spread from 2 to 0. The above assumes that the soybean contracts are for the same crop year.

The interesting thing about spreads is the protection they provide in the event that expectations do not materialize. The protection comes from the fact that contracts of different maturities tend to move in the same direction pricewise, although not necessarily with equal vigor. Thus what may be lost on the short position will be made up for (partially or totally) on the long position, and vice versa.

To further drive the point home, contrast a spread with an open position in the commodity. Assume, for example, that the expectations of the bull spreader in the above example did not materialize on February 28, 1983 and that he closed his position at the following prices:

February 28, 1983

Sell one July soybean at	620
Buy one November soybean at	625

Profits/Losses

Profit on long position	$= 620 - 613¼ = ¢6¾$
Losses on short position	$= 625 - 615¼ = ¢9¾$
Net loss per bushel of soybeans	**($0.03)**

Had the trader established a short position in November soybean without a long position in July soybean, his loss would have amounted to 9¾ cents. One can argue, however, that a long position in July soybean would have been the best of all alternatives. This is so under perfect hindsight.

$P_D < P_N$ or Inverted Market

In an inverted market, a bull spread would still require a long position in the near contract and a short position in the distant one and would produce profits if the spread strengthened.

Bull Spread

Strategy	Buy near wheat	3.70	
			$P_D - P_N = -0.20$
	Sell distant wheat	3.50	
After	Sell near wheat	3.80	
			$P_D - P_N = -0.25$
	Buy distant wheat	3.55	

Profits in long position	$= 3.80 - 3.70 = \$0.10$
Losses in short position	$= 3.50 - 3.55 = \underline{\$0.05}$
Net profits	**\$0.05**

The profits result from the strengthening of the spread, $-0.25 < -0.20$.

Bear Spread

Once again, a bear spread calls for a short position in the near contract and a long position in the distant one. Profits will accrue as the spread weakens.

Strategy	Sell near	3.70	
			$P_D - P_N = -0.20$
	Buy distant	3.50	
After	Buy near	3.60	
			$P_D - P_N = -0.15$
	Sell distant	3.45	

Profits in short position	$= 3.70 - 3.60 = \$0.10$
Losses in long position	$= 3.50 - 3.45 = \underline{0.05}$
Net profits	**\$0.05**

The profits result from the weakening of the spread, $-0.20 < -0.15$.

Intermarket Spreads

Intermarket spreads attempt to capitalize on "unwarranted" price disparities between two contracts on the same commodity that have the same maturity month but are traded on two different exchanges.

From Table 5.6 we see that the March 83 wheat contract on the Chicago Board of Trade (CBT) was trading at 345(¾) cents per bushel and the same contract was trading at 379½ cents per bushel on the Kansas City Board of Trade (KC). This difference in prices can be explained, partially or totally, by the difference in the quality of deliverable wheat against each of the contracts and by transportation and other costs.

Assume, however, that a trader observing this spread concludes that it is too wide and is likely to narrow. The spread strategy would, therefore, call for the following:

January 17, 1983

> Buy March 83 CBT wheat at   345(¾) cents
> Sell March 83 KC wheat at   379½ cents

If profits are to be realized, the CBT contract should appreciate in price and the KC contract should depreciate in price. By, say, February 9, 1983, if the expectations had materialized, the following would be executed:

February 9, 1983

> Sell March 83 CBT wheat at   350 cents
> Buy March 83 KC wheat at   370 cents

Net profit $= (350-345(¾)) + (379½-370) =$ **13.75** (cents per bushel)

Intercommodity Spreads

Intercommodity spreads are intended to capitalize on "unwarranted" price differentials between futures contracts with similar maturities on two commodities considered to be close substitutes. For example, intercommodity spreads can be used on oats and corn contracts, for both commodities are used as feed grain.

Table 5.6 shows that on January 14, 1983, a July 83 corn contract traded at 271.5 cents per bushel while a July 83 oats contract traded at 185.25 cents per bushel. After close study and much deliberation, a trader decides that the gap (spread) is too wide and is bound to narrow. Thus, the following spread is established:

January 17, 1983

> Sell July 83 CBT corn at   271.5 cents
> Buy July 83 CBT oats at   185.25 cents

If the traders' expectations materialize, the above transaction is reversed.

March 23, 1983

> Buy July 83 CBT corn at   260 cents
> Sell July 83 CBT oats at   200 cents

Net profits $= (271.5 - 260) + (200 - 185.25)$
$$= \textbf{26.25} \text{ cents}$$

We now move to the discussion of a commodity-product spread.

Commodity-Product Spreads

The commodity-product spread attempts to capitalize on the changes in the price differential between a commodity futures contract of a certain maturity (or a different maturity) and that on a product or products derived from it. For example, a commodity-product spread could involve a long position in November soybean and a short position in October soybean oil.

In order to achieve approximate weight equivalency between contracts, the nature and results of the conversion process from commodity to product must be kept in mind. The crushing of a 60-pound bushel of soybeans produces 11 pounds of soybean oil and 48 pounds of soybean meal, with one pound wasted. The achievement of weight equivalency in contracts would require 50,000 bushels of soybeans (10 contracts), 50 contracts of soybean oil, and 12 contracts of soybean meal.

The nature of the commodity-product spread depends to a large degree on the profit margins realized from processing the commodity. The difference between the contracts, say soybean and soybean oil, should approximate the cost of processing soybeans into soybean oil. This cost should include a reasonable rate of return on the processing activity.

If the price differential is considered by the trader to be a bit low and the expectation is that soybean futures prices will fall while soybean oil prices appreciate, a spreader may enter the following order:

Buy 50 July 83 soybean oil at   17.50 cents
Sell 10 July 83 soybean at   613¼ cents

A nonprocessor spreader may not be concerned with weight equivalence and may well establish the above spread independent of the processing margins. The spread would yield profits if the price of soybean oil rose and that of soybeans rose by less (in percentage terms) than that of soybean oil, or if the price of soybeans stayed the same, or even better yet, fell.

A more complex commodity spread is used by commodities processors. It involves a short (long) position in the commodity (soybean, for example) and a long (short) position in the finished products derived from that commodity (oil and meal in the case of soybeans). A soybean-based spread of this type is referred to as a BOM (beans-oil-meal) spread. To understand BOM spreads, one must understand "board" or gross processor margin.

To arrive at a gross processor margin, begin with the prices from Table 5.6 for soybeans, soybean oil, and soybean meal July 83 contracts. We find the following prices:

July 83 soybean/bushel $6.1325
July 83 soybean oil/pound $0.1750
July 83 soybean meal/ton $185.30

We now convert oil and meal prices into prices per bushel, using the weight equivalence factors cited earlier as a benchmark

1. Multiply oil prices by 11.

    $0.1750 \times 11 = \$1.925$ per bushel.

2. Find price of soybean meal per pound (a short ton of meal is 2,000 pounds):

$$\frac{185.30}{2000} = 0.09265$$

3. Convert the price of soybean meal to a price per bushel:

$$0.09265 \times 48 = \$4.4472$$

4. Calculate the gross processor margin:

oil price + meal price − soybean price =
$$\$1.925 + \$4.4472 - \$6.1325 = \$0.24$$

Therefore, the products are at a premium in relation to the commodity and that premium is equal to 0.24. Figure 5.4 shows the history of this premium for the various harvest seasons. The \$0.24 represents a positive "crush." Had the margin been negative, we would have had a "reverse crush" and processors would have had no incentive to produce oils or meals.

FIGURE 5.4.   MAR products futures over/under MAR soybean future.

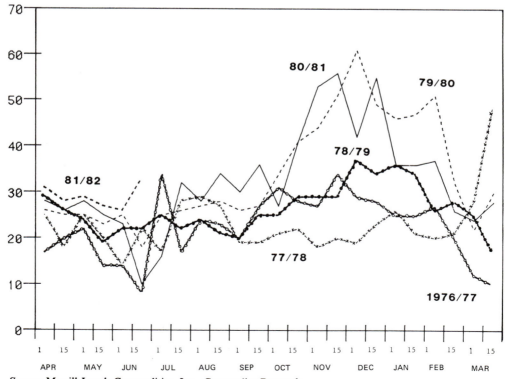

Source: Merrill Lynch Commodities, Inc., Commodity Research.

A speculator may find the $0.24 margin too high (average margins equal to $0.15) and may wish to enter the following order:

Buy 10 July 83 soybean
Sell 50 July 83 soybean oil
Sell 12 July 83 soybean meal

Again, the distribution of the number of contracts may be different. Profits will accrue if soybean prices rise and those of soybean products fall or do not rise as much in percentage terms.

After observing a reasonable premium between, say, July and September contracts, a soybean processor, on the other hand, would enter the following order:

Buy 10 July 1983 soybeans
Sell 50 September 1983 soybean oil
Sell 12 September 1983 soybean meal

With this order, the processor would have hedged the position by locking in the cost of the soybean and the selling price of the derivative products if the plan was to sell them in September.

Other spread strategies are used. To cover them is beyond the scope of this book.

5.13 PORTFOLIO AND OTHER CONSIDERATIONS

The size of the commitment to commodities in any given portfolio depends to a large extent on the risk profile of the portfolio owner and on the expected return and riskiness of the commodities. The long-term trends as well as the shorter-term trends in commodity prices are shown in Figure 5.5. The price performance of commodities does not appear to surpass that of stocks but appears to have provided an adequate hedge against inflation. The inflation hedge is normal, for during inflationary periods investors shift from fiat money to commodities, that is, from a depreciating to an appreciating asset.

The extent to which commodities allow for portfolio risk diversification depends largely on the correlation coefficient between the rate of return on commodities and that on the remainder of the portfolio. The closer the value of ρ is to $+1$, the lower the risk-diversification potential. When $\rho = 1$, there is no diversification possibility.

Portfolio managers generally recommend that 10 percent of the portfolio be invested in commodities. The less risk-averse the investor is, the greater this percentage should be.

5.14 IMPACT OF FUTURES MARKETS ON CASH MARKETS

The impact of futures markets on the cash markets is of importance because any destabilizing impact on the cash market by futures trading could hurt borrowers and lenders in the cash market and reduce the efficiency of this market. In the process some skilled speculators may well succeed in expropriating the wealth of the less knowledgeable.

The impact of futures markets on cash markets was acknowledged by the U.S. Congress in 1958 when it outlawed futures trading in onions on the grounds that it was responsible for the price instability in the cash onion market.

FIGURE 5.5. Commodity prices, stock prices, wholesale, & consumer prices.

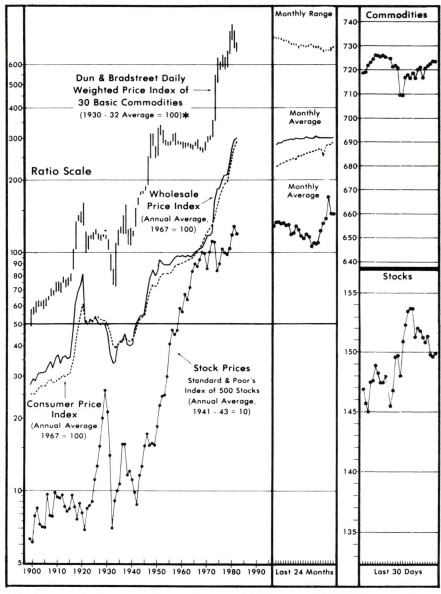

* Yearly ranges based upon daily prices for years 1950 to present; 1932–1949 ranges based upon monthly averages; 1899–1931 ranges based upon an early Dun & Bradstreet Commodity Index (Spliced to Current Index by this publication)

Source: The Media General Financial Weekly, March 21, 1983.

Before discussing the empirical evidence, we must note the two principal functions of futures markets. The futures markets allow producers and processors to hedge, that is, to shift price level risk onto professional risk takers and allow for a mechanism for price discovery. In the latter sense the futures market serves as an information (forecasting) tool.

The weight of the evidence suggests that futures markets have, under normal conditions, contributed to the stability of the cash market and in the process improved the profitability of farmers and processors. This result was achieved by the increased market information that futures markets provide to these economic agents.

Among the more recent empirical tests are those by J. Cox,[30] B. Gardner,[31] S. Grossman,[32] A. Peck,[33] and S. Turnovsky.[34]

The Cox study presented evidence in support of the hypothesis that the futures markets have increased the efficiency of spot markets. The primary reason was the increased flow of information. Gardner's evidence supports that of Cox for the soybean and cotton markets. S. Grossman, again emphasizing the informational role of futures markets, argued convincingly that since futures prices and spot prices represent the results of interaction among informed traders, the uninformed trader benefits from that price information and the intertemporal allocation of resources is enhanced as a result. A. Peck also offered evidence about the stabilizing effects of futures markets. The effect on nonstorable commodities (like cattle) was surprisingly higher than that on storable commodities (like wheat). S. Turnovsky offered further evidence about the stabilizing role of the futures market and concluded that it facilitated the production and storage decision. Once again, the effect on nonstorable commodities was more pronounced.

We can, therefore, conclude that the effect of futures markets on the spot markets is generally positive.

CONCLUSION

Commodities futures contracts are an excellent vehicle for preserving wealth, for accumulating wealth, and also for losing it. Any trader who is not willing to spend the needed time to study, to understand, and to follow the markets should avoid commodities unless he or she is willing to rely on the advice of a broker who has been thoroughly investigated in terms of performance record and attention to customer needs.

---

[30] J. C. Cox, "Futures Trading and Market Information," *Journal of Political Economy,* vol. 84 (1976), pp. 1215–1237.

[31] G. L. Gardner, "Futures Prices in Supply Analysis," *American Journal of Agricultural Economics,* (1976), pp. 81–84.

[32] S. J. Grossman, "The Existence of Futures Markets, Noisy Rational Expectations and Informational Externalities," *Review of Economic Studies,* vol. 44 (1977), pp. 431–449.

[33] A. E. Peck, "Futures Markets, Supply Response, and Price Stability," *Quarterly Journal of Economics,* vol. 90 (1976), pp. 407–423.

[34] S. J. Turnovsky, "Futures Markets, Private Storage, and Price Stabilization," *Journal of Public Economics,* vol. 12, pp. 301–327.

QUESTIONS

1. Discuss the differences and the similarities between the normal backwardation theory and the storage theory.

2. Few commodities futures contracts are ever delivered against. What does this reveal about the nature of the market?

3. What roles do commodities futures contracts play in the U.S. and the world economy? Justify your answer.

4. "Hedging is always a speculation." Comment.

5. What are the differences and the similarities between a futures and a forward contract?

6. What role does the CFTC play in the futures market? What are the implications on market efficiency?

7. Do you think that the daily price limits on futures contracts retard or enhance speculation? What are the possible implications on market efficiency?

8. Outline the mechanics of a BOM spread. Who could use it?

9. The profitability of intermonth commodity spreads depends on the behavior of the basis. What must the basis do for a bear spread to realize a profit in an inverted market? In a noninverted market?

10. An inverted market is not a common occurrence. Outline the conditions under which an inverted market may prevail.

11. "A stop order on a commodities futures contract works in exactly the same way as a stop order on a common stock." Do you agree?

12. "Commodities markets are too speculative, stay out of them." Comment.

13. How important a role do speculators play in the commodities markets?

14. The commodities exchanges are quite concerned about "excessive speculation." Discuss some of the tools used by the exchanges to limit speculative fevers.

PROBLEMS

1. On January 7, 1983, Hillsman's Coffee Inc., a Chicago based company, forecasts a need for coffee beans of 187,500 lbs. by December 1983. Concerned with possible increases in the price of coffee, Hillsman's Coffee Inc. decides to hedge in the futures market.
   a. What type of hedge would it establish?
   b. What are the consequences of the basis's weakening by 10 percent?
   c. What are the consequences of the basis's strengthening by 10 percent?
   d. Comment on the results above.

2. R. B. O'Neill, head of an Iowa corn-farming family, fears a fall in the price of corn by harvest time (September). R. B. expects 100,000 bushels. On January 7, 1982, the spot price for corn is $2.63¼/bu. and the September futures price is $2.94¼/bu. R. B. decides to hedge in the futures market.

a. What type of hedge would he establish?

b. What are the consequences of the basis's weakening by 15 percent?

c. What are the consequences of the basis's strengthening by 15 percent?

d. Comment on the results of the strategy.

Glossary

arbitrage: The simultaneous purchase and sale of similar financial instruments or commodity futures in order to benefit from an anticipated change in their price relationship.

bear: One who believes prices will move lower. (See *bull.*)

bear market: A market in which prices are declining.

bid: An offer to purchase at a specified price. (See *offer.*)

break: A rapid and sharp price decline.

bull: One who expects prices to rise. (See *bear.*)

bull market: A market in which prices are rising

buy in: To cover, offset or close out a short position. (See *evening up, liquidation, offset.*)

buy on close: To buy at the end of the trading session at a price within the closing range.

buy on opening: To buy at the beginning of a trading session at a price within the opening range.

car: A loose quantity term sometimes used to describe a contract, e.g., "a car of bellies." Derived from the fact that quantities of the product specified in a contract used to correspond closely to the capacity of a railroad car.

cash commodity: The actual physical commodity as distinguished from a futures commodity.

CFTC: The Commodity Futures Trading Commission is the independent federal agency created by Congress to regulate futures trading. The CFTC Act of 1974 became effective April 21, 1975. Previously, futures trading had been regulated by the Commodity Exchange Authority of the USDA.

clearinghouse: An adjunct to a futures exchange through which transactions executed on the floor of the exchange are settled using a process of matching purchases and sales. A clearing organization is also charged with the proper conduct of delivery procedures and the adequate financing of the entire operation.

clearing member: A member firm of the clearinghouse or organization. Each clearing member must also be a member of the exchange. Not all members of the exchange, however, are members of the clearing organization. All trades of a nonclearing member must be registered with, and eventually settled through, a clearing member.

Note: This glossary was compiled by the Chicago Mercantile Exchange from a number of sources. The definitions are not intended to state or suggest the correct legal significance or meaning of any word or phrase. The sole purpose of this compilation is to foster a better understanding of futures.

close, the: The period at the end of the trading session. Sometimes used to refer to the closing price. (See *opening, the.*)

closing range (or range): The high and low prices, or bids and offers, recorded during the period designated as the official close. (See *settlement price.*)

commission (or round-turn): The one-time fee charged by a broker to a customer when a position is liquidated either by offset or delivery.

commission house: (See *futures commission merchant, omnibus account.*)

commitment: A trader is said to have a commitment, when he assumes the obligation to accept or make delivery on a futures contract. (See *open interest.*)

contract: A term of reference describing a unit of trading for a financial commodity future. Also, actual bilateral agreement between the buyer and seller of a futures transaction as defined by an exchange.

contract month: The month in which futures contracts may be satisfied by making or accepting a delivery. (See *delivery month.*)

cover: The purchase of futures to offset a previously established short position.

day order: An order that is placed for execution, if possible, during only one trading session. If the order cannot be executed that day, it is automatically canceled.

day trading: Refers to establishing and liquidating the same position or positions within one day's trading.

deferred futures: The most distant months of a futures contract. (See *nearby.*)

delivery: The tender and receipt of an actual commodity or financial instrument or cash in settlement of a futures contract.

delivery month: (See *contract month.*)

delivery notice: The written notice given by the seller of his intention to make delivery against an open, short futures position on a particular date. (See *notice day.*)

delivery points: Those points designated by futures exchanges at which the financial instrument or commodity covered by a futures contract may be delivered in fulfillment of such contract.

delivery price: The price fixed by the clearinghouse at which deliveries on futures are invoiced, also the price at which the fu-tures contract is settled when deliveries are made.

discretionary account: An account over which any individual or organization other than the person in whose name the account is carried, exercises trading authority or control.

equity: The residual dollar value of a futures trading account, assuming its liquidation at the going market price.

evening up: Buying or selling to offset an existing market position. (See *buy in liquidation offset.*)

first notice day: The first date, varying by contracts and exchanges, on which notices of intention to deliver actual financial instruments or physical commodities against futures are authorized.

floor broker: A member who is paid a fee for executing orders for clearing members or their customers. A floor broker executing customer orders must be licensed by the CFTC.

floor trader: A member who generally trades only for his own account, for an account controlled by him or who has such a trade made for him. Also referred to as a "local."

futures: A term used to designate all contracts covering the sale of financial instruments or physical commodities for future delivery on a commodity exchange.

futures commission merchant: A firm or person engaged in soliciting or accepting and handling orders for the purchase or sale of futures contracts, subject to the rules of a futures exchange and, who, in connection with such solicitation or acceptance of orders, accepts any money or securities to margin any resulting trades or contracts. The FCM must be licensed by the CFTC. (See *commission house, omnibus account.*)

give up: At the request of the customer, a brokerage house which has not performed the service is credited with the execution of an order.

hedge: The purchase or sale of a futures contract as a temporary substitute for a transaction to be made at a later date. Usually it involves opposite positions in the cash

market and the futures market at the same time. (See *long hedge, short hedge.*)

hedger: One who hedges.

initial margin: (See *security deposit—initial.*)

inverted market: A futures market in which the nearer months are selling at premiums to the more distant months. (See *premium.*)

last trading day: The final day under an exchange's rules during which trading may take place in a particular delivery futures month. Futures contracts outstanding at the end of the last trading day must be settled by delivery of underlying physical commodities or financial instruments, or by agreement for monetary settlement if the former is impossible.

limit price: (See *maximum price fluctuation.*)

limit order: An order given to a broker by a customer which has restrictions upon its execution. The customer specifies a price and the order can be executed only if the market reaches or betters that price.

liquidation: Same as evening up or offset. Any transaction that offsets or closes out a long or short position. (See *buy in, evening up, offset.*)

long: One who has bought a futures contract(s) to establish a market position and who has not yet closed out this position through an offsetting sale; the opposite of *short.*

long hedge: The purchase of a futures contract(s) in anticipation of actual purchases in the cash market. Used by processors or exporters as protection against an advance in the cash price. (See *hedge, short hedge.*)

margin: A cash amount of funds that must be deposited with the broker for each futures contract as a guarantee of fulfillment of the contract. Also called *security deposit.*

maintenance margin: A sum, usually smaller than—but part of—the original margin, which must be maintained on deposit at all times if a customer's equity in any futures position drops to, or under, the maintenance margin level, the broker must issue a "margin call" for the amount of money required to restore the customer's equity in the account to the original margin level. (See *margin call, security deposit—maintenance.*)

margin call: A demand for additional cash funds because of adverse price movement. (See *maintenance margin; security deposit—maintenance.*)

mark to market: The daily adjustment of an account to reflect profits and losses.

market order: An order for immediate execution given to a broker to buy or sell at the best obtainable price.

maximum price fluctuation: The maximum amount the contract price can change, up or down, during one trading session, as fixed by exchange rules. (See *limit price.*)

minimum price fluctuation: Smallest increment of price movement possible in trading a given contract. (See *point.*)

M.I.T.: Market if touched. A price order that automatically becomes a market order if the price is reached.

nearby: The nearest active trading month of a financial or commodity futures market. (See *deferred futures.*)

nominal price: Price quotations on futures for a period in which no actual trading took place.

notice day: A day on which notices of intent to deliver pertaining to a specified delivery month may be issued. (See *delivery notice.*)

offer: Indicates a willingness to sell a futures contract at a given price. (See *bid.*)

offset: (See *buy in, evening up, liquidation.*)

omnibus account: An account carried by one futures commission merchant with another futures commission merchant in which the transactions of two or more persons are combined and carried in the name of the originating broker, rather than designated separately. (See *commission house, futures commission merchant.*)

open contracts: Contracts which have been bought or sold without the transaction having been completed by subsequent sale or purchase, or by making or taking actual delivery of the financial instrument or physical commodity. (See *position.*)

open interest: Number of open futures contracts. Refers to unliquidated purchases or sales.

open order: An order to a broker that is good until it is canceled or executed.

opening, the: The period at the beginning of

the trading session officially designated by the exchange during which all transactions are considered made "at the opening." (See *close, the.*)

opening price (or range): The range of prices at which the first bids and offers were made or first transactions were completed.

original margin: The margin needed to cover a specific new position. (See *security deposit—initial.*)

P&S: Purchase and sale statement. A statement provided by the broker showing change in the customer's net ledger balance after the offset of a previously established position(s).

point: (See *minimum price fluctuation.*)

position: An interest in the market, either long or short, in the form of open contracts. (See *open contracts.*)

premium: The excess of one futures contract price over that of another, or over the cash market price. (See *inverted market.*)

primary market: The principal underlying market for a financial instrument or physical commodity.

rally: An upward movement of prices following a decline, the opposite of a *reaction.* (See *recovery.*)

range: The high and low prices or high and low bids and offers, recorded during a specified time.

reaction: A decline in prices following an advance; the opposite of *rally.*

recovery: Usually describes a price advance following a decline. (See *rally.*)

registered representative: A person employed by, and soliciting business for, a commission house or futures commission merchant.

round-turn: Procedure by which the long or short position of an individual is offset by an opposite transaction or by accepting or making delivery of the actual financial instrument or physical commodity.

scalp: To trade for small gains. It normally involves establishing and liquidating a position quickly, usually within the same day.

security deposit: (See *margin.*)

security deposit (initial): Synonymous with the term *margin,* a cash amount of funds that must be deposited with the broker for each contract as a guarantee of fulfillment of the futures contract. It is not considered as part payment or purchase. (See *initial margin, original margin.*)

security deposit (maintenance): A sum usually smaller than, but part of, the original deposit or margin that must be maintained on deposit at all times. If a customer's equity in any futures position drops to or below the maintenance level, the broker must issue a call for the amount of money required to restore the customer's equity in the account to the original margin level. (See *maintenance margin, margin call.*)

settlement price: A figure determined by the closing range which is used to calculate gains and losses in futures market accounts. Settlement prices are used to determine gains, losses, margin calls, and invoice prices for deliveries. (See *closing range.*)

short: One who has sold a futures contract to establish a market position and who has not yet closed out his position through an offsetting purchase; the opposite of a *long.*

short hedge: The sale of a futures contract(s) to eliminate or lessen the possible decline in value of ownership of an approximately equal amount of the actual financial instrument or physical commodity. (See *hedge, long hedge.*)

short selling: Establishing a market position by selling a futures contract.

short squeeze: A situation in which a lack of supply tends to force prices upward.

speculator: One who attempts to anticipate price changes and, through buying and selling futures contracts, aims to make profits; does not use the futures market in connection with the production, processing, marketing or handling of a product.

spread: Refers to simultaneous purchase and sale of futures contracts for the same commodity or instrument for delivery in different months, or in different but related markets.

stop order (or stop): An order to buy or sell at the market when a definite price is reached, either above or below the price that prevailed when the order was given.

switching: Liquidating an existing position and

simultaneously reinstating a position in another futures contract of the same type.

tender: To offer for delivery against futures.

tick: Refers to a change in price, either up or down.

trend: The general direction of the market.

volume: The number of transactions in a futures contract made during a specified period of time.

wire house: A firm operating a private wire to its own branch offices, or to other firms, commission houses and brokerage houses.

CHAPTER

6

Interest Rate Futures, Stock Index Futures, and Their Options

6.1 INTRODUCTION

Recent developments in the U.S. money and capital markets have been dramatic. The 1970s have witnessed, as never before, sustained sharp fluctuations in the rate of interest combined with occasional and at times caustic assaults on the ability of the Federal Reserve System to control the money supply. Changes in interest rates meant reciprocal changes in bond prices and hence changes in the wealth of investors. Bondholders watching their wealth shrinking and expanding frequently and unexpectedly had to seek refuge somewhere. The creation of the financial futures markets provided one answer.

The introduction of futures contracts on financial instruments came about 100 years after the first futures contract on commodities was traded. The reason was that prior to the early 1970s the volatility of interest rates was not sufficiently high to warrant the presence of the market.

The recent interest-rate gyrations are depicted in Figures 6.1 and 6.2. The largest average weekly fluctuation in 13-week T-bill auction rates was recorded in 1974. The size of the fluctuation was 33.4 basis points[1] that followed a 22.4 basis-point average weekly fluctuation in 1973. It is not a mere coincidence, therefore, that the Chicago Board of Trade began trading financial futures in the fall of 1975. Bondholders who watch rising interest rates (falling bond values) are concerned with the value of their assets, although they may intend to hold the bonds until maturity and expect to receive face value. This is so because changing interest rates affect the reinvestment rate for coupon bonds. The face value to be received is also worth less in real terms as interest rates rise, primarily because of revised expectations about the price level.

Rising interest rates also affect decision makers who expect to be net borrowers in the future. They would seek protection against escalating interest costs through various hedging mechanisms, which we shall explore in detail.

Falling interest rates, on the other hand, are of concern to lenders and to bondholders wishing to roll over their investments. Their concern is with the reinvestment of their

---

[1] A basis point is 0.01 percent.

FIGURE 6.1.   Long-term interest rates—monthly averages.

Monthly Averages of Daily Figures

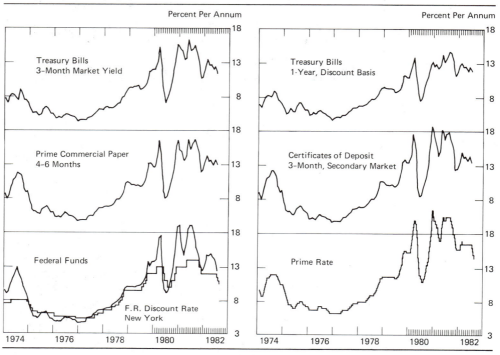

Source: *Federal Reserve Chart Book*, August 1982, p. 72.

funds at advantageous rates (roughly equal to those prevailing currently in the market-place). A hedging mechanism is needed in this case as well.

All the economic agents mentioned above and many others are concerned with the stability and predictability of interest rates.

6.2 THE INTEREST-RATE FUTURES MARKET

The interest-rate futures market is currently the most widely used avenue for hedging price and credit risks. The number of financial futures markets contracts traded on the various exchanges rose from 605,000 in 1977 to 28,825,112 in 1982, with no sign of abating (see Table 6.1a). This trading level accounted for 25.65 percent of all trading in all futures contracts on all the futures exchanges. The percentage for 1980 was only 13.5 percent (see Table 6.1a). Many market observers expect trading in futures contracts to dominate trading in any commodity group by the mid 1980s. The center of trading activity remains the CBT, although the CME is making major gains. In 1982 the CBT accounted for about 43 percent of all trading in futures contracts, down from about 50 percent in 1981 (see Table 6.1b).

The financial futures market provides a centralized, orderly market where standardized contracts are traded in accordance with prescribed rules that are backed by the needed guarantees.

FIGURE 6.2. Long-term interest rates—monthly averages of daily figures.

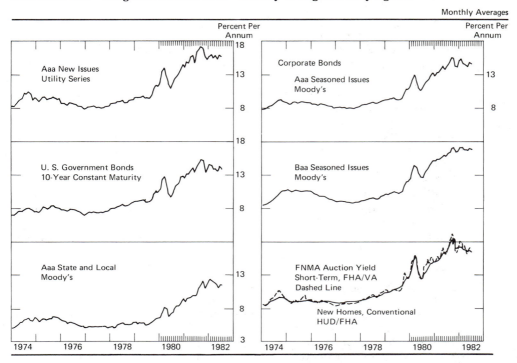

Source: *Federal Reserve Chart Book*, August 1982, p. 73.

Financial Futures Contract

A financial futures contract is an agreement (an obligation) to buy or sell a specified amount of a certain financial instrument at some future date at a price determined today. The net effect is to lock in the price and the interest rate on the financial instrument for that period of time to begin sometime in the future (the expiration date of the futures contract). Simply, it is the purchase (sale) of a financial instrument to be received (delivered) at a specified time in the future at the agreed-upon price. The results are a reduction in the investors' concerns about future bond price levels, which could have adverse effects on their financial and mental welfare.

Historical Background

As the prices of financial instruments rivaled the volatility of commodity prices, the emergence of a futures market in interest rates was inevitable. Building on its vast experience in dealing with futures contracts, the Chicago Board of Trade (CBT) became the first organization to provide an interest-rate futures market in October of 1975. The trading vehicle was the Government National Mortgage Association (GNMA or Ginnie Mae) certificate, representing a pool of government-insured mortgages. The success of the CBT with the Ginnie Mae futures encouraged other organizations to enter the interest-rate futures market. The first to follow was the International Monetary Market (IMM), a division of the Chicago Mercantile Exchange. Futures trading on

TABLE 6.1a
Futures Contracts Traded by Commodity Groups

Rank	Commodity Group	1982 Contracts		%
			1982	
(1)	Agricultural commodities		46,310,209	41.21
	Soybean complex	15,528,665		13.82
	Grain	14,263,908		12.69
	Livestock, products, and poultry	11,702,487		10.41
	Imported agricultural commodities	3,276,512		2.92
	Other agricultural commodities 1	1,538,637		1.37
(2)	Financial instruments		28,825,112	25.64
(3)	Precious metals		18,809,458	16.73
(4)	Foreign currency		8,690,285	7.73
(5)	Stock indexes		4,911,121	4.37
(6)	Nonprecious metals		2,362,625	2.10
(7)	Petroleum products		1,875,414	1.67
(8)	Lumber products		616,655	.55
	Total		**112,400,879**	**100.00**
			1981	
(1)	Agricultural commodities		50,381,053	51.15
	Grain	17,915,624		18.18
	Soybean complex	17,431,221		17.70
	Livestock, products, and poultry	9,406,687		9.55
	Imported agricultural commodities	3,562,613		3.62
	Other agricultural commodities 1	2,064,908		2.10
(2)	Financial instruments		22,864,613	23.20
(3)	Precious metals		15,690,495	15.93
(4)	Foreign currency		6,122,002	6.21
(5)	Nonprecious metals		1,647,383	1.67
(6)	Petroleum products		1,005,160	1.02
(7)	Lumber products		811,665	.82
	Total		**98,522,371**	**100.00**

1 Cotton, eggs, orange juice, potatoes, and sunflower seeds

Rank	Commodity Group	1980 Contracts		%
			1980	
(1)	Agricultural commodities		59,134,754	64.2
	Grain	20,349,023		22.1
	Soybean complex	19,207,489		20.9
	Livestock, products, and poultry	11,639,519		12.6
	Imported agricultural commodities	4,886,416		5.3
	Other agricultural commodities	3,052,307		3.3
(2)	Precious metals		13,171,816	14.3
(3)	Financial instruments		12,469,878	13.5
(4)	Foreign currency		4,222,820	4.6
(5)	Nonprecious metals		1,848,108	2.0
(6)	Lumber products		1,010,424	1.1
(7)	Petroleum products		238,309	0.3
	Total		**92,096,109**	**100.0**

Source: Futures Industry Association, Washington, D.C., Feb. 1983.

TABLE 6.1b
Futures Volume Highlights, 1982 in Comparison with 1981

Rank	Exchange	1982 Contracts	%	1981 Contracts	%	Rank
1.	Chicago Board of Trade	48,206,790	42.89	49,085,763	49.82	(1)
2.	Chicago Mercantile Exchange	33,574,286	29.87	24,527,020	24.89	(2)
3.	Commodity Exchange, Inc.	17,520,712	15.59	13,293,049	13.49	(3)
4.	Coffee, Sugar, and Cocoa Exchange	3,252,512	2.89	3,562,613	3.62	(4)
5.	New York Mercantile Exchange	2,649,941	2.36	1,781,407	1.81	(7)
6.	Mid-America Commodity Exchange	2,397,721	2.13	2,588,540	2.63	(5)
7.	Kansas City Board of Trade	1,493,558	1.33	1,181,884	1.20	(8)
8.	New York Cotton Exchange	1,479,781	1.32	1,802,891	1.83	(6)
9.	New York Futures Exchange	1,451,442	1.29	290,585	.29	(10)
10.	Minneapolis Grain Exchange	346,264	.31	372,624	.38	(9)
11.	New Orleans Commodity Exchange	27,872	.02	35,995	.04	(11)
		112,400,879	**100.00**	**98,522,371**	**100.00**	

Source: Futures Industry Association, Washington, D. C., February 1983.

the IMM in 90-day (13-week) T-bills began on January 6, 1976. Buoyed by its immediate success (110,223 contracts changing hands between January 6, 1976, and December 31, 1976), the IMM introduced one-year T-bill futures contracts on September 11, 1978, and contracts on four-year T-notes on July 10, 1979. Unfortunately, neither of the last two contracts met with sufficient market acceptance.

The IMM was later to drop the futures contract on four-year T-notes. Trading in the contract on one-year T-bills was halted during 1981 and 1982. The IMM planned to reintroduce the one-year T-bill contract in November 1983 upon moving to its new building. At the same time, the IMM also planned to introduce a futures contract on six-month T-bills. Other successful contracts currently traded on the IMM are the three-month Eurodollar time deposit futures contract introduced on December 9, 1981, and the three-month domestic certificate of deposit (CD) introduced on July 29, 1981. These contracts and that on the 90-day U.S. T-bill were the only financial futures contracts traded on the IMM as of February 1983. The specifications of the three contracts appear in Table 6.2.

The CD and particularly the Eurodollar contract merit further discussion. A Eurodollar is simply a dollar on deposit outside the United States. American banks are active participants in this market both on the demand and on the supply side. The size of the futures contract on Eurodollars is $1,000,000. Delivery against the contract, should it become necessary, will be made in cash. This is a new feature for this and a few other futures contracts. Cash delivery has become acceptable. Previously it was looked upon, and incorrectly so, as a form of gambling. The final settlement price on the contract is a bit difficult to arrive at. The Clearing Corporation determines on the last day of trading the appropriate London Interbank Offered Rate (LIBOR). That determination is made by a random sampling at two different points in time during the last

TABLE 6.2
Summary of Contract Specifications: Three-Month Eurodollar Time Deposit, Three-Month Certificate of Deposit, and 90-Day Treasury Bill

Specifications	Three-Month Eurodollar Time Deposit	Three-Month Domestic Certificate of Deposit	90-Day U.S. Treasury Bill
Size	*$1,000,000*	*$1,000,000*	*$1,000,000*
Contract grade	1. Cash settlement	1. "No-name" CDs. Deliverable banks announced 2 business days before 15th day of delivery month. Deliverable CDs determined by polling of dealers 2. CDs must mature between 16th and last day of the month 3 months after delivery month 3. Deliverable maturity range approx. 2½ to 3½ months 4. CDs with no more than 185 days accrued interest 5. Variable rate and discount CDs are deliverable if and when yields are equivalent to "no-name" run	1. Treasury bills with 91 days to maturity
Yields	Add-on[1]a	Add-on	Discount
Hours	7:30 am-2:00 pm[b]	7:30 am-2:00 pm[1b]	8:00 am-2:00 pm[b]
Months traded	Mar, Jun, Sep. Dec. & Spot Month	Mar, June, Sep, Dec	Jan, Mar, Apr, Jun, Jul, Sep. Oct, Dec
Clearing house symbol	ED	X1	T1
Ticker symbol	ED	DC	TB
Minimum fluctuation in price	0.01 (1 basis pt)($25/pt)	0.01 (1 basis pt)($25/pt)	0.01 (basis pt)($25/pt)
Limit move	1.00 (100 basis pts)($2,500) No spot month limit	0.80 (80 basis pts)($2,000)	0.60 (60 basis pts)($1,500)
Last day of trading	2nd London business day before 3rd Wednesday	Last business day *before* last delivery day	2nd day following 3rd weekly Treasury bill auction in contract month. (Effective with June '83 contract, the day before the first delivery day)
Delivery date	Last day of trading	15th through last day of month	1st Thursday after 3rd weekly bill auction in the delivery month
Minimum margins	I $2000[2]c	M $1500	I $2000	M $1500	I $2000	M $1500
CD/T-Bill spread			I $ 500	M 400	I $ 500	M $ 400
Eurodollar/CD spread	I $ 500	M $ 400	I $ 500	M $ 400		
Eurodollar/T-Bill spread	I $ 700	M $ 600			I $ 700	M $ 600
Spread margins	I $ 400	M $ 200	I $ 400	M $ 200	I $ 400	M $ 200
Delivery month margins	I $2000	M $1500	I $2000	M $1500	I $2000	M $1500
Delivery month spread margins	I $ 400	M $ 200	I $ 400	M $ 200	I $ 400	M $ 200

(1)a Interest is added onto the $1,000,000 principal

b Chicago Time

(2)c Minimum payment at the time of purchase

Source: Inside Eurodollar Futures, 1982, p. 17. Reprinted with the permission of the International Monetary Market, a division of the Chicago Mercantile Exchange.

trading days of at least 20 approved banks in the London Eurodollar market. Quotations from 12 banks in the sample on three-month Eurodollar deposits are tabulated. The two extreme values on each side are dropped and the arithmetic average of the remaining eight is calculated. The settlement price would equal 100 minus the average rate rounded to the nearest 1/100th of a percentage. The settlement price is paid to (short position) the Clearing Corporation and is received (long position) from it.

The CD market has proven to be most valuable in the management of bank liabilities. The futures market on CDs was a natural extension in order to allow banks direct hedging opportunities and much flexibility in the management of their portfolios. The eligible CDs for delivery are specified in Table 6.2.

The success of the CBT with its GNMA contract brought along other contracts. On August 22, 1977 the CBT introduced futures contracts on $100,000 of Treasury bonds. On May 3, 1982, the CBT introduced a futures contract on $100,000 of 10-year T-notes. Its last product was a contract on $100,000 of 2-year Treasury notes introduced on January 21, 1983. No other financial futures contracts are currently contemplated by the CBT.

The success experienced by the IMM and the CBT in interest futures coupled with increasingly wider surges in interest rates (8.46 percent range between December 1976 and February 1980) brought additional competitors to the marketplace. In September 1978, the American Stock Exchange began trading GNMA futures through its affiliate the American Commodities Exchange (ACE). Its success was not impressive, and the ACE stopped trading in interest-rate futures in August 1980. The ACE transferred all its business to the newly formed New York Futures Exchange (NYFE), a wholly owned subsidiary of the New York Stock Exchange. In the fall of 1979, the Commodity Exchange Inc. (COMEX) inaugurated a three-month T-bill futures contract, but was later to drop it because of insufficient volume. And on August 7, 1980, the New York Futures Exchange inaugurated trading in 90-day T-bills (with January, April, July, and October delivery months) as well as in T-bonds that have a 20-year maturity (with February, May, August, and November delivery months).

All NYFE contracts proved unsuccessful and were subsequently withdrawn. The exchange is currently trading options on the New York Futures Index and futures contracts on the index.

On October 22, 1982, the Chicago Board Options Exchange introduced an option on T-bonds. This option serves the same needs as the futures contract and thus is a source of competition. The other options on cash instruments also represent instruments that compete with futures contracts on the same instrument.

A call T-bond option allows the holder to purchase T-bonds at any time during the life of the option at a predetermined striking (exercise) price. The option holder does not have to exercise the option. For this right, the option holder pays a market determined price called the premium.

A put T-bond option, on the other hand, allows the holder to sell T-bond securities at any time during the life of the option at a striking price set today. The price of this right is the put premium.

Interest options are competitors to financial futures contracts because of several interesting features. Among them are:

1. The financial futures contract represents an obligation to deliver or to take delivery of a financial instrument unless the position is reversed prior to expiration date. The options contract allows its holder a choice. The holder of an options contract can simply let the contract expire.

2. The maximum loss to an option holder is limited to the premium paid, as we discussed in the stock option case. The loss on a futures contract does not have a maximum set limit.

3. The futures contract, as we discuss below, requires marking to the market and

daily settlement; that is, it releases or requires cash on a daily basis as interest rates fluctuate. The option buyer, on the other hand, has a fixed cash outflow limited to the size of the premium that is paid when the contract is purchased.

It remains to be seen whether financial futures contracts can live side by side with financial options. Those recently introduced and contemplated instruments are a confirmation of the usefulness of futures markets and of increased sophistication of financial markets and of market participants.

The contracts discussed above are not the sole methods for hedging. Prior to the introduction of futures contracts, several methods for reducing or eliminating interest rate risk were available, but none were as effective and as flexible. The currently available hedging vehicles are as follows:

1. Purchase of insurance.
2. A hedge in the cash market.
3. Use of the repurchase agreement.
4. Interest-rate futures markets.
5. Debt options (covered in the latter part of this chapter).

Purchase of Insurance

Protection against various types of risks—theft, fire, explosion, and others—is provided by insurance companies against the payment of a premium. The losses and the operating costs of insurance companies are spread over the policyholders in the form of a premium. In so doing, the insurance company is not assuming the risk but rather functioning as an agent for spreading the incidence of the risk among the insured population so that one's premium pays for another's losses, and so on. In short, the losses have been "socialized" that is, spread out through the insured segment of the population.

Insurance companies have not yet devised a mechanism for socializing losses that result from price changes or from changes in the creditworthiness of the issuer of a security. Not even Lloyd's of London sells insurance that protects investors against losses in a stock or a bond position. The insurance option is, therefore, not available to provide investors with protection against changes in interest rates—although such changes can cause losses that are more devastating than those resulting from insurable casualties. However, option bonds guaranteeing a resale price to the holder (the guarantee is provided by the issuer or his investment banker) and interest options that are currently available to investors represent two forms of insurance schemes.

The Cash Market

Investors who wish to lock in the rate of interest implied in the yield curve—that is, to earn the forward rate—can achieve their goal in the cash (spot) market by an appropriate combination of bond purchase and sale. An investor who wishes to realize the one-year forward rate to prevail one year hence, would sell (short)[2] a one-year bond, and

---

[2] A short position begins with the sale of a borrowed security followed by a purchase of the same security. The securities bought are then returned to the party who initially loaned them. Profit accrues if the sale price is higher than the purchase price; losses accrue if the opposite is true.

buy a two-year bond. The forward rate on this one-year investment to begin one year into the future is equal to

$$_1F_1 = \frac{(1+R_2)^2}{(1+R_1)^1} - 1$$

where, F_1 = one-year (second subscript) rate to prevail one year from now (first subscript)

R_2 = current two-year rate (expressed in annual rates)

R_1 = current one-year rate

The general formulation for the forward rate is

$$_{t+N-1}F_1 = \frac{(1+{}_tR_N)^N}{(1+{}_tR_{N-1})^{N-1}} - 1$$

The short one-year position offsets the one-year return on the long position in the two-year bond. The investor is left with the second-year interest on the two-year bond.

For this strategy to be of economic consequence, it must be possible. The facts are that:

1. Only securities dealers can expect to assume short positions in the bond market on a reasonably consistent basis.

2. The short positions are not likely if the underlying bond is thinly traded. Dealers cannot do much about this. A short position in certificates of deposit, for example, is not possible even for dealers. Also, it is not always possible to go short on another bond whose returns are close to perfectly positively correlated with those on the thinly traded bond.

3. No dealer can borrow bonds to deliver against a short position on a long-term basis. The argument that the dealer can enter the market continuously and establish a short position is not workable. Interest-rate differentials may shift and transactions costs can become prohibitive.

The argument by certain dealers that they could do in the cash market whatever one can do in the futures market is not very potent. Hedging in the cash market, like the other hedging tools we shall discuss, is used as an alternative. At times hedging in the cash market acts as a complement to the classical hedging method, which consists of matching up size and maturity of cash assets and liabilities on the balance sheet.

The Repurchase Agreement

An investor wishing to secure a certain rate of return on a T-bill beginning three months from now can do so in the cash market by entering into a repurchase agreement— that is, buying a six-month bill and selling it with a proviso that the buyer will sell it back three months to date at a specified price (yield). The difference in yields will be the cost of the hedge. The risk due to changes in interest rates is being borne by the buyer, otherwise known as the speculator. Risk has not been dissipated throughout

society as in the insurance case; rather, it has been shifted from the investor to the speculator. The repurchase agreement is not very feasible, however:

1. The repurchase market is basically a dealer market. Small investors hardly participate, since brokerage houses do not provide such facilities to them.

2. The repurchase market is not a centralized market.

3. The repurchase market does not have a standardized contract backed by a third party. Transactions are consummated over the telephone, which is hardly reassuring to investors of a lesser market significance.

4. The repurchase market does not have a centralized agency capable of performing clearing functions for all transactions.

5. As Marcelle Arak[3] argues, the repurchase market offers lower after-tax rates of return than the equivalent position in the futures market.

6. The repurchase agreement does not offer the needed time flexibility for the establishment of a hedge.

6.3 MECHANICS OF FUTURES TRADING

Trading in the futures markets is regulated by the Commodity Futures Trading Commission (CFTC), an independent five-member agency of the U.S. government.[4] The CFTC requires the registration of futures commission brokers and approves the exchanges where futures contracts are traded, the type of contract traded, its terms, and any changes thereof.

All contracts on an underlying security are standardized as to size, maturity, type of deliverable security against the position, delivery time or period, minimum and maximum daily fluctuation, and the way the price is quoted.

For illustration purposes, we shall use T-bill contracts to explain the mechanics of futures trading. Covering every type of contract is far beyond the scope of this chapter.

An investor interested in purchasing a T-bill contract contacts a broker who is a member of the exchange on which the contract is traded (assume the IMM). The message is wired to the floor broker. The floor broker at the IMM enters the trading pit and signals and shouts out the bid. Another broker with an order to sell does likewise, and if both can agree on a price, a transaction is consummated. Once the agreement is reached, the IMM clearinghouse (each major exchange has its own clearinghouse) steps in and assumes responsibility for the contract by interposing itself between the buyer and the seller. The buyer's and the seller's contracts are with the clearinghouse and not with each other. The clearinghouse guarantees delivery and demands receipt of T-bills. It is the "pay-and-collect" agency.

The contract delivery procedure for **IMM**-listed futures contracts (a typical procedure) is shown in Figure 6.3. In order to maintain its financial integrity, the clearinghouse requires member firms to post margin on each contract and marks them to the market

---

[3] See **Marcelle Arak,** "Taxes, Treasury Bills, and Treasury Bill Futures." Federal Reserve Bank of New York (March 26, 1980).

[4] As of June 1982, the halls of the U.S. Congress were filled with rumors that the CFTC would be abolished, or its duties sharply curtailed. The jurisdictions of the SEC, the competing agency, were expected to expand. None of this materialized. The mandate of the CFTC was renewed, although for a limited period.

FIGURE 6.3 **Delivery procedure for International Money Market-futures contract.**

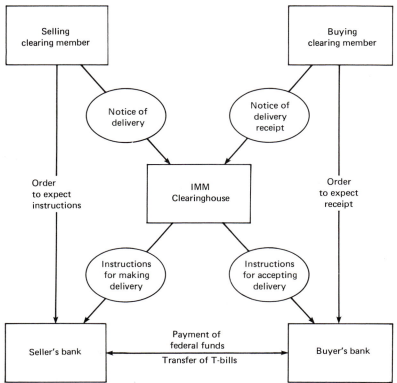

Source: *Opportunities in Interest Rates Treasury Bills Futures,* November 1977. Reprinted with the permission of the International Monetary Market, a division of the Chicago Mercantile Exchange.

at the end of each business day. Each clearing firm must, by using cash, a letter of credit, or an approved security, pay the clearinghouse its previous day's debit balance or receive the previous day's profit based on that day's settlement price.

Financial futures contracts are traded on an exchange. None are traded over the counter. Each contract has a buyer (long) and a seller (short). Futures contracts have a specific maturity date, or a settlement date determined by the seller. The delivery of securities against a futures contract is not frequent. Almost 95 percent[5] of all financial futures contracts are closed out by an offsetting transaction (long if short originally, or short if long originally) prior to their last delivery date.

Short positions in the futures market (contrary to the cash market) always equal the long positions. Short positions, unlike their counterpart in the stock market, do not have to be preceded by an uptick. Furthermore, no securities will have to be borrowed against a short position in the futures market because delivery would not have to be

---

[5] The 5 percent delivery—a high percentage relative to agricultural commodities (3 percent)—is explained by the fact that delivery can be a good way for dealers to liquidate securities with a thin cash market and by the difficulty of closing out arbitrage positions in the cash market.

effected until the expiration date of the contract, if at all. A futures contract is a future obligation and does not involve an immediate exchange of title. The absence of the need to borrow securities obviously helps the investor to avoid interest costs as well as dividends, which are owed by the short seller to the individual or brokerage house that lent the securities for the short position in a stock. Additionally, while the short position in a stock has unlimited downside risk on any given day, the short position in the futures market can incur only a maximum loss set by the daily price-limit change allowed by the exchange (provided that covering the short position is possible at any time).

T-bill contracts are quoted by using the difference between 100 and the actual T-bill yield. A T-bill yielding 8 percent would be quoted at 92(100–8). This form of quoting prices allows prices on futures contracts to be quoted in a manner consistent with that of other financial instruments listed on other exchanges—that is, with a bid price lower than the ask (offer) price. Had T-bills been quoted on a yield basis, the bid would be higher than the ask because the buyer wants the highest possible yield and the seller wants to give up the lowest possible yield.

Minimum price fluctuations on T-bill futures are quoted in multiples of 0.01 or one basis point ($\frac{1}{100}$ of 1 percent). The dollar value of the minimum price fluctuation, given that the face value or the size of the T-bill contract is $1 million, is equal to

$$1,000,000 \times \left(\frac{1}{100}\right)(1\%) \times \text{¼} \left(\frac{90 \text{ (days)}}{360}\right) = \$25$$

The 90 days is used because the contracts are for 90-day T-bills. The maximum daily price fluctuation is 100 basis points or 1 percent for NYFE and 60 basis points for IMM.

The leverage possibilities on the financial futures market are truly remarkable. On a $1 million par value of T-bills, the initial margin requirement is $2,000 on the IMM. The maintenance margin for the same contract is $1,500. This means that if the market yields change in a direction unfavorable to the position of the investor by more than $500, a margin call will be made by the brokerage house. If, on the other hand, market yields move in a favorable direction, the margin account of the trader will be credited by the full profit realized on that day. A margin call must be met in cash and a credit may be withdrawn in cash. This process is referred to as "mark to the market" and is done daily. The minimum margin requirements on futures contracts are set by the exchange (the Federal Reserve System in the cash market for stocks and bonds) and may be revised at the discretion of the exchange. Some brokerage firms require higher margins. Margins are considered a "good faith" deposit and not a downpayment on the price of the contract because the remaining value of the contract is likely never to be paid. Margins are required for both long and short positions and are strongly related to the daily price limits in effect. We will focus further our discussion on T-bills.

An investor having to make a delivery against a 90-day T-bill contract can either deliver a three-month bill, a six-month T-bill with three months to run, or a one-year T-bill with three months to run. (The one-year T-bill used to be deliverable only against T-bill futures contracts traded on the New York Futures Exchange.)

The popularity of T-bill futures contracts as hedging, speculative, and arbitrage vehicles has been spectacular. On a typical day in 1982, $25 billion in face-value three-month

TABLE 6.3
Relationship Between Yields on 90-Day T-Bills and Other
Short-Term Instruments (Monthly 1968 Through 1979)

Financial Instrument	Coefficient of Correlation with 90-Day T-Bills
Six-month T-bill rate	0.994
One-year T-bill rate	0.981
90-day CD rate	0.961
Four- to six-month commercial paper rate	0.963

Source: Calculated from Federal Reserve Board data.

T-bills (each contract having $1 million face value at maturity) was transacted on the IMM alone, with all indications pointing toward even higher volumes.

Corporations wishing to lock in borrowing costs prior to the actual financing date, investors interested in earning today's rate beginning at a certain time in the future, and other hedgers may not be able to sell a futures contract on the specific asset they are trying to protect. Then what is the usefulness to these economic agents of having T-bill futures contracts? To the extent that T-bill rates are highly correlated with those rates on the financial instruments for which protection is sought, T-bill futures can achieve the desired objective. The fact is that the correlation between T-bill rates and other rates are high and significant, as shown in Table 6.3.

T-bills have many other attractive if not peculiar features that make them prime candidates for trading in the futures markets. Among them are the following:

1. *Liquidity.* T-bills enjoy a very highly developed secondary market with considerable depth. The primary market (new issues) is equally strong, with approximate weekly offerings of $3 billion. These features are essential if the investor is to guard against a delivery squeeze.

2. *Security.* T-bills are backed by the full faith and credit of the U.S. government. They are considered riskless.

3. *Homogeneity.* All T-bills are alike in terms of quality, unlike other financial instruments issued by private parties or even by federal agencies. The only difference among T-bills is in their maturity.

4. *Familiarity and ease of delivery.* Investors of varied level of sophistication and nationality are usually familiar with T-bills. The Federal Reserve wire transfer system is used for the quick and efficient transfer of T-bills.

With all of these qualities, the marked success of T-bill futures as a prime vehicle for hedging in the futures market should not surprise any observer.

Another financial instrument issued by the U.S. government that has found considerable popularity on the futures markets is the T-bond. T-bill and T-bond contracts are currently the most actively traded in the futures markets. We shall, therefore, concentrate on the features of these futures contracts, on the differences and similarities in the requirements and trading rules of the major exchanges on which the contracts are traded, and on the determinants of the contract prices.

TABLE 6.4
Features of CBT T-Bond Futures Contracts

Contract size = $100,000

Deliverable security: a T-bond with a minimum of 15 years to maturity or a 15-year call protection.

Invoice pricing mechanism: based on price maintenance determined by factors.[a]

$$\text{Invoice price } (IP) = \text{settlement price } (SP) \times \text{factor } F$$
$$IP = SP \times F$$

Price fluctuations:

Minimum 1/32 of 1%
Maximum 64/32 (2 points)

Margin requirements (set by the exchange and subject to change at any time)

	Initial	*Maintenance*
Hedgers	$1,500	$1,500
Speculators	$2,000	$1,500

Delivery months: March, June, September, and December

Delivery can be made on any business day of the delivery month.

[a] A factor F is an invention of CBT. It is the price of a bond as if yielding 8 percent divided by 100. If the coupon rate on delivered bond is higher than 8 percent, the factor is greater than 1, otherwise, $F \leq 1$; $0.5 \leq F \leq 1.5$.

Features of T-Bond and T-Bill Contracts

The main features of T-bill futures contracts were summarized in Table 6.2. Those on CBT T-bond futures are summarized in Table 6.4. A few entries in these tables warrant further elaboration.

Since November 1, 1979, one-year T-bills have been auctioned and issued the Thursday of every fourth week. Given the auction cycle, a one-year T-bill can be delivered against a 91-day T-bill futures contract on one or two Thursdays of the delivery month. The delivery day on IMM-listed T-bill futures contracts is always on the third Thursday of the delivery month.

On the T-bond side, the most important issue deals with invoice pricing on the CBT. The next section deals with this issue. Another important concern is the delivery date. Any business day during the delivery month is a delivery date on the CBT. Trading in the futures contract ends on the eighth business day before the end of the month, however. The notice day[6] is two business days prior to delivery date. The short—who decides when it is most advantageous for him to deliver—must give notice of his intentions to deliver by 8:00 P.M. (CST). However, if the delivery is to be made on the last business

---

[6] The notice date is the day on which notice of intent to deliver is made by the seller.

day of the delivery month, the short has until 2:00 P.M. (CST) of the day preceding delivery day to notify the clearing corporation.

6.4 MATHEMATICS OF TREASURY FUTURES CONTRACTS

The pricing of futures contracts is both simple and confusing. Table 6.5a shows the price quotations on T-bond and T-bill futures contracts traded on the major exchanges—Table 6.5b shows price quotations for cash T-bonds.

The yields reported in Table 6.5a are based on the settlement price. This price is generally calculated by using the highest and lowest prices during the closing period of a trading day. It could equal the last price (the closing price), but very infrequently. It is the settlement price which is used by brokers for valuing portfolios and for calculating

TABLE 6.5a Futures and Spot Prices

–FINANCIAL–

	Open	High	Low	Settle	Chg	Yield Settle	Yield Chg	Open Interest
EURODOLLAR (IMM)–$1 million; pts of 100%								
Mar83	90.92	91.00	90.90	90.93	+ .03	9.07	– .03	9,853
June	90.52	90.61	90.52	90.55	+ .05	9.45	– .05	7,289
Sept	90.19	90.24	90.18	90.18	+ .04	9.82	– .04	2,632
Dec	89.90	89.93	89.88	89.89	+ .06	10.11	– .06	161
Est vol 1,425; vol Wed 1,609; open int 19,935, +136.								
GNMA 8% (CBT)–$100,000 prncpl; pts. 32nds. of 100%								
Mar83	71-20	72-11	71-20	71-27	+ 13	12.741	– .095	15,889
June	70-27	71-13	70-27	71-01	+ 13	12.918	– .089	6,237
Sept	70-13	70-26	70-13	70-17	+ 13	13.028	– .097	3,879
Dec	69-26	70-11	69-26	70-02	+ 11	13.132	– .091	2,502
Mar84	69-22	69-30	69-21	69-21	+ 12	13.233	– .085	3,275
June	69-20	69-20	69-11	69-11	+ 10	13.294	– .085	2,003
Sept	69-09	69-10	69-01	69-02	+ 12	13.358	– .078	1,979
Dec	69-02	69-06	68-27	68-27	+ 11	13.408	– .071	1,829
Mar85	....	....	....	68-21	+ 9	13.451	– .065	105
June	....	....	....	68-16	+ 9	13.487	– .065	78
Est vol 6,500; vol Wed 6,423; open int 37,776, +208.								
TREASURY BONDS (CBT)–$100,000; pts. 32nds of 100%								
Mar83	77-08	77-16	76-29	76-31	– 1	10.841	+ .005	77,334
June	76-18	76-26	76-09	76-10	– 1	10.941	+ .005	17,130
Sept	76-00	76-08	75-25	75-25	– 1	11,023	+ .005	16,912
Dec	75-19	75-25	75-11	75-11	– 1	11.092	+ .005	21,539
Mar84	75-09	75-13	75-00	75-00	– 1	11.146	– .005	22,235
June	75-00	75-03	74-24	74-24	– 1	11.186	+ .005	9,846
Sept	74-25	74-28	74-17	74-17	– 1	11.221	+ .005	2,661
Dec	74-21	74-23	74-11	74-12	– 1	11.246	+ .005	3,447
Mar85	74-19	74-19	74-08	74-08	– 1	11.266	+ .005	341
June	74-15	74-15	74-04	74-04	– 1	11.286	+ .005	164
Sept	74-11	74-11	74-00	74-00	– 1	11.306	+ .005	35
Est vol 50,000; vol Wed 47,768; open int 171,674, +648.								
TREASURY NOTES (CBT)–$100,000; pts. 32nds of 100%								
Mar83	85-12	85-19	85-07	85-07	+ 3	10.414	– .017	6,263
June	84-19	84-20	84-11	84-11	+ 3	10.574	– .017	315
Sept	....	....	....	83-24	+ 3	10.684	– .017	38
Est vol 2,500; vol Wed 2,543; open int 6,616, +173.								
TREASURY BILLS (IMM)–$1 mil.; pts. of 100%								
	Open	High	Low	Settle	Chg	Discount Settle	Discount Chg	Open Interest
Mar83	92.46	92.56	92.45	92.45	+ .03	7.55	– .03	33,347
June	92.07	92.20	92.07	92.00	+ .06	7.89	– .06	9,811
Sept	91.70	91.81	91.70	91.75	+ .08	8.25	– .08	3,868
Dec	91.39	91.46	91.37	91.38	+ .06	8.42	– .06	1,574
Mar84	91.06	91.11	91.06	91.08	+ .06	8.92	– .06	557
June	90.84	90.84	90.83	90.83	+ .06	9.17	– .06	530
Sept	90.63	90.63	90.63	90.63	+ .06	9.37	– .06	114
Dec	....	....	....	90.45	+ .08	9.55	– .08	24
Est vol 9,237; vol Wed 8,788; open int 49,825, –854.								
BANK CDs (IMM)–$1 million; pts. of 100%								
Mar83	91.54	91.65	91.54	91.57	+ .04	8.43	+ .04	8,734
June	.9.15	9.21	9.14	9.14	+ .06	8.86	– .06	2,080
Sept	90.70	90.80	90.70	90.73	+ .05	9.23	– .05	1,333
Dec	90.40	90.45	90.40	90.42	+ .07	9.58	– .07	128
Est vol 1,832; vol Wed 1,869; open int 12,273, +208.								

TABLE 6.5b Futures and Spot Prices

Treasury Bonds

Rate	Mat. Date		Bid	Asked	Bid Chg.	Yld.
11¾s,	2001	Feb.	107.23	107.31	+ .13	10.74
13⅛s,	2001	May	117.21	117.29	+ .6	10.85
8s,	1996-01	Aug	80.5	80.21	+ .3	10.37
13⅜s,	2001	Aug	119.20	119.28	+ .7	10.86
15¾s,	2001	Nov	138.28	139.12	+ .4	10.81
14¼s,	2002	Feb	126.28	127.4	+ .6	10.86
11⅝s,	2002	Nov	106.31	107.7	+ .7	10.74
10¾s,	2003	Feb	100.30	101.2	+ .5	10.63
8¼s,	2000-05	May	81.18	81.26	+ .8	10.35
7⅝s,	2002-07	Feb	76.30	77.6	+ .11	10.18
7⅞s,	2002-07	Nov	79.2	79.10	+ .4	10.18
8⅜s,	2003-08	Aug	82.9	82.17	+ .7	10.33
8¾s,	2003-08	Nov	84.21	84.29	+ .9	10.45
9⅛s,	2004-09	May	87.28	88.4	+ .9	10.46
10⅜s,	2004-09	Nov	98.19	98.27	+ .9	10.50
11¾s,	2005-10	Feb	107.26	108.2	+ .10	10.78
10s,	2005-10	May	95.14	95.22	+ .7	10.48
12¾s,	2005-10	Nov	115.25	116.1	+ .8	10.84
13⅞s,	2006-11	May	125.8	125.16	+ .9	10.85
14s,	2006-11	Nov	126.22	126.30	+ .11	10.82
10⅜s,	2007-12	Nov	99.14	99.22	+ .4	10.41

Source: The Wall Street Journal, January 14, 1983.

the size of the margin call (if any). The column titled "Change" shows the difference between the settlement price of the day minus the settlement price of the preceding day. The open interest column indicates the total number of contracts outstanding.

Table 6.5b reports the cash prices on T-bonds. The bid column gives the midafternoon bid price at which dealers were willing to buy the issue that day. The naked column gives the dealer selling price. The yield column reports yields to maturity (the effective return on the investment) on the bond issue. How these futures prices are determined and what relationship they have to each other and to the cash market are the subjects of this section.

Pricing of T-Bonds

A competitive economy precludes, through arbitrage, perfect substitutes from selling at different prices. It is the arbitrage mechanism that cements the relationship among the various futures contracts and between the futures and the cash markets.

A short position in the CBT–June 1983 T-bond futures established on January 14, 1983 will require delivery of T-bonds by Thursday, June 30, 1983 at the very latest. Four options are available in fulfilling the delivery requirements:

1. Borrow money now, buy T-bonds, and deliver them on June 30 or any other business day during June.
2. Buy a March '83 CBT contract (the last contract month available on any futures exchange before the June '83 contract month) and take delivery of the bonds, and deliver them against the short position.
3. Wait until June and buy T-bonds in the cash market for delivery against the short position.
4. Make no delivery; that is, close the position by buying an equivalent contract on the CBT.

Options 3 and 4 are not suitable for arbitrage for they do not provide any coverage at the time the short futures are established. Options 1 and 2 are suitable if one is arbitraging between the cash and futures markets or between one futures maturity and another. We shall attempt to price futures contracts off the cash market.

An investor wishing to lock in interest rates for June 1983 could purchase a bond today and carry it until June or buy a futures contract on which he expects to take delivery. The two options should be equivalent, otherwise an arbitrage opportunity would present itself. If the futures price (*FP*) is higher than the cash price plus the net carry charges, an arbitrageur would sell futures and buy cash. The opposite strategy would be employed if the opposite conditions hold (*FP* < cash price + net carry charges).

The pricing of T-bonds futures should consider all the cash inflows and cash outflows for the cash and the futures position. The method is simple:

Let IP = invoice price (futures contract)

  SP = settlement price (futures contract)

   F = the factor

   $IP = SP \times F$

  CC = gross carrying charges

cc = net carrying charges

P^B = cash price of T-bond

The steps are:

1. Determine which T-bonds are deliverable against the June '83 T-bond futures contract. Every bond appearing in Table 6.5b is deliverable except the 8s, 1996–01. The list varies over time as the life to call or to maturity for some bonds shrinks to less than 15 years.

2. Determine which among the deliverable bonds is the "cheapest to deliver." The bond that is cheapest to deliver is the one which gives the short futures the maximum advantage. Since the arbitrageur is buying in the cash market to deliver in the futures market, he or she would want the difference between the adjusted futures price and the cash price to be as low (absolute value) as possible as shown in the example below:

$$\text{Cheapest to deliver} = SP \times F - P^B \qquad (6.1)$$

TABLE 6.6
Calculation of the "Cheapest to Deliver" Treasury Bond Issue Against the June '83 Futures Contract with a Settlement Price of 76 10/32 on January 14, 1983

Treasury Bond Issue Meeting Delivery Requirements	Time to call or maturity (Yrs. + qtrs.)	F^b	Conversion Value = 76.10/32 $\times$ F	Midafternoon T-bond Asking Quote	Conversion Value Minus Asking Quote
11 3/4S 2001 Feb	18	1.3545	103.365	107.31	−3.95
13 1/8S 2001 May	18¼	1.4872	113.492	117.29	−3.80
13 3/8S 2001 Aug	18½	1.5145	115.575	119.28	−3.71
15 3/4S 2001 Nov	18¾	1.7458	133.226	139.12	−5.90
14 1/4S 2002 Feb	19	1.6052	122.497	127.40	−4.90
11 5/8S 2002 Nov	19¾	1.3566	103.526	107.70	−4.17
10 3/4S 2003 Feb	20	1.2722	97.085	101.20	−4.11
8 1/4S 2000–05ᵃ May	17¼	1.2130	78.068	81.26	−3.19
7 5/8S 2002–07 Feb	19	.9637	73.542	77.60	−4.06
7 7/8S 2002–07 Nov	19¾	.9875	75.359	79.10	−3.74
8 3/8S 2003–08 Aug	20½	1.0375	79.174	82.17	−3.0
8 3/4S 2003–08 Nov	20¾	1.0751	82.044	84.29	−2.25
8 1/8S 2004–09 May	21¼	1.0125	77.266	88.40	−11.13
10 3/8S 2004–09 Nov	21¾	1.2427	94.830	98.27	−3.44
11 3/4S 2005–10 Feb	22	1.3853	105.716	108.20	−2.48
10 S 2005–10 May	22¼	1.2061	92.041	95.22	−3.18
12 3/4S 2005–10 Nov	22¾	1.4938	114.00	116.10	−2.10
13 7/8S 2006–11 May	23¼	1.6155	123.283	125.16	−1.88
14 S 2006–11 Nov	23¾	1.6333	124.641	126.30	−1.66
10 3/8S 2007–12 Nov	24¾	1.2540	95.696	99.22	−3.52

[a] 2,000 is the year when the bond may be called by the issuer
2005 Feb are the year and the month of maturity

[b] Using conversion factors tables.

From Table 6.6 we see that the cheapest bond to deliver is the 14S 2006–11 Nov. The "cheapest" could be purchased at the ask price of 126.30 per $100 face value and delivered against the June '83 futures contract at $124.64 per $100 face value.

Before we go much farther we should note how a factor is calculated:

$$F = \frac{\sum_{t=1}^{N} \dfrac{C_t}{(1 + .04)^t}}{100{,}000} \tag{6.2}$$

C_t = Value of semiannual coupon per $100,000 face value, paid at time t.

N = Number of periods = Number of years $\times$ 2 to call or to maturity.

This factor is the price of one dollar of bond with C coupon and N periods to maturity to yield 8 percent.

The calculation of each factor in Table 6.6 was not necessary because tables exist for this purpose. A sample is shown in Table 6.7.

3. Having determined the cheapest to deliver, you should recognize that all futures contracts should be priced in relation to it if markets are operating efficiently.

4. Look at the cash outflows and inflows from the arbitrage position.

Outflows

a. Ask price on the "cheapest" U.S. T-bonds at time t plus accrued interest. All bonds are sold with accrued interest added.

$$\text{Purchase price} = P_t^B + A_t$$

where A_t = accrued interest. (6.3)

b. Carry costs $(CC) = (P_t^B + A_t) \times \dfrac{\text{No. of days carried}}{360} \times R$

where R = Repurchase (Repo) rate prevailing at time t.

Securities dealers ordinarily borrow in the Repo market.

c. Opportunity cost (OC), assuming cash is used, on the margin requirement for T-bond futures. The current margin is $2,000.

$$OC = 2{,}000 \times \frac{\text{No. of days carried}}{360} \times R_B \tag{6.4}$$

where R_B = yield on U.S. Treasury bills maturing with the futures contract.

The opportunity cost could be adjusted upward (if additional margin is required when prices move contrary to expectations) or downward (if margin is released because futures price movements are consistent with expectations). Since the price movements and the related margins are unpredictable and are likely to cancel each other, we can ignore them in our calculations.

Inflows

a. The total coupon income is equal to the first coupon payment plus the coupon that would accrue if the position is closed (at τ) before the next coupon payment.

TABLE 6.7
U.S. Treasury Bond Futures Conversion Factor to Yield 8.000% (Coupon Rates)

TERM	8%	8 1/8%	8 1/4%	8 3/8%	8 1/2%	8 5/8%	8 3/4%	8 7/8%
15	1.0000	1.0108	1.0216	1.0324	1.0432	1.0540	1.0648	1.0757
15-3	.9998	1.0107	1.0216	1.0325	1.0434	1.0543	1.0652	1.0761
15-6	1.0000	1.0110	1.0220	1.0330	1.0440	1.0550	1.0660	1.0769
15-9	.9998	1.0109	1.0220	1.0330	1.0441	1.0552	1.0663	1.0774
16	1.0000	1.0112	1.0223	1.0335	1.0447	1.0559	1.0670	1.0782
16-3	.9998	1.0111	1.0223	1.0336	1.0448	1.0561	1.0678	1.0786
16-6	1.0000	1.0118	1.0227	1.0340	1.0454	1.0567	1.0681	1.0794
16-9	.9998	1.0112	1.0226	1.0341	1.0455	1.0569	1.0683	1.0798
17	1.0000	1.0115	1.0230	1.0345	1.0460	1.0575	1.0690	1.0805
17-3	.9998	1.0114	1.0230	1.0346	1.0461	1.0577	1.0693	1.0809
17-6	1.0000	1.0117	1.0233	1.0350	1.0467	1.0583	1.0700	1.0817
17-9	.9998	1.0115	1.0233	1.0350	1.0468	1.0585	1.0702	1.0820
18	1.0000	1.0118	1.0236	1.0355	1.0473	1.0591	1.0709	1.0827
18-3	.9998	1.0117	1.0236	1.0355	1.0474	1.0592	1.0711	1.0830
18-6	1.0000	1.0120	1.0239	1.0359	1.0479	1.0598	1.0718	1.0837
18-9	.9998	1.0118	1.0239	1.0359	1.0479	1.0600	1.0720	1.0840
19	1.000	1.0121	1.0242	1.0363	1.0484	1.0605	1.0726	1.0847
19-3	.9998	1.0120	1.0241	1.0363	1.0485	1.0607	1.0728	1.0850
19-6	1.0000	1.0122	1.0245	1.0367	1.0490	1.0612	1.0734	1.0857
19-9	.9998	1.0121	1.0244	1.0367	1.0490	1.0613	1.0736	1.0859
20	1.0000	1.0124	1.0247	1.0371	1.0495	1.0619	1.0742	1.0866
20-3	.9998	1.0122	1.0247	1.0374	1.0495	1.0620	1.0744	1.0868
20-6	1.0000	1.0125	1.0250	1.0375	1.0500	1.0625	1.0750	1.0875
20-9	.9998	1.0124	1.0249	1.0375	1.0500	1.0626	1.0751	1.0877
21	1.0000	1.0126	1.0252	1.0378	1.0505	1.0631	1.0757	1.0883
21-3	.9998	1.0125	1.0251	1.0378	1.0505	1.0632	1.0758	1.0885
21-6	1.0000	1.0127	1.0255	1.0382	1.0509	1.0637	1.0764	1.0891
21-9	.9998	1.0126	1.0254	1.0382	1.0509	1.0637	1.0765	1.0893
22	1.000	1.0128	1.0257	1.0385	1.0514	1.0642	1.0771	1.0899
22-3	.9998	1.0127	1.0256	1.0385	1.0514	1.0643	1.0772	1.9091
22-6	1.0000	1.0130	1.0259	1.0389	1.0518	1.0648	1.0777	1.0907
22-9	.9998	1.0128	1.0258	1.0388	1.0518	1.0648	1.0778	1.0908
23	1.0000	1.0131	1.0261	1.0392	1.0522	1.0653	1.0783	1.0914
23-3	.9998	1.0129	1.0260	1.0391	1.0522	1.0653	1.0784	1.0915
23-6	1.0000	1.0132	1.0263	1.0395	1.0526	1.0658	1.0789	1.0921
23-9	.9998	1.0130	1.0262	1.0394	1.0526	1.0658	1.0790	1.0922
24	1.0000	1.0132	1.0265	1.0397	1.0530	1.0662	1.0795	1.0927
24-3	.9998	1.0131	1.0264	1.0397	1.0530	1.0663	1.0795	1.0928
24-6	1.0000	1.0133	1.0267	1.0400	1.0534	1.0667	1.0800	1.0934
24-9	.9998	1.0132	1.0266	1.0399	1.0533	1.0667	1.0801	1.0935
25	1.0000	1.0134	1.0269	1.0403	1.0537	1.0671	1.0806	1.0940
25-3	.9998	1.0133	1.0267	1.0402	1.0537	1.0671	1.0806	1.0941
25-6	1.000	1.0135	1.0270	1.0405	1.0540	1.0676	1.0811	1.0946
25-9	.9998	1.0134	1.0269	1.0405	1.0540	1.0675	1.0811	1.0946
26	1.0000	1.0136	1.0272	1.0408	1.0544	1.0680	1.0816	1.0951
26-3	.9998	1.0134	1.0271	1.0407	1.0548	1.0679	1.0816	1.0952
26-6	1.000	1.0137	1.0273	1.0410	1.0547	1.0684	1.0820	1.0957
26-9	.9998	1.0135	1.0272	1.0409	1.0546	1.0683	1.0820	1.0957
27	1.0000	1.0137	1.0275	1.0412	1.0550	1.0687	1.0825	1.0962
27-3	.9998	1.0136	1.0274	1.0411	1.0549	1.0687	1.0825	1.0963
27-6	1.0000	1.0136	1.0276	1.0415	1.0553	1.0691	1.0829	1.0967
27-9	.9998	1.0137	1.0275	1.0414	1.0552	1.0691	1.0829	1.0968

Source: Reprinted from *Treasury Bond and Note Futures Conversion Factors,* 1980, Financial Publishing Company, Boston, Massachusetts, pp. 8, 9.

TABLE 6.7 (*Continued*)

TERM	8%	8 1/8%	8 1/4%	8 3/8%	8 1/2%	8 5/8%	8 3/4%	8 7/8%
28	1.0000	1.0139	1.0278	1.0417	1.0555	1.0694	1.0833	1.0972
28-3	.9998	1.0137	1.0276	1.0416	1.0555	1.0694	1.0833	1.0972
28-6	1.0000	1.0140	1.0279	1.0419	1.0558	1.0698	1.0837	1.0977
28-9	.9998	1.0138	1.0278	1.0418	1.0557	1.0697	1.0837	1.0977
29	1.0000	1.0140	1.0280	1.0421	1.0561	1.0701	1.0841	1.0981
29-3	.9998	1.0139	1.0279	1.0419	1.0560	1.0700	1.0841	1.0981
29-6	1.0000	1.0141	1.0282	1.0422	1.0563	1.0704	1.0845	1.0986
29-9	.9998	1.0139	1.0280	1.0421	1.0562	1.0703	1.0844	1.0986
30	1.0000	1.0141	1.0283	1.0424	1.0566	1.0707	1.0848	1.0990
30-3	.9998	1.0140	1.0281	1.0423	1.0565	1.0705	1.0848	1.0990
30-6	1.0000	1.0142	1.0284	1.0426	1.0568	1.0710	1.0852	1.0994
30-9	.9998	1.0140	1.0282	1.0425	1.0567	1.0709	1.0851	1.0994
31	1.0000	1.0143	1.0285	1.0428	1.0570	1.0713	1.0855	1.0998
31-3	.9998	1.0141	1.0284	1.0426	1.0569	1.0712	1.0855	1.0997
31-6	1.0000	1.0143	1.0286	1.0429	1.0572	1.0715	1.0858	1.1001
31-9	.9998	1.0141	1.0285	1.0428	1.0571	1.0714	1.0858	1.1001
32	1.0000	1.0144	1.0287	1.0431	1.0574	1.0718	1.0861	1.1005
32-3	.9998	1.0142	1.0286	1.0429	1.0573	1.0717	1.0861	1.1004
32-6	1.0000	1.0144	1.0288	1.0432	1.0576	1.0720	1.0864	1.1008
32-9	.9998	1.0142	1.0287	1.0431	1.0575	1.0719	1.0864	1.1008
33	1.0000	1.0145	1.0289	1.0434	1.0578	1.0723	1.0867	1.1012
33-3	.9998	1.0143	1.0287	1.0432	1.0577	1.0722	1.0866	1.1011
33-6	1.0000	1.0145	1.0290	1.0435	1.0580	1.0725	1.0870	1.1015
33-9	.9998	1.0143	1.0288	1.0433	1.0579	1.0724	1.0869	1.1014
34	1.0000	1.0145	1.0291	1.0436	1.0582	1.0727	1.0872	1.1018
34-3	.9998	1.0144	1.0289	1.0435	1.0580	1.0726	1.0872	1.1017
34-6	1.0000	1.0146	1.0292	1.0437	1.0583	1.0729	1.0875	1.1021
34-9	.9998	1.0144	1.0290	1.0436	1.0582	1.0728	1.0874	1.1020
35	1.0000	1.0146	1.0292	1.0439	1.0585	1.0731	1.0877	1.1074
35-3	.9998	1.0144	1.0291	1.0437	1.0584	1.0730	1.0876	1.1023
35-6	1.0000	1.0147	1.0293	1.0440	1.0586	1.0733	1.0880	1.1026
35-9	.9998	1.0145	1.0292	1.0438	1.0585	1.0732	1.0879	1.1025
36	1.0000	1.0147	1.0294	1.0441	1.0588	1.0735	1.0882	1.1029
36-3	.9998	1.0145	1.0292	1.0439	1.0587	1.0734	1.0881	1.1028
36-6	1.0000	1.0147	1.0295	1.0442	1.0589	1.0737	1.0884	1.1031
36-9	.9998	1.0146	1.0293	1.0440	1.0588	1.0735	1.0883	1.1030
37	1.0000	1.0148	1.0295	1.0443	1.0591	1.0738	1.0886	1.1034
37-3	.9998	1.0146	1.0294	1.0441	1.0589	1.0737	1.0885	1.1033
37-6	1.0000	1.0148	1.0296	1.0444	1.0592	1.0740	1.0888	1.1036
37-9	.9998	1.0146	1.0294	1.0442	1.0591	1.0739	1.0887	1.1035
38	1.0000	1.0148	1.0297	1.0445	1.0593	1.0742	1.0890	1.1038
38-3	.9998	1.0146	1.0295	1.0443	1.0592	1.0740	1.0889	1.1037
38-6	1.0000	1.0149	1.0297	1.0446	1.0594	1.0743	1.0892	1.1040
38-9	.9998	1.0147	1.0296	1.0444	1.0593	1.0742	1.0880	1.1039
39	1.0000	1.0149	1.0298	1.0447	1.0596	1.0745	1.0894	1.1042
39-3	.9998	1.0147	1.0296	1.0445	1.0594	1.0743	1.0892	1.1041
39-6	1.0000	1.0149	1.0298	1.0448	1.0597	1.0746	1.0895	1.1044
39-9	.9998	1.0147	1.0297	1.0446	1.0595	1.0745	1.0894	1.1043
40	1.0000	1.0149	1.0299	1.0448	1.0598	1.0747	1.0897	1.1046

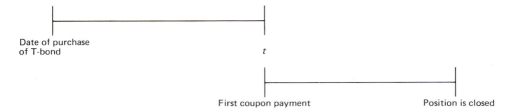

Date of purchase
of T-bond

t

First coupon payment   Position is closed

C_t = value of semiannual coupon

$C_{\tau-t}$ = accrued coupon = value of coupon $\times \dfrac{\tau - t}{360}$

$C_\tau = C_t + C_{\tau-t}$

b. If t is less than τ, the arbitrageur will be able to invest C_t at a rate R_B. The income from reinvestment of C_t is equal to:

$$IR = C_t \times \frac{\tau - t}{360} \times R_B \tag{6.5}$$

In Equation 6.5, τ may not be as easy to determine as it seems. If interest costs are higher than interest revenue ("negative carry") settlement on the CBT contract would be made the first day of June. If, on the other hand, the interest costs are lower than the interest revenues ("positive carry"), the arbitrageur would wish to deliver the last day possible, which is the last business day of the contract month. If he simply wants to close out the short futures position, he would have to do this by the eighth business day before the end of the delivery month.

In the June '83 futures contract case, the last trading day is Monday, June 20, 1983. We will assume that τ is determined by the last trading day.

5. Determine the invoice price (*IP*) of the futures contract.

$$IP + C_\tau + IR = (P_t^B + A_t) + CC + OC$$
$$IP = (P_t^B + A_t) + CC + OC - C_\tau - IR$$
$$IP = (P_t^B + A_t) + cc \tag{6.6}$$

The method for valuing T-bond futures summarized in Equation 6.6 is very similar to that of valuing commodities futures when the futures price is equal to the cash price plus net carry costs. The value, *IP*, derived from 6.6 is the theoretically correct value. If the market observed *IP* is different, then the futures contract is incorrectly priced.

Example

Assume we wish to value the June CBT T-bond futures contract on January 14, 1983 where the cheapest to deliver is 14S 2006–11.

$$P_t^B = 126.30 \times 100,000 = \$126,300$$

   Coupon payments on Treasury bonds coincide ordinarily with the months in which the U.S. Treasury sells long-term T-bonds: February, May, August, and November.

   A bond issued in November pays interest in May and November; thus its accrued interest on January 14, 1983 is

$$A_t = \frac{\dfrac{14\% \times 1000}{2} \times 60}{180} = \$23.34$$

   The accrued interest on 100 bonds is equal to \$2,334. Therefore:

$$P_t^B + A_t = \$126,300 + \$2,334 = \$128,634.$$

$$CC = (P_t^B + A_t) \times \frac{\text{No. of days carried}}{360} \times R$$

   No. of days carried = Jan/14/83–June/20/83 = 158 days

$$R \approx 7.8\%$$

$$CC = \$128,634 \times \frac{158}{360} \times \frac{7.8}{100} = \mathbf{\$4,403.57}$$

$$OC = \$2,000 \times \frac{158}{360} \times \frac{7.7}{100} = \mathbf{\$67.59}$$

$$C_t = \frac{14}{200} \times 100,000 = \mathbf{\$7,000}$$

$$C_{\tau-t} = \frac{14}{200} \times 100,000 \times \frac{36 \text{ days}}{180} = \mathbf{\$1,400}$$

$$C_\tau = \$7,000 + 1,400 = \mathbf{\$8,400}$$

$$IR = \$7,000 \times \frac{36}{360} \times \frac{7.7}{100} = \mathbf{\$53.90}$$

Therefore:

Theoretical $IP = \$128,634 + \$4,403.57 + \$67.59 - \$8,400 - \$53.90$
$$= \mathbf{\$124,651}$$

Market determined $IP = $ futures prices $\times F \times 1,000$
$$= \mathbf{\$124,641}$$

   The June CBT T-bond contract appears to be correctly priced.
   We now demonstrate how T-Bill futures contracts are priced.

6.5 PRICING T-BILL FUTURES CONTRACTS

The price of a T-bill futures contract can be determined, as in the T-bond case, on the basis of the arbitrage relationship between the spot market and the futures market. Our model is based on the work of W. Poole[7] as well as on that of R. Rendleman and C. Carabini.[8] Poole determined the upper and lower price limits of the T-bill futures contract. Using essentially a similar approach, Rendleman and Carabini arrive at similar upper and lower bounds and at a formula for determining the IMM index value assuming no transactions costs. In both papers, the upper and lower limits are determined by transactions costs and the margin requirements on IMM contracts.

The term arbitrage will be used rather loosely in this section, without necessarily meaning pure arbitrage. A pure arbitrage opportunity results in a return on a riskless position that requires no commitment of funds. Pure arbitrage is not always possible in T-bill futures contracts because maturities cannot always be matched. This is so because of the marking to the market requirements that generate opportunity losses to those on the wrong side of the market and because the borrowing rate is not uniform for all borrowers. Therefore, the arbitrage we speak of is not necessarily risk-free and may require commitment of funds.[9]

The pricing of futures T-bill contracts is rather simple. Consider the case of an investor faced with the following choice: (1) invest in 182-day T-bill or (2) invest in a 91-day bill and buy a futures contract maturing 91 days hence.

In a perfect market, the investor should be indifferent between the two options because both offer equivalent returns.

Let K_m = yield on a 91-day T-bill

K_n = yield on a 182-day T-bill

$K_{Ft,m}$ = yield on a futures contract maturing m days from now

$K_{FW,n-m}$ = implied forward rate on a T-bill with a life equal to $n - m$.

Therefore, if the market is in equilibrium

$$((1 + K_m)(1 + K_{Ft,m}))^{1/n} = ((1 + K_m)(1 + K_{FW,n-m}))^{1/n} = (1 + K_n) \qquad (6.7)$$

Arbitrage presents itself when

$$K_{Ft,m} \gtreqless K_{FW,n-m}$$

$$K_{Ft,m} > K_{FW,n-m} \qquad (i)$$

---

[7] **William Poole,** "Using T-Bill Futures to Gauge Interest Rate Expectations." *Federal Reserve Bank of San Francisco Economic Review* (Spring 1978), pp. 7–19.

[8] **Richard J. Rendleman** and **Christopher E. Carabini,** "The Efficiency of the Treasury Bill Futures Market." *Journal of Finance,* vol. 34 (September 1979), pp. 895–914.

[9] See **Douglas T. Breeden,** "Comments on Selected Articles Concerning T-Bill Futures Efficiency" and "The Effect of Interest Rate Futures on the Variations in Spot Rates." Center for the Study of Futures Markets, Columbia Business School, p. 198.

Assume that the six-month T-bill rate is 9 percent and the three-month T-bill rate is 10 percent. The implied three-month forward rate is, therefore equal to

$$K_{FW,3} = \frac{(1+0.09)^2}{(1+0.10)} - 1 = 8 \text{ percent}$$

An arbitrageur observing that the futures rate is above the 8 percent forward rate would employ the following strategy:

1. Borrow money long term at 9 percent. This assumes that the borrowing and the lending rates are equal.
2. Buy a three-month T-bill.
3. Simultaneously, go long (buy) one T-bill futures contract with a three-month maturity.

The spot and futures T-bill positions have the effect of creating a synthetic six-month T-bill with a yield exceeding that realized on the six-month T-bill. If the futures rate is equal to 9 percent, the six-month annualized rate on the "synthetic" position is

$$\sqrt{(1+0.10)(1+0.09)} - 1 = 9.50\%$$

The 9.5 percent is larger than the 9 percent that could be realized on a six-month T-bill bought in the spot market.

$$K_{Ft,m} < K_{FW,n-m} \tag{ii}$$

Assume that the rates in the preceding example were reversed; the forward rate would then be equal to

$$K_{FW,3} = \frac{(1+0.10)^2}{(1+0.09)} - 1 = 11\%$$

An arbitrageur who observes this forward rate and judges the difference between it and the futures rate to be too high would undertake the following:

1. Borrow money for three months
2. Buy longer-term (six-month) T-bills
3. Simultaneously go short (sell) one (or more) T-bill futures contract with a three-month maturity.

The long bill will be delivered against the short contract upon maturity of the futures contract. The debt will be repaid from the proceeds on the short position. The arbitrage profit would equal the profit on the short futures position less net borrowing costs.

From Equation 6.7 we can derive the theoretical price of the T-bill futures contract. Taking the inverse of Equation 6.7, we get

$$\left[\frac{1}{(1+K_m)}\right]\left[\frac{1}{(1+K_{Ft,m})}\right] = \frac{1}{(1+K_n)^n}$$

or

$(P_m)(P_F) = P_n = $ price of a T-bill that pays \$1 maturity

Therefore:

$$P_F = \frac{P_n}{P_m} \tag{6.8}$$

where $P_F = $ price of a futures contract using the bankers' discount method of pricing T-bills — price equals the difference between \$100 and the annualized discount from par assuming 360 days in a year

$P_n = $ spot price of an n-day T-bill

$P_m = $ spot price of an m-day T-bill

Equation 6.8 assumes no commission costs and zero bid-ask dealer spread. If these transactions costs are accounted for, the price of the forward contract will have to fall in the following range—assuming \$6 or \$0.006 per \$100 of par round-trip commission costs:

$$100 \frac{P_n^A}{P_m^B} - 0.006 \leq P_F \leq 100 \frac{P_n^A}{P_m^B} + 0.006 \tag{6.9}$$

where $P_n^A = $ asking price

$P_m^B = $ bid price

$0.006 = $ \$60 round commission on a \$1 million contract

Subtracting both sides of Equation 6.9 from 100, then multiplying by 360/91 days to arrive at the annualized discount from par and subtracting from \$100 to arrive at the IMM index value, we get the following range:[10]

$$100 - 395.6\left(1 - \frac{P_n^B}{P_m^A}\right) - 0.0237 \leq P_F \leq 100 - 395.6\left(1 - \frac{P_n^A}{P_m^B}\right) + 0.0237 \tag{6.10}$$

Example
What should be the theoretical price of an IMM March '83 contract as of January 14, 1983, if the deliverable bill against the futures contract is a June 16, 1983 T-bill with a bid price of 7.75 and asked price equal to 7.65, or an average price of 7.70?

Answer
1. Determine the T-bill rate applicable to the m period—the period between January 14, 1983 and the third Thursday of March when the T-bill is deliverable. This period is equal to 62 days.
2. Find the price on a T-bill maturing 62 days hence (March 17, 1983). From *The Wall Street Journal* January 14, 1983 issue, we read that the bid price is 7.68 and the ask is 7.54, yielding an average price of 7.61.

---

[10] **Rendleman** and **Carabini,** pp. 898–899.

3. Calculate

$$P_F = \frac{100 - (7.70 \times (153/360))}{100 - (7.61 \times (62/360))} =$$

$$= \frac{100 - 3.27}{100 - 1.31} = \frac{96.73}{98.69} = 0.9801$$

Therefore:

$$100 - 98.01 = 1.99$$

$$\text{the annualized yield} = 1.99 \times \frac{360}{91} = 7.87$$

$$P_F = 100 - 7.87 = \mathbf{92.13}$$

TABLE 6.8
91-Day U.S. Treasury Bills

		91-Day Bills					91-Day Bills		
IMM Index	Disc. Rate	Coupon Equiv.	Disc. on $1,000,000	Price	IMM Index	Disc. Rate	Coupon Equiv.	Disc. on $1,000,000	Price
91.61	8.39	8.691	21,208.06	978,791.94	92.12	7.88	8.152	19,918.89	980,081.11
91.62	8.38	8.680	21,182.78	978,817.22	92.13	7.87	8.141	19,893.61	980,106.39
91.63	8.37	8.670	21,157.50	978,842.50	92.14	7.86	8.131	19,868.33	980,131.67
91.64	8.36	8.659	21,132.22	978,867.78	92.15	7.85	8.120	19,843.06	980,156.94
91.65	8.35	8.648	21,106.94	978,893.06	92.16	7.84	8.110	19,817.78	980,182.22
91.66	8.34	8.638	21,081.67	978,918.33	92.17	7.83	8.099	19,792.50	980,207.50
91.67	8.33	8.627	21,056.39	978,943.61	92.18	7.82	8.088	19,767.22	980,232.78
91.68	8.32	8.617	21,031.11	978,968.89	92.19	7.81	8.078	19,741.94	980,258.06
91.69	8.31	8.606	21,005.83	978,994.17	92.20	7.80	8.067	19,716.67	980,283.33
91.70	8.30	8.596	20,980.56	979,019.44	92.21	7.79	8.057	19,691.39	980,308.61
91.71	8.29	8.585	20,955.28	979,044.72	92.22	7.78	8.046	19,666.11	980,333.89
91.72	8.28	8.574	20,930.00	979,070.00	92.23	7.77	8.036	19,640.83	980,359.17
91.73	8.27	8.564	20,904.72	979,095.28	92.24	7.76	8.025	19,615.56	980,384.44
91.74	8.26	8.553	20,879.44	979,120.56	92.25	7.75	8.015	19,590.28	980,409.72
91.75	8.25	8.543	20,854.17	979,145.83	92.26	7.74	8.004	19,565.00	980,435.00
91.76	8.24	8.532	20,828.89	979,171.11	92.27	7.73	7.994	19,539.72	980,460.28
91.77	8.23	8.522	20,803.61	979,196.39	92.28	7.72	7.983	19,514.44	980,485.56
91.78	8.22	8.511	20,778.33	979,221.67	92.29	7.71	7.972	19,489.17	980,510.83
91.79	8.21	8.500	20,753.06	979,246.94	92.30	7.70	7.962	19,463.89	980,536.11
91.80	8.20	8.490	20,727.78	979,272.22	92.31	7.69	7.951	19,438.61	980,561.39
91.81	8.19	8.479	20,702.50	979,297.50	92.32	7.68	7.941	19,413.33	980,586.67
91.82	8.18	8.469	20,677.22	979,322.78	92.33	7.67	7.930	19,388.06	980,611.94
91.83	8.17	8.458	20,651.94	979,348.06	92.34	7.66	7.920	19,362.78	980,637.22
91.84	8.16	8.448	20,626.67	979,373.33	92.35	7.65	7.909	19,337.50	980,662.50
91.85	8.15	8.437	20,601.39	979,398.61	92.36	7.64	7.899	19,312.22	980,687.78
91.86	8.14	8.426	20,576.11	979,423.89	92.37	7.63	7.888	19,286.94	980,713.06
91.87	8.13	8.416	20,550.83	979,449.17	92.38	7.62	7.878	19,261.67	980,738.33
91.88	8.12	8.405	20,525.56	979,474.44	92.39	7.61	7.867	19,236.39	980,763.61
91.89	8.11	8.395	20,500.28	979,499.72	92.40	7.60	7.856	19,211.11	980,788.89
91.90	8.10	8.384	20,475.00	979,525.00	92.41	7.59	7.846	19,185.83	980,814.17
91.91	8.09	8.374	20,449.72	979,550.28	92.42	7.58	7.835	19,160.56	980,839.44
91.92	8.08	8.363	20,424.44	979,575.56	92.43	7.57	7.825	19,135.28	980,864.72
91.93	8.07	8.352	20,399.17	979,600.83	92.44	7.56	7.814	19,110.00	980,890.00
91.94	8.06	8.342	20,373.89	979,626.11	92.45	7.55	7.804	19,084.72	980,915.28
91.95	8.05	8.331	20,348.61	979,651.39	92.46	7.54	7.793	19,059.44	980,940.56
91.96	8.04	8.321	20,323.33	979,676.67	92.47	7.53	7.783	19,034.17	980,965.83
91.97	8.03	8.310	20,298.06	979,701.94	92.48	7.52	7.772	19,008.89	980,991.11
91.98	8.02	8.300	20,272.78	979,727.22	92.49	7.51	7.762	18,983.61	981,016.39
91.99	8.01	8.289	20,247.50	979,752.50	92.50	7.50	7.751	18,958.33	981,041.67
92.00	8.00	8.278	20,222.22	979,777.78	92.51	7.49	7.741	18,933.06	981,066.94
92.01	7.99	8.268	20,196.94	979,803.06	92.52	7.48	7.730	18,907.78	981,092.22
92.02	7.98	8.257	20,171.67	979,828.33	92.53	7.47	7.720	18,882.50	981,117.50
92.03	7.97	8.247	20,146.39	979,853.61	92.54	7.46	7.709	18,857.22	981,142.78
92.04	7.96	8.236	20,121.11	979,878.89	92.55	7.45	7.698	18,831.94	981,168.06
92.05	7.95	8.226	20,095.83	979,904.17	92.56	7.44	7.688	18,806.67	981,193.33
92.06	7.94	8.215	20,070.56	979,929.44	92.57	7.43	7.677	18,781.39	981,218.61
92.07	7.93	8.205	20,045.28	979,954.72	92.58	7.42	7.667	18,756.11	981,243.89
92.08	7.92	8.194	20,020.00	979,980.00	92.59	7.41	7.656	18,730.83	981,269.17
92.09	7.91	8.183	19,994.72	980,005.28	92.60	7.40	7.646	18,705.56	981,294.44
92.10	7.90	8.173	19,969.44	980,030.56	92.61	7.39	7.635	18,680.28	981,319.72
92.11	7.89	8.162	19,944.17	980,055.83	92.62	7.38	7.625	18,655.00	981,345.00

Source: 91-Day U.S. Treasury Bills, International Monetary Market, Chicago Mercantile Exchange.

Table 6.8 shows relevant T-bill data available from the IMM. It allows for easy translation of an IMM index into the actual value (price) of a contract.

6.6 USES OF T-BILL AND T-BOND FUTURES

The investment strategies that T-bill futures afford can be devised, the reader should be reminded, using other vehicles (forward contracts,[11] repurchase agreements, the cash markets, etc.), as was discussed earlier in this chapter. The futures markets, however, allow for greater convenience, greater flexibility, greater liquidity, and lower transactions costs in implementing the strategies.

Futures contracts are generally used to hedge risk and to speculate. The speculation is either on the level of the interest rate or on the relationship among rates. Thomas A. Hieronymus makes clear in his book that the distinction between hedging and speculating is misleading.

> *It is sometimes said that hedging is the opposite of speculation. This is not so. They are different kinds of the same thing. The thing that is usually identified as speculation, that is, long or short positions in futures contracts, is speculation in changes in price level. The thing that we identify as hedging, that is, long cash and short futures or vice versa, is speculation in price relationships.*[12]

With this qualifier, we proceed in the analysis of various hedging and speculative strategies.

Hedging

In futures, hedging is "The assumption of a position in futures . . . opposite to an already existing or immediately anticipated cash position . . . to hedge is to insulate one's business activities from price level speculation while retaining the opportunity to speculate in basis variation."[13] In effect, hedging exchanges absolute market risk for basis risk. The difference and similarities between the two definitions should become obvious from the examples to follow.

The particular situation of an investor could dictate one of two possible hedging strategies: a short hedge (referred to at times as "long the basis"), or a long hedge (referred to at times as "short the basis"). The short hedge involves the sale (a short position) of a futures contract, and the long hedge involves the purchase (a long position) of a futures contract.

Short Hedge

The purpose of a short hedge is to offset risk in a cash position. Consider the case of a bank with a $5 million holding of government securities. The bank investment committee expects a rise in the yield on government bonds within the next two months and a

---

[11] A forward contract is a cash contract with a deferred delivery.

[12] **Thomas A. Hieronymus,** *Economics of Futures Trading for Commercial and Personal Profit,* Commodity Research Bureau, Inc., New York, p. 150.

[13] Ibid., p. 149. A "basis" is the difference between the yield on the futures contract and on a cash contract.

leveling off thereafter. That is, the investment committee expects a capital loss on the bank holdings of government bonds. The futures market, it was decided, should be used to hedge against the expected depreciation. The process involves the following:

Date	Cash Market	Futures Market
January 14, 1983 (today's date)	No transaction. Average price of bonds is equal to $5,000,000 × 92.2% = $4,610,000.	Sell 50 ($100,000 each)[14] March '83 T-bonds contracts on the CBT. Invoice price IP = settlement price SP × conversion factor CF The CF for a 10¾ bond (assumed deliverable bond) is 1.2922. Therefore $IP = 0.76968 \times 1.2922$ $\quad = 0.99458$ per $1 of contract. Total value $= IP \times$ contract size × no. of contracts. Total value $= 0.99458 \times \$100,000 \times 50 = \$4,972,900$. (This sum is not received in cash, only the appreciation on the short position is credited daily to the bank's account.)
March 1, 1983	No transaction; average price of bond is equal to $5,000,000 × 90.2% = $4,510,000.	Cover short position (buy 50 March contracts). Invoice price = 0.97458. Total value $=$ $0.97458 \times \$100,000 \times 50 = \$4,872,900$
	$4,610,000 −4,510,000 Book loss $ (100,000)	$4,972,900 −4,872,900 Gain $ 100,000

In this example, the book loss is offset exactly by the gain in the futures market. This is an example of a perfect hedge.[15] The net gains (losses) are zero. The bond holdings have been fully protected against rising interest rates. The example ignores transactions costs, which are not very significant (about $60 round-trip costs per contract).

---

[14] The sale of futures contracts is not necessarily done on a one-to-one basis, as we discuss later in this chapter. This form of hedging is referred to as a naive hedge.

[15] Lest the reader be misled, the T-bond futures contract used here is a good hedge only against 8 percent 20-year government bonds. Any other coupon or maturity requires the application of a factor to improve the basis; this is conveniently ignored in this example.

The full protection results from an equal movement in price in the cash and the futures market. That is, the basis—the differential between the yield on the futures contract and the yield on a cash contract—has remained constant between January 14, and March 1, 1983 (assuming a flat yield curve). Such occurrences are rare, however, in the real world. The basis may shrink or expand with advantageous or harmful results to the bank. If the yield on futures contracts rises faster than its cash counterpart, the bank stands to realize a profit from the hedge. If, on the other hand, the yield on futures contracts rises more slowly than its cash counterpart, the bank will not realize a gain in the futures market sufficiently large to offset the losses in the cash market. The bank, under these circumstances, is not fully hedged. The implications of the changes in the basis will become more obvious as more examples are given below. Three additional considerations must be noted:

1. The $100,000 gain in the futures market is not realized all at once, as may be deduced from the example above. Brokers are required to mark their clients to the market on a daily basis. If a profit in the short position accrues, the client's account is credited the full amount on a daily basis. This credit can be withdrawn and invested elsewhere, a possibility that is ignored here.

2. The hedge in this case, basis concerns aside, works well because there exists a futures contract on the exact bond that the bank is trying to protect. Were the bank the owner of corporate bonds instead of government bonds, for example, the extent of the protection provided by the futures market would depend on the degree of correlation between the yields on corporate bonds and that on futures T-bonds contracts. Shorting the T-bond futures contract in this case is referred to as a "cross hedge", which offers less protection than the exact hedge.

3. In the event that the expectations of the investment committee do not materialize, a real loss would be incurred on the short position, offset (partially or totally) by gains in the cash position. Thus the aversion of some portfolio managers to interest rate futures.

The inevitable conclusion to be drawn from the above observations is that the strategy of always hedging is not always optimum. Additionally, the strategy of hedging 100 percent of the exposed assets is also not always optimum.

A short hedge can also be used to manage the liability side of the balance sheet. A bank expecting to issue $1 million in one-year certificates of deposits (CDs) three months from now is obviously concerned with rising interest rates. In order to "lock-in" today's CD rate, the bank could enter the following transactions:

Date	*Cash Market*	*Futures Market*
January 14, 1983	No transaction CD rate = 9%	Sell one 90-day June U.S. T-bill* on IMM (current settlement price = 92.00) Proceeds** = $1,000,000 - (91/360 \times 8/100 \times 1,000,000) = $979,777.78.

Date	Cash Market	Futures Market
April 5, 1983	Issue $1 million of CDs at 10 percent. Additional annual interest costs =	Cover the short position (June contract quoted at 90.00) Costs = 1,000,000 − (91/360 × 10/100 × 1,000,000) = $974,722.23 Profit on short position =
	1/100 × 1,000,000 = **$10,000**	$979,777.78 − $974,722.23 = **$5,055.55**

* The banker could obviously hedge using bank CDs futures contracts traded on the IMM. We are using T-bill futures to illustrate a cross hedge and to show that it is possible and sometimes desirable to occasionally use the T-bill futures market for it may have greater depth and liquidity.

** The funds are not actually received. In fact, the short seller would have to pay the margin requirement on the contracts. We use this concept here to simplify presentation.

The profits realized in the futures market were clearly insufficient to offset the losses (the increased costs) in the cash market. The bank could have elected to short two futures contracts instead of one, had it correctly anticipated the narrowing in the basis.

A short hedge is sometimes referred to by practitioners as "long the basis": a long position in the cash market and a short position in the futures market. For profits to accrue, the cash price must appreciate more or depreciate less than the futures price by the maturity date of the futures contract. Upon maturity, the futures contract is equivalent to a cash contract.

The opposite of a short hedge is a long hedge, referred to sometimes as "short the basis."

Long Hedge

The long hedge is the opposite of a short hedge. The intent is the same; however, the long hedge is established in order to offset risk in an actual or prospective cash position. A pension fund manager expecting to receive $5 million in three months is concerned about falling yields requiring him to invest at a much lower rate in the future than he presently could. In order to lock in today's rate, the manager decides to go long 50 futures T-bond contracts. The process is as follows:

Date	Cash Market	Futures Market
January 14, 1983	No transaction. Average yield on long-term bonds is 10.25 percent.	Buy 50 June T-bond futures contracts on the CBT. Settlement price = 76. 10/32. This price is based on the delivery of an 8 percent coupon bond. Assuming that such a bond is available and cheapest to deliver the cost of 50 contracts is: 50 × .763125 × $100,000 = $3,815,625.

Date	Cash Market	Futures Market
		(The pension fund manager is only obligated to pay the margin requirement per contract and is expected to be ready to meet the margin calls). The cost is the financial commitment required if the manager takes delivery of the bonds when the futures contract matures.
April 5, 1983	Invest the $5 million at 9.50 percent. Opportunity loss = 0.75 percent per year or 0.0075 × $5,000,000 = **$37,500**	Sell 50 June T-bonds futures contracts at 80. The proceeds are = 50 × $100,000 × 0.80 = $4,000,000
	This opportunity loss will be incurred over the life of the investment, which can well exceed a year in the case of a pension fund.[16]	Profits = $4,000,000.00 −3,815,625.00 $ 184,375.00 This is a one-time gain.

The long hedge demonstrates once again the dependence of the hedge strategy on the basis. This turns the hedge into a speculation on the size of the basis. Understanding the basis behavior is paramount to establishing a successful hedging strategy. Once again, fundamentalists look for an economic rationale for basis behavior and chartists look at past trends, hoping to cash in on their recurrence. The fundamentalists argue that the basis is determined primarily by market expectations concerning interest rates and by dealer behavior.

Interest rate expectations are embodied in the yield curve. A flat yield curve (see Figure 6.4a) implies a constant basis. Figure 6.4b shows a rising yield curve, although at a diminishing rate. The farther we move along the t axis, the smaller the basis. The problem lies in correctly defining the basis. The optimum way is to think of the basis as the difference between the futures yield and the yield on a six-month T-bill to be delivered three months from now against the futures contract. Therefore, as we move through time and each futures contract turns into a cash contract as its life shrinks

---

[16] The actual value of the loss due to a one-time drop in interest rates is equal to the present value of the annual losses. This value is equal to:

$$PV = \sum_{t=1}^{n} \frac{L_t}{(1 + 0.1025)^t} = \$37,500 \times PVDF_a$$

where L_t = loss at time t.

Assuming a 20-year time horizon: $PV = \$37,500 \times 8.40 = \$315,000$. Assuming a constant basis, the bank would have had to buy $315,000/$184,375 ≈ 1.71 times the value of the investment in the cash market.

FIGURE 6.4.   Price-sensitivity strategy.

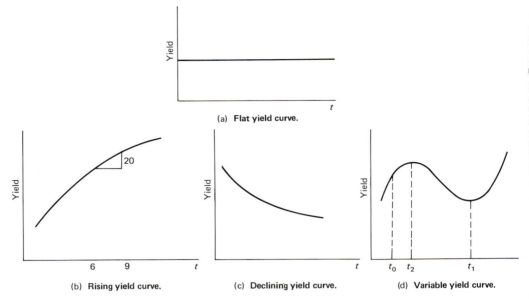

(a) Flat yield curve.

(b) Rising yield curve.   (c) Declining yield curve.   (d) Variable yield curve.

to zero, the basis shrinks. The size of the shrinkage depends on the size of the rate of change in the yield.

Figure 6.4c shows the declining yield curve. Again, the changes in the basis will depend on the size of the change in the slope of the curve.

Figure 6.4d is most interesting in that it describes the conditions under which basis trading could bring sizable gains or losses, depending on the starting point and the established hedge strategy. A hedger at time t_0, expecting a reversal in the yield curve and judging its size correctly, is obviously at an advantage when compared with a hedger anticipating an upward-sloping yield curve. A correctly anticipated yield-curve slope is most helpful in timing a hedge. The maximum basis size is between t_2 and t_1, suggesting to the hedger standing at time t_0 to wait until time t_2 to establish a hedge provided that the particular situation allows.

The maximum swings in the basis are more likely to occur with yield curves changing slopes. The factors influencing the behavior of bond dealers also affect the basis. The influence emanates from the cost of financing the inventory of corporate and government bonds—a cost determined by the relationship between short and long rates. The higher short rates are in relation to long rates, the higher the inventory carrying costs and the higher the price quotations are on deferred contracts. The lower the short rates are in relation to long rates, the larger the profits from carrying bond inventory and the lower the price on deferred contracts.

No matter how well conceived a hedging strategy is, it is not always superior to a no-hedge position. Real losses in a futures position established to hedge against interest-rate risks in the cash market are offset (partially or totally) by gains in the cash market. A no-hedge position, on the other hand, would have produced only gains in the cash market and zero losses in the futures market. Furthermore, as the reader must have noted by now, depending on expectations, hedging may require a long or a short position

in the futures market equal to a fraction of that in the cash market. Once again, the ability to predict the behavior of the basis should dictate the hedge ratio. The operating constraint, however, is that futures contracts are not divisible. Only multiples of the standard contract size on the particular exchange are achievable.

Determination of the Hedge Ratio

The ideal hedge is the one that produces gains that exactly offset losses. Stated mathematically, a perfect hedge is

$$\Delta P_i + \Delta P_J(N) = 0 \tag{6.11}$$

where ΔP_i = change per unit in the value of bond i to be hedged.

$\quad\quad \Delta P_J$ = change per unit in the value of a futures contract J

$\quad\quad N$ = number of units of a futures contract

If Equation 6.11 holds, the wealth of the hedger will be unaffected by changes in the interest rate.

Studies on the hedge ratio have traditionally emphasized that a way to arrive at a perfect hedge (or an approximation thereof) is to equate the face value of the securities to be hedged with those used to hedge.[17] This, unfortunately, works only under very limited assumptions, such as the equality of coupons and maturity between the hedged and hedging instrument.

A new method divised by Kolb and Chiang offers greater but limited promise. The new method "takes account of differences between the maturity and coupon structures of the hedged and hedging instruments."[18] The new method was dubbed by Kolb and Chiang as the price-sensitivity (PS) strategy.

Using PS, the number of futures contracts necessary to hedge a cash position is arrived at as follows:

$$N = -\frac{\bar{R}_J P_i D_i}{\bar{R}_i FP_J D_J} \times \frac{(d\bar{R}_i/dR_F)}{(d\bar{R}_J/dR_F)} \tag{6.12}$$

where $\quad R_F$ = 1 + the risk-free rate

$\quad\quad \bar{R}_J$ = 1 + expected yield to maturity on the asset underlying futures contract J

$\quad\quad \bar{R}_i$ = 1 + expected yield to maturity on asset i

$\quad\quad FP_J$ = agreed upon price to the bond underlying J

$\quad\quad P_i$ = the expected price of asset i when the hedge is terminated

$\quad\quad D_i$ = the duration of asset i expected at the end of the hedge period

$\quad\quad D_J$ = the duration of the asset underlying contract J expected at the end of the hedge period

---

[17] See for example, **P. Bacon** and **R. Williams**, "Interest Rate Futures: New Tools for the Financial Manager." *Financial Management* (Spring 1976), pp. 32–38.

[18] **Robert W. Kolb** and **Raymond Chiang**, "Improving Hedging Performance Using Interest Rate Futures." *Financial Management* (Autumn 1981), p. 77.

While Kolb and Chiang took a major step forward, their model has very limited applications. It produces a perfect hedge only when the yield curve is flat and changes in interest rates are "infinitesimal."

Another method for computing the hedge ratio is extensively used by Salomon Brothers, Inc. It is the regression-determined hedge ratio. It is quite effective and involves three simple steps:

1. Determine the yield volatility of the asset to be hedged relative to that of the futures contract. This is done using regression analysis. If a 12 basis-point change in *B*, the security to be hedged, is associated with a 10 basis-point in the appropriate futures contract (*A*), the relative yield volatility is then 1.2 to 1.

2. Determine the price value change per basis-point, that is, the change in dollar price of the asset to be hedged and the hedging instrument corresponding to a change of one basis-point in yield. Assume that

Price value change per basis-point for $A = 0.055$
Price value change per basis-point for $B = 0.061$

Therefore, a one basis-point change in A's yield produces a dollar price change of 0.055. The dollar price change in B is, therefore, equal to $1.2 \times 0.061 = 0.0732$.

3. Determine the hedge ratio.

$$\text{Hedge ratio} = \frac{\text{volatility of security to be hedged}}{\text{volatility of futures contract}}$$

$$= \frac{0.0732}{0.055} = 1.33$$

Thus, one futures contract unit, in this example, is needed to hedge 1.33 units of *A*.

The problem of determining the hedge ratio that produces a perfect hedge under varying states of the world has yet to be completely resolved. Meanwhile, every hedge remains a speculation on the basis.

Speculation[19]

The financial futures markets offer interesting opportunities for speculators. They are characterized by high leverage possibilities, very high liquidity, low transactions costs, a large body of information on the behavior (past, actual, and expected) of the underlying security, and a special tax treatment of the results of speculative strategies. Long-term capital gains (if any) on financial futures contracts are established only after a six-month holding period, compared with a one-year holding period for the underlying financial asset. Market participants may speculate on the level of the rate or on the relationship among rates.

---

[19] The coverage of speculation is intended to give the reader a general idea on how to capitalize on certain opportunities using futures contracts. It is not a comprehensive analysis.

Rate-Level Speculation

Speculators are hedgers without offsetting positions in the cash market. They simply bet on the direction of the yield curve and the size of the change by holding an open futures position. If a drop in yields is expected (a rise in the price of bonds), a long position is established. If a rise in yields is expected, on the other hand, a short position is established.

These rate-level speculations are less widespread than those on rate relationships, which we examine next.

Rate-Relationship Speculation

Rate-relationship speculations are known as spreads. They are varied in kind and in level of sophistication.

A spread involves the concurrent sale of one contract and the purchase of another. The most frequently used spreads are the intermonth and interinstrument spreads. The intermonth spread involves the sale (a short position) of one delivery month contract and simultaneously the purchase (a long position) of another delivery month contract on the same financial instrument. The interinstrument spread involves the sale of one contract month on one instrument (say March '85, GNMA) and the purchase of the same contract month on another (say March '85 T-bonds). If the contract month is different, then the spread becomes both an intermonth as well as an interinstrument spread.

The purpose of spreads is to capitalize on aberrations in relationships among futures contracts traded in the financial futures markets.

Intermonth Spreads

The intermonth spread, as stated in the stock option case, involves the purchase of one contract month and the sale of another on the same underlying instrument. The speculator is betting that the yield on the contract bought will fall by more than (or rise by less than) the yield on the contract sold.

The empirical evidence on the price behavior of financial futures contracts suggests that near contracts (contracts with shorter maturities) are generally affected to a larger degree by a set of events than are distant contracts (contracts with longer maturities). A bullish spreader would, therefore, buy the near contract and sell the distant contract. The bearish spreader would do precisely the opposite. Profits will accrue, depending on whether the market is inverted (price of near contract P_N > price of distant contract P_D) or is noninverted ($P_N < P_D$) and on whether the spread strengthens or weakens.

1. $P_D > P_N$ (noninverted market) with $P_D - P_N > 0$.
   a. If $P_D - P_N$ approaches zero, the spread is strengthening (narrowing).
   b. If $P_D - P_N \gg 0$, the spread is weakening (widening).
2. $P_D < P_N$ (inverted market) with $P_D - P_N < 0$.
   a. If $P_D - P_N \ll 0$, the spread is strengthening.
   b. If $P_D - P_N$ approaches zero, the spread is weakening.

The price differentials reported on spreads are not absolute values. Practitioners prefer absolute values, however. We believe that our method is easier and can be consistently

used across futures contracts regardless of the underlying commodity, as demonstrated in this and the previous chapter.

To illustrate the various intermonth strategies and their consequences, we begin with the bull spread in the noninverted market case.

Noninverted Market

	Yield	Price
Assume: Distant contract (D, six-month)	11.60	88.40
Near contract (N, three-month)	11.80	88.20

Bull Spread

Strategy: Buy near   88.20
$$\rightarrow P_D - P_N = 0.20$$
Sell distant   88.40

The near contract is expected to appreciate by more than the distant contract. Otherwise, no profit will accrue from the position. Thus, a profitable bull spread.

After (with greater appreciation):
Sell near   88.30
$$\rightarrow P_D - P_N = 0.15$$
Buy distant   88.45

Profit on near = 88.30 − 88.20 = 0.10
Loss on distant = 88.40 − 88.45 = (0.05)
Net profit = 0.10 − 0.05   = **0.05**

Profits can also accrue if the near contract, for whatever reason, depreciates by less. (with less depreciation):

Near   88.15
$$\rightarrow P_D - P_N = 0.15$$
Distant   88.30

Loss on near = (0.05), profit on distant = 0.10,
Net profit = 0.10 − 0.05 = 0.05
The spread has strengthened: 0.20 > 0.15.

Bear Spread

	Yield	Price
Assume: Distant	11.60	88.40
Near	11.80	88.20

$\rightarrow P_D - P_N = 0.20$

Strategy: Sell near   88.20
$$\rightarrow P_D - P_N = 0.20$$
Buy distant   88.40

The near contract is expected to depreciate by more.

After: Buy near   88.10
$$\rightarrow P_D - P_N = 0.25$$
Sell distant   88.35

The spread has weakened (widened), thus the profitability of the bear spread.

Profit on near $= 88.20 - 88.10 \quad = 0.10$
Loss on distant $= 88.40 - 88.35 = (0.05)$
Net profit $= 0.10 - 0.05 \qquad = \textbf{0.05}$

We now discuss the bull and bear spreads under inverted market conditions.

Inverted Market

An inverted market is quite normal for financial futures.

	Yield	Price
Assume: Distant (six month)	11.80	88.20
Near (three-month)	11.60	88.40

Bull Spread

Strategy: Buy near   88.40
$$\to P_D - P_N = 0.20$$
Sell distant   88.20

Expect the near contract to appreciate more

After: Sell near   88.55
$$\to P_D - P_N = -0.30$$
Buy distant   88.25

The spread has strengthened $-0.30 < -0.20$, thus the profitability of a bull spread in an inverted market.

Profit near $= 88.55 - 88.40 \quad = 0.15$
Loss on distant $= 88.20 - 88.25 = (0.05)$
Net profit $= 0.15 - 0.05 \qquad = \textbf{0.10}$

Bear Spread

Strategy: Sell near   88.40
$$\to P_D - P_N = -0.20$$
Buy distant   88.20

After: Buy near   88.30
$$\to P_D - P_N = -0.15$$
Sell distant   88.15

The basis has weakened $-0.15 > -0.20$, which explains the profitability of the bear spread in an inverted market.

Profit on near $= 88.40 - 88.30 \quad = 0.10$
Loss on distant $= 88.20 - 88.15 = (0.05)$
Net profit $= 0.10 - 0.05 \qquad = \textbf{0.05}$

We now use an example to further illustrate the intermonth spreads.

Example

The current (January 14, 1983) price spread between the June '83 T-bill contract listed on the IMM and the December '83 contract is −0.62(91.38 − 92.00) defining an upward sloping yield curve. The yield on the near contract (100 − 92.00 = 8.00) is lower than the yield on the distant contract (100 − 91.38 = 8.62). If, as a result of the budget cuts by the Reagan Administration, inflationary expectations are dampened considerably, and if, in addition, the Federal Reserve System pursues a less stringent monetary policy, the speculator may anticipate a change in the slope of the yield curve. If the expected price differential (the spread) is +0.20 ($P_D - P_N$), the yield on the near contract would have to rise faster than that on the distant contracts (prices on nearby contracts falling faster than those on distant contracts.) The speculator would, therefore, set up a bear spread, for he expects the spread to weaken.

1. Sell the June '83 contract.
2. Simultaneously, buy the December '83 contract.

If expectations materialize, large profits would accrue. Margin requirements on the spread = $1,000 (less than one-third the margin requirement on either the long or the short position separately).

Returns = 82 basis points × 1,000,000 = $8,200

Interinstrument Spread

From the diary of a financial futures trader, we quote the following scenario and associated trading strategy. We think this is the easiest way to understand interinstrument spreads. The date is September 26, 1979.

> Currently, the GNMA market has been in a state of disarray. Demand has completely dried up and of course as a result an excess of supply has developed. This weak demand can be explained by several conditions.
>
> 1. The current coupon is 9½ percent and the market is anticipating an increase to 10 percent coupon rate.
>
> 2. When GNMAs are selling at a discount they become attractive to investors because of the monthly paydown characteristic. Since all paydowns occur at par, the purchaser of a discounted GNMA hopes for as much paydown results in a capital gain which increases the overall yield on the GNMA investment. The current situation is that housing turnover has slowed because of a slowing economy and higher interest rates which make homeowners reluctant to give up their low-interest mortgages and assume new mortgages at today's rates.
>
> 3. The spike in interest rates since Volcker took office as Chairman of the Federal Reserve and his announced intention to continue any necessary tightening has created a cautious atmosphere in the debt market. This skepticism leads to less institutional buying of long-term securities and what buying is done tends to occur in the safest issues. As a result, Treasury bonds experience strength relative to GNMAs.
>
> 4. Technical factors have created a shortage of collateral in some of the Treasury bond issues. This also has resulted in strength in the T-bond market relative to the GNMA market.
>
> As a result of this market activity since early August, the spread relationship between Treasury bonds and GNMA futures has widened from its normal

2–4 point range—6.4/32–12.8/32—to a record 5½ points—17.6/32. While there is little reason to suggest that this spread will return to its normal range within the next 30 days, I feel that the risk reward level on the trade is rapidly becoming attractive. If the conditions which have created this aberration normalize, one would expect the spread relationship to come into 3 points— 96/32 by June 1980.
Specifically one might:

Buy June 80 GNMAs.
Sell June 80 Treasury bonds.
Price difference—5½ points.

Because I see nothing to create an improvement in this technical situation before the November refunding, I would commit only half of available funds now and the other half in late October. I view the profit potential by June of 80 as being $2500/ct—read 2,500 per contract. I view the risk as $1000/ct. The margin requirement for this trade is $500/ct. The round trip commission cost is $140/ct. This trade should be profitable not as a function of any change in direction of interest rates, but as a function of a correction in technical factors. [20]

6.7 EFFICIENCY OF FINANCIAL FUTURES MARKETS

The futures markets play a dual role. They allow investors to hedge and they provide a mechanism for price discovery—information on expected future spot prices on financial instruments. The efficiency question deals with how well futures rates predict spot rates to prevail in the future; that is, are futures prices unbiased predictors of future interest rates?

In an efficient market, perfect substitutes should sell at the same price. Donald J. Puglisi[21] tested this hypothesis for T-bill futures. His investor is presented with two options.

1. Buy nearby T-bill.
2. Buy distant T-bill and short a futures contract.

In an efficient market, the investor should be indifferent between 1 and 2 and between

3. Buy distant T-bill.
4. Buy nearby T-bill and go long a futures contract.

Puglisi tested whether the difference between alternatives 4 and 2 and alternatives 3 and 1 are substantially different from zero, using returns on futures contracts with nine months or less to maturity. His results led him to conclude that "the T-bill futures market is inefficient." While the major inefficiencies occurred early in the life of the

---

[20] From **Frank Mickel,** Vice President, E. F. Hutton, New York.

[21] **Donald J. Puglisi,** "Is the Futures Market for Treasury?" *Journal of Portfolio Management* (Winter 1978).

new commodity futures and have ebbed as the market has continued to mature, the systematic mispricing of T-bill futures has not been corrected over time."[22]

To arrive at this conclusion, Puglisi relied on the sign test to measure whether the mean difference between the investment strategies was significantly different from zero. He found that it was significantly different in six of the seven futures contracts examined. The sign test, however, does not take into account the economic significance of the signs, that is, the size of the deviations. The use of autocorrelations would have been far superior, for they would have measured reversals in the mean difference of returns on the two strategies—reversals that could be significant enough to negate earlier returns.

Anthony J. Vignola and Charles J. Dale used tests different from those of Puglisi, as well as different data sources, to measure the efficiency of the T-bill futures market. Based on the values of the t statistics, they concluded that the T-bill futures market is inefficient and that "inefficiency has not diminished with the maturation of the market."[23]

William Poole tested the efficiency of the T-bill futures market by assuming that the arbitrageur holds a long-term T-bill, and that no interest is earned on margin deposited (an incorrect assumption for those investors who use T-bill to meet margin requirements). After developing an upper and a lower limit on the price of a T-bill futures contract traded on the IMM, he wanted to test whether futures rates fell within this quasi-arbitrage band. His conclusion was that "quotes on the nearest maturity in the bill futures market can, therefore, be interpreted for all practical purposes as the market's unbiased estimates of the future spot rates on 13-week bills."[24]

Poole's analysis implied that the conclusion above applied to all maturities. Richard W. Lang and Robert Rasche set out to disprove this. Their results "do not support these conclusions about the relationship between futures rates and forward rates for futures contracts, except for the ones closest to delivery, which were the ones investigated by Poole."[25] Their null hypothesis (that the futures rate is equal to the associated forward rate) was tested by measuring if the mean absolute difference is significantly different from zero for each category. The categories used were determined by the time period between the spot market and the maturity date of the futures contract. Their tests led them to the following statement: "On the basis of this evidence, we cannot conclude that the differences between the futures and forward rates have been narrowing consistently over time as the futures market for Treasury bills has become more developed."[26]

Starting with an excellent data base and using a superior t-statistic, which takes autocorrelation into account, Richard Rendleman and Christopher Carabini tested if the observed IMM index values fall within their price range—a range equivalent to that derived by Poole. Their conclusion was

> *To the extent that quasi-arbitrage (arbitrage involving transactions costs and commitment of funds) opportunities have existed in the market, there appears*

[22] Ibid., p. 57.

[23] **Anthony J. Vignola** and **Charles J. Dale,** "Is the Futures Market for Treasury Bills Efficient?" *Journal of Portfolio Management* (Winter 1979), p. 62.

[24] **Poole, William,** "Using T-bill Futures to Gauge Interest Rate Expectations," *Federal Reserve Bank of San Francisco Economic Review* (Spring 1978), p. 12.

[25] **Richard W. Lang** and **Robert H. Rasche,** "A Comparison of Yields on Futures Contracts," *Journal of Portfolio Management* (Winter, 1979), p. 62.

[26] Ibid., p. 25.

to have been a tendency for the market to become less efficient over time. The pricing of the third contract has become more efficient. However, it is doubtful that these efficiencies have been large enough to induce portfolio managers to alter their investment policies. [27]

The most recent study of the efficiency of the T-bond futures market was commissioned by the CBT and undertaken by B. Resnick and E. Hennigar.[28] Using daily data covering the period January 2, 1979 to May 15, 1981 on CBT T-bond futures and on the underlying T-bond, they tested for the presence of arbitrage opportunities. Their findings were that, "It is doubtful that many arbitrage opportunities exist . . . that the T-bond futures market was less efficient when T-bill yields, or the riskless borrowing rate, was high."[29]

6.8 EFFECTS OF THE T-BILL FUTURES MARKET ON THE CASH T-BILL MARKET

The effects of the T-bill futures market on the cash T-bill market is of great concern to policymakers. If futures markets increase the volatility of the cash markets, investors would demand a larger risk premium on cash T-bills and consequently the cost to the borrower, the government of the United States, increases. Observers of the government securities market report a rising demand for T-bills in months in which futures contracts mature.[30]

Richard Gardner ran various regression tests to measure the impact of T-bill futures on the stability of cash T-bill rates. His conclusion is that "The regression results strongly indicate that Treasury bill futures have not destabilized the Treasury bill cash market. In addition, the systematic and random variability of cash T-bill rates was reduced in the period after futures trading and cash T-bill rates became more efficient in a capital market theory sense."[31]

The problem with Gardner's conclusion lies in the nature of the statistical technique he employs. While regression analysis measures the relationship among variables, it says nothing about causation. It is not possible to isolate the impact of the introduction of futures contracts on the financial markets. The reduction in "random variability" could be due to factors other than futures contracts. Gardner's conclusion about the impact of futures markets on stability must be considered tentative.

A study dealing with the GNMA futures market and its impact on the cash GNMA market was undertaken by K. C. Froewiss.[32] His findings were that the GNMA futures market had indeed contributed to the stability of the GNMA cash market by significantly

---

[27] **Richard J. Rendleman** and **Christopher E. Carabini,** "The Efficiency of the Treasury Bill Futures Market." *Journal of Finance,* vol. 34, (September 1979) p. 913.

[28] **Bruce G. Resnick** and **Elizabeth Hennigar,** "The Relationship Between Futures and Cash Prices for U.S. Treasury Bonds," Chicago Board of Trade, 1982.

[29] Ibid., p. 21.

[30] See *Financial Times* (August 7, 1980).

[31] **Richard M. Gardner,** "The Effects of the T-Bill Futures Market on the Cash T-Bill Market." Working Paper, Chicago Mercantile Exchange, (April 1979).

[32] **K. C. Froewiss,** "GNMA Futures: Stabilizing or Destabilizing?" *Federal Reserve Bank of San Francisco–Economic Review* (Spring 1978) pp. 20–29.

reducing the random fluctuations in spot prices. Further research on this whole issue is still needed.

6.9 TAX CONSIDERATIONS

In November 1978, the IRS ruled that T-bill futures are capital assets.[33] As capital assets, they enjoy a very peculiar feature. Gains or losses on T-bill futures contracts are considered long-term only after a six-month holding period.[34] The ruling by the IRS also disallowed the deductibility of losses from spreads unless a real economic loss is incurred. Prior to the ruling, investors set up spreads in order to reduce tax liability. Before the end of the tax year (1983), investors would, for example:

1. Buy March '84 contracts.
2. Simultaneously, sell September '84 contracts.

Assuming the yields on both contracts are highly correlated, and they usually are, the loss (gain) on one contract should offset the gain (loss) on the other.

When the end of 1983 arrives, the spreader would close the position that produced a loss. The other half of the spread will be closed in 1984. Spreads of this kind, intended to reduce the tax liability, would not produce tax-deductible losses under the 1978 rule.

Investors are advised to seek competent legal advice before establishing positions in the futures markets, particularly for the complex ones.

6.10 STOCK INDEX FUTURES

A stock index futures contract is an agreement between the clearing corporation of the futures exchange and the seller and the buyer of the contract to deliver or take delivery of funds equal to the value of an underlying market index (times a set multiple) at the end of a specified period.

Like all other futures contracts, the primary functions of the stock index futures contract are twofold: price discovery and hedging.

Three stock index futures contracts are currently being traded and a fourth is contemplated. The first stock index futures contract was introduced by the Kansas City Board of Trade on February 24, 1982. The contract is based on the Value Line Stock Index. This index (1961 = 100) represents the geometric average of the approximately 1700 stocks followed by the Value Line Investment Service. The index is computed once every three minutes during any trading day. The price quotation is equal to the Value Line Average Composite Stock Index multiplied by 500. The available contract months are March, June, September, and December. This stock index futures contract is purchased like any other futures contract. The initial margin requirement is $6,600 and the maintenance margin requirement is $2,000 for speculative transactions. Hedge transactions have an initial margin requirement of $3,000 and a maintenance margin requirement of $1,500. These margin requirements are set by the exchange with the Federal

---

[33] Rev. Rul. 78–414, 1978–42 CB 213.

[34] Only long positions qualify, however. All gains and losses on short positions are short-term, regardless of the holding period.

Reserve Board in this case, playing a coercive role to make these margins the highest among futures contracts.

The margin requirement is not a downpayment on the futures contract. It is a performance bond. If prices move in an unfavorable direction, the contract holder is required to put up additional funds if the loss causes his margin balance to fall below the maintenance margin requirement. In this eventuality the contract holder must deposit the additional margin before trading opens on the next business day. A margin deposit, it must be noted, does not represent an equity position in the contract or in the underlying security(ies).

The maturity date for the Kansas City Board of Trade Value Line Index (KBT-VLI) is the last trading day of the contract month. KBT-VLI contracts have a required minimum price change of 0.01 or $50 in the value of the contract.

Trading of the KBT-VLI has been quite active, particularly for the near contract. The average daily volume in April 1983 was 2500 contracts, up from 1894 in March 1982.

The stock index futures contract, like all futures contracts, is guaranteed by the Clearing Corporation of the Exchange. The Clearing Corporation interposes itself between the buyer and the seller of the contract so in effect every purchase is from the Clearing Corporation and every sale is to the Clearing Corporation. The delivery and the payments are made in cash. This is a peculiar feature of the contract because the underlying instrument is a collection of securities with each security making up a fraction of the index. The delivery of fractions of securities is simply not feasible. It would not help the liquidity of the contract. Deliveries are guaranteed by the Clearing Corporation and ultimately by the capital of the member firms. Stock index futures contracts are practically default-free instruments.

The second exchange to introduce stock index contracts was the Chicago Mercantile Exchange (CME), through its subsidiary the Index and Option Market. The underlying index to the CME contract is the S&P 500-stock index. The base year of the index is 1941–1943 and the base value is 10. The value of the contract is equal to the value of S&P at a point in time multiplied by 500.* All other operating details are similar to those of KBT-VLI. The S&P 500 Stock Index Futures Contract is the most active of index contracts as far as volume is concerned. (See Table 6.9.)

The third exchange to introduce stock index contracts was the New York Futures Exchange (NYFE) on May 6, 1982. The underlying index to the contract was the New York Stock Exchange Index, which is a weighted average of the 1525 common stocks listed on the New York Stock Exchange. The weight used is the market value of the stock. The contract months are September, December, March, and June.

The fourth exchange to consider stock index futures contracts was the Chicago Board of Trade. The contract was to be based on the Dow Jones 30 Industrial Average. Progress was stalled when the Dow Jones Co. filed suit to bar the CBT from using the Dow Jones Average as a base for its futures contracts. The reason was that Dow Jones Co. did not wish its name to be associated with what it considered a highly speculative (a gambling) instrument. The offer by the CBT to pay for the privilege of using the Dow Jones name was turned down.

All the indexes on which futures contracts are based are supposedly "representative" of the market. The fact is that some are more representative than others and some are

---

* This multiplier was reduced to $100 on August 15, 1983.

TABLE 6.9
Stock Index Futures Prices

The Kansas City
Board of Trade

4800 MAIN STREET, KANSAS CITY, MO 64112
VALUE LINE AVERAGE STOCK INDEX FUTURES
July 1, 1982

	Open	High	Low	Settle	Change
Sept82	120.00-120.50	120.50	117.95	118.10	−1.40
Dec82	120.00	120.00	117.50	117.50	−1.85
Mar83	119.90	120.00	117.80	117.80	−1.75
June83	119.45	119.80	118.60	118.60	−1.60
Sept83	.....	....	....	118.80	−1.75
Dec83	.....	....	....	....	.....
VLIC	120.58	120.58	119.75	119.76	− .81

Est. Vol: 2,085; Vol: Wed., 2,377; Open Int: Wed. 4,250, −645.

Index and Option Market

DIVISION OF CHICAGO MERCANTILE EXCHANGE
S&P 500 Stock Index Futures
(Contract Size 500 Times Index)
July 1, 1982

	Open	High	Low	Settle	Change
Sept82	111.50	111.75	109.75	109.85	−165
Dec82	111.75	112.00	110.25	110.25	−160
Mar83	112.25	112.30b	110.70a	110.65	−150
June83	....	113.00b	111.20a	111.20a	−150
S&P 500 Stock					
Index (prelim)	109.52	109.63	106.62	108.71	− 90

Est. Vol: 9,786; Vol. Wed., 11,783; Open Int Wed., 9,603, +1,184.

N.Y. Futures Exchange

(Subsidiary of the New York Stock Exchange)
NYSE COMPOSITE INDEX FUTURES CONTRACT
(CONTRACT SIZE 500 TIMES INDEX)
July 1, 1982

	Open	High	Low	Settle	Chge.
Sep82	64.15	64.30	63.15	63.20	− .85
Dec82	64.50	64.50	63.40	63.45	− .85
Mar83	64.55	64.55	64.00	63.75	− .85
Jun83	64.80	64.80	64.45	64.05	− .85
NYSE INDEX	63.02	63.02	62.47	close 62.51	− .51

Vol: 5,374 Vol: Wed. 6,375 Open Int: Wed. 4,384 +175.

Source: The Wall Street Journal, July 2, 1982.

better constructed. The Value Line Index covers more companies than any of the others and is unweighted, that is, each of the 1700 stocks has an equal weight in the index. The Dow Jones industrial average, the S&P, and the NYSE index are all weighted, which gives the heavily capitalized companies undue influence over the direction of the index. Because of these constraints and of the type and number of stocks included in each of these indexes (averages), their performance could vary substantially. The correlation between these indexes is, in many cases, substantially different as shown in Table 6.10.

Fundamental Motivation for Stock Index Futures

The riskiness of a security (portfolio) can be broken down into two components: the systematic and the unsystematic risk. The systematic risk is the risk that results from the covariability between the returns on the security and those on the market. This

TABLE 6.10
Correlations Among the Four Major Indices Daily
(February 1, 1971–March 31, 1982)

	S&P 500	Value Line	NYSE	DJIA
S&P 500	1.000	—	—	—
Value Line	0.882	1.000	—	—
NYSE	0.989	0.928	1.000	—
DJIA	0.729	0.507	0.644	1.000

Source: Data Resources, Lexington, Ma., copyright © 1982. Reprinted by permission.

risk is not diversifiable, that is, the addition of more securities to the portfolio will not reduce the portfolio's systematic risk. Unsystematic risk, on the other hand, is diversifiable. Risk of this kind is inherent in the nature of the firm's operations and can be made to disappear if less than perfectly positively correlated securities of different industries and geographic locations are included in the portfolio. It usually requires about ten securities selected at random to reduce unsystematic risk to zero as shown in Figure 6.5.

Mathematically, the components of total risk can be easily explained. From the Capital Asset Pricing Model we have

$$R_{i,t} = a + b_i R_{M,t} + \epsilon_{i,t} \tag{6.13}$$

where $R_{i,t}$ = rate of return on security i

b_i = beta = systematic risk of security i

$R_{M,t}$ = rate of return on a market index

The variance of Equation 6.13 is

$$\sigma_i^2 = b_i^2 \, \sigma_M^2 + \sigma_\epsilon^2 \tag{6.14}$$

The σ_ϵ^2 component approaches zero as the number of securities in the portfolio increases. Thus the risk of greatest concern to portfolio managers is the systematic risk ($b_i^2 \, \sigma_M^2$).

FIGURE 6.5.   **Reduction of unsystematic risk through diversification.**

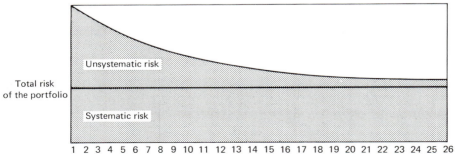

Total risk of the portfolio

Unsystematic risk

Systematic risk

1 2 3 4 5 6 7 8 9 10 11 12 13 14 15 16 17 18 19 20 21 22 23 24 25 26

Number of securities in the portfolio

FIGURE 6.6.   **S&P 500 stock index.**

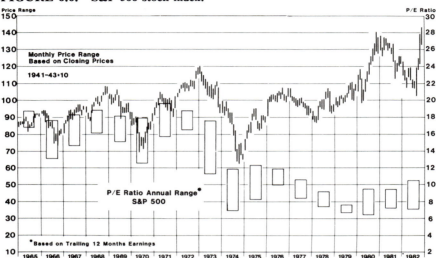

Stock index futures contracts are intended to hedge precisely against this risk. The market variability as measured by the S&P 500 has been high as shown in Figure 6.6.

The gyrations of the market could have a dramatic impact on the riskiness of securities and portfolios, depending on the beta value of the security or the portfolio. The higher the beta value, the greater the systematic risk. A beta of 1.6 means that a one percent appreciation (depreciation) in the market (measured usually by using the S&P 500 as a proxy) would lead to a 1.6 percent appreciation (depreciation) in the rate of return on the security or portfolio.

The extent of the success of stock index futures contracts will largely depend on the correlation between the index on which the contract is based and the typical portfolio. Also of importance is the liquidity of the contract. The Chicago Mercantile Exchange calculates, for example, that a well-diversified portfolio of 50 stocks has a correlation of about 0.90 with the S&P 500. The S&P index and other broadly based indexes should prove to be potent tools in hedging systematic risk.

The justifications for a stock index futures contract are, as explained above, similar to those of any other futures contract. Namely, futures contracts are used as a mechanism for price discovery and for hedging. The major difference between a stock index futures contract and the futures contracts that preceded it is the settlement in cash. This method of settlement has led many market observers and regulators to charge that this type of futures contract is a disguised form of gambling. The charge is not very defensible because of the following reasons.

1. A cash delivery is the only logical form of delivery in this case. The alternatives would have been to deliver fractions of shares that make up the underlying index, or shares in a mutual fund invested strictly in the companies that make up the index. Neither of the alternatives is feasible or desirable.

2. The fact that over 95 percent of futures contracts on any commodity are never delivered against means that cash settlement is, indeed, the dominant form. Net profits (losses) from offsetting transactions in the futures market are collected (paid) in cash.

3. Futures contracts are a mechanism for shifting an existing risk, at a price, from one party to another. Gambling, on the other hand, creates artificial risk situations with odds typically against the player (in favor of the house) and does not allow for price discovery. The outcome from spinning a roulette wheel serves no economic purpose and helps in no way in predicting future outcomes. Even if it did, one questions what benefit accrues to society from such information.

The enthusiasm for the arguments in favor of cash settlement on stock index futures contracts must be tempered by the fact that the price discovery function is valuable if and only if the futures price is an accurate, on the average, predictor of the future spot price. In addition, the hedging function is legitimized if a significant number of hedgers (the expected type) is active in the market. The April 5, 1983 issue of *The Wall Street Journal* had some startling disclosures on the identity of market participants. One of the frequent hedgers, significant by the number of contracts involved, in the stock index futures market is Ladbrokes of London. Ladbrokes runs the largest bookmaking operation in the world. Ladbrokes has been accepting bets on the Dow Jones averages since 1964 and has recently found the stock index futures markets to be a convenient vehicle for hedging any imbalance (bulls > bears, bears > bulls) in its portfolio of accepted bets. The *Journal* also reported that, of the 182 portfolio managers surveyed by Yankelovich, Skelly & White in 1982, only 1 percent were "very likely" to hedge through the index futures markets during 1983. This suggests that the market is the domain of speculators, which gives some credence to the gambling argument.

Users of Stock Index Futures

Users of stock index futures contracts are most likely to be portfolio managers, particularly those who are risk-averse. Mutual funds and pension funds managers will lead the way. Equity market makers would also be interested in using these contracts to hedge their cash positions in the securities they make markets in or just hold positions in. Underwriters who carry large inventories of yet-to-be-issued securities are interested in hedging against unexpected shifts in the market that may leave them with large losses. Losses of these kinds may wipe out the underwriting spread (the difference between the underwriting price and the selling of a new issue or a secondary offering).

Specialists on the floors of the stock exchanges hold positions in the securities they specialize in, which could be adversely affected if expectations do not materialize. Stock index futures contracts could help cushion, if not avoid, the losses altogether. The stock index futures markets should encourage specialists to increase the size of their position and further stabilize the cash market.

Uses of Stock Index Futures

Stock Index Futures Contracts are used either as speculative or as hedging vehicles. A speculator may speculate on the short or on the long end of the market. A hedger may establish a long or a short hedge to protect a position (actual or prospective) in the cash stock market or in the option market. Examples will follow.

Arbitrageurs can also use stock index futures contracts. Their arbitrage could be across time or across space. Arbitrage across time attempts to capitalize on an unwarranted price differential between contracts with different maturity months that trade

on the same or on different exchanges. Arbitrage in space attempts to capitalize on an unwarranted price differential between one contract month traded on one exchange and the same contract month traded on another, taking into consideration the different makeup of the indexes. More complex arbitrage strategies can and have been devised. Suffice it to say that a pure arbitrage position involves zero risk, no commitment of funds, and yields the risk-free rate.

We now illustrate basic speculative and hedging positions.

Basic Bear Speculation

A basic bear speculation involves simply the sale of a stock index futures contract in the hope of covering it later at a lower price. The speculator is expecting a drop in the value of the stock index.

A short position in the futures market is not the same as that in the stock market. In the futures market a short position does not require the borrowing of securities to be sold, because delivery is either deferred or may never occur. A short stock index position is simply the sale of a commitment to pay a sum of money at a point in time in the future. The value of the commitment is determined at the time it is made by an open auction system.

Basic Bull Speculation

A basic bull speculation represents the speculator's optimism about the future. It is simply a long position in the stock index futures contract. If the speculator's expectations do materialize, he would have bought low and sold high.

Long Hedge

An investor with a net short position in stocks, or who has intentions to purchase stocks at a specified time in the future, or who has established a short call (stock option) position or a long put position, can hedge using a stock index futures contract. A long position in the stock index futures contract is established with the hope that any loss in the cash or options positions will be offset by gains realized on the futures contract.

We now offer two examples. On July 2, 1982, a pension fund manager who expects to receive $75,000 in contributions in September 1982 and to invest this sum in a portfolio of select common stocks is concerned that the price of the stocks will appreciate by the time he is ready to invest. To hedge against such a possibility, he would buy, say, a September 1982 S&P 500 stock index futures contract for 109.85 (Table 6.9), which represents a total commitment of 109.85 × 500 = $54,925. The expectation is that if stock prices appreciate, the appreciation in the value of the futures contract will offset the increased cost of acquiring the desired securities in September.

Several issues should be of concern here. The first deals with the size of the futures contract vis-à-vis the size of the cash position. In this example, the hedger could only buy one or two futures contracts to achieve a hedged position. Fractions of futures contracts are not available. The implication here is that the position could be overhedged or underhedged depending on the number of futures contracts purchased. No one, however, should draw the conclusion that if the size of the futures contract is equal to that of the actual or prospective cash position, the hedger would have a perfect hedge

(the gains on the futures offset exactly the losses in the cash). The results depend on the movement of futures prices in relation to the price movement in the cash position. An adequate hedge ratio must, therefore, be determined.

The determination of the hedge ratio begins with the calculation of the beta of the security or the weighted beta of the portfolio, b_p:

$$b_p = \sum_i W_i b_i \tag{6.15}$$

where b_p = weighted beta (systematic risk) of the portfolio

W_i = weight of security i in the portfolio

b_i = beta of security i

Assume $b_p = 1.6$. On July 2, 1982 S&P September stock index futures contracts were selling for 109.85. The expected dollar value of the portfolio is $75,000. Therefore, the hedge ratio, the appropriate number of futures contracts necessary to equate the sensitivity of the market to that of the portfolio, is calculated as follows

$$\text{Hedge ratio } (HR) = \frac{\$ \text{ value of portfolio}}{\$ \text{ value of contract}} \times \frac{\text{weighted beta}}{\text{of portfolio}} \tag{6.16}$$

In our example, the hedge ratio is equal to

$$HR = \frac{\$75,000}{54,925} \times 1.6 = 2.18 \text{ contracts.}$$

If 2.18 contracts could have been purchased, a one percent gain in the futures contract will offset a one percent loss in the cash. Since only round lots can be purchased in the futures market, the hedger is advised here to buy two S&P stock index futures contracts in order to hedge, assuming a sufficiently well-diversified portfolio.

A long hedge can also be used to hedge a short call position in the following manner

July 2, 1982

GM call option: 5½, GM stock: 44¼
(Sept. '82, strike price = 40)

Options Position
Sell 50 GM call
options: 550 × 50 = $27,500
(5,000 underlying shares)

Futures market
Buy four Sept. S&P 500
stock index futures contracts: 109.85
Value = 4 × 109.85 × 500 = $219,700
Value of shares underlying the
options: 5,000 × 44.25 = **$221,250**

September 30, 1982

GM call: 9½

GM stock: 49¼
S&P 500/Sept. = 122.25

Options Position	**Futures market**
Buy 50 GM call at 9½	Sell four S&P/Sept '82:
Total cost = $47,500	4 × 122.25 × 500 = $244,500
Gain (loss) on Options	Gain (loss) on Futures
$47,500 − $27,500 = ($20,000)	$244,500 − $219,700 = **$24,800**

Net Results from Hedge

Loss on options	= $(20,000)
Gain on futures	= 24,800
Net gain before transactions costs	**$ 4,800**

We now look at the short hedge.

Short Hedge

A short hedge protects (partially or totally) a long position in a stock portfolio, a long call position, and a short put position. The profits from the short (sell) position in the futures market are expected to offset the losses in the cash or option position. We offer two examples.

A portfolio manager with a $2,000,000 portfolio with a weighted beta of 1.4 is concerned with the significant probability of a market weakness over the next three months. To hedge his position he would

July 2, 1982

Cash Market	**Futures Market**
No transaction market value of portfolio = $2,000,000	$HR = \dfrac{2,000,000}{54,925} \times 1.4 = 51$
	Sell 51 Sept. '82 S&P 500 stock index futures for 109.85
	Total value:
	51 × 109.85 × 500 = $2,801,175

September 10, 1982

Market value = $1,825,000 of portfolio	Buy 51 Sept. contracts at 106.7
Book loss = $2,000,000 − $1,825,000 =	Total value = 106.7 × 51 × 500 = $2,720,850
	Profit = $2,801,175 − 2,720,850 =
($175,000)	**$80,325**

The book loss in the cash market was partially offset by the gain in the futures market and the impact of the decline in stock values was dissipated. It is worth noting that the profits in the futures market are not realized all at once. The sum $80,325 is the balance of margin debits and credits during the period when the contract is outstanding.

We now look at how a short put position can be hedged in the stock index futures market.

July 2, 1982

IBM put = 5, IBM: 60⅝
(October 82, striking price = 65) stock

Options Market
Sell 20 GM put options:
500 × 20 = $10,000
(2,000 underlying shares)

Futures Market
Sell two Sept. '82 S&P 500 stock
    index futures contracts at:
    2 × 109.85 × 500 = $109,850
Value of shares underlying the
    options = 2,000 × 60⅝ = **$121,250**

September 15, 1982

IBM put = 1

IBM stock: 70⅝

Options Market
Buy 20 GM put options at:
100 × 20 = $2,000

Futures Market
Buy two Sept. '82 S&P 500 for:
2 × 127 × 500 = 127,000

Gain (Loss) on Put Options
$10,000 − 2,000 = $8,000

Gain (Loss) on Futures
$127,000 − 109,850 = (17,150)

Net Gains or Loss

(17,150) − 8,000 = **($9,150)**

It is apparent from the above example that the put seller would have been better without the hedge. This is hindsight, however. The loss incurred in this hedge is a real loss. This partially explains the hesitancy of some portfolio managers to hedge by using futures contracts. Contracts of these kinds look good when futures prices go in the right direction, but are terrible when prices go in the wrong direction. Hedging is not always desirable or, indeed, possible.

We now discuss another popular strategy in the stock index futures market.

Spreads

A spread consists of a simultaneous long position in one futures contract month and a short position in another contract month. The intent is to capitalize on an unnatural price differential between the contracts.

Spreads could be bull or bear spreads. A bull spread requires a long position in the contract that is expected to move upward most vigorously; that is, usually the near contract. A bear spread, on the other hand, requires a short position in the contract that is expected to move downward most vigorously; that is, usually the near contract also. We now illustrate a bull spread.

Morning of July 2, 1982

Buy S&P 500 Sept. '82	111.50
Sell S&P 500 March '83	112.50
Spread	**1.00**

September 15, 1982

Sell S&P 500 Sept. '82	112.00
Buy S&P 500 March '83	112.70
	0.70

Profit on September contract = 112.00 − 111.50 = $0.50
Loss on March '83 contract = 112.70 − 112.50 = (0.20)
Net Profit (before transactions costs)   **$0.30**

The profit in the bull spread results from the narrowing of the spread from 1.00 to 0.70 (narrowing of spreads produces a loss in a bear spread).

The reader may infer from the above example that a long position in the S&P 500 Sept. '82 contract would have been the best position. This is hindsight. The short position is intended to be a hedge against an incorrect anticipation of market moves.

We must also note that the margin requirement on spreads is much lower than that on two separately established short and long positions. This is so precisely because of the lower risk of spreads.

The Pricing of Stock Index Futures

The pricing of stock index futures is the work of Bradford Cornell and Kenneth French[35] with considerable reliance on the work of G. M. Constantinides.[36]

The Cornell-French model (C&F) allows for the pricing of futures contracts on the S&P 500 and the New York stock exchange composite index. That is, it works only for futures contracts on value-weighted averages because the rate of change in the underlying index would be equal to the returns from holding the component stocks. The C&F model does not apply, therefore, to futures contracts on the Value-Line Index that are currently traded on the Kansas City Board of Trade.

The assumptions underlying the final version of the model are

1. Forward and futures prices are equal.
2. No restrictions on short sales and perfect divisibility of assets.

The development of the model begins with some further simplifying assumptions such as no taxes and transactions costs, borrowing and lending at the risk-free rate, and no dividends. These assumptions are then gradually relaxed to arrive at the final solution to the model.

---

[35] **Cornell Bradford and Kenneth French,** "The Pricing of Stock Index Futures." Center for the Study of Futures Markets, Columbia Business School, Working paper series No. CSFM-43.

[36] **G. M. Constantinides,** "Capital Market Equilibrium with Personal Tax." *Econometrica* (1983).

An investor who wishes to acquire a stock could do so in the spot market at time t or in the futures market at time T, which coincides with the maturity date of a futures contract purchased at time t. If he or she opts for a deferred purchase, he or she could invest the funds which would have been invested in the cash market at the risk-free rate (minimally). Thus, the futures price of a stock should equal the current spot price plus the interest.

$$F(t,T) = P(t) \times e^{r(T-t)} \tag{6.17}$$

where $F(t,T)$ = futures price at time t for a contract maturing at time T.

$\qquad P(t)$ = market price of stock purchased at time t.

$\qquad r$ = risk-free rate of interest prevailing at t.

Equation 6.17 assumes that the stock does not pay dividends between t and T because if it did, the benefit of buying early (at time t) would be to receive the dividend. This cash inflow would largely offset the cash flows in the form of interest payments on a stock position established at time t and carried until T—the equivalent of a futures position. The futures price adjusted for dividends is, therefore equal to

$$F(t,T) = P(t) \times e^{(r-d)(T-t)} \tag{6.18}$$

where d = size of the dividend payment

Equation 6.18 assumes, however, that dividend flows are constant, that interest rates are nonstochastic, and that we are operating in the unrealistic world of no taxes.

If we drop these assumptions and introduce both ordinary income taxes (i) and capital gains taxes (g), the valuation model is transformed to the following

$$F(t,T) = \left\{ P(t)[e^{(1-i)r(t,T)(T-t)} - g] - \int_t^T (1-i)D(w)e^{(1-i)R(t,W,T)(T-W)}dw \right\}/(1-g) \tag{6.19}$$

where $\quad D(W)$ = instantaneous dividend payout at time W

$\qquad R(t,W,T)$ = the forward rate on a loan considered at time t, booked at time W, and carried until time T.

The variables following the integration sign represent the offsetting nature of dividend payments that are adjusted for the fact that they are taxable and that the interest costs represented by $R(t,W,T)$ are deductible for tax purposes. This leaves a net aftertax interest cost of $(1-i)R(t,W,T)(T-W)$.

Equation 6.19 allows for the standard introduction of taxes in valuation models. This is not a fully adequate method, however, because the "timing option" referred to by Constantinides was ignored. The current tax laws allow an individual to realize losses on a stock position when it suits him to do so and to defer capital gains to a more suitable period. This option is not available to a holder of a futures contract because of its limited life. Therefore, the holder of a long stock position receives all the benefits of a futures contract plus the option to defer any capital gains taxes. By looking at a long position in the stock as a portfolio of two assets we get

$$P(t) = S(t) + C(t) \tag{6.20}$$

where $S(t)$ = value of a "truncated" security

= value of a stock position with similar benefits as those of a futures position

$e(t)$ = value of the timing option when $P_t > P_T$

The new valuation model is

$$F(t,T) = S(t) \frac{\left[e^{(1-i)r(t,T)(T-t)} - g - \int_t^T (1-i)d(W)e^{(1-i)R(t,W,T)(T-W)}dW \right]}{(1-g)}$$

where $d(W) = \dfrac{D(W)}{S(t)} = \dfrac{\text{dividend payment per one dollar investment}}{\text{in the truncated security}}$ \hfill (6.21)

Equation 6.21 is very similar to Equation 6.19 except that $S(t)$ replaces $P(t)$. Letting the terms in [ ] equal Z and recognizing that $C(t) = P(t) - S(t)$, we get

$$\begin{aligned} F(t,T) &= [P(t) - C(t)]Z \\ &= [1 - c(t)]P(t)Z \end{aligned} \tag{6.22}$$

where $c(t) = \dfrac{C(t)}{P(t)}$

therefore $c(t) = 1 - \dfrac{F(t,T)}{P(t)Z}$

While a closed form solution is possible for $F(t,T)$, it is not possible for $c(t)$. It can be demonstrated that $c(t)$ is

$$c(t) = f(\sigma^2, T, d) \tag{6.23}$$

$$\frac{\delta c(t)}{\delta \sigma^2} > 0, \ \frac{\delta c(t)}{\delta T} > 0, \ \frac{\delta c(t)}{\delta d} < 0$$

where σ^2 = variance of stock return

T = maturity of the truncated security

d = dividend yield

C&F estimated $c(t)$ as a fraction of the stock price, using $i = 50\%$, $g = 20\%$, and found significant changes in $c(t)$ from one contract month to another. The changes could not be explained by the model. The estimates for the timing option were "positively biased when the market falls and negatively biased when the market rises." (p. 20).

The validity of the C&F model requires further testing. Meanwhile, it is the only

model that comes close to approximating the true market price of a stock index futures contract.

6.11 OPTIONS ON FUTURES CONTRACTS

The CBT—the first exchange to introduce interest rate futures contracts in 1975—was the first exchange to introduce options on futures contracts on October 1, 1982. The instrument underlying that first option contract was a U.S. Treasury bond futures contract. Other options on futures contracts were later introduced by the CBT and other exchanges, as was detailed in Chapter one, but none covered financial futures contracts on interest-bearing instruments. We shall, therefore, place our primary focus in the balance of this chapter on option contracts on T-bond futures and our secondary focus on options on stock index futures contracts—keeping in mind that options covering other futures contracts are used in essentially similar ways.

Definitions

A call option on a Treasury bond futures contract gives its holder, for a price-called premium, the right to assume a long position in one T-bond futures contract, at a striking price set by the exchange, at any time between the purchase date and the expiration date of the option contract.

A put option, on the other hand, gives its holder for a price-called-premium the right to establish a short position in the underlying futures contract (sell a T-bond futures contract) at a striking price set by the exchange, anytime between the purchase date and the expiration date of the option contract.

Similarly, a call option on a stock index futures contract gives the holder the same rights with the same conditions to buy (a call) or to sell (a put) a futures contract on a designated stock index. The Chicago Mercantile Exchange began trading options on the S&P 500 stock index futures on January 28, 1983, and the New York Futures Exchange began trading on option contract on the NYSE index futures on the same day. The CBT began trading an option on the Value-Line stock index futures on March 4, 1983, not on its floors but on the Kansas City Board of Trade. This option faded quickly after a good start.

All of these contracts serve essentially the same goal: the limitation of investment risk. We shall discuss some of the various ways such options can be used. First, we present a few important details about the nature and the mechanics of these instruments.

The trading unit of an option on a T-bond futures is $100,000 face value of a U.S. Treasury bond futures contract. For example, if a call option is exercised, the call holder would acquire a long position in a futures contract on $100,000 face value of T-bonds.

The exercise price (strike price) of an option on Treasury bond futures is set by the exchange in a multiple of two points ($2\% \times 100,000 = \$2,000$) per T-bond futures contract. For example, exercise prices may be 76, 74, 72. The market price of these options is quoted in increments of $\frac{1}{64}$ of 1 percent of $100,000 of a T-bond futures contract. The dollar value of this increment is $15.63.

While stock options are completely unconstrained in their price movement, options on T-bond futures are constrained because of the daily price limit set by the futures exchange on the futures contract. The price of an option on T-bond futures can, under currently prevailing rules, move up or down by a maximum of two points ($2,000)

from the previous day's settlement price. These limits are those set by the CBT on the movement of T-bond futures prices and may be changed when the exchange deems that market conditions warrant.

The expiration cycle for options on T-bond futures is the same as T-bond futures. If the cycle for futures is March, June, September, December, that of options thereon would be the same. Options expire on the first Saturday following the last day of trading. This day is the first Friday preceding, by at least five business days, the first notice day for the corresponding T-bond futures contract. The reader should keep in mind that trading in options always ceases in the month prior to the delivery month on the futures contract.

The exercise, if one is opted for, of an option on T-bond futures follows a very straightforward procedure. An option holder may exercise the option on any business day prior to expiration. A notice to the Clearing Corporation must be given by 8:00 P.M. This is so because the Clearing Corporation is the middleman in every option transaction and because buyers and sellers of options are not matched at the time the transaction is consummated. That is, for every buyer for whom there is no specific seller designated to deliver the futures contract, the Clearing Corporation assigns the notice to exercise to an option seller usually by a random process.

We now look at the characteristics of an option on the S&P futures contract. The expiration cycle of calls and puts on the S&P 500 is the same as that of the underlying futures contract. S&P 500 futures expiring in March, June, September and December will have options expiring in these same months.

Exercise prices for options on S&P futures are initially set around the current price of the S&P futures contract. New ones are introduced as market conditions in the underlying futures change. Market prices are quoted in points, with each point worth $500. For example, 2.80 points correspond to a value of $2.8 \times 500 = \$1,400$.

Pricing Options on T-bonds and S&P Futures

The development of pricing models for options on T-bonds and stock index futures is still in process. Clearly two factors remain as components of option prices. They are intrinsic value and time premium. The value of an option on a futures contract (W_f) is

$$W_f = \text{Intrinsic value} + \text{time premium}$$

The intrinsic value (IV) is simply the difference between the market price (MP) of the option and the exercise price (E). In the case of a call, if $MP > E$, the option is in-the-money—that is, the option can be exercised profitably. If $MP < E$, the option is out-of-the-money and an exercise would produce a loss. The opposite is true for puts. A put is in-the-money if $MP < E$ and out-of-the-money if $MP > E$.

The time premium is, as the name implies, a function of the time to expiration. The longer that period is, the larger the probability that the option will become profitable. When intrinsic value is zero or negative, the time premium is the only component value. It must be this because the value of an option cannot be negative. That time value decreases with time is because the option is a decaying asset.

The primary focus in option pricing must be on the determinants of the market value of the underlying instrument. In the options on T-bond futures, the primary determi-

nant of option prices is interest rates. In the options on stock index futures, the primary determinant is the movement in stock prices making up the index. The more volatile the price of the underlying stocks is, the higher the price of the option.

Strategies in Options on Futures

Straightforward options strategies will be presented here for options on stock index futures. Similar and more advanced strategies for options on T-bond futures will be presented later.

Calls on S&P Index Futures

The two sides of the call market on S&P Index futures (the long and the short) have different uses and risk characteristics.

An investor expecting a surge in the market would buy a call to participate in this rise. Once the expectations are realized, the option is closed by simply selling it in the market where it was purchased.

The choice of the option is not the only one available to the investor. The investor could alternatively have purchased the underlying futures contract, or shares in a fund that was indexed to the S&P 500 or highly correlated with it. He or she could have purchased the shares that make up the index. The latter option is cumbersome and could be very costly in terms of transactions costs. The index fund option allows for no leverage possibility—that is, contrary to the futures contract case, it requires full commitment of funds. The choice of the option, instead of the futures, contract itself is based on two very important factors:

1. Limited risk: The maximum loss in the event expectations do not materialize is the call premium.
2. Settlement in the futures market is required on a daily basis.

Therefore, if on any given day the price of a futures contract moves in an unfavorable direction, the holder of the contract will receive a margin call that will require deposit of additional funds. No such thing ever occurs in the options market. The option buyer simply pays the option price (plus transactions costs) at the time the option is purchased and can sell anytime he chooses. No additional cash on that same option is ever required during its life. Therefore, an option on a futures contract allows for a full participation in the futures markets without any of the sometimes painful restrictions that a holder of a futures contract must live with.

Calls can also be used to protect a short position in the underlying futures contract. A short position in a June '83, S&P 500 futures contract would incur losses if the S&P 500 appreciates in value. A call option bought against the same futures contract represents a form of insurance, the cost of which is the call premium. If the S&P 500 appreciates in value, the profits on the call would offset—partially or totally depending on whether the option is in- or out-of-the-money and how far in or out—the losses on the futures position. If the S&P 500 falls in value as expected, the depreciation must be larger than the price of the call before profits accrue to the short in the futures market. The holder of the call may decide to sell it (offset the position) well before it expires as he becomes more definite about the downward direction of the market. By this maneuver the holder of the call reduces the cost of insurance.

A short call position on an S&P 500 stock index could be a valuable hedging or speculative tool, depending on whether it is covered or naked. An option is covered when the writer owns the underlying futures contract. An option is naked when the writer does not own the underlying futures contract.

A long position on an S&P futures contract purchased at, say, 138 could be protected by a short June S&P 500 call with a striking price of, say, 140. If the market value of the call is 4.00 its total cost would be $2,000. This sum, $2,000, would serve as a cushion should futures prices fall. If, on the other hand, futures prices rise above 144, the call option would be exercised against the long futures position and the covered call writer would only realize the difference between 144 and 138. The writer would miss, in the process, any gains resulting from a price appreciation beyond 144. This sum is his opportunity loss. If futures prices fall below $140 - 4 = 136$, the loss in the long futures position would be real. Therefore, a covered short call position provides a limited (to the size of the premium) downside protection while it limits the upside potential of the long futures position.

A naked short call, on the other hand, is established only when futures prices are expected to remain stagnant or to decline. If one writes a call without a long position in the S&P 500 futures contract, he would be required to deliver the contract should the call become profitable to exercise. Assume an exercise price of 140 (premium = 4) and a futures price movement to 150, the naked call writer would have to purchase a S&P 500 futures contract at 150 and sell it at 140 for a loss of $10 - 4 = 6$ points. The higher futures prices go, the higher the loss unless the naked call option writer enters an offsetting transaction. The premium received in this case represents, therefore, the maximum profit while losses could be substantial.

Puts on S&P 500 Index Futures

The thinking and the strategies here are opposite those of calls both on the short and on the long side.

A put can be used to profit from an expected decline in futures prices. Also, it can be used to protect a long position in an S&P 500 index futures contract. The cost of protection is limited to the put premium in the event futures prices fall. If prices rise, on the other hand, the gains in the futures contract will be reduced by the cost of insurance (put premium) and net gains will accrue after the premium is fully recovered.

A long put can also be used to "fix" a future sale price of a portfolio of stocks that is highly correlated with the S&P 500. The profit on the put position would offset partially or totally the losses in the underlying securities in the event of a price decline.

A short put position is used primarily for two purposes: to establish a purchase price below current market price and to protect a short futures position.

A bullish investor who wishes to purchase an S&P 500 index futures contract, but judges its current market price a bit too high, could sell a put contract with the expectation it would be exercised against him at the strike price. Upon exercise the put writer becomes the owner of a long futures contract on the S&P 500 index futures. Losses, if any, from the exercise could partially or totally offset the put premium received.

A short put intended to protect a short futures position provides protection, in a rising market, limited to the option premium. In a down market the put negates any gains in the futures position that are larger than the option premium received.

Calls on T-bond Futures Contracts

The strategies presented in the sections to follow rely on actual prices reported in Table 6.11. Two positions, each with several strategies, are possible, a long position and a short position.

Long calls on T-bond futures contracts. A speculator who expects the decline in interest rates that began in mid-1982 to continue could purchase a call option on T-bond futures. Depending on how bullish he or she is on bond prices, he or she may buy in-the-money or out-of-the-money options. Assume that on January 28, 1983 the June/74 call option (Table 6.11) was purchased for 1–60 points or $1,937.50. The call is a bit out-of-the-money because the underlying June futures contract is settling at $73^{17}/_{32}$. If interest rates fall, the call could appreciate and a profit would be realized.

The alternatives to the speculator would have been to speculate in the cash market or simply in the futures markets. The margin requirement on $100,000 investment in cash bonds is $10,000, reducing the leverage potential. The speculation in the futures market compared with the call option market was discussed earlier in this chapter.

A pension fund manager who expects on January 28, 1983 to receive funds by June '83 and who wishes to lock in today's higher rates would buy a June/74 contract. If interest rates fall, the profits from the call option will compensate partially or totally for the lower interest income on the position in the cash market to be established in June 1983.

Long calls can also be used as indicated earlier to hedge a short position in the futures market.

Short calls on T-bond futures contracts. Short call positions, on the other hand, can be used to enhance the return on a long futures position or as a speculative device

TABLE 6.11
Futures Options   Futures

Thursday, January 27, 1983

Chicago Board of Trade

TREASURY BONDS—$100,000; points and 64ths of 100%

Strike Price	Calls—Last Mar	Jun	Sep	Puts—Last Mar	Jun	Sep
64	....	....	....	0-01	....	....
66	....	....	....	....	....	....
68	6-20	5-50	....	0-01	0-21	....
70	4-22	4-05	....	0-05	0-52	....
72	2-32	2-55	....	0-15	1-32	....
74	1-05	1-60	....	0-47	2-35	....
76	0-22	1-12	....	2-03	3-43	....
78	0-05	0-43	....	3-52	5-05	....
80	0-02	0-28	....	5-48	6-60	....

Est. total vol. 4,000
Calls: Wed. vol. 3,235; open int. 12,548
Puts: Wed. vol. 3,057; open int. 8,713

TREASURY BONDS (CBT)—$100,000; pts. 32nds of 100%

	Open	High	Low	Settle	Change	Lifetime High	Low	Open Interest
Mar83	74-02	74-12	73-17	74-09	+ 17	11.261	− .086	79,062
June	73-10	73-20	72-28	73-17	+ 16	11.382	− .083	19,749
Sept	72-26	73-01	72-15	73-00	+ 15	11.470	− .078	16,270
Dec	72-15	72-21	72-04	72-20	+ 15	11.532	− .079	21,407
Mar84	72-09	72-12	71-24	72-10	+ 14	11.584	− .074	22,492
June	71-19	72-06	71-19	72-02	+ 13	11.626	− .069	9,107
Sept	71-13	71-30	71-13	71-23	+ 8	11.685	− .043	2,157
Dec	71-22	71-25	71-11	71-23	+ 13	11.685	− .069	3,267
Mar85	71-15	71-20	71-12	71-19	+ 13	11.706	− .070	347
June	71-11	71-16	71-08	71-15	+ 13	11.728	− .069	173
Sept	71-07	71-12	71-04	71-11	+ 13	11.749	− .070	33

Est vol 58,000; vol Wed 84,652; open int 173,704, +4,344.

Source: The Wall Street Journal, January 28, 1983.

if they are naked. The strategies and their consequences are exactly as described in the options on stock index futures. The options to be written could be in-, out-, or at-the-money depending on investors' expectations. The more out-of-the-money the option is, the greater the margin of safety but the lower the premium received. An option-writing program works best when little or no movement is expected in interest rates over the life of the option.

Long and short put positions.   The strategies used with long and short put positions are similar to those used in options on stock index futures. The only substitution to be made is that in this case we have a futures contract on a homogeneous instrument (T-bonds) instead of a collection of stocks.

Straddles on T-bond futures contracts.   The straddle strategies on T-bonds futures contracts are the same as those on common stock discussed in Chapter 3. We shall reintroduce some of the strategies for the purpose of illustration.

A straddle is a combination of a put and a call with the same strike price and maturity. A long straddle position is established when interest rates and hence bond prices are expected to be very volatile and the trader is incapable or unwilling to guess the direction of the change.

A trader may purchase a June/74 call for 1 60/64 and a June/74 put for 2 35/64 (Table 6.11). The total cost is

June/74 call	$1,937.50
June/74 put	2,546.87
Total cost (4 31/64)	**$4,484.37**

The settlement price of the underlying T-bond futures contract on the same date (1/28/83) is $73^{17}\!/_{32}$. This makes the call an out-of-the-money call and the put an in-the-money put.

This type of straddle is biased toward an upward movement in interest rates and a downward movement in bond prices because the put option is in-the-money.

Let us trace the effects of bond price changes on the long straddle position.

1. Future price moves to 79

June/74 call exercised or sold	5 28/64
June /74 Put	0
Gross profit	5 28/64
Straddle Premium	4 31/64
Net profit (before commission)	**61/64**

2. Futures prices remain the same

Call expires worthless	–0–
Put is exercised or sold profitably	
$(74 - 72.\ ^{02}\!/_{32})$	$1^{60}\!/_{64}$
Gross profit	$1^{60}\!/_{64}$
Straddle premium	4 31/64
Net profit (before commission)	**(2 35/64)**

3. Future prices move to 70

Call expires worthless	–0–
Put is exercised or sold for	4
Gross profit	4
Straddle premium	4 31/64
Net loss (before commission)	**(31/64)**

We can conclude, therefore, that unless the movement in the price of the underlying T-bond futures contract exceeds a certain range, the long straddle position will produce a loss. The range is

Strike price ± straddle premium:
74 ± 4 31/64 = 69 33/64 to 78 31/64

Within the range the long straddle will lose part or all of the premium paid. Beyond the range, profits can be made. The farther prices move from the range limits, the larger the profits.

The trader could have purchased a put and a call with a different strike price and/ or expiration month. This is called a *combination*. The more bullish he or she is, the more the call the trader purchases will be in-the-money, and the more bearish, the more in-the-the-money the put will be. An example of a combination is

Buy March/72 call	2 32/64
Buy June/72 put	2 35/64

Combinations give the trader much more flexibility than straddles do whenever the trader is undecided but is leaning in a certain direction (bullish or bearish) despite the indecision.

The purchase of a straddle or a combination is not necessarily a frozen position until both components of the transaction are liquidated. The trader may well decide to close out the put or the call side once the direction of the market is better known (the risk of owning one put or one call and not both is higher). Or, the trader may wish to substitute one call for another or one put for another.

A short straddle position is established for reasons opposite those of a long straddle. Here the investor is expecting little movement in interest rates. Profits accrue if the price of T-bonds futures remains in the range and losses accrue if prices move outside the range. A short straddle position could be

Sell June/74 call	$1,937.50
Sell June/74 put	$2,546.87
	$4,484.37

If the price of T-bonds futures contracts remains in the $69^{33}\!/_{64}$–$78^{31}\!/_{64}$ range, the straddle seller will realize part or all of the premium. If, on the other hand, the price of T-bonds futures moves beyond the range, a real loss would accrue in both the short put or in the short call if the call position is naked. If the short call position is covered, the loss would be an opportunity loss. The option writer would have missed a portion of the appreciation in the value of the T-bond futures contract against which the option

was written. The maximum gain would equal the value of the premium received both on the call and on the put.

Depending on his expectations, an investor may wish to establish a short position in a combination instead of a straddle. The more bullish he is the more the out-of-the-money the call written is and the more in-the-money the put written is. The opposite is true if he is bearish.

We now discuss a prevalent strategy among traders: spreading.

Spreads

Spreads can be established with calls or with puts. They may be either bear or bull spreads. A spread, as discussed in Chapter 3, is a simultaneous purchase and sale of a call or put with the same contract month and different strike price (a vertical spread). It can also be the simultaneous purchase and sale of a call or put with the same strike price and different contract month (a horizontal or time spread).

Bull Call Spreads

An investor who expects falling interest rates (rising bond prices) and wishes to limit his risk could establish a bull call spread. The bullishness is an inducement for a net commitment of funds by the spreader. The intent here is not only to capitalize on an upward movement of bond prices, but also on the differential movement in the price of calls.

An example of a vertical bull call spread would be (Table 6.11).

Buy T-bond futures/June/70	4 05/64
Sell T-bond futures/June/74	1 60/64
Net cost (debit to spreader account)	**2 9/64**

Since the settlement price of the underlying T-bond futures contract is $73^{17}\!/_{32}$, the June/70 is an in-the-money call option and the June/74 is out-of-the-money.

If by March 1983 the expectations of the spreader are realized and the price of T-bond futures moves to, say, 78, the spreader will reverse his position. He or she realizes

Sell T-bond futures/June/70[37]	8
Buy T-bond futures/June/74	4
Net proceeds	**4**

The return on the spread is, therefore, equal to

$$4 - 2\ 9/64 = 1^{55}\!/_{64}$$

The $2\%_{64}$ investment represents the maximum exposure (loss) of the spreader no matter what happens in the T-bond futures market.

---

[37] The price movement of an in-the-money option is more in tandem with that of the underlying security than an out-of-the-money option.

After looking at the numbers in the example, you may conclude that the investor would have been better off without the spread and with simply a long call position. This is hindsight and it destroys the fundamental premise for establishing a spread position. The short call position was intended to cut the losses of the spreader if his expectations do not materialize. The simple call position could lose $4\%_{64}$, but the maximum loss on the spread is $2\%_{64}$. The size of the protection is the premium received from the sale of the call ($1^{60}\!/_{64}$).

The maximum profit on this vertical bull call spread is equal to the difference in strike prices less the net premium paid, that is

Maximum profit = $(74 - 70) - 2\ 9/64 =$ **1 55/64**

The risk reward ratio is, therefore, equal to

$$\frac{2\ 9/64}{1\ 55/64} = 1.15$$

Bear Call Spreads

An investor who expects a rise in interest rates (falling bond prices) and wishes to capitalize on that possibility, while limiting his risk, would establish a bear call spread. The bearish outlook on bond prices prevents the spreader from committing any funds to the spread. A bear call spread results, therefore, in a credit balance in the account of the spreader.

A horizontal (calendar) bear call spread on T-bond futures established on January 28, 1983 could be as follows

Buy T-bonds futures/March/74	1 05/64
Sell T-bond futures/June/74	1 60/64
Credit Balance	**55/64**

If expectations materialize and bond futures prices fall to, say, 68 from their 72.02 level on January 28, 1983, the spreader would reverse his position.

Sell T-bond futures/March/74	5/64
Buy T-bond futures/June/74	8/64
Net cost	3/64

Profit on the spread position = 55/64 − 3/64 = 52/64

The credit balance on the calendar bear call spread, it must be noted, represents the maximum profit the spreader can realize from his spread.

Bull Put Spreads

The put spreads require a thought process opposite that of call spreads. They are as easy to understand and establish, however.

An investor who expects interest rates to fall (bond prices to rise) and who wishes

to limit exposure could set up a bull put spread. Unlike the bull call spread, this spread results in a credit in the account of the spreader.

A vertical bull put spread from Table 6.11 could be

Buy T-bond futures/March/74 *P*	47/64
Sell T-bond futures/March/78 *P*	3 52/64
Net proceeds	3 5/64

If expectations materialize and T-bond futures prices move to 82, the spreader would reverse his position as follows

Sell T-bond futures/March/74 *P*	1/64
Buy T-bond futures/March/78 *P*	10/64
Net Cost	**9/64**

Profit from spread = 3 5/64 − 9/64 = $2^{60}\!/_{64}$

The maximum profit on a vertical bull put spread is the premium received, $3\frac{5}{64}$. The maximum loss is the difference in strike prices and the net premium received. That maximum is

Maximum loss = (78–74) − 3 5/64 = **59/64**

The risk/return tradeoff here is much more desirable than that of the vertical bull call spread.

Bear Put Spreads

An investor with the opposite expectations of a bull put spreader would establish a bear put spread. An example from Table 6.11 would be

Buy T-bond futures/June/74	2 35/64
Sell T-bond futures/June/72	1 32/64
Net premium paid	1 3/64

The reader should note that, unlike a bear call spread, the bear put spread requires a net commitment of funds. The net premium paid represents the maximum loss. The maximum gain, as should be verified under various states of the world, is equal to

Maximum gain = (74–72) − 1 3/64 =
2 − 1 3/64 = **61/64**

The risk return tradeoff of this strategy is

$$\frac{1\frac{3}{64}}{61\!/_{64}} = \textbf{1 09 to 1}$$

CONCLUSION

The interest of hedgers and speculators in financial futures continues to increase steadily. While mindful of the advantages of the financial futures market, a trader should be careful of the pitfalls.

Stock index futures contracts owe their existence to the volatility of the stock market and to the nonexistence of insurance contracts on stock portfolios. The strategies in and the tax implications of stock index futures contracts can be very complex, however.

Option strategies on T-bond futures or T-bond cash contracts or stock index futures are the same as those on common stock. The major differences between the various options are the determinants of their price movement and the instrument underlying the option contract. Interest options contracts could enhance the liquidity, the efficiency, and the attractiveness of the financial futures market for they allow for a multitude of ways to limit risk and expand the investment and speculative opportunities. Options on futures contracts complement the futures market but do not compete with it as options on cash instruments do.

The interested reader should study far beyond this introductory analysis.

QUESTIONS

1. "The presence of more than one commodity exchange is socially undesirable, for it contributes to the decentralization of the market." Comment.

2. How does interest rate volatility affect the investor? What opportunities do current wide gyrations offer that were not available in past stable conditions?

3. There are several alternatives to the financial futures market. What are they? Why have they not been very successful as a hedging or a speculative tool?

4. The profitability of an intermonth financial futures spread depends on the behavior of the basis. What must the basis do for a bull spread to realize a profit in a noninverted market?

5. Spreading is quite popular among speculators. What are the special characteristics that will make spreads more attractive than other strategies?

6. What type risk does a stock index futures contract hedge against? Why? How effective is the hedge?

7. Show the easiest and most correct way for pricing a financial futures contract.

8. What opportunities do stock market index futures offer investors? What effects should they have on the stock market itself?

9. A strategy known as "cash and carry" is gaining popularity among bond traders. It involves a short position in a financial futures contract and owning a U.S. government bond that is deliverable against the contract. What requirements concerning a bond's deliverability make the strategy possible? Might this strategy explain a flat yield curve beyond 15 years?

10. What properties do T-bills have that make them an ideal instrument upon which to write futures contracts?

11. To what factors would you attribute the growth of futures markets, Index Futures in particular?

12. What options does an investor have to close out a short position in the futures market?

13. An investor feels she may have made an unwise purchase of a T-bill. How might that be dealt with? Look at the various choices.

14. Define the "basis." What are its implications to futures strategies?

15. How might speculators use futures markets? What opportunities, otherwise unavailable, do they offer?

16. How would a banker use stock index futures to manage his assets?

17. Why would one choose an option on a futures contract instead of the futures contract itself? Be specific.

18. "Stock index futures are a disguised form of legalized gambling." Comment.

19. How do margin requirements for stock index futures compare with margin requirements for other futures contracts? Why the difference? What does the margin requirement represent?

20. "Stock index futures allow an investor to hedge against total risk." Comment.

21. Why is the weighted beta of the portfolio included in the calculation of the hedge ratio?

22. How does the relationship between the basis and carrying costs offer a profit potential to speculators?

23. Based on the evidence presented in the preceding chapter, what can you conclude about the efficiency of the futures market? What would be the implications of proof that futures markets affect the cash markets?

24. What are the essential ingredients of a model to price options on a stock index futures?

PROBLEMS

1. What is the maximum daily price fluctuation for a $1 million T-bill future selling on the IMM? What implications do these restrictions have?

2. An arbitrageur observes that a 91-day T-bill yields 9.20 percent, a 182-day bill yields 9.80 percent, and a futures contract requiring delivery of a 91-month T-bill three months hence is priced so as to yield 10.2 percent. What action would he take?

3. Calculate the theoretical price (on April 1) of a futures contract to deliver a six-month T-bill on October 1. A one-year bill maturing in six months (on October 1) yields 10.3 percent and a newly issued one-year T-bill currently yields 10.8 percent.

4. On January 12, 1983, a banker intends to roll over $10 million in CDs (liability) maturing in three months. He is obviously concerned with changes in interest rates and decides to protect his position. The current quotation on the closest contract to his time horizon (the June 1983 contract) is 86.67 (settlement price).
   a. Would he establish a long or a short position?
   b. How many contracts? Justify.
   c. Calculate his profits or losses on April 12, 1983, if the spot T-bill rate is now 86.0 and if the basis weakens by 10 basis points. Recalculate if the basis strengthens by 10 points.

PART
THREE

International
Dimensions

CHAPTER 7   Foreign Exchange Markets

7 | Foreign Exchange Markets

AN OVERVIEW

The international monetary system has evolved through the years into its present form. The Gold Standard prevailed between 1870 and 1914. International settlements were made in gold. Countries with balance of payments deficits lost gold, which led to lower income and prices. Countries with balance of payments surplus increased their gold reserves with resulting increases in income and prices. International disequilibrium was thus eliminated through the price system, leaving the exchange rates (value of currency in terms of gold) intact.

The second international economic system was agreed to by the participants at the Bretton Woods Conference in 1944. Under this agreement all currencies were pegged to gold, but only the dollar was convertible into gold. Exchange rates were allowed to fluctuate within ±1 percent of par value (value in terms of U.S. dollars). The system worked well until the 1960s when it showed major signs of weakness. The confidence in the dollar was waning at a time when world trade was expanding, necessitating a larger supply of a common denominator for international payments. This would have necessitated continued and increasing U.S. balance of payments deficits.

Despite various attempts at patching up the system, the central bankers of the world finally rediscovered the free market system. Today certain (major) currency prices are determined, although not always, by the forces of supply and demand. Governments do intervene from time to time in order to "stabilize" the foreign exchange market.

7.1 DEFINITIONS

Foreign Exchange

Foreign exchange is the price of one currency in terms of another. A foreign exchange contract is like any commodity contract that specifies the delivery of one good (currency) for another. However, commodity contracts in most economies do not specify the price of one commodity in terms of another, but rather in terms of a common denominator (a currency).

A foreign exchange contract consists of an entry on the books of a market maker (almost always a bank) that reflects a transaction in the spot (immediate delivery) market or in the forward (future delivery) market.

Foreign Exchange Market

The foreign exchange market is where currencies are traded. It is not a centralized market in the sense of a trading floor where all buyers and sellers meet to transact business. Transactions are effected over the Telex wire or over the telephone. Face to face contact is hardly ever necessary. London, Tokyo, Frankfurt, Amsterdam, Zurich, Paris, Brussels, Milan, New York, and Toronto are the financial centers through which the majority of transactions flow. These centers are connected by sophisticated communications networks. The market is a continuous market with no opening or closing hours, particularly with Hong Kong and Singapore becoming important centers for currency trading. It is a very competitive market, some argue *the* most competitive.

7.2 SIZE OF MARKET

No one really knows how large the market is. Many studies have attempted to estimate the size of the foreign exchange market. The range of estimates is very wide indeed. An official of the Federal Reserve Bank of New York estimated the size of the market to be $30 trillion (yes, trillion) for 1977.[1] Citibank's estimate is $50 trillion[2] for the same period. The latest estimate is provided by Ian Giddy.[3] Giddy puts the size of the market at $29 trillion per annum. The estimating procedure used by Giddy is worth summarizing. Using the transactions flowing through the Clearing House Interbank Payments System (CHIPS)—the dominant channel for international transactions calling for fund transfer—and adjusting for "nonforeign exchange transfers through CHIPS for forward and book transfer transactions that do not go through CHIPS, and for foreign exchange transactions not involving the U.S. dollar," Giddy arrived at the $29 trillion for the year 1977, or an average daily volume of $118 billion.

Although the growth of the foreign exchange market is impressive, it was certainly not very smooth. The market was severely jolted by the failures of the Herstatt Bank and the Franklin National Bank in 1974. Much of the speculation was curtailed as banks attempted to keep their foreign exchange exposure to a minimum. Early in 1975 volume began to pick up once again and continued a steep rise through the early 1980s.

7.3 MARKET PARTICIPANTS

The major participants in the foreign exchange market are commercial banks, central banks, and nonbanking institutions. The distribution of the foreign exchange activity among the participants is depicted in Figure 7.1. As Figure 7.1 makes clear, 82 percent of the activities are motivated by speculation and arbitrage opportunities. Only 3 percent of the total volume is motivated by commercial transactions. The distribution of nonbank activities is shown in Figure 7.2. The largest activity is that of commodity dealers,

---

[1] *The Wall Street Journal* (January 15, 1979).

[2] See **James H. Wooden,** "U.S. Multinational Banks—Foreign Exchange Operations." *Merrill Lynch Institutional Report* (July 1979).

[3] **Ian H. Giddy,** "Measuring the World Foreign Exchange Market." *Columbia Journal of World Business* (Winter 1979), pp. 36–48.

FIGURE 7.1.   **The international dollar payments system.**

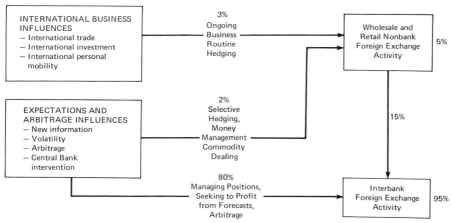

Source: Ian H. Giddy, "Measuring the World Foreign Exchange Market," *Columbia Journal of World Business* (Winter 1979), p. 40.

particularly those in the metals markets. These activities are predominantly speculative in nature.

While interbank trading dominates the foreign exchange market, it must be remembered that the motivating force behind the market is those transactions associated with the movement of goods and capital. It is these transactions which create the legitimate need for foreign exchange and to which the banking system must ultimately answer. The speculative and arbitrage activities by commercial banks are the result of attempts by banks to protect and to maximize the rate of return on positions held to accommodate

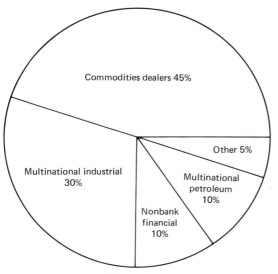

FIGURE 7.2.   Nonbank participants in foreign exchange trading.

Source: Ian H. Giddy, "Measuring the World Foreign Exchange Market," *Columbia Journal of World Business* (Winter 1979), p. 43.

trade and capital transactions. Note further that speculative and accommodating transactions are not always undertaken by banks for their own account.

7.4 CURRENCY COMPOSITION

The currencies playing major roles in the foreign exchange markets are those of countries with well-developed markets characterized by minimal interference by the indigenous government in the market mechanism and by liberal policies regarding conversion and flow of capital across national borders. The strength of these markets is not always derived from the strength of the indigenous economy or from the country's position in international trade. The political and economic role of the United States in the world and the size and strength of its economy account for the dominant role of the dollar. The strength of the ties between many European countries and developing nations (which began during the industrial revolution and which solidified during periods of colonialism) have certainly contributed to the role played by some European currencies, such as the Dutch guilder and the British pound. The Swiss case is most peculiar; the position of the Swiss franc in the world market stems from the strength of the Swiss economic and political system and from the peculiar position Switzerland enjoys in world politics.

Currencies that are allowed to float freely or jointly, as opposed to being pegged, account for approximately 70 percent of the denomination of world trade. So, while history is important, economics and institutional constraints play an overriding role. This view is supported by the relatively weak role played by the Japanese yen because of the interference of the Japanese government in the foreign exchange market.

TABLE 7.1
Estimated Currency Composition of Foreign Exchange Trading

Currency	Percentage of Total Transactions
U.S. dollar	99%
German mark	40
British pound	15
Swiss franc	18
Canadian dollar	5
Japanese yen	5
French franc	6
Dutch guilder	5
Belgian franc	2
Italian lira	1
Swedish krona	1
Other	3
Total	**200%**

Note: Total adds to 200 percent because two currencies are involved in every foreign exchange transaction.

Source: Ian H. Giddy, "Measuring the World Foreign Exchange Market." *Columbia Journal of World Business* (Winter 1979), p. 41.

FIGURE 7.3. **The international dollar payments system.**

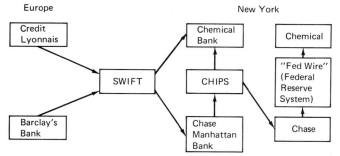

Steps in the transfer of funds resulting from a foreign exchange transaction:

1. Barclay's Bank buys German marks from Credit Lyonnais; to consummate this it must transfer funds in the U. S. to Credit Lyonnais' account in Chemical Bank, New York.

2. Barclay's uses SWIFT, a worldwide financial communications network, to instruct Chase to transfer funds out of the Barclay's account.

3. Chase debits Barclay's account and transfers the funds through CHIPS, the payments clearing system for international transactions. In effect, it sends an electronic check to CHIPS. Then "clearing house funds" get credited to Chemical on the same day. Night falls.

4. Next day, the net amount is settled between Federal Reserve member banks by transfers in "Fed funds"—deposits held at the various federal Reserve banks. This is done through the domestic interbank clearing system, the "Fed wire."

5. Chemical credits Credit Lyonnais' account and notifies Credit Lyonnais, again through the SWIFT network.

Source: Ian H. Giddy, "Measuring the World Foreign Exchange Market," *Columbia Journal of World Business* (Winter 1979), p. 40.

The relative importance of each currency in the foreign exchange market is summarized in Table 7.1. The roles played by the dollar, the German mark, the British pound, and the Swiss franc far exceed those played in international trade by their respective countries.

7.5 TRADING MECHANICS

Trading in the foreign exchange market almost invariably involves the U.S. dollar. Giddy's work indicates that 99 percent of the value of foreign exchange transactions involve the U.S. dollar.[4] Transactions between two European currencies, for example, are almost never direct. They are indirect transactions involving the U.S. dollar because of the depth of the dollar–foreign currency market and the associated lower transactions costs. (A British importer wishing to buy German marks to pay a German exporter would likely sell pounds for dollars and then buy German marks with the proceeds.) What the bank would do in a foreign exchange transaction is illustrated in Figure 7.3.

Intricate as Figure 7.3 may appear, transactions are executed effectively and quickly.

---

[4] Ibid., p. 39.

Electronic communications have considerably facilitated the movement of funds. We must note, however, that no currency of whatever nationality has changed hands here. The foreign exchange contract is simply a bookkeeping entry. The correspondent banks in the United States called upon to execute foreign exchange transactions are usually New York banks. The twelve largest U.S. banks, anchored in New York, constitute the totality of the U.S. market. These banks, by arbitraging their own foreign exchange position and that of their clients, in a currency or across currencies provide a continuous marketplace for currencies. Banks trading in New York deal through a broker in order to preserve anonymity and to centralize the communication network.

The role of the central bank is not always a passive one (a transfer agent) in foreign exchange transactions (Figure 7.1). Central banks intervene in order to maintain an orderly market. They do so by trading with commercial banks or with each other. The greater the role of the central bank, the less freedom commercial banks enjoy, and the less the foreign exchange rate is truly market-determined.

7.6 NECESSARY DEFINITIONS

Forward Exchange

A forward exchange contract is an agreement to buy (sell) a certain amount of foreign currency at a specified date in the future (one, two, three, six, and twelve months, usually) at a price determined today.

Spot Exchange

A spot exchange contract is a special condition of a forward contract where the time period shrinks to a few days (two days or less, usually).

Futures Contract

A foreign exchange futures contract is an obligation to buy or sell a specified amount (standard for all customers) of a foreign currency at a specified time (set by the exchange) in the future at a price determined today.

Swap Transaction

A swap is the simultaneous purchase and sale of spot and forward exchange or two forward transactions of different maturities.

7.7 EXCHANGE RATE QUOTATIONS

The Wall Street Journal and several other daily publications report daily quotations on 45 different currencies (Table 7.2). The activity in the spot market centers around a handful of currencies. Few currencies are widely traded in the forward market (6) as well as in the futures market (5). The other currencies have either very thin forward markets or none at all. In the forward market the life of the contract is generally

standardized. Tailored contracts can be devised and are usually more expensive. All futures contracts are standardized as to maturity.

7.8 EXCHANGE QUOTATIONS

Spot rates are quoted in either of two ways: direct or indirect. The direct quote gives the price of a unit of the foreign currency in terms of domestic currency—that is, the direct quote states how many dollars it takes to buy, say, a Lebanese pound; it took $0.2262 according to the first column of numbers in Table 7.2 (A). The indirect quote gives the price of a unit of domestic currency in terms of foreign currencies. That is, the indirect quote states how many Lebanese pounds it takes to purchase a dollar. The answer according to Table 7.2 (A) is 4.42 on Wednesday, October 6, 1982. The direct quote is referred to as the U.S. basis; the indirect quote is referred to as the European basis. The reader may have noted that the indirect quote is the inverse of the direct quote (4.42 is the inverse of 0.2262). Each quote must reflect both sides of the market: the sell side (ask) and the buy side (bid).

Forward rates are also quoted the direct and indirect way with an interesting and sometimes confusing twist. A trader in New York may quote the DM spot, 1 month, 3 month, and 6 month as follows:

0.4000–0.4003   12–19 (or 12/19, or 12 to 19), 45–64, 95–130

The bid/ask spread on the forward rates is referred to as points. A point is the fourth digit to the right of the decimal—for example, 12 is equivalent to .0012. These quotes correspond to the following rates:

Maturity	Buy	Sell
Spot	0.4000	0.4003
1 Month	0.4012	0.4022
3 Month	0.4045	0.4067
6 Month	0.4095	0.4133

Since the forward rate is higher than the spot rate, we can say that the DM is selling at a premium. The size of the premium for one month is 0.0019 on the sell side, or 0.0019/0.4003 (the spot rate) = 0.474 percent or an annual rate of 5.69 percent (0.474 × 12). A possible reason for this premium is that the market expects the spot rate that prevails one month from now to be higher than the current spot rate.

Whenever the currency is selling at a premium, the quote from the trader will have a smaller number (12, bid) followed by a larger number (19, ask). These numbers must be added to the spot rate quotation in order to arrive at the outright forward rate. When a currency is selling at a discount, the trader's quote will be flashed in reverse order, with the larger number (the bid) preceding the smaller number (the ask). These numbers will have to be *subtracted* from the spot quotation to arrive at the outright forward rate.

The preceding is based on the direct quotation (the U.S. point of view) system. Using the European indirect quotation, we arrive at an opposite and important conclusion: the U.S. dollar is selling at a discount. The size of the discount (in percentage terms) would not equal that of the premium on the opposing currency simply because of the nature of the arithmetic. For the DM case the European quotations on the ask side

TABLE 7.2a

Spot and Forward Markets—Foreign Exchange

Wednesday, October 6, 1982
The New York foreign exchange selling rates below apply to trading among banks in amounts of $1 million and more, as quoted at 3 p.m. Eastern time by Bankers Trust Co. Retail transactions provide fewer units of foreign currency per dollar.

Country	U.S. $ equiv. Wed.	Tues.	Currency per U.S. $ Wed.	Tues.
Argentina (Fincl)	.000026	.000026	39.000	39.000
Argentina (Peso)	.000036	.000036	27.540	27.540
Australia (Dollar)	.9460	.9451	1.0571	1.0581
Austria (Schilling)	.0565	.0559	17.70	17.90
Belgium (Franc)				
Commercial rate	.0204	.0202	49.00	49.50
Financial rate	.0193	.0193	51.75	51.75
Brazil (Cruzeiro)	.0048	.0048	206.72	206.72
Britain (Pound)	1.6955	1.6910	.5898	.5914
30-Day Forward	1.6971	1.6929	.5892	.5907
90-Day Forward	1.7010	1.6968	.5879	.5893
180-Day Forward	1.7095	1.7063	.5850	.5861
Canada (Dollar)	.8081	.8071	1.2375	1.2390
30-Day Forward	.8066	.8058	1.2398	1.2410
90-Day Forward	.8046	.8039	1.2429	1.2439
180-Day Forward	.8026	.8022	1.2459	1.2466
Chile (Official-Rate)	.0169	.0169	59.00	59.00
China (Yuan)	.5076	.5063	1.9700	1.9750
Colombia (Peso)	.0151	.0151	66.27	66.27
Denmark (Krone)	.1122	.1121	8.9100	8.9225
Ecuador (Sucre)	.0302	.0302	33.15	33.15
Finland (Markka)	.1967	.2053	5.0850	4.8700
France (Franc)	.1391	.1389	7.1900	7.2000
30-Day Forward	.1385	.1386	7.2225	7.2175
90-Day Forward	.1369	.1372	7.3025	7.2900
180-Day Forward	.1353	.1351	7.3900	7.4000
Greece (Drachma)	.0139	.0139	71.75	72.000
Hong Kong (Dollar)	.1546	.1548	6.4700	6.4600
India (Rupee)	.1030	.1031	9.7100	9.7000
Indonesia (Rupiah)	.0015	.0015	659.50	659.50
Ireland (Punt)	1.3415	1.3400	.7454	.7463
Israel (Shekel)	.0347	.0346	28.70	28.90
Italy (Lira)	.00070	.00070	1433.00	1435.25
Japan (Yen)	.003654	.003656	273.65	273.50
30-Day Forward	.003669	.003672	272.57	272.30
90-Day Forward	.003697	.003700	270.50	270.27
180-Day Forward	.003740	.003744	267.40	267.10
Lebanon (Pound)	.2262	.2262	4.4200	4.4200
Malaysia (Ringgit)	.4207	.4207	2.3770	2.3770
Mexico (Peso)	z	z	z	z
Netherlands (Guilder)	.3596	.3587	2.7805	2.7875
New Zealand (Dollar)	.7200	.7135	1.3889	1.4015
Norway (Krone)	.1425	.1428	7.0200	7.0020
Pakistan (Rupee)	.0805	.0805	12.4278	12.4278
Peru (Sol)	.0013	.0013	780.62	780.625
Philippines (Peso)	.1151	.1151	8.6890	8.6890
Portugal (Escudo)	.0120	.0120	83.00	83.00
Saudi Arabia (Riyal)	.2908	.2908	3.4390	3.4390
Singapore (Dollar)	.4513	.4523	2.2160	2.2110
South Africa (Rand)	.8650	.8892	1.1561	1.1246
South Korea (Won)	.0013	.0013	742.65	742.65
Spain (Peseta)	.0088	.0087	114.25	115.30
Sweden (Krona)	.1580	.1587	6.3300	6.3010
Switzerland (Franc)	.4579	.4558	2.1840	2.1940
30-Day Forward	.4610	.4591	2.1690	2.1780
90-Day Forward	.4668	.4647	2.1422	2.1520
180-Day Forward	.4751	.4731	2.1050	2.1135
Taiwan (Dollar)	.0251	.0251	39.87	39.87
Thailand (Baht)	.0435	.0435	23.00	23.00
Uruguay (New Peso)				
Financial	.0757	.0757	13.204	13.204
Venezuela (Bolivar)	.2329	.2329	4.2938	4.2938
W. Germany (Mark)	.3933	.3925	2.5425	2.5480
30-Day Forward	.3946	.3939	2.5340	2.5388
90-Day Forward	.3975	.3967	2.5160	2.5205
180-Day Forward	.4020	.4015	2.4875	2.4905
SDR	1.06763	1.06625	.936658	0.937871

Special Drawing Rights are based on exchange rates for the U.S., West German, British, French and Japanese currencies. Source International Monetary Fund.

TABLE 7.2b

Futures Market—IMM

	Open	High	Low	Settle	Change	Lifetime High	Low	Open Interest
BRITISH POUND (IMM) –25,000 pounds; $ per pound								
Dec	1.6945	1.6990	1.6920	1.6925	– .0015	1.9350	1.6855	14,856
Mar83	1.7040	1.7080	1.7020	1.7020	– .0020	1.8500	1.6950	1,113
June				1.7110	– .0030	1.7550	1.7280	12
Est vol 2,484; vol Tues 2,593; open int 15,981, +110.								
CANADIAN DOLLAR (IMM) –100,000 dlrs.; $ per Can $								
Dec	.8050	.8055	.8035	.8039	– .0006	.8350	.7618	11,697
Mar83	.8024	.8030	.8010	.8017	– .0005	.8150	.7282	2,880
June	.7995	.8000	.7995	.7995	+ .0025	.8085	.7810	149
Est vol 2,870; vol Tues 6,022; open int 14,726, +1123.								
JAPANESE YEN (IMM) 12.5 million yen; $ per yen (.00)								
Dec	.3677	.3688	.3664	.3665	– .0023	.4505	.3664	13,997
Mar83	.3723	.3732	.3706	.3708	– .0025	.4400	.3706	625
June				.3755	– .0023	.3966	.3778	8
Est vol 3,344; vol Tues 3,270; open int 14,630, –416.								
SWISS FRANC (IMM) –125,000 francs-$ per franc								
Dec	.4624	.4652	.4623	.4626	+ .0002	.5920	.4608	15,283
Mar83	.4707	.4732	.4707	.4709	+ .0002	.5680	.4682	870
June				.4795	...	.5069	.4770	9
Est vol 6,296; vol Tues 5,548; open int 16,162, –262.								
W. GERMAN MARK (IMM) –125,000 marks; $ per mark								
Dec	.3957	.3966	.3949	.3951	– .0005	.4675	.3942	14,811
Mar83	.4004	.4011	.3998	.3998	– .0003	.4220	.3987	550
June				.4045	...	.4450	.4045	14
Est vol 3,441; vol Tues 3,951; open int 15,375, –186.								

Source: The Wall Street Journal, October 7, 1982.

are 2.4981 and 2.4863, respectively, for the spot and the 30-day forward rate. This yields a discount on the dollar equal to

$$\frac{2.4863 - 2.4981}{2.4981} = \frac{0.0118}{2.4981} = 0.00472 \text{ or } 0.472 \text{ percent.}$$

This is equivalent to an annual rate of 5.664 percent (0.472 × 12). If the quotations were reversed—that is, the forward rate is equal to 2.4981 and the spot equal to 2.4863—the monthly premium would equal 0.475 percent or an annual premium of 5.7 percent.

Forward rates in London are quoted with the ask price first. The 12–19 forward rate quote on the DM in New York will come over the wire from London as 19–12, to be used as 0.0019–0.0012.

All quotations in futures contracts are of the direct type. The December contract on a British Pound closed at $1.6925 (settlement price) on October 6, 1982 (Table 7.2 (B)). On October 6, 1982 14,856 December contracts, each covering 25,000 British pounds, were outstanding, of which 2,484 were estimated to have traded on the same day. All futures contracts are traded on the International Monetary Market (IMM), which is located in Chicago.

7.9 BUYING FOREIGN EXCHANGE

A corporate executive who wishes to purchase or sell foreign exchange does so directly with his bank. No broker is needed. The bank acts as a dealer, realizing its profits from the spread—the difference between the bid and the ask. It is advisable to check with several banks before an investor decides to enter into a transaction. The bank selling a forward contract does not have to keep an open position with its attending risks. The bank can turn around and buy a forward contract to match the one sold. If Citibank sells a DM forward contract to an American corporation, it buys, to cover itself, a forward contract, say, from a German bank. In turn the German bank finds a German customer buying U.S. goods who needs to buy dollars forward (sell German DM forward) to sell the contract to. Citibank can also engage in a swap transaction in order to avoid exchange risk.

It is instructive to remember that the spread earned by the bank is not the equivalent of an insurance premium. The bank is not insuring the foreign exchange contract buyer against foreign exchange risk. By matching its buy and sell positions, the bank assumes no risk. The example above points out how risk is dissipated through the foreign exchange system as a whole.

7.10 USES OF FORWARD EXCHANGE

The forward exchange market is used for several purposes.

Covering Commercial Transactions

A U.S. exporter who expects to receive foreign currency sells the currency forward in order to lock in a certain exchange rate. Alternatively, he may insist that he be paid in dollars, thereby eliminating risk altogether. However, in that case the buyer may offer a lower price.

A U.S. importer expecting to make payments in DM for his imports from Germany may buy DM forward to avoid higher costs that result from the appreciation in the value of the DM.

Hedging

The foreign exchange market is used to hedge against reduction of value of assets and/ or earnings subject to foreign exchange risk.

Arbitrage

Arbitrageurs who use the foreign exchange market attempt to capitalize on interest rate differences across national boundaries. An extensive discussion of this topic follows later.

Speculation

A speculator is a person trying to outguess the market. He is actually betting that the expected spot rate implied by the forward rate will be different from the spot rate that will prevail at the end of the period covered in the forward contract.

The speculator has a preference for the forward market because little or no capital is required. Speculation in the spot market requires commitment of 100 percent of the value of the contract. The speculator can buy foreign currency with the hope of selling it later at a profit. If he expects the spot rate to drop, he borrows the depreciating currency, sells it immediately and buys back the currency in the market to repay the loan when the loan matures or when he deems the time is right. The speculator profits if the currency depreciates and loses if it appreciates.

7.11 CONSISTENCY IN THE FOREIGN EXCHANGE MARKET

Two consistencies are required of the foreign exchange market: one across markets for a given currency and the other across currencies.

Consistency Across Markets

Across-market consistency requires that the price of the dollar in New York should be the same as that in, say, London. If not, an arbitrage opportunity would present itself, leading to a flow of funds across borders. If the value of the pound were $1.90 in New York and $1.80 in London, the arbitrageur would sell pounds in New York where the value is high and receive $190 (assuming he holds 100 pounds). In London the $190 are sold for sterling where they fetch 105.55 pounds. The gross gain from this arbitrage transaction is 5.55 pounds. The gain will be less if transactions costs are accounted for. With minimal transactions costs and no impediments to the flow of funds, the price of one currency in terms of another should be the same.

Consistency Across Currencies (Consistent Cross Rate)

If the equilibrium rate between the U.S. dollar and the British pound were $2 to 1 pound, that between the dollar and the franc $0.25 to Fr 1, the equilibrium rate between the franc and the British pound would then have to be 1 pound = Fr 8. Restated, the equilibrium rates are

$1 = £0.5   £ = Fr 8   Fr 1 = $0.25

The product of the right hand side of the equalities is 1, as it must be. Otherwise, arbitrage opportunities would present themselves. Had the pound sold for 10 French francs, an arbitrageur would sell dollars for pounds and pounds for francs. Starting, say, with $100 we buy 50 pounds, sell the pounds for francs and get 500 francs. Then we exchange the francs for $125 for a net profit of $25. As this process continues, the price of the pound will fall until consistency across exchange rates is established.

7.12 TYPES OF FOREIGN EXCHANGE RISK

Citibank, in a 1979 study, classified foreign exchange risk into three categories:

1. Rate Risk. This type of Risk results from an unexpected exchange rate movement.
2. Credit Risk. Risk of this type results from imminent bankruptcy of the party that issues the foreign exchange contract before the contract matures.
3. Liquidity Risk. Risk of this variety results from high transaction costs and/or high discount on the contract, which may have to be accepted because of the thinness of the futures market at the time of liquidation.

7.13 RELATIONSHIP BETWEEN SPOT AND FORWARD RATES

Suppose we have the following prices

$P$$ Current prices of $ and £ for current (P) or future
$F$$ (F) delivery. Prices are defined in terms of some
$P£$ standard tradable commodity that can be bought
$F£$ in either country.

Given these four prices, three independent prices must exist. The obvious two are

$$S = \frac{P\$}{P£} = \text{spot rate}$$

and

$$F = \frac{F\$}{F£} = \text{forward rate}$$

The third price is

$$\frac{F\$}{P\$.} = 1 + i_{\text{U.S.}}$$

or

$$\frac{F\pounds}{P\pounds} = 1 + i_{\text{U.K.}}$$

The equality of the ratio of the forward price of the dollar ($F\$$) to the spot price of the dollar ($P\$$) to the interest rate in the United States ($i_{\text{U.S.}}$) covering the same period as the forward contract may not be intuitive. The $\dfrac{F\$}{P\$}$ ratio represents the future value of a unit of currency in relation to its current value in terms of the standard commodity. The sum $1 + i_{\text{U.S.}}$ represents the future value of one dollar in relation to the current value ($\$1$) if invested at the interest rate $i_{\text{U.S.}}$. If markets are efficient the two returns must be equal to each other, otherwise domestic arbitrage opportunities will present themselves.

We can rewrite the preceding relationships as follows:

$$\frac{1 + i_{\text{U.S.}}}{1 + i_{\text{U.K.}}} = \frac{\dfrac{F\$}{P\$}}{\dfrac{F\pounds}{P\pounds}} = \frac{F\$}{P\$} \times \frac{P\pounds}{F\pounds} = \frac{(F\$)\,(P\pounds)}{(F\pounds)\,(P\$)}$$

$$= \frac{1 + i_{\text{U.S.}}}{1 + i_{\text{U.K.}}} = \frac{F_{\$,\pounds}}{S_{\$,\pounds}} = \frac{\text{Forward rate of the British pound in terms of the U.S. dollar}}{\text{Spot rate of the British pound in terms of the U.S. dollar}} \qquad (7.1)$$

In general

$$\frac{1 + i_d}{1 + i_f} = \frac{F}{S} \qquad (7.2)$$

when i_d = domestic rate of interest

i_f = foreign rate of interest

F = forward rate

S = spot rate

Equation 7.2 is referred to as the interest rate parity theorem (IRPT).

7.14 INTEREST RATE PARITY THEOREM

The equilibrium shown in Equation 7.2 among the current exchange rate, the forward exchange rate, the domestic interest rate, and the foreign rate of interest is realized through the process of arbitrage according to IRPT. This arbitrage is referred to as investor arbitrage or borrower arbitrage.

Investor Arbitrage

Consider a world made up of the United States and Britain and assume

1. No government intervention in the flow of funds across national borders.
2. Tax treatment of arbitrage profits is the same in both countries.
3. Flexible exchange rates without limit.

A disequilibrium in Equation 7.1 brings about arbitrage opportunities. To see how, let us rewrite Equation 7.1. Subtracting 1 from both sides of the equation, we get

$$\frac{F_{\$,£}}{S_{\$,£}} - 1 = \frac{1 + i_{U.S.}}{1 + i_{U.K.}} - 1$$

$$\frac{F_{\$,£} - S_{\$,£}}{S_{\$,£}} = \frac{1 + i_{U.S.} - 1 - i_{U.K.}}{1 + i_{U.K.}}$$

or

$$\frac{F_{\$,£} - S_{\$,£}}{S_{\$,£}} = \frac{i_{U.S.} - i_{U.K.}}{1 + i_{U.K.}} \tag{7.3}$$

Equation 7.3 represents the no arbitrage case. The left-hand side of the equation is referred to as the implicit rate, the right hand side as the interest rate differential.

$$\frac{F_{\$,£} - S_{\$,£}}{S_{\$,£}} - \frac{i_{U.S.} - i_{U.K.}}{1 + i_{U.K.}} = AM \text{ (Arbitrage Margin)}$$

Note that the arbitrage margin can exist although the interest differential is equal to zero.

Example

From Table 7.2 we find the spot German mark at 0.3933 and the 90-day German mark forward rate at 0.3975. The U.S. three-month treasury bill rate is 8.50 percent and the German three-month treasury bill rate is, say, 8 percent. Is there an arbitrage opportunity? In what direction would money flow?

Arbitrage Opportunity?

$$\frac{F_{\$,DM} - S_{\$,DM}}{S_{\$,DM}} - \frac{i_{U.S.} - i_{Ger}}{1 + i_{Ger}} = AM$$

$$\frac{0.3975 - 0.3933}{0.3933} - \frac{0.02125 - 0.02}{1.02} = (0.01068) - (0.00125)$$

$$= 1.068\% - 0.1225\% = 0.946\%$$

The implicit rate is positive and equal to 1.068 percent. The interest rate differential favors the United States. The German mark is selling at a forward premium, that is, the U.S. dollar is selling at a forward discount. This condition in the foreign exchange market is favorable to Germany, as will be shown in detail below. The numbers thus far indicate that an arbitrage opportunity exists and funds must flow out of the United States (a negative *AM* would have required a flow of funds in the direction of the United States).

A U.S. investor observing this would decide to invest in Germany. Owning German securities, however, is owning DM-denominated assets with attending foreign exchange risk. This risk is eliminated through the forward market. The process is as follows:

The Mechanics

Assume the U.S. investor has $10,000 invested in U.S. treasury bills (or may be willing to borrow funds in the United States at $i_{U.S.}$). Considering the arbitrage opportunity that exists between the United States and Germany, he would do the following:

1. Sell the U.S. treasury bills.
2. Buy DM in the spot market.

   Net proceeds = 10,000 / 0.3933 = DM 25,426

3. Buy German T-bills for DM 25,426.
4. Calculate the total exposure in DM.

$$\text{Total exposure} = 25,426 \left(1 + \frac{0.08}{4}\right) = \text{DM } 25,934.5$$

5. Sell DM 25,934.5 forward to eliminate foreign exchange exposure. (Note that this high DM forward rate translates itself into a higher transaction cost (a reduced incentive for buying German securities.)) Expected proceeds in 90-days are

   (25,934.5) (0.3975) = $10,309

The U.S. investor has just realized $309 on a three-month investment in risk-free German securities. Had he purchased U.S. treasury bills, his total return would have been $10,000 (0.02125) = $212.50. His gross profits from looking at world opportunities as opposed to domestic (U.S.) opportunities is $309 − $212.50 = $96.50.

In order to generalize the results of the preceding example, we state the general version of Equation 7.2.

$$a[1 + i_{U.S.}(90)] = \frac{a}{S_{\$,DM}} [1 + i_{Ger}(90)] \times F_{\$,DM}(90) \tag{7.4}$$

$a[1 + i_{U.S.}(90)] = $ dollar return on U.S. investment of $\$a$.

$\dfrac{a}{S_{\$,DM}} = $ DM the U.S. arbitrageur gets upon converting his dollars

$\dfrac{a}{S_{\$,DM}} [1 + i_{Ger}(90)] \times F_{\$,DM}(90) = $ dollar return on covered investment in Germany

From Equation 7.3 or Equation 7.4, one can easily derive the equilibrium (or no arbitrage) forward rate.

$$F^*_{\$,DM}(t) = \frac{1 + i_{U.S.}(t)}{1 + i_{Ger}(t)} \times S_{\$,DM} \tag{7.5}$$

If Equation 7.5 holds, no funds will move from either country to the other. Knowing the values of the exogenous variables $i_{U.S.}$, i_{Ger}, and $S_{\$,DM}$, we can easily calculate $F_{\$,DM}$. If $F_{\$,DM}$ is different from $F^*_{\$,DM}(t)$, funds will flow from one country to another.

Impact Analysis

Let us briefly examine the consequences of the flow of funds from the United States to Germany.

The U.S. rate of interest will rise as investors sell their U.S. securities and substitute them for German securities. The German rate of interest will decline as U.S. investors increase the demand for German securities and in the process raise their price. This will increase the interest rate differential between the two countries.

As the dollar is sold in the spot market, that is, as the German DM is bought, the spot rate will move against the dollar in favor of the German mark.

The forward rate on the dollar improves as arbitrageurs buy dollars forward. The opposite is true for the forward rate on DM.

With the spot DM rising and the forward DM falling, the implicit rate is shrinking. The process continues until the implicit rate is equal to the interest rate differential between the two countries and the no arbitrage position is reached.

Domestic interest rates, it must be noted, are affected by many factors other than those suggested above. Considering that both domestic money markets and the foreign exchange markets do not have the same degree of depth, most of the adjustment would take place in the forward exchange market. It is, therefore, the case that interest parity relationships determine the forward exchange rate.

Interest Rate Parity Theory—A Graphical Illustration

Referring again to equation (7.2),

$$\frac{F_{\$,DM} - S_{\$,DM}}{S_{\$,DM}} = \frac{i_{U.S.} - i_{Ger}}{1 + i_{Ger}}$$

If $i_{U.S.} > i_{Ger}$, then $F_{\$,DM}$ must be greater than $S_{\$,DM}$ by an offsetting amount for equilibrium to prevail. The reverse must also be true.

Anywhere along the interest parity line, $F = F^*$ and no funds will flow from either country to the other. If the interest rate differential were at c and the implicit rate at a so that market conditions were represented by point d, (Figure 7.4), $Oc > Oa$ and the investor will clearly be interested in shifting funds from Germany to the United States. The process will continue until a new equilibrium is reached where $F = F^*$ and we are once again back on the interest parity line. The adjustments in the money and foreign exchange markets will be along the lines described earlier. We can, therefore,

FIGURE 7.4.   Interest rate parity theory: a graphical illustration.

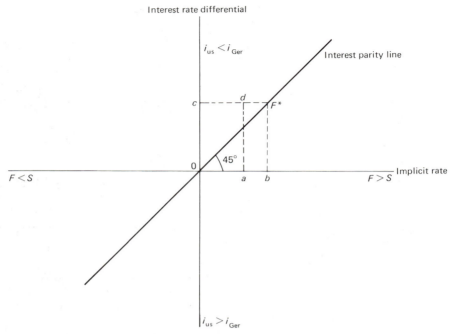

conclude that forward rates lying above the interest parity line cause a flow of capital into the United States and those below the line will cause flows in the opposite direction.

Problems with the Interest Rate Parity Theory

The interest rate parity theory is limited in many ways by its own assumptions and by market considerations. Its weaknesses are

1. IRPT considers only the behavior of arbitrageurs and looks at the adjustment process as one determined by their behavior in the marketplace; that is a consequence of the covered interest arbitrage activity. In so doing, IRPT ignores the activities of speculators, hedgers, and traders. Speculators' activities could have a dramatic impact on exchange rates both in the spot and in the forward markets.

2. Borrowers and lenders may face different interest rate schedules. The borrowing rate is not always equal to the lending rate.

3. IRPT looks only at the level of the rate, but not at the risk associated with that rate. Holding investment vehicles in more than one country may be desirable from a risk diversification point of view.

4. While the comparison of short-term rates among countries such as the United States and England or Germany is quite possible because of the similarity of instruments in terms of maturity and risk profile, this is not the case across all countries because of the difficulty of specifying short-term interest rates.[5]

[5] **M. Adler** and **B. Dumas,** "Portfolio Choice and the Demand for Forward Exchange," *American Economic Review* (May 1976), pp. 332–339.

5. IRPT ignores transactions costs associated with covered interest arbitrage. These costs can be significant and are incurred (following an example earlier in this section) when the U.S. securities are liquidated, when the swap transaction in the foreign exchange market is affected, and when the foreign currency-denominated securities are purchased. Direct measures of these transactions costs are always possible. A worthwhile attempt was made by J. Hilley, C. Beidleman, and J. Greenleaf.[6] These authors divided transactions costs into two categories: those related to the spread in foreign exchange transactions (bid-ask), and nonspread costs. The U.S. investor in our example would, therefore, buy DM at the ask and sell them forward at the bid. This would take care of the spread costs. The nonspread costs are summarized in the following equation:

$$K = (1 - t)(1 - t^*)(1 - t_s)(1 - t_f)$$

where t = percent transaction cost arising from brokerage fees and costs of information involved in selling a dollar-denominated asset.

t^* = percent transaction cost of buying a DM-denominated asset.

t_s = percent transaction cost of purchasing spot DM.

t_f = percent transaction cost of selling DM forward.

Accounting for both K costs and the spread costs, the IRPT equilibrium condition would look as follows:

$$\frac{F_b - S_a}{S_a} = \frac{(1 + i_{\text{U.S.}}) - K(1 + i_{\text{Ger}})}{K(1 + i_{\text{Ger}})} \tag{7.6}$$

where F_b = Forward exchange rate (bid)

S_a = Spot exchange rate (ask)

Empirical tests run on Equation 7.6 show, consistent with other empirical studies, that the K factors are significant. Tests also show that "covered interest arbitrage dominates in the foreign exchange markets."[7]

7.15 THE MODERN THEORY OF FORWARD EXCHANGE RATE

The modern theory of forward exchange rate (*MT*) states that the behavior of arbitrageurs, determined by the IRPT and that of speculators, influenced by their expectations with regard to the spot rate, determine the foreign exchange rate. In other words, *MT* states that the forward rate is a weighted average of two rates: one resulting from the behavior of arbitrageurs alone, the other from the behavior of speculators alone.

---

[6] **John Hilley, Carl Beidleman,** and **James Greenleaf,** "Does Covered Interest Arbitrage Dominate in Foreign Exchange Markets." *Columbia Journal of World Business* (Winter 1979), pp. 99–107.

[7] Ibid., p. 103.

The Arbitrageur's Schedule

Our objective here is to determine conditions under which the arbitrageur would supply forward contracts or demand forward contracts and the impact this has on the forward rate. Consider a world made up of two countries, Germany and the United States, and assume that the exchange rate is quoted the direct way and that the interest rate differential is given.

At $F^*_{\$,DM}$ no funds will flow in either direction (Figure 7.5). Hence there is no supply of or demand for forward contracts by arbitrageurs. For equilibrium to prevail, the interest rate in the United States must be higher than that of Germany because $F^*_{\$,DM} > S_{\$,DM}$. If the forward rate is quoted at $F'_{\$,DM}$, then the forward premium on DM, that is, the forward discount on the dollar, is higher than the interest rate differential and funds will flow from the United States to Germany. This will require a swap transaction involving the spot sale of a dollar for DM and simultaneously the sale of DM forward. That is, arbitrageurs will be selling forward contracts (OK's worth). If, on the other hand, the forward rate is quoted at $F''_{\$,DM}$, the forward discount on the dollar is lower than the interest rate differential and funds will flow into the United States. This will require the forward sale of dollars, that is, the forward purchase of DM (OJ's worth).

The Speculator's Schedule

The speculator is an investor who, expecting a certain rate of return, exposes himself to foreign exchange risk. Speculation is achieved in the spot or in the forward market. Expecting the spot rate to rise, a speculator would purchase foreign currency in the spot market and would wait until its price rises. When it does, he sells and realizes a profit. If the speculator expects the DM to drop in price, he borrows DM and converts them into dollars. When the DM depreciates in value, he closes the loan transaction. His profit is the change in value of the DM net of interest cost and transactions costs. Either the long or the short position requires a commitment of funds (his own or borrowed). Usually, less costly and more profitable opportunities present themselves in the forward market. However, the margin requirement on a forward contract is about 10 percent of the face value of the contract and can be as low as 2 percent.

FIGURE 7.5.

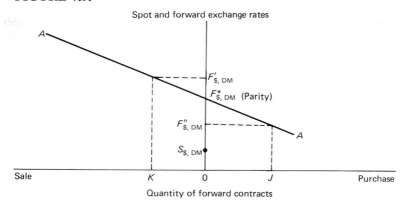

FIGURE 7.6.

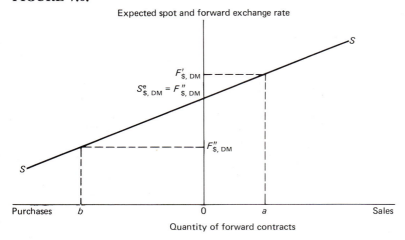

The speculator operating in the forward market (as in the spot market) expects to cash in on the probability that he is wiser than the market. His concerns are not with the current spot rate, but rather with the forward rate as compared with the expected spot rate $[S^e_{\$,DM}(t)]$ to prevail concurrently with the expiration of the forward contract.

The decision by the speculator to be on the supply or the demand side of forward contracts is, therefore, a function of the differential between the prevailing forward rate on DM and the expected spot rate at the end of the period covered by the forward contract.

$$K_s(t) = f[F_{\$,DM}(t) - S^e_{\$,DM}(t)]^8 \tag{7.7}$$

where $K_s(t) =$ supply of forward DM contracts.

If $K_s(t) < 0$, the speculator would buy DM forward. If his expectations proved right, that is, if the spot rate forecasted by the forward rate proves incorrect, the speculator would take delivery of the DM and sell the proceeds in the spot market at a higher price than that specified in the forward contract.

If $K_s(t) > 0$, the speculator would sell DM forward. The reason is simple. The speculator would sell when the rate $[F_{\$,DM}(t)]$ is high and buy at $[S^e_{\$,DM}(t)]$, a lower price (if expectations prove to be correct) to deliver against the forward contract.

Figure 7.6 depicts the speculators' schedule. At $F'_{\$,DM}$, $F'_{\$,DM}$ is $> S^e_{\$,DM}$ and the speculator would sell forward contracts $(0a)$ hoping to deliver against those contracts by buying in the future at the lower expected spot rate. At $F''_{\$,DM}$, $S^e_{\$,DM} > F''_{\$,DM}$ and the speculator would purchase forward DM $(0b)$ with the hope of selling them at a higher price. The larger the difference between $F_{\$,DM}$ and $S^e_{\$,DM}$, the larger the sale or purchase commitment by the speculator.

---

[8] This equation assumes a certain relationship among the variables. The shape of the curve may well be curvilinear because of transactions costs, risk of exchange controls, and the risk profile of the speculator.

FIGURE 7.7.   **Equilibrium forward rate.**

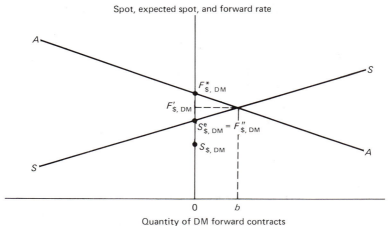

Spot, expected spot, and forward rate

Quantity of DM forward contracts

Determination of the Equilibrium Rate

If we superimpose Figure 7.5 on Figure 7.6, we can easily arrive at the equilibrium forward rate. This is depicted in Figure 7.7.

At $F'_{\$,DM}$ we have an equilibrium forward rate. Arbitrageurs would buy Ob of DM forward contracts and speculators would sell the exact amount. Arbitrageurs are net buyers because the forward rate $F^*_{\$,DM}$ is above the spot rate and the forward premium is less than the interest differential. That is, the forward rate is below the interest parity level. Funds flow into the United States, requiring the sale of forward dollars or the purchase of DM forward contracts to cover this flow against exchange losses. Noting that the market forward rate $F'_{\$,DM}$ is higher than $S^e_{\$,DM}$, speculators would be net sellers of forward contracts. The reader must note that $F'_{\$,DM}$ is lower than $F^*_{\$,DM}$ because of the role of the speculator. Equilibrium was possible only at F^* under IRPT.

Who Dominates the Market Place?

The identification of which of the market participants ultimately dominate the market—that is, determine the forward rate—depends on the elasticity (sensitivity) of the AA and SS schedules. We examine three cases shown in Figure 7.8.[9]

Figure 7.8 part (a) shows two schedules with approximately equal elasticity. Both speculators and arbitrageurs determine the forward rate. In Figure 7.8 part (b), the arbitrageur dominates the market. His supply/demand schedule is much more elastic than that of the speculator. If arbitrageurs were the only market participants, the forward rate would be at $F^1_{\$,DM}$ (Figure 7.8(b)) which is much closer to $F'_{\$,DM}$ than $F^2_{\$,DM}$. Figure 7.8(c) depicts the opposite case of Figure 7.8(b). The size of the elasticity is the measure of responsiveness to price changes. For very small changes in price, the speculator will be willing to supply (demand) much more than the arbitrageur in Figure 7.8(c)—hence,

---

[9] Based on **Houston H. Stokes** and **Hugh Neuburger**, "Interest Arbitrage, Forward Speculation, and the Determination of the Forward Exchange Rate." *Columbia Journal of World Business* (Winter 1979), pp. 86–95.

FIGURE 7.8. **Three market situations.**

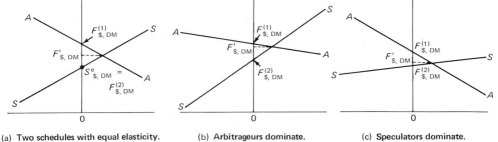

(a) Two schedules with equal elasticity.   (b) Arbitrageurs dominate.   (c) Speculators dominate.

the control over the market. Were the speculators the only market participants, the equilibrium rate would be at $F^2_{\$,DM}$, which is much closer to $F'_{\$,DM}$ than $F^1_{\$,DM}$ is in Figure 7.8(c).

Empirical evidence referred to earlier (J. Hilley, C. Beidleman, and J. Greenleaf) and additional evidence provided by H. Stokes and H. Neuburger, shows, in support of many previous studies, that Figure 7.8(b) correctly depicts the foreign exchange market—that is, the arbitrageur dominates.

It may be worthwhile at this juncture to mention reasons for speculators being on the opposite side of the market from arbitrageurs. When arbitrage funds are flowing into the United States, for example, the dollar is being sold forward, forecasting a lower spot rate in the future. If speculators agreed with the market, they would have nothing to speculate on and may well become arbitrageurs themselves. It is only when speculators consider market expectations to be erroneous that they begin speculating. The gambler betting on a roulette wheel is aware that the odds of winning are 1/36. When the wheel is spun, the gambler's attitude is that his chance of winning is a lot higher than 1/36. In fact he believes that he has picked the winning number. That is, he has outsmarted the house. The speculator similarly feels that he is outguessing the market as it forecasts the future spot rate through the forward rate.

Causes for Shifts in the *AA, SS* Schedules

Shifts in the arbitrageurs' schedule (*AA*) or the speculators' schedule (*SS*) are caused by market forces and/or government intervention. Changes in the spot rate and the interest rate differential between the United States and Germany can shift the *AA* schedule up or down because they change the value of F^*, the no-arbitrage forward rate. Changes in the forward rate, or some economic or political development, may cause the speculator to revise his/her expectations about the expected spot rate at time t. Such revision will obviously impact on the size of the speculators' forward commitments, long or short. If the expected spot rate is revised upward, the difference between it and the forward rate will shrink and the speculator would supply (demand) less (more) forward contracts.

The reader should take notice of the fact that a movement in one variable is not independent of the movement in another. A rise in the interest rate in the United States ($i_{U.S.}$) will cause larger flows of funds into the United States, assuming the starting point is F^*. Associated with these flows are the spot sale of the foreign currency and

the forward sale of the dollar. The value of the dollar will appreciate in the spot market and will fall in the forward market.

The analysis above also assumes an unlimited ability on the part of the arbitrageur to raise funds and willingness to shift from, say, a U.S. asset to a foreign asset or vice versa. A sudden shift in the arbitrage equation indicating the need to shift funds to Germany may go unheeded depending on whether the arbitrageur has a capital gain or loss in the U.S. securities he holds, or whether he has sufficient investment funds and/or ability to borrow at a rate he considers advantageous. The liquidation of existing holdings may further be complicated by the size of transactions costs.

Another important assumption is that of freely fluctuating exchange rates. An examination of the actions of the Federal Reserve Bank of New York reported quarterly in the *Federal Reserve Bulletin* would quickly reveal that the government rarely leaves the foreign exchange market to market forces. The Fed's actions are referred to as the dirty float. We now examine the nature and the impact of the dirty float.

7.16 DIRTY FLOAT

The Federal Reserve made clear in 1980 that the age of routine interventions in the foreign exchange market for dollars was over. Some observers questioned whether this resolve would endure if the dollar came under pressure. It did not. The Fed did intervene in June 1982, albeit after a long respite. The issues treated in this section are: Was the experiment in dirty floating since 1973 a failure? Did a convincing theoretical justification for the Fed's intervention develop? We first look at the sources of the funds used by the Fed for intervention in the foreign exchange market.

Sources of Intervention Funds

Intervention by the U.S. Government in the foreign exchange markets is undertaken by the Federal Reserve Bank of New York on behalf of the U.S. Treasury. The U.S. Treasury has the following sources of funds:[10]

1. Borrow from the IMF against the U.S. quota and up to the limit determined by the IMF.
2. Sell Special Drawing Rights (SDRs) to build positions in foreign currencies.
3. Sell securities denominated in foreign currencies.
4. Sell gold.
5. Use its own reserves bought in the open market when conditions were favorable.
6. Pressure other countries to use their resources to intervene in the direction desired by the Fed.

The Fed's source of funds is the swap network. It works as follows:

> A swap contract is written at the end of each day that Federal Reserve swap intervention takes place. To write a contract the Federal Reserve calculates the dollar amount of the intervention and receives sufficient foreign exchange

---

[10] This section is based on **Sarkis J. Khoury,** "Dirty Float: Nature, Impact, and Validity." *Proceedings,* Asia-Pacific Dimension of International Business, Academy of International Business (1982).

to cover its dollar purchases. *The foreign bank's dollars are then invested in a nonnegotiable U.S. Treasury certificate of indebtedness until the swap is retired.*

Swaps mature in 90 days. They are retired by purchasing the foreign bank's dollars at the original exchange rate.[11]

Intervention Methods

The Fed intervenes in the foreign exchange market in three ways:

1. *The Direct Method.* The Fed deals directly with banks. It makes offers to buy or sell a specific currency.
2. *The Indirect Method.* Commercial banks act as agents of the Fed operating within specified guidelines.
3. *Creating an Atmosphere of Imminent Action.* The Fed, through various releases and actions, attempts to dissuade speculators from a course of action.

In the direct method the intervention is accomplished by buying or selling the currency the value of which the Fed wishes to modify, or through third currencies. The Fed may intervene in the market of French francs and effectuate changes in the DM market through arbitrage, which insures consistent cross rates among currencies.

Intervention can take place in the spot and/or the forward market. The Fed may choose to intervene to shore up forward rates on the dollar for fear that low forward rates may increase speculation against the dollar as they foretell a weak future spot rate. The efficient market hypothesis implies, some argue, that the forward rate be an unbiased predictor of the future spot rate.

Intervention in the forward market is not frequently used despite some advantages of forward intervention. To effectuate an upward movement in the forward rate of the dollar in the hope of revising expectations about future spot rates, the Fed would purchase forward dollar contracts. These purchases do not require the Fed to tap any of its reserves immediately, and in fact, may never do so because the forward contract can be easily reversed later. The constraining force, however, is that a massive (even a substantial) intervention may not be possible and/or achievable discretely. Banks, which sell the contracts, may not be willing to trade up to the requirements of the Fed. Additionally, if the Fed succeeds in raising the forward rate, it may adversely affect the balance of payments. A higher forward rate, *ceteris paribus,* leads to lower capital inflows. This is so because the higher rate increases the cost of forward cover and leads to less exports, for the cost of forward cover by traders will also increase. (These concerns are not peculiar to forward rates.)

Conditions for Intervention

A thorough review of the events preceding intervention by the Fed in the foreign exchange markets, reported on a quarterly basis in the *Federal Reserve Bulletin,* leads to the conclusion that the leading indicators for Fed action are not much different from those which foretell currency depreciation or appreciation. These indicators have been

---

[11] **Richard Abrams,** "Federal Reserve Intervention Policy." *Economic Review,* Federal Reserve Bank of Kansas City (March 1979), p. 16.

1. Balance of trade deficits (e.g., caused by high oil prices).
2. Budget deficits coupled with high growth rates in the money supply, foretelling higher rates of inflation compared with other countries.
3. Size of the differential in real interest rates, which actually translate into considerable capital inflows or outflows.
4. Price-level announcements that are high relative to expectations and to prices in other countries.
5. "Excessive" speculation against a certain currency (March 1974 is an example). We further discuss this point below.
6. Pressures from other countries whose currencies have experienced significant appreciations or depreciations.
7. Political events like the attempted assassination of President Reagan.

The intervention of the Fed is officially justified on the basis that speculative activities in the market are either insufficient or "unwarranted." In either situation while activities of speculators are essential to the efficiency of the foreign exchange market, they can lead to temporary and unwarranted disequilibrium situations. Bureaucrats, who are usually very risk-averse and much inclined to exert influence, are fearful that short-run phenomena could produce panic in the marketplace and generate problems, the solutions of which require a long period of adjustment. Bureaucrats, therefore, often opt for intervention.

The issues with regard to intervention policy are: how does the Fed go about determining what is warranted or not, and how does it determine the size of the intervention fund? Faced with a complete information blackout from the Fed in this regard, we hypothesize that the Fed generates its own forecast of the exchange rate using some model like:

$$S_{\text{Fed}}^{W12} = f \text{ (differential inflation rate, differential real rates of interest, exports–imports, net capital flows, differential growth rate in the money supply)}$$

where $S_{\text{Fed},t}^{W}$ = warranted spot rate (by the Fed) to prevail at time t.

where the Fed intervention policy is a function of:

$$I_t = f[\lambda^e, (S_{\text{Fed},t}^e - S_{\text{Fed},t}^W)] \tag{7.8}$$

where I_t = size of the intervention

λ^e = expected speed of adjustment in the foreign exchange market from current levels to the expected levels.

$\dfrac{\partial I_t}{\partial \lambda^e} > 0$ The faster the expected speed of adjustment, the larger the intervention by the Fed in order to keep its commitment to smoothing fluctuations in exchange rates.

---

[12] The reader should note that the problem with warranted exchange rate is rather new. The Fed had clear guidelines for intervention under the fixed exchange rate system: As soon as the currency value hit its upper or lower limits, intervention was signaled.

$S^e_{\text{Fed},t}$ = The expected spot rate to prevail at time t. The Fed here looks at the current spot rate and at the average change in that spot rate (ΔS_{t0}) if the current level of activity by speculators persists in the absence of intervention.

$$= S_{t_0} + \overline{\Delta S_{t_0}}$$

If $S^e_{\text{Fed},t} \simeq S^W_{\text{Fed},t}$, the Fed will only intervene to smooth a decline. It would not intervene to counter the trend in the foreign exchange market even if the trend indicates a considerable appreciation or depreciation in the value of the dollar.

In order to better understand the action of the Fed, one must understand its preoccupation with exchange patterns that could be characterized as "disorderly." Disorderly is not well-defined in the Fed's literature, but there seems to be a general understanding that a time path characterized by oscillations that are both frequent and of great amplitude is disorderly and unwanted. Thus, perhaps it would be agreed that of the two time paths depicted below, the one drawn in solid lines is less disorderly than the one drawn in dotted lines (see Figure 7.9).[13] Although price fluctuations certainly serve a purpose in a market economy—and one would not wish to forbid a price to go up just because there was a certain prospect that some day it would come down again—nevertheless most theorists would probably agree that the "orderly" time path is likely to be associated with higher social welfare (and healthier profits for the Fed as well) than the "disorderly" time path. If the Fed had a theoretical reason to believe that it could change the time path of the exchange rate from the dotted line to the solid line with no (or little) impact on other macroeconomic goals, it would probably have sufficient theoretical justification for its intervention.

As to the size of the intervention fund, once a decision to intervene is made, it is gauged in accordance with the estimated excess supply or demand for a given currency as estimated by the Fed.

The next set of issues deals with whether a "warranted" intervention is indeed warranted.

Warranted Intervention?

Inefficiencies in the foreign exchange market are a prime justification for intervention by the Fed. The issue of whether the foreign exchange markets are efficient or not is still unsettled.[14] What is settled, however is the following:

1. An inefficient market implies that profitable opportunities have gone unexploited, or that profitable opportunities have been systematically exploited by a group or an entity at the exclusion of other participants in the marketplace, and

---

[13] There is perhaps not as much agreement about the following two time paths:

[14] See **Richard Levich**, "The Efficiency of Markets for Foreign Exchange: A Review and Extension," in *International Financial Management Theory*, Donald Lessard, ed., Warren Gorham and Lamont, Boston (1979).

FIGURE 7.9. Federal reserve interventions.

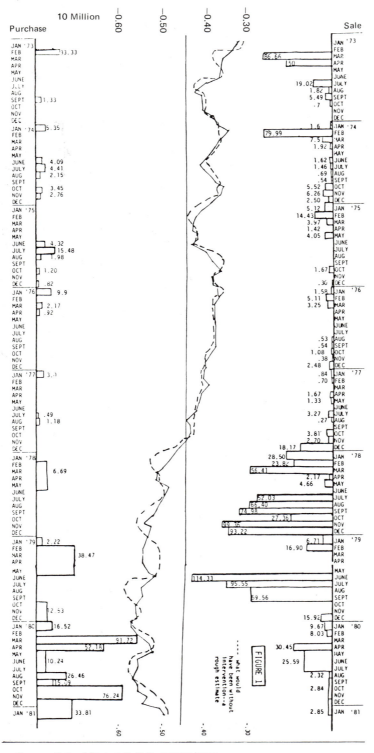

2. The information markets and the transactions markets are not competitive, preventing the foreign exchange market from reaching equilibrium.

While we do not wish to enter the controversy surrounding the efficient market hypothesis, we make the following points:

1. An inefficient market is one where excess profits can be realized. This is so because
   a. A speculator or a group of speculators have acquired a monopoly position in the marketplace;
   b. The information available, if porperly received and interpreted, indicates excess profit opportunities that were not exploited either out of ignorance or sheer stupidity. The latter case is inconsistent with the concept of economic rationality on which economic theory if founded. The former (ignorance) may be due to high transactions cost in the collection of information, or to the inability to interpret information—that is, speculators were not able to read the signals correctly. In this case the level of speculative activity would not be sufficient to bring prices to equilibrium as arbitrage opportunities remain outstanding. This slack in speculative activity can be eliminated by government intervention in the foreign exchange market. This is the conclusion of David Longworth with regard to the Canadian–U.S. exchange market:

   Speculators looking at economic variables such as deviations from purchasing power parity and relative money supplies would have made extraordinary profits in the case of the Canadian dollar, as those two variables indicated that it was overvalued in 1976. This is the type of apparent inefficiency that is of direct concern to policy makers. In the absence of sufficient speculative funds with a long-term horizon, a case can be made for official intervention in the foreign exchange market.

With respect to monopoly powers prevailing in the marketplace, whether temporary or permanent, the government may choose, through intervention in the foreign exchange market, to balance actual or potential market domination. In so doing it would eliminate the artificiality of prices that result from cornering the market. If, as a result, the government realizes a profit, then its intervention contributes to the stability of the market and if a loss is realized then the intervention is destabilizing.

This can be explained by Samuelson's propositions:[15]

Proposition 1. If a speculator stabilizes prices, he earns a profit and the rest of society gains.

Proposition 2. If a speculator loses, prices are destabilized and the rest of society gains.

The issue with regard to proposition 2 is whether the losses outweigh the gains or vice versa. Samuelson argues that the losses always outweigh the gains. The concern with a dirty float is, therefore, who pays the losses. If the government loses, society must worry about the losses for it ultimately is responsible for them. Losses by the

---

[15] **Paul H. Samuelson**, "The Consumer Does Benefit From Feasible Price Stability." *Quarterly Journal of Economics* (August 1972), pp. 476–93.

government may lead to higher taxes, lower government expenditures, and/or higher monetary growth and all of their attending consequences.

The conditions for stabilizing speculation are[16]

1. Risk neutrality by speculators. The speculator operates on the basis of expected value.
2. Ability by speculators to detect profitable opportunities and to take appropriate action (buy when the exchange rate is low and sell when it is high).
3. Willingness by speculators to move funds across borders in response to changes in expected yield.

Profits realized by the Fed, while stabilizing, must be carefully distinguished from those realized by speculators. The Fed does not consider intervention as a speculative activity and is thus likely to cover swap lines sooner than expected. The Fed may be knowingly a suboptimizer. In addition, when the Fed intervenes in a declining market in an attempt to reduce the steepness of the drop, it may purposely take losses.

While profits per se are not the goal, the conclusions remain the same; unless the results of intervention are profitable, it cannot be a stabilizing factor.

When the government takes an action opposite that of speculators or assumes a position that is much larger than that of speculators (but in the same direction) is it acting on "inside" information? If so, would it be better for the government to share the information which speculators and stay completely out of the foreign exchange markets? The answer to this is "yes" and lies in the fact that government monopoly is no more desirable than private monopoly and the manipulation of the foreign exchange market by the Fed is no more desirable than that by any other economic agent.

The profitability of the Fed foreign exchange operations leads invariably to increased market efficiency, hence it is desirable. The latest report by the Fed shows, unfortunately, that as of January 31, 1981, valuation profits and losses on outstanding assets and liabilities of the Fed that are foreign-exchange-related were -150.6 million. The Treasury did not do much better. As of the same date, its net loss was $45.2 million.

7.17 FOREIGN EXCHANGE FUTURES

The forward market lost its monopoly on foreign exchange contracts for future delivery on May 16, 1972 when the International Monetary Market (IMM), a subsidiary of the Chicago Mercantile Exchange, began trading futures contracts in seven currencies. Two currencies were later added (the French franc and the Dutch guilder) and one was dropped (the Italian lira). Today an active market exists only for five currencies: the British pound, the Canadian dollar, the Japanese yen, the Swiss franc, and the West German mark.

A futures contract obligates the buyer (the seller) to buy (sell) a certain amount of foreign exchange at a specified price (negotiated today) at some future date. The contract is not between the buyer and the seller, but between the buyer and the Clearing Corporation (CC) and the seller and the Clearing Corporation of the IMM. It is the CC which

---

[16] See **J. R. Artus and A. D. Crockett,** "Floating Exchange rates and the Need for Surveillance." *Essays in International Finance,* no. 127, International Finance Section, Princeton University, Princeton, N.J. (May 1978).

TABLE 7.3
IMM Currency Contracts Specifications

International Monetary Market of the Chicago Mercantile Exchange	Currencies:	Trading Months	Trading Hours (Central Time)	Contract Size	Price Quoted in	Minimum Price Fluctuation	Daily Limit
	British pound	Jan/Mar/Apr/Jun/ Jul/Sept/Oct/Dec & Spot	7:30–1:24	25,000 £	¢/£	0.0005/£ = $12.50 (1 pt = $12.50)	5¢ = $1,250 (100 pts)
	Canadian dollar	Jan/Mar/Apr/Jun/ Jul/Sept/Oct/Dec & Spot	7:30–1:22	100,000 CD	¢/CD	0.0001/CD = $10.00 (1 pt = $10.00)	¾¢ = $750 (75 pts)
	Deutsche-mark	Jan/Mar/Apr/Jun/ Jul/Sept/Oct/Dec & Spot	7:30–1:20	125,000 DM	¢/DM	0.0001/DM = $12.50 (1 pt = $12.50)	0.0100 = $1,250 (100 pts)
	Japanese yen	Jan/Mar/Apr/Jun/ Jul/Sept/Oct/Dec & Spot	7:30–1:26	12,500,000 Yen	¢/Yen	0.000001/Y = $12.50 (1 pt = $12.50)	0.0001 = $1,250 (100 pts)
	Swiss franc	Jan/Mar/Apr/Jun/ Jul/Sept/Oct/Dec & Spot	8:45–1:13	125,000 SF	¢/SF	1/100¢/SF = $12.50 (1 pt = $12.50)	⅜¢ = $1,875 (150 pts)

Source: Reprinted with the permission of the International Monetary Market, a division of the Chicago Mercantile Exchange.

guarantees payments (delivery) on foreign exchange futures contracts traded on its exchange.

On August 7, 1980, the New York Futures Exchange (NYFE), a wholly owned subsidiary of the New York Stock Exchange, began trading futures contracts in five currencies: British pounds, Canadian dollars, Deutsche marks, Japanese yen, and Swiss francs. The success of NYFE was so limited that all contracts are currently inactive leaving the entire currency futures market in the hands of the IMM.

The specifications of the IMM contracts are summarized in Table 7.3. From Table 7.3 we can see the months for which currency futures contracts are available, the size of each contract, the method used for price quotation, and the minimum and the maximum daily price fluctuations per currency unit and per contract.

The IMM Foreign Exchange Contract

The IMM uses the direct quotation system: the price of a unit of foreign currency in terms of domestic currency. A point is not the same for every contract. A point for a Canadian dollar contract is 0.0001 of a CD, while a point is 0.000001 of a yen. Table 7.3 illustrates the point system and the equivalent dollar value per contract. All contracts have a high degree of liquidity and allow for a very high leverage possibility. The initial margin requirement on a British pound contract covering $25,000 is only $1,500. The maintenance margin requirement is $1,000, which means that if the value of the futures contract drops by more than $500, the contract holder is called upon to bring this deposit up to $1,000. The settlement (for both pofits and losses) is done on a daily basis. Contracts are guaranteed by the Clearing Corporation, which is in turn guaranteed by the capital of a defaulting firm. As a last resort, contracts are guaranteed by the collective capital of the members of the Exchange who encompass most major securities and commodities firms. It is this very high level of safety, the standard size of the contracts, the centralized nature of the market, and depth and breadth (all major curren-

cies with several maturity months are covered) which account for the high level of liquidity the contracts enjoy.

While futures contracts accomplish the same economic ends as forward contracts, there exist several distinguishing elements in the two vehicles that give the futures contract

TABLE 7.4
Comparison of Futures Market and Forward Market

	Forward	Futures
Size of contract	Tailored to individual needs.	Standardized.
Delivery date	Tailored to individual needs.	Standardized.
Method of transaction	Established by the bank or broker via telephone contact with limited number of buyers and sellers.	Determined by open auction among many buyers and sellers on the exchange floor.
Participants	Banks, brokers, and multinational companies. Public speculation not encouraged.	Banks, brokers, and multinational companies. Qualified public speculation encouraged.
Commissions	Set by "spread" between bank's buy and sell price. Not easily determined by the customer.	Published small brokerage fee and negotiated rates on block trades.
Security deposit	None as such, but compensating bank balances required.	Published small security deposit required.
Clearing operation (financial)	Handling contingent on individual banks and brokers. No separate clearing house function.	Handled by exchange clearing house. Daily settlements to the market.
Marketplace	Over the telephone worldwide.	Central exchange floor with worldwide communications.
Economic justification	Facilitates world trade by providing hedge mechanism.	Same as forward market. In addition, it provides a broader market and an alternative hedging mechanism.
Accessibility	Limited to very large customers who deal in foreign trade.	Open to anyone who needs hedge facilities, or has risk capital with which to speculate.
Regulation	Self-regulating	April 1975—Regulated under the Commodity Futures Trading Commission.
Frequency of delivery	More than 90 percent settled by actual delivery.	Theoretically, no deliveries in a perfect market. In reality, less than 1 percent.
Price fluctuations	No daily limit.	Daily limit imposed by exchange with a rule provision for expanded daily price limits.
Market liquidity	Offsetting with other banks.	Public offset, Arbitrage offset.

Source: Understanding Futures in Foreign Exchange, August 1979. Reprinted with the permission of the International Monetary Market, a division of the Chciago Mercantile Exchange.

the competitive advantage. Prices in both markets should not differ significantly, however; otherwise arbitrageurs would step in and bring the prices into equality. The differences and the similarities between the two vehicles are summarized in Table 7.4. Substantial evidence on the superiority of the futures contract in terms of liquidity and transactions costs have been provided by Janis Petersen[17] in her doctoral dissertation on the subject. Using transactions costs required on forward market contracts in British pounds, Canadian dollars, Swiss francs, and Deutsche marks, and comparing them with transactions costs on futures contracts in the same currencies, Petersen concluded that the futures market is more efficient. She rationalized:

> *One reason why transactions costs are lower in the futures market may be because the futures market is the more perfect market, that is, it more closely resembles a perfectly competitive market. Costs (commissions) are determined by the forces of competition. Customers can "shop around" among brokerage firms to find the lowest price. This tends to keep transactions costs down.*
>
> *In the forward market, banks deal with other banks using a foreign exchange broker as middleman. The fee for using the services of a foreign exchange broker is the bid-ask spread in the interbank market. When the bank deals with its customers, it widens the spread, which results in a higher price to the customer. Thus, the element of monopolistic competition results in slightly higher costs in the forward market.[18]*

Uses of the Futures Market

Hedgers and speculators can use the futures market in a manner similar to that using the forward market. The hedger enters the futures market to offset a cash position, expecting that the profits in the futures market offset the losses (if any) in the cash market. As in the interest rate futures case, the effectiveness of the hedge is determined by the movement in the basis: the difference between the futures price and the cash price.

The relationship between the futures market and the cash market is complex and not very easy to predict. The basis is influenced by interest rate differentials among countries (and, consequently, by the arbitrage opportunities they create), by investors' expectations, and by a host of government actions ranging from exchange controls to interest rate manipulations for domestic or international equilibrium purposes. Expectations could have most dramatic effects on the exchange rate. If speculators anticipate a weakness in the dollar, as they did in 1971, they will shift funds out of dollars into a stronger currency like the Deutsche mark. The results are a cheaper dollar and a dearer DM. As discussed earlier in this chapter, speculators can manifest their expectations in the spot or in the forward market. Speculators prefer the forward or futures market, however, because of the vary low margin requirements and lower transactions costs. Their transactions affect the relationship between prices of future delivery and those of spot delivery and consequently the effectiveness of the hedged position.

We now offer an example of a long and a short hedge.

---

[17] **Janis Petersen,** *A Study of Transactions Costs in the Forward and Futures Exchange Markets During the Years of Floating Exchange Rates.* Doctoral Dissertation, Department of Economics, University of Notre Dame, May 1980.

[18] Ibid., p. 176.

Short Hedge

A short hedge involves a long position in the spot market and simultaneously a short position in the futures market. The easiest way to illustrate the short hedge is to resurrect the interest arbitrage examples presented earlier in this chapter. The arbitrage margin was positive and favored Germany, thus creating an arbitrage opportunity requiring investment in German securities. In order to invest in Germany, the arbitrageur would have to sell dollars for DM and simultaneously sell his DM forward. Alternately, he would sell a futures contract—short a contract—on DM that will mature in the contract month equal to or nearest his time horizon.

Consider now the case of an American tool maker with a German subsidiary in need of cash to meet operating expenses. The cash infusion into the subsidiary requires the sale of dollars for DM and simultaneously the sale of a DM futures contract with a maturity that coincides with the debt repayment date (to the extent possible). The objective is to lock in today's exchange rate no matter how the exchange rates move in the future. The transactions will be as follows.

Cash (Spot) Market	Futures Market
October 7, 1982	October 7, 1982
Buy 1,000,000 DM at 0.4000	Sell 8 March '83 DM* contracts at 0.4004 (Table 7.4B)
Cost $400,000	Expected proceeds** $400,400
January 17, 1983	January 17, 1983
Case 1 $/DM = 0.4200	*Case 1* $/DM = 0.4100 (January 17 price of the March '83 contract)
Sell 1,000,000 DM	Buy the 8 March '83 contracts back
Proceeds $420,000	Cost = 410,000
Profit (420,000 − 400,000) = $20,000	Profit (400,400 − 410,000) = $(9,600)

Net Profit = 20,000 − 9,600 = **$10,400**

Case 2 $/DM = 0.3900	*Case 2* $/DM = .4000
Sell 1,000,000 DM	Buy 8 March '83 contracts
Proceeds $390,000	Costs $400,000
Profit (400,000 − 390,000) = ($10,000)	Profit (400,400 − 400,000) = $400

Net Profit = (10,000) − 400 = **($9,600)**

---

* The sale of futures contracts which face value equals the total commitment in the cash market is referred to as a naive hedge. The matching of face values is not necessarily an optimal strategy as should become obvious from our examples.

** The "proceeds" here are really fictitious and are used to simplify the presentation. Acutally, the sale of 8 March contracts requires meeting the margin requirement per contract 8 times. Futures contracts require margin commitments both on the long and the short positions.

Cash (Spot) Market	**Futures Market**
Case 3 $/DM = 0.3850	*Case 3* $/DM = 0.3800
Sell 1,000,000 DM	Buy 8 March '83 contracts
Proceeds $385,000	Cost $380,000
Profit (400,000 − 385,000) = ($15,000)	Profit (400,400 − 380,000) = $20,400

Net Profit = 20,400 − 15,000 = **$5,400**

Before we comment on the preceding transactions and their consequences, let us review the alternative strategy of hedging in the forward market.

Cash (Spot) Market	**Forward Market**
October 17, 1982	October 17, 1982
Buy 1,000,000 DM	Sell 1,000,000 DM forward for delivery on January 17, 1981 at 0.4004[19]
Cost $400,000	

Case 1

Spot rate (January 17, 1983) = 0.4200

The hedger will simply deliver 1,000,000 DM at 0.4004. The profits from foreign exchange transactions are equal to:

400,400 − 400,000 = 400.

Profits result from the fact that the DM was selling at a forward premium. Because of the forward commitment, the hedger is unable to fully capitalize on the rise in the spot rate. His opportunity loss is 20,000 − 400 = $19,600.

Case 2

Spot rate (January 17, 1983) = 0.3900

The hedger simply delivers his DM at 0.4004 and avoids the $9,600 loss which would have been incurred in the futures market.

Case 3

Spot rate (January 17, 1983) = 0.3850

No matter how low the spot rate turns out to be, the hedger will sell his DM at 0.4004. His gains are equal to $400. The gains in the futures market would have been $20,400 − $15,000 = $5,400.

---

[19] The forward rate of 0.4004 corresponds to the futures rate for the same period. Deviations between the forward rate and the futures rate will be eliminated by arbitrage if markets are perfectly efficient.

The conclusion is that the forward market represents a true hedge by locking in $400 in profits, regardless of the direction of the spot rate. There are no such guarantees in the futures case, although there is a probability that the profits resulting from a spot futures hedge would equal $400. The speculative nature of a futures market hedge must once again be emphasized.

As the short futures hedge transactions make obvious, the profits (losses) in the cash market may more than offset the losses (profits) in the futures market. Cases 2 and 3 illustrate that the net profit from a short hedge is very much dependent on the size of the basis—that is, the differential between the futures rate and the spot rate on January 17, 1983. A "perfect" hedge would have resulted in zero net loss or gain (long-short position profits or losses) no matter what the direction of the exchange rates. Given the hedger's expectations about the basis it may not be necessary, therefore, for him to offset the cash position on a one-to-one basis by a futures position. Only 15/20 of the 8 futures DM contracts would have produced profits large enough to almost cover the loss in the spot market (case 3) had the change in the basis been correctly anticipated.

We can, therefore, conclude that profits (losses) from a short hedge depend to a great degree on the basis, and that it may be best not to hedge at all—the case of the spot rate moving above 0.4004. The reader must have observed that it is quite possible to use a certain foreign exchange rate so that, using 8 futures DM contracts, the hedge produces zero net profits. The reader must have also noted that the calculations in the preceding example do not account for the very small transactions costs. Also, the reader must observe that the smaller (stronger) the basis, the larger the net profits in a short hedge. The weakening of the basis in case 2 $[(0.4000 - 0.3900) > (0.4004 - 0.4000)]$ produced a loss. The opposite is true in a long hedge. Since perfect hedges are not always possible, given indivisibilities in the market and noncoinciding maturities, the hedger is always a speculator on part or all of his assets. Net exposure is positive with the attending rewards and penalties.

Long Hedge

A long hedge consists of a short position in the cash market and a long position in the futures market—the opposite of the short hedge.

Using the preceeding example of the German subsidiary with excess cash and its U.S. parent in need of it, the transactions will be as follows.

Cash (Spot) Market	**Futures Market**
October 7, 1982	October 7, 1982
Sell 1,000,000 DM	Buy 8 March '83 DM contracts
January 17, 1983	January 17, 1983
Buy 1,000,000 DM	Sell (offset) 8 March '83 DM contracts

The gains (losses) in the futures position should offset (partially or totally) the losses (gains) in the cash position in a manner similar to that described in the preceding section.

Speculation in the Futures Market

The futures markets have many features that are attractive to speculators: low commissions, low margin requirements, and very high liquidity.

Speculators who expect the DM to fall in value in relation to the dollar would sell a futures DM contract and buy it back at a lower price once their expectations are realized. If, on the other hand, speculators anticipate the DM to strengthen against the dollar, they would purchase a DM futures contract and sell it at a higher price once the currencies are realigned in the expected direction. In either case, speculators have the option of closing out their position in the futures market if their expectations do not materialize.

Speculators can also speculate in currency futures in a manner similar to that in T-bills futures. They may use spreads. Three types of spread positions can be utilized: intermonth, intermarket, and intercurrency. The intermonth spread involves the short position in one contract month and simultaneously a long position in another contract month on the same currency. The intermarket spread involves a long position in a currency contract on one exchange and a short position on another exchange involving the same currency. The intercurrency spread involves a short position in one currency and a long position in another in the same market and on the same exchange.

7.18 CURRENCY OPTIONS

December 10, 1982 marked the birth of a new hedging vehicle for exchange rate risk: currency options. These options were introduced by the Philadelphia Stock Exchange.* Currency options are valuable hedging and speculative instruments because of the peculiar features they possess. They add to the flexibility of any hedging program.

A currency option is a right to buy (a call option) or to sell (a put option) a designated quantity of a foreign currency at a specified price (exchange rate), called the striking price, during a designated time period.

The above definition is that of an American option. A European option, on the other hand, has the same characteristics except it is only exercisable on maturity (expiration) date. The trading details of currency options are summarized in Table 7.5. This table contains data on currency futures for comparison purposes.

Options on five currencies are currently traded on the Philadelphia Stock Exchange. The size of the sterling contracts is £12,500, that of Swiss francs is 62,500, that of Deutsche marks 62,500, that of Canadian dollars 50,000, and that of Japanese yens 6,250,000. All of these contracts are half the size of those in the currency futures markets. The reason for this is to keep the option premiums in their traditional range. It must be noted that only the specified contract size is available. Fractions of an option contract cannot be purchased.

Currency option premiums are quoted using the direct quotation (U.S. basis) method. All premiums are expressed in cents per unit of currency except for the Japanese yen, where it is expressed in hundredths of a cent per unit of currency. The March call option on the British pound, for example, would cost (before commissions) 0.05 ×

---

* The Philadelphia stock exchange could get a new competitor soon. The CME has filed (April, 1983) with the CFTC for permission to trade an option on Deutsche mark physicals.

TABLE 7.5

Foreign Currency Options at the Philadelphia Exchange

Underlying Currency	Strike Price	Calls—Last			Puts—Last		
		Mar	June	Sept	Mar	June	Sept
12,500 British pounds	150	5.00	....	....	0.40	....	....
Pound open int. 1705				Pound spot close 1.5449			
		Mar	June	Sept	Mar	June	Sept
62,500 Swiss francs	48	2.37	....	....	0.04	....	....
	50	....	....	....	0.71	....	....
	52	0.22	1.37	....	2.02	....	....
Franc open int. 619				Franc spot close .5000			
		Mar	June	Sept	Mar	June	Sept
62,500 West German marks	38	3.83	....	....	....	....	....
	42	0.77	....	....	....	....	....
Mark open int. 162				Mark spot close .4169			
50,000 Canada dollars		(NO TRADES)					
Dollar open int. 196				Dollar spot close .8168			

Premium expressed in hundredths of a cent per unit of currency.

		Mar	June	Sept	Mar	June	Sept
6,250,000 Japanese yen	40	2.87	....	....	0.10	....	....
	42	1.30	2.10	....	0.41	0.96	....
	44	0.34	1.24	....	1.52	1.99	....
	46	0.08	....	....	....	....	....
Yen open int. 983				Yen spot close .004276			
Total volume 467							

— FINANCIAL —

BRITISH POUND (IMM)—25,000 pounds; $ per pound

Mar83	1.5420	1.5470	1.5395	1.5425	....	1.8500	1.5065	16,820
June	1.5370	1.5425	1.5320	1.5360	− .0005	1.7550	1.5020	3,986
Sept	1.5330	1.5380	1.5320	1.5320	− .0015	1.6360	1.4995	565
Dec	1.5320	1.5370	1.5305	1.5305	− .0015	1.6425	1.5000	631

Est vol 4,951; vol Thur 4,054; open int 22,002, +391.

CANADIAN DOLLAR (IMM)—100,000 dlrs.; $ per Can $

Mar83	.8161	.8169	.8159	.8163	− .0001	.8196	.7282	10,748
June	.8156	.8164	.8153	.8158	....	.8190	.7810	4,196
Sept	....	....	....	.8154	....	.8175	.7960	1,146
Dec	....	....	....	.8147	....	.8170	.8015	37

Est vol 1,688; vol Thur 2,488; open int 16,127, −152.

JAPANESE YEN (IMM) 12.5 million yen; $ per yen (.00)

Mar83	.4274	.4299	.4274	.4281	− .0024	.4438	.3622	26,290
June	.4307	.4330	.4305	.4311	− .0024	.4467	.3650	8,743
Sept	.4350	.4360	.4340	.4340	− .0025	.4380	.4210	112

Est vol 13,376; vol Thur 16,298; open int 35,145, −113.

SWISS FRANC (IMM)—125,000 francs-$ per franc

Mar83	.5024	.5049	.5007	.5013	− .0039	.5680	.4546	28,081
June	.5103	.5125	.5080	.5084	− .0045	.5355	.4616	6,943
Sept	.5193	.5193	.5163	.5163	− .0042	.5428	.4635	314
Dec	.5285	.5285	.5240	.5240	− .0050	.5450	.4815	76

Est vol 17,614; vol Thur 15,068; open int 35,414, −671.

W. GERMAN MARK (IMM)—125,000 marks; $ per mark

Mar83	.4167	.4186	.4167	.4180	− .0002	.4319	.3882	14,580
June	.4208	.4225	.4207	.4219	− .0003	.4450	.3915	5,573
Sept	.4255	.4264	.4255	.4256	− .0005	.4370	.4115	87
Dec	.4298	.4305	.4298	.4301	− .0009	.4400	.4163	72

Est vol 6,711; vol Thur 9,746; open int 20,312, +578.

Source: The Wall Street Journal, February 22, 1983.

12,500 = $625. The striking price for the March contract on the pound is $1.50. Striking prices may vary. They are set by the exchanges around the prevailing spot price (±2¢ in the case of the Swiss franc, for example). Additional striking prices may be introduced by the options exchange as spot exchange rates change significantly.

The available contract months for currency options are March, June, September, and December. Every contract matures on the third Wednesday of the contract month.

The default risk on an option contract is practically nonexistent. Options are guaranteed by the Options Clearing Corporation (OCC), which interposes itself between every buyer and every seller. Every sale is, therefore, a sale to the OCC and every purchase is a purchase from the OCC. No buyer should have to worry about the party on the

other side of the transaction. The same holds true for the seller. The OCC guarantees the outstanding options by its own capital and ultimately by the capital of the member firms.

Distinguishing Features of Currency Options

Call and put contracts give their holder the "option" to do what he or she pleases; one may exercise the option, sell it, or simply let it expire. There is no obligation to deliver or take delivery as in the case of forward and futures contracts.

Another advantage of currency options is the absence of margin calls. Every futures contract requires a deposit (margin) at the time it is sold or purchased. This margin is set by the exchange and is intended to provide some protection in the event the market moves in a direction opposite that expected by the buyer or the seller of the futures contract. As such, the margin serves as a performance bond. If the market moves appreciably contrary to expectations, additional margin will have to be deposited by the position holder. The settlement must be done on a daily basis. If, on the other hand, the expectations of the position holder do materialize, a credit will be made in his account on a daily basis. It is, therefore, a requisite that holders of futures positions have sufficient liquidity in the event they are called upon to deposit the additional margin known as a "variation margin." This, incidentally, is not required for forward contracts.

Considering that 100 percent of the option premium is paid in advance, no additional commitment will be called for during the life of the option. The option premium represents the maximum commitment and consequently the maximum loss.

The above indicates, however, the negative side of options when compared with futures contracts. That is, option contracts require the payment of the full premium, which can be lost in its entirety.

Uses of Options Contracts

We shall satisfy ourselves in this section with the discussion of the simple, yet most prevalent uses of currency options. We leave the more advanced strategies for the reader to explore by using more specialized sources.

Figure 7.10 summarizes the positions we shall be discussing.

Long Calls

A long call position is established when the investor purchases a call. The call premium is the maximum that can be lost. The gain is theoretically unlimited.

An investor/speculator who is bullish on a currency could purchase the currency

FIGURE 7.10. Possible option positions.

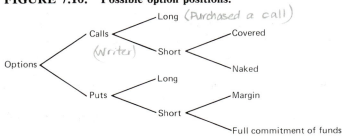

itself, a forward contract, a futures contract, or a call option. The consequences of a long call option are best illustrated by using an example. From Table 7.5, assume that the March 1983 DM call option with the 42 strike price is purchased. The option is out-of-the-money because the strike price exceeds the market price of the DM (0.4169). No one wants to buy DM at the 42¢ strike price if it could be purchased for 41.69¢ in the market place. An out-of-the-money option will lose money if it is exercised. The opposite is true for an in-the-money option. The premium on the DM/March/42 is equal to DM 62,500 × 0.77¢ = **$481.25.**

Assume three possible prices following the purchase of the DM/March/42 call option:

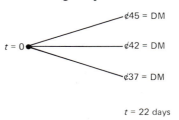

$$t = 22 \text{ days}$$

If the DM trades at 42, the option will expire worthless. If the DM increases in value to 45¢ the call will be in-the-money and it could be exercised or sold profitably. Typically, a long option position is closed out by a sale. If the DM drops to 37¢ the call option will again expire unexercised. No one wants to exercise an option that would lose her money.

Covered Short Calls

A short call position represents an obligation to the seller (the writer) of the option. By selling a call option, the seller is committing himself to sell his shares at the striking price whenever the buyer chooses to do so during the life of the option contract. For this commitment the seller is compensated by a premium.

It is important to note here the difference in the expectations of the buyers (the long) and the sellers (the short) of the call options. While the buyer hopes for a maximum upward movement in the value of the DM, the covered seller (the seller with a long position in the underlying DM) wishes that no price movement will occur. A downward movement in the value of the DM, while not resulting in the exercise of the option, will produce a loss in the underlying cash position. The loss is obviously cushioned by the premium received.

A covered option writer, therefore, is one who is expecting no, or little, movement in the value of the underlying currency and who wishes to earn an income on what otherwise is a nonincome-generating asset, or an asset with a limited income.

Let us now examine the consequences of a short call position assuming the same price movements indicated above. If the DM moves to 45¢, the option is exercised. The option writer would earn the full premium, which means that he effectively succeeded in selling his DMs for 42 + 0.77 = 42.77¢ while the DM market price at the time the short position was established was only 41.69¢. However, had the short option seller not sold the call, he would have been able to sell it at the new 45¢ market price. The opportunity loss is equal to 45¢ − 42.77 = 2.23¢ per DM.

If the value of the DM remains at 42¢, the full premium is realized by the short seller with no loss in the long cash position.

A drop in the value of the DM to 37¢ would lead to no option exercise but would produce a book loss of 41.69 − 37 or 4.69¢ per DM. This obviously assumes that the long cash position was established at the same time the option was written.

The above demonstrates the importance of price stability (constancy) to the option writer.

Naked Short Calls

A naked or uncovered short call is much riskier than a covered short call because the writer does not have a position in the underlying security to deliver in the event the option is exercised. The risk here is that if the DM rises in value to, say, 50¢ the naked writer would have to buy DMs at 50¢ and deliver them to the exercising call holder at the 42¢ strike price. However, the naked writer does not have to wait for the DM to reach 50¢. He may, and in many cases should, buy a call to offset the short position. The purchased call may have the same strike price or a different strike price and/or maturity.

Let us further explore the consequences of a naked short call, assuming the earlier price movements. A DM movement to 45¢ is not desirable for it requires, as indicated earlier, the purchase of the DM at 45¢ and its sale at 42¢. The loss is real and is equal to 3¢ minus the call premium. If the DM stays at about 42¢ or better yet falls, the naked writer earns the full premium and avoids the book loss of his covered counterpart. Therefore, the naked writer expects currency values to remain constant or to fall, while the covered writer is counting on their constancy.

Long Puts

A long put position is intended to capitalize on a downward movement in the value of a currency. It can also be used, among other things, to protect a long position in a currency as a call option is used to protect a short position in a currency. A put gives the holder an option to sell at a fixed price. If the value of the currency falls below the strike price, the put is in-the-money (a situation opposite that of a call) and if it rises above the strike price, the put is out-of-the-money because no one would want to buy at the high market price and sell at the lower strike price.

A put holder would lose the full premium if currency values rise appreciably and would make money if currency values fall. Currency values would have to fall beyond the strike price minus the put premium if a profit is to be realized from the exercise of the option.

A sterling/March/150 put could have been purchased for 0.40¢ × 12,500 = $50 on February 22, 1983. The put is out-of-the-money because the strike price (1.50) is below the spot price (1.5449). If during the remaining life of the put, the pound does not fall below $1.50, the full put premium would be lost. If the fall occurs, on the other hand, a profit could be made.

Short Put Options

A short put position creates an obligation for the seller to buy whenever the underlying currency is "put" to him during the life of the option. For the commitment the option writer is paid a premium. The full premium is earned if the market value remains at

or higher than the strike price and a loss is realized (cushioned by the premium received, of course) if the market value of the currency falls below the strike price. A put option writer would, therefore, write an option only when expecting the value of the currency to remain the same or to rise.

The potential financial commitment that would have to be made by the option writer in the event of an exercise requires some evidence on the writer's current ability to perform. This evidence is typically provided through a margin deposited with the broker by the option writer. The full potential liability may also be deposited or kept on hand, but this is rarely done.

Having examined the simple but common strategies in currency options, we now discuss the manner in which they are priced. Our discussion relies on the work of Ian Giddy[20] and that of F. Black and M. Scholes (B&S).[21]

Pricing Call Options

The pricing of currency call options is similar to that of common stocks, provided the assumption that exchange rates are log-normally distributed with constant variance is acceptable (defensible). The empirical evidence[22] suggests that such is, unfortunately, not necessarily the case. The distribution of exchange rate changes is not consistent with a log-normal distribution and their variance is not very stable.

Ignoring the above reservations, the B&S model may be used to price currency call options.

$$C_t = SN(d_1) - \frac{E}{e^{\rho t}} N(d_2)$$

(7.9)

$$\text{where } d_1 = \frac{\ln(S/E) + (\rho + \frac{1}{2}\sigma^2)t}{\sigma\sqrt{t}}$$

$$d_2 = d_1 - \sigma\sqrt{t}$$

and where C_t = market price of a currency call option at time t

S = spot exchange rate (direct quotation)

E = strike price of the option

$e = 2.71828$

t = time to expiration

ρ = riskless rate = $\ln(1 + r)$ = treasury bill rate over t.

$N(\cdot)$ = The cumulative normal probability of the unit normal variate d_1, d_2. It is approximated by the values in Table A in the appendix.

σ = Instantaneous standard deviation

---

[20] **Ian H. Giddy**, "Foreign Exchange Options." Center for the Study of Futures Markets, Colombia Business School, Working paper series No. CSFM 47, 1983.

[21] **Fisher Black and Myron Scholes**, "The Pricing of Options and Corporate Liabilities," *Journal of Political Economy*, vol. 81 (May/June 1973), pp. 637–659.

[22] See **Richard Rogalski and Joseph Vinso**, "Empirical Properties of Foreign Exchange Rates." *Journal of International Business Studies*, vol. 9 (Fall 1978), pp. 69–79.

Based on the call pricing model and on other relationships in the foreign exchange markets, a put pricing model may be easily derived.

Pricing Put Options

The pricing of put options requires an understanding of what Giddy calls the "Put-Call-Forward Exchange Parity."

Assume the price of a call and that of a put are sunk costs. A call will earn a profit if $S > E$. If $S < E$, a short put will lose money because the put writer would have to buy at E from the exercising put holder and sell at the lower S. The gains and losses in the option positions are equal whether the options are sold or are exercised if option prices and transactions costs are ignored. The long call and the short put, when held jointly, produce the results similar to a long forward contract. The gain on the contract will equal the difference between the higher S and the contracted forward rate (F), $S - F > 0$, and the loss would equal $S - F$. The equivalency of a combined long call and short put position to the long forward contract requires that $F = E$, and the sunk-cost assumption.

The Put-Call-Forward Exchange theory advanced by Giddy is

$$C_t - P_t = \frac{F - E}{(1 + r)^t}$$

(7.10)

where P_t = price of a put

Equation 7.10 says that the difference between the price of a call and that of a put is the discounted value of the difference between the forward rate and the strike (exercise) price.

A hedger could choose the forward market or the options market. The cost of acquiring currency in the forward market is equal to F. That of acquiring currency through the combined long call and short put positions is

$$\text{Total cost} = E + (C_t - P_t)(1 + r)^t$$

(7.11)

Equation 7.11 assumes that the difference between C_t and P_t (the net cost of the call option) is fully financed at r over time t. The cost of acquiring foreign exchange by using either method should be the same, otherwise a risk-free arbitrage profit would exist and would equal

$$\text{Profit} = F - \{E + (C_t - P_t)(1 + r)^t\}$$

(7.12)

In an efficient market the arbitrage profit would equal zero. Setting Equation 7.12 equal to zero and solving for the Put-Call-Forward Exchange relationship, we get Equation 7.10:

$$C_t - P_t = \frac{F - E}{(1 + r)^t} \quad \text{or} \quad P_t = C_t - \frac{F - E}{(1 + r)^t}$$

Equation 7.10 proves that the relationship between call and put prices is no more complex than that in the stock price.

Pricing Call and Put Options—An Example

Let us attempt to price the £/March/150 shown in Table 7.5.
The following values are known:

$S = 1.5449$

$E = 1.50$

$t =$ February 22, 1983, to March 16, 1983 $= 22$ days

$\quad = \dfrac{22}{360} = 0.061$ year

$\rho = \ln(1 + r)$

$\quad = \ln(1 + 0.0793) = 0.0763$, $r = 7.93\% =$ the applicable T-bill rate.

$\sigma = 0.1270$ calculated using the standard deviation of $\ln\left(\dfrac{S_t}{S_{t-1}}\right)$ using end-of-month

spot exchange rates.

Therefore

$$d_1 = \frac{\ln\left(\dfrac{1.5449}{1.50}\right) + (0.0763 + \frac{1}{2}(0.1270)^2)0.061}{0.1270\sqrt{.061}}$$

$\quad = 1.105$

$d_2 = 1.105 - 0.0314 = 1.0736$

$N(d_1) = N(1.10) = 0.8643$ (From Table A-1)

$N(d_2) = N(1.07) = 0.8575$ (From Table A-1)

$C_t = 1.5449(0.8643) - \dfrac{1.50}{e^{0.0046}}(.8575)$

$C_t = 1.33 - 1.28 = \mathbf{5}\cancel{c}$

This theoretical price of a call is equal to the market price of the £/March/1.50 as shown in Table 7.7. The call appears, therefore, to be correctly priced.

It must be noted, however, that the price of the call is very sensitive to the value of σ. It appears that we have correctly gauged the value of σ in this case.

The value of the put is calculated as follows (given $F = 1.5462$):

$$P_t = C_t - \frac{F - E}{(1 + r)^t}$$

$$P_t = 0.05 - \frac{1.5462 - 1.50}{(1.0793)^{0.061}} = \mathbf{\$0.004}$$

Once again the put appears to be correctly priced. (See Table 7.4b.)

This concludes our limited coverage of options. The interested reader should go beyond the scope of this presentation.

CONCLUSION

The floating of exchange rates increased the uncertainty in the foreign exchange markets and, consequently, the need to hedge through the forward or the futures market. More volatile and more complex markets increase speculative opportunities in the market place, however. This chapter looked at the various options available to investors and to speculators in the foreign exchange market and at the advantages and the pitfalls of each.

QUESTIONS

1. Discuss in detail the effects of interest arbitrage on interest rates and exchange rates.

2. Explain how a BOP surplus or deficit was eliminated under the gold standard.

3. Compare and contrast the foward and the futures foreign exchange market. Be specific.

4. What is a foreign exchange contract?

5. What are the primary motivating forces behind the foreign exchange market?

6. What are the reasons for the dominant role played by the U.S. dollar in the foreign exchange market?

7. Suggest reasons for the arbitrageur schedule's negative slope.

8. Describe the process that would have to occur for a French bank to buy German marks from a Brazilian bank.

9. Who appears to dominate the foreign exchange market: arbitrageurs or speculators What is the deciding factor?

10. Why might an exporter being paid in a foreign currency at some time in the future use forward contracts to hedge foreign exchange risk? How would he or she do this?

11. Outline the limitations of the IRPT. How serious are they? Explain.

12. The following exchange rates are given: $1 = 200 yen, £1 = $2, 1 yen = £0.0025. Is there consistency across currencies? How do you know?

13. An arbitrageur in the United States calculates the interest differential between the United States and England to be 0.9 percent and the implicit rate between the three-month forward pound to be 1.15 percent.
    a. Explain the course of action that the arbitrageur would take, given this data.
    b. According to the interest rate parity theory, what effect would this have on U.S. and English financial markets and exchange rates?

14. Discuss the reasons why the interest differential and the implicit rate between two countries usually are not equal, as predicted by the interest rate parity theory.

15. Differentiate between arbitrage and speculation.

16. How does the modern theory of foreign exchange rates differ from the interest rate parity theory?

17. Distinguish between a real rate of interest and a nominal rate of interest; does this distinction explain the discount (1976–1980) on the U.S. dollar relative to the DM, despite higher interest rates in the United States?

18. "The best way to forecast exchange rates is to flip a coin." Comment.

19. Under what market conditions is the forward rate the ultimate forecasting tool? Why?

20. Explain the major considerations of foreign exchange investors when deciding between buying a forward contract or a futures contract.

21. How do you suppose a commercial bank uses currency options?

22. What are the advantages of currency options when compared with currency futures?

23. What factors determine the value of a currency call option?

PROBLEMS

1. Given that £1 = $1.50, state the New York direct quote and indirect quote.

2. The following New York ticker quotes for the French franc are given:
   0.2376–0.2378   19–14,   57–46,   78–63
   a. State the bid and ask quotes for the spot and forward rates.
   b. Are the forward French francs selling at a premium or a discount? How can you tell?
   a. What is the annualized premium/discount on the buy side of the three-month forward franc?

3. The following exchange rates are given: $1 = DM 2, DM1 = £0.25, £1 = $1.60.
   a. What transactions would an arbitrageur with $100 undertake? What would his profit be?
   b. What would happen to the exchange rates as this process continued?

4. Given the spot pound at $1.4800 and the 30-day forward pound at $1.4830, the U.S. one-month T-bill rate is 12.30 percent and the British T-bill rate is 8.4 percent.
   a. Calculate the arbitrage margin.
   b. What are the implications of this margin?
   c. Assuming an investor had £1,000 invested in British T-bills, what steps would she take to capitalize on this arbitrage opportunity?
   c. What would be the consequences of similar actions taken by a number of people, assuming that interest rates did not change?

5. A DM spot rate of 0.52, a German 90-day T-bill rate of 12 percent, and U.S. 90-day T-bill rate of 10.5 percent are given.

a. What is the equilibrium forward rate?

b. Would the 90-day DM sell at a discount or premium?

6. The following are given: an ask on the spot French franc of 0.2250, a 90-day U.S. T-bill rate of 8 percent, a 90-day French T-bill rate of 8.8 percent, and these transactions costs:

   1 percent on sale of dollars
   1 percent on purchase of spot francs
   1 percent on purchase of franc-denominated asset
   1 percent on sale of 90-day forward francs

   Find the price of the 90-day French franc at which arbitrageurs would no longer find it profitable to move funds from the United States to France.

7. The spot British pound is selling for $2.00 and the one-year forward pound is selling for $2.15. The annual interest rate in the United States is 20 percent, 10 percent in England. Speculators expect the spot rate for the British pound to be $2.15 in one year.

   a. Outline the steps that an English arbitrageur with £10,000 would take.

   b. What actions would a speculator in the forward market take and what would be his profit if his expectations were met?

   c. What are the implications of the actions of the arbitrageur and the speculator for the price of the forward contract?

8. A U.S. multinational owns a subsidiary in France which requires 1 million French francs from June 18 to Oct. 14. The June 18 spot rate for the French franc is 0.2198 and the October futures contract is 0.2234. Assume that the delivery date for the futures contract is Oct. 21.

   a. Calculate the implied futures contract rate on Oct. 14. Why can it be assumed that a forward contract for Oct. 14 will have the same rate?

   b. If the spot rate on Oct. 14 is 0.2230, calculate the profit/loss for hedging in both the futures market and the forward market, assuming the implied October 14 futures rate holds.

   c. Calculate the profit/loss for hedging in the futures market and for hedging in the forward market if the implied rate does not hold and if on Oct. 14 the spot rate is 0.2233 and the futures rate is 0.2225.

   d. Calculate the profit/loss for hedging in the futures market and for hedging in the forward market if the implied rate does not hold and if on Oct. 14 the spot rate is 0.2220 and the futures rate is 0.2229.

   e. What are the implications of these findings?

Cumulative Probability Distributions

Values of $N(x)$ for Given Values of x for a Cumulative Normal Probability Distribution with Zero Mean and Unit Variance

x	N(x)	x	N(x)	x	N(x)	x	N(x)	x	N(x)	x	N(x)
		−1.00	.1587	1.00	.8413	−2.00	.0228	.00	.5000	2.00	.9773
−2.95	.0016	−.95	.1711	1.05	.8531	−1.95	.0256	.05	.5199	2.05	.9798
−2.90	.0019	−.90	.1841	1.10	.8643	−1.90	.0287	.10	.5398	2.10	.9821
−2.85	.0022	−.85	.1977	1.15	.8749	−1.85	.0322	.15	.5596	2.15	.9842
−2.80	.0026	−.80	.2119	1.20	.8849	−1.80	.0359	.20	.5793	2.20	.9861
−2.75	.0030	−.75	.2266	1.25	.8944	−1.75	.0401	.25	.5987	2.25	.9878
−2.70	.0035	−.70	.2420	1.30	.9032	−1.70	.0446	.30	.6179	2.30	.9893
−2.65	.0040	−.65	.2578	1.35	.9115	−1.65	.0495	.35	.6368	2.35	.9906
−2.60	.0047	−.60	.2743	1.40	.9192	−1.60	.0548	.40	.6554	2.40	.9918
−2.55	.0054	−.55	.2912	1.45	.9265	−1.55	.0606	.45	.6736	2.45	.9929
−2.50	.0062	−.50	.3085	1.50	.9332	−1.50	.0668	.50	.6915	2.50	.9938
−2.45	.0071	−.45	.3264	1.55	.9394	−1.45	.0735	.55	.7088	2.55	.9946
−2.40	.0082	−.40	.3446	1.60	.9452	−1.40	.0808	.60	.7257	2.60	.9953
−2.35	.0094	−.35	.3632	1.65	.9505	−1.35	.0885	.65	.7422	2.65	.9960
−2.30	.0107	−.30	.3821	1.70	.9554	−1.30	.0968	.70	.7580	2.70	.9965
−2.25	.0122	−.25	.4013	1.75	.9599	−1.25	.1057	.75	.7734	2.75	.9970
−2.20	.0139	−.20	.4207	1.80	.9641	−1.20	.1151	.80	.7881	2.80	.9974
−2.15	.0158	−.15	.4404	1.85	.9678	−1.15	.1251	.85	.8023	2.85	.9978
−2.10	.0179	−.10	.4602	1.90	.9713	−1.10	.1357	.90	.8159	2.90	.9981
−2.05	.0202	−.05	.4801	1.95	.9744	−1.05	.1469	.95	.8289	2.95	.9984

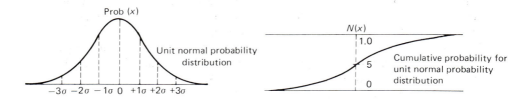

Prob (x)

Unit normal probability distribution

−3σ −2σ −1σ 0 +1σ +2σ +3σ

N(x)

1.0

Cumulative probability for unit normal probability distribution

CHAPTER
8 | Gems and Collectibles

8.1 INTRODUCTION

The massive literature (in relative and in absolute terms) on stocks and bonds may lead the uncritical reader to conclude that the promising investment opportunities are limited to these investment vehicles. Salomon Brothers reports, however, that since 1970, gold, stamps and coins, Chinese ceramics, diamonds, and other precious stones have been steady, if not spectacular winners. During 1980 gold appreciated 1562 percent, U.S. stamps 718 percent, Chinese ceramics 561 percent, and U.S. coins 441 percent. The appreciation in precious stones over the 1976–1981 period is shown in Table 8.1.

These phenomenal returns are not without risk and cannot necessarily be duplicated in future time periods. It is the characteristics of these investment vehicles, their risk profile, and the nature of their markets which are the heart of this chapter.

TABLE 8.1
How Prices Have Moved in Precious Stones

	Wholesale Cost per Carat (Thousands of Dollars)					
	1976	1977	1978	1979	1980	2/25 1981
Diamond (one-carat, D-flawless)	$6.7	$7.7	$18	$22	$60	$44
Diamond (one-carat, F-flawless)	4.6	4.8	9	10	21	24
Ruby (three-carat Burma)	9	11	18	32	33	33
Ruby (three-carat Thai)	2	3.5	12	15	16	16.5
Emerald (three-carat Colombian)	8	10	17	19	21	22
Sapphire (10-carat Ceylon)	2	3	7	8	9.5	9.5
Sapphire (10-carat Kashmir)	5	7	14	21	22	27

Source: "Precious Stones Newsletter." Reprinted from the March 16, 1981 issue of *Business Week* by special permission, © 1981 by McGraw-Hill, Inc.

8.2 DIAMONDS

The focus of this section is on precious stones, diamonds in particular.

Diamonds—An Historical Perspective

The continuing inability of developed and developing nations to control inflation and to dampen inflationary expectations has revived the memories of the German experience after World War I. Rampant inflation destroys the fabric of the economic system and demonstrates in the process the unscrupulous power of government to devalue the wealth of individuals—particularly that wealth held in the form of paper currency. The ability of governments to create inflation is determined by the speed at which its printing presses can turn out money. The more money that is printed, the less is the value of money held, hence, the need for protection. Precious stones have provided and continue to provide an excellent hedge against inflation. Their supply is limited. The more that are extracted, the lower the deposit levels become, and the higher the value of the stones. Additionally, the appreciation in the value of precious stones, when and if their existence is known, does not take place under the close scrutiny of the tax collector. This is an inducement to some investors seeking to maximize their aftertax rate of return.

Ever since their discovery thousands of years ago, diamonds have fascinated men and women everywhere. The reasons for the fascination are embodied in the name. Diamond is a derivative of the Greek word *adamas* which means "invincible."

Investors have committed funds to precious gems for thousands of years. Centuries ago Marco Polo, probably the most famous gem dealer, told entertaining stories to Kubla Khan (the Mongol leader) for which he received gifts of turquoise, jade, and rubies mined in Burma and sapphires from Ceylon.

Later on, in the sixteenth century, Louis XIV was reported to wear colored gems—that is, rubies, sapphires, and emeralds in the daytime—and colorless diamonds at night. He felt that the diamond "fire" added magic to his candlelit ballroom.[1]

After World War I a lost 137.27 carat diamond, the Florentine, became part of history as the imperial family of Austria was forced to leave the country.

Harry Winston, probably the most famous modern day gem dealer, made headlines when he donated the Hope diamond to the Smithsonian Institute in Washington, D.C. This 44.5 carat, deep blue diamond is among the three most valuable in the world (the others being the Star of Africa and the Cullinan II). The Smithsonian Institute received its gift via the U.S. Postal Service.

Major diamond discoveries, sales, and auctions have historically been of great interest. Among the more notable are the discovery in 1893 of the 969-carat Excelsior diamond in South Africa, the discovery of the largest diamond in the Soviet Union (342.5 carats) in the Yakutia region toward the end of 1981, the sale by auction on November 24, 1980 at Christie's of the 41.28 carat Polar Star diamond for a record total price ($4.6 million) and a record price per carat ($112,268), and the failure to sell the fifth largest diamond (234.65 carats), the DeBeers, for the minimum price of $3.5 million set by the owner at a Sotheby Parke Bernet auction held on May 6, 1982, in Geneva, Switzerland.

---

[1] "Glitter of Diamonds," *Barron's* (October 24, 1977).

The illustrative and complex history of the diamond industry giant, DeBeers Diamond, Ltd., is reflective of the problems and the glories of the diamond trade.

Diamonds have also been a symbol of great love and at the center of political controversy. Richard Burton contributed to the glamour of diamonds when he gave a 69.22 carat Cartier diamond to Elizabeth Taylor, who was later to charge a $2,500 inspection fee for potential buyers. President Valery Giscard d'Estaing of France had to put out many political fires in early 1981 as a result of having accepted gifts in diamonds from Jean-Bedel Bokassa, the deposed emperor of the Central African Republic.

The illustrious history of diamonds and their performance as an investment medium should not be overlooked by portfolio managers. We discuss next the supply of diamonds.

The Supply of Diamonds

Diamonds are a highly pressured form of carbon. Their supply can be classified into two broad categories, the supply of natural diamonds and the supply of synthetic diamonds. The supply of natural diamonds in the world is tightly controlled by DeBeers Consolidated Mines through its marketing arm, the Central Selling Organization (CSO) in London. CSO markets about 85 percent of the diamonds produced in the world, including some of the Russian production. World production of natural diamonds in 1981 was approximately equal to 48 million carats. The control over the diamond market by the South African company owes its origin to the diamond rush in 1869 after the discovery of the Kimberley Hole in South Africa. The mining of diamonds in South Africa remained chaotic until Cecil Rhodes organized the Kimberley diamond fields. This led to the development of the DeBeers Company in 1887—which today controls the diamond industry, either directly or indirectly, from mining to distribution. The countries involved in the production of natural diamonds and their relative weight in the market are shown in Table 8.2.

DeBeers Consolidated is the world's largest diamond producer and retailer of rough diamonds. Its net production of natural diamonds does not always translate itself into a net supply, however, because of the monopolistic position of CSO. Using its large reserves of rough stones and of accumulated cash,[2] CSO decides on the size of the net supply it is willing to bring to the market.

DeBeers is truly a multinational corporation with huge financial resources. It owns $3 billion in assets outside the diamond industry. Its largest holding is a 38 percent interest in Anglo-American Corp., which produces gold, steel, and coal and owns real estate and insurance subsidiaries. DeBeers is also part owner of Phibro-Salomon (a commodities/investment banking firm), Englehard Corp., Consolidated Gold Fields, and Hudson Bay Mining and Smelting of Canada. The financial powers DeBeers possesses proved of critical importance in allowing it to maintain its firm hold on the diamond market. In 1982 DeBeers ranked 339 among the *Fortune*'s 500 largest industrial corporations. This ranking represented, however, a large drop from a 169 ranking the preceding year, reflecting the sorry state of the diamond industry in the early 1980s.

The control over the supply of natural diamonds is effected through control over the size of production and the quantity and quality of diamonds offered by CSO, the value of the privileged access, "the license," which DeBeers grants a limited number

---

[2] CSO earned $2.72 billion in profits in 1980 and $2.6 billion in 1979.

TABLE 8.2
Diamond (Natural): World Production, by Country and Type[1]
(Thousand carats)

Country	1977 Gem	1977 Indus-trial	1977 Total	1978 Gem	1978 Indus-trial	1978 Total	1979 Gem	1979 Indus-trial	1979 Total	1980[2] Gem	1980[2] Indus-trial	1980[2] Total	1981e Gem	1981e Indus-trial	1981e Total
Africa:															
Angola	265	88	353	r488	r162	r650	630	211	841	1,125	375	1,500	1,050	350	1,400
Botswana	404	2,287	2,691	r420	r2,379	r2,799	659	3,735	4,394	765	4,336	5,101	744	4,217	[2]4,961
Central African Republic	178	119	297	199	85	284	205	110	315	227	123	350	200	100	300
Ghana	230	1,717	1,947	142	1,281	1,423	125	1,128	1,253	126	1,132	1,258	100	900	1,000
Guinea^e	25	55	80	25	55	80	27	58	85	12	26	38	12	26	38
Ivory Coast	r20	r19	[2]39	r22	r23	r45	24	24	48	—	—	.	—	—	—
Lesotho	39	3	42	62	5	67	48	4	52	50	4	54	49	4	[2]53
Liberia[3]	163	163	326	128	180	308	170	132	302	123	175	298	117	169	[2]286
Namibia	1,901	100	2,001	1,803	95	1,898	1,570	83	1,653	1,482	78	1,560	1,186	62	[2]1,248
Sierra Leone	423	538	961	353	426	779	419	436	855	317	275	592	320	275	595
South Africa, Republic of:															
Finsch Mine	r365	r2,061	2,426	r403	r2,227	2,630	465	2,120	2,585	465	2,442	2,907	1,002	3,463	[2]4,465
Premier Mine	r378	r1,632	2,010	r380	r1,603	1,983	468	1,613	2,081	407	1,632	2,039	510	1,530	[2]2,040
Other De Beers properties[4]	r1,216	r1,441	2,657	r1,254	r1,395	2,649	1,850	1,370	3,220	1,550	1,489	3,039	1,603	1,069	[2]2,672
Other	r372	r178	550	r320	r145	465	403	95	498	391	44	435	314	35	349
Total	r2,331	r5,312	7,643	r2,357	r5,370	r7,727	3,186	5,198	8,384	2,813	5,607	8,420	3,429	6,097	r9,526

Country															
Tanzania	204	204	408	r141	r141	r282	157	157	314	137	137	274	140	140	280
Zaire	533	10,681	11,214	640	10,603	11,243	294	8,440	8,734	345	9,890	10,235	260	7,240	7,500
Other areas:															
Australia	—	—	—	—	—	—	—	—	—	—	48	48	21[2]	184[2]	205[2]
Brazil	r236	r384	r620	236	r384	r620	236	384	620	253	414	667	228	372	600
Guyana	7	10	17	7	10	17	6	10	16	4	6	10	4	6	10
India	15	3	18	14	2	16	14	2	16	e12	e2	e14	12	2	14
Indonesia[e]	3	12	15	3	12	15	3	12	15	3	12	15	3	12	15
U.S.S.R.[e]	2,100	8,200	10,300	2,150	8,400	10,550	2,200	8,500	10,700	2,250	8,600	10,850	2,120	8,480	10,600
Venezuela	204	483	687	r271	r549	r820	247	556	803	238	483	721	102[2]	388[2]	490[2]
Total	**r9,281**	**r30,378**	**r39,659**	**r9,461**	**r30,162**	**r39,623**	**10,220**	**29,180**	**39,400**	**10,282**	**31,723**	**42,005**	**10,097**	**29,024**	**39,121**

Source: *Minerals Yearbook*, Centennial Edition, United States Department of the Interior, 1981, p. 362.

e Estimated. p Preliminary. r Revised.

1 Table includes data available through May 7, 1982. Total diamond output (gem plus industrial) for each country is actually reported except where indicated by a footnote to be estimated. In contrast, the detailed separate data for gem diamond and industrial diamond are Bureau of Mines estimates in the case of every country except Australia (1980–81), Central African Republic (1977–78), Liberia (1977–78), Sierra Leone (1977–78), and Venezuela (1978–81), for which source publications give details on grade as well as totals. The estimated distribution of total output between gem and industrial diamond is conjectural, and for most countries is based on the best available data at time of publication. China also produces some natural diamond, but output is not reported.

2 Reported figure.

3 Total exports.

4 All company output from the Republic of South Africa, except for that credited to the Finsch and Premier Mines for the years indicated; excludes De Beers Group output from Botswana, Lesotho, and Namibia.

of diamond dealers and cutters with the attending power to cajole and coerce, and through price surcharges imposed by CSO.

Rough diamonds are sold by CSO through 10 annual "sights" at which 300 dealers and cutters are given plain paper boxes of rough stones for examination in private rooms. DeBeers sells 20 to 30 million carats of diamonds a year through these sights. The sales are held at 17 Charterhouse Street, in London's diamond district. The diamonds offered at the sights are on a "take-it-or-leave-it" basis. Dealers who wish to continue doing business with DeBeers accept whatever DeBeers offers on whatever terms. Nothing is negotiable. This procedure allows DeBeers to engineer regular price increases to finance the South African economy and in the process that of the Soviet Union and several African countries.

DeBeers and the Central Selling Organization regulate the supply and the price of diamonds in accordance with prevailing and projected economic conditions. Supplies are released into the market during economic boom periods, and are restricted during periods of economic slowdown. Supplies, for example, were restricted during the 1973–1974 U.S. recession. Each year the DeBeers annual report carries the following statement:

> *"The policy of DeBeers, as a leader of the diamond industry, is to maintain a high degree of price stability for gem diamonds at all times."*[3]

The absolute monopoly power DeBeers has over the market is evidenced by the fact that since 1934—the date marking the formation of the DeBeers London Selling Organization—the price of rough diamonds at the sightings rose consistently until 1980, without a single year of decline, staying well ahead of increases in the general price level.

DeBeers further demonstrated its power over the market in the Spring of 1978 following a period of frenzied activity in the diamond market. Sightholders had decided to hoard the rough diamonds purchased at the sightings and not send the whole supply to diamond cutters. Cutters and dealers offered premiums upward of 100 percent on boxes of unopened rough diamonds[4] in order to keep a steady supply and preserve their businesses. DeBeers responded with surcharges on the rough diamonds it marketed. This action forced the hoarders to bring the diamonds to the market. Following a series of surcharges, DeBeers put an end to speculation by imposing a permanent 30 percent surcharge on all rough diamonds marketed at the March 1978 sight. This series of actions effectively put a temporary end to speculation. The cartel had survived the challenge.

The year 1979 brought yet another rush to buy diamonds. The price of a one-carat D-flawless diamond rose steadily until it reached $63,000 by March 1980. Fueling the rise was a new policy of the Israeli government. Israel, a major center for cutting diamonds, permitted its banks to cut interest rates charged diamond cutters by 25 percent from current market rates. Wishing to hedge against high inflation in Israel, diamond cutters bought all the diamonds they could and hoarded them. The size of the hoard was high enough to constitute an inventory of 12 to 18 months.

The Israeli buying spree spread to other centers, leading to even higher prices. As prices rose, DeBeers's ability to control the market diminished. Dealers had to pay

---

[3] "The Diamond Game," *The New Leader* (June 5, 1978).

[4] "The Diamond Hustle," *Forbes* (September 18, 1978).

increasingly higher prices for diamonds brought to the market by diamond cutters and dealers. What DeBeers was offering was below what diamonds could fetch on the open market. Some members of the cartel began to see opportunities in breaking away from DeBeers. The "solution" offered by DeBeers was a price surcharge. The market cooled off only to be reignited later by a 30 percent price increase by DeBeers. Speculators were convinced that the best was yet to come.

Meanwhile DeBeers's inventory kept climbing, reaching about $1 billion during 1980. DeBeers was close to the breaking point in terms of its ability to control supply. Hoarders were trying to capitalize on historic price levels beyond the ability of the market to absorb this new source of supply. Prices began to fall, causing a snowball effect.

Signs of considerable weakness in CSO's hold on the market began to emerge toward the end of 1980. DeBeers's ability to absorb excess supply was shown to be limited indeed. The cracks in DeBeers's market dominance began to appear toward the end of 1980. During the September–November 1980 period, DeBeers began to sell fewer diamonds at its sights, but diamond prices continued to weaken. By the end of 1980 the Soviet Union sold large quantities of diamonds directly to dealers at a 15 percent discount in order to finance grain imports and its invasion of Afghanistan.

By March 22, 1981, DeBeers announced that it would reduce the supply of stones it sold at sights in London by 65 percent. DeBeers's efforts to stabilize prices failed as prices continued to plummet. By the end of 1981 the value of DeBeers's diamond stockpile had increased to $1.3 billion. The September 21, 1981, issue of *Business Week* reported that DeBeers was thought to "be holding a stockpile equal to 90 percent of a year's sales, its largest stockpile ever." The stockpiling continued in 1982. Despite these huge inventories, the price of polished diamonds dropped by 40 percent between September 1980, and September 1981. The dramatic change in diamond prices for all grades is illustrated in Table 8.3. As a result of these price declines DeBeers's operating results for 1981 were the worst since the Great Depression—reflecting themselves in the market value of DeBeers stock. Sales by CSO fell 45 percent in 1981 to $1.47 billion. Dividends on DeBeers's South African shares were cut for the first time since the 1940s. By May 27, 1982, DeBeers was forced to cut the production of diamonds as a last resort for controlling supply. Further weakening DeBeers's hold on the diamond market was the announcement by Zaire on May 12, 1981, that, henceforth, it would sell its diamonds through four European dealers and not through DeBeers. On June 2, 1981, Zaire, the largest supplier of diamonds (by weight) in the noncommunist world, sold 620,000 carats (about 10 percent of Zaire's 1981 output) to dealers. The significance of such a sale must be put in perspective, however, for Zaire accounts for only 5 to 10 percent of world gem diamond production. The predominant share of Zaire's production consists of low-quality industrial diamonds.

The defection of Zaire could have had a dramatic long-run impact, had it represented the beginning of a trend. Some dealers speculated that Tanzania, Lesotho, and even Namibia, where 60 percent of DeBeers' finest stones are mined might be encouraged by Zaire's success to break away from CSO. The Russians could have pulled away because of economic and political considerations. Being a partner with the South Africans is not good politics in third world countries where the Soviet Union has significant military, strategic, political, and economic stakes. Yet another threat to supplies and to the market power of CSO could have come from Botswana which accounts for 40 percent of South Africa's diamond production. The fiercely independent Botswana could have caused serious problems for CSO if not to South Africa as a whole. DeBeers's

TABLE 8.3
Prices of U.S. Cut Diamonds, by Size and Quality

Carat Weight	Description, Color[1]	Clarity[2] (GIA Terms)	Price Range per Carat 1981		Median price per carat[3]	
					December 1980	Early December 1981
0.04–0.08	G–I	VS$_1$	$375–	$650	$570	$467
.04– .08	G–I	SI$_1$	325–	550	520	400
.09– .16	G–I	VS$_1$	475–	750	655	550
.09– .16	G–I	SI$_1$	400–	615	585	470
.17– .22	G–I	VS$_1$	600–	1,205	1,080	837
.17– .22	G–I	SI$_1$	510–	1,045	975	687
.23– .28	G–I	VS$_1$	750–	1,375	1,385	900
.23– .28	G–I	SI$_1$	640–	1,215	1,150	800
.29– .35	G–I	VS$_1$	875–	1,795	1,550	1,200
.29– .35	G–I	SI$_1$	740–	1,535	1,375	917
.46– .55	G–I	VS$_1$	1,300–	2,285	2,738	1,800
.46– .55	G–I	SI$_1$	1,000–	2,000	1,950	1,500
.69– .79	G–I	VS$_1$	1,600–	3,010	3,556	2,300
.69– .79	G–I	SI$_1$	1,200–	2,420	2,530	1,850
1.00–1.15	D	FL		(4)	^{5}53,000	26,500
1.00–1.15	E	VVS$_1$	10,000–	16,050	^{5}23,000	11,250
1.00–1.15	G	VS$_1$	4,600–	8,480	^{5}8,600	5,075
1.00–1.15	H	VS$_2$	3,500–	5,700	^{5}5,650	3,800
1.00–1.15	I	SI$_1$	2,600–	4,000	^{5}3,550	2,750

Source: Minerals Yearbook, Centennial Edition, United States Department of the Interior, 1981, p. 354.
[1] Gemological Institute of America (GIA) color grades: D—colorless; E—rare white; G-I—traces of color.
[2] Clarity: FL—no blemishes; VVS$_1$—very, very slightly included; VS$_1$—very slightly included; VS$_2$—very slightly included, but more visible; SI$_1$—slightly included.
[3] Jewelers' Circular-Keystone, v. 152, No. 1, January 1981, p. 124; v. 153, No. 2, February 1982, p. 150. These figures represent a sampling of net prices that diamond dealers in various U.S. cities charged their customers during the month.
[4] Not enough sales reported to quote prices. Last quoted as $36,000–$44,000 in July 1981 Jewelers' Circular-Keystone. Quoted at yearend in The Diamond Registry Bulletin, New York, N.Y., as $20,000–$25,000.
[5] Representative of early November 1980 sales. December sales are nonrepresentative.

greatest producing mines lie outside South Africa, the Orapa mine in Botswana and C.D.M. in Namibia.

The defection of Zaire was the acid test for DeBeers. The future of the cartel was in balance. DeBeers began dumping bort (low quality industrial diamond powder) on the market, undercutting the $3 a carat Zaire was charging. Zaire was unable to meet head-on the brute force of DeBeers. The other more important players in the diamond industry, Botswana and the Soviet Union, found it in their interest to keep their partnership with DeBeers intact.

Another recently discovered source of diamond supply was to present a new challenge to DeBeers's supremacy: Lake Argyle mine in Western Australia. The mine was discovered in January 1980. Its output potential was estimated to be 20 to 25 million carats

by the year 1986. DeBeers and the Australians were quick to reach an agreement, however. The agreement calls for the CSO to market the entire gem quality output of Argyle and 75 percent of its industrial diamonds. This less than complete hold on the marketing of the output of a diamond-producing country represented an unusual step by DeBeers. *The Wall Street Journal* reported in its April 28, 1983 issue the sale of the first diamond from the Australian mine by the CSO. The value of the diamonds sold was put at $1.9 million.

Investors must, however, keep in mind that 75 percent of the world diamonds come from Communist or African countries: the Soviet Union and South Africa. The leading producer is South Africa. DeBeers of South Africa alone produced 14.7 million carats in 1980. Most of the diamond-producing areas are politically and economically unstable. A national emergency could flood the diamond market (diamond holders cashing in their stones to live overseas, or new governments selling stones to insure the continued functioning of the state) or could dry it up. Shortages could occur as mining operations are disrupted and as people fleeing the country or concerned with its future, accumulate easily storable (hideable) and transportable wealth. Experts argue that the latter event has a greater probability of occurrence.

Two additional problems/developments should concern DeBeers and therefore, the investor. The first is diamond smuggling. Of the 48 million carats produced in the world in 1981, 4 to 6 million carats were smuggled, finding their way mostly to Israel. The second development deals with the fact that the General Electric Co. should be able to produce gem quality artificial diamonds by 1990 at the latest. This development could seriously destabilize the diamond industry and substantially reduce the role of diamonds as an investment vehicle.

Thus far, we have concentrated on natural gem diamonds. Of the 50 million carats of diamonds produced annually, 80 percent are used for industrial application in tool systems designed for grinding, sawing, polishing, and so forth. The remaining 20 percent are polished to produce gem stones. Only 2 percent of the rough stones polished is in a form suitable for investment purposes.

Natural diamonds used in industry are in competition with synthetic diamonds. About two thirds of all commercial abrasive diamond is man-made. The production of man-made diamonds began in 1955 when the General Electric Co. Research Laboratories in Schenectady, N.Y., succeeded in manufacturing the first diamond, which it called, appropriately, "Man-Made." By 1980, General Electric produced 100 million carats (44,000 pounds) of diamond in its Worthington, Ohio plant—about one half of the world's synthetic diamond production. The remaining 50 percent is produced by DeBeers, Ireland, Sweden, Japan, West Germany, and the Soviet Union. A new plant owned by SDT, Inc. will produce synthetic diamonds in South Bend, Indiana, by 1984.

In summary, the investor must keep in mind that the stability of the supply of diamonds in the future is quite suspect even under the best of world political circumstances.

Marketing Diamonds

Once the diamonds are purchased by brokers, they travel through various channels before they reach the investor. The flow is described in Figure 8.1.

The cutting phase is handled by approximately 200 diamond manufacturers in nine cutting centers: New York, Antwerp, Tel Aviv, Amsterdam, London, Zurich, Vienna,

FIGURE 8.1.

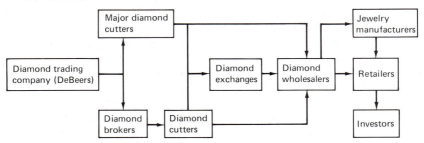

Johannesburg and Bombay. Because of its high labor costs, New York handles the costlier diamonds.

Cutters sell their diamonds to diamond wholesalers on the worldwide exchanges. The leading exchanges are located in Antwerp, Belgium. The exchanges operate in a peculiar fashion. Only members of the exchanges or visiting professionals are admitted to the exchanges. Sellers exhibit their diamonds and buyers shop around for the most suitable collection at the best possible price. Pits for shouting brokers are nowhere to be seen. Jewelry manufacturers are also buyers from the exchanges or from wholesalers. They mount stones in jewelry pieces for resale.

In addition to the new supply of diamonds, existing diamonds held by the public can influence total supply. Widowers, wives, even divorcees are never willing to part with their diamonds, however. Investors who sell their diamonds have but an insignificant impact on the supply and hence the price.

It can be said in conclusion that the supply of diamonds is quite stable and is a function of the actions of CSO.

The Demand for Diamonds

The demand for gem quality diamonds comes from consumers of jewelry items and from investors. The interest of investors is in unmounted stones which are handled by investment houses and discount brokers, and increasingly by retail jewelers.

The demand for diamonds by investors is increasing steadily as inflationary pressures build, as stock markets prove to be inadequate places for hedging against inflation, as more professional money managers recognize the important role diamonds can play in the investment portfolio, and as diamond funds, which make the ownership of diamonds easier and more rewarding, spread. It is estimated that the demand for diamonds in the United States alone has increased by 300 percent since World War II.[5] Since the middle of 1980, the effectiveness of diamonds as a hedge against inflation has become suspect, however.

The traditional focus of pension funds and investment trusts on stocks and bonds and other paper securities has been gradually shifting into "hard assets" like diamonds. Paper securities did not produce the expected risk/return results, which necessitated the search for an alternative. On July 13, 1979, the Senior Deputy Comptroller for bank supervision pronounced in the Banking Circular No. 15 that

---

[5] See *Pension World,* September 1979.

investing in these "hard assets" is permissible for pension funds and investment trusts if it is done in a prudent manner. The prudence of each investment decision should be judged with regard to the role that the proposed investment or investment course of action plays within the overall portfolio. The use of diamonds as an investment is permissible when consistent with the rule of prudence. [6]

The Employee Retirement Income Security Act of 1974 (ERISA) confirms the fundamental position of the comptroller for it allows funds managers to seek prudent alternatives to stocks and bonds consistent with reasonable risk and high returns.

Trust companies have increasingly been accepting diamonds as part of their portfolios as pressures build from participants in the Individual Retirement Accounts and Keogh plans. Now "the pressure to include diamonds in IRA and Keogh plans is coming from individuals searching for ways to build a retirement nest-egg in a high inflationary period."[7]

Investment quality gems—and there are now 5,000 varieties—have also been used as tax shelters. In a properly administered tax shelter program, diamonds purchased at wholesale can be appraised according to retail prices and donated to charitable and educational institutions.[8]

Industrial users have also begun purchasing gem quality diamonds. They have discovered that although higher quality stones are much more expensive, they last a lot longer than industrial diamonds that are full of inclusions and consequently are more susceptible to cracking under pressure.

The demand for diamonds is distributed as follows: 80 percent for industry use, 19 percent for jewelry, and the remaining 1 percent for loose stones used for investment purposes. The demand for diamonds is very sensitive to political stability and to economic conditions. Soft prices are typically experienced during recessions, such as those of 1973–1974 and 1980–1982, and whenever CSO has problems managing the supply of diamonds.

The increasing literature on diamonds and other precious stones, the increased experience of professional money managers in investing in diamonds, the substantial strength CSO still holds in the market, and the increased availability of diamond-based mutual funds should provide some degree of stability to the diamond market in the long run.

Price of Diamonds

The impressive price increases realized in the diamond industry up to June 1980 speak for the relationship between supply and demand and parenthetically for the market power of DeBeers. Throughout the 1970s the average compounded annual rate of return on diamond was 16 percent. Figure 8.2 and Table 8.4 show the price performance of diamonds relative to other investment vehicles and the price levels for various quality diamonds as of April 10, 1980. The price of the highest grade (D-flawless) one-carat diamond as of February 1981, was reported by *The Wall Street Journal* (February 17, 1981) to equal $45,000, down from $63,000 in March of 1980, and up from $6,500 in

---

[6] Trust Banking Circular no. 15, July 13, 1979.

[7] "Investing in Gems." *Business Week* (October 2, 1978).

[8] "Investment Factsheet." *Gemma Corporation,* no. 2, p. 1.

1976. Diamond prices dropped further, reaching only $20,000 per carat for a D-flawless diamond in May 1982. Price stability has long since left the market.

Based on the assumption that no new major discoveries of diamonds are made, prices can take either of the following courses:

1. At current production levels, diamond prices can be very stable.
2. If production is increased and if competition intensifies, diamond prices could become very unstable in the short run, with a downward direction.

FIGURE 8.2.   Diamonds versus gold, stocks, and other indices.

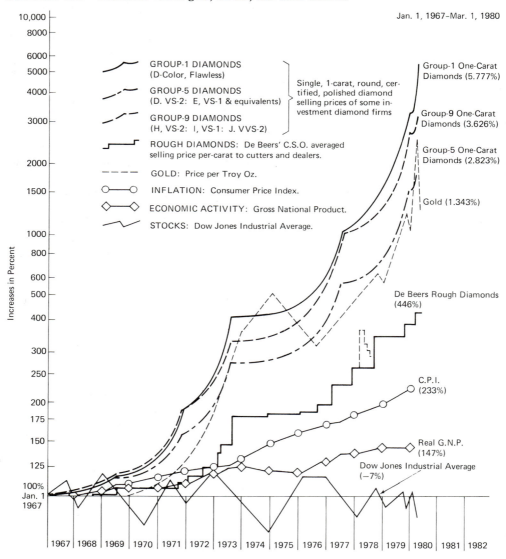

Source: Jack B. Backer & Co., 1980.

3. If production is cut substantially, and CSOs hold on the market is not diminished, the price of diamonds is likely to rise but not at its historic rate.

The most likely course is the first because DeBeers continues to be able to flex its muscle in the market place. Diamonds could be a desirable investment vehicle for those who are well versed in the operations of the market.

TABLE 8.4
Official Price Index

VVS	Average Low	Average High	Minimum Deposit
¼ carat	$860	$1170	$1040
⅓ carat	$1535	$1835	$1700
½ carat	$3620	$5100	$4530
¾ carat	$5975	$8660	$7510
1 carat		Priced individually	
2 carats		Priced individually	

VS	Average Low	Average High	Minimum Deposit
¼ carat	$820	$1035	$945
⅓ carat	$1315	$1740	$1540
½ carat	$3215	$4410	$3830
¾ carat	$5025	$7355	$6600
1 carat		Priced individually	
2 carats		Priced individually	

Melange[a]	Per Carat Price
0.02–.07	$1020
0.08–.12	$1240
0.13–.17	$1860
0.18–.22	$2330

Source: Gemological Institute of America

[a] Melange diamonds are not individually fingerprinted and are graded to general specifications and sold by carat weight. Because the merchandise is relatively inexpensive, there is no requirement to grade the material outside the parameters of the original supply parcel and the price per carat and point. This standard method of grading melange merchandise is pervasive throughout the diamond trade and will serve as the basis for repurchase at the time liquidation takes place through the IDC Brokerage Service.

Note: This pricing index supplies price zones for the most popular weights of diamonds. Heavy weight categories such as ¾, ⅝ and ⅞, light ½ carats and some others are not provided in the price chart. Therefore, some stones in the price zone may be lower than the low indicated, and heavy weight, color and clarity combinations may be slightly higher than the average high. The price index has been prepared with computer assistance, using average figures from the widest band of selling prices actually in place at the present time. This price index supersedes all other price indexes.

Buying Diamonds—The Four Cs

Investment in diamonds is difficult for the uninitiated. Few investors have a mastery of the range that quality diamonds have and of the methods for differentiating between one diamond and another. The Gemological Institute of America (GIA) has developed a grading scale for diamonds which offers a systematic approach to evaluating diamonds. The European counterpart to GIA is the European Gemological Laboratory (EGL) located in Antwerp, Belgium. Both GIA and EGL use essentially similar grading scales and have equally high professional standards. Diamonds are evaluated in terms of carat, color, clarity, and cut—the four Cs.

Carat

The carat is a measure of weight. It is equal to 200 mg ($\frac{1}{5}$ of a gram). The relationship between weight and value is an exponential relationship: four one-quarter-carat stones are less valuable than a one-carat stone, and a two-carat stone is usually three or four times as valuable as a one-carat stone. The larger the stone, the more rare and expensive it becomes and the greater its potential for appreciation. The marketability of a large stone decreases, however, as we shall later demonstrate. In evaluating diamonds, "points" are used to specify the size. One hundred points are equivalent to one carat.

Color

The color of a diamond is critical in the determination of its grade. The more color the diamond has, the less valuable it is. Colorless and slightly blue diamonds are the most valuable. The color scales shown in Table 8.4 are those developed by GIA, and are universally accepted. A "D" color is most valuable and V is least valuable. Diamonds graded F are worth about 50 percent less than those graded D and 30 percent less than those graded E. The classification by color is not very accurate, however.

Clarity

Clarity also has a large effect on the value of the investment. All diamonds have inclusions (impurities or flaws in the stone) which form during the development of the gem. It is the relative occurrence of these imperfections which determines the clarity scale assigned the stone. The internal flaws of a diamond influence its ability to diffuse and diffract light. The clarity grades shown in Table 8.5 range from the flawless (the highest grade) to the flawed that is visible to the naked eye (a P grade).

Cut

The cut of the stone involves taking the rough diamond and cutting it down into gem form. The cut is intended to accentuate the internal brilliance of the stone, and is measured relative to the "ideal" cut developed by a mathematician named Marcel Tokowsky. Diamond cutters occasionally sacrifice cut for carat. Diamonds are usually cut in the

TABLE 8.5

Color Scales			Clarity Scales	

GIA

Colorless	D E F	Blue White
Nearly Colorless	G H I J	Fine White White Comm. White Top Silver Cape
Slight Tint	K L M N	Silver Cape Light Cape
Very Light Yellow Light Yellow Yellow	O P Q R S T U V	Cape Dark Cape

GRADES	SUBGRADES
FL	FL
IF	IF
VVS	VVS^1
	VVS^2
VS	VS^1
	VS^2
SI	SI^1
	SI^2
P(I)	P^1
	P^2
	P^3

Source: Gemological Institute of America.

FL = Flawless
IF = Internally flawless
VVS = Very very slight imperfection
VS = Very slight imperfection
SI = Slight imperfection
P = Visible with naked eye

round brilliant form for optimal results and highest investment value. This is shown in Figure 8.3.

Another C

Recently a fifth C was added to the evaluation process: Certification. The certification is essential if the investor is to be assured of the quality of his investment. A sample of the certification form issued by GIA appears in Figure 8.4. The investor should be cautioned, however, that the standards for grading diamonds differ from one lab to another. Also, certificates never mention the dollar value of the investment, that is, they do not provide the appraisal value.

The error factor in certification, usually thought to be 5 percent, is apparently a lot higher. The September 7, 1981 issue of *Barron's* reported that of 145 sample certificates experts found that in "72 cases . . . the labs had awarded the stone a higher grade than it deserved." Investors are advised to ask for the opinion of more than one expert.

FIGURE 8.3.   Round brilliant cut for a diamond.

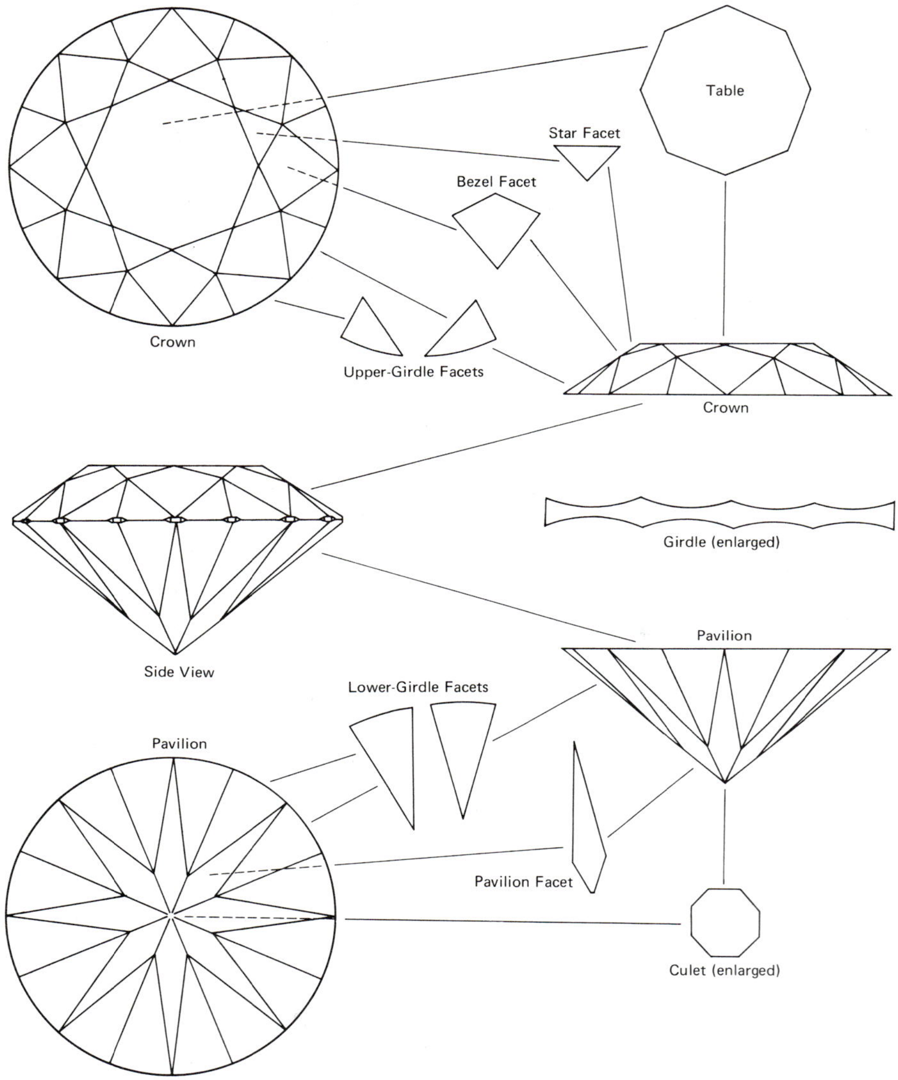

Table

Star Facet

Bezel Facet

Crown

Upper-Girdle Facets

Crown

Side View

Girdle (enlarged)

Pavilion

Lower-Girdle Facets

Pavilion

Pavilion Facet

Culet (enlarged)

Source: GIA assignment #24. Courtesy of the Gemological Institute of America.

Advantages and Pitfalls of Diamond Investments

Some of the advantages of investing in diamonds have been mentioned earlier. We repeat them here and complete the list. They are

1. Risk diversification. To the extent that rates of return on diamonds are not perfectly, positively correlated with those rates of return on investment vehicles traditionally held by investors (stocks and bonds), an opportunity for risk diversification exists. Many investors and professional portfolio managers have been using diamonds to diversify

FIGURE 8.4. A sample GIA certificate.

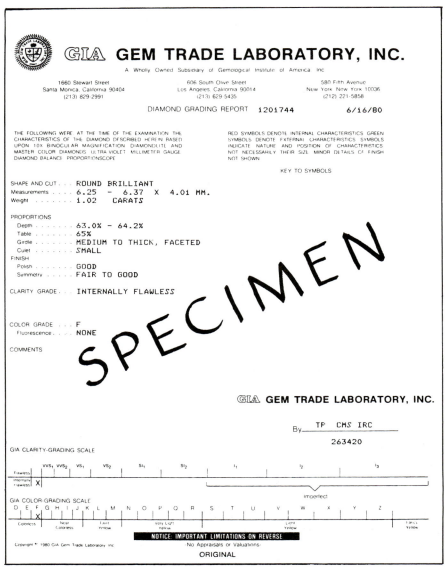

their portfolios. Jean Francois Moyersohn[9] calculated the risk/return profile of five hypothetical portfolios and found portfolios with a larger proportion of funds invested in diamonds to have a better risk/return profile (see Table 8.6).

2. High returns. Returns on diamond investments have very frequently been positive and have on the average exceeded the prevailing rate of inflation.

3. Relative Market Stability. The control CSO holds over the market has almost always worked to stabilize the market and has thus decreased the risk. During periods

---

[9] **Jean-Francois Moyersohn,** *Investing in Diamonds.* Gem Reports, New York, N.Y., 1981.

TABLE 8.6
Portfolio Strategies

Investment Type	Portfolio A (%)	Portfolio B (%)	Portfolio C (%)	Portfolio D (%)
Long-Term Bonds	33.9	50.9	43.1	
Stocks	6.7			
Gold	3.7	.6		
Diamonds	1.6	35.7	52.7	65
Treasury Bills	32.5			
Swiss Franc	21.5	12.8	4.2	
Deutsche Mark				
Silver				35
Expected Return	10.4	20	25	50
Expected Risk	1.1	7.2	11.6	68
95% percent Chance that Return will be within Range	+ 8.2 and + 12.6	+ 5.6 and + 34.4	+ 1.8 and + 48.2	−86 and + 186

Source: Jean-Francois Moyersohn, *Investing in Diamonds.* Gem Reports, New York, N.Y.

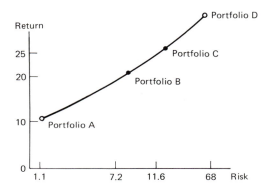

An investor can choose among these portfolios to get the best
fit between his attitude towards risk and his expected return.

of recession (1948–1949, 1953–54, 1957–58, 1960–61, 1969–70, and 1974–1976) diamonds have maintained or increased their value at the wholesale level. The recent troubles experienced by CSO have reduced investor's confidence, but recovery is underway.

4. Value per gram. Diamonds represent the most concentrated form of wealth. They are small, light, and easily transported or stored. Diamonds are a form of an international currency that is "legal tender" in any country of the world.

5. Privacy. Ownership of diamonds is private and anonymous, and is free of government control. Diamonds are mobile and hideable.

With high returns and other advantages come various pitfalls. They are as follows:

1. Information. The diamond markets are still a mystery to many investors despite the recent increase in the flow of literature. They are not regularly reported on in the financial journals.

2. Liquidity. This represents the most serious of problems related to diamond investment. There exists no central market where investors can readily buy/sell their diamonds. The liquidity discount is currently estimated to be in the range of 8 to 10 percent. The most likely organization to purchase a diamond from an investor is that from

which the stone was originally purchased. In this case the commission may be less than 10 percent. Another avenue for selling a diamond is through the big auction houses. Again the commission is approximately 10 percent, both on the buy and on the sell side. Top quality diamonds can command top prices if offered at Christie's or Sotheby Parke Bernet.

The Securities and Exchange Commission and the Federal Trade Commission prohibit any gem investment company from guaranteeing repurchase prices. Diamond dealers may guarantee a "best effort" in their attempts to locate a diamond buyer. Most wholesale brokers offer rebrokerage services at a commission ranging from 5 to 15 percent. Liquidity costs are still high, particularly when compared with those of stocks and bonds.

3. Limited cash flows. Investments in diamonds do not yield periodic cash flows as, for example, stocks and bonds do in the form of dividends and interest, respectively. All cash flows are one-time cash flows realized at the end of the holding period. Diamond investors, who necessarily have long-run horizons because of high transaction costs, must wait a long time before they taste the fruits of their investment.

4. Political instability of producing countries. The dominant share of diamond production comes from politically unstable countries in the African continent. Internal turmoil in South Africa spells potentially devastating effects on the diamond markets. The breakup or the nationalization of DeBeers can destroy the stability and the predictability of the diamond market. Furthermore, as inflation takes its toll on many government budgets, new sources of revenues will be sought. A tax on luxury items like diamonds (if the tax agent can find them) is usually the first of considerations.

5. Risk of theft or loss. Yes! Diamonds are insurable. Elizabeth Taylor had to be accompanied by an army of security agents whenever she wore her diamond. Small and valuable as a diamond is, its loss is quite possible and potentially devastating financially.

Guidelines for Investing in Diamonds

The guidelines proposed by experts for investing in diamonds are as follows:

1. Know the seller of diamonds and carefully scrutinize the buy-back offer.
2. Buy loose, cut, and polished quality diamonds.
3. Buy the highest affordable quality. The recommended size is between 0.5 and 2.0 carats; the color is between D and H, no lower; the clarity is flawless (FL) to very slight flawed (VS), no lower; and the cut is round and brilliant. Committing all speculative funds to one large stone is not recommended primarily for liquidity reasons.
4. Diversify the size of diamonds in order to improve liquidity.
5. Do not purchase stones set in jewelry.
6. Make sure that all purchases are certified. GIA or its overseas counterpart the European Gemological Laboratory (EGL) provide excellent services. In addition you may wish to ask for an additional certification from the dealer. Insurance may be purchased from companies like Northbrook Excess and Surplus Insurance Co. (an Allstate Insurance Co. subsidiary) to insure against incorrect certification of diamonds (weight, color, clarity). The policy limits in 1982 were $100,000 per stone and $500,000 in the aggregate annually.
7. Always insure the investment up to its full market value.

8. Consider the services of companies like the Zale Corporation which work with insured owners of lost or stolen diamonds to provide similar or exact replacements.

9. Use gemprints. This process employs a laser photographic process to record the unique light pattern of a diamond. Gemprints improve the chance of recovering a stolen or lost diamond, and lower the insurance premium on the diamond.

10. Shop around for diamonds. Prices may vary considerably as may commission costs (between 10 and 15 percent). Information on diamonds and other jewelry items is found in *The Wall Street Journal* and in the *Jewelers Circular-Keystone,* a trade publication.

8.3 OTHER PRECIOUS STONES

Rubies

Rubies are a rare form of aluminum oxide. Rubies range from Castilean red to purple, the various shades depending on the amount of chromium contained in the stone. The color is very important in evaluating the stone and determining the price.

Rubies are mined in Burma, Thailand, Brazil, Colombia, and Kenya. The rubies are found by digging wells and scraping through the dirt along riverbeds. The primitive mining process is due to several factors: first, it is difficult to locate underground mining areas; second, many of the rubies are found along riverbeds where the river has carried them away from their origin; and third, the miners are not organized, which reduces the efficiency of the mining process.

The worldwide supply of rubies is extremely low. Burmese rubies, the most prized, are almost completely mined; only a few fine-quality stones remain. The Ceylon, Siamese, and African rubies are also in small supply. This scarcity causes rubies to be identifiable, stone by stone. So few rubies are in circulation that dealers and experts often remember previously viewing a particular stone.

In determining the value of rubies, the four Cs are used. The color is critical in judging the origin of the stone and its fair market value. The shades of red must be remembered because there is no system of grading the color, as there is with diamonds. The Burmese ruby is the finest shade of red. This deep red, often called "pigeon's blood,"[10] is rare and commands top price. Rubies from other parts of the world are different shades of red, which range from a pinkish Ceylon ruby to a brownish African ruby. The differentiation of these colors is not always easy. Disputes over color are common as shades of some rubies approach other shades of rubies with different origins.

The number and length of inclusions in the cut stone affect the value. These inclusions can also affect the redness of the ruby. Inclusions, however, can be evaluated to distinguish rubies from spinels, which are lower in quality and value.

The carat weight of rubies is important because a ruby that weighs in excess of five carats is extremely rare. Larger rubies command much higher prices than their weight equivalent in smaller stones.

The limited supply of and the increasing demand for rubies have resulted in substantial price increases. A three-carat Burma stone which sold for $9,000 per carat in 1975 commanded a market price of $27,000 per carat by February 1981.

---

[10] **Benjamin Zucker,** *op. cit.,* p. 20.

Sapphires

Sapphires are primarily blue but can also be yellow, green, or purple. The blue is caused by iron impurities within the stone, different amounts of iron leading to various tints of blue. The tints range from gray-blue to blackish-blue.

The major source of sapphires is Ceylon, which produces stones with grayish or violet tints. Ceylon has been the major stone producer for the last 3000 years.[11] The second major source is Thailand. Some sapphires are found in Montana and Cowee Creek, North Carolina, but not on a large scale.

Mining of sapphires is similar to the mining of rubies. The gems are found in the ground and along riverbanks. Miners search for sapphires which are then purchased by merchants and shipped to a cutting center. Ceylon's government is trying to nationalize the precious stone industry in order to provide better results.

In determining value, color is again critical. In some stones the color radiates from one portion of the stone while the rest remains pale. Royal Burmese sapphires and Kashmir sapphires are the finest quality.

The inclusions and the cut also add to the value of the stone. The fewer the inclusions within the stone, the more valuable the stone is.

Sapphires are not as valuable as rubies. A fine ten-carat sapphire sold for $9,000 per carat in 1976. By Feburary 1981, the same sapphire sold for $25,000 per carat.

Emeralds

Emeralds are another aluminum oxide formation. The green tint, which is caused by chromium, varies from dark to light green. The color, which denotes the emerald's origin, has a great deal to do with the price of the stone.

The first emeralds were found in Egypt and were of lower quality than more recent discoveries. Sources of emeralds include Colombia, Russia, Austria, and India, and recent discoveries have been made in Brazil, Rhodesia, Zambia, and Afghanistan.

Mining techniques for emeralds are different from those of rubies and sapphires, since they are found imbedded in rocks rather than along river beds. This increases the price of the gems. The work is slow and must be done by hand, since any blasting will destroy the stone. Typically, emeralds discovered first are bigger and of higher quality than deeper stones, which often are not of gem investment quality.

Emeralds are usually cut into melees, which are smaller than a carat. Melees account for the bulk of trade volume because of the rarity of larger high-quality stones.

As with most colored stones, the color of an emerald is the primary price determinant. Darker and deeper green stones are of greater value. The most valuable emeralds are the Colombian ones, which are a deep green, and the Indian stones, which are a blue-green. The pale green stones from Russia and Brazil command a lower price.

The inclusions present in emeralds are more pronounced than those in rubies and sapphires, and even though they reduce the clarity of the stone, the effect on value is not as great as it would be for other colored stones. The traditional cut of an emerald is distinctive because it is cut in a rectangular form with a flat top and faceted edges.

---

[11] **Zucker**, *Op. cit.*, p. 27.

The supply of large emeralds is dwindling and there are few quality emeralds being mined today. This shortage, combined with complex mining procedures, causes emeralds to be highly valuable. Larger carat sizes are extremely rare and the suggested investment size for stones is larger than one carat.

Emerald prices have also appreciated considerably. A three-carat quality emerald sold for $12,000 per carat in 1976 and for $20,000 per carat in February 1981.

It can be said in conclusion that an investment in precious stones is risky and requires very careful study. Investors should watch for artificial gems. Chatham Created Gems, Inc., and Cerez Corporation produce artificial emeralds, rubies, sapphires, and so forth. It is the natural gems that are worth one's investable funds. Additionally, an investor must carefully consider the portfolio implications of a gem investment. Some commitment of funds to gems may reduce the riskiness of the portfolio and/or improve its rate of return.

We now look at investment in art.

8.4 INVESTMENTS IN ART

Investors' perception of the possible inadequacy of the stock market as a hedge medium against inflation sent investors looking for other alternatives. Investors turned to tangibles such as art and collectible assets. This shift has generally borne substantial fruit.

The magic of art grows by leaps and bounds as the press reports the truly incredible prices paid for certain masterpieces. The "Self-portrait: Yo Picasso" by Picasso brought $5.3 million on May 22, 1981, up from $650,000 in 1975.[12] These and other stories increase the interest in art investment and possibly the rewards derived therefrom.

The income from art is in a considerable part a psychic income. The beauty of the painting, regardless of the appreciation potential, may be all the investor desires. Since psychic income is so hard to measure and since it differs from one investor to another, we shall, therefore, concentrate on the economic income derived from collecting art.

Valuation of Paintings

The determination that a painting is "investment quality art" requires in general that the artist meets all of the following criteria: (1) be of European nationality; (2) be decreased; (3) be listed in the Benezit and/or other recognized reference books, and (4) be traded reasonably frequently on the international art market.[13] There are surely exceptions to this general rule. Living American artists like Andy Warhol, Andrew Wyeth, and Le Roy Nieman have seen many of their paintings rise in price at a phenomenal rate.

The factors that must be taken into consideration in evaluating a painting are

1. Attribution. Attribution refers to the degree of certainty concerning the authenticity of a given painting.

---

[12] The sale price is a record price for a twentieth century painting. The record for any painting is held by a nineteenth century English artist, J. M. W. Turner, for "Juliet and Her Nurse." Turner's painting sold in 1980 for $6.4 million.

[13] See **S. K. Clark**, "Fine Art: Advertising This Valuable Stock Asset." *Trusts and Estates* (March 1978).

2. Age. It is of importance for only certain paintings.

3. Condition of the piece of art.

4. Rarity. The scarcity of important works by the great masters adds tremendously to their value.

5. Provenence. Provenence includes such things as "signature of the artist or firm attributions to an artist by several scholars, appearance of the object in authoritative art historical literature, its appearance in exhibits, and its ownership by prominent collectors of the past.[14]

6. Historical interest. The association of a given work with famous names as creators or owners, or with historical events, can increase its value.[15]

7. Fashion (taste). Current fashions can increase or decrease the value of a given object, depending on whether or not it fits in with the trend.

All of these factors are reflected in the demand for and the supply of paintings. The principal sources of demand for paintings are (1) private individuals; (2) museums, which make up a large part of the total demand in the art market; (3) corporations, which represent the fastest-growing segment of demand in the art market; and (4) international art investment trusts, which pool the resources of relatively wealthy individuals to purchase expensive art works that the participants could not have afforded individually.

The main source of supply of "investment value" painting is the private collector. The reasons for private collectors to sell vary considerably. They range from boredom with the object to the desire to cash in the value of the object and realize the capital gains. Museums have increasingly become suppliers of paintings of investment value.

The interesting thing about the art market is that each new purchase lowers the supply available in the market. In most cases, a painting is held for at least two or three years before the investor realizes any appreciable gain. This restricts the supply at any point in time. In addition, many art buyers keep their collections for a lifetime purely for aesthetic enjoyment. Financial gains are of no interest. In fact, many art collectors end up donating the works of the greatest artists to museums, which effectively removes them from the open market.

The art market is a segmented market, each with its own supply and demand characteristics. The Old Masters constitute the smallest of the art markets in relation to the number of pieces sold. Traditionally, they comprised the most elegant and aristocratic field of collecting where one must be a connoisseur. In the last year only two first-level pieces were sold at auction: *The Resurrection,* by Dieric Bouts, for $3,740,000; and *Samson and Delilah* by Sir Peter Paul Rubens, for $5,400,000, the third highest price ever paid for a work of art. Only large museums, galleries, and private collectors can afford to compete in this field because skyrocketing prices have resulted from a market chasing a dwindling supply of top quality art. The second level of Old Masters, a considerably larger field, also enjoys a strong demand. They are much more affordable, with representative prices ranging between $100,000 and $200,000.

The market for Impressionist and Post-Impressionist works is also considered to be

---

[14] **James Winjun,** and **Joanne Winjum** "The Art Investment Market." *The Michigan Business Review* (November 1974), p. 313.

[15] See **S. Dorn,** *The Insider's Guide to Antiques, Art, and Collectibles.* New York: Doubleday and Co., Inc., 1974, p. 15.

highly sophisticated. Here, the majority of buyers and sellers are private collectors and galleries, and the transactions are frequently private. In this rich man's field the market is characterized as being conservative. A select handful of artists (e.g., Paul Cezanne, Pierre August Renoir, Henri Toulouse-Lautrec, Vincent Van Gogh, and Edgar Degas) have dominated this market for the past quarter century. Paintings by these artists are representative of a market for lovers of quality art who are willing to invest on the basis of personal aesthetic gain. Of the fourteen paintings sold at auction in 1980 for more than $1,000,000, ten were from the Impressionist and Post-Impressionist periods. Even so, one fourth of the offerings from these categories failed to sell.

One of the great successes in the art market has been in the demand for nineteenth century European paintings (exclusive of the Impressionists), which are characterized as "storytelling pictures." (In January 1980, record prices were set for no less than nineteen artists.) Many of these paintings originally had been purchased by American collectors from European salons. While American tastes for these works waned in favor of the Impressionists, demand for them has significantly increased among European collectors, especially those from Germany, the Netherlands, and Belgium.

Representative of twentieth century art are the Surrealist and Abstract styles of paintings. Surrealist art may be considered as a new investment alternative, which came into existence with the recent sale of the William N. Copley collection. This collection of 130 paintings, assembled from 1948 to 1968, has made the name "Copley" synonymous with the international Surrealist school. Since most of these works had not gone through the public salesroom before, there was no means of ascertaining their original costs and, therefore, their investment value.

As of yet, there are very few collectors of American contemporary art, mainly because, it would seem, of the need for a special "taste" for these works. Both Sotheby and Christie's have been unable to reach their desired level of transactions with this style. (Sotheby fell short by 37 percent in 1980, selling only 50 of 79 lots). Record prices have been set, yet this is an extremely volatile market, resulting in a high degree of risk.

Contemporary and nineteenth century American artists appear to be gaining favor with art investors. The nineteenth century Hudson River School (1860–1910) seems to be experiencing a phenomenal growth. Paintings by artists like Frederick Church and Asher B. Durand are fetching prices well over $100,000. Marine paintings of the same period by artists like J. E. Buttersworth and James Gale Tyler are fetching prices upward of $50,000. Leading impressionist painters (1890–1940) like Mary Cassatt and Theodore Robinson have had their work sell for $50,000 and over. Paintings by Western artists like Frederick Remington sold for over $100,000 in 1982. Even contemporary Western artists like Dan Bodelson and Eric Sloane have seen interest in their work rise dramatically in the last few years.

Prints of art works have become a major market in their own right, especially for investors who lack the expertise to enter the more sophisticated parent markets. This market provides opportunities for every purse, with prices of quality prints ranging from $2,000 to $150,000 over the past year. Dominanting that market have been Rembrandt, Goya, Tolouse-Lautrec, and Picasso.

The maze of investment quality paintings makes it hard, if not impossible, for a novice to determine the real quality of a painting and the reasonableness of its price. The authenticity of a work of art can be checked against its entry in a *Catalogue Raissonae*. This is a reference book that describes in detail individual works of art of a given

TABLE 8.7
The Sotheby Index®

Category	April 26	April 19	Sept. 1982	Sept. 1981
Old master paintings	212	212	199	199
19th century European paintings	185	185	183	176
Impressionist and Post-Impressionist paintings	267	267	255	239
Modern paintings (1900–1950)	245	245	245	232
American paintings (1800-pre-WW II)	452	452	459	424
Continental ceramics	266	266	266	299
Chinese ceramics	440	440	460	459
English silver	209	209	183	160
Continental silver	139	139	134	143
American furniture	239	239	213	209
French and continental furniture	239	239	234	218
English furniture	282	282	263	270
Weighted aggregate	257	257	251	244

Sept. 1975 = 100.
© 1983 Sotheby Parke Bernet Inc.

Source: Barron's, May 2, 1983.

The data reflected in the Sotheby Index are based on results of auction sales by affiliated companies of the Sotheby Parke Bernet Group and other information deemed relevant by Sotheby's. Sotheby's does not warrant the accuracy of the data reflected therein. Nothing in any commentary furnished by Sotheby's nor any of the Sotheby's Indices is intended or should be relied upon as investment advice or as a prediction, warranty or guaranty as to future performance or otherwise. All individual prices quoted in this review are aggregate prices, inclusive of the buyer's premium.

artist. Simply checking the watermark of an old print against its entry in the catalogue can often uncover a fake.[16] Specialized catalogues of auction houses like Christie's and Sotheby Parke Bernet and many reference books available at public libraries should prove invaluable in the determination of the authenticity and of the market value of a painting. For modern art pieces, an investor can rely on William Bongard's *Kunst Kompass,* which assigns points to artists and their works and helps in the determination of the reasonableness of prices.

Another source for the value of paintings (and other investments) is the "Sotheby Index" published by Sotheby Parke Bernet Group PLC of London and appearing in *Barron's* as shown in Table 8.7. The index is widely followed and is based on the latest auction returns of Sotheby and affiliated and significant enterprises.

There are two types of dealers:[17] those dealing almost exclusively with art of living artists and the others who deal in the work of dead artists as it passes from collection to collection. The latter type relies on private collections and/or on public auctions as a source of supply. Many dealers have opted, in some cases, to act as advisors for clients and earn a commission (about 10 percent) for their expertise and efforts.

[16] **R. Ricklefs,** "Tips on Collecting Art and Antiques," *The Wall Street Journal* (October 1, 1979), p. 46.

[17] See **J. R. Taylor** and **B. Brooke,** *The Art Dealers.* New York: Scribner's, 1969, p. 62.

The auction houses are playing an increasingly important role as intermediaries between buyers and sellers. The publicity that auction houses have received from the sale of major paintings has contributed to their elevation as the dominant force in the art auction market. The auction house functions strictly as a broker for objects of art that they obtain on consignment. The services provided include cataloguing the price of art, offering expert opinion on many art works, and assisting the seller in setting a reserve price. A reserve price is simply a price below which the painting will not be sold. If no one in an auction is willing to bid up to the reserve price, a representative of the house will; that is, the work is bought in. The owner will then pay a commission of 2 to 15 percent of the highest public bid.[18]

Having set the reserve price and issued the catalogue, the auction house must publicize the upcoming sale and arrange an auction preview. This preview gives prospective buyers the chance to examine and evaluate the merchandise so that they can determine their appropriate bids before the actual sale.

In return for all of the services offered by the auction house, it commonly charges a commission of 10 percent of the purchase price to both the buyer and the seller, although this percentage can vary with the value of the article. Lower fees can usually be negotiated for the costliest auction items.

The leading auction house for art in the world is Sotheby Parke Bernet PLC, which was founded in 1944. Sotheby received much coverage in the press in early 1983 when it became a takeover target by General Felt Industries, Inc. on April 12, 1983. In December 1982 General Felt bought a 14 percent interest in Sotheby. The bid for the remaining 86 percent was met with great resistance in British circles and particularly from the 133 auction experts employed by Sotheby. What prompted the move by General Felt was the poor performance by Sotheby in 1982. Sotheby lost $4.6 million on revenue of $80.5 million in 1982. About half of the total revenue came from North American interests. Americans owned about half of Sotheby's outstanding shares at the time of the takeover bid. The winner of the battle for Sotheby was A. Alfred Taubman, an American. The decision was made by Sotheby's senior art experts in September, 1983.

Advantages and Pitfalls of Investing in Paintings

There are many advantages and disadvantages to investing in paintings which investors must consider before venturing into the complex world of art.

Advantages

The advantages of art ownership are numerous and are discussed below.

High Rate of Return. Prices in the international art market for paintings doubled between 1950 and 1955, tripled from 1955 to 1960, tripled again from 1960 to 1970, and more than doubled from 1970 to 1975. The rate of return from 1960 to 1975 was 800 percent, as compared with 154 percent for the stock market.[19] An investment of

---

[18] P. Keresztes, "Collecting for Profit: Art, Antiques Market Is Booming, but Gains Can Be Illusory." *The Wall Street Journal* (March 13, 1978).

[19] S. K. Clark, "Fine Art: Administering This Fine Asset." *Trust and Estates* (March 1978), pp. 133–134.

$1,000 made in 1974 in a portfolio consisting of the composition of the Dow Jones Industrial Average would have been worth $1,333 in January 1980 for a return of 5.92 percent, whereas that same $1,000 invested in a portfolio of European nineteenth paintings would have appreciated to $2,230 for a 17.4 percent return. The potential of art is summarized in the words "Art is the currency of the infinite that never can be devalued."[20]

The rate of return on art works has consistently been higher than inflation rates, which make them an excellent hedge vehicle.

Psychological Returns. The beauty and the prestige of art provide a strong incentive for investment when compared with other investment vehicles.

Tax Advantages. The tax implications of art ownership can be placed in three categories: (1) the taxation of gains realized upon the sale of the object; (2) the tax deductions available from donating works of art to museums, colleges, or other institutions; and (3) estate taxes.

Taxation of Gains. Profits on paintings sold after a one-year holding are taxed at the long-term capital gains rate. The maximum tax is 20 percent.

In the case of losses, the distinction must be made between a "collector" and an "investor." This distinction is important because an investor can write off losses on a sale, which a collector may not. Normally, the investor must both show a reasonable profit from his investments in two out of the past five years and limit the items he buys and sells to his personal use. Commissions paid when purchasing art are not deductible by the investor at the time of purchase, but are added to the cost of the property at the time the gain or loss on its sale is determined. Likewise, commissions paid in selling property are not deductible. They are subtracted from the selling price when calculating the gain or loss on the sale. (This does not apply to dealers, who may deduct commissions as an expense.) Furthermore, if an investor becomes so good at buying and selling art that he quits his job and turns full-time to it, the Internal Revenue Service may decide that he is, for tax purposes, a dealer. In this case, gains are taxed as ordinary income.

Donations. Donations have become the most prominent form of tax shelters in art. The taxpayer acquires a work of art, holds it for at least one year and one day and then donates it to a qualified organization. The tax deduction the donor receives is equal to the fair market value at the time of donation, which is equal to the purchase price plus the interim capital appreciation. The taxpayer must be cautious in the use of this tactic, as the IRS may consider the donor to be a dealer in property (if said donor trades too frequently) and therefore disallow the amount of gain.[21]

The second sophisticated method in using art as a tax shelter is to donate partial interest in a work of art to a qualifying organization, thereby gaining the advantage of a tax shelter.

---

[20] **S. Feldman,** "From Art in Banking to Banking in Art." *The Bankers Magazine* (September 1980), p. 88.

[21] **S. Feldman,** "Tax Shelters Under Attack Again." *CPA,* (September 1980), pp. 58–59.

As an example: If you live in Palm Beach and you have a $300,000 Monet, you can donate a third of the painting to a museum, stipulating that the museum will have possessory interest for one third of the year. In Palm Beach you might let the museum have the painting for the summer months when, of course, you will be in Newport or the Riviera. [22]

Incidentally, the museum's insurance would cover the Monet for the period during which it has possession, thus reducing your personal household expenses to some extent.

Estate Taxes.   Prior to 1976, when an asset passed from one owner to another at death, it took on a new tax basis—its market value at the time of the owner's death. Under the new tax law, the basis is the value at the end of 1976 (or the cost of acquisition if acquired after 1976). This means that, when the heir sells the asset, he will have to pay tax on any post-1976 appreciation. In addition, the estate will have to pay estate taxes on the market value of the item. The tax considerations are based on a new unified schedule which increases, under the Economic Recovery Tax Act of 1981, the size of the estate that is exempt from tax to $600,000 by 1987. The schedule also reduces the maximum estate tax rate to 50 percent by 1985.

The effect of this new taxing method is likely to snowball with time and inflation, since post-1976 appreciation will make up an ever-increasing proportion of the objects market value. Therefore, the larger the original cost can be documented to be, the less the capital gain on which taxes will eventually be paid.

Because of the tax laws, it will become increasingly cheaper to sell appreciated art and antiques rather than to leave them in an estate. But, if owners are determined to keep their collections within the family, lifetime gifts can still create tax savings. The $10,000 yearly gift tax exclusion ($20,000 for married couples) can be taken advantage of. This means that, for example, a husband and wife can give up to $20,000 a year in cash or goods to as many individuals as they wish, usually without subjecting the value of the gifts to any gift or estate taxes. However, the value of the gifts made within three years of death will be included in the dead donor's taxable estate.

Pitfalls

There are many pitfalls in investing in paintings that no investor can afford to overlook. Among them are high transaction and ownership costs and doubtful liquidity.

High transaction and ownership costs.   The costs at the time of purchase include sales tax, appraisal fee, research costs, packing costs, and commissions or fees. During the ownership period, the costs incurred include insurance, cleaning and repair, research, storage (on occasion), and the foregone periodic income the investor could have earned from financial assets in the form of dividends or interest.

The selling costs include commission fees, advertisements, photographs, price guides, auction catalogues, appraisal fees, telephone and postage costs, packing and repair or refinishing to improve sales appeal.

Liquidity?   Many collectors' items cannot be turned into cash as easily as securities. Finding the right buyer can take months, and during that time the value may change as tastes and fashions change.

---

[22] G. Mahon, "Investing in Art." *Barron's* (July 16, 1979).

CONCLUSIONS

The investment vehicles discussed in this chapter do not exhaust the list of investment opportunities. Investors have found stamps, antique autos, photographs, etchings, lithographs, silk-screened works, antique rugs, antique furniture, Chinese ceramics, African ivory, and other vehicles to be very attractive and financially rewarding.

The broad issues and warning signals offered here are quite translatable, however, to many of the aforementioned vehicles and should assist the investor in making enlightened decisions. A complete discussion of each and every investment vehicle is far beyond the scope of this book. However, one cannot overstate the risks involved in all of these investment vehicles. The rewards are there; but they are realized by those who *very carefully* study these markets. The novice can be very easily taken advantage of.

QUESTIONS

1. Discuss the factors that contribute to the conclusion that the supply of diamonds is quite stable.

2. Identify and discuss the four Cs of diamond evaluation.

3. Describe the characteristics of an investment grade diamond.

4. Why are portfolio managers diversifying into diamonds and other hard assets? What factors must they be careful to take into consideration when making such an investment decision?

5. Discuss the advantages and disadvantages of investing in paintings.

6. "The certification process is a *perfect* way to *guarantee* the quality of the diamond." Comment.

7. What are the pitfalls of investments in diamond?

8. How will the improving technology of manufacturing artificial diamond affect the diamond market? Submarkets? Why?

9. When would an investor consider a diamond investment despite the knowledge that its rate of return is lower than that of any other available investment.

10. The monopoly of DeBeers over the diamond market is no longer slipping. Is this a good or a bad sign for the individual investor?

11. State precisely how diamonds can be used to reduce the investor's tax burden.

12. What must an investor look for in a painting?

13. "The role played by firms like Sotheby and Christie in auctioning art is similar to that of an exchange (like the stock exchange)." Comment.

14. How do you see diamonds, objects of art, and other precious objects fitting in a portfolio of various types of investors (in terms of income levels, taste, and background)?

CHAPTER 9 | Gold and Gold Futures

9.1 A BRIEF HISTORICAL PERSPECTIVE

The history of gold is replete with political, economic, military, and personal accounts and events. Gold played an important role in the economic life of nations as early as the 6th century B.C. King Croesus of Lydia (modern day western Turkey) minted pure gold coins to be used as currency, ending the barter system of trading. For 3500 years gold and silver coins served as the basis for the monetary system of nations.

The movement away from gold currency toward gold-backed paper currency began in 1717 when Sir Isaac Newton, the Master of Mint in England, fixed the value of the pound sterling at 0.24 ounces of gold. This marked the beginning of the age of the gold standard which lasted 200 years. The United States adopted the gold coin standard in 1834. The value of currencies in circulation was tied to the amount of gold in the country's coffers. The international economic order was characterized during that period by free trade and free convertibility from paper into gold.

The full gold standard was followed by the gold-bullion standard when nations redeemed their paper currency with gold bullion. The gold bullion standard was different from the gold coin standard in that it only had one coin; a 400-ounce ingot of gold.

World War I, the great depression, and a combination of other factors shocked the financial systems worldwide and a new system for international payment settlement emerged. It was dubbed the gold-exchange standard. Under this new standard international settlements were made in dollars or in gold. The value of the dollar was set in terms of gold (35 dollars to an ounce of gold). In 1933 the right of American citizens to hold gold was revoked, thus turning the convertibility of dollars into gold into a privilege granted only to nations and foreign nationals.

The Bretton Woods conference in 1944 strengthened the gold exchange standard and the role of the dollar. The U.S. dollar became the standard value against which other currencies were measured and was convertible into gold at $35 an ounce.

The new international monetary order worked with considerable success for a period, but began to show signs of weakness in the late 1960s. In 1968 a two-tier gold pricing system was adopted, fixing the official price of gold at $35 and allowing the market system to determine the price of gold for consumers and industrial users.

The persisting balance of payments deficits experienced by the United States in the late 1960s and the early 1970s led to two devaluations of the dollar in terms of gold, namely, in the spring of 1971 (to 1/38th of an ounce of gold) and in February 1973 (to 1/42nd of an ounce of gold). President Richard Nixon ended the convertibility of the dollar into gold on August 15, 1971. No one could convert dollars into gold any longer. The year 1973 ushered in the flexible exchange rate system where the market system determines the price of currencies in terms of others.

The 1970's witnessed the emergence of Special Drawing Rights (SDRs) as an alternative international currency. SDRs, referred to as paper gold, are a synthetic currency, created by the IMF in 1968, consisting of entries on its books. The value of an SDR is currently determined in relation to five currencies: the dollar (42 percent), the German mark (19 percent), the Japanese yen (13 percent), the French franc (13 percent), and the British pound (13 percent). SDRs are allocated to IMF member countries in accordance with each country's quota with the IMF. The United States has the lion's share.

The abandonment of the gold standard and the adoption of the flexible exchange rate system did not really end the official role of gold. The European Currency Unit (ECU), a grid of nine European currencies, is backed by gold and is convertible into the metal. Because of this vestige of the gold standard, no country in the world has decided to sell (voluntarily) every ounce of gold it owns because of the international "irrelevance" of gold. At the end of August 1981 the world's "official gold stock amounted to nearly $500 billion."[1]

Gold, as we discuss later in this chapter, has many other uses beside the official use. Gold has fascinated man since the days of the Egyptian Pharaohs. Ornaments placed in Egyptian tombs in 2500 B.C. were still in perfect shape when discovered in the twentieth century. In addition to its indestructible nature, gold is nonrusting, malleable, ductile, and has a low melting point and high density. Gold is also beautiful and has been valued for centuries as a symbol of love, security, and wealth. A close examination of Table 9.1 reveals a great deal about the history of gold both on the demand and on the supply side.

We now discuss the nature and the composition of the supply of gold.

9.2 THE SUPPLY OF GOLD

The nondestructible nature of gold makes its supply cumulative. Some claim that the first ounce of gold mined is still around somewhere, perhaps in the bottom of an ocean. In fact, of the 1182 metric tons of gold supplied in 1981, 197 metric tons, or 17 percent of the world supply, were from scrap recovery. The source of this scrap was new scrap—gold resulting from various production processes—and old scrap—previously fabricated gold being melted down.

Much of the gold supply is hoarded by governments, by industry, or by individuals. The world's private gold holdings are estimated to equal 50 to 150 percent of the $500 billion held by official institutions as of August 1981.[2]

Hoarding or rather dishoarding is only one source of gold supply. As Table 9.2 shows, dishoarding is an unstable source of supply and can at times be a significant one. In 1980 dishoarding accounted for 20.33 percent of world supply. The primary

---

[1] **Henry C. Wallich,** "The Financial System: Gold and the Dollar." *Commodity Journal* (March–April 1982), p. 12.

[2] *Ibid,* **Wallich,** p. 12.

TABLE 9.1
World Production, Distribution, and Stocks of Gold, 1800–1980
(Metric Tons)

For Decade Ending	(1) Cumulative World Mine Production	(2) Increment in World Mine Production	(3) Monetary Stock	(4) Increment in Monetary Stock	(5) Official Reserves	(6) Increment in Official Reserves
1800	3,515.4					
1810	3,697.4	182.0	1,203.4			
1820	3,816.2	118.8	1,297.4	94.0		
1830	3,961.7	145.5	1,399.1	101.7		
1840	4,166.1	204.4	1,449.1	50.0		
1850	4,698.6	532.5	1,691.8	242.7		
1860	6,706.7	2,008.1	3,184.8	1,493.0		
1870	8,607.2	1,900.5	4,089.6	904.8		
1880	10,367.0	1,759.8	4,729.4	639.8	1,505.4	
1890	11,996.3	1,629.3	5,295.8	566.4		
1900	15,156.8	3,160.5	7,274.7	1,978.9	3,732.5	
1910	20,899.2	5,742.4	10,636.1	3,361.4	6,320.4	2,587.9
1920	27.318.5	6,419.3	14,475.6	3,839.5	10,917.6	4,597.2
1930	33,109.2	5,790.7	18,299.5	3,823.9	16,469.7	5,552.1
1940	42,927.8	9,818.6			26,059.1	9,589.4
1950	51,814.0	8,886.2			33,570.8	7,511.7
1960	61,593.8	9,779.8			37,950.2	4,379.4
1970	75,600.0	14,006.2			38,311.0	360.8
1980	88,847.9	13,247.9			37,471.2	− 839.8

Source: Above-Ground Stocks of Gold, Amounts and Distribution, International Gold Corporation, October, 1982, pp. 4–5.

Note:

e = ECS estimate

Source by Column

[1] Statistical Compendium of *The Report to the Congress of the Commission on the Role of Gold in the Domestic and International Monetary Systems* (Gold Commission Report), March 1982, Table SC-6, pp. 195–196. Includes Soviet mine production.

[2] Calculated from (1).

[3] Monetary gold stock includes both official gold reserves and bank and nonbank holdings of gold coins.
 1810–1910 Statistical Compendium of the *Gold Commission Report*. Table SC-7, p. 198.
 1920–1930 League of Nations *Interim Report of the Gold Delegation of the Financial Committee* (Geneva, 1930) Table B, pp. 82–84 (converted from monetary pounds to ounces by dividing by 4 2287 pounds per fine ounce).

[4] Calculated from (3).

[5] These figures represent physical gold in the form of bullion or coin, held either at home or abroad by central banks and governments and international organizations. All the estimates include Soviet reserves.
 1880–1900: Estimates from *Short-Term Capital Movements Under the Pre-1914 Gold Standard* by Arthur I. Bloomfield Princeton Studies in International Finance, No. 11, 1963, p. 15. Estimates are actually given for 1880 and 1903. Our 1900 figure (120.0 million ounces) is estimated from Bloomfield's 1903 figure of $2.6 billion 125.8 million ounces).
 1910 Estimate from *Key Currencies and Gold: 1900–1913* by Peter H. Lindert, Princeton Studies in International Finance, No. 24, 1969, p. 25.
 1920–1980: Estimates from Statistical Compendium of the *Gold Commission Report* Table SC-8, p. 199, compiled from *Banking and Monetary Statistics 1914–1941, 1941–1970* Board of Governors of the Federal Reserve System, pp. 544–48 and pp. 913–22, from *International Financial Statistics,* IMF; and *Gold Statistics and Analysis,* Dec. 1981/Jan. 1982, J. Aron & Co.

(7) Cumulative Absorption in Fabricated Products	(8) Increment in Absorption in Fabricated Products	(9) Residual Coin and Bullion in Private Hands (1)-(5)-(7)	(10) Increment in Residual	(11) Accumulation of Gold in Karat Jewelry Since 1900	(12) Increment in Jewelry Holdings	(13) Percentage Change in Real Gold Price From Beginning to End of Decade
2,493.9						− 1.51
2,518.8	24.9					+ 23.47
2,562.7	43.9					+ 16.46
2,717.0	154.3					+ 2.16
3,006.8	289.8					+ 6.63
3,521.9	515.1					− 4.68
4,517.6	995.7					− 20.75
5,637.6	1,120.0	3,224.0				+ 17.27
6,700.5	1,062.9					+ 22.08
7,882.1	1,181.6	3,542.2		141.2		+ 0.34
10,263.1	2,381.0	4,315.7	773.5	2,227.4	2,086.2	− 20.39
12,842.9	2,579.8	3,558.0	− 757.7	4,451.3	2,223.9	− 54.46
14,809.6	1,966.7	1,829.9	−1,728.1	6,655.4	2,204.1	+ 78.75
15,450.4	640.8	1,418.3	− 411.6	7,090.2	434.8	+ 86.45
16,485.8	1,035.4	1,757.4	339.1	8,200.9	1,110.7	− 50.49
21,441.7	4,955.9	2,201.9	444.5	12,376.7	4,175.8	− 13.81
32,060.7	10,619.0	5,228.3	3,026.4	20,745.3	8,368.6	− 11.74
41,485.2	9,424.5	9,891.5	4,663.2	27,351.2	6,605.9	+601.81

The Federal Reserve series was used for all years except 1980, for which the IMF estimate was used. Soviet reserves were not reported from 1918 to 1921, but they were probably minimal as of 1920 as gold was sold to finance the war effort reported Soviet reserves in 1922 were only $2.6 million (125,786 troy oz). The last time Soviet reserves were reported was September 1935. This figure ($838.3 million—24 million ounces) was included as an estimate in the 1940 total. From 1950–1980, J. Aron's estimates of Soviet reserves were added to the Gold Commission statistics to reach a total.

[6] Calculated from (5).

[7] Net absorption of gold in *all* fabricated products.

1810–1930: Cumulative figures derived as difference between cumulative production in (1) and monetary stocks in (3). Increments calculated from these figures.

1940–1950: Estimates of increments from *Annual Reports of the Director of the Mint*, U.S. Treasury Department, various years. Increments then added to update cumulative total.

1960–1980: Increments from *Gold Statistics and Analysis.* Dec. 1981/Jan. 1982, J. Aron & Co.; figures for jewelry and industrial demand from 1950–1968 include coins and medallions, so estimates of official gold coinage for these years from *Gold Coins,* Federal Coin & Currency, Inc., Switzerland, 1973 were subtracted. Increments added to update cumulative total.

[8] Calculated from (7).

[9] Residual = Cumulative World Mine Production (1) minus Official Reserves (5) minus Cumulative Absorption in Fabricated Products (7). This column represents the theoretical maximum amount of gold coin and bullion held by private individuals and banks.

[10] Calculated from (9).

[11] This is a subset of column (7), absorption in fabricated products. It represents holdings of karat jewelry in private hands which are considered potentially accessible to the market.

[12] Calculated from (11).

[13] Calculated from Statistical Compendium of the *Gold Commission Report.* Table SC-16, pp. 219–223, in which the real price of gold is calculated using the United States wholesale price index, with 1967 = 100.

TABLE 9.2
Gold: The Supply-Demand Picture

Tonnes Supplies	1980	1979	Offtake	1980	1979
Non-Communist world					
production	960	968	Investment	655	505
Of which South			Of which official		
Africa	(675)	(703)	purchases[a]	(425)	(126)
Soviet sales	80	230	Coin manufacture	225	280
IMF sales	69	173	Of which krugerrand	(98)	(153)
Other official sales	86	464	Jewelry	400	700
Of which US	—	(365)	Industrial use	220	260
Gross dishoarding	305	—	Other	—	90
	1,500	1,835		1,500	1,835

[a] Includes retentions of gold production by South Africa and other non-Communist producers
Source: Samuel Montagu and *The Banker,* May 1981.

and more reliable source of supply of gold are South African mines which consistently provide more than 50 percent of the world gold output (see Table 9.3). The second largest supplier of gold in the world markets is the Soviet Union, which accounts for an estimated 25 percent of the world supply. The Soviet Union produced 300 million metric tons in 1981 and accounted for most of the 283 metric tons net sales by communist countries in the world markets. The Soviet Union does not release production data, which explains the reasons for inferring production data from sales data. The 300 million metric tons figure is the best estimate of Consolidated Gold Fields PLC.

The supply of gold by the Soviet Union is quite unpredictable. It is largely a function of their political commitments overseas and their need for food imports. In the summer of 1981, after a complete absence from the market, which lasted approximately 9 months, the Soviet Union suddenly sold 100 tons of gold in four weeks at an average price of $425. It is estimated that Russia sold between 70 and 100 tons of gold in 1980 and approximately 200 metric tons in 1981.

The sale of Soviet gold is effected by Moscow's Zurich-based bullion-marketing subsidiary, Wozchod Handelsbank. The Soviet subsidiary engages often in simultaneous buy and sell transactions and in "location swaps" (delivering one quality of gold in one market and taking delivery of a different quality of gold in another market) in order to confuse market observers as to its intentions and the net size of its transactions.

The Soviet Union markets its gold directly, mainly in Zurich and London, but occasionally uses gold dealers to sell its gold. The South Africans, on the other hand, primarily use Zurich banks who are always ready to buy gold. The Russians cooperate with the South Africans in the management of gold supply in the world markets.

The country that holds the third rank in gold production is Canada, followed by Brazil and the Philippines. Canada's output is approximately 5 percent of world output. (see Table 9.3.)

The South African gold production is controlled by the Chamber of Mines of South Africa (CMSA), which has controlled gold production in South Africa since the 1930s. In addition, CMSA controls the operating policies of member mines, labor practices, refining methods and extent, and the marketing of gold. Its practices are intended to

TABLE 9.3
Gold Mine Production in the Non-Communist World
(Metric tons)

	1971	1972	1973	1974	1975	1976	1977	1978	1979	1980	1981
South Africa	976.3	909.6	855.2	758.6	713.4	713.4	699.9	706.4	705.4	675.1	657.6
Canada	68.7	64.7	60.0	52.2	51.4	52.4	54.0	54.0	51.1	50.6	49.5
USA	46.4	45.1	36.2	35.1	32.4	32.2	32.0	30.2	30.2	27.6	40.6
Other Africa:											
Ghana	21.7	22.5	25.0	19.1	16.3	16.6	16.9	14.2	11.5	12.8	13.6
Zimbabwe	15.0	15.6	15.6	18.6	18.6	17.1	20.0	17.0	12.0	11.4	11.6
Other	2.5	1.7	1.7	1.5	1.5	1.5	1.5	2.0	2.5	8.0	12.0
Zaire	5.4	2.5	2.5	4.4	3.6	4.0	3.0	1.0	2.3	3.0	3.2
Total Other Africa	44.6	42.3	44.8	43.6	40.0	39.2	41.4	34.2	28.3	35.2	40.4
Latin America:											
Brazil	9.0	9.5	11.0	13.8	12.5	13.6	15.9	22.0	25.0	35.0	35.0
Colombia	5.9	6.3	6.7	8.2	10.8	10.3	9.2	9.0	10.0	17.0	17.7
Dominican Republic	—	—	—	—	3.0	12.7	10.7	10.8	11.0	11.5	12.8
Chile	8.2	9.0	3.2	3.7	4.1	3.0	3.0	3.3	4.3	6.5	11.4
Other	3.0	2.6	4.7	2.2	1.9	5.0	5.0	5.2	4.2	3.5	5.4
Peru	4.7	4.6	2.6	2.7	2.9	3.0	3.4	3.9	4.7	5.0	7.2
Mexico	3.3	2.8	4.2	3.9	4.7	5.4	6.7	6.2	5.5	5.9	5.0
Nicaragua			2.8	2.4	1.9	2.0	2.0	2.3	1.9	1.5	1.6
Total Latin America	34.1	34.8	35.2	36.9	41.8	55.0	55.9	62.7	66.6	85.9	96.1
Asia:											
Philippines	19.7	18.9	18.1	17.3	16.1	16.3	19.4	20.2	19.1	22.0	24.9
Japan	8.2	7.8	6.2	4.5	4.7	4.5	4.8	4.7	4.2	3.4	3.1
India	3.7	3.3	3.3	3.2	3.0	3.3	2.9	2.8	2.7	2.6	2.6
Other	2.1	2.7	2.7	2.7	2.7	3.0	3.0	3.0	3.0	3.0	3.8
Total Asia	33.7	32.7	30.3	27.7	26.5	27.1	30.1	30.7	29.0	31.0	34.5
Europe	7.6	13.2	14.3	11.6	11.0	11.4	13.2	12.5	10.0	8.6	8.5
Oceania:											
Papua/New Guinea	0.7	12.7	20.3	20.5	17.9	20.5	22.3	23.4	19.7	14.3	17.2
Australia	20.9	23.5	17.2	16.2	16.3	15.4	19.2	20.1	18.3	17.0	16.2
Other	2.8	3.2	2.8	2.2	2.2	2.3	1.8	1.1	1.0	1.0	1.1
Total Oceania	24.4	39.4	40.3	38.9	36.4	38.2	43.3	44.6	39.0	32.3	34.5
Total	1235.8	1181.8	1116.3	1004.6	952.9	968.9	969.8	975.3	959.6	946.3	961.6

Source: Consolidated Gold Fields PLC, *Gold 1982*, May 1982, p. 16.

TABLE 9.4
Gold Fabrication and Net Changes in Investment Holdings
(Metric tons)

	1971	1972	1973	1974	1975	1976	1977	1978	1979	1980	1981
A. Total gold bullion supply	1386	1244	1397	1245	1111	1439	1640	1747	1703	806	985
Fabricated gold in developed countries											
Carat jewellery	553	702	428	278	317	471	540	593	552	273	373
Electronics	86	105	126	91	66	75	76	88	97	84	84
Dentistry	59	61	64	54	58	73	78	85	82	60	61
Other industrial/ decorative uses	62	65	67	64	55	59	59	71	71	66	62
Medals, medallions and fake coins	33	32	19	12	10	20	22	21	16	18	13
Official coins	44	44	36	209	221	145	125	256	242	170	151
B. Total	837	1009	740	708	727	843	900	1114	1060	671	744
Fabricated gold in developing countries											
Carat jewellery	511	297	90	−54	206	464	463	415	186	−150	221
Electronics	—	—	1	1	1	1	1	2	2	2	1
Dentistry	4	5	4	3	4	4	4	4	4	2	1
Other industrial/ decorative uses	6	5	4	3	4	4	5	7	6	4	4
Medals, medallions and fake coins	20	10	3	−4	11	31	30	30	18	−2	15
Official coins	10	19	18	78	30	37	17	31	48	15	50
C. Total	551	336	120	27	256	541	520	489	264	−129	292
D. Total fabricated gold (B + C)	1388	1345	860	735	983	1384	1420	1603	1324	542	1036
E. Bullion holdings* (A–D)	−2	−101	537	510	128	55	220	144	379	264	−51

Source: Gold 1982, Consolidated Gold Fields PLC, p. 32.

* This category excludes coins, but includes hoarding of bars and all other forms of bullion investment.

preserve the integrity of the gold market as well as the long-run political and economic interests of South Africa. The selling arm of South African gold is the South African Reserve Bank.

The other source of gold supply is the occasional sale by official institutions. The International Monetary Fund began selling its gold holdings from members' quotas in 1978. Its sale program ended in May 1980. The sale of gold bullions by the U.S. government ended earlier, in November 1979. No government today seems ready to dispose of the nation's heirloom. The trend, however, appears to be moving in the direction of selling official gold holdings in the form of gold coins minted by the government. We shall discuss some of the popular official coins later in the chapter.

It can be concluded, therefore, that the understanding of gold supply factors requires careful scrutiny of Russian and South African production and sales strategies. The prevailing gold prices, world economic conditions, world political stability, and the Russian and South African internal and external policy requirements must also be carefully watched in order to understand the factors influencing gold supply, as we shall demonstrate later in this chapter.

9.3 THE DEMAND FOR GOLD

The world demand for gold may be broken down into four—although overlapping—categories: investment demand, coin demand, jewelry demand, and industrial demand. Table 9.2 shows that about 44 percent of the gold sold in 1980 was used as an investment vehicle for individuals or as a security blanket for the treasuries of many nations. The distribution of fabricated gold for developed and developing countries across the various industries appears in Table 9.4. The table makes clear that the jewelry industry dominates the worldwide fabricated use of gold, followed by the minting of official coins. The demand for jewelry is a function of gold prices, income levels, and of cultural factors. The distribution of the supply and the demand for gold on the U.S. level appears in Table 9.5. Once again the use for jewelry is dominant, followed closely by the industrial use where the U.S. electronics industry dominates.

TABLE 9.5
Salient U.S. Gold Statistics
(In thousands of troy ounces)

Year	Mine Production	Value Mil. $	Refinery Prod. New (Domestic)	Secondary	Exports²	General Imports²	Stocks Dec. 31 Treas. Dept.	Futures Exch.	Industrial	Dental	Consumption Industrial³	Jewelry & Arts	Total	Price $ Per Troy Oz.⁴
1969	1,733	71.9	1,717	2,920	338	5,861			4,158	710	2,560	3,839	7,109	41.51
1970	1,743	63.4	1,750	2,780	1,074	6,652			3,984	658	1,975	3,340	5,973	36.41
1971	1,495	61.7	1,437	2,202	1,339	7,201			4,375	750	1,884	4,299	6,933	41.25
1972	1,450	85.0	1,478	2,107	1,472	6,126			4,407	750	2,191	4,344	7,285	58.60
1973	1,176	115.0	1,210	1,779	2,985	3,845			4,498	679	2,577	3,473	6,729	97.81
1974	1,127	180.0	1,021	1,926	3,963	2,651			5,670	509	1,740	2,402	4,651	161.08
1975	1,052	169.9	1,093	2,696	3,496	2,662	275	530	788	595	1,059	2,080	3,993	161.49
1976	1,048	131.3	954	2,504	3,531	2,656	275	320	928	694	1,233	2,562	4,648	125.32
1977	1,100	163.2	956	2,454	8,671	4,454	278	1,835	1,976	728	1,209	2,658	4,863	148.31
1978	999	193.3	962	3,085	5,509	4,690	276	2,752	1,672	706	1,313	2,651	4,738	193.55
1979	970	298.3	795	2,883	16,499	4,630	265	2,473	868	646	1,406	2,688	4,785	307.50
1980¹	951	582.8	773	3,824	6,119	4,542	264	4,998	872	341	1,287	1,505	3,215	612.56
1981⁵	1,304		801	3,288	6,438	4,652	264	2,449	571	272	1,226	1,641	3,161	459.64

Source: Bureau of Mines in 1982 Commodity Year Book, Commodity Research Bureau, Inc., New York, p. 156.

¹ Preliminary ² Excludes coinage. ³ Including space & defense ⁴ Engelhard selling quotations. ⁵ Estimate.

TABLE 9.6
Gold Reserves
(End of Period, Millions of Fine Troy Ounces)

Country or Area	1973	1974	1975	1976	1977	1978	1979	80Q3	80Q4	81Q1	81Q2	81Q3	81Q4
World	1017.0	1015.5	1014.3	1009.5	1024.4	1027.1	934.95	935.98	937.54	939.03	939.13	940.13	936.94
Afghanistan	0.93	0.93	0.93	0.93	0.94	0.95	0.96	0.96	0.96	0.96	0.96	0.96	0.96
Algeria	5.47	5.47	5.47	5.47	5.50	5.53	5.58	5.58	5.58	5.58	5.58	5.58	5.58
Argentina	4.00	4.00	4.00	4.00	4.18	4.28	4.37	4.37	4.37	4.37	4.37	4.37	4.37
Australia	7.37	7.38	7.38	7.36	7.65	7.79	7.93	7.93	7.93	7.93	7.93	7.93	7.93
Austria	20.88	20.88	20.88	20.88	20.99	21.05	21.11	21.11	21.11	21.11	21.11	21.11	21.11
Bahamas	—	—	—	—	0.01	0.01	0.02	0.00	0.00	0.00	0.00	0.00	0.00
Bahrain	0.24	0.24	0.15	0.15	0.15	0.15	0.15	0.15	0.15	0.15	0.15	0.15	0.15
Bangladesh	—	—	—	—	0.05	0.03	0.05	0.05	0.05	0.05	0.05	0.05	0.05
Belgium	42.17	42.17	42.17	42.17	42.45	42.59	34.21	34.18	34.18	34.18	34.18	34.18	34.18
Benin	—	—	—	0.00	0.01	0.01	0.01	0.01	0.01	0.01	0.01	0.01	0.01
Bolivia	0.41	0.41	0.41	0.41	0.60	0.64	0.68	0.75	0.76	0.78	0.80	0.82	0.83
Brazil	1.33	1.33	1.33	1.33	1.51	1.61	1.70	1.81	1.88	1.95	2.02	2.08	2.20
Burma	0.20	0.20	0.20	0.20	0.23	0.24	0.25	0.25	0.25	0.25	0.25	0.25	0.25
Burundi	0.00	0.00	0.00	0.00	0.01	0.01	0.01	0.02	0.02	0.02	0.02	0.02	0.02
Canada	21.95	21.95	21.95	21.61	22.01	22.13	22.18	21.11	20.98	20.92	20.91	20.75	20.46
Central African Rep.	—	—	—	0.00	0.01	0.01	0.01	0.01	0.01	0.01	0.01	0.01	0.01
Chad	—	—	—	0.00	0.01	0.01	0.01	0.01	0.01	0.01	0.01	0.01	0.01
Chile	1.38	1.44	1.30	1.34	1.36	1.39	1.52	1.69	1.70	1.70	1.70	1.70	1.70
China	—	—	—	—	12.80	12.80	12.80	12.80	12.80	12.80	12.80	12.80	12.70
Colombia	0.43	0.43	1.13	1.41	1.73	1.96	2.32	2.79	2.79	3.05	3.11	3.25	3.37
Congo	—	—	—	0.00	0.01	0.01	0.01	0.01	0.01	0.01	0.01	0.01	0.01
Costa Rica	0.06	0.06	0.06	0.06	0.07	0.08	0.09	0.09	0.09	0.09	0.00	0.01	0.03
Cyprus	0.43	0.43	0.43	0.43	0.44	0.44	0.46	0.46	0.46	0.46	0.46	0.46	0.46

Democratic Yemen	0.02	0.02	0.02	0.02	0.03	0.03	0.04	0.04	0.04	0.04	0.04	0.04	0.04
Denmark	1.81	1.81	1.81	1.92	1.98	1.64	1.63	1.63	1.63	1.63	1.63	1.63	1.63
Dominican Republic	0.09	0.09	0.09	0.10	0.10	0.11	0.12	0.13	0.13	0.13	0.13	0.13	0.14
Ecuador	0.39	0.39	0.39	0.40	0.41	0.41	0.41	0.41	0.41	0.41	0.41	0.41	0.41
Egypt	2.43	2.43	2.43	2.43	2.47	2.47	2.43	2.43	2.43	2.43	2.43	2.43	2.43
El Salvador	0.49	0.49	0.49	0.50	0.50	0.51	0.52	0.52	0.52	0.52	0.52	0.52	0.52
Ethiopia	0.26	0.27	0.27	0.29	0.29	0.29	0.31	0.31	0.26	0.26	0.26	0.26	0.26
Fiji	—	—	—	0.01	0.01	0.01	0.01	0.01	0.01	0.01	0.01	0.01	0.01
Finland	0.82	0.82	0.82	0.90	0.94	0.99	0.99	0.99	0.99	0.99	0.99	0.99	1.27
France	100.91	100.93	100.93	101.67	101.99	81.92	81.85	81.85	81.85	81.85	81.85	81.85	81.85
Gabon	—	—	—	0.01	0.01	0.01	0.01	0.01	0.01	0.01	0.01	0.01	0.01
Germany, Fed. Rep.	117.61	117.61	117.61	118.29	118.64	95.25	95.18	95.18	95.18	95.18	95.18	95.18	95.18
Ghana	0.16	0.16	0.16	0.20	0.22	0.22	0.24	0.25	0.28	0.25	0.27	0.27	0.31
Greece	3.50	3.61	3.63	3.73	3.77	3.81	3.83	3.83	3.84	3.84	3.85	3.85	3.85
Guatemala	0.49	0.49	0.49	0.51	0.51	0.52	0.52	0.52	0.52	0.52	0.52	0.52	0.52
Haiti	0.00	0.00	0.00	0.01	0.01	0.02	0.02	0.02	0.02	0.02	0.02	0.02	0.02
Honduras	0.00	0.00	0.00	0.01	0.01	0.01	0.02	0.02	0.02	0.02	0.02	0.02	0.02
Iceland	0.03	0.03	0.03	0.04	0.04	0.05	0.05	0.05	0.05	0.05	0.05	0.05	0.05
India	6.95	6.95	6.95	7.36	8.36	8.56	8.56	8.59	8.59	8.59	8.59	8.59	8.59
Indonesia	0.06	0.06	0.06	0.17	0.22	0.28	1.79	2.39	2.78	3.10	3.10	3.10	3.10
Iran (Islamic Rep. of)	3.74	3.74	3.74	3.78	3.82	3.90	—	—	—	—	—	—	—
Iraq	4.10	4.10	4.10	4.14	—	—	—	—	—	—	—	—	—
Israel	1.10	1.10	1.10	1.16	1.17	1.23	1.17	1.19	1.22	1.20	1.19	1.19	1.19
Italy	82.48	82.48	82.48	82.91	83.12	66.71	66.67	66.67	66.67	66.67	66.67	66.67	66.67
Ivory Coast	—	—	0.00	0.02	0.03	0.04	0.04	0.04	0.04	0.04	0.04	0.04	0.04
Jamaica	—	—	—	0.01	0.00	0.01	0.00	0.00	0.00	0.00	0.00	0.00	0.00
Japan	21.11	21.11	21.11	21.62	23.97	24.23	24.23	24.23	24.23	24.23	24.23	24.23	24.23
Jordan	0.80	0.80	0.80	0.81	0.81	0.82	0.97	1.02	1.05	1.05	1.05	1.07	1.07
Kenya	0.00	0.00	0.00	0.02	0.07	0.08	0.08	0.08	0.08	0.08	0.08	0.08	0.08

For general note and footnotes, see end of table.

TABLE 9.6 *(Continued)*

Country or Area	1973	1974	1975	1976	1977	1978	1979	80Q3	80Q4	81Q1	81Q2	81Q3	81Q4
Korea, Republic of	0.11	0.11	0.11	0.11	0.15	0.27	0.29	0.30	0.30	0.30	0.30	0.30	0.30
Kuwait	2.85	3.50	3.99	5.58	2.51	2.52	2.54	2.54	2.54	2.54	2.54	2.54	2.54
Lebanon	9.22	9.21	9.21	9.21	9.22	9.22	9.22	9.22	9.22	9.22	9.22	9.22	9.22
Libyan Arab Jamah	2.44	2.44	2.44	2.44	2.45	2.45	2.46	2.67	3.08	3.52	3.54	3.58	3.58
Malawi	—	—	—	—	0.01	0.01	0.01	0.01	0.01	0.01	0.01	0.01	0.01
Malaysia	1.66	1.66	1.66	1.66	1.74	1.89	2.13	2.29	2.32	2.33	2.33	2.33	2.33
Mali	—	—	—	—	0.01	0.01	0.02	0.02	0.02	0.02	0.02	0.02	0.02
Malta	0.35	0.35	0.35	0.35	0.36	0.36	0.37	0.40	0.43	0.43	0.45	0.45	0.46
Mauritania	—	—	—	—	0.01	0.01	0.01	0.01	0.01	0.01	0.01	0.01	0.01
Mauritius	—	—	—	—	0.01	0.03	0.04	0.04	0.04	0.04	0.04	0.04	0.04
Mexico	4.63	3.66	3.66	1.60	1.75	1.89	1.98	2.05	2.06	2.17	2.13	2.25	2.26
Morocco	0.60	0.61	0.61	0.61	0.63	0.68	0.70	0.70	0.70	0.70	0.70	0.70	0.70
Nepal	0.13	0.13	0.13	0.13	0.13	0.15	0.15	0.15	0.15	0.15	0.15	0.15	0.15
Netherlands	54.33	54.33	54.33	54.33	54.63	54.78	43.97	43.94	43.94	43.94	43.94	43.94	43.94
Netherlands Antilles	0.55	0.55	0.55	0.55	0.55	0.55	0.55	0.55	0.55	0.55	0.55	0.55	0.55
New Zealand	0.02	0.02	0.02	0.02	0.04	0.07	0.05	0.02	0.02	0.02	0.02	0.02	0.02
Nicaragua	0.01	0.02	0.02	0.02	0.03	0.03	—	—	—	—	—	—	—
Niger	—	—	—	0.00	0.01	0.01	0.01	0.01	0.01	0.01	0.01	0.01	0.01
Nigeria	0.57	0.57	0.57	0.57	0.63	0.63	0.69	0.69	0.69	0.69	0.69	0.69	0.69
Norway	0.98	0.98	0.98	0.98	1.08	1.13	1.18	1.18	1.18	1.18	1.18	1.18	1.18
Oman	0.01	0.03	0.03	0.05	0.10	0.19	0.19	0.19	0.21	0.22	0.26	0.27	0.27
Pakistan	1.59	1.59	1.59	1.62	1.62	1.72	1.82	1.82	1.82	1.82	1.85	1.85	1.85
Papua New Guinea	—	—	—	—	0.03	0.04	0.05	0.06	0.06	0.06	0.06	0.06	0.06
Paraguay	0.00	0.00	0.00	0.00	0.01	0.01	0.04	0.04	0.04	0.04	0.04	0.04	0.04
Peru	1.00	1.00	1.00	1.00	1.00	1.00	1.16	1.40	1.40	1.40	1.40	1.40	1.40
Philippines	1.06	1.06	1.06	1.06	1.06	1.51	1.70	1.84	1.92	1.99	1.54	2.05	1.65
Portugal	27.54	27.84	27.72	27.67	24.11	22.13	22.13	22.16	22.17	22.17	22.17	22.16	22.14
Qatar	0.19	0.19	0.19	0.19	0.18	0.25	0.27	0.45	0.47	0.55	0.60	0.67	0.71

Country													
Romania	2.27	2.45	2.60	2.75	3.06	3.35	3.53	3.68	3.71	3.74	3.71	3.69	3.59
Saudi Arabia	3.09	3.08	3.08	3.08	3.08	4.54	4.57	4.57	4.57	4.57	4.57	4.57	4.57
Senegal	—	—	—	0.00	0.01	0.02	0.03	0.03	0.03	0.03	0.03	0.03	0.03
Somalia	0.00	0.00	0.00	0.00	0.01	0.01	0.01	0.02	0.02	0.02	0.02	0.02	0.02
South Africa	18.99	18.25	17.75	12.67	9.72	9.79	10.03	12.03	12.15	12.25	12.28	12.36	9.29
Spain	14.27	14.27	14.27	14.27	14.44	14.52	14.61	14.61	14.16	14.61	14.61	14.61	14.61
SriLanka	—	—	—	—	—	0.04	0.06	0.06	0.06	0.06	0.06	0.06	0.06
Suriname	0.15	0.15	0.15	0.15	0.15	0.05	0.05	0.05	0.05	0.05	0.05	0.05	0.05
Sweden	5.79	5.79	5.79	5.79	5.93	6.00	6.07	6.07	6.07	6.07	6.07	6.07	6.07
Switzerland	83.20	83.20	83.20	83.28	83.28	83.28	83.28	83.28	83.28	83.28	83.28	83.28	83.28
Syrian Arab Republic	0.80	0.79	0.79	0.79	0.81	0.81	0.83	0.83	0.83	0.83	0.83	0.83	0.83
Thailand	2.34	2.34	2.34	2.34	2.40	2.43	2.45	2.45	2.49	2.51	2.49	2.49	2.49
Togo	—	—	—	0.00	0.01	0.01	0.01	0.01	0.01	0.01	0.01	0.01	0.01
Trinidad and Tobago	—	—	—	—	0.03	0.04	0.05	0.05	0.05	0.05	0.05	0.05	0.05
Tunisia	0.13	0.13	0.13	0.13	0.15	0.16	0.17	0.19	0.19	0.19	0.19	0.19	0.19
Turkey	3.57	3.57	3.57	3.57	3.63	3.67	3.76	3.76	3.77	3.77	3.77	3.77	3.77
United Arab Emirates	0.00	0.00	0.00	0.54	0.57	0.58	0.58	0.58	0.58	0.58	0.67	0.67	0.68
United Kingdom	21.00	21.03	21.03	21.03	22.22	22.83	18.25	18.73	18.84	18.88	18.89	18.97	19.03
United Rep. Cameroon	—	—	—	—	0.01	0.01	0.03	0.03	0.03	0.03	0.03	0.03	0.03
United States	275.97	275.97	274.71	274.68	277.55	276.41	264.60	264.51	264.32	264.18	264.17	264.13	264.11
Upper Volta	—	—	—	0.0	0.01	0.01	0.01	0.01	0.01	0.01	0.01	0.01	0.01
Uruguay	3.54	3.54	3.54	3.54	3.58	3.64	3.31	3.38	3.42	3.39	3.39	3.39	3.39
Venezuela	11.17	11.18	11.18	11.18	11.32	11.39	11.46	11.46	11.46	11.46	11.46	11.46	11.46
Yemen	0.00	0.00	0.00	0.00	0.00	0.01	*0.01	*0.01	0.01	0.01	0.01	0.01	0.01
Yugoslavia	1.46	1.47	1.46	1.47	1.51	1.63	1.72	1.85	1.85	1.86	1.86	1.86	1.86
Zaire	1.46	0.50	0.26	0.26	0.26	0.31	0.25	0.28	0.30	0.30	0.32	0.34	0.36
Zambia	0.20	0.17	0.17	0.17	0.17	0.20	0.22	0.22	0.22	0.22	0.22	0.22	0.22
Zimbabwe	0.75	0.50	0.35	0.26	0.15	0.16	0.26	0.26	0.35	0.36	0.40	0.42	0.47

Source: International Monetary Fund and *Monthly Bulletin of Statistics*, United Nations, March 1983, pp. 254–258.

The industrial demand for gold is based primarily on the unique properties of the metal, its conductibility in particular. Gold is used in television sets, pocket calculators, electronic games, and so forth. The demand for gold in 1981 exceeded production for the first time since 1972 according to a report in *The Wall Street Journal* (May 27, 1982), yet prices still declined because speculators had deserted the market. The increased demand, *The Wall Street Journal* reports, "came from greater use of gold for fabrication into jewelry, gold coins, dental work, and industrial products. There was also a big jump, the report said, in the purchase of gold bars and coins by small hoarders . . . total consumption amounted in 1981 to 1,036 tons, valued at $12 billion. Sales of new gold from South Africa and the Soviet Union was estimated at 985 tons, valued at $11.4 billion."

Official institutions have substantial holdings of gold and are active participants in the gold market. The distribution of official gold ownership throughout the world is shown in Table 9.6. By the end of the fourth quarter of 1981, the United States owned 28 percent of the 937 millions of fine troy ounces owned by all governments that are members of the IMF. The feeling of security that gold provides to both individuals and institutions (public or private) must be considered a powerful return on investment— hence, a demand stimulus, nonpecuniary as the return may be. The individual purchasers of spot gold, it must be noted, are not all investors. Speculators are very active in the gold market. Their demand is a function of the relationship between the expected return on gold and that on alternative forms of investment. Speculators, however, are much more likely to speculate in the futures gold market than in the spot gold market because of the leverage, liquidity, and lower transactions costs the futures market offers. The characteristics and the opportunities in the gold futures market are explored later in this chapter.

The demand for gold coins is satisfied by private as well as official organizations. The largest private mint in the United States is the Franklin Mint, which is engaged in the production of high quality coins and medals, and which covers the entire production process from the melting stage to the polishing and packaging stage.

9.4 THE PRICE OF GOLD

The price of gold has been characterized by considerable instability ever since December 31, 1974 when private ownership of gold by U.S. citizens was legalized. The behavior of cash gold prices in the London market is shown in Figure 9.1

The price of an ounce of gold reached an $850 high in January 1980, up from $217 in September 1978, only to fall to $500 at the end of March 1980. These developments took place while the U.S. dollar was showing considerable strength in the world foreign exchange markets. Between September 1978 and January 18, 1980, the price of an ounce of gold changed by 285 percent. The average monthly standard deviation of gold rose from $2.17 per ounce in 1977 to $4.95 in 1978, to $10.47 in 1979. This volatility continues in the 1980s.

The most often referred to price of gold is the London daily price fixing. The price of an ounce of gold is fixed twice daily in London, (10:30 A.M. and 3:00 P.M., London time). Five gold-trading houses bring to the London Gold Market bids and offers from their banking and industrial clients. A price that clears the market—a price acceptable to all parties—is then set. This price, the London Gold Fix, is shown in Figure 9.1.

FIGURE 9.1. Weekly high, low, and close (based on daily earnings and afternoon quote).

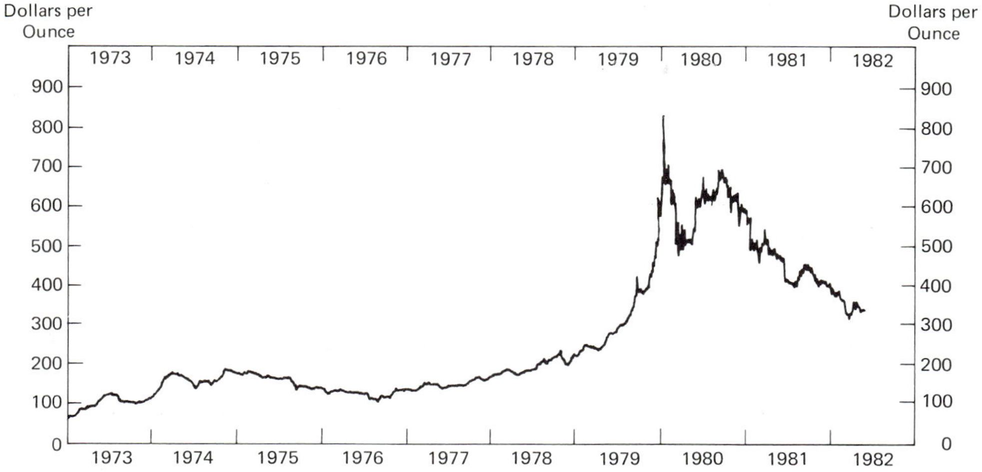

Dollars per Ounce

Dollars per Ounce

Source: 1982 Commodity Year Book, Commodity Research Bureau, Inc., New York, p. 160.

The Determinants of Gold Prices

Gold prices are influenced by political as well as economic factors. The universal acceptance of gold makes it a preferred "currency," particularly when compared with the holdings of indigenous currencies in third world countries. The Egyptian Guineh is practically worthless outside Egypt, but gold held by Egyptians is salable anywhere, provided it can be transported outside the country. Furthermore, political turmoil invites economic chaos and consequently a depreciation in the value of the national currency and in the wealth denominated in that currency. As the value of a national currency drops, the value of hard assets, such as gold, appreciates. This explains the importance of gold to citizens in times of trouble. It is tangible and represents visible evidence of well being that cannot be reduced to nothing by government fiat.

The responsiveness of gold prices to political turmoil has been documented repeatedly. Libya converted some of its holdings in European and U.S. currencies into gold after the Chad conflict erupted. Gold prices increased by $13.50 after the Israeli attack on Iraq's nuclear installation and gold prices also increased after the crisis over the Falkland Islands developed. Gold prices jumped $17 an ounce on June 8, 1982 as Israel invaded southern Lebanon. These are but a few of the cases that demonstrate a positive relationship between gold prices and political turmoil.

Another relationship, observed repeatedly, is between economic instability and gold prices. There exists a high correlation between gold prices and inflation—one measure of economic instability.

The price of gold is also influenced by the rate of return on alternative investments. Gold pays no interest or dividends, although an indirect investment in gold through bonds or stocks issued by gold mining firms realizes interest or dividend. The return from actual ownership of gold consists of capital gains (losses).

A comprehensive study on the determinants of the price of gold was conducted by Barbara Young and I. Using monthly data covering the period January 1975–December

1978—a period that precedes the unprecedented, if not alarming, volatility in gold prices—we obtained the following results:

$$Y = -751.373 - 2.889X_1 - .31X_2 + .3253X_3 + .00592X_4 + 679.798X_5$$
$$\quad\;\;(-4.47)\quad\;(-1.97)\quad(-1.95)\quad\;(1.965)\quad\;\;(2.23)\quad\quad(8.47)\qquad\qquad(9.1)$$

$$R^2 = .94, \; \bar{R}^2 = .935$$
$$\text{D.W.} = 1.91$$

Values in parentheses are t values. The variables are

Y = price of one troy ounce of gold.

X_1 = treasury bill rate minus the rate of inflation lagged by one period to reflect expectations.

X_2 = the rate of return on the S&P 500 composite index. Used here as a proxy for return on alternative investments.

X_3 = real income in the United States. Used as a measure of investable funds that may end up in gold investments.

X_4 = average monthly foreign exchange holdings of major official participants in the gold market. This measures potential demand, particularly from the OPEC nations.

X_5 = monthly U.S. consumer price index. Used to test the hypothesis that gold is a hedge vehicle against inflation.

All the regression coefficients were significant at the 95 percent confidence level and had the theoretically correct sign.

Another study on the determinants of the price of gold by Eugene J. Sherman appeared in *Commodity Journal,* March–April 1982. Sherman used monthly data covering two periods: one from January 1968 to March 1980 and the other from January 1972 to March 1980. He first estimated the demand function for commercial use (jewelry, dentistry, medicine, art, electronics) and arrived at the following results:

log of quantity of commercial = -0.71 $-$ 1.24 log of real + 2.94 log of real
use   gold price   world gross
$\qquad\qquad\qquad\qquad\qquad\qquad$ $(-0.34)\quad(-6.45)$ $\qquad\qquad$ (4.80) domestic
$\qquad\qquad\qquad\qquad\qquad\qquad\qquad\qquad\qquad\qquad\qquad\qquad\qquad\qquad$ product

$$R^2 = 0.8270 \quad (9.2)$$

The values in parentheses are t values. Sherman does not report the value of the Durbin-Watson statistics.

The price equation was estimated using the following independent variables:

U.S. money supply: $M1B$
World money supply: $M1$
World liquidity: $(M1)$ + (net Eurocurrencies)
Eurodollar interest rate

(real Eurodollar rate) = nominal Eurodollar rate − rate of change in the consumer price index for industrial countries for the trailing six months, annualized.

U.S. real gross national product
U.S. dollar trade-weighted exchange rate
Hudson Institute Index of Political Tension

The data on gold prices consisted of the daily average of the London afternoon fixing price.

For the period 1968–1980 two sets of regressions were run, using U.S. data and world data, respectively. Real GNP (U.S.) was used as a proxy variable for world output in the world regression. Two measures of inflationary pressures were used: the first is the log of U.S. money supply in U.S. regressions and world money supply in world regressions; the second is excess money growth—money over real GNP. The results for the 1968–1980 period regressions are shown in Table 9.6a. Equation 21 in Table 9.6a appears to be the better equation for U.S. data, as does Equation 4 for the world data.

Table 9.6b uses monthly data covering the period 1972–1980, a period that followed the "Nixon Shock" of 1971 when the convertibility of dollars into gold was suspended.

TABLE 9.7a
Gold Price Regressions: Monthly, 1968 to 1980*

	U.S.		World	
	1	2	3	4
Constant	−23.95	−29.06	21.63	−23.94
	(−3.22)	(−5.39)	(−2.68)	(−3.19)
Log Money**	1.01	—	1.04	.711
	(2.10)		(3.63)	(2.05)
Log Eurodollar Rate	−.14	—	—	—
	(−1.50)			
Log Real GNP (US)	3.08	4.63	−.778	3.56
	(2.03)	(5.68)	(−.68)	(2.81)
Real Eurodollar Rate	—	−.018	−.017	−.046
		(−2.01)	(−.87)	(−1.96)
Real Eurodollar Rate Lagged One Month	—	—	.003	.002
			(.13)	(.94)
Log Exchange Rate	—	—	−3.47	—
			(−8.63)	
Money Real GNP (US)	—	1.07		
		(1.98)		
R²	.8855	.8816	.9282	.8907
Standard Error of Estimate	.2486	.2525	.2161	.2656

* Dependent variable is log gold price. Values in parentheses are t-values.
** U.S. money supply in U.S. regressions, world money supply in world regressions.

TABLE 9.7b
Gold Price Regressions Monthly, 1972 to 1980*

	U.S.			World		
	1	2	3	4	5	6
Constant	−12.30	−5.06	−27.44	−7.52	−15.10	15.31
	(−2.09)	(−1.35)	(−2.48)	(−.60)	(−1.29)	(1.56)
Log Real GNP (US)	2.45	1.84	3.65	.881	2.14	.448
	(3.03)	(2.23)	(3.05)	(.43)	(1.12)	(.30)
Log (Money Real GNP (US))	1.61	1.80	1.39	—	—	—
	(4.03)	(4.55)	(3.18)			
Real Eurodollar Rate	−.062	−.062	−.057	−.008	−.017	−.039
	(−6.12)	(−6.26)	(−5.66)	(−.47)	(−1.09)	(−3.16)
Political Tension	—	.005	.182**	—	.010	.005
		(2.54)	(3.12)		(4.15)	(2.50)
Log World Money	—	—	—	1.32	.933	.765
				(2.63)	(1.98)	2.08)
Log Exchange Rate	—	—	1.27	—	—	−3.78
			(1.97)			(−7.95)
R^2	.8216	.8324	.8414	.7177	.7611	.8572
Standard Error of Estimate	.2464	.2401	.2345	.2962	.2739	.2129

Source: Eugene J. Sherman, "New Gold Pricing Model Explains Variations." *Commodity Journal* (March–April 1982), p. 18.

Equation 3, using U.S. data, shows the best results (significant *t* values, and high R^2), as does Equation 6, using world data. The best results in Table 9.6b are those of Equation 6.

The results reported by Sherman, although based on data from a different time period and using a logarithmic structure, are not substantially different from those in the Khoury-Young study. (See Table 9.7.) Inflation, real economic activity, alternative rates of return, and political stability are the factors to consider when examining the gold markets in order to formulate price expectations.

9.5 INVESTING IN SPOT GOLD

There are six major ways for investing in gold: gold bullion, gold certificates, gold mining shares, numismatic coins, jewelry items, and gold futures contracts. We shall discuss each method briefly and spend the rest of the chapter discussing gold futures contracts and the various strategies therein.

The motives for investing in gold are really two: price appreciation and risk diversification. The latter motive is based on the fact that the inclusion of gold in a portfolio of securities will reduce the total variance of the portfolio. That is, the inclusion will achieve risk diversification if the rates of return on gold are not perfectly positively correlated

with those on the other securities in the portfolio. The variance of a portfolio with gold is calculated as follows:

$$\sigma_p^2 = W_o^2 \sigma_o^2 + W_G^2 \sigma_G^2 + 2 W_o W_G \sigma_{o,G} \tag{9.3}$$

where W_o = percentage of investable funds committed to the other securities.

W_G = percentage of funds committed to gold.

σ_o^2, σ_G^2 = variance of rates of return on the other investments and on gold, respectively.

$\sigma_{o,G}$ = covariance between the rates of return on the other investments and on gold.

Other returns that investors derive from gold are nonpecuniary in nature. The feeling of security that gold allows and the beauty of the metal represent a substantial return on investment to many people. Wise and calculating portfolio managers largely ignore these aspects of an investment in gold, however.

Gold Coins

Gold coins were an integral part of nations' monetary systems until the eighteenth century. Toward the end of the seventeenth century every European nation was minting and using gold coins. The gold coin was the currency. In this age of paper currency, gold coins are only an investment vehicle. The old coins are beyond the financial reach of many investors. The coins of greatest interest to American investors are the South African coins (the Krugerrand) and the new Canadian Maple Leaf.

The Canadian Maple Leaf was approved for production by the Canadian government in February 1979. One million coins consisting of one ounce of fine (0.9999 pure) gold were minted in 1979. The production levels for 1979 and 1981 were 2 million coins per year. The Maple Leaf shows a Maple Leaf on one side and Queen Elizabeth II on the other. The face value of the Canadian Maple Leaf is $50 Canadian.

The South African Krugerrand also contains one ounce of gold. The coin is an alloy consisting of 90 percent gold. The Krugerrand has a much higher production and circulation level than the Maple Leaf. In 1979 alone, 4,700,511 Krugerrands were produced and sold. The coin derives its name from the portrait of Paul Kruger on one of its sides. The other side has a portrait of a running springbok gazelle.

Among the popular American gold coins are the Double Eagle and the Eagle. The first pure gold American coin was minted in 1787 and is called the Brasher Doubloon. A list of popular coins appears in Table 9.8.

New competitors to the popular coins are being provided by the U.S. Treasury. They are the U.S. gold medallions and are being marketed for the first time by a private corporation: J. Aron & Company, one of the world's leading precious metal dealers. The medallions were authorized in 1978 and were initially sold by mail through the U.S. Postal Service. J. Aron & Company changed the method of sale by setting up a new distribution network for the medallions. A total of ten different gold medals is authorized under the American Arts Gold Medallion Act. During 1982 the U.S. Mint struck 420,000 one-ounce medals and 360,000 half-ounce pieces. The one-ounce medal

TABLE 9.8
Popular Gold Coins

Krugerrand   South Africa
1 troy ounce fine gold
33.1903 grams. $916\frac{2}{3}/1000$
31 mm diameter

Sovereign   Great Britain
7.9881 grams. $916\frac{2}{3}/1000$ fine gold
22 mm diameter

Hall sovereign   Great Britain
3.9940 grams. $916\frac{2}{3}/1000$ fine gold
19 mm diameter

Double Eagle   United States
20 dollar gold piece
33.4370 grams. 900/1000 fine gold
34 mm diameter

Eagle   United States
10 dollar gold piece
16.7185 grams. 900/1000 fine gold
27 mm diameter

Ducat   Austria
3.4909 grams. $986\frac{2}{3}/1000$ fine gold
20 mm diameter

Sovrano   Austria
11.060 grams. 919/1000 fine gold
28.5 mm diameter

50 Pesos piece   Mexico
41.6666 grams. 900/1000 fine gold
37 mm diameter

20 Pesos piece   Mexico
16.6666 grams. 900/1000 fine gold
27 mm diameter

10 Pesos piece   Mexico
8.3333 grams. 900/1000 fine gold
22 mm diameter

100 Schillings   Austria
23.5240 grams. 900/1000 fine gold
33 mm diameter

10 Soles   Peru
4.68 grams. 900/1000 fine gold
18 mm diameter

Vreneli (or 20 Francs)   Switzerland
6.4516 grams. 900/1000 fine gold
21 mm diameter

10 Francs   Switzerland
3.2258 grams. 900/1000 fine gold
19 mm diameter

Chervonetz   Soviet Union
8.6026 grams. 900/1000 fine gold
22.5 mm diameter

20 Francs   France
Known as Napoleon
6.4516 grams, 900/1000 fine gold
21 mm diameter

20 dollars   Canada
18.2733 grams. 900/1000 fine gold
27 mm diameter

20 Francs   Belgium
Known as Lator
6.4516 grams. 900/1000 fine gold
21 mm diameter

20 Lira   Italy
Also known as Lator
6.4516 grams. 900/1000 fine gold
21 mm diameter

Source: Peter Robbins and Douglass Lee, *Guide to Precious Metals and Their Markets.* Van Nostrand
Reinhold, 1979, p. 46.

carries the likeness of Louis Armstrong and the one-half-ounce piece that of Frank
Lloyd Wright. Thus far the two coins have met with limited success.

The factors determining the value of a gold coin are gold content, beauty and condition
of the coin, face value, the theme the coin represents (e.g., Olympics), rarity, country
where the coin was minted and issued, and whether the coin was privately or government
minted. Political and economic factors also influence the value of all coins, as indicated
earlier in this analysis.

Investors in gold coins must be aware of the following:

1. Coins do not yield periodic income.
2. Coins may be stolen or lost.
3. Coins are not very liquid. The liquidity of coins is ordinarily assured at considerable discount. The average transaction costs on a coin purchase or sale is 3 percent.
4. Information on coins and their prices is not very current and is often spotty.

Some of these problems have recently been alleviated by the creation of an exchange specializing in trading gold coins.

The American Gold Coin Exchange

The increasing interest in gold coins evidenced by the fivefold increase in gold coin purchases between 1977 to 1980 led to the creation of a centralized market for trading the more popular gold coins.

The American Gold Coin Exchange (AGCE), a subsidiary of the American Stock Exchange, began operations in January 1982. AGCE currently (1983) trades five coins: the Austrian 100 Corona, the Canadian Maple Leaf, the Mexican 50 Peso, the Mexican One Ounce, and the South African Krugerrand. All trades are on a cash basis. Settlement is required within two business days. No short sales are permitted and no leverage (margin) is possible.

Trading on the AGCE is supervised by the Exchange itself and is not subject to the scrutiny of the SEC or the CFTC. Trading on the floor is similar to that of trading stocks. Once an order is received by the floor broker, it is taken to the specialist (Mocatta Metals) who makes a two-way market in the coins. Both offers and bids are much better than those available in the over-the-counter market. The specialist is, as in stock exchanges, charged with maintaining an orderly and liquid market. The responsibility for liquidity requires the maintenance of firm bids and offers by the specialist. The quotations reported on the electronic machines available to stockbrokers and investors are good for a minimum of five coins and a maximum of 100.

All trades on AGCE are cleared through the Securities Industry Automation Corporation (SIAC). Coin purchases are delivered at the Bank of Delaware (the depository institution) and stored under the name of the member exchanges or their customers. The buyer has a choice: he may take delivery or keep his coins on deposit with the bank. If delivery is opted for, a resale on the AGCE cannot take place until the coins have been authenticated by the Bank of Delaware. This requires shipment of the coins to the bank and a waiting period, which could have serious consequences in a volatile market. Additionally, a delivery will require the payment of shipping charges and two types of taxes: use tax and a state sales tax. Some investors may still opt for delivery, however, because of the psychic gain they derive from having the physical coin instead of a receipt. The delivery of the coins is realized by notifying the broker who fills out a standard form and sends it to SIAC. SIAC then records the change in the customer account and notifies the Bank of Delaware by mail.

The emergence of AGCE improved the efficiency of the gold coin market by increasing its competitiveness both in terms of the price of the coin and the transactions costs involved in acquiring it or disposing of it. The gold coin market is now more liquid, highly visible, and offers a unique opportunity for trading gold coins that never existed before. An investor/speculator can now trade coins without ever taking possession of them.

TABLE 9.9

GOLD COINS			
		Premium Over the Value of the Gold Contained in Coin	
NAME OF COIN	Price	In $ Per Coin	As a % of Gold Value
Krugerrand	446.00	15.00	3.48
Maple Leaf	445.00	14.00	3.25
Mexican 1 oz	445.50	14.50	3.36
Mexico Peso	533.30	13.89	2.67
Austria Crown	421.00	−1.47	−0.35
Sovereign	106.00	4.54	4.47

MOCATTA'S spot Gold price $431.00.
 Wholesale dealer offering price on Friday.
Source: Mocatta Metals Corp.

To improve the prospects of an investment in gold coins, the investor should exercise great care before the commitment of funds. Care in investment means information and a careful synthesis thereof. The American Numismatic Association (ANA) provides a coin authentication service and publishes the *Blackbook Price Guide of the United States Coins*. This guide reports bid and ask prices on various grades of coins. Other publications of value are the *R. S. Yeoman's Guide Book of Unites States Coins*, and *The Handbook of United States Coins*. The guide provides information on retail prices and the handbook provides information on dealer prices. An even better and more timely price data source is *The Coin Dealer Newsletter*, which furnishes dealer-to-dealer prices on a weekly basis. Of great value also are the services of *Paramount Modern Coin Exchange*, which provides information on coins and attempts to match buyers and sellers. The most recent source of price information, albeit on a small number of coins is the AGCE.

While the purchase of gold coins may be intricate, that of gold bullions is considerably simpler. The value of gold bullion is a function of its size and the purity of the gold. Price is determined, as in all free markets, by supply and demand. The price of popular gold coins quoted in the May 2, 1983 issue of *Barron's* appears in Table 9.9.

Gold Stocks

Stocks in gold mining companies solve many of the problems associated with investments in gold coins and bullions, but they introduce new ones as well. Information on gold mining companies—those listed on the national exchanges in particular—and on the prices of their shares is extensive and readily available at minimal costs. Gold stocks offer two possible returns: price appreciation and dividends. Gold stocks can be registered and left on deposit with one's broker, and can be purchased and liquidated at minimal transaction costs (about 1 percent of total value). Gold stocks are not subject to storage costs or risks and thus do not have to be insured. Gold stocks could be a safer investment in a down market, because their value does not always drop in tandem with the value of gold. Several gold mining companies are sufficiently diversified that they are not at the mercy of gold prices exclusively.

The new complications that gold stocks introduce into gold investment are:

1. While a dividend is likely, it is very unstable, almost as unstable as gold prices.

2. In a bull gold market the appreciation potential of gold stocks is not ordinarily as high as that of gold coins or bullions.

3. The value of a gold stock is not only dependent on the production rate and the prevailing gold price. Other factors affecting value depend on the reserves of gold left in the ground—and the future cash flows to accrue therefrom—on the efficiency of the mining process, the efficiency of the marketing and sales force, and on the position of the company in the industry.

The relationship between gold prices and gold share prices, while not perfect, is certainly very significant. It is estimated that the after-tax profits of Homestake Mining, the largest producer of gold in the United States, varies by about $1 million for every $5 upward or downward move in the price of gold. Gold accounted for 53 percent of Homestake's operating earnings in 1982, down from 77 percent a year earlier.

4. Many of the important gold mining companies are outside the United States. Most of them are in potentially explosive South Africa. The major South African shares sold in the form of American Depository Receipts (ADRs) appear in Table 9.10.

5. Gold mining shares are generally thinly capitalized. The combined market value of all South African shares is less than 40 percent of that of IBM.

6. Gold stocks are defensive (countercyclical) stocks. To invest in them in a very bullish market is not the intelligent thing to do unless the investor is attempting to reduce the beta of his/her portfolio.

7. The range of U.S. gold mining stocks is very limited. Only five U.S. corporations with gold mining operations are publicly owned. A list of gold mining companies in

TABLE 9.10

SOUTH AFRICAN ADR's

Closing prices of selected issues in U.S currency.

April 29, 1983

Name of Stock	Week's Close	Week's Change
Bracken	3.55	+ .05
Deelkraal	4.10	− .05
Doornfontein	28.25	− 2.50
Durban Deep	34.50	− 3.00
ERPM	18.75	− .75
Elandsrand	12.75	+ .25
Elsburg	4.10	− .05
ERGO	9.125	+ .125
Gen Mining	25.50	− 3.50
Grootvlei	17.00	− .25
Harmony	21.00	− .75
Hartebeestfontein	83.00	− 4.00
Impala Platinum	11.625	− .25
Kinross	25.25 ·	− 3.50
Leslie	20.75	− 1.00
Libanon	39.00	. . . .
Loraine	7.10	− .25
Lydenburg Platinum	5.625	− .50
Palabora Mining	17.75	+ .25
Randfontein	160.00	− 4.00
Rustenburg Platinum	7.75	. . . .
So. African Breweries	7.00	− .625
Southvaal	61.00	− 1.50
Stilfontein	17.00	− 1.00
Unisel	14.25	− 1.00
Venterspost	18.00	− 3.00
Western Areas	6.50	. . . .
West Rand Cons	9.50	− .50
Winkelhaak	41.00	− 3.50
Zandpan	14.00	− .25

x-Ex-Dividend.
Source. Akroyd & Smithers Inc.

Source: Barron's, May 2, 1983.

TABLE 9.11
Gold Ores in the United States

Cortez Gold Mines #1 California St. San Francisco, CA 94111	Bar Resources, Inc. 50 Mi E. of Carlin Carlin, NV 89822
Homestake Mining Co.[a] 650 California St. San Francisco, CA 94108	McCravey, David L. 816 Sunset Williamsburg, NM 87942
Golden Cycle Corp. 228 No. Cascade Ave. Colorado Springs, CO 80901	Carlin Gold Mining Co., Inc. 300 Park Ave. New York, N.Y. 10022
Minerals Engineering Co.[a] 950–17th St. Denver, CO 80202	Neptune Mining Co.[a] 120 Broadway New York, NY 10005
Callahan Mining Corp. 1120 Post Rd. Darien, CT 06820	Rosario Resources Corp. 375 Park Ave. New York, NY
Goldfield Corp De 65 E. NASA Blvd. Melbourne, FL 32901	Standard Metals Corp. 645 Fifth Ave. New York, N.Y.
Golden Eagle Mines, Inc. R#2, Box 55 C-Z Grangeville, ID 83530	Pennzoil Co.[a] Pennzoil Bldg. Houston, TX 77001
United Silver Mines, Inc. 208 So. Wilson Ave. Oakley, ID 83346	Bamok[a] 359 So. State Salt Lake City, UT
Day Mines, Inc. Day Building Wallace, ID 83873	

Source: Dun & Bradstreet Million Dollar Directory, 1981.
[a] Indicates that the firm is a corporation.

the United States appears in Table 9.11. Several of these companies are not exclusively in gold.

The choice among gold stocks and between gold stocks and gold coins must be carefully made. The preferences, the expertise, and the risk profile of the investor are at the heart of the choice process.

Gold Certificates

Gold certificates represent ownership interest in the metal without actual physical possession and the associated problems and costs—they are the equivalent of a warehouse receipt. A major bank is usually involved in the issuance of gold certificates. The gold is on deposit in a safe, insured place and is administered by the bank for a fee of ½ to 1 percent of the value of the gold. The certificates usually have a minimum denomination of $1,000 and are negotiable. Their liquidity is higher than that of the metal and

carries a transactions cost of approximately 3 percent. The return on gold certificates are in the form of appreciation in the value of the underlying gold. Gold certificates are marginable, that is, they allow for considerable leverage, although few banks are willing to make the loans. Seventy percent of the value of the gold certificate may be borrowed.

Before we begin discussion of another method for participating in the gold market, gold futures, we should mention the French gold-indexed bond. Here the return on the bond is indexed to the price of gold. Few Americans participate in this market, which has not escaped the attention of many astute portfolio managers.

The gold portion of a portfolio should itself be diversified among the various instruments available for participation in the gold market. A gold portfolio made up of 40 to 50 percent coins or bullions (or gold certificates), 30 to 40 percent South African shares, 5 to 10 percent North American shares, and some French gold indexed bonds is considered advisable for most investors. No portfolio manager should automatically rule out or rule in gold. The particular circumstances and goals of the fund as well as expectations about gold prices should determine the extent of the participation and its nature.

9.6 GOLD FUTURES

Trading in gold futures contracts began on December 31, 1974, coinciding with the first day on which American citizens were permitted once again to own gold. The nature, extent, structure, and trading strategies in gold futures contracts are the subject of this section.

Definition

A gold futures contract is a commitment to deliver (take delivery of) a set quantity (100 ounces) and quality of gold at a specified time in the future, at a price agreed upon today. The price is determined by a competitive auction process on the floor of the exchange.

Gold Exchanges

Two major exchanges: the International Monetary Market—a division of the Chicago Mercantile Exchange in Chicago—and the Commodity Exchange Inc. (COMEX) in New York account for practically all the trading in gold futures contracts.[3] Comex is the largest metals futures exchange in the world and accounts for the largest share of gold futures trading (Table 9.12).

Both exchanges use the auction system to arrive at a price. Floor brokers step into a designated trading ring, and, by using hand signals and open outcry, they indicate their intention to buy or sell and at what price.

The exchanges do not buy or sell futures contracts directly. They merely provide the space where trading takes place under specified rules and regulations and by approved personnel. In so doing they further the centralization of the market, increase the liquidity of the market, and improve its operating efficiency, which is reflected in lower transactions

---

[3] The Chicago Board of Trade trades gold futures with minimal success.

TABLE 9.12
Gold Futures Contract Volume

Year	IMM	COMEX
1974	2,131	2,550
1975	406,968	393,517
1976	340,921	479,363
1977	908,180	981,551
1978	2,812,870	3,742,378
1979	3,558,960	6,541,893
1980	2,543,419	8,001,410
1981	2,518,435	10,373,706

Source: International Monetary Market and Commodity Exchange, Inc. (COMEX) research departments. Data provided on June 4, 1982.

costs. The exchanges derive their income primarily from the sale of their price quotations the world over to dealers and brokers in the commodities traded on their floor. The exchanges also charge their members a fee for the privilege of association. The clearing corporation of each of the exchanges interposes itself between the buyer and the seller. In effect, every sale is a sale to the clearing corporation and every purchase is a purchase from the clearing corporation. The buyer, therefore, does not have to know the identity of the person on the other side of the transaction and obviously does not have to worry about that person's credit worthiness. The contract is guaranteed by the clearing corporation and ultimately by the capital of the exchange members. Unfortunately, the guarantee does not cover price movements. In addition, the clearing corporation marks all traders to the market on a daily basis—that is, it demands payment from those traders with losses in their accounts and makes payments to those traders with gains in their accounts. All accounts must be settled by the opening bell of the next business day. The marking to the market applies to both short and long positions.

A long position represents a purchase of a futures contract—that is, the purchase of an obligation of the clearing corporation to sell 100 ounces of gold at the agreed-upon price. It bears noting that a smaller contract is now available. The Chicago Board of Trade began trading a new gold futures contract on April 12, 1983, covering 32 troy ounces of gold—a minimarket. The early signs were very encouraging as the contract drew considerable interests from investors and speculators. The Mid-American Commodity Exchange in Chicago trades these minicontracts as well. A short position represents a sale of a futures contract. However, a short position in the futures market is not the same as one in the stock market. No security is being borrowed to be sold with the expectation that prices will drop. A short position in the futures market is simply a commitment to deliver a set amount of the underlying commodity (gold, here) at a specific price during a certain period of time. No uptick is required, as in the stock case for the transaction to be consummated on the exchange.

The futures exchanges set the margin requirements on the futures contract. In the case of gold, it is $2,000 initial margin for speculative transactions and $1,200 for hedging transactions on the COMEX. The maintenance margin is 75 percent of either value. The margin requirements on the IMM are $2,000 for speculative transactions ($1,500

maintenance) and $1,000 for hedging transactions ($1,000 maintenance). This margin requirement represents a performance bond and is not a downpayment on the contract. It is required on both the short and the long positions and serves to offset the losses on the contract on any given day. The losses result from an adverse movement in the price. The maximum loss is set by the daily price limit, which is determined by the exchange. The maximum daily price fluctuation on the COMEX is $25 per troy ounce above or below the previous day settlement price.

It should be apparent by now that the characteristics of the futures market are quite distinct from those of the spot market. A summary on the characteristics of both markets appear in Table 9.13.

Trading Gold Futures

To buy or sell a futures contract is not much different from buying a listed stock, since all futures contracts are traded on futures exchanges with standardized order execution procedures. The anatomy of a futures transaction appears in Figure 9.2.

A customer may place different types of orders. A limit order is an order to buy or sell at a set price or a better price. A market order is an order to buy or sell at the best possible available price at the time the order is being filled.

The critical person in processing orders is the floor broker on the exchange. He acts as a broker's broker filling orders for the member firms or their clients. Another important operator is the floor trader who acts as a market maker and trades for his own account. The floor trader increases the liquidity and ensures the continuity of the market by making sure that bids and offers are always available.

The preponderance (99 percent) of futures contracts does not result in actual delivery. The contracts are offset prior to expiration—that is, the holder of a long position sells a futures contract for the same contract month. This results in a no position, and the trader with a short position buys a futures contract, which also results in a no position. The delivery process is both cumbersome and costly. Unless one needs the physical gold, delivery should be avoided.

Another method for closing out a position involves an Exchange for Physical (EFP). An EFP is an arrangement entered into by two parties where the physical commodity (gold) held by one party is exchanged for the appropriate (size, maturity) futures contract(s). A trader with a long futures position would look, in an EFP, for a person holding gold physical and exchange his futures contract for the gold. A trader who is long spot gold and short gold futures would look for another trader with a long position in the gold futures market in order to exchange his spot gold for the long futures contract.

We now examine the various trading strategies in gold futures beginning with arbitrage. A necessary prerequisite, however, is a discussion on the determinants of futures gold prices.

Determinants of Futures Prices

The difference between the futures gold price for a given delivery month and the spot price of gold is practically equal to the interest costs necessary for carrying an inventory of physical gold for the length of the futures contract. This is so because in an efficient

TABLE 9.13
Characteristics of the Gold Futures Market and the Dealer (cash) Market

IMM Futures Market	Dealer (Cash) Market
1. Participants are either buyers or sellers at a single specified price at any given point in time.	1. Participants make two-sided markets (quoting two prices that indicate a willingness to buy at the lower price and to sell at the higher price).
2. Non-member participants deal through brokers, who represent them on the IMM floor.	2. Participants deal on a principal-to-principal basis.
3. Market participants are usually unknown to one another, except where a firm is trading its own account through its own brokers on the IMM trading floor.	3. Participants in each transaction always know who is on the other side of the trade.
4. Trading is conducted in a competitive arena by "open outcry" of bids, offers, and amounts.	4. Trading is done by telephone or telex with customer orders coming into each dealer's trading room.
5. Participants include those who are in the gold business as well as those who are not, including large and small "retail" or individual speculators and investors.	5. Trading is dominated by participants in the precious metals business; access for individuals is limited.
6. Daily price and volume statistics are disseminated publicly by the IMM.	6. Actual prices are not publicly available (applies to daily trading; fixes are exceptions) and no data are available on total volume.
7. The Exchange's Clearing House becomes the opposite side to each cleared transaction; therefore, the credit risk for a futures market participant is always the same and there is no need to analyze the credit of other market participants.	7. Each party with whom a dealer does business must be individually examined as a credit risk and credit limits must be set for each. There may be a wide range in the credit capabilities of participants.
8. Margins are required of all participants.	8. Margins are not always required, depending upon a dealer's assessment of each counterpart to a transaction.

market where no arbitrage opportunities exist two alternatives for fixing the delivery price of gold in the future should be equivalent. These alternatives are

1. Buy (sell) a futures contract.

2. Instead of a long position, say, in the futures market, a trader may borrow the necessary funds at prevailing interest rates, buy spot gold, and store it (storage and transportation costs must be included) until he needs it. The sum of interest costs and storage and transportation costs is referred to as carrying charges (*cc*). Any deviation between *cc* and the basis represents, as we shall show below, an arbitrage opportunity. Therefore

$$FP = SP + cc \qquad (9.4)$$

TABLE 9.13 (*Continued*)

IMM Futures Market	Dealer (Cash) Market
9. Settlements are made daily via the Exchange's Clearing House. Gains on position values may be withdrawn and losses are collected.	**9.** Settlement takes place two days after spot transactions. For forward transactions, settlement occurs two days after the maturity date.
10. A small percentage of contracts is delivered against.	**10.** The majority of contracts are delivered against.
11. Generally trading is in contracts for future delivery.	**11.** The bulk of trading is spot.
12. Long and short positions are easily liquidated.	**12.** Forward agreements are not easily offset or transferred to other participants.
13. Standardized dates are used for delivery of gold in the spot month and/or the quarterly months of March, June, September, and December.ᵃ	**13.** Forward contracts can be delivered at any date agreed upon between the buyer and seller.
14. Contract size is 100-troy ounces of .995 fineness.	**14.** Dealers normally trade 400-ounce bars of .995 fineness, though other weights and qualities are available.
15. Pricing basis is for Chicago or New York delivery. Specifications of IMM gold contracts allow delivery at seller's option in designated warehouses in either Chicago or New York.	**15.** Pricing basis is normally for London delivery, though delivery charges for other locations may be included by dealers at customer request.
16. A single round-turn (in and out of the market) commission is charged. It is negotiated between broker and customer and is relatively small in relation to the value of the contract.	**16.** No commission is charged, but the dealer's cost of making the transaction is built into the price and often substantially exceeds that of the futures market commission.

Source: Gold Futures Trading for Bullion Dealers, International Monetary Market, Chicago, Ill., 1980, pp. 6, 7, and 8. Reprinted with the permission of the International Monetary Market, a division of the Chicago Mercantile Exchange.

ᵃ The Board of Governors may add additional contract months from time to time. Spot months are opened at each interval between the regular contract months.

where FP = futures price

SP = spot price

cc = carrying charges

$$cc = (\text{borrowing costs}) \left(\frac{\text{days to maturity of futures contract}}{360} \right)(SP)$$

$+$ storage costs $+$ transportation costs.

Storage and transportation costs per ounce of gold, as the examples below demonstrate, are minimal. Interest costs dominate *cc*.

FIGURE 9.2.   Elements of a typical futures transaction.

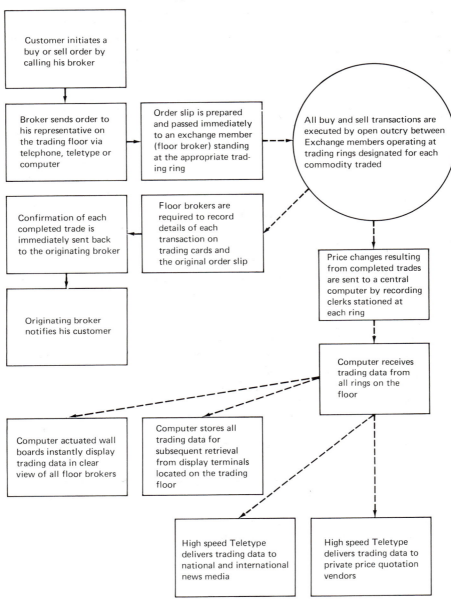

Source: Gold Futures, Comex, pp. 2–3.

Trading and Hedging Strategies

We begin our strategy discussion with arbitrage.

Arbitrage

Arbitrage can be classified into two broad categories: space arbitrage, which attempts to capitalize on unwarranted price differences between two places, and price arbitrage, which attempts to capitalize on an unwarranted relationship in prices in a given location.

Space Arbitrage. Our discussion, heretofore, has been based on the futures and spot prices in Table 9.14. An arbitrageur who observes that the price differential between, say, the September '82 IMM contract and the October '82 COMEX gold futures contract is too great, given his carry charges, would

Buy Sept/82 (IMM) 343.70
$$\left.\begin{array}{l}\text{Buy Sept/82 (IMM)} \quad 343.70 \\ \\ \text{Sell Oct/82 (COMEX)} \quad 348.00\end{array}\right\rangle \text{COMEX} - \text{IMM} = 4.30$$

TABLE 9.14
Spot and Futures Markets

	Fri.	Thu.	Yr. Ago
Gold, troy oz			
Engelhard indust bullion 333.25		331.00	485.00
Engelhard fabric prods 349.91		347.55	504.40
Handy & Harman base price 333.25		331.00	485.00
London fixing AM 331.75 PM 333.25		331.00	485.00
Krugerrand, whol a349.00		342.00	493.00

	Open	High	Low	Settle	Change	Lifetime High	Low	Open Interest
GOLD (CMX) — 100 troy oz.; $ per troy oz.								
May	335.00	335.00	335.00	338.20	+ 6.60	370.00	319.50	112
June	333.50	341.50	333.50	340.00	+ 6.50	925.00	319.00	44,894
July	....	....	....	343.60	+ 6.50	347.00	336.00	9
Aug	341.00	348.50	340.80	347.30	+ 6.50	887.00	327.00	24,190
Oct	348.00	355.50	347.50	354.60	+ 6.60	842.00	333.09	21,316
Dec	355.40	363.00	355.20	361.90	+ 6.50	666.50	340.00	10,791
Fb83	366.50	371.00	366.50	369.50	+ 6.50	642.00	347.50	18,025
Apr	373.00	377.30	373.00	377.30	+ 6.50	604.00	355.50	10,999
June	....	....	....	385.30	+ 6.50	596.00	365.00	3,231
Aug	....	....	....	393.40	+ 6.50	515.50	371.00	1,775
Oct	....	....	....	401.60	+ 6.50	500.00	388.00	770
Dec	408.00	408.00	408.00	309.90	+ 6.50	495.00	385.00	110
Fb84	....	....	....	418.20	+ 6.50	454.00	411.50	5
Est vol 30,000; vol Thu 17,809; open int 136,227, −599.								
GOLD (IMM) — 100 troy oz.; $ per troy oz.								
June	333.00	341.80	333.00	339.80	+ 6.40	920.00	318.80	6,258
Sept	343.70	353.00	343.70	350.80	+ 6.50	948.00	329.50	2,540
Dec	354.50	363.00	354.50	361.90	+ 6.60	974.00	341.00	3,228
Mr83	371.00	373.20	371.00	373.20	+ 6.60	887.20	353.00	2,377
June	....	....	....	384.80	+ 6.60	674.50	365.50	1,067
Sept	395.50	398.00	395.50	396.70	+ 6.60	626.20	388.00	164
Est vol 2,845; vol Thu 3,437; open int 15,634, −400.								

Source: The Wall Street Journal, May 17, 1982.

After the prices have adjusted to their equilibrium values, (possibly after a few minutes or an hour), the above transaction is reversed:

Sell Sept/82 (IMM)   345.30
> COMEX − IMM = 2.80
Buy Oct/82 (COMEX)   348.10

1. Profit (loss) on Oct/82 (COMEX), that is, on the short position = 348.10 − 348.00 = (0.10)
2. Profit (loss) on Sept/82 (IMM), that is, on the long position = 345.30 − 343.70 = 1.60
3. Net profit (loss) on arbitrage strategy = 1.60 − (0.10) = $1.50

Difference in price across exchanges for the same maturity month presents arbitrage opportunities. An arbitrageur might have entered the following transaction:

Buy Dec/82 on IMM   354.50
> COMEX − IMM = 0.90
Sell Dec/82 on COMEX   355.40

As soon as prices adjust sufficiently the arbitrageur reverses the transaction above. If the position remains open for a long period of time, the arbitrageur runs the risk of having the COMEX contract exercised against him. The probability of this happening is practically nonexistent, because arbitrage positions are typically very short-lived.

When the transaction is later reversed, the arbitrageur would:

Sell Dec/82 on IMM   355.50
> COMEX − IMM = 0.20
Buy Dec/82 on COMEX   355.70

Profit (loss) on Dec/82 IMM   355.50 − 354.50 = 1.00
Profit (loss) on Dec/82 COMEX   355.40 − 355.70 = (0.30)
Net profit (loss)   0.70

Thus far we have concentrated on arbitrage across exchanges within the same country. Arbitrage can also take place between, say, the U.S. futures exchange and the London futures exchange. Prices must be adjusted for the cost of forward cover in the foreign exchange market and for the transportation costs of gold bullions across the Atlantic.

Price Arbitrage. The formula for the calculation of carrying charges (cc):

$$cc = (\text{borrowing costs}) \frac{\text{days to maturity}}{360} (\text{spot price})$$

$$+ \text{storage costs} + \text{transportation costs}.$$

Typically the arbitrageur has lower borrowing costs than the market. Thus, the basis he calculates will usually be smaller than that determined by the entire market. Hence,

the typical arbitrage strategy involves a long cash position and a short futures position. On May 17, 1982 the arbitrageur observes:

Borrowing costs = 14%
Storage costs per ounce per month = 0.05
Transportation costs per ounce = 0.45

He determines the applicable carrying charges to the August '82 contract as follows (assume delivery on August 17, 1982):

$$\text{basis} = (0.14)\left(\frac{90}{360}\right)(333.25) + \left(\frac{90}{30}\right)(0.05) + 0.45 = \$12.26$$

The arbitrageur would thus be willing to buy gold in the spot market, carry it, and deliver the gold against an August futures contract at any price greater than 333.25 + 12.26 = 345.51. Thus, on May 17 he would:

Buy spot   333.25
Sell August   347.30

As spot gold is purchased, its price will increase; as August contracts are sold, their price will decrease. Ultimately, the arbitrage opportunity will disappear. The arbitrageur will buy spot and sell futures as long as some arbitrage profit exists. However, as the price of the futures drops and the opportunity closes, the profit realized per transaction (i.e., buy spot, sell futures) will obviously decrease also. When the market adjusts, the arbitrageur will reverse his position:

Sell Spot   334.00
Buy August   346.00

The profit realized equals

Profit (loss) on long position   334.00
                                    333.25
                                      0.75

Profit (loss) on short position   347.30
                                    346.00
                                      1.30

Net profit (loss) on arbitrage strategy
                                      0.75
                                      1.30
                                    $2.05

Had the market underestimated the carrying charges and thus the price of the futures contract, the arbitrageur will go short in the spot market and long in the futures market. After the prices have adjusted, the transaction will be reversed.

Hedging in the Futures Market

Hedging in the futures market is intended to reduce, if not eliminate, exposure to price changes in an actual or prospective cash position. Two types of hedges are discussed here: the long hedge and the short hedge.

Long Hedge. The best way to gain understanding of a long hedge is through an example.

Consider a jeweler who, on May 17, 1982 realizes that he will need 100 troy ounces of gold for jewelry manufacturing by November 15, 1982. Concerned about the possibility that gold will increase in price in the intervening period, he decides to hedge his position in the futures market.

	Cash Market	Futures Market
May 17, 1982	Anticipated need for spot gold Spot price = $333.25/oz.	Buy one Dec/82 futures contract for $335.40/oz.
November 15, 1982	Buy 100 ounces of gold at $373.25	Sell futures contract for $376.20
Gains (losses)	Opportunity Loss = $373.25 − $333.25 = **($40.00)**	Profit = $376.20 − $355.40 = **$20.80**

As is apparent, the position in the futures market allowed for $20.80 worth of protection against price increases. The net opportunity loss is equal to $40 − $20.80 = $19.20.

Had the spot price of gold dropped to, say, $315.00 and that of the Dec/82 futures contract to, say, $318.50, the opportunity gain in the spot market would be $333.25 − $315 = $18.25 and the real loss in the futures market would be $355.40 − $318.50 = $36.90. The net real loss is equal to $36.90 − $18.25 = $18.65. The net cost to the jeweler, however, is $315.00 + $36.90 = $351.90.

It must be pointed out that opportunity losses and real losses are very different from the jeweler's point of view, the accountant's point of view, and the Internal Revenue Service's point of view. Opportunity losses do not appear on the corporate records. They simply represent lost opportunities. Real losses, however, do appear on the records of the firm and are deductible for tax purposes. It is the probability of real, visible losses which discourages many executives from establishing positions in the futures market.

The important lessons to draw from this example are:

1. The effectiveness of the hedge (gains in the futures market offsetting higher spot prices) depends on the relationship between the movements in spot and in futures prices. That is, effectiveness of the hedge depends on the behavior of the basis. If the basis strengthens, that is, if the value of the basis decreases, the effectiveness of a long hedge is diminished. The gains in the futures market will not offset the higher prices in the spot market. Had the basis weakened sufficiently (gotten larger), the long hedge would have more than paid for the increase in the price of spot gold.

2. Regardless of the direction in the movement of gold prices, the probability of a perfect hedge (gains in futures = appreciation in spot price) is very low if the futures

contract must be offset before its maturity. A long hedge, therefore, remains a speculation on the basis.

Had the jeweler been able to predict the behavior of the basis, he would have sold two instead of one futures contract. The gain, where gold prices appreciated, would have been $41.60, which exceeds the opportunity loss in the spot market ($40.00).

The number of futures contracts to buy (sell) against actual or prospective cash positions is referred to as the hedge ratio. This ratio is not easy to figure out because the behavior of the basis appears to be random. Many traders, however, rely on past relationships between movements in spot and futures prices in the determination of a hedge ratio.

Short Hedge. A short hedge is intended to protect against falling prices. A gold dealer, or a gold mining company expecting to sell, say, 100 troy ounces of gold in January 1983 would obviously be concerned about a drop in gold prices. To protect against this expected drop, a short position is established in the futures market as follows:

	Cash Market	**Futures Market**
May 17, 1982	Hold spot gold Spot price = $333.25	Sell one February/83 futures Contract for $336.50
January/13/1982	Sell gold at $315.75 per ounce	Buy Feb/83 Futures Contract at $318.0 per ounce
Gains (losses)	Opportunity loss = $333.25 − $315.75 = $17.50	Actual profit = $336.50 − $318.00 = $18.50

Net profits = $18.50 − $17.50 = **$1.00**

Clearly, in this example, the actual profits do exceed the opportunity loss. The gold holder has in fact succeeded in selling his gold for $315.75 + $18.50 = $334.25, while the current spot price is only $315.75.

Once again, the results depend on the behavior of the basis. Here the basis strengthened. A strengthening of the basis produces net profits in a short hedge, while a weakening of the basis produces a net loss in a short hedge.

Several of South Africa's 37 gold mines have been using the gold futures market to hedge against price declines. The August 16, 1982, issue of *Business Week* reported that such hedging has become a matter of survival for many mines that need to sell their gold at about $400 in order to break even. *Business week* quoted a South African expert who opined that "hedging is putting some pressure on the spot price."

We now discuss an often used trading strategy: spreading.

Spreading

A spread involves simultaneous short and long positions in two contract months. The objective is to take advantage of a movement in the spread (the price difference between one contract month and another). Prices of different contract months move in the same direction, but not necessarily with equal vigor. The ability to chart the course of the

spread is, therefore, critical if positive and significant returns are to be earned. When contrasted with an open long or short position, the spread has considerably less risk. What the spreader loses on one side of the spread, he partially recovers on the other if his expectations do not materialize. The initial expectation, obviously, is that the profits on one side more than offset the losses on the other.

The difference between the price of the distant contract (P_D) and that of the near contract (P_N) represents, as indicated earlier, the carry charges. Those charges consist primarily of interest costs. The spread is, therefore, the implied interest rate for that relevant time period. An investor who wants to lend at that implied rate would simply buy the near contract and sell the distant one. This practice is referred to as a lending spread. If borrowing at the implied rate is desired, the spreader will sell the nearby contract and buy the distant. Since the distant price is almost always higher than the near price for gold futures, the lending spread will earn a positive return and the borrowing spread will incur a net cost.

The lending spread is so characterized because the spreader would deliver the gold he had acquired from the near contract against the distant contract and earn the interest rate implied for the time period covered. The opposite is true for the borrowing spreader because he bought high and sold low. The position of the lender is more advantageous, however, given the delivery mechanism in the gold futures market. Delivery in this market is at the option of the seller. Since the lending spreader holds a short position in the distant contract, he therefore decides when it is most advantageous for him to make delivery. The borrower, on the other hand, is at the mercy of the seller. He does not know the exact borrowing period and consequently his risk is higher than that of the lender.

Another risk that both lending and borrowing spreaders face results from the possibility that the short position may have to be closed prior to its maturity date. This may happen if the clearing corporation calls on our spreader to deliver gold against his short position because the person on the other side of the transaction wishes to take delivery of gold. The selection is a random process.

Other risks faced by spreaders result from the possibility that they may need the funds committed to the spread before the spread expiration date or that they may have to liquidate their spread position because of their inability to meet margin calls.

The profitability of a spread depends on the price behavior of both sides of the spread, that is, on whether the spread narrows or widens and on whether the futures market is inverted ($P_D < P_N$) or noninverted ($P_N < P_D$). We shall concentrate on the noninverted market case because the history of the gold futures market shows only this type of market. We examine both bull and bear spreads.

Bull Spreads. A bull spread requires a long position in that contract which is expected to appreciate most in price. According to Paul Samuelson,[4] the volatility of futures price changes per unit of time increases as the time to maturity decreases. This hypothesis has been disputed by several studies,[5] but appears to hold in the gold futures case. This suggests that a bull spread should consist of a long position in the near contract

---

[4] **Paul A. Samuelson,** "Proof That Properly Anticipated Prices Fluctuate Randomly." *Industrial Management Review.* Vol. 6 (1975), pp. 41–49.

[5] See for example, **Ronald W. Anderson,** "The Determinants of the Volatility of Futures Prices." Paper presented at the meeting of the American Economic Association (December 1981).

and a short position in the distant contract. We now use an example to show the mechanics and the consequences of a bull spread.

On May 17, 1982, a spreader observed what he perceived to be an unjustifiable relationship between the Feb/83 and the April/83 COMEX contracts. (See Table 9.12.) Expecting the prevailing spread to narrow, that is, to strengthen, the spreader would

Buy Feb/83 $366.50

Sell April/83   373.00 $> P_D - P_N > = 6.50$

On June 1, 1982, after the market has adjusted, the spreader would reverse the above transaction.

Sell Feb/83 $374.00

Buy April/83   374.50 $> P_D - P_N = 0.50$

Profit (loss) per ounce on the Feb/83 long position

$\$374.00 - \$366.50 = \$7.50$

Profit (loss) per ounce on the April/83 short position

$\$373.00 - \$374.50 = (\$1.50)$

Net profit (loss) on the spread $= \$7.50 - \$1.50 = \mathbf{\$6.00.}$

Bear Spread. In a bear spread, the spreader establishes a position in the contract month that is expected to depreciate the most, the near month. We now offer an example.

On May 17, 1982, the spreader observes an unwarranted spread between Oct/82 and Dec/82 gold futures contracts and, expecting the spread to weaken, that is, to widen (in value), would:

Sell Oct/82   348.00

Buy Dec/82   355.40 $> P_D - P_N = \$7.40$

After the prices have adjusted in the desired direction the spreader would, say, on June 3, 1982, reverse the initial transaction

Buy Oct/82   343.90

Sell Dec/82   353.00 $> P_D - P_N = 9.10$

Profit (loss) on the Oct/82 short position

$\$348.00 - \$343.90 = \$4.10$

Profit (loss) on the Dec/82 long position

$353.00 − $355.40 = ($2.40)

Net Profit (loss) on the bear spread

$4.10 − $2.40 = **$1.70**

The net profit resulted from the weakening of the spread from $7.40 to $9.10. Had the spread strengthened instead, the spread position would have produced a loss.

We now discuss "tails" as a method for removing price risk.

Tail. A tail consists of a (or several) spread(s) and an additional futures contract for the near month. Its purpose is to equalize the change in the value of the spread with that of the change in the price of the near contract.[6]

Having shown earlier that the spread represents an implied interest rate, we can state that

$$P_{D,t} = P_{N,t} + R_t P_{N,t}$$

where

$$\text{subcript } t = \text{time period } t$$
$$R_t P_{N,t} = \text{value of the spread at time } t$$
$$R_t = \text{implied interest rate at time } t$$
$$P_{D,t} = \text{price of distant } (D) \text{ contract at time } t$$
$$P_{N,t} = \text{price of near } (N) \text{ contract at time } t$$

therefore

$$P_{D,1} = P_{N,1} + R_1 P_{N,1}$$
$$P_{D,2} = P_{N,2} + R_2 P_{N,2}$$

and

$$P_{D,1} - P_{N,1} = R_1 P_{N,1}$$

or

$$P_{D,2} - P_{N,2} = R_2 P_{N,2}$$
$$S_1 = R_1 P_{N,1}$$
$$S_2 = R_2 P_{N,2}$$

Therefore

$$S_2 - S_1 = R_2 P_{N,2} - R_1 P_{N,1}$$

---

[6] The analysis here is based on a series of studies prepared by COMEX.

If interest rates are constant, that is, $R_2 = R_1$:

$$S_2 - S_1 = R_1(P_{N,2} - P_{N,1}) \tag{9.5}$$

or

$$\frac{(S_2 - S_1)}{R_1} = P_{N,2} - P_{N,1}$$

Equation 9.5 establishes the fact that a change in the spread is solely a function of a change in the price of the near contract. That is why the tail is a near contract. The second important conclusion from Equation 9.5 is that for a one-point change in the value of the near contract, it is necessary to have $1/R$ spreads to achieve an equivalent move in the value of the spread. This conclusion, it must be noted, is based on the assumption of constancy of interest rates.

The correct ratio of spreads to achieve equivalency if the six-month rate is 10 percent ($R = 10\%$) is equal to $1/0.10 = 10$ spreads and one near contract. The overall position would consist, therefore, of 11 near contracts and 10 distant contracts.

In terms of a hedging strategy, the preceding discussion suggests that a hedge against a change in the price of gold requires that the total value of the near contracts should equal the value of the investment in gold. A $500,000 investment in gold is completely hedged with ten near futures contracts and nine distant contracts if the near futures price is $500 per ounce. This assumes, however, that the maturity of the near contract coincides with that of the investment. If not, the hedger should pick that near contract with the closest maturity to that of the investment.

We now discuss yet another method for participating in the gold market.

9.7 GOLD OPTIONS

In October 1982, the Commodity Exchange Inc. began trading options on gold futures contracts. These options work in exactly the same way as any other option on a futures contract discussed in the earlier chapters. These options limit the exposure of the speculator, because the maximum loss is limited to the size of the premium both on the call and the put side. Also these options avoid margin calls because the full cost of the option is paid up front.

Another interesting option offered by Mocatta Metals Corp. is the "lookback option." Mocatta offers through International Trading Group, Ltd. an option to buy 100 ounces of gold anytime during periods of three and six months. The striking price is a "floating" one.

At the end of the option period, the option holder can look back and pick the lowest price that was quoted during the option period. This price will be the price paid for the 100 ounces of gold.

Alternatively, the option can be exercised prior to maturity or sold to another party. In so doing the option holder locks in (accepts) a certain profit (loss) or locks in a certain price of gold. This type option is ideal in a very volatile market but there is no free lunch. The price of this option is about 80 percent higher than a standard option traded on the exchange would cost. In September 1982 a lookback option traded for $13,500.

CONCLUSION

The gold market is rather complex and intimidating to many investors. To ignore it is probably to allow for a suboptimal portfolio. To participate in it without careful analysis is to be foolish. We trust that this chapter has provided the reader with the necessary foundation to further explore the exciting world of gold.

QUESTIONS

1. Discuss the nature of the supply of gold and explain the reasons for the related instabilities.

2. What are the primary uses for gold?

3. What are some of the determinants of the price of gold? Discuss any relationships between the price of gold and economic and political factors.

4. Discuss two ways of investing in gold. How should all of the gold investment instruments be combined in a given portfolio?

5. Given the many pitfalls to investing in gold, why would an investor include gold in his portfolio?

6. What are the differences between a short sale in the gold futures market and the stock market? What are the implications for the investor?

7. What do the carrying costs implicit in gold futures prices represent?

8. What are the differences between space and price arbitrage?

9. Discuss the various pitfalls of investing in gold. Are all of the six major ways for investing in gold equally susceptible to these pitfalls?

10. Compare and contrast the advantages and disadvantages of direct investment in gold versus the purchase of gold certificates.

11. Explain the advantages of investing in the gold futures market instead of investing directly in gold bullion.

12. Discuss how the leading gold futures exchanges reduce the risk of a buyer or a seller in the gold futures market.

13. "The greatest danger in gold investments lies in the thinness of the market." Do you agree? Explain.

14. How does the AGCE increase the efficiency of the gold coin market?

PROBLEMS

1. You are a gold dealer in New York. On April 15, the spot rate of gold is $525, the prime rate is 19.5 percent, the storage cost per ounce of gold is $0.04/month, and the shipping cost from London to New York is $0.50/oz.

    a. Calculate the theoretical price of an August futures contract (delivery on August 15).

    b. What strategy would you follow if the actual August contract's price is $548?

    c. Why should the market adjust to this price?

2. The March 15 spot rate for gold is $485, the prime rate is 18 percent, the storage cost per ounce of gold is $0.05/mo., and the shipping cost from London to New York is $0.40/oz. What action would a speculator undertake if the March 15 price of a June gold futures contract is $525?

3. A jeweler needs 100 ounces of gold on August 20. The spot price for gold on February 24 is $363.80. The jeweler is worried about an increase in the price of gold. The price of an August gold futures contract is $384.10. How could the jeweler hedge against an anticipated price increase? What would be his commitment? (Assume 10 percent margin requirement.) Under what circumstances would he undertake such a hedge?

4. You are an investor with 500 ounces of gold in your portfolio on February 23; you wish to dispose of this gold but cannot sell it until June 15. You anticipate that the price of gold will fall over the next four months. What strategy would you employ to hedge in the futures market?

5. On May 17, 1982 a jeweler realizes he will require 300 troy ounces of gold for jewelry production by January 23, 1983. Given the spot and futures prices in Table 2.12, and given that the jeweler is afraid that the spot price for gold will rise by the middle of January, construct a long hedge that would protect the jeweler. If by 1/23/82, the spot price for gold is $381.75 and the Feb/83 futures contract is selling for $389.75, what is the net result of the hedge? If the spot price falls to $289.50 and the Feb/83 futures contract falls to $303.25, what is the net result of the hedge? Was it possible for the jeweler to construct a perfect hedge? Why or why not?

6. On May 17, 1982, the C. Johnson Gold Mine Co. decides to sell 200 troy ounces of gold in September 1982. Construct, from Table 9.12, a short hedge to protect the firm from an expected decline in the price of gold. If on September 22 the spot price for gold is $308.75 and the price for an October futures contract is $315.00, what is the net result of the hedge? If instead the spot price rises to $347.75 and the October futures price rises to $356.75, what is the net result of the hedge?

7. On May 17, 1982, a spreader observes what he perceives to be an unjustifiable relationship between the October/82 and December/82 COMEX gold futures contract. If he believes the spread will narrow, what spread position would he take? Is this a bull or a bear spread? If the price of the October/82 contract rises $2.00 and the December/82 contract falls $3.25 what is the net gain or loss from the spread? If the price for the October/82 contract remains constant and the December/82 contract rises $1.50, what is the net gain or loss from the spread? If instead the spreader believes that the spread will widen, what spread would he establish and what would be his gains or losses from the above price movements?

CHAPTER 10 | Investing in Real Estate

Man may buy land, speculate in land, fight over land, enslave fellowman through land but, in the end, the land reclaims the man.

—Joseph S. Khoury

10.1 INTRODUCTION

The fascination with real estate goes back to the origin of man. Even animals have their preferred habitat, which they guard with their lives. Land and property represent a visible and tangible endowment; the kingdom of their owner. The preservation of this kingdom and its expansion have led to court suits, wars, and to big fortunes. It is the fortunes that this chapter focuses on.

Real estate investments are but one element in the investment portfolio of individuals, corporations, or other groups or entities. Real estate investment opportunities are not homogeneous. Each has its own characteristics and its risk/return tradeoff and is thus suitable for investors with a certain profile. In general, however, real estate investments have the following characteristics.

1. They allow for a substantial use of leverage with its associated advantages and disadvantages.

2. Real estate investments provide a tax shelter through the tax deductibility of interest, depreciation, and losses.

3. Real estate investments are generally not very liquid and are characterized by high transactions costs.

4. Real estate investments generally require a considerable outlay of capital relative to the income and the savings of most investors.

5. Real estate investments have provided historically a good hedge against inflation.

6. Real estate investments carry considerable risk and are heavily influenced by economic cycles. Wide gyrations in real estate values are part of America's history:

- *Land that had been purchased in the booming young town of Chicago in 1836 for $11,000 an acre could not fetch $100 an acre in 1840.*

- *But the Florida market peaked, too, mostly because speculation had driven prices to levels far above what people were willing to pay. In the aftershock, several banks that had overextended their credit failed, and some two dozen Florida cities defaulted on their bonds.*

- *The Great Depression of 1929–33 brought another real estate slump.*

- *In August 1976, more than a thousand projects worth $250,000 each or more had failed in Dade and Broward counties, which embrace Miami and Fort Lauderdale, and nearly 32,000 condominiums were going begging. Meanwhile, the index price per share of publicly traded REITs [Real Estate Investment Trusts] plunged 83 percent from February 1972 to December 1974.* "[1]

Against these horror stories there are many stories of remarkable successes in real estate. *The Wall Street Journal,* commenting in its May 18 issue on the explosion of real estate prices in Manhattan, cited the case of an art dealer who had purchased a townhouse for $750,000 in 1975 and sold it for $4.3 million in 1981. Similar if not more extravagant cases are heard from Los Angeles, Florida, and other locations in the United States. With a limited supply of choice real estate, demand is increasing by leaps and bounds, fueled by foreign capital seeking a safe political haven in the United States. The flood of foreign capital has produced several restrictions on foreign ownership of United States land and property, however.

Real estate investment is to many Americans the only meaningful investment they ever undertake and accounts for the largest share of their wealth. We shall, therefore, concentrate our analysis on home ownership, investment in income property, and real estate investment trusts (REITs).

10.2 HOME OWNERSHIP

Home ownership is to many a part of the "American Dream." Unless carefully done, however, the ownership of a home could turn into a nightmare. It is the intent of this section to identify the special characteristics of home ownership and its advantages and disadvantages.

Government and Housing

Governments on all levels—federal, state, and local—are extensively involved in the housing market. In their drive to increase access to home ownership by all Americans, governments have passed housing laws and regulations and have provided grants and subsidies for the housing industry.

The Federal Government provides funds for building and financing housing projects throughout the United States. Some of them will be discussed below. The tax deductibility of interest expenses and of property taxes are yet another form of subsidy to the housing market.

Among the major Federal laws dealing with the housing market are

---

[1] *U.S. News & World Report,* July 21, 1980.

1. *The Equal Credit Opportunity Act.* This Act forbids discrimination in the granting of credit on the basis of sex or marital status.
2. *The Fair Credit Reporting Act.* This Act provides the applicant for a mortgage with the right to receive a summary of the report on his creditworthiness and affords him the right to challenge its contents.
3. *Fair Housing Act.* The Fair Housing Act, enacted in 1968 as part of the Civil Rights Act, outlaws discrimination in housing (purchase, rent, or lease transactions) on the basis of race.
4. *Anti Red-lining Law.* The law was intended to outlaw the practice by bankers of not making loans to "high-risk," usually black, neighborhoods.

The objective of these and other laws is to reduce, if not eliminate, the obstacles to decent housing in any community in which individuals *choose* to live regardless of their sex, religion, or race.[2]

State governments are involved in the housing markets through various laws affecting building codes and sales practices. States are also involved in the financing of housing projects primarily as administrators of federally funded programs. State housing codes reinforce Federal housing codes and occasionally provide for stiffer penalties.

States can also assist those acquiring property through their power of eminent domain. This power is usually exercised in conjunction with the mission of state housing authorities. In addition, states issue industrial revenue bonds to help finance public housing projects.

County and city governments are extensively involved in the housing market through zoning laws, rent controls, housing and building codes, and property taxes from which the major share of their income is derived. County and city governments have historically provided significant subsidies to the housing market through the installation of sewage lines, the building of roads, the distribution of water, and lately through the issuance of municipal bonds, the proceeds from which are used to finance mortgages at rates well below prevailing market rates. The trends, however, point towards lower subsidies as local governments force the privatization of costs or impose user fees. The full cost under these arrangements will be borne by the property owner, not by the taxpayers.

Home Ownership: Advantages and Disadvantages

The advantages from home ownership are many. They include the following:

1. *Security for self and the family.* A home is a commitment (temporary as it may be) to a community and embodies some form of stability.
2. *The freedom of use.* A home can be remodeled and used any way the owner pleases, subject to the applicable laws and regulations. The use of a rented property is much more restricted.
3. *Forced saving.* The equity built up every time a mortgage payment is made and the appreciation thereon represent a dependable security net in the event of future need.

---

[2] For a lucid, nontechnical discussion of Federal laws, programs, and policies, we suggest: **John L. Weicher,** *Housing: Federal Policies and Programs.* Washington, D.C.: American Enterprise Institute, Studies in Economic Policy, (1980).

4. *Fixed mortgage payments.* These payments represent a gradually declining percent of an increasing earned income over time.

5. *An inflation hedge.* Real estate values have provided an impressive hedge against inflation.

6. *Tax shelter.* The interest component of mortgage payments, property taxes, and depreciation on that part of the home used for business are all deductible for federal tax purposes. Furthermore, the appreciation on the value of the property and that resulting from upkeep and improvements is taxable at the lower capital gains rate.

Among the disadvantages of homeownership are

(a) The relatively high maintenance costs.
(b) The investment risks. Homeownership brings risk of illiquidity, risk of *depreciation* in the value of the property because of change in the character of the neighborhood, risk of not being able to meet a fixed obligation, and risk of incurring a damage not adequately covered by insurance.

Types of Housing

There exists a wide range of housing options available to prospective home owners, consistent with their financial and other requirements.

Single-Family Homes

Single-family homes are the preferred form of housing for most Americans. Sales of single-family homes are expected to rebound to 2,700,000 units in 1983, up from 1,990,000 units in 1982 (Figure 10.1) but far below the record set in 1978—3,986,000 units. The total value of all single-family homes sold in 1982 was $160.2 billion. The average price of a single-family home in 1982 was $67,000 and the expected average price for 1983 is $69,300.

The average mortgage rate paid to finance housing purchases in 1982 was approximately 15.3 percent (Table 10.1) and the average monthly mortgage payment in 1982 was $700, representing 36 percent of monthly median family income of $1,940. By March 1983 the Housing Affordability Index (HAI) stood at 81.8 percent, indicating that a family with the median income of $24,150 was earning "81.8 percent of the income needed to qualify for the purchase of a median-priced existing single-family home." Of all the single-family homes sold in March 1983 the dominant percentage was of the three-bedroom category (53.5 percent) followed by four bedrooms or more (27.3 percent) and two bedrooms or less (19.2 percent).

The largest share of single-family housing in the United States sold in 1982 went to married couples with dependents followed by married couples without dependents, single males, and single females. The percentages for Los Angeles, for example, were 42, 27, 12, and 7 percent, respectively. The largest share of the houses go to buyers in the 25 to 34 years age group (48 percent in Los Angeles, 65 percent in Pittsburgh, 57 percent in Baltimore). The preferred housing characteristic, about 60 percent nationwide, is the existing detached single-family home with considerable variation across metropolitan areas.

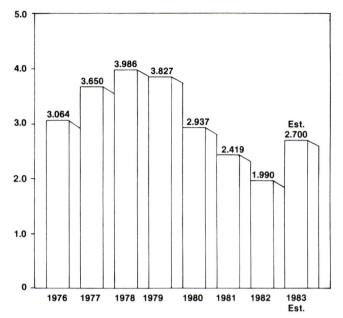

FIGURE 10.1. Existing single-family home sales for the United States (millions of units).

Source: Federal Home Loan Bank Board Journal, Annual Report 1982, vol 16., no. 4 (April 1983).

The relationship between reported sales prices and the true value of the home in residential transactions is measured by the price overstatement factor. This factor represents the interaction between the price of the house and the mortgage rate. For example, the price of a house could be increased if advantageous financing terms could be offered. The figures for 1982 are shown in Table 10.2.

The market for single-family homes began to recover in 1983 after two turbulent years. One measure of the recovery is the number of months' supply of homes on the market. By March 1983 that number stood at 10.5 months. (See Table 10.3.) The recovery of the housing market continues as the U.S. economy improves and as mortgage rates drop. The average mortgage rate in March 1983 was 13 percent, down from a high of 16.11 percent in May 1982. The downward trend is expected to continue. The behavior of mortgage rates in the early 1980s is depicted in Figure 10.2.

We now discuss another form of housing that is steadily gaining popularity, particularly in large cities, condominiums.

Condominiums

Condominiums give the dweller a title to the interior space he occupies and a common interest in the common areas and facilities of the complex, such as tennis courts, golf courses, basketball courts, hallways, and so forth.

The financial obligations of a condominium owner consist of his mortgage payments and monthly maintenance fees for the common interest property. The fees are paid to the condominium association, which consists of condominium owners and which manages the affairs of the complex.

The condominium owner assumes no responsibility for the financial obligations of any other condominium owner in the same complex. He arranges for his own mortgage and pays his own property taxes and utility bills.

TABLE 10.1
Housing Affordability

Year	Median-Priced Existing Single-Family Home	Mortgage Rate*	Monthly P & I Payment	Payment as % Income	Median Family Income	Qualifying Income**	Affordability Index
1977	$42,900	9.02%	$277	20.7%	$16,010	$13,279	120.6
1978	48,700	9.58	330	22.4	17,640	15,834	111.4
1979	55,700	10.92	422	25.7	19,680	20,240	97.2
1980	62,200	12.95	549	31.3	21,023	26,328	79.9
1981	66,400	15.12	677	36.3	22,388	32,485	68.9
1982	67,800	15.38	702	35.4	23,800	33,713	70.6
1982							
Mar	$67,000	15.65%	$706	37.2%	$22,741	$33,873	67.1
Apr	67,100	16.00	722	37.9	22,859	34,650	66.0
May	67,800	16.11	734	38.3	22,976	35,242	65.2
Jun	69,400	15.56	727	37.8	23,094	34,893	66.2
Jul	69,200	15.52	723	37.4	23,212	34,707	66.9
Aug	68,900	15.59	723	37.2	23,329	34,706	67.2
Sep	67,300	15.27	692	35.4	23,447	33,236	70.5
Oct	66,900	14.95	675	34.4	23,565	32,380	72.8
Nov	67,700	14.29	654	33.1	23,682	31,401	75.4
Dec	67,800	13.95	641	32.3	23,800	30,609	77.4
1983							
Jan	$68,100	13.54%	$626	31.4%	$23,917	$30,035	79.6
Feb[r]	68,200	13.40	621	31.0	24,033	29,791	80.7
Mar[p]	69,300	13.04	615	30.6	24,150	29,520	81.8

Source: Monthly Report, National Association of Realtors, April 1983, p. 12.

[r] Revised

[p] Preliminary

* Effective rate on loans closed on existing home—Federal Home Loan Bank Board

** Based on current lending requirements of the Federal National Mortgage Association using a 20 percent downpayment.

There are many advantages to condominiums. Among them are (1) Price affordability; condominoums sell in some cases for one-half the price of an equivalent single-family home; (2) freedom from maintenance chores; (3) access to a wide range of recreation facilities, which foster socializing and decrease recreation costs; (4) security—many condominium complexes have rather elaborate security systems, which make them particularly attractive to the elderly; (5) the usual proximity to downtown areas and to shopping centers; and (6) marketability.

The disadvantages of condominiums are (1) the density of people surrounding one's living quarters, (2) the required involvement in the condominium association if one is keen about protecting his rights and privileges in the property, and (3) the rising maintenance fees over which one condominium owner may have no control.

A new and innovative method for selling condominiums has emerged recently. It is referred to as "time-sharing condominiums." Under this arrangement an individual pur-

TABLE 10.2
Extent of Price
Overstatement[1] In Recent
Residential Transactions
(Percentage Distribution)

.........0........	6.3%
.1% — 4.9%........	10.2%
5% — 9.9%........	12.7%
10% — 14.9%........	15.0%
15% — 19.9%........	14.9%
20% — 24.9%........	22.2%
25% — 29.9%........	11.1%
30% or more........	7.7%
...Total........	100.0%
Average........	16.5%

Source: Real Estate Quarterly, vol. 2, no. 1, Winter 1983, p. 4.

[1] These estimates assume a market rate of interest of 17 percent, a marginal personal income tax rate of 32 percent, a before tax yield on alternative investments of 14 percent, and an 8 year holding period. Methodology available upon request.

chases one period (week, month, etc.) share in a condominium. During this period the owner has exclusive use of the property. Taxes, utilities, and maintenance fees are charged to a share owner in accordance with his proportionate ownership. This arrangement is prevalent in resort areas and is used by many as a form of limiting vacation expenses. A secondary market in time shares has emerged wherein an owner of a time-sharing condominium in Colorado, for example, may trade his share with a time-share holder in the same condominium for a different period, or with a time-share owner in another complex or city.

The growth of condominiums has been slowed a bit by angry renters who saw their apartment buildings converted into condominiums and by various laws regulating the conversion process. The future is very promising, however. In the first quarter of 1983, 169,000 condominiums and cooperatives were sold in the United States (Table 10.4). The largest share (37 percent) was sold in the Northeast.

Cooperative Housing

The person occupying a unit in a cooperative housing is the owner of a proportionate share in a nonprofit corporation which holds legal title to the building. The shareholder effectively leases his unit from the corporation and pays in consideration thereof his proportionate share of the mortgage on the entire building, of the utilities, of the maintenance expenses, of the taxes, and of other expenses. The shareholder is additionally responsible for covering the shortfall in income resulting from the failure of other members to meet their financial commitments to the corporation.

TABLE 10.3
United States Summary

		Existing Single-Family Home Sales (Seasonally Adjusted Annual Rates)	Number of Homes Available for Sale (End of Period)	Months Supply of Homes on the Market	Median Sales Price of Existing Single-Family Homes
	1976	3,064,000	n/a	*	$38,100
	1977	3,650,000	n/a	*	42,900
	1978	3,986,000	n/a	*	48,700
	1979	3,827,000	n/a	*	55,700
	1980	2,973,000	n/a	*	62,200
	1981	2,419,000	n/a	*	66,400
	1982	1,990,000	1,910,000	*	67,800
1982	Mar	2,030,000	n/a	n/a	$67,000
	Apr	1,960,000	n/a	n/a	67,100
	May	1,920,000	n/a	n/a	67,800
	Jun	1,980,000	1,950,000	11.8	69,400
	Jul	1,910,000	1,930,000	12.2	69,200
	Aug	1,860,000	2,120,000	13.7	68,900
	Sep	1,910,000	2,190,000	13.8	67,300
	Oct	1,990,000	2,290,000	13.8	66,900
	Nov	2,150,000	2,200,000	12.3	67,700
	Dec	2,260,000	1,910,000	10.2	67,800
1983	Jan	2,580,000	2,300,000	10.7	$68,100
	Feb[r]	2,460,000	2,480,000	12.1	68,200
	Mar[p]	2,700,000	2,370,000	10.5	69,300

Source: Monthly Report, National Association of Realtors, April 1983, p. 5.

[r] Revised   n/a not available
[p] Preliminary   *   not applicable

Cooperative housing does not allow for the flexibility of condominiums. Substantial modifications in the unit require the permission of the corporation, as does the sale, rental, or subleasing of the unit.

Mobile Home

During 1982, 243,000 mobile home units were shipped. Mobile homes represent the least expensive form of single-family dwellings. In addition to the price advantage, mobile homes are usually subject to lower property taxes because some states tax them as vehicles instead of homes. A problem with mobile homes has been zoning laws which preclude them from many neighborhoods. Many states, such as California, have passed laws permitting mobile home owners much greater flexibility in site selection.

Basic Considerations in Home Ownership

The successful choice of a home requires attention to many factors, the most important of which we shall enumerate here.

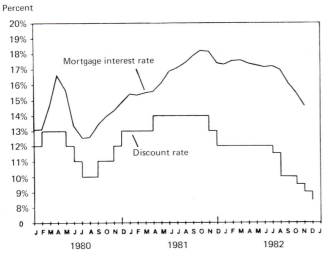

FIGURE 10.2. Mortgage and discount rates.

Source: *Real Estate Quarterly,* vol. 2, no. 1, Winter 1983, p. 1.

The trends in a neighborhood are an important consideration in the determination of appreciation potential. A neighborhood with a high percentage of owner-occupied homes and a tradition of neighborhood pride is most desirable.

The site of the house should be considered in terms of nearness to water; nearness to railroad tracks; nearness to schools, shopping centers, medical services; and in terms of the privacy and of the view it affords. Equally important is the nature of the land making up the site and its ability to hold water. The relationship between the house level and the water table is very important to those homes with a basement.

TABLE 10.4
Apartment Condo and Co-op Sales
(Seasonally Adjusted Annual Rates)

	Year	United States	Northeast	North Central	South	West
	1978	213,000	60,000	54,000	57,000	42,000
	1979	221,000	61,000	56,000	61,000	44,000
	1980	186,000	52,000	46,000	55,000	37,000
	1981	153,000	45,000	33,000	46,000	28,000
	1982	130,000	45,000	26,000	39,000	20,000
1982	I	128,000	42,000	26,000	39,000	21,000
	II	127,000	44,000	25,000	38,000	20,000
	III	127,000	45,000	25,000	37,000	19,000
	IV	140,000	50,000	28,000	42,000	20,000
1983	Iᴾ	169,000	59,000	37,000	50,000	23,000

Source: *Monthly Report,* National Association of Realtors, April 1983, p. 15.

ᴾ Preliminary

Property taxes and utility bills are also important considerations. A prospective owner should ask for previous utility bills and should carefully check the quality and the extent of the insulation of the home.

Other considerations deal with the exterior appearance of the home; the extent of the renovation necessary to suit the taste of the new owner; the quality and accessibility of fire and police protection; the size of the house in relation to the buyer's needs; the crime rate in the neighborhood; the level of noise and air pollution; zoning laws which can prevent the addition of an apartment over the garage or having a tenant; the distance from congested and/or unpleasant areas; and the structural soundness of the house. The latter may be determined by a professional inspection and by a termite inspection.

On the financial side, the considerations are as follows:

1. Buy only a home you can afford. It is recommended that the price of the house not exceed 2.5 times gross annual income, and that the mortgage payments not exceed 25 percent of monthly income. While the affordability of the house is being determined, the closing costs must be kept in mind because they must be made in their entirety along with the down payment. These costs include title insurance fees (average of $200 to $300), fire insurance (¼ percent of sale price), service charges on the mortgage (about 2 percent of a loan), appraisal fees (about $100), escrow fee, legal fees, and the recording fee (about $10). It must be remembered that closing costs differ from one bank to another.

2. The fairness of the asking price for the property must be determined. One easy way is to compare the asking price with the sale price of a similar home recently sold. Another way is to look at the rental value of the property and multiply by a factor appropriate to the community and to the type of property. A rental of $5,000 a year and a factor of ten yield a market value of $50,000. The services of a professional appraiser can alternatively be used.

The home buyer should note that a new home is not necessarily superior in value to an older home with otherwise similar characteristics. Also, the brokerage fee charged the seller is really paid by the buyer. Buying a house directly from the seller could save a considerable sum. Brokerage fees average 7 percent of the sale price. Also, foreclosed property (property repossessed by the lender) is usually cheaper to purchase than other properties, but care must be taken in selecting the property. The likelihood of neglect (little or no maintenance) prior to foreclosure is very real.

Listed prices on a property are usually inflated prices and allow considerable room for bargaining. This bargaining can also carry to the items included in the property such as curtains, refrigerators, washers and dryers, and so forth.

3. Check on liens[3] on the property. Liens may retard the transfer of ownership, if not preclude it.

4. Purchase adequate home insurance with an inflation clause (coverage rising with inflation) if possible.

5. Watch for the liquidity of the property. A house you are considering that has not sold for a long time is likely to present the same problem when you decide to sell it.

6. Pick the appropriate financing arrangement. This is discussed in the next section.

---

[3] A lien is a legal claim on the property for the satisfaction of a debt.

7. Once agreement is reached and the mortgage is arranged, the *deed must be recorded.* This secures the absolute right of the buyer to the property.

Home Mortgages

The level of interest rates and their volatility, since 1978 in particular, have increased the significance of mortgages in the housing investment decision.

A mortgage creates an interest in a property as security for the payment of debt. The party pledging the property (the borrower) is referred to as the mortgagor, and the lender is referred to as the mortgagee.

Before discussing the types of mortgages available, we offer some general recommendations.

1. The size of the mortgage should not exceed 2.5 times current gross income.

2. The borrower must compare mortgages before making a commitment. Lending institutions do not always offer the same terms. Closing costs must be carefully compared.

3. A mortgage should be assumable, that is, transferrable from the current borrower to the new borrower at the same or at advantageous terms (compared with prevailing market conditions). Homeowners with assumable mortgages have found it easier to sell their property at the desired price, particularly when the differential between prevailing mortgage rates and the rate at which the mortgage is assumable is considerable. Unfortunately, assumable mortgages are no longer made by lending institutions with Federal charters. FNMA no longer accepts them in their auctions which practically eliminates the secondary market for this type of mortgage.

4. A mortgage should be open-ended, that is, allowing the borrower to borrow more in the future without having to rewrite the mortgage agreement. The only change will be in the amount borrowed and in the monthly payments calculated at the time the additional financing is provided using prevailing market rates.

5. A mortgage should permit the mortgagor to prepay the full amount borrowed without penalty. If a penalty is required, it should be very reasonable in relation to the size of the loan.

Types of Mortgages

Mortgages come in various types. Their diversity has been increasing dramatically as mortgage funds remain tight and mortgage rates remain high. The new mortgages available have developed as a result of pressures by buyers and sellers alike to maintain accessibility and liquidity.

Conventional Mortgages. A conventional mortgage is one secured by the underlying property and by the financial integrity of the mortgagor.

This type of mortgage has a life of 20 to 30 years, and can be as high as 95 percent of property value (some claim 100 percent). The monthly payments include principal and interest and could, in addition, include property taxes and insurance premiums. If the latter two items and other similar items are included, the mortgage is referred to as a budget mortgage.

FHA-Insured Mortgage. The U.S. federal government has several programs designed to stimulate homeownership among middle and lower income families. Among these programs are those administered by the Federal Housing Authority (FHA) under the

jurisdiction of the Department of Housing and Urban Development.

FHA loans are *insured* by the Federal Housing Authority. The mortgagor pays an insurance premium of up to ½ of 1 percent of the value of the loan. A mortgage inflation fee of up to one percent is also allowed.

The maximum sums that can be borrowed as of April 1983, are

> $67,500 for one-family dwellings,
> $72,000 for two-family dwellings,
> $94,000 for three-family dwellings, and
> $108,000 for four-family dwellings.

The loan amount is figured on the basis of 97 percent of the first $25,000, and 95 percent of the excess over $25,000 (for an owner-occupied dwelling) up to the maximum allowed.

FHA loans are made at a rate usually lower than the prevailing market rate. When market conditions are tight, however, lenders are allowed to add "points" to the loan in order to increase the effective rate of return on the mortgage. A point is equal to one percent of the mortgage size and is assessable against the buyer or the seller, or both. Three points on a $50,000 loan means that $1,500 (50,000 × 3%) will be deducted from the $50,000 when the mortgage agreement is signed. The net effects are that the interest rate is calculated on the basis of $50,000, while only $48,500 has been received.

V.A. Guaranteed Mortgage.   The Veterans Administration (V.A.) is also involved in the housing market. Military personnel, active or retired, may qualify for a V.A.-*guaranteed* loan. The V.A. guarantee is currently (April 1983) the lesser of $27,500 or 60 percent of the loan. The maximum amount that can be borrowed without a down payment is $110,000. This maximum can increase to $135,000, provided the borrower pays 25 percent of the difference between $135,000 and $110,000. The recipient of the loan must live in the mortgaged property, however (similarly for FHA-guaranteed loans).

The rate charged on V.A. loans is equal to that on FHA loans. The "point" system is operational here as well. All V.A. loans may be prepaid without incurring any penalty.

Purchase-Money Mortgage.   In a purchase-money mortgage the seller finances part of the sale price. He is said to "take back" the mortgage. The net result is that the house will have two mortgages: the first mortgage and the junior mortgage. The junior mortgage is subordinated (takes second seat to) the first mortgage in the event of default and liquidation of the underlying property.

Purchase-money mortgages are ordinarily used to finance part of the downpayment on a house.

Wraparound Mortgage.   A wraparound mortgage is possible only when the existing mortgage is assumable. It is achieved by wrapping the interest on the second mortgage around the existing mortgage. This type of mortgage is offered by sellers or lenders. In a seller wraparound mortgage the seller continues to make mortgage payments on the existing mortgage and finances the buyer with a second mortgage. The second mortgage combines the existing balance on the mortgage owed by the seller and the additional financing needed. The seller would charge one rate, which is higher than the one he is

paying on his mortgage and lower than the market rate the home buyer would have had to pay on the new financing.

A wraparound mortgage from a lender requires the home buyer to assume the outstanding mortgage and to finance the additional funds needed. Both mortgages (the new and the old) are combined and only one rate is applicable: the wraparound rate.

Participation Mortgage—Shared Appreciation for Equity (*SAFE*). In a participation mortgage the lender shares in the income, capital appreciation, or both of an income property; or in the capital appreciation of a privately owned and occupied home. The lender is ordinarily a home seller who is not in need of the entire equity in the property. In return, the home buyer is afforded lower down payment and/or lower interest rates.

This type of mortgage, sometimes referred to as shared appreciation for equity, is very popular among young homeowners in areas characterized by high property values.

The share of the lender in the appreciation of the property is determined in advance as is the maximum length of the time period when the property must be sold or its market value calculated for the purpose of settlement with the lender. The house may be sold prior to this date, however. If the property is not sold, its value is usually determined by averaging two appraisals with appropriate adjustments for improvements and damages. The lender runs the risk of lower than expected appreciation, and the borrower the risk of having to refinance the property at higher rates when the contract expires.

Ground Lease. In a ground lease arrangement the buyer acquires a mortgage on the house only and leases the land. This separation between land and home allows prospective homeowners in areas characterized by high land values greater access to homeownership. Ground leases are popular in California, Nevada, Florida, and Colorado.

Other Arrangements. Young homebuyers, those who are single in particular, are increasingly opting for joint ownership. The mortgage is in the names of the two or more parties involved. They share the downpayment and the mortgage payments burden as well.

Paying the Mortgage

There are various ways to meet mortgage obligations. We shall discuss those that are most prevalent.

Fixed Payment Schedule. The fixed payment schedule, the most common of alternatives, calls for a fixed payment made periodically, usually monthly, to the lender. The rate on the mortgage is a fixed rate determined at the time the mortgage is drawn up.

Fixed Payments with a Balloon. This arrangement calls for a fixed mortgage payment during a short period of time (3 to 5 years) and for a balloon payment at the end of the designated period. The last payment (or balloon) will consist of the last monthly mortgage payment plus the balance of the principal owed.

This payment schedule results when the mortgage is of the rollover or renegotiated rate type. At the end of the designated period the mortgage rate is renegotiated. In Illinois, for example, the renegotiated rate cannot rise by more than half a point a

year. The intent behind this type loan, however, is to renegotiate a loan at a lower rate. This accounts for the popularity of the arrangement during 1980–1981 when mortgage rates were at an all-time high. Many homebuyers who expected a reversal in interest rate trends opted for short-term mortgages in the hope of capitalizing on lower future rates.

Mortgage Payment with a Price-Level Adjustment. This arrangement calls for a periodic mortgage payment that is tied to a specified price index. The interest rate on the mortgage remains constant during the life of the mortgage. The monthly payment would vary with the price index.

Variable Rate Mortgage. Variable rate mortgages become very popular. Indeed, some savings and loan institutions issue predominantly variable rate mortgages. Both the mortgage rate and the periodic payments are variable. The mortgage rate and consequently the payment are tied to a certain market rate of interest, usually the prime rate. If the prime rate rises, the mortgage rate rises by a certain percentage determined by a mutually agreed-upon formula.

This payment schedule could be very advantageous if mortgage rates are high and are expected to trend downward. The variable rate permits the borrower considerable flexibility in that he would not have to borrow at a fixed rate now, while still holding onto this option for a time in the future when mortgage rates are at a lower level.

The Federal National Mortgage Association (Fannie Mae) currently makes eight types of adjustable-rate mortgages (ARM) (see Table 10.5). According to a survey by the National Association of Realtors conducted in 1983, the most popular plan is plan eight. Borrowers seem to have a strong preference for ARMs with a ceiling on payment changes and for those where the rate charged is tied to a rate perceived as "stable."

TABLE 10.5
Features of Fannie Mae ARM Plans[a]

Plan	Interest Rate Index	Interest Rate Adjustment Period	Payment Adjustment Period	Maximum Interest Rate Adjustment (cap)	Maximum Payment Adjustment (cap)
1	6-mo. T-Bill	6 mos.	6 mos.	—	7½%
2	6-mo. T-Bill	6 mos.	3 yrs.	—	—
3	1 yr. T-Security	1 yr.	1 yr.	—	7½%
4	3 yr. T-Security	2½ yrs.	2½ yrs.	—	18¾%
5	3 yr. T-Security	2½ yrs.	2½ yrs.	5%	—
6	5 yr. T-Security	5 yrs.	5 yrs.	—	—
7	FHLBB Contract Rate	1 yr.	1 yr.	—	—
8	FHLBB Contract Rate	1 yr.	1 yr.	2%	—

Source: Housing Finance, National Association of Realtors, vol. 3, no. 4, April 1983, p. 2.

[a] Fannie Mae allows graduated payment options with Plans 2, 4 and 6. However, ARMs with this option were not discussed with respondents.

Graduated Payment. Graduated payment mortgages are designed to have the periodic mortgage payments grow with the income of the mortgagor. The terms of the mortgage and the rate remain fixed throughout the life of the mortgage, but the periodic payments increase at regular intervals (every year, for example).

The intent of this arrangement is to make home buying easier for younger homebuyers who have little saved for down payment and who expect much higher levels of income in the future.

Borrowers opting for this program must realize that under certain payment schedules, the "negative amortization" of the principal is possible. That is, the indebtedness of the mortgagor increases in the early years rather than decreases. The early payments would not even cover the full interest expenses for the period; thus, the increase in indebtedness. This may be the only reasonable alternative to certain home buyers, however.

Rollover Mortgage. A rollover mortgage is a long-term mortgage requiring refinancing at specified short-term intervals. The entire balance of the mortgage (the balloon) comes due after a certain period and must be refinanced at then prevailing rates. This type of mortgage is very advantageous during a period of declining mortgage rates.

Zero-Rate Financing. Zero-rate financing is a form of financing requiring no explicit interest payment. It is a common offer made by home builders. The down payment on this type of financing is high (30 to 40 percent) and the life of the mortgage is very short. The Internal Revenue Service recognizes the implicit rate (imputed rate) charged by the builder and allows for its deduction for tax purposes.

Taxes and Home Ownership

The provisions of the tax law dealing with home ownership are numerous and occasionally complex. We shall be satisfied here in providing a brief outline.
Homeownership is a tax-sheltering device resulting from:

1. The tax deductibility of interest costs.
2. The tax deductibility of property and other home-related taxes.
3. The taxability of the appreciation in the value of the property at the preferred capital gains rate if the property is sold after a holding period of a year. The maximum capital gains rate is currently 20 percent compared with 50 percent for income other than wages.

No capital gains tax is owed if another house of equal or higher value is purchased within two years after the sale or is built within two years. The tax liability is not abolished but is deferred until the last property held is sold.

No capital gains tax is owed if at least one spouse is 55 years of age or older on the day the title to the property is transferred. The maximum exclusion (appreciation not subject to capital gains taxes) of $125,000 can only be taken once in a lifetime, and applies to both *husband and wife*. A married couple *cannot* exclude $250,000 if both are 55 or older, are selling a house for the first time, and file a joint return. An additional requirement is that the home must have been the main home for at least three of the last five years prior to its sale.

The calculation of the taxable gain requires the following steps:

1. Calculate the cost basis of the home.

   Cost basis = original cost + expenses (brokerage fees, etc.) + county and city assessments (for roads, sewers, etc.).

2. Net sale price = sale price − fix-up expenses − selling costs.
3. Taxable gain = net sale price − cost basis.

The gain is fully taxable during the tax year when the home is sold, if another property is not purchased within 24 months and if the sale does not qualify for the tax exemption.

If a portion of the home were used for business purposes, the sale of the property must be treated as two separate transactions: One for the business portion, another for the residence portion. The cost basis will also be divided accordingly with the cost of the business portion reduced by the accumulated depreciation. If one-fifth of the house is used for business, then one-fifth of the sale price and of the cost basis go to the business portion. The capital gains tax owed on the business portion must be paid the year the property is sold.

Two additional methods for reducing the tax burden must be examined:

1. The installment sale method allows the seller of a home to sell the property with the sale price paid over a period of time. Effectively, the seller is financing the sale of his property. Only the differential between the net sale price received during a given year and the corresponding cost basis is subject to capital gains tax. The interest income from the mortgagor is subject to regular income taxes, however.

2. An exchange of one property for another of at least equal value is considered a tax-deferred exchange. No tax is owed on the appreciation in the value of the property being exchanged. This can be used in a transaction involving a home or residence or an income property. In the latter case the saving would consist of the capital gains tax, the tax on the recapture of depreciation, and any alternative minimum tax.

The problem in this type transaction is to find the appropriate property for the exchange, which is not always easy.

10.3 INCOME-PRODUCING REAL ESTATE

The discussion in this section centers on the evaluation of the investment value of an apartment building. The logic and the methodology offered are easily adaptable to other real estate investment projects, such as shopping centers and the like.

To illustrate the evaluation process, we use an example taken from the files of a prominent real estate firm in a Midwestern city. Table 10.6 gives detailed description of the property under consideration. Table 10.7 gives the operating income statement for the property as of December 31, 1981. Our objective is to arrive at a market price or range of prices for the property that is consistent with a required rate of return or a range of required rates of return.

TABLE 10.6
Jefferson Blvd. Property Data
(December 1981)

Legal:	Lots 123–124–125–126 Jefferson Blvd.
Lot Size:	176′ × 176′
Number of Units:	15 efficiencies
Current Rents:	$146–$187 (2 apts. at $146/month) (4 apts. at $158/month) (8 apts. at $162/month) (2 apts. at $187/month)
Personal Property:	All units are supplied with stove, refrigerator, disposals and unit air conditioners
Laundry:	On premises—two washers/two dryers Leased Owner takes 40% of gross
Built of:	Brick and Cedar—two story
Heat:	Electric baseboard. Separately metered and paid by tenants
Water:	City—paid by owner
Air Conditioning:	Unit air conditioners in each apartment
Roof:	Asphalt/shingle—good condition
Year Built:	1972
Assessed Value:	Land 4490 Improvements $41,080 Total $45,570
Security:	Controlled access and intercom system
Parking:	Off-street for 18 cars
Annual Tax Rate:	$10.4630 per $100 of assessed value
Annual Taxes:	$3,772.43
Rental History:	Only three vacancies have occurred in the last three years of ownership
Existing Financing:	First Bank balance approximately $125,000, 9½%, 25 years, $1,135.81 per month. Call provision in August 1984
Reason for Sale:	Owners have other interests. Investment has served its purpose.
Price and Terms:	$225,000. First mortgage may be assumed or wrapped. Owner will carry a second mortgage. Creative terms will be considered.

Evaluating Income Property—The Financial Aspects

The evaluation of a real estate investment opportunity, like any capital-budgeting problem, requires the forecasting of the periodic net cash flows that the investment is expected to generate, the determination of the holding period, the forecasting of the selling price at the end of the holding period, and the calculation of the appropriate discount factor. These considerations are summarized in the following equation.

TABLE 10.7
Jefferson Blvd. Property
Operating Income Statement
(December 31, 1981)

Income:	
Gross Annual Receipts—Rent	$28,500
Interest Income	143
Misc. Income—Laundry	458
Total Rents	$29,101
Expenses:	
Supplies	415
Repairs and Decorating	1,028
Utilities	2,087
Advertising	94
Scavenger and Snow Removal	929
Management Fee	480
Miscellaneous	138
Accounting and Attorney's Fee	150
Insurance	715
Taxes	3,800
Total Expenses	$ 9,836
Net operating income	**$19,265**

$$PV = \sum_{t=1}^{n} \frac{NCFAT_t}{(1+K)^t} + \frac{NSP}{(1+K)^N} \tag{10.1}$$

where PV = present value or market value of the property

      $NCFAT$ = net cash flows after taxes

          NSP = net selling price at time N

            K = appropriate discount factor

            N = investment horizon = length of the holding period

It is hoped that the reader is already familiar with the present value and with the internal rate of return concepts. If not, a review of a basic finance text is required.

An alternative formulation of Equation 10.1 allows for the calculation of the internal rate of return.

$$-C + \sum_{t=1}^{n} \frac{NCFAT_t}{(1+K^*)^t} + \frac{NSP}{(1+K^*)^n} = 0 \tag{10.2}$$

where C = asked price for the property

       K^* = the internal rate of return

For a given K (required rate of return), an investment is acceptable if

  1. $PV < C$, or
  2. $K^* > K$

Both Equations 10.1 and 10.2 should yield the same accept/reject decision. Real estate investors find it easier to speak in terms of rates of return. Hence, they prefer for Equation 10.2. We shall, however, use Equation 10.1 in the development of the model.

The model we present here is an abbreviated version of a much larger and complex model developed by the author in cooperation with Khalil Matta. The essential considerations in the evaluation of a real estate investment opportunity are all included, however.

We begin the evaluation process by showing how net cash flows after taxes are arrived at.

Gross Annual Rent	=	rent per unit × number of units
− vacancy	=	a certain percent × gross rent
− bad debts	=	a certain percent × gross rent
Net gross Income		
− operating expenses (see Table 10.7)		
Net operating income (NOI)		
− mortgage payments (interest + principal, (annualized)).		
Cash flows		
+ principal payments	(principal payments are not deductible for tax purposes, this must be added back)	
Adjusted cash flows		
− depreciation (annual)		
Taxable income		
− taxes (assume a fixed rate = 50%)		
Cash flows after taxes		
− principal	(to permit accounting for principal amortization)	
+ depreciation	(must be added back because it is not a cash expense)	
Net cash flows after taxes		

The net cash flow after taxes differs from one period to another. The reasons are

1. Gross annual rent is not constant. Many lease arrangements have automatic escalator clauses indexed to the rate of inflation or requiring a certain percentage increase in rent. The model allows the investor to pick a growth rate consistent with his expectations.

$$GR_t = GR_o(1 + g_1)^t$$

The calculation presented later is based on a value of $g_1 = 10$ percent.

2. The vacancy rate is assumed to fall within 0 percent to 20 percent. The computer program breaks the interval into five values (0%, 5%, 10%, 15%, 20%).

3. The bad debts are not constant. The range used in our calculations is 0 percent to 6 percent. The computer program picks three values (0 percent, 3 percent, and 6 percent).

4. Operating expenses are assumed to increase at a constant rate. The one utilized here is 5 percent.

$$OE_t = OE_o(1 + g_2)^t$$

where OE_o = operating expenses at time zero

g_2 = growth rate in operating expenses

5. The mortgage payments are constant but their components change from one period to another. As the reader must be aware, the interest on a mortgage is paid on the remaining outstanding balance. Thus each successive payment will have a higher principal component and a lower interest component. At the beginning of the mortgage period practically the whole periodic payment is in the form of interest and toward the end of the mortgage period, the largest component of the payment is the principal.

As the interest component of mortgage payments decreases, the tax shelter resulting from leverage decreases as well and, consequently, the tax liability.

6. The addition of the principal amount is necessary because principal payments are not deductible for tax purposes. This sum varies from one period to another. It increases over time.

7. The depreciation expenses are another source of tax shelter. The use of the accelerated method of depreciation could help increase this tax shelter. The Internal Revenue Service has specific guidelines on the methods of depreciation that can be used for each type of property. Investment in land and personal use property cannot be depreciated while investment in income-producing property can be depreciated.

The computation of the tax-deductible depreciation expense is somewhat complicated. The applicable tax laws depend on when the property was acquired. Depreciable tangible property acquired prior to December 31, 1980 may be depreciated by using straight line, sum-of-the-years digits, or one of the declining balance methods of depreciation as shown below.

Type of Property	Acquisition Date	Allowable Method
Residential Rental (new)	After 7/24/69	Declining balance at twice straight line.
Residential Rental (used)	After 7/24/69	Declining balance at 1¼ times straight line.

The method specified does not have to be used, provided that another one of the accepted methods is chosen and that it yields a smaller first-year depreciation than the specified method.

The calculation of accelerated depreciation on a property similar to the one under consideration proceeds as follows:

A. First year:

$$\frac{\text{Cost of Property} - \text{assessed value of land}}{\text{estimated life of building}} = \text{S.L. depreciation}$$

Straight line depreciation/(cost of property − assessed value of land) = percent of property depreciable using straight line (SLD)

Using declining balance, the depreciation would equal

$$(\text{SLD} \times 1.25)\ (\text{cost of property} - \text{assessed value of land}) = (\text{SLD} \times 1.25)\ (\text{net building cost basis})$$

B. Second year (SLD × 1.25) (net building cost basis − first year depreciation) and the process goes on until the last year of the estimated life of building.[4]

The Economic Recovery Tax Act of 1981 changes radically the above provisions for property acquired after December 31, 1980, regardless of when the property was constructed. The Act eliminates the useful life concept [based on either asset depreciation range (ADR) or facts and circumstances], the estimation of salvage value, the differential treatment for used and new assets, and component depreciation. Under the Act real estate used in business, as an investment, or as a tax shelter can only be depreciated in either of two methods under the accelerated cost recovery system (ACRS):

1. 175 percent declining balance method for 15-year real property (200 percent for low-income housing), or
2. straight line depreciation using a 15, 35, or 45 year recovery period.

The above election could be made on a property-by-property basis. Once the election is made, it becomes irrevocable. The 175 percent declining balance method is summarized in a Table provided by the U.S. Treasury. (See Table 10.8.) This table allows for a switch to straight line at the optimum point during the general recovery period. The introduction of ACRs increases the size of the tax shelter derived from a real estate investment because it lowers the recovery period and increases the allowable percentage for the declining balance method. The theory behind this accelerated recovery of an investment is that a higher tax shelter increases the incentive to invest.

Some readers may erroneously conclude that real estate investors would always opt for the declining balance method. This is not so because of the recapture provision in the tax law. This provision requires the taxation as ordinary income of any gain from the sale of a nonresidential real property up to the full depreciation if the accelerated method was used. Had the straight line method been used, none of the gain would be taxed as ordinary income.

The case of a residential property is different. The law requires that only the difference between the higher depreciation using the accelerated method and the depreciation obtained had the straight line method been used be taxed as ordinary income. We use an example to illustrate the recapture provision.

Consider two properties, one residential and the other nonresidential acquired for

---

[4] The shorter the estimated life of the building, the larger the depreciation allowance for each period, and consequently, the larger the tax shelter. Thus, the investor would be most interested in as short a life as possible. The IRS, however, is not very accomodating. The larger the depreciation allowance, the less the tax revenue. The accepted minimum life for a residential property was 20 years under the old tax laws.

TABLE 10.8
ACRS Tables for Real Estate (other than low-income housing)

If the Recovery Year is:	The applicable percentage is: (Use the column for the month the property is placed in service)											
	1	2	3	4	5	6	7	8	9	10	11	12
1	12	11	10	9	8	7	6	5	4	3	2	1
2	10	10	11	11	11	11	11	11	11	11	11	12
3	9	9	9	9	10	10	10	10	10	10	10	10
4	8	8	8	8	8	8	9	9	9	9	9	9
5	7	7	7	7	7	7	8	8	8	8	8	8
6	6	6	6	6	7	7	7	7	7	7	7	7
7	6	6	6	6	6	6	6	6	6	6	6	6
8	6	6	6	6	6	6	5	6	6	6	6	6
9	6	6	6	6	5	6	5	5	5	6	6	6
10	5	6	5	6	5	5	5	5	5	5	6	5
11	5	5	5	5	5	5	5	5	5	5	5	5
12	5	5	5	5	5	5	5	5	5	5	5	5
13	5	5	5	5	5	5	5	5	5	5	5	5
14	5	5	5	5	5	5	5	5	5	5	5	5
15	5	5	5	5	5	5	5	5	5	5	5	5
16	—	—	1	1	2	2	3	3	4	4	4	5

$300,000 each in January 1981 and sold for $500,000 each in January 1984. The depreciation schedule using the declining method and the straight line method would be

	Residential			Nonresidential	
Year	Declining	S. Line	Excess	Declining	S. Line
1	$36,000	20,000	16,000	$36,000	20,000
2	$30,000	20,000	10,000	$30,000	20,000
3	$27,000	20,000	7,000	$27,000	20,000
	$93,000	**$60,000**	**$33,000**	**$93,000**	**$60,000**

Realized gains are as follows:

1. Residential = 500,000 − (300,000 − 93,000) = **$293,000**
2. Nonresidential = 500,000 − (300,000 − 93,000) = **$293,000**

The $293,000 capital gains on the residential property will be taxed as follows: $33,000 (the excess) as ordinary income and $260,000 as long-term capital gains. The gains on the nonresidential property will be taxed as follows: $93,000 (the full depreciation from the declining balance) as ordinary income and $200,000 as long-term capital gain. Clearly, the residential property is at an advantage.

The recapture provision leads, as many tax and finance experts have demonstrated, to superior aftertax results using straight line versus the declining balance method under most circumstances.

An additional consideration with regard to depreciation deals with the "at risk" provision. Briefly, the at-risk provision limits the deduction of losses from an investment to the amount the taxpayer actually has at risk. This provision does not apply to real estate. An investor with a share in a limited real estate partnership is allowed to deduct losses according to his share of the cost basis in the property. The cost basis is determined by the taxpayer's contributions of equity and his share of the purchase price that was financed through nonrecourse debt. This allows investors in limited partnerships to deduct losses in excess of the amount of risk.

A limited partner who invested, say, $10,000 (the price of a unit) in a real estate partnership with a $20,000 mortgage per unit has an asset value of $30,000, which can be depreciated although the loan may never be paid. The $20,000 is ordinarily a nonrecourse debt settled, in the event of bankruptcy, by the mortgage holder taking over the property instead of requiring the partners to pay.

The tax rate will be assumed to equal 50 percent.
The size of the tax shelter (that part of income protected from taxation because of the tax deductibility of interest costs and depreciation) is calculated as follows.

Tax shelter = net operating income − taxable income

We now look at the net sale price.

Net Sale Price

The net sale price from a real estate income property is equal to

NSP = expected sale price (SP) − sales expenses (commissions, etc.) − unpaid mortgage (principal) − capital gains taxes − other taxes (if any)

The capital gains taxes are calculated as follows:

$$\text{CGT} = \left[\text{NSP (except capital gains taxes)} - \left(C - \sum_{t=1}^{n} \text{Dep.} \right) \right] T_{cg} \tag{10.3}$$

where Dep. = periodic (annual in our case) depreciation expenses.

T_{cg} = Capital gains tax rate. We shall assume that it is equal to 20 percent [40 percent (the maximum taxable portion of the gain) × 50 percent (the maximum tax bracket of the individual)].

The sales expenses will be assumed to equal 6 percent of the expected sale price.
The unpaid mortgage will equal zero, as we assume (to simplify the presentation) that the property is sold concurrently with the expiration of the mortgage.[5]
Since the expected sale price is not known with certainty, the computer program was so structured to allow the user to assign three possible growth rates in the value

---

[5] It must be noted that most investors in real estate liquidate their position within 5 years because the tax shelter would have been dissipated by then.

of the property and to attach a probability to each of the growth rates. The model works as follows:

(1) Cost of property at time zero	(2) Assumed compound growth rate in value	(3) Probability of growth rate	(4) Expected growth rate	(5) CVIF 6% 15 yrs.	(6) SP (6) = (1)(5)
$225,000[1]	0%[2]	0.10	0		
	5%	0.60	3.0		
	10%	0.30	3.0		
$225,000		1.00	6.0%	2.397	$539,325

[1] Assumed cost.
[2] Could use any three values.

The net sales price can now be calculated. The task is made deliberately easier by assuming that the property is sold at a time when the mortgage is fully paid off and the property fully depreciated. Full depreciation deserves a comment here. The Internal Revenue Service does not permit any property, regardless of the method of depreciation used, to be depreciated below a reasonable salvage value other than zero. The generally accepted rule is that the salvage value of a residential property is approximately 10 percent of the cost basis.

The net sale price is, therefore, equal to

$$NSP = SP - (SP \times 6\%) - CGT \tag{10.4}$$

where   SP = expected sale price
        SP × 6% = sales commissions and other sales expenses
        CGT = capital gains taxes

Equation 10.4 assumes that the unpaid mortgage is equal to zero and that "other expenses" are also equal to zero.

We now discuss the discount factor K.

The Discount Rate

The appropriate discount factor can be arrived at in various ways.

The first way is to use the borrowing cost to the individual investor or the cost of capital to an entity in which the investor is a participant. If the entity is a corporate entity, the cost of capital could be calculated as follows (assuming debt and equity are used in financing the investment project):

$$K_c = W_e K_e + W_d K_d (1 - T_c)$$

where K_c = cost of capital

K_e = cost of equity = $\frac{D}{MP} + g$ where D = dividend on stock, MP = market price of stock and g = growth rate in dividends

K_d = cost of debt. The current rate, as opposed to the historic rate, should be used

T_c = corporate tax rate

The second route is to use an appropriate opportunity cost. If the funds committed to the investment project could have earned a certain rate of return in an alternative investment with similar risk characteristics, then use this rate as a discount factor.

The third route is to use the capital asset pricing model,

$$K_i = R_F + \beta(K_M - R_F)$$

where K_i = required rate of return on investments

K_M = rate of return on a market index

R_F = risk-free rate = rate on a three-month Treasury bill

$$\beta = \frac{\text{Cov}(K_i, K_M)}{\sigma^2(K_M)} = \frac{\begin{array}{c}\text{the covariance of the rate of return} \\ \text{on investment } i \text{ (or on an investment} \\ \text{with similar characteristics) with} \\ \text{the rate of return on a market index}\end{array}}{\begin{array}{c}\text{variance of the rate of return on} \\ \text{a market index}\end{array}}$$

The market index could consist of the index of rates of return on income-producing residential real estate in the United States or another index with which it is highly correlated, perhaps the Standard & Poor's Composite Index.

The fourth route is to use various hurdle rates, the lowest of which represent the minimum rate of return acceptable to the investor and the highest representing the most realistically desirable rate.

We have opted for the fourth method. Our computer program allows the user to specify a range, say 15 to 25 percent, and selects the lowest value, the highest value, and the medium value. The range picked by the investor is presumed to be consistent with investment opportunities currently available in the market and consistent with the investment's risk characteristics.

Present Value of the Property

Having calculated the net cash flows after taxes for each of the years during the life of the investment, having selected the range for K, and having estimated the net selling price, we are now ready to calculate the range of present values—that is, the range of bid prices, each of which is consistent with a given rate of return.[6] This requires the application of Equation 10.1. An alternative form to Equation 10.1 preferred by practitioners because of its emphasis on the tax shelter elements in a real estate property, is as follows:

---

[6] This rate represents the aftertax rate of return because taxes are already accounted for in the numerator and because double taxation does not apply in this case.

$$PV = \sum_{t=1}^{n} \frac{\text{NOI}_t - (I + Pr)_t}{(1+K)^t} + \sum_{t=1}^{n} \frac{\text{Dep}_t(T)}{(1+K)^t}$$

$$+ \sum_{t=1}^{n} \frac{I_t(T)}{(1+K)^t} + \frac{\text{NSP}}{(1+K)^n} \qquad (10.5)$$

where NOI_t = net operating income at time t

$\quad\quad I_t$ = interest payments at time t

$\quad\quad Pr_t$ = principal payments at time t

$\quad\text{Dep}_t$ = depreciation allowance at time t

$\quad\quad\quad T$ = the personal tax rate

$\quad\text{NSP}$ = net selling price

$\quad\quad\quad K$ = rate of return on the real estate investment

The computer model developed by the author follows Equation 10.5. It also provides data on the size of the shelter in each period.

Applying the computer program to the data on the Jefferson Blvd. Property (see Tables 10.6 and 10.7) using the values indicated earlier for the time period, the growth rates, the vacancy and bad debt rates, and the discount factors, we obtained the results shown in Tables 10.9 (a sample of the output when the vacancy rate and the bad debt rate are equal to zero percent), and 10.10.

For a given value of K an investor can calculate the probability of loss, given various rates of occupancy and bad debts and given that a certain price has been paid for the property. Similarly, for given vacancy and bad debt rates, the probability of not realizing the average rate of return can be calculated.

If the actual price paid for the property is $225,000, the probability of realizing a loss because of paying a price higher than the mean value, given a rate of return after taxes, is calculated as follows:

1. From Table 10.10 calculate the mean value of the property for the 10 percent aftertax rate of return (could use any of the rates).

$E(PV) = 209,594.62$

2. Calculate the standard deviation of the values in the 10 percent column (Table 10.10).

$\sigma = \sqrt{E(X^2) - (E(X))^2} = 14{,}495$

3. Calculate the standard normal variate (the Z score).

$$Z = \frac{225{,}000 - 209{,}594.62}{14{,}495} = 1.06$$

4. Look in Table 1 in the Appendix of this chapter to find the probability corresponding to $Z = 1.06$.

$P(0 \le Z \le 1.06) = 14.46\%.$

The 14.46 percent represents the increased probability of realizing a rate of return lower than that of K used as a discount factor (the required after tax rate of return).

TABLE 10.9

```
**** VACANCY RATE OF    0 % ******

**** BAD DEPT RATE      0 % ******
```

YEAR	1982	1983	1984	1985	1986
GROSS ANNUAL RENT:	28500.00	31350.01	34485.02	37933.53	41726.90
LESS VACANCY 0 %:	0.0	0.0	0.0	0.0	0.0
LESS BAD DEBTS 0 %:	0.0	0.0	0.0	0.0	0.0
EFFECTIVE GROSS INCOME:	28500.00	31350.01	34485.02	37933.53	41726.90
LESS OPERATING EXPENSES:	6021.00	6322.05	6638.15	6970.06	7318.56
NET OPERATING INCOME:	22479.00	25027.96	27846.87	30963.47	34408.34
LESS MORTGAGE PAYMENTS:	32119.67	32119.67	32119.66	32119.66	32119.66
PRINCIPLE:	3678.30	4269.64	4956.07	5752.83	6677.67
INTEREST:	28441.37	27850.02	27163.60	26366.82	25441.99
CASH FLOWS:	-9640.67	-7091.71	-4272.80	-1156.18	2288.61
PRINCIPLE:	3678.30	4269.64	4956.07	5752.83	6677.67
ADJUSTED CASH FLOW:	-5962.37	-2822.07	683.27	4596.65	8966.35
LESS DEPRECIATION:	16874.99	15468.74	14179.68	12998.04	11914.86
TAXABLE INCOME:	-22837.36	-18290.80	-13496.41	-8401.39	-2948.52
LESS TAXES:	-11418.68	-9145.40	-6748.20	-4200.69	-1474.26
CASH FLOWS AFTER TAXES:	5456.31	6323.34	7431.47	8797.34	10440.61
LESS PRINCIPLE:	3678.30	4269.64	4956.07	5752.83	6677.67
DEPRECIATION:	16874.99	15468.74	14179.68	12998.04	11914.86
CASH FLOW AFTER TAX:	18653.00	17522.43	16655.08	16042.54	15677.80
TAX SHELTER:	45316.36	43318.76	41343.27	39364.86	37356.85

YEAR	1987	1988	1989	1990	1991
GROSS ANNUAL RENT:	45899.60	50489.58	55538.55	61092.43	67201.69
LESS VACANCY 0 %:	0.0	0.0	0.0	0.0	0.0
LESS BAD DEBTS 0 %:	0.0	0.0	0.0	0.0	0.0
EFFECTIVE GROSS INCOME:	45899.60	50489.58	55538.55	61092.43	67201.69
LESS OPERATING EXPENSES:	7684.49	8068.71	8472.14	8895.75	9340.54
NET OPERATING INCOME:	38215.11	42420.87	47066.41	52196.68	57861.15
LESS MORTGAGE PAYMENTS:	32119.65	32119.65	32119.66	32119.66	32119.65
PRINCIPLE:	7751.18	8997.27	10443.67	12122.58	14071.41
INTEREST:	24368.47	23122.38	21675.98	19997.07	18048.24
CASH FLOWS:	6095.46	10301.21	14946.76	20077.02	25741.50
PRINCIPLE:	7751.18	8997.27	10443.67	12122.58	14071.41
ADJUSTED CASH FLOW:	13846.64	19298.48	25390.43	32199.61	39812.91
LESS DEPRECIATION:	10921.96	10011.79	9177.48	8412.68	7711.62
TAXABLE INCOME:	2924.68	9286.69	16212.95	23786.92	32101.29
LESS TAXES:	1462.34	4643.34	8106.47	11893.46	16050.64
CASH FLOWS AFTER TAXES:	12384.30	14655.14	17283.95	20306.14	23762.27
LESS PRINCIPLE:	7751.18	8997.27	10443.67	12122.58	14071.41
DEPRECIATION:	10921.96	10011.79	9177.48	8412.68	7711.62
NET CASH FLOW AFTER TAX:	15555.08	15669.66	16017.76	16596.25	17402.48
TAX SHELTER:	35290.43	33134.18	30853.46	28409.76	25759.86

YEAR	1992	1993	1994	1995	1996
GROSS ANNUAL RENT:	73921.87	81314.06	89445.44	98390.00	108229.00
LESS VACANCY 0 %:	0.0	0.0	0.0	0.0	0.0
LESS BAD DEBTS 0 %:	0.0	0.0	0.0	0.0	0.0
EFFECTIVE GROSS INCOME:	73921.87	81314.06	89445.44	98390.00	108229.00
LESS OPERATING EXPENSES:	9807.57	10297.95	10812.84	11353.48	11921.16
NET OPERATING INCOME:	64114.31	71016.06	78632.56	87036.50	96307.81
LESS MORTGAGE PAYMENTS:	32119.65	32119.65	32119.66	32119.67	32119.67
PRINCIPLE:	16333.52	18959.25	22007.10	25544.85	29651.30
INTEREST:	15786.13	13160.39	10112.56	6574.82	2468.33
CASH FLOWS:	31994.66	38896.41	46512.91	54916.83	64188.14
PRINCIPLE:	16333.52	18959.25	22007.10	25544.85	29651.31
ADJUSTED CASH FLOW:	48328.18	57855.67	68520.00	80461.62	93839.41
LESS DEPRECIATION:	7068.99	6479.91	5939.91	5444.92	4991.11
TAXABLE INCOME:	41259.18	51375.76	62580.09	75016.69	88848.22
LESS TAXES:	20629.59	25687.88	31290.04	37508.34	44424.12
CASH FLOWS AFTER TAXES:	27698.59	32167.79	37229.96	42953.28	49415.31
LESS PRINCIPLE:	16333.52	18959.25	22007.10	25544.85	29651.30
DEPRECIATION:	7068.99	6479.91	5939.91	5444.92	4991.18
NET CASH FLOW AFTER TAX:	18434.06	19688.44	21162.77	22853.35	24755.18
TAX SHELTER:	22855.12	19640.30	16052.48	12019.81	7459.56

```
*** ENPV 1:    234273.31 AT A RATE OF RETURN OF 10.00 % ******

*** ENPV 2:    153348.25 AT A RATE OF RETURN OF 15.00 % ******

*** ENPV 3:    108100.19 AT A RATE OF RETURN OF 20.00 % ******
```

TABLE 10.10
Present Value of the Property Under Different Assumptions

Discount rate Vacancy rate Bad debt rate	10 percent (After-tax rate of return)	15 percent (After-tax rate of return)	20 percent (After-tax rate of return)
0 percent (Vacancy) 0 percent (Bad debt)	$239,273.31	$153,348.25	$108,100.19
0 3	$228,443.75	$149,187.44	$104,984.19
0 6	$222,614.00	$145,026.81	$101,868.25
5 0	$224,556.25	$146,413.56	$102.906.94
5 3	$219,019.19	$142,460.87	$ 99,946.81
5 6	$213,481.06	$138,508.12	$ 96,986.62
10 0	$214,841.31	$139,479.06	$97,713.75
10 3	$209.594.69	$135,734.25	$94,909.44
10 6	$204,348.12	$131,989.62	$ 92,105.12
15 0	$205,125.37	$132,544.37	$ 92,520.62
15 3	$200,170.12	$129,007.75	$ 89,872.00
15 6	$195,215.06	$125,471.06	$ 87,223.50
20 0	$195,409.37	$125,609.81	$ 87,327.37
20 3	$190,745.69	$122,281.25	$ 84,834.56
20 6	$186,082.06	$118,952.56	$ 82,341.81

The probability of the actual price exceeding a price that results from a specific set of circumstances (a certain value for the occupancy rate and the bad debt rate) could be calculated in a manner similar to that just discussed.

The calculations reported in Tables 10.9 and 10.10 are based on many assumptions, which we shall summarize again. The critical ones are

1. The growth rate in rental income is 10 percent and is constant throughout the life of the project.

2. The growth rate in operating expenses is 5 percent and is constant throughout the life of the project.

3. The chosen K is constant throughout the project.

4. No major repairs will be needed on the property, that is, no new roof, no new appliances, no new air conditioning, and so forth will be needed during the holding period. This somewhat unrealistic assumption could be rationalized on the basis that if any of these expenditures become necessary, they will be met by a proportional increase in rent.

5. The depreciation rate is 125 percent of straight line depreciation.

6. The liquidation date of the property, the expiration date of the mortgage, and the depreciable life of the property are all equal.

7. The mortgage is on 85 percent of the asked price for the property and the mortgage rate is 15 percent.

These assumptions, while restrictive, are not intended to dilute the analysis, but simply to make it more manageable. The expanded version of the computer program does reduce, if not eliminate, some of these restrictions, but it is too complex to report in this text.

The Full Analysis

The preceding section dealt with the financial aspects of a real estate project. This is only one part of the full analysis. Table 10.11 shows in great detail the many necessary steps for a deliberate, careful, and complete analysis of an investment project. The reader is urged to scrutinize it carefully and to consult the sources of the table for further details.

TABLE 10.11
Real Estate Market Analysis

I. Delineation of the market area, geography, and climate

A. Metropolitan area

  1. Name of standard metropolitan statistical area (SMSA)
  2. Identification of entire area
     a. County or counties
     b. Principal incorporated and unincorporated urbanized areas (10,000 or more population)
  3. Geography
     a. Size (land area)
     b. Major topographical features
  4. Climate
     a. Rainfall
     b. Temperature changes (monthly, seasonal)
     c. Relative humidity

  5. General urban structure; location of facilities
     a. Significant geographic sub-markets in SMSA
     b. Employment areas
     c. Shopping areas (central-business-district, regional and community shopping centers)
     d. Principal transportation facilities (air, highway, rail, water)
     e. Educational facilities
     f. Community facilities (religious, cultural, recreational)
  6. Direction of city growth
  7. Commuting patterns (journey to work)
  8. Any major community developments and/or special features or

TABLE 10.11 *(Continued)*

characteristics germane to the
market analysis

II. Demographic analysis
  A. Population
    1. Most recent estimate for total pop-
       ulation
    2. Past trends in population growth
    3. Estimated future population
       a. 1980, 1985, 1990, 1995 totals
          and average annual rate of
          growth
       b. Changes in population due to
          (1) Net natural increase
          (2) Migration
    4. Distribution by age groups
       a. 1970 census
       b. Most recent estimates
  B. Households
    1. Most recent estimates for house-
       hold formations
    2. Past trends in household forma-
       tions
    3. Estimated future total households
       and average annual rate of growth
    4. Current trends in household size
       (increasing, decreasing)

III. Economy of the market area
  A. Economic history and characteristics
    1. General description
    2. Major economic activities and de-
       velopments
       a. Before 1970
       b. Recent and present
  B. Employment, total and nonagricul-
     tural
    1. Current estimates (1975 annual
       data, 1976 monthly)
    2. Past trends: 1960, 1970, 1971,
       1972, 1973, 1974
    3. Distribution by industry groups
       a. For each period, past and pres-
          ent
       b. Numerical and as percent of all
          employment
    4. Estimated future employment
       a. Total
       b. By industry groups
    5. Trends in labor participation rate

6. Trends in female employment
  C. Unemployment
    1. Current level
    2. Past trends
  D. Economic-base analysis
    1. Shift-share analysis: metropolitan
       area compared to national and
       state employment data
    2. Alternative: location quotients
    3. Discussion of principal employers
       a. Primary industries (manufac-
          turing, construction, mining)
       b. Secondary industries (TCU,
          trade, FIRE, services, govern-
          ments)
       c. Location and accessibility
    4. Payroll data (census of manufac-
       turers, trade, services, govern-
       ments)
  E. Income data
    1. Personal income by major sources
       a. By type: wage and salary, pro-
          prietors
       b. By industry: farm, nonfarm,
          government
    2. Per capita personal income
    3. Family-income distribution
       a. All families
       b. Owner households
       c. Renter households
       d. Households and female heads
    4. Projections for growth in personal
       income

IV. Construction and real estate activity
  A. Building and construction industry
    1. Residential building by type (sin-
       gle-family, multifamily, rental or
       sales)
       a. Historical and recent trends
          (past 10 years)
       b. Building permits: monthly for
          current and previous year
       c. Conversions and demolitions
    2. Nonresidential construction
       a. Commercial
       b. Industrial
       c. Institutional
    3. High-rise building activity (mini-
       mum height of five stories above
       ground)

TABLE 10.11 *(Continued)*

a. Residential
b. Commercial (offices, stores, hotel and motels, multiple-use)
c. Other (governmental, schools, hospitals)
4. Heavy engineering construction
B. Demand-and-supply analysis for properties other than residential
   1. General demand factors in metropolitan area
      a. Number of potential new employees
      b. Number of potential new tenants or owner-users
      c. Movement of firms in and out of the area
      d. Recent trends in replacement ratios
   2. Existing inventory, by property type
      a. Price: sale or rental rates
      b. Quantity: net leasable square footage
      c. Year built: before 1960, 1960–1975, new
      d. Competitive status
      e. Vacancy factors
   3. Project production, by property type
      a. Price: sale or rental rates
      b. Quantity: net leasable space
      c. Probable conditions (financing, marketing, absorption rates)
C. Housing inventory, by type (single-family, multifamily)
   1. Most recent estimates
   2. Past trends including 1970 census
      a. Index of housing values and rents
   3. Principal characteristics
      a. Tenure of occupancy
      b. Value of houses and monthly contract rent
      c. Type of structure
      d. Year built
      e. Vacancy ratios: percent of total units (total, homeowner, rental)
D. Residential sales and rental markets
   1. General market conditions
   2. Major subdivision activity

a. Current
b. Past trends
3. Trends in sales prices or monthly rentals
   a. Existing units
   b. New units
   c. Sales prices or monthly rentals adjusted to square-foot basis
4. Unsold inventory of new sales housing
   a. Price ranges
   b. Number of months unsold
   c. Absorption rates
   d. Environmental ratings
   e. Competitive status with other sales properties
5. New rental housing
   a. Date of completion
   b. Type of units and rental ranges
   c. Marketing experience to date
   d. Absorption rates
   e. Environmental ratings
   f. Competitive status with existing rental housing
6. Residential units under construction
   a. Volume
   b. Types of units
   c. Probable environmental ratings
   d. Probable marketing schedules
E. Other housing markets
   1. Public and government subsidized housing
      a. Identification and location
      b. Existing and planned
   2. Specialized submarkets for housing demand and supply
      a. College or university housing
      b. Housing for the elderly
      c. Military housing
F. Real estate loans and mortgage markets
   1. Sources and availability of funds
   2. FHA, VA, FNMA, GNMA
   3. Interest rates and terms of mortgages
   4. Recordings of mortgages and/or deeds of trust
   5. Foreclosures
      a. Overall trend
      b. Conventional, FHA, other

TABLE 10.11 (*Continued*)

V. Political and legal aspects
  A. Land-use planning
    1. Regional
    2. County(ies)
    3. Incorporated cities in SMSA
  B. Zoning
    1. Review of present zoning ordinances for county(ies) and cities
    2. Zoning history and present attitudes of zoning authority
    3. Identify raw land presently zoned for land use of subject property
  C. Ordinances, codes, regulations
    1. Subdivisions
      a. Submission procedures
      b. Requirements for improvements
    2. Building codes
    3. Health and public safety
    4. Allocation of land for schools, recreational areas, open space
  D. Municipal services
    1. Public safety
      a. Fire
      b. Police
    2. Hospitals and health care
    3. Utilities
  E. Ecological
    1. Environmental-impact studies
    2. Limited growth policies
    3. Floodplains and flood control
    4. Solid-waste disposal

  F. Property taxation
    1. Tax rate per $1,000 valuation
    2. Assessment ratio as percent of market value
    3. Special assessment districts

VI. Identify sources of information
  A. Population
  B. Employment
  C. Personal income
  D. Planning
  E. Building
  F. Zoning
  G. Other pertinent

VII. Qualifications of the real estate market analyst(s)

VIII. Visual materials
  A. Metropolitan area road map (major traffic arteries)
  B. Topographical maps
  C. Land-use planning maps (present and future uses)
  D. Map(s) showing present urban structure and location of facilities
  E. Subdivision plots
  F. Aerial photographs of area(s)
  G. Area map showing location of subject property(ies) and comparables
  H. Photographs of comparable properties

Source: U.S. Department of Housing and Urban Development. *FHA Techniques of Housing Market Analysis.* Washington, August 1970. Jordan E. Glazov, "A Market Analysis for Land Assemblage," *Real Estate Today,* March 1975, pp. 32–36, and William R. Beaton and Robert J. Bond. *Real Estate,* Goodyear Pacific Palisades, Calif., 1976 in Paul E. Wendt and Alan R. Cerf, *Real Estate Investment Analysis and Taxation,* 2 Ed., New York, McGraw-Hill, Inc., 1979.

Real Estate and Portfolio Analysis

A real estate investment must not be considered in isolation, but as an element in the portfolio of investments held by an investor. The reasons are risk diversification and return maximization.

The variance of a portfolio is calculated as follows.

$$\sigma_p^2 = \sum_{i=1}^{n} W_i^2 \sigma_i^2 + 2 \sum_i \sum_{i<j} W_i W_j \sigma_{i,j}$$

where σ_p^2 = variance of the rates of return on the portfolio

W_i = weight of each type security in the portfolio.

σ_i^2 = variance of the rate of return on security type i in the portfolio.

$\sigma_{i,j}$ = the covariance between the rate of return on security type i, and the rate of return on security type j.

The rate of return on the portfolio is calculated as follows.

$$E(R_p) = \sum_i W_i E(R_i)$$

Where $E(R_p)$ = expected rate of return on the portfolio.

$E(R_i)$ = expected rate of return on security type i.

An investor may wish to know how a certain percentage of his total resources invested in real estate affects the riskiness and the rate of return on the total portfolio. This can be easily determined using a computer simulation technique. P. Wendt and A. Cerf[7] simulated a portfolio consisting of varied percentages of municipal bonds, Standard and Poor's 500 stocks, and real estate investments (not only residential income property), and obtained the results shown in Table 10.12.

The results show that the more real estate investment accounts for the total portfolio, the more stable the portfolio is (a lower standard deviation), and the higher its rate of return. The reader should not, however, rush to the erroneous conclusion that 100 percent investment in real estate is optimal.

The results of Wendt and Cerf are not very robust, for they are based on a restrictive set of assumptions under certain states of the world. They are indicative, however, of the type of analysis necessary to establish a comprehensive, coherent investment strategy and of the constructive role real estate can play in an investment portfolio.

TABLE 10.12
Estimated After-tax Yields on Three Hypothetical Portfolios, 1977–1981

Type of investment	Portfolio (percent)		
	A	B	C
Municipal-bond fund	25 %	20 %	15 %
Standard and Poor's 500	50	40	35
Real estate investments	25	40	50
Estimated mean average aftertax return	10.3	11.0	11.5
Standard deviation of portfolio returns	5.27	3.28	2.49
Range:			
±1	5.03 to 15.57	7.72 to 14.28	9.01 to 13.99
±2	−0.24 to 20.84	4.44 to 17.56	6.52 to 16.48

---

[7] **Paul E. Wendt** and **Alan R. Cerf**, *Real Estate Investment Analysis and Taxation*, 2 Ed. McGraw-Hill, Inc., New York, 1979.

Thus far we have discussed risk diversification across investment vehicles. Diversification is also possible, indeed desirable, within the real estate portion of a portfolio. The investor can achieve this diversification (across types of real estate property and across geographic areas) on his own by buying a share in or a complete set of real estate projects. The rates of return on these projects must not be perfectly positively correlated for risk diversification to result. This strategy requires, however, a substantial commitment of funds and considerable expertise in a wide range of real estate projects, which are beyond the reach of most investors. A suitable diversification alternative is available through real estate investment trusts, which we discuss next.

10.4 REAL ESTATE INVESTMENT TRUSTS

Real estate investment trusts (REITs) are closed-end investment companies that sell a *fixed* number of shares and debt instruments to the public and use the proceeds to invest in income-producing real estate projects and in real estate mortgages.

Types of REITs

There are two basic types of REITs: Equity REITs and Mortgage REITs.

Equity REITs are investment companies that invest the bulk of their equity and debt capital in the ownership of income properties.

Mortgage REITs, on the other hand, use the bulk of their equity and debt capital to supply financing to the real estate market.

Within these broad categories of REITs there exist a wide array of options. Some equity REITs specialize in office buildings, shopping centers, hotels, warehouses, or apartment buildings. Others may specialize in joint ventures (with builders) or in land purchase-leaseback arrangements.[8]

Mortgage REITs may specialize in long-term first mortgages, second mortgages, short-term construction and development loans, and other type of mortgages. Depending on the maturity of their portfolios, mortgage REITs are distinguished into two groups: long-term mortgage trusts that hold 20-year or longer mortgages, and short-term mort-

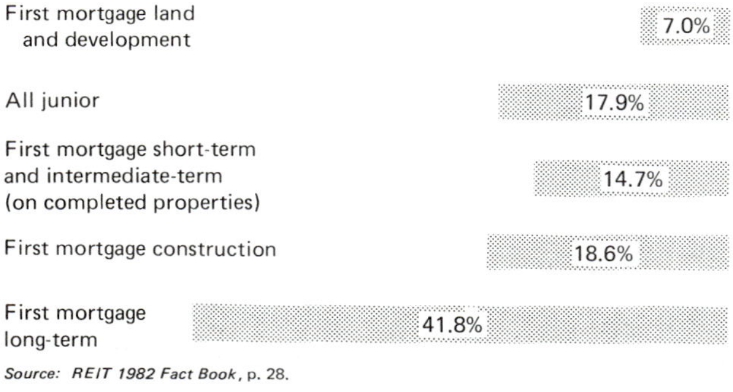

First mortgage land and development	7.0%
All junior	17.9%
First mortgage short-term and intermediate-term (on completed properties)	14.7%
First mortgage construction	18.6%
First mortgage long-term	41.8%

FIGURE 10.3.   Mortgage loans of REITs (year end 1982).

Source: *REIT 1982 Fact Book*, p. 28.

---

[8] A land purchase-leaseback is an arrangement whereby the REIT purchases the land on which a property is built and leases it back to the property owner. The benefits are that the owner of the property would have disposed of an undepreciable property, and the REIT would have an income-producing property with an appreciation potential.

gage trusts, which hold mortgages of shorter maturity. The distribution of the mortgage loans made by REITs is shown in Figure 10.3.

Equity REITs accounted for the majority of the industry assets until the late 1960s. By 1973, mortgage REITs accounted for over 80 percent of the industry assets. After a serious setback in the mid-1970s, the industry rebounded and shifted its emphasis to equity participation. Mortgage holdings accounted for less than 40 percent of the REIT industry assets by January 1, 1983. (See Table 10.13.)

A Brief Historical Overview

The first REIT was organized in Massachusetts during the middle of the nineteenth century.

> . . . the business trust form of organization was utilized in Massachusetts for pooled ownership of real estate. The business trust, or "Massachusetts Trust," was favored because it possessed characteristics common to corporations, i.e., limited liability for shareholders, transferable ownership interests, centralized management, and continuity of life. [9]

The issue to arise later dealt with the taxation of the trust as an entity. Considering its similarity to a corporate structure, the early laws oscillated between taxability and nontaxability. It was not until September 14, 1960, when bill H.R. 10960 was signed into law by President Eisenhower and became Public Law 86–779 that the REIT industry was launched. The purpose of the law was to allow the small investor access to large

TABLE 10.13
December 31, 1982
REIT Industry Balance Sheet*
($ millions)

Assets		Liabilities	
First mortgages:		Commercial paper	$ 428.7
Land and development	$ 195.4	Bank borrowings	576.4
Construction	523.5	Senior non-convertible debt	268.0
Completed properties:		Sub. non-convertible debt	26.5
0–10 years	411.6	Convertible debt	371.9
10 + years	1,170.3	Mortgage on property owned	2,043.2
Junior mortgages	501.6	Other liabilities	325.7
Loan loss allowance	(68.9)		4,040.4
Property owned	4,152.2		
Cash & other assets	645.8	Shareholders' equity	3,491.1
	$7,531.5		$7,531.5

Source: REIT 1982 Fact Book, p. 34.

* The most recently published financial statements of all REITs of which NAREIT has any record. The totals in this table and all other REIT tables do not necessarily equal the sum of their parts due to rounding. Joint venture and partnership interests are also included in "property owned" at the amounts reported on REIT balance sheets.

[9] **Donald J. Valechi,** "REITs: An Historical Perspective." *The Appraisal Journal* (July 1977), p. 449.

real estate projects from which he was barred by the limited size of his equity. The access is provided through the pooling principle for the purpose of participation in real estate ownership or financing under the watchful eyes of the SEC. By the end of 1982, 121 REITs were in existence with assets exceeding $7.5 billion. (See Table 10.14.) REITs are managed by their trustees with the help of employees and frequently of outside advisors. Several (48) REITs operate without advisors and had assets equal to $2.5 billion or 33.33 percent of the industry assets by the end of 1982. REITs are structured either as trusts (the dominant form) or as corporations. The first issues shares of beneficial interest and the latter issues common stock.

The law effectively treats a REIT like any other investment company. REITs are not taxable as an entity provided

1. At least 95 percent of taxable income is distributed to shareholders.
2. 75 percent or more of the trust's assets must be real estate-related.
3. 75 percent or more of the trust's income is derived from real estate-related assets.
4. The trust does not hold property primarily for sale, and the property held is managed by other than the employees or the advisor of the trust.
5. There are 100 or more shareholders where no five shareholders or less own more than half the outstanding shares during the second half of the taxable year.

The elimination of double taxation—one at the level of the trust, the other at the level of the shareholder receiving a distribution from the trust—coupled with a strong economy led to a remarkable increase in the assets of the REIT industry. Between 1968 and 1972 alone, the total assets of the REIT industry increased from $1.03 billion to $14.18 billion. The lion's share of the growth came from the newly discovered mortgage

TABLE 10.14
REIT Assets by Type of Advisor
(Year-end 1982)

Category	Number of REITs	Total Assets ($ millions)	Percent of Assets
Commercial bank	4	$ 668.7	8.9%
Independent mortgage banker, broker, or real estate-oriented co.	26	1,332.9	17.7
Advisor owned by individuals	14	886.5	11.8
Life insurance company	3	254.3	3.4
Conglomerate	6	986.5	13.1
No advisor	48	2,523.5	33.5
Other including unknown	19	845.8	11.2
Totals	121	$7,531.5	100.0%

Source: REIT 1982 Fact Book, p. 11.

Note: In many instances indirect ties, overlaps, and partial ownership of the advisor impede efforts to place an advisor in any one category. Any REIT whose advisor was at least 50 percent owned by a bank, bank holding company, or bank holding company subsidiary was considered to fall into the "commercial bank" category. Similar yardsticks were employed in classifying REITs into the other categories of advisor affiliation.

FIGURE 10.4. NAREIT share price index: Dec. 1981—76.53; Dec. 1982—88.89. (The December, 1982 index figure is up 16.2% from a year ago 1981.)

	1982						
Jan.	74.52	Apr.	73.19	July	70.76	Oct.	84.42
Feb.	72.46	May	72.06	Aug.	75.16	Nov.	87.86
Mar.	72.41	June	69.06	Sept.	77.39	Dec.	88.89

(Share price index adjusted /1/83)

Source: National Association of Real Estate Investment Trusts.

REITs, which were largely sponsored by the banking industry. The banks considered REITs as an appropriate vehicle for relieving the mortgage market from the credit crunch of 1968–1972. Bankers borrowed heavily in the money markets to satisfy the loan demand.

This euphoria came to an abrupt end in 1974 after the real estate market had softened considerably. The results were devastating to the REIT industry as reflected in the NAREIT (National Association of Real Estate Investment Trusts) share price Index. (See Figure 10.4.) Huge losses were taken and many bank-sponsored REITs were threatened by bankruptcy. The Chase Manhattan Mortgage and Realty Trust, the largest bank-sponsored REIT, was hit hardest. Despite heroic efforts by the parent company, Chase Manhattan Bank, to save it, it filed for protection under Chapter XI of the bankruptcy law on January 22, 1979. Its assets had fallen from $941 million in 1975 to merely $270 million by filing time.

The reasons for the demise of the REIT industry, those bank-sponsored REITs in particular, were documented by Clarence C. Elebash.[10] They are

1. The impact of the 1973–1975 recession. Hardest hit was the state of Florida where REIT lending was concentrated.

2. The too rapid growth pace which led to inefficiencies and recklessness.

---

[10] **Clarence C. Elebash,** "Bank REITs: A Continuing Embarrassment." *The Appraisal Journal* (April 1980).

3. Incompetent asset managers who merely collected the rent and offered little, if any, advice on real estate trends and strategy.

4. Excessive leverage by REITs proved disastrous. Toward the end of 1973, 40 percent of the bank-sponsored REITs equity and debt was in commercial paper. The high interest rates required refinancing at increasingly higher rates, which exceeded the projected rate of return on the property. Unable to renew commercial paper or to sell new equity, and forced to distribute 90 percent of their earnings to maintain their tax-exempt status, many REITs were forced to liquidate their properties at substantial losses.

5. The riskiness of the projects being financed and the nature of the financing was grossly underestimated. Inexperience and greed finally took their toll.

In addition to the liquidation of property, REITs needed sources of funds which came from revolving credit arrangements, debt structuring, and asset swaps. The latter involved trading loans and property for debt forgiveness and cash.

The lesson of the 1973–1974 period has not been lost. The 11 bank REITs that survived those years had substantially restructured their portfolios by 1978, as is shown in Table 10.15.

Loans were deemphasized in favor of property ownership and commerical paper was downgraded considerably as a source of funds. The current structure of the industry balance sheet is shown in Table 10.13. The historical balance sheet developments are shown in Table 10.16.

The REIT industry has reemerged strong and confident after years of indecision and self-examination. A casual look at Figure 10.4 should confirm this. Other evidence suggests that a brighter future lies ahead. During 1982 the REIT industry raised $453.6 million in new capital, using public offering and private placement. By the end of 1982, 25 REITs had yields in excess of 10 percent, with four in excess of 15 percent. The total yield on REITs' price changes plus dividends exceeded 26 percent in 1982, up from −.10 percent in 1978. (See Table 10.17.) Total dividend to payouts in 1982 reached $274 million, up 13 percent from 1981. Eighty REITs increased their dividends in 1982.

TABLE 10.15
Combined Balance Sheets
11 Bank REITs
($ millions)

	1973	1978	Change
Total assets	$2,956	$1,240	− 58%
Loans	2,699	561	− 79
Property	51	606	+ 1088
Other assets	206	73	− 65
Total liabilities and equity	2,956	1,240	− 58
Commercial paper	1,281	108	− 92
Bank loans	442	699	+ 58
Other debts	439	285	− 35
Other liabilities	157	31	− 80
Equity	637	117	− 82

Source: REIT financial statements in *Appraisal Journal*, April 1980, © 1980 by *The Appraisal Journal*. Reprinted by permission.

TABLE 10.16

Aggregate Balance Sheet Data for REITs

($ billions, year-end data)

	1968	1969	1970	1971	1972	1973	1974	1975	1976	1977	1978	1979	1980*	1981	1982
Assets															
Land, development, and construction loans	$0.26	$0.85	$2.58	$4.25	$7.56	$10.74	$ 9.47	$ 3.86	$1.97	$1.25	$1.04	$1.07	$0.83	$0.71	$0.72
Other loans	0.12	0.26	0.64	1.51	3.07	4.13	6.78	3.28	2.67	2.13	2.03	1.85	1.89	1.93	2.08
Loan loss reserves	—	—	—	—	—	—	(0.73)	(0.76)	(0.64)	(0.37)	(0.21)	(0.14)	(0.06)	(0.05)	(0.07)
Property owned	0.55	0.70	0.95	1.35	2.47	3.29	4.06	4.74	5.08	4.24	3.99	3.88	3.77	3.89	4.15
Other assets	0.10	0.22	0.56	0.61	1.07	1.74	0.90	0.89	0.62	0.45	0.42	0.54	0.57	0.59	0.65
Total assets	$1.03	$2.03	$4.73	$7.72	$14.17	$19.90	$20.48	$12.01	$9.70	$7.70	$7.27	$7.20	$7.00	$7.07	$7.53
Liabilities															
Bank borrowings and commercial paper	$0.09	$0.23	$0.80	$2.24	$6.21	$10.31	$10.29	$6.13	$3.96	$2.39	$1.79	$1.59	$1.21	$1.11	$1.01
Mortgages on property owned	0.36	0.43	0.55	0.68	1.15	1.45	1.58	1.51	2.00	1.81	1.96	1.95	1.91	1.93	2.04
Other liabilities	0.11	0.13	0.49	0.83	1.70	2.36	3.95	1.21	1.10	0.89	0.92	0.87	0.96	0.94	0.99
Total liabilities	$0.56	$0.79	$1.84	$3.75	$9.06	$14.12	$15.82	$8.85	$7.06	$5.09	$4.67	$4.41	$4.08	$3.98	$4.04
Shareholders' Equity	0.47	1.24	2.89	3.97	5.11	5.78	4.66	3.16	2.64	2.61	2.60	2.79	2.92	3.09	3.49
Total assets	$1.03	$2.03	$4.73	$7.72	$14.17	$19.90	$20.48	$12.01	$9.70	$7.70	$7.27	$7.20	$7.00	$7.07	$7.53

Source: REIT 1982 Fact Book, p. 33.

* 1982 balance sheet figures are preliminary.

TABLE 10.17
Total Performance of REITs

Year	Change in Prices (%)[a]	Divident Yield (%)[b]	Total Yield (%)
1977	10.08	8.01	18.09
1978	−8.53	8.43	−0.10
1979	17.97	10.67	28.64
1980	10.46	9.68	20.14
1981	−0.21	9.48	9.27
1982	16.15	9.88	26.03

Source: REIT 1982 Fact Book, p. 21.
[a] Percent change in the REIT share price index from year end to year end.
[b] Annual dividend yield for all REITs included in the REIT share price index, weighted by the market value of each REIT. The 1982 data includes 78 REITs.

Advantages and Disadvantages of REITs

The advantages of a carefully selected REIT are

1. Risk diversification. REIT assets are usually invested in different types of real estate property in various regions of the United States. To the extent that the rates of return on the properties held are not perfectly positively correlated, risk diversification would obtain.

2. Experienced management. The investment strategies and policies of REITs are set by their trustees in accordance with the objectives of the trust. The day-to-day operations of the trust are managed by a separate entity contracted by the trustees. The management includes both assets and liabilities. The manager (advisor) is ordinarily an affiliate of the same parent company that sponsors the REIT.

3. Liquidity. REIT shares have an active secondary market affording investors a much higher liquidity than outright ownership of real estate property. REIT shares are traded on the exchanges or over-the-counter.

4. Flexibility. REITs have been increasingly innovative in responding to market needs and in devising strategies to improve their rate of return and reduce their risk. Among these strategies are (a) joint ventures with builders when the REIT provides the necessary cash and financing in return for an equity position in the property usually at an advantageous price. The builder (developer) provides the construction and management expertise; (b) leaseback arrangements, (c) floating rate mortgages, rollover loans, and loans with an equity conversion clause.[11]

5. Inflation hedge. Property values have historically provided a good hedge against inflation.

6. Tax shelter. A REIT provides a tax shelter in two ways: (a) the distribution to shareholders in excess of current net income is considered a return of capital and is

---

[11] An equity conversion clause allows the lender to convert the loan into equity ownership in the underlying property.

not subject to income tax, (b) a distribution of a gain from the sale of a property is taxed at the preferred capital gains rate—a maximum of 20 percent.

7. High yield. Current yields on REITs are well over 10 percent.

These advantages must be considered against the following disadvantages.

1. The permission granted REITs under the Tax Reform Act of 1970 to carry their losses forward for eight years, coupled with the fact that many REIT assets are valued at substantially less than market value, have made them prime takeover candidates. Once acquired, the property of a REIT is liquidated at a considerably higher price than the purchase price. These gains are not realized by the original shareholder. Investors considering REITs must carefully assess the value of their properties.

2. Operating losses, taxes, interest deductions, and depreciation expenses in excess of operating income are *not* of direct benefit to the shareholder. If a REIT has, for example, $20,000 in operating income and $20,000 in depreciation, and it distributes $20,000 to the shareholders, the $20,000 is not taxable. If, on the other hand, operating income is zero and depreciation is equal to $20,000, the $20,000 *cannot* be used by the shareholder as a deduction from his current income.

3. High interest rates increase the cost of acquiring property and thus decrease its liquidity. A shareholder expecting a substantial capital gains distribution must take the costs of illiquidity into consideration. These costs are reflected in the market price of the share.

4. Real estate remains an investment with considerable risk. Professional managers have already proven the extent to which they can miscalculate. History may repeat itself.

Another form allowing ownership of real estate is the limited partnership real estate tax shelter.

10.5 REAL ESTATE SYNDICATION

Syndication represents a vehicle for participation in the real estate market. A syndication allows for the pooling of funds under professional management (the syndicator or sponsor) for the purpose of acquiring, developing, managing, operating, or marketing real estate or any combination of the above. As such, a real estate syndicate becomes a vehicle for smaller investors to invest in real estate projects which otherwise would be well beyond their reach. These projects may include shopping centers, office buildings, apartment complexes, and so forth. Some of the largest real estate and brokerage firms are involved in syndications as sponsors. The largest are: The Balcor Co., Consolidated Capital Co., Fox & Carskadon Corp., Integrated Resources, Inc., JMB Realty Corp., The Robert A. McNeil Corp., and Merrill Lynch, Hubbard.

Syndications are typically organized as limited partnerships with the sponsor acting as a general partner. These partnerships are of two types: private and public.

Private Limited Partnerships

A limited partner in a partnership has a risk exposure limited to his financial commitment to the partnership. The commitment is created through the purchase of a unit. The minimum value of a unit in a private limited partnership is now $35,000. The range

of minimum participation requirements is $35,000 to $150,000. This makes private limited partnerships the domain of the rather affluent. The minimum cash investment does not have to be paid all at once, however. Typically, it is paid in annual installments over five years which effectively translates into early years' cash flows, primarily from the tax shelter, providing enough cash to meet the payments in the latter years.

Private limited partnership deals, consistent with their target market, emphasize the tax shelter aspect of real estate rather than cash income. In addition, capital gains from the sale of property, occurring typically five to eight years after the partnership is formed, are emphasized.

Recently, established real estate limited partnerships have been providing equity help to prospective home buyers against a share in the tax benefits and/or in the appreciation of the value of the property. Equity capital is also being provided to build factories and other commercial/industrial structures.

Limited partners in a private partnership are of two types: accredited and nonaccredited. Accredited partners must meet high "suitability" requirements. Their annual income must be over $100,000 and their net worth about $750,000. Nonaccredited partners, on the other hand, must meet less stringent requirements. Their income must exceed $30,000 and their net worth $100,000. These requirements are a response to Regulation D of the Securities Exchange Commission (SEC) which governs investors in private unregistered partnerships. Registration with the SEC, however, is required if the number of nonaccredited partners exceeds 35. Registration of the securities with state authorities is required regardless of the number of nonaccredited partners.

Public Limited Partnerships

Public limited partnerships are intended to allow for a larger number of participants at affordable unit prices ($5,000 minimum unit price, ordinarily). They require registration with the SEC and the issuance of a prospectus. They operate on a blind pool concept— that is, as soon as a set level of funds is reached, the acquisition of property begins. Public partnerships have one-fifth the muscle of private ones. We now explore the advantages and the risks of limited real estate partnerships.

Advantages

Limited partnerships are legal entities which make it possible for tax losses and cash flows to pass through to the individual limited partner. The partnership itself is not subject to taxation. The aim is to generate large tax losses in the early years and significant income levels in the later years of the partnership.

The tax benefits were explained in detail earlier in this chapter. The largest benefit in the early years accrue from the accelerated depreciation taken on the total cost of the property, although the investor's equity is only a fraction of that total. The difference between the total cost and the investor's equity is a nonrecourse loan which the investor or the partnership may never pay. This is a very important advantage when compared with the consequences of debt when the investor ventures alone into real estate. Additional advantages result from the taxability of the profits that are realized on the sale of partnership property at the preferred capital gains rate (maximum of 20 percent).

The other advantages of a limited partnership are as follows:

1. Permanence. A limited partnership in a real estate syndicate does not necessarily end with the death, insanity, or retirement of the general partner.

2. Professional management. The management expertise is provided by the general manager whose importance should never be underestimated by any limited partner.

3. Limited liability. The limited partner's total liability is limited to his investment.

4. Risk diversification. This results from spreading partnership assets across several properties of different types and in different locations.

5. Limited partnerships may be the only way for small investors to participate in large real estate deals.

6. Specialization. Syndication is likely to lead to specialization in certain types of property. The economies of scale may be significant.

7. Freedom. Limited partnerships give the investor freedom from management, bookkeeping, records, and so forth.

The benefits to the syndicator are also numerous. The first is the fees for the syndicator's services, generally in the range of 8 to 10 percent payable up front. The second lies in the diversification of the portfolio of income-producing ventures. The third lies in the possibility of selling property that is held by the general partner or by a firm in which he has an interest to the limited partnership. These advantages are not without risks.

Risks in Real Estate Partnerships

The risks in real estate limited partnerships are numerous. The most significant is that of illiquidity. Limited partnership units are characteristically illiquid almost by design. The illiquidity results from the heterogeneity of the units across syndications and the limited number of homogeneous units in a partnership (lack of depth). Added to this is the suitability requirement and the requirement that a buyer of an already outstanding unit must be acceptable to the general partner. These and the securities laws that prohibit a liquidating partner from advertising or making solicitations to prospective buyers limit the size of the market.

The process of liquidating a unit remains difficult even if a purchaser is identified. The determination of the economic worth of a partnership interest is not an easy matter. The methods used for gauging value are the replacement cost method, the market value of a comparable unit, and the discounted value of the income stream. The latter method is the one most often used, yet it is applicable to a limited range of property types. The peculiarity of certain projects requires the use of different valuation techniques. Government-assisted housing projects, for example, have limitations on cash distributions and cannot be sold or refinanced until held for the mandatory period.

The liquidity problem is particularly acute when liquidation is absolutely necessary. This is so in cases of divorce, death, retirement, radical changes in financial position, and so forth. There is hope, however. A new San Francisco-based company, Liquidity Fund Investment Corp., was created solely to buy previously-owned real estate limited partnership units of both the public and the private type. The unfortunate reality is that the reach of this corporation is very limited.

The other risks faced by limited partners are

1. Insufficient emphasis on several important factors besides the tax shelter.

2. The partnership investments may turn out to be unprofitable.

3. The recapture provision of the tax laws diminishes the attractiveness of the units as discussed earlier in this chapter.

4. Natural disasters not accounted for in the insurance contracts may wipe out entire projects.

5. The success of the partnership depends largely on the judgement, skills, and ethics of the general partner. Some or all of these may be absent.

6. Tax losses may run ahead of the limited partner's income, triggering an IRS audit which investors do not appreciate.

7. Construction of new projects may not be completed on time because of labor and other problems.

8. Detrimental changes in the tax law can occur at any time, wiping out some, if not all, of the advantages currently enjoyed.

Some of the risks listed above cannot be hedged against. Others can be reduced, if not eliminated, by carefully checking the qualifications (experience) and financial position of the general partner, by checking the value of the properties owned or under consideration, by checking the syndicate's fee structure and the projections and assumptions made by the syndicator, by examining the location where most of the properties held are concentrated, and most importantly, by checking the reputation of the sponsoring firm and its track record.

We now look at some vehicles for participating in real estate financing.

10.6 FINANCING REAL ESTATE—INVESTMENT OPPORTUNITIES

Investors/speculators interested in participating in the financing of real estate may choose to buy shares in savings and loans, in mortgage companies, and even in banks that have heavily invested in mortgages. Alternatively, they may decide to issue their own mortgages to prospective borrowers and assume the role and the responsibility of a mortgage banker. Another easy and very popular way is to buy debt instruments linked to real estate financing, such as Government National Mortgage Association (GNMA) and Federal National Mortgage Association (FNMA) securities.

Federal National Mortgage Association

The Federal National Mortgage Association (FNMA or "Fannie Mae") is a profit-making corporation wholly owned by its stockholders. FNMA is supervised by a fifteen-member board of directors, five of whom are appointed by the President of the United States; the remaining ten are elected annually by the stockholders.

FNMA was formed in 1954 under the FNMA Act. Its function is to provide liquidity in the secondary market for mortgages and to provide special assistance in the mortgage area as may be requested by the President or the Congress.

FNMA's 56 million outstanding shares are actively traded on the New York Stock Exchange. Institutions servicing mortgages on behalf of FNMA must own FNMA stock.

Although classified as Federal Agency Securities (Table 10.18), debt instruments issued by the FNMA are neither federal government obligations nor federally guaranteed. However, FNMA has authority to borrow up to $2.25 billion from the U.S. Department of the Treasury. Interest on these securities is taxable on the federal, state, and local levels.

The primary function of FNMA is to supplement the secondary market for residential mortgages. It does so by injecting funds into the mortgage market when conditions are not very accomodating to home buyers, home builders, and mortgage lenders. The funds used to increase the availability of mortgage money are raised by borrowing from private sources. These funds would not have flowed to the mortgage market otherwise.

FNMA buys outstanding mortgages from approved lenders at yields determined by auction. The approval of lenders by FNMA is based on their financial positions and their ability to service residential mortgage loans. The major suppliers of mortgages to FNMA are savings and loan associations, commercial banks, mutual savings banks, life insurance companies, and mortgage bankers. Total FNMA debt outstanding equals $70.05 billion; this represents 28.3 percent of all debt outstanding for federal and federally sponsored agencies in December 1982. The FNMA mortgage and loan portfolio accounts for approximately 6 percent of total residential mortgage debt in the United States.

FNMA issues various types of securities, among them FNMA discount notes (30- to 360-day maturity tailored, as to maturity date, to the specific need of investors); secondary-market notes and debentures with maturities ranging from 1.5 to 25 years and with denominations of $10,000, $25,000, $50,000, $100,000, and $500,000; and mortgage-backed bonds secured by mortgages, some guaranteed by the Government National Mortgage Association (a U.S. government agency). The minimum denomination on mortgage-backed bonds is $25,000.

Government National Mortgage Association

The Government National Mortgage Association (GNMA or "Ginnie Mae") was created in 1968 to assume programs that were originally part of FNMA: (1) special assistance functions like the extension of financial aid to certain types of housing programs of the federal government and (2) management functions relating to existing FNMA mortgage portfolios. GNMA made possible the origination of federally insured and guaranteed mortgages at below-market rates; that is, it allowed for the subsidization of home ownership.

Securities issued by GNMA are taxed on the federal, state, and local levels. Three types of securities are issued by GNMA:

1. Mortgage-backed securities. These securities are backed by a pool of FHA or VA-insured mortgages.
2. Participation certificates. These certificates are issued against loan assets of government agencies whose mortgage management was taken over by GNMA from FNMA.
3. GNMA modified passthroughs. These securities are created when a mortgage originator, often a mortgage banker or a savings and loan association, assembles a pool ($500,000 minimum) of mortgages insured by the Federal Housing Administration (FHA) or the Farmers Home Administration, or guaranteed by the Veterans Administration (VA) with identical maturities and interest rates and consisting of mortgages on homes in one geographical area, and deposits them at a custodial bank.

Upon submission of all necessary documents by the originator to GNMA and approval by the latter, the originator issues securities against the mortgage pool and assumes

TABLE 10.18
Federal and Federally Sponsored Credit Agencies Debt Outstanding
(Millions of dollars, end of period)

				1982						
Agency	1978	1979	1980	June	July	Aug.	Sept.	Oct.	Nov.	Dec.
1 Federal and federally sponsored agencies¹	137,063	163,290	193,229	238,787	242,565	243,623	246,050	245,698	243,634	247,218
2 Federal agencies	23,488	24,715	28,606	32,274	32,302	32,280	32,606	32,713	32,772	33,055
3 Defense Department²	968	738	610	419	408	399	388	377	364	354
4 Export-Import Bank³,⁴	8,711	9,191	11,250	13,939	13,938	13,918	14,042	14,000	13,999	14,218
5 Federal Housing Administration⁵	588	537	477	358	353	345	335	323	311	288
6 Government National Mortgage Association participation certificates⁶	3,141	2,979	2,817	2,165	2,165	2,165	2,165	2,165	2,165	2,165
7 Postal Service⁷	2,364	1,837	1,770	1,471	1,471	1,471	1,471	1,471	1,471	1,471
8 Tennessee Valley Authority	7,460	8,997	11,190	13,715	13,760	13,775	14,010	14,185	14,270	14,365
9 United States Railway Association⁷	356	436	492	207	207	207	195	192	192	194
10 Federally sponsored agencies¹	113,575	138,575	164,623	206,513	210,263	211,343	213,444	212,985	210,862	214,163
11 Federal Home Loan Banks	27,563	33,330	41,258	61,883	62,058	61,747	61,251	60,904	60,356	61,447
12 Federal Home Loan Mortgage Corporation	2,262	2,771	2,536	3,099	3,099	3,099	3,099	3,099	3,099	3,099
13 Federal National Mortgage Association	41,080	48,486	55,185	62,660	65,563	65,733	68,130	67,916	66,852	70,052
14 Federal Land Banks	20,360	16,006	12,365	8,217	7,652	7,652	7,652	6,813	6,813	6,813
15 Federal Intermediate Credit Banks	11,469	2,676	1,821	926	926	926	926	926	926	926
16 Banks for Cooperatives	4,843	584	584	220	220	220	220	220	220	220
17 Farm Credit Banks¹	5,081	33,216	48,153	64,506	65,743	65,657	65,553	66,449	65,877	65,014
18 Student Loan Marketing Association	915	1,505	2,720	5,000	5,000	6,307ʳ	6,611ʳ	6,657	6,718	6,591
19 Other	2	1	1	2	2	2	2	1	1	1

MEMO:

20 Federal Financing Bank debt[1,8]	51,298	67,383	87,460	120,241	121,261	122,623	124,357	125,064	125,707	126,424

Lending to federal and federally sponsored agencies

21 Export-Import Bank[4]	6,898	8,353	10,654	13,829	13,829	13,823	13,954	13,954	13,954	14,177
22 Postal Service[7]	2,114	1,587	1,520	1,221	1,221	1,221	1,221	1,221	1,221	1,221
23 Tennessee Valley Authority	5,635	7,272	9,465	11,990	12,035	12,050	12,285	12,460	12,545	12,640
24 United States Railway Association[7]	356	436	492	207	207	207	195	192	192	194
Other Lending[9]										
25 Farmers Home Administration	23,825	32,050	39,431	52,346	52,711	53,311	53,736	53,661	53,661	53,261
26 Rural Electrification Administration	4,604	6,484	9,196	15,454	15,688	15,916	16,282	16,600	16,750	17,157
27 Other	6,951	9,696	13,982	20,194	20,570	21,095	21,684	26,976	27,384	27,774

Source: Federal Reserve Bulletin, March 1983, p. A35.

[1] In September 1977 the Farm Credit Banks issued their first consolidated bonds, and in January 1979 they began issuing these bonds on a regular basis to replace the financing activities of the Federal Land Banks, the Federal Intermediate Credit Banks, and the Banks for Cooperatives. Line 17 represents those consolidated bonds outstanding, as well as any discount notes that have been issued. Lines 1 and 10 reflect the addition of this item.

[2] Consists of mortgages assumed by the Defense Department between 1957 and 1963 under family housing and homeowners assistance programs.

[3] Includes participation certificates reclassified as debt beginning Oct. 1, 1976.

[4] Off-budget Aug. 17, 1974, through Sept. 30, 1976; on-budget thereafter.

[5] Consists of debentures issued in payment of Federal Housing Administration insurance claims. Once issued, there securities may be sold privately on the securities market.

[6] Certificates of participation issued prior to fiscal 1969 by the Government National Mortgage Association acting as trustee for the Farmers Home Administration; Department of Health, Education, and Welfare; Department of Housing and Urban Development; Small Business Administration; and the Veterans Administration.

[7] Off-budget.

[8] The FFB, which began operations in 1974, is authorized to purchase or sell obligations issued, sold, or guaranteed by other federal agencies. Since FFB incurs debt solely for the purpose of lending to other agencies, its debt is not included in the main portion of the table in order to avoid double counting.

[9] Includes FFB purchases of agency assets and guaranteed loans; the latter contain loans guaranteed by numerous agencies with the guarantees of any particular agency being generally small. The Farmers Home Administration item consists exclusively of agency assets, while the Rural Electrification Administration entry contains both agency assets and guaranteed loans.

the responsibility for making monthly payments of interest and principal to holders of GNMAs. If the payment date coincides with that of the underlying mortgages, the securities are referred to as straight GNMA passthroughs. If, on the other hand, the payment date does not coincide with that of the underlying mortgages—that is, the originator makes payments on GNMA securities prior to or after the receipt of payments from the underlying mortgages—the securities are referred to as GNMA modified passthroughs. What GNMA guarantees, therefore, is the payment of interest and principal on a given date. The guarantee against default on the mortgage is provided by the VA or FHA.

Yields on GNMA passthroughs are closely tied to mortgage interest rates. They offer great opportunities for investors interested in the mortgage market while increasing the liquidity of the market and the participating financial institutions. Since their introduction in 1970, GNMA passthroughs have been most popular with thrift institutions, which currently hold about 30 percent of outstanding securities.

GNMA mortgage-backed securities are quoted in terms of percentage of unpaid principle balance; with fractions quoted in increments of thirty-seconds of a percentage point. The average life of the pool of mortgages underlying the GNMA securities is about 12 years. Yield quotations on GNMA certificates are based on the assumption of prepayment in the twelfth year. The minimum denomination on GNMA modified passthroughs is $25,000.

The advantages associated with ownership of GNMA passthroughs are as follows:

1. Participation in the mortgage market without the paperwork and the service requirements associated with mortgage investing.
2. Practically risk-free assets.
3. Monthly cash-flows of interest and principal payments guaranteed regardless of whether payments on the underlying mortgages are made or not.
4. The collateral value of the securities, since GNMA passthroughs qualify as a real estate asset and meet the regulations of the FSLIC.
5. High liquidity.

GNMA and FNMA securities afford the investor higher returns than generally available on investments with comparable risk and maturity while avoiding many of the administrative requirements associated with direct issuance of mortgages.

The interest of pension funds in these instruments remains surprisingly miniscule. Pension fund assets in 1980 equalled $650 billion. GNMA holdings included in government bonds (Figure 10.5), accounted for only 3 percent of total assets. The interest can only increase, however, when the pension fund managers realize that the yield on GNMAs has historically been higher than on corporate bonds by one percentage point despite the fact that GNMAs have no default risk and are more liquid than many corporate bonds.

CONCLUSION

Real estate may be the only investment undertaken by many Americans. If not, it should certainly be an integral part of a comprehensive investment strategy. The options we present here are but a few of several opportunities involving real estate.

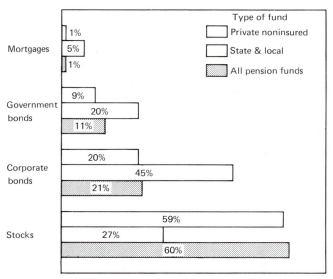

FIGURE 10.5. Pension fund asset holdings by type of fund.

Type of fund
☐ Private noninsured
☐ State & local
▨ All pension funds

Mortgages: 1% / 5% / 1%
Government bonds: 9% / 20% / 11%
Corporate bonds: 20% / 45% / 21%
Stocks: 59% / 27% / 60%

Source: Real Estate Quarterly, vol. 2, no. 2, Winter 1983, p. 21.

Questions

1. Describe the characteristics of real estate investments. How do they compare with other investment vehicles?

2. Discuss how the government subsidizes, directly and indirectly, home ownership in the U.S.

3. What must a potential homeowner consider before buying a house? What must he or she do when financing a house? Why is insurance so important?

4. How does owning a home "force" saving?

5. Compare and contrast condominiums and cooperatives.

6. How do the FHA and the VA increase access to home ownership? For whom?

7. Outline the various types of mortgages and payment plans. Which might best suit a young couple?

8. Explain, in light of recent interest rate changes, the reluctance of S&Ls to provide fixed-rate mortgages. Do you perceive VRMs as a solution? Explain.

9. Why is it essential to understand the variability of cash flows on an income property? How does investing in income property resemble any other business investment?

10. Discuss the major expense items of investing in an income property. How are these items estimated?

11. Show and explain how to calculate taxable income for investments in income property.

12. Explain the decline in popularity of mortgage REITs and the concurrent resurgence of equity REITs.

13. How have changes in REIT portfolios since the late 1970s enhanced their soundness as an investment?

14. What alternatives besides an equity position allow an investor to participate in the real estate market?

15. What are the basic advantages of syndication? Disadvantages?

16. How are syndications different from REITs?

17. What is the difference between FNMA and GNMA?

18. What are the most interesting features of GNMA passthroughs?

Problems

Go to a local real estate broker, obtain information on an apartment complex for sale. Use the model in the chapter to estimate its value.

Areas Under the Normal Curve

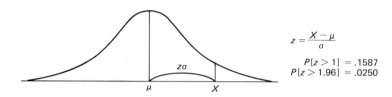

$$z = \frac{X - \mu}{\sigma}$$

$$P[z > 1] = .1587$$
$$P[z > 1.96] = .0250$$

Normal Deviate z	.00	.01	.02	.03	.04	.05	.06	.07	.08	.09
0.0	.5000	.4960	.4920	.4880	.4840	.4801	.4761	.4721	.4681	.4641
0.1	.4602	.4562	.4522	.4483	.4443	.4404	.4364	.4325	.4286	.4247
0.2	.4207	.4168	.4129	.4090	.4052	.4013	.3974	.3936	.3897	.3859
0.3	.3821	.3783	.3745	.3707	.3669	.3632	.3594	.3557	.3520	.3483
0.4	.3446	.3409	.3372	.3336	.3300	.3264	.3228	.3192	.3156	.3121
0.5	.3085	.3050	.3015	.2981	.2946	.2912	.2877	.2843	.2810	.2776
0.6	.2743	.2709	.2676	.2643	.2611	.2578	.2546	.2514	.2483	.2451
0.7	.2420	.2389	.2358	.2327	.2296	.2266	.2236	.2206	.2177	.2148
0.8	.2119	.2090	.2061	.2033	.2005	.1977	.1949	.1922	.1894	.1867
0.9	.1841	.1814	.1788	.1762	.1736	.1711	.1685	.1660	.1635	.1611
1.0	.1587	.1562	.1539	.1515	.1492	.1469	.1446	.1423	.1401	.1379
1.1	.1357	.1335	.1314	.1292	.1271	.1251	.1230	.1210	.1190	.1170
1.2	.1151	.1131	.1112	.1093	.1075	.1056	.1038	.1020	.1003	.0985
1.3	.0968	.0951	.0934	.0918	.0901	.0885	.0869	.0853	.0838	.0823
1.4	.0808	.0793	.0778	.0764	.0749	.0735	.0721	.0708	.0694	.0681
1.5	.0668	.0655	.0643	.0630	.0618	.0606	.0594	.0582	.0571	.0559
1.6	.0548	.0537	.0526	.0516	.0505	.0495	.0485	.0475	.0465	.0455
1.7	.0446	.0436	.0427	.0418	.0409	.0401	.0392	.0384	.0375	.0367

Normal Deviate z	.00	.01	.02	.03	.04	.05	.06	.07	.08	.09
1.8	.0359	.0351	.0344	.0336	.0329	.0322	.0314	.0307	.0301	.0294
1.9	.0287	.0281	.0274	.0268	.0262	.0256	.0250	.0244	.0239	.0233
2.0	.0228	.0222	.0217	.0212	.0207	.0202	.0197	.0192	.0188	.0183
2.1	.0179	.0174	.0170	.0166	.0162	.0158	.0154	.0150	.0146	.0143
2.2	.0139	.0136	.0132	.0129	.0125	.0122	.0119	.0116	.0113	.0110
2.3	.0107	.0104	.0102	.0099	.0096	.0094	.0091	.0089	.0087	.0084
2.4	.0082	.0080	.0078	.0075	.0073	.0071	.0069	.0068	.0066	.0064
2.5	.0062	.0060	.0059	.0057	.0055	.0054	.0052	.0051	.0049	.0048
2.6	.0047	.0045	.0044	.0043	.0041	.0040	.0039	.0038	.0037	.0036
2.7	.0035	.0034	.0033	.0032	.0031	.0030	.0029	.0028	.0027	.0026
2.8	.0026	.0025	.0024	.0023	.0023	.0022	.0021	.0021	.0020	.0019
2.9	.0019	.0018	.0018	.0017	.0016	.0016	.0015	.0015	.0014	.0014
3.0	.0013	.0013	.0013	.0012	.0012	.0011	.0011	.0011	.0010	.0010

Index